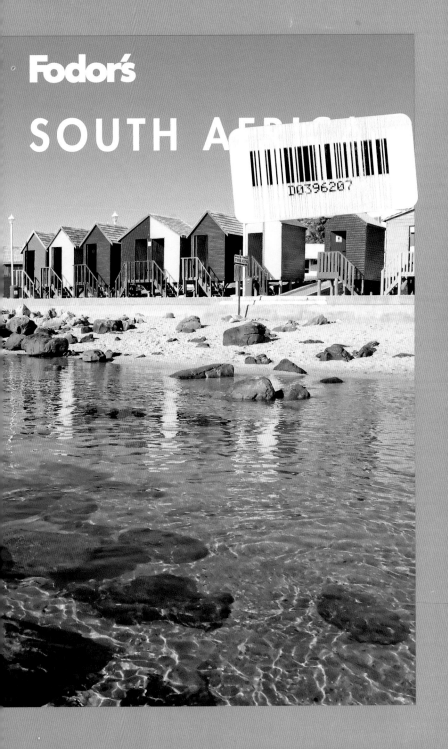

Fodor's

SOUTH AFRICA

D0396207

WELCOME TO SOUTH AFRICA

Everything about Africa that stirs the imagination is concentrated in its southernmost country. Lions freely roam vast game reserves such as Kruger National Park, vineyards stretch across the Cape Winelands, and mountains cascade into the sea along miles of beaches. In addition to dream safaris and romantic honeymoons, South Africa offers modern cities with thriving arts and dining scenes. South Africans are welcoming, and the country's emergence from a turbulent past provides a dramatic history lesson and the promise of something new every time you visit.

TOP REASONS TO GO

★ **Wildlife:** The "Big Five"—lion, elephant, rhino, leopard, Cape buffalo—and many more.

★ **Scenery:** Landscapes from the soaring Drakensberg Range to the endless Kalahari desert.

★ **Cities:** Cape Town, Johannesburg, and Durban are among Africa's most vibrant places.

★ **Wine:** World-renowned viticulture, beautiful Cape Dutch architecture, and charming hotels.

★ **Beaches**: Surf, sand, endangered penguins, and abundant whale-watching from the shore.

★ **African Culture:** A diverse population (Zulu and Xhosa predominate) speaks 11 languages.

12
TOP EXPERIENCES

South Africa offers terrific experiences that should be on every traveler's list. Here are Fodor's top picks for a memorable trip.

1 Cape Town

South Africa's "Mother City" spreads magnificently around Table Mountain. Its popular Victoria & Albert Waterfront is a vibrant setting for many of the city's top hotels and restaurants. *(Ch. 2)*

2 Nelson Mandela's Legacy

See his grave in the Eastern Cape, the cell where he was imprisoned for 18 years on Robben Island, and the house where he lived in Soweto *(pictured)* until 1961. *(Ch. 8)*

3 Cape Winelands

Known for Pinotage and Chenin Blanc varietals, as well as striking Cape Dutch architecture, South Africa's famous wineries are near Stellenbosch, Franschoek, and Parl. *(Ch. 3)*

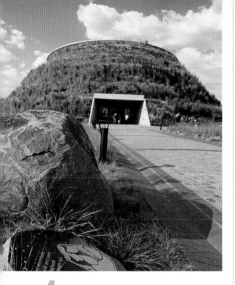

4 Cradle of Humankind

The bones of our ancient ancestors have been found in the complex of limestone caves that comprise this impressive World Heritage Site west of Johannesburg. *(Ch. 8)*

5 Garden Route

The 130-mile stretch of coast from Mossel Bay to Storms River has spectacular scenery and quaint towns, and it's one of the country's top draws for driving and hiking. *(Ch. 5)*

6 Kalahari Desert

The Northern Cape, the country's least-populated province, is home to the native San people and a vast, semi-arid savannah that stretches into Namibia and Botswana. *(Ch. 4)*

7 Whale Watching

South Africa is a top spot to see whales and dolphins. At Plettenberg Bay, the country's premier beach resort, you can see them by boat or right from the beach. *(Ch. 5)*

8 Drakensberg Range of KwaZulu-Natal

The Zulu call this World Heritage Site the *uKhahlambra* ("Barrier of Spears"). It offers some of the most dramatic landscapes and best hiking in South Africa. *(Ch. 7)*

9 Safaris

Whether in Kruger National Park or a private wildlife reserve, seeing the "Big Five" (lion, elephant, rhino, leopard, and buffalo) in the wild is awe-inspiring. *(Ch. 9)*

10 Cape Point

Just over 40 miles south of Cape Town, near the southernmost point of Africa, you can look out to the sea where the waters of the Atlantic meet the Indian Ocean. *(Ch. 2)*

11 South African Culture

Every June and July, South Africa's National Arts Festival brings a roster of contemporary and traditional dance, theater, and music performances to Grahamstown. *(Ch. 6)*

12 Shopping

Masks, carvings, clothing, bowls, and other crafts: you'll find an amazing variety of authentic items in the large African crafts markets in Cape Town, Johannesburg, and Durban. *(Ch. 6)*

CONTENTS

CONTENTS

ABOUT THIS GUIDE

Fodor's Recommendations

Everything in this guide is worth doing—we don't cover what isn't—but exceptional sights, hotels, and restaurants are recognized with additional accolades. **Fodor's Choice★** indicates our top recommendations; and **Best Bets** call attention to notable hotels and restaurants in various categories. Care to nominate a new place? Visit Fodors.com/contact-us.

Trip Costs

We list prices wherever possible to help you budget well. Hotel and restaurant price categories from $ to $$$$ are noted alongside each recommendation. For hotels, we include the lowest cost of a standard double room in high season. For restaurants, we cite the average price of a main course at dinner or, if dinner isn't served, at lunch. For attractions, we always list adult admission fees; discounts are usually available for children, students, and senior citizens.

Hotels

Our local writers vet every hotel to recommend the best overnights in each price category, from budget to expensive. Unless otherwise specified, you can expect private bath, phone, and TV in your room. For expanded hotel reviews, facilities, and deals visit Fodors.com.

Top Picks	Hotels &
★ **Fodor's**Choice	**Restaurants**
	⊞ Hotel
Listings	⇗ Number of
⊠ Address	rooms
⊠ Branch address	⫮◎⫮ Meal plans
☎ Telephone	✕ Restaurant
🖷 Fax	⟿ Reservations
⊕ Website	𝄢 Dress code
✉ E-mail	▭ No credit cards
🗲 Admission fee	⑤ Price
⊙ Open/closed	
times	**Other**
Ⓜ Subway	⇨ See also
⊹ Directions or	☞ Take note
Map coordinates	🏌 Golf facilities

Restaurants

Unless we state otherwise, restaurants are open for lunch and dinner daily. We mention dress code only when there's a specific requirement and reservations only when they're essential or not accepted. To make restaurant reservations, visit Fodors.com.

Credit Cards

The hotels and restaurants in this guide typically accept credit cards. If not, we'll say so.

EUGENE FODOR

Hungarian-born Eugene Fodor (1905–91) began his travel career as an interpreter on a French cruise ship. The experience inspired him to write *On the Continent* (1936), the first guidebook to receive annual updates and discuss a country's way of life as well as its sights. Fodor later joined the U.S. Army and worked for the OSS in World War II. After the war, he kept up his intelligence work while expanding his guidebook series. During the Cold War, many guides were written by fellow agents who understood the value of insider information. Today's guides continue Fodor's legacy by providing travelers with timely coverage, insider tips, and cultural context.

EXPERIENCE
SOUTH AFRICA

WHAT'S WHERE

Numbers refer to chapters.

2 Cape Town and the Peninsula. Backed by Table Mountain, Cape Town anchors a stunning coastline: mountains cascading into the sea, miles of beaches, and inland wineries.

3 Western Cape. The Cape Winelands make popular day trips from Cape Town. A region of tranquil farms and popular beach resorts, the Overberg is also a developing wine region. Whale-watching is guaranteed along the southern Cape coast.

4 Garden Route and the Little Karoo. The aptly named Garden Route is more than 100 miles of forested mountains, waterways, and beaches. The Little Karoo, through which threads the awesome R62, is separated from the coast by the Outeniqua Mountains, famous for their ostrich farms and the hugely impressive Cango Caves.

5 Northern Cape. South Africa's emerging tourist region offers seriously off-the-beaten-track adventures. The Namaqualand spring flowers should be a must-see for any global traveler, because this is the country's last remaining wilderness, the rugged Richtersveld.

6 Eastern Cape. One of South Africa's most populated and diverse provinces offers seaside family getaways on the Wild Coast (where Nelson Mandela was born), the country's lesser-publicized but fascinating battlefields, and the nation's premier elephant reserve, Addo Elephant National Park.

7 Durban and KwaZulu-Natal. Inland from Durban, a bustling port city with a tropical feel, are the battle-fields where Boers, Britons, and Zulu fought to control the country; the province also has the beautiful Drakensberg mountains, a sanctuary for hikers. Wildlife-viewing in the far north reserves rivals that at Kruger.

8 Johannesburg. This historic gold town is orbited by the capital of Pretoria and the Soweto township. See some of the world's oldest human fossils at the nearby Cradle of Humankind.

9 Mpumalanga and Kruger National Park. South Africa's premier wild-life destination is packed with epic battle and gold-rush history, not to mention any animal you might wish to see.

Kgalagadi Transfrontie Park

Bokspits

NAMIBIA

Vioolsdrif

Orange Riv

NAMAQUALAND

ATLANTIC

OCEAN

Laaiplek

Wellington

Cape Town

Cape of Good Hope

3

2

GREAT

CAPE FOLDED
MOUNTAINS

Mossel Bay

Cape Agulhas

10 **Victoria Falls.** The Zambezi River joins Botswana's Chobe River here to form the vast plunge between Zambia and Zimbabwe.

NEED TO KNOW

AT A GLANCE

Capital: Pretoria, Cape Town, Bloemfontein

Population: 48,375,645

Currency: Rand

Money: ATMs common, credit cards widely accepted

Language: Afrikaans, English, Ndebele, Northern Sotho, Sotho, Swazi, Tswana, Tsonga, Venda, Xhosa, and Zulu

Country Code: ☎ 27

Emergencies: ☎ 10111 ☎ 10177

Driving: On the left

Electricity: 220v and 230v/50 cycles; plugs have three round prongs

Time: 7 hours ahead of New York

Documents: Up to 90 days with valid passport

Mobile Phones: GSM (900 and 1800 bands), UMTS (2100 band), LTE (1800 band)

Major Mobile Companies: Vodacom, MTN, Cell C

WEBSITE

South Africa: ⊕ www.southafrica.net

GETTING AROUND

✈ **Air Travel:** Johannesburg, Cape Town, and Durban have the main airports.

🚌 **Bus Travel:** Budget-minded travelers can use Baz Bus, which makes regular stops between Cape Town and Johannesburg.

🚗 **Car Travel:** Roads are good, and it's easy to drive between Johannesburg and Kruger, and from Cape Town through the Winelands and Garden Route.

🚆 **Train Travel:** Luxury trains run between Pretoria and Cape Town; regular trains take the same routes. Other trains are not considered safe for tourists or locals.

PLAN YOUR BUDGET

	HOTEL ROOM	MEAL	ATTRACTIONS
Low Budget	R1,500	R300	National Gallery, R15
Mid-Budget	R3,200	R700	Theater ticket, R150
High Budget	R7,000	R1,100	Birding, R500

WAYS TO SAVE

Grab a bunny. One of the cheapest and most substantial take-out options is the bunny chow, a hollowed-out loaf of bread loaded with curried meat.

Self-cater. Cape Town and Johannesburg have huge selections of self-catering accommodation options with full kitchens that are usually much cheaper than hotels.

Get a bus pass. Many of the country's bus companies offer money-saving passes good for varying numbers of travel days.

Take a tour. A full-day ticket for City Sightseeing South Africa's Blue Mini Peninsula Tour takes you to 14 diverse stops for just R170 (less if bought online).

PLAN YOUR TIME

Hassle Factor	Medium. Direct flights are still long (15 to 16 hours). Connections through Europe increase travel time.
3 Days	Explore Cape Town and Robben Island, and take a trip to Cape Point.
1 Week	Kruger National Park, the Mpumalanga Panoramic Route back to Johannesburg for two days before heading on to Cape Town.
2 Weeks	Spend 3 days in Cape Town then another 2 in the Winelands. Next take the Garden Route drive to Port Elizabeth, then spend three days on safari before heading to Victoria Falls.

WHEN TO GO

High Season: Cape Town is busy from November through January, with glorious sunshine and very late sunsets. Johannesburg summers are sunny and hot but never humid, with short afternoon thunderstorms.

Low Season: May through August is unpredictable, with cold, windy, rainy days but also some sun. Johannesburg winter days are bright and sunny, but nights can be frosty. Winter is the best time to go on safari—vegetation is sparse, and water is scarce, so game congregates around photo-friendly water holes.

Value Season: Cape Town's best weather is between February and March, and September and October can still be great months to go on safari. Hotel prices during these months will not be at their lowest, but they'll be off their summertime peaks.

BIG EVENTS

January: Kaapse Klopse, also called Tweede Nuwe Jaar, sees some 13,000 minstrels take to the streets of Cape Town on January 2.

June–July: The 10-day National Arts Festival in Grahamstown is the oldest and largest of its kind in South Africa. ⊕ www.nationalartsfestival.co.za.

July: The popular Knysna Oyster Festival not only celebrates the oyster, but raises money for charity. ⊕ www.oysterfestival.co.za.

October: Bloemfontein's MACUFE, the Mangaung African Cultural Festival, showcases African music, theater, dance, fine art, and crafts. ⊕ www.macufe.co.za.

READ THIS

■ **Cry, the Beloved Country,** Alan Paton. A black priest searches for his son in 1940s race-divided Johannesburg.

■ **The Power of One,** Bryce Courtenay. An English boy faces harsh treatment from the Boers during World War II.

■ **A Dry White Season,** André Brink. A white schoolteacher in Jo'burg sees the brutality of apartheid.

WATCH THIS

■ **Tsotsi.** A grim look at the violent life of a Johannesburg teenage gang leader.

■ **Invictus.** Nelson Mandela uses rugby to unite a race-divided nation.

■ **Sarafina!** The 1976 Soweto uprising—as told through music.

EAT THIS

■ **Biltong:** air-dried meat, often made from venison

■ **Bobotie:** piced ground meat and raisins, with egg-based topping

■ **Boerewors:** a beef, lamb, and/or pork sausage

■ **Bunny chow:** a bread loaf filled with curried meat

■ **Koeksister:** a doughnut, twisted and sweet or egg-shaped and spicy

■ **Pap:** fluffy cornmeal porridge, similar to polenta

SOUTH AFRICA TODAY

The Rainbow Nation

The "Rainbow Nation" of South Africa is one in which people intermingle racially far more than they did in the past. You can expect to find a once-segregated population living side by side as equals: as guests in game lodges, dining together in air-conditioned malls, and in the workplace.

However, vast economic disparities and racial tensions still exist. The physical legacy of apartheid remains, with large shantytowns inhabited by black South Africans; for many of the country's poor, things have not changed substantially since the 1990s. Black ownership of businesses has increased, but the wealth has often been transferred to a new black elite (former unionist leader Cyril Ramaphosa, for example). The tourism industry has begun evolving partnerships to improve the economic fortunes of rural communities and residents, who increasingly have shares in the lodges they work for. You'll find it's easier to meet South African blacks on an equal footing in Johannesburg than in Cape Town.

More than 80% of South Africans are Christians (the Zion African Church has the largest following). About 3% follow other religions, including Hinduism, Islam, and Judaism. About 13% of the population claim no affiliation.

Performing Arts

Cape Town, Durban, and Johannesburg all have lively arts scenes. Annual festivals, such as the National Arts Festival in Grahamstown in late June and/or early July, are great places to experience innovative performing- and visual-arts trends in the country.

On the music front, singer/songwriter Johnny Clegg, Jazz musician Hugh Masekela, and a cappella group Ladysmith Black Mambazo have all gained international fame; however, they are slowly being replaced internationally by the likes of Afro-fusion band Freshlyground and the dance music duo Goldfish.

Dance companies postapartheid have begun to use movement as a form of expression to explore the country's legacy. The dance form called Afro-fusion, named by Moving Into Dance Company's Sylvia Glasser, combines classic and traditional movements. Cape Town's Jazzart Dance Theatre, the oldest in the country, experiments with styles and expression.

Local theaters feature international as well as homegrown authors such as Athol Fugard, who often returns "home" from his residence in San Diego to direct his own works at the recently opened Fugard Theatre in Cape Town's District Six.

Literature

Most South African literature is published in English and Afrikaans, predominately because indigenous languages were not recognized and African experiences were not valued. Increasingly, however, works are being translated into other languages, often for a foreign market.

Fiction writers like Deon Meyer, Mike Nicholls, and Lauren Beukes have joined Nobel Prize winners Nadine Gordimer and J. M. Coetzee (who has also won the Booker Prize twice) in successfully flying the local literary flag in the international literary fiction market. Much of apartheid-era writing in the recent past tended toward realism and such themes as the white minority's sense of psychological and physical alienation and the black struggle living under the apartheid regime—but such topics are gradually fading away.

SOUTH AFRICA'S HISTORY

The First Known Inhabitants
Two-million-year-old hominid fossils of the earliest known prehuman ancestors were found in South Africa, at the Sterkfontein Caves, about an hour's drive from Johannesburg. This area is now known as the Cradle of Humankind.

Among the descendants of these prehistoric Africans were the San, Stone Age hunter-gatherers. From AD 200 to 400, people speaking various Bantu/Nguni languages moved into the area that is now South Africa's Eastern Cape and KwaZulu-Natal provinces, bringing with them Iron Age culture. Between AD 500 and the 1300s, the Khoikhoi—pastoralists and nomadic cattle herders—moved south and interacted, as well as clashed, with the San, as did a later group of farmers from the north. As the population increased, powerful kingdoms developed.

European Colonization
The Portuguese were the first to land in the Cape—in 1487—when pioneering a sea route to India, but it was the Dutch who decided to set up a refreshment station in 1652. Station commander Jan van Riebeeck later established a permanent settlement and imported a large number of slaves, mostly from the East Indies. The Cape Colony started to expand outward, and the Khoikhoi, who were living in the Cape, were no match for the might of the Europeans, and in the process lost most of their livestock, grazing areas, and population; those who remained became marginalized servants. The Afrikaans language slowly evolved (in 1925 it became an official language) from the Dutch mother tongue, with a smattering of words and sounds from the languages of other European settlers, slaves, and San and Khoikhoi servants thrown in, too.

Over the next 100 years, the Dutch pushed farther inland, sometimes clashing with indigenous inhabitants. Official control seesawed between the Dutch and the British until the region was formally recognized by the 1815 Congress of Vienna as a British colony.

The Great Trek
The British government subsequently annexed the Cape Colony and outlawed slavery in 1834. The Boers, or Afrikaners, fled inland, setting up new communities and drawing up constitutions explicitly prohibiting racial equality in church and state.

Also known as the Voortrekkers (or pioneers), the Boers traveled into lands occupied by Bantu-speaking peoples, including the Zulu kingdom. Ruled by Shaka, the Zulus evolved during the 1820s into the most powerful black African kingdom in southern Africa and occupied most of what is now KwaZulu-Natal.

Between 1837 and 1838, Afrikaner farmer and businessman Piet Retief attempted to negotiate a land agreement with the Zulu king, Dingane. Deceit entered the frame, and the Zulus killed Retief and more than 500 Voortrekkers.

In retaliation, a Boer raiding party defeated the Zulus at the Battle of Blood River in 1838 and set up the independent Republic of Natalia, now roughly the province of KwaZulu-Natal. Also around that time, two Boer republics were established: the South African Republic (now Mpumalanga, North West, and Limpopo provinces) and the Orange Free State (now Free State).

Prosperity and Conflict
The discovery of diamonds in Kimberley in 1867 and then gold in 1886 outside Johannesburg changed South Africa's

fortunes forever. The economic center moved from the British-controlled Cape to the Boer republics and transformed an agricultural society into an urbanized, industrial one.

Mining companies required a great deal of labor, supplied by black, male migrant workers, who by the 20th century were forced to live in single-sex hostels or compounds. Workers had to carry passes, and their movements were tightly controlled. The British, with financial interest in the mines, wanted to control the entire country and thus its mineral wealth. To this end, they took over Natalia and invaded Zulu territory. They next turned their attention to the two Boer republics.

To preempt an invasion by the British, the Boers declared war in 1899. The Anglo-Boer war (now called the South African War, as it involved all races) lasted until 1902. A "scorched earth" policy by the British meant farms were burned and women and children were put into concentration camps. The Boers eventually surrendered, but bitterness toward the British remained. By 1910 the former British colonies were united as the Union of South Africa, and Afrikaners were appointed to government positions in an attempt to reconcile English and Afrikaans speakers.

Apartheid

In 1913, the Natives Land Act divided the country into black and white areas. Blacks were given less than 10% of land, so many became migrant workers on white-owned farms and mines. Black political leaders established the South African Native National Congress in 1912, a forerunner to the African National Congress (ANC), to protest against such measures.

During World War I, South Africa, as part of the British Empire, was at war with Germany, and invaded German South West Africa (later Namibia). White Afrikaners tried to exploit this opportunity to win back their country but failed. Between the World Wars, the country was ruled by an Afrikaner-dominated government. The ANC continued to peacefully protest, with little success.

Once World War II began, the Union voted to support the British by a small majority; many Afrikaners openly supported Nazi Germany. The National Party won the 1948 election on the platform of pro-apartheid policies, the cornerstone of which, the 1950 Population Registration Act, classified all South Africans according to race and established separate schools, universities, residential areas, and public facilities.

Opposition to Apartheid

The government in turn introduced severe penalties for opposition to apartheid and banned the ANC and Pan Africanist Congress (PAC)—a faction of the ANC, which went underground or into exile.

ANC leaders, Nelson Mandela among them, were arrested in 1952 and, after a lengthy detention and trial, sentenced to life imprisonment on Robben Island in 1964.

By the mid-1970s the anti-apartheid struggle was revived, aided by condemnation from other countries, including South Africa's neighbors, who were no longer sympathetic to the white regime. In 1976 several thousand black African schoolchildren marched through the township of Soweto to protest Afrikaans becoming the language of instruction. During what became known as the Soweto Uprising, police opened fire on the crowds, killing between 200 and 500 people and injuring thousands. After this, the government was increasingly forced to rely on force to crush resistance and impose order; it never fully regained control.

By the 1980s, international condemnation of, and reaction to, apartheid had reached fever pitch: celebrities avoided South Africa, its sports teams were shunned abroad, and U.S. college students held rallies demanding that their universities divest their assets from the country. Despite this, the government continued to arrest South African journalists, students, and other opponents, detaining them without trial. Prominent apartheid opponents were killed in neighboring countries. However, sanctions, boycotts, strikes, and campaigns by the liberation organizations were damaging the economy, and business began to be badly affected.

The Dawn of Democracy

F. W. de Klerk became president of South Africa in December 1989, and in his first speech to Parliament two months after his election, he made the unexpected and astonishing announcement: Mandela and other political prisoners were to be released and the ANC and PAC were to be unbanned. Talks began between government and the liberation movements, although racial tensions remained. In 1994, South Africa had its first democratic election, and Mandela became president. It was a time of great joy and exultation for many, and South Africa rejoined the rest of the world on the political stage, resuming full participation in the United Nations and the Commonwealth, and sending its first racially integrated team to the Olympics.

A government-appointed panel called the Truth and Reconciliation Commission, headed by Desmond Tutu, an Anglican archbishop, began public hearings across the country to probe human-rights violations during the apartheid years. People could talk about their experiences, and the full extent of apartheid atrocities came to light; many considered this to be an important healing process.

Mandela was succeeded in 1999 by Thabo Mbeki, a Sussex (UK) university-educated intellectual who continued to guide the transformation process from a white-dominated, apartheid government to a democratic one.

The Present

In 2008, the populist Jacob Zuma became leader of the ANC and succeeded Mbeki as president in 2009. South Africans hope for continued progress toward a better future under Zuma—and that his populist utterances will translate into action that will improve the lives of people, the majority of whom still live in poverty. Despite South Africa's modern economy, prosperous gold and diamond mines, and the export of raw materials, the country continues to face numerous problems, including an unskilled labor force, a threat to media freedom, failing infrastructure, violent crime, chronic unemployment, and the highest rate of HIV infection in the world. A symbol of Zuma's rule has been the country's increasing closeness to China; the Dalai Lama was refused entry (for the second time) into South Africa in late 2014 because it would irritate the Chinese. As a sign of the country's "development" since the end of apartheid, former archbishop Desmond Tutu—the same who rallied against apartheid—has become the Zuma government's most vociferous critic.

IF YOU LIKE

Drop-Dead Luxury

Not into roughing it? No problem. Our favorite luxe properties will tempt you to defect from the real world and live like kings and queens.

Bushmans Kloof Wilderness Reserve, Western Cape. This Relais & Châteaux lodge is one of South Africa's gems. Set in a phenomenal, otherworldly mountain landscape, it offers beautiful views of nature, wildlife, and birdlife, as well as proximity to the country's finest collections of Bushman rock art found in the mountains.

Lion Sands, Sabi Sands Reserve. Family-owned and family-operated for more than 80 years, the camp, which sits across the Sabi River from Kruger National Park, guarantees awesome animal sightings from just about every vantage point, including your plush king-size bed. Your every need will be catered to from the moment you arrive.

One&Only Cape Town. In the heart of the V&A Waterfront, the hotel's large rooms, swimming pool, name-brand restaurants, and view of Table Mountain remain part of this experience.

Rovos Rail, Cape Town, Johannesburg, and Durban. Some travelers just can't bear to stay put when on a journey. For them, Rovos Rail's plush cars are the best way to stay pampered while on the move.

Tswalu Kalahari Reserve, Northern Cape. Big skies, superb accommodation, wonderful wildlife, and miles from anyone else—this, plus the fact that it's owned by the Oppenheimers, distinguishes it from most other game lodges. Unique belongs here, the largest private game reserve in South Africa.

Rubbing Shoulders with Locals

South Africa's rich cultural offerings run from the rhythms of Soweto to the jazz riffs of Cape Town's clubs. Crafts, drama, and dance combine to form the rich cultural mosaic of South Africa, where native beats mingle with European traditions. Step out like a local, or visit some locals and soak it in.

Cape Town Stadium. For a soccer or rugby match or even a music concert, this is one of the country's best places to meet South Africans. In fact, any of the country's stadiums built for the FIFA 2010 World Cup are excellent.

Jazz Tours, Cape Town. Join like-eared aficionados for a tour that will show you the roots of jazz and expose you to some local ear candy.

Jazzart Dance Theatre, Cape Town. The country's oldest modern dance company has a range of programs and teaches in disadvantaged communities.

Kirstenbosch National Botanical Gardens, Cape Town. The 1,304 acres feature indigenous southern African plants that captivate even the locals. Come for lawn picnics in the shadow of Table Mountain, and stay to listen to the Winter Concert Series.

Market Theatre, Johannesburg. With its rich legacy, this is one of the country's renowned venues, and showcases new works. During the era of apartheid it was one of South Africa's only venues where all races could watch together.

Sisal Cooperative, Madikwe. Learn how locals turn sisal fiber into acid-free paper used for colorful gift tags and cards in this workshop adjacent to a mill.

The Beach

South Africa's coastline stretches from tiny towns to desolate windswept acres, and most beach lovers can find exactly what they're after, be it a private cove or an endless stretch of sand.

Boulders Beach, Simon's Town, Cape Peninsula. The sparkling coves ringed by dramatic boulders are also home to a colony of seriously threatened African penguins. Share your spot in the sand with these curious creatures; it's quite unique.

Camps Bay, Cape Town. A broad Atlantic beach backed by looming Table Mountain and a street full of umbrella-shaded cafés is the perfect place to watch a sunset or take a stroll. But it's a bit too cold for swimming.

Lookout Beach, Plettenberg Bay. Washed away (literally) a few years ago, it's back. South Africa's ultimate playtime beach has perfect bodysurfing waves, with dolphins often joining in, not to mention the most awesome, mountain-fringed setting.

Rocktail Bay, KwaZulu-Natal. If you're in the mood for pristine beaches, surf fishing, snorkeling, or sunbathing, then coming to the lodge nestled on the Maputaland Coastal Reserve that will surely be the perfect beach getaway after your safari.

St. James, Cape Town. Just south of Kalk Bay's shops, St. James's colorful changing cabanas are photo icons. The gentle surf and tidal pool on False Bay are perfect for kids.

Second Beach, Port St Johns, Eastern Cape. Probably the country's most picture-perfect subtropical beach, fringed by bush and hills, this is for the adventurous—but it's so very worth it.

Getting Out of the Vehicle

Game drives are thrilling and often action packed, but sometimes, particularly if you are a second-time visitor to Africa and have ticked off your Big Five, you'll be interested in the more interactive aspect of safari, getting up close and personal with the African bush and its inhabitants. Here are some of the best ways to really get down to nature.

Elephant Safaris. Whether people should ride elephants is the subject of debate, but if you prefer your wildlife a bit more tame, visit the Addo Elephant Sanctuary, where you'll meet some trained African elephants available for short rides, walks, petting, and feeding.

Rhino Tracking. Seeing a rhino on foot is quite a different experience from viewing one from a jeep. Depending on your level of interest, you can organize a walking safari within a special area of Kruger for several hours or several days. Along the way, the guide will point out interesting grasses and smaller animals.

Stargazing Safaris. Ask if your lodge has a guide trained in astronomy for a night safari of the Southern Hemisphere's sky. The west is best, but Sutherland in the Northern Cape may be a highlight.

Turtle-Watching. From St. Lucia to Kosi Bay, join a safari to look for loggerhead and leatherback turtles laying their eggs for a few months starting in October.

Walking Safaris. For some, feeling the grass on their legs and hearing the rustle under their feet is the best way to experience the land. Amble with trained guides for several hours to gain a new perspective on creatures large and small—you may spot the "little five" up close in many locations throughout the country.

Kid-Friendly Destinations

More and more families want their kids to share in their safari experience, and more lodges are catering to kids with programs designed especially for them. Always find out in advance which camps welcome kids, as some still won't allow children under 12. You can try for one of the malaria-free reserves to avoid the added worry of antimalarial medication, although that will restrict your options.

Berg-en-Dal Rest Camp, Kruger National Park. This is a government-operated camp, so there are no children's programs. However, kids can explore in safety at this attractive, fenced camp, which has a great pool and curio shop. Get them to walk around the camp's perimeter and spot game.

Jaci's Lodges, Madikwe. This could well be the original lodge to have made an art of child-friendly safaris (after 9/11, because of the slump in global travel, many lodges started inviting children). Jaci van Heterem celebrates children with jungle drives for the littlest adventurers and family drives for Mom and Dad, too.

Pafuri Camp, Kruger National Park. This lovely camp in Kruger's far north has a superb children's program and special family accommodations that give everybody privacy. It's close to Crooks Corner, where baddies-on-the-run used to hide.

Phinda Reserve, KwaZulu-Natal. Staff are dedicated to entertaining children at this excellent game lodge. The kids even get to make pizzas in the kitchen.

Sanbona Wildlife Reserve. Great for families, Gondwana Lodge inside the reserve is dedicated to children. It's the sort of place where children yelping at dinner isn't frowned upon. There's a wonderful playroom, and it's excellent for younger kids.

Game-Viewing at Smaller Reserves

Kruger Park may well be the granddaddy of game-viewing in South Africa, but smaller reserves attract visitors seeking boutique accommodations, a special sense of place, or a particular type of game.

Kwandwe Private Game Reserve. Excellent, especially for nocturnal wildlife, this reserve is close to the Fish River Valley near Grahamstown. Clean, modern lines take the place of animal skins and trophies in the lodge.

MalaMala, Mpumalanga. Retaining that genuine bushveld feel of bygone days, MalaMala, which adjoins Kruger National Park, is the largest privately owned Big Five game area in South Africa. The animal-viewing is unbeatable, probably because it was the first of the lodges in the Sabi Sands, and animals have learned historical familiarity.

Mattanu Private Game Reserve, Northern Cape. This small reserve—once a farm—was established in the early 1990s to breed rare and endangered antelope species from Zimbabwe. It has offered accommodations since 2006.

Phinda Reserve, KwaZulu-Natal. Seven ecosystems, superb, varied accommodations, and a wide variety of wildlife draw animal lovers to this luxurious retreat, which offers everything from glass-enclosed suites in the forest to a family lodge with a private butler and chef.

FLAVORS OF SOUTH AFRICA

South Africa's rich cultural legacy comes alive on the plate, in the array of flavors and tastes influenced by the mélange of people who have made South Africa their home, as well as in the global cuisine that has arrived with international chefs settling here in the past two decades. Local restaurants score well in global awards and subscribe to the highest food-safety standards.

BBQ Traditions

South Africans love to *braai* (rhymes with rye)—that is, barbecue—at any opportunity. In black townships, literally hundreds of people meet and socialize around an outdoor fire at recreational sites after purchasing meat from nearby butchers and drinks from a corner *shebeen* (neighborhood tavern). But it's in the homes of South Africans that the braai comes to life.

Boerewors (pronounced boo-rah-vors)—beef-and-pork sausage with heady doses of coriander seed, lamb chops, and chicken pieces—is a braai staple. *Sosaties* (so-*sah*-teez), skewers of meat with fruit or vegetables, are also popular. Potatoes and sweet potatoes, known as *patats* (pah-*tutzz*), are often wrapped in foil and cooked among the coals. Rooster*Brood* (roosta-brewat) are sandwiches (typically onion and tomato) cooked on the fire to the perfect consistency: crisp on the outside, moist on the inside. A *potjie* (poy-kee) is a three-legged cast-iron pot as well as the name of the dish typically prepared in it: meat on the bone is layered with vegetables (potatoes, onions, garlic, dried beans) and cooked over low coals for hours (think paella).

During the grape harvest (March and April) a soft, sweet bread is made from the grape must. Called *mosbolletjies*

(*mohss*-ball-eh-keys), it's irresistible if purchased fresh from the oven.

Indigenous South African Dishes

Pap (pronounced pup; also known as *samp*) is made from maize meal and cooked to varying consistencies—*krummel* (*kruh*-muhl) is dry and crumbly, whereas *stywe* (*stay*-ver) is like a stiff porridge. A staple, it's served alongside stewed vegetables or meats and is extremely filling. The texture is like couscous, and the flavor is mild enough that it goes with everything. Other vegetables abundant in South African recipes include gem squash, butternut squash, pumpkin, green beans, tomatoes, and cabbage. You may also come across the following confusing terms: rocket (arugula), peppadew (a cross between a pepper and cherry tomato), or *waterblommetjiebredie* (literally flower stew, made from the buds of a Western Cape flower).

For dessert expect *malva* (muhl-vah) pudding, its sweet and sour notes created by pouring an apricot-jam-and-vinegar sauce over sponge cake. *Melktert* (melk-tet) is a thick custard typically dusted with cinnamon or nutmeg. *Koeksisters* (cook-sis-ter) is braided sweet dough boiled in cinnamon-spiced syrup (finger-shape coconut doughnuts available at Cape Malay restaurants or at carnivals are also called koeksisters).

Immigrant Influences

Despite the name, the cuisine of Cape Town's Malay community is not Malaysian, but instead mixes the flavors, spices, and preparations of Indonesia, China, Africa, and Europe. *Bobotie*, curried, chopped beef with raisins, topped with a savory custard mixture, most closely resembles English shepherd's pie—with a kick. *Bredie* is another way of saying stew and is often made with tomatoes. You'll find *samoosas* (samosas—pronounced sah-*moo*-sah here) at every corner café. *Rootis* (rotis—pronounced *root*-ee), a soft, griddled flatbread, when filled with curry-mince is called a *salomi* (pronounced sah-*low*-me). The Gatsby is a long roll packed with lettuce, tomatoes, french fries, and melted cheese; a sausage or steak is added and then topped with anything from mayonnaise to *peri-peri* (fiery tomato-and-chili sauce that originated in Mozambique). You will find them at roadside cafés in half or full portions. "Bunny chow," made famous in Durban by indentured Asian laborers who couldn't sit down to eat, is a half or quarter white-bread loaf that's hollowed out, filled with biryani, and capped by the leftover bread. Top your snacks with *chakalaka* (a spicy vegetable relish) or peri-peri, which is perfect with grilled seafood.

Beyond Beef

Similar to beef jerky, biltong is a popular snack that's found just about everywhere from roadside stands to high-end markets. Types range from beef and ostrich to game (kudu is a favorite) and can be flavored with spices. "Wet" biltong is moist (usually beef), whereas game is dry. *Frikkadels,* mini–lamb *rissoles* (small croquettes), are occasionally wrapped in cabbage leaves and flavored with nutmeg, reminiscent of Eastern European stuffed cabbage dishes or the little Greek meatballs called *keftedes*.

Many restaurants serve game such as ostrich and springbok but also wildebeest, impala, and kudu. Karoo lamb is the most delicious lamb you will find, on account of the wild herbs the animals eat in the arid Karoo region. The meat has an almost perfumed quality to it.

Succulent Seafood

In a country surrounded on three sides by water, it's no surprise that a major source of protein comes from the sea. As with the rest of the world, local fish stocks are under tremendous threat, and every decent seafood restaurant will have a sustainable-seafood guide, explaining what on the menu is okay to eat. Once used as bait, rock lobster (also known as crayfish) is now highly sought after and closely resembles New England lobster. Costly perlemoen, or abalone, which is almost on the brink of extinction, is tough and best described as similar to calamari steak. Local fish include kingklip (a firm white fish), hake (a flaky, white fish called haddock once smoked), and snoek (pronounced snook), an oily fish with many long bones. Line-caught fish includes Cape salmon (also known as *geelbek*), which isn't salmon at all but is sure to be on the menu. You may come across *kabeljou* (*cabal*-yoh), also known as kob, a flaky fish similar to kingklip. Tuna is often seared; it's divine with a pepper crust. Unexpectedly, the best seafood can be found in landlocked Johannesburg, as merchants send their best quality to the biggest market.

Eating on Safari

Since most, if not all, of the ingredients must be flown in or grown locally in small quantities, you might expect meals to be limited. However, you'll usually have a choice of entrée options (two to three), and you'll be amazed at the delicious and innovative creations that come out of the kitchen. You'll also have plenty of opportunity to try new varieties of fish or game and South African wines. Breads and pastries are generally fresh baked, and any dietary concerns are catered to if possible. Don't be surprised if you gain a few pounds. It's not unheard of to eat six or seven times a day. Dining is truly a pastime on safari. Stopping for coffee and rusks (rustic biscotti, which often include raisins and seed kernels) under an acacia tree, with wild animals surrounding you, is a morning game-drive highlight.

Taste at Your Own Risk

Odd-sounding treats are often presented on a township tour. Two of the most common are *smileys* (sheep's heads cooked in the fire) and *walkie-talkies*, which, appropriately enough, are made from chicken heads and feet. You may also be offered Mopane worms, a tofulike, protein-rich staple that tends to take on the taste of other ingredients; it's typically cooked with tomatoes and onions. More Afrikaner than African, *skilpadjies* (skul-*pai*-keys) is calf liver covered by caul fat, and *poffaddertjies* (*pohf*-aader) is liver and kidneys stuffed into a sheep's intestine and cooked on the braai.

Wetting Your Whistle

South Africa's world-renowned wines generally offer great quality for lower prices than those in the U.S. and Europe. Pinotage, a cross between Pinot Noir and Cinsaut, is a native cultivar and widely available. Grassy or mineral-y Sauvignon Blanc is a very good (white meat) food wine, and the newer vineyards that receive ocean breezes (as in False Bay and closer to Agulhas and Elgin) are comparable to New Zealand's best. Local Cabernet Sauvignon, Shiraz, and Pinot Noir have been excelling in international competitions.

Much as in wine-growing regions from California to Australia and New Zealand, the dining emphasis is on the freshest greens, light flavors, and experimental dishes that complement the relaxed atmosphere. Many vineyards have cafés

attached so you can eat a light meal between tastings if you plan ahead.

South Africans consume more beer than any other nation in Africa; this area was settled by the Dutch, Germans, and English, after all. South African Breweries (SAB Miller) became the world's second-largest brewer when it was bought by Miller of the United States, and controls most of the beer market here, with operations throughout Africa and throughout the world. Its most popular brew is Castle Lager. You'll also find Windhoek lager, a Namibian beer, and a rapidly increasing number of craft beers, mostly in Cape Town but also in Johannesburg and Durban. In fact, the first craft beers were made in the village of Nottingham Road, on KwaZulu-Natal's Midlands Meander. Hunters Gold and Savanna Dry are hard commercial ciders.

South Africans have created a variety of nectars from Muscadels (Muscatels) filled with intense fruits, to creamy liqueurs best served over ice under a full moon. Amarula, South Africa's unique creamy fruit liqueur with the elephant on the label, is popular. Some say it's similar to Bailey's Irish Cream. South Africa's brandy regularly beats cognacs in blind tastings.

Teetotalers might prefer to quaff *rooibos* (pronounced *roy*-boss), the unique South African red bush tea. Ginger beer, a carbonated soft drink, is another tasty option. Appletiser (a pure, unsugared carbonated drink) and LiquiFruit (noncarbonated) are wildly successful exports. Top-quality fruit is always available at supermarkets. The *naartjie* (*nah*-chee) is an easy-peeling small citrus, and melons like *spanspek* (*spun*-speck) and pawpaw (papaya) are available elsewhere and are usually served at breakfast.

GREAT ITINERARIES

SOUTH AFRICA IN 7 DAYS

With only one week, you can still enjoy the best of South Africa, including Johannesburg and Cape Town highlights, as well as a short safari.

3 Days: Kruger National Park

Spend your first afternoon recovering from your international flight by lazing at a luxury lodge, but take a short game drive if one is offered. Meals are all arranged for you, and bedtime is early.

Experience your first full safari on Day 2. A quick caffeine jolt at sunrise before setting out on a game drive (usually with a stop for morning coffee and snack) sets the tone for your stay—you'll love the sheer wildness. Return to the lodge for lunch and a rest during the midday heat. Depending on where you stay, you may be able to arrange for a massage or spa treatment during this time (it helps with the jet lag). After a hearty and proper afternoon tea of sweet and savory options, you're off in the vehicle again. Having sundowner drinks at sunset is an experience you'll never forget. After the evening drive, it's back to the lodge for cleanup, drinks, and dinner, where guests and guides share tales.

You'll fit in a morning game drive before departing the camp on Day 3. Head back to Johannesburg by car so you can stop at the sites along the Mpumalanga Panoramic Route through Blyde Canyon's breathtaking scenery, arriving in Johannesburg late in the day. Shoppers might select a small B&B or guesthouse in the thick of things (for example, the Melville or Parkhurst neighborhoods); those looking for retail therapy will have the Rosebank shopping malls a short drive away. To experience life outside the cloistered environment and walk down a street or sit at a café, Melville is the bohemian choice, whereas Parkhurst tends toward chic shopping and eating.

Logistics: To make the most of your time, take a direct flight from O. R. Tambo Airport to a safari lodge at one of Kruger's fly-in reserves. International flights arrive in the early morning, making it easy to board the daily midmorning South African Airlink flight to an airfield servicing one of the private reserves making up the Greater Kruger National Park, like Timbavati and Sabi Sands. Rent a car for your return trip.

1 Day: Johannesburg

Prearrange a township tour to Soweto to learn about the roots of apartheid and the way entrepreneurs are changing lives within the community. A tour of Alexandra township will be just as informative but off the beaten track. Include a stop at the Apartheid Museum for a full taste of the country's history. Catch a late-afternoon or early-evening flight to Cape Town, where you'll spend the next two nights.

Logistics: Arrange a township tour of your choice in advance; choose a company that offers a pickup at your hotel so you don't have to drive (return the rental car on arrival in Jo'burg and take a taxi to your hotel).

1 Day: Cape Town

You can stay at the V&A Waterfront at one of the numerous hotels, or if you prefer quiet, try something like the historic and beautiful Cellars-Hohenort in the wooded Constantia Valley. Whichever you choose, dinner will feature Table Mountain looming behind you.

On the following morning, take the first boat to Robben Island to see where Nelson

Mandela spent decades, and inhale that bracing, fresh sea air. When you return, grab a taxi to the base of Table Mountain and ride up on the cable car for magnificent views. You can walk a few miles on one of the trails up there to stretch your legs. If you're a shopper, you could spend the rest of the afternoon browsing African curios in Greenmarket Square and then grab a snack in one of the bohemian Long Street cafés. The Cape Quarter in Greenpoint offers more chic shopping and cafés. Alternatively, you could rent a car to visit Kirstenbosch National Botanical Gardens to see magnificent protea plants—the national flower—and views (in summer there are concerts on the lawns). You may even have time to dip into some nearby wine-tasting rooms before heading to Camps Bay for sunset cocktails and a light dinner, followed by a stroll along the beach.

Logistics: Your day in Cape Town will be busy and hectic; be sure to plan it in advance, and book a guided tour if possible to maximize your time.

1 Day: Cape Winelands
Head out early to the university town of Stellenbosch, less than an hour from Cape Town, on Day 6. Check out the historic downtown's Cape Dutch architecture

TIPS

■ Think how many times you will visit South Africa: it's probably worth splurging on a luxury fly-in camp in Kruger.

■ In Cape Town, always prepare for sudden weather changes, especially on Table Mountain. A sweater or raincoat is mandatory.

■ Be flexible in your plans; if the morning weather is good, head to the mountain first and do Robben Island in the afternoon. And depending on your time in the city, take the cable car; hiking up affords stunning views but eats up time. Squeezing too much into a CT visit will spoil the experience.

before settling into a typical South African B&B (La Petit Ferme in Franschhoek has standout views). Book some spa time wherever you stay. Stop for some wine tastings at Fairview wine estate toward Paarl or Boschendal, famous for its picnics and Blanc de Noir, just outside Franschhoek to finish off the day.

Logistics: You don't have to rent a car to do this trip, and don't have to spend a night in the Winelands; there are plenty of companies that offer tours that will allow you to taste wines with impunity.

1 Day: Cape Peninsula

Get an early start on your last morning, but there's no point in exhausting yourself. Take in False Bay village gems like Kalk Bay (for its harbor) and Simon's Town for the fantastic penguins at Boulders. Visit Cape Point before finishing up at Cape Town's airport for a flight home that evening.

Logistics: You can do all of this exploring on a guided tour if you don't want to drive yourself.

SOUTH AFRICA IN 10 DAYS

With 10 days you can spend the majority of your time on safari and finish up with highlights of the Cape.

2 Days: Johannesburg

Commence your journey with a didactic experience in the City of Gold. A variety of excellent accommodation and activities are a highlight in this place colloquially known as "Jozi" (or Jo'burg). Many new developments within the central business district, such as the Maboneng precinct, offer a great variety of local eateries and opportunities to walk the city streets, discovering the history and evolution of this rejuvenated South African icon. The museums and outdoor educational tours on offer—from paleo-anthropological interests to South Africa's more modern heritage, including the evolving Soweto and Alexandra townships and a gold-mining experience—are captured in this city. On Day 2, a trip to the Cradle of Humankind would also be worthwhile.

Logistics: Don't drive in Johannesburg. You can do all your local exploring on guided tours, which will maximize your time and your safety. But do rent a car and drive to Madikwe. It's only three hours on good roads; alternatively, you can arrange a transfer.

2 Days: Madikwe Game Reserve

Madikwe Game Reserve on the border with Botswana is smaller than Kruger National Park but still large. Additionally, it was one of the largest relocation projects in South Africa's conservation history and offers a slightly different safari experience. The camps are all private, but this is still Big Five country and offers a wider variety of birdlife and varying accommodation options, all within a significant landscape. Spend the early afternoon of your arrival day visiting a community program just outside the reserve's gates, then relax and enjoy the still air and hot breeze of the middle of the day from a private balcony or a luxury lodge's plunge pool. Night drives may bring out the elusive leopard or lions feasting on a kill. Go on a morning safari on your second day before heading to Kruger that afternoon, with an overnight en route in Dullstroom, which is in misty-morning highland trout country with excellent accommodation and a beautiful change in landscape. The early part of the drive will give you views of contemporary African villages in the country's platinum-mining belt, as well as the distant Waterberg and Pilanesberg ranges, which add awesome vistas to the drive.

Logistics: It's a long trip to Kruger from Madikwe, so if you don't want to drive, you may want to return to Jo'burg and fly to Kruger so you can have three nights there.

3 Days: Kruger National Park

If you decided to stop over in Nelspruit or elsewhere, rise early on Day 5, so you can meander through the scenic Blyde River Canyon with views of the distant eastern Drakensberg Range. Consider visiting the Three Rondavels and God's Window, a lookout where you can see clear to Mozambique some days. Stop for lunch in quaint Pilgrim's Rest, a former mining town. Remember to get through Kruger's gates long before sundown (check times) so you can settle in at your accommodation and avoid the fines for driving after dark. Choose either a national park accommodation (there are some awesome locations) or a luxury lodge—which number in the hundreds and offer the options of spas, walking safaris, and local community interaction in addition to game drives—or split your stay.

On your first full day in Kruger, take an organized guided trip at a rest camp to get your bearings and learn how to spot game. Book a dinner at a *boma* under the stars or a stargazing safari for a memorable only-in-Africa experience. Your final day should be spent exploring the park in detail, viewing your favorite animals for as long as you wish.

TIPS

■ Three nights inside a park or reserve allows you much more flexibility to relax and take in the experience. If you stay two nights at a game lodge, you'll have at most four drives.

■ You can split your stay between more than one lodge in Kruger, but the best plan is to base yourself in one place and visit others during the day.

■ This is a country laced with adventure, so don't be afraid to make an unexpected stop or just enjoy the countryside on the long drive from Madikwe.

Logistics: It's a nine-hour drive from Madikwe to Kruger along the more direct N4. In less than seven hours (without stops) you can get to Nelspruit. It's only about two hours from Nelspruit to Pilgrim's Rest, but leave plenty of time to watch the scenery, and stop frequently for the views. It's a long trip back to Jo'burg by car; rather, drop your car off in Nelspruit and fly back.

3 Days: Cape Town

After arriving in Cape Town and dropping your bags, you should have enough time for a stroll along the Mouille Point promenade or around the Waterfront harbor precinct, followed by a sundowner or a sunset cruise. If you choose sightseeing, book dinner at any excellent city restaurant (the V&A Waterfront by night lacks soul). You can shop late in the arts-and-crafts collective, which benefits local artists. For a low-key option, dine next to the beach at the foot of the Twelve Apostles mountain range.

Head out early on the next morning to see the highlights outside of town. The funicular and beaches at Cape Point demand a visit (but don't feed the baboons; it makes them aggressive and can end badly). Simon's Town is a beautiful period-piece village, with many hidden, niche attractions (like a brilliant toy museum). Stop for fish-and-chips in Kalk Bay. Finish your long day with a walk along the long beach at Camps Bay and dinner at one of the many establishments across the road.

On your final day, plan to visit both Table Mountain and Robben Island. Lace up your hiking shoes and fit in enough walking before your lengthy flight home. There's no better place to do it.

Logistics: Whether driving or flying, make sure you get back to Johannesburg in time for an early-afternoon flight to Cape Town. For convenience, base yourself at a V&A Waterfront hotel in Cape Town, or if you want a more relaxing experience, get a hotel in Camps Bay in the Southern Suburbs. If you don't want to rent a car in Cape Town, there are plenty of tour companies to show you the Cape Peninsula and the city. Most flights to the United States leave in the early evening, so you can have a full day of sightseeing before your departure.

SOUTH AFRICA IN TWO WEEKS

Depending on where your inbound flight lands, you can begin or end with Cape Town. Most long-haul flights allow you to start and end wherever you wish.

4 Days: Cape Town and Environs

In four days, you can enjoy Cape Town's attractions at a leisurely pace. Take two days to explore the city's outdoor spaces and fabulous markets. Live music and laid-back days are enjoyed in most open spaces in summer—including the almost legendary Kirstenbosch National Botanical Gardens on the backside of Table Mountain, and the Company's Garden in the city center—surrounded by museums and the anti-apartheid political landmark, St. George's Cathedral.

On Day 3, get an early start and take a day-pack hike, allowing you to take in the scenery of Table Mountain and recharge, far away from a car. If you don't do Table Mountain, Lions Head is a good option if time is tight, because both offer spectacular views. Lunch could be a leisurely picnic on the lawn of the Roundhouse in the Glen, right below Lions Head, overlooking Camps Bay. Then try a restaurant along the Mouille Point promenade for dinner. Use Day 4 to make a full loop of the Cape Peninsula, heading out of town through Hout Bay, over Chapman's Peak Drive (one of the world's most spectacular), then making for Simon's Town for a walk along the boardwalk among the penguins at Boulders Beach. Be sure to make it to Cape Point for a walk around Cape Peninsula National Park.

Logistics: If you don't want to drive yourself around Cape Town, then tours can get you to all the same places. For a longer stay, pick a more relaxing location for your hotel than the V&A Waterfront. There are plenty of inviting guesthouses and B&Bs.

3 Days: The Garden Route via the Cape Winelands

Heading out from Cape Town on Day 5 you'll have plenty of time to linger over culinary tastings in Stellenbosch, dine on gourmet French food in Franschhoek, and stroll alongside Paarl's mix of Cape Dutch, Edwardian, Victorian, and art deco architecture lining the main street. With so many excellent guesthouses to choose from, part of the fun is deciding which fantasy accommodation suits you best (and in which town)—from tranquil lakeside to mountain or historic main street cottages in Stellenbosch, Paarl, or Franschhoek.

Begin Day 6 with a drive to Hermanus for lunch, where you can watch whales from the shore—or if your sea legs are up to it, try a little shark-cage diving around the corner in Gansbaai. Spend the night in remarkable accommodation at the scenic Grootbos Private Nature Reserve.

Next day, head for Africa's southern-most point, Cape Agulhas, also called the Cape of Storms, with its own standout vineyards and shipwreck history. Five

TIPS

■ You know it already, but don't cram in too much. If you have two weeks, savor what you do rather than rushing to your next appointment. Even if it's your first visit, you'll likely be back.

■ Read up on your next destination. There's a compelling history behind every place you visit.

■ Walk as much as you can. Moving slowly (not driving) allows you to take in this new experience.

minutes around the corner from the rocks is Stilbaai, with 30 km (19 miles) of empty sandy beaches, gentle surf, and seafood. Spend the night in Knysna or Plettenberg Bay. The former is packed with history, standout golf courses, forest, and water sports; the latter has some of the best swimming beaches in the country, framed by mountain ranges and the ocean.

Logistics: Rent a car in Cape Town for the remainder of your trip. You could accomplish everything with guided tours, but it's nicer to go at your own pace.

5 Days: Eastern Cape Safari Parks

An early start from your accommodation will see you cruise past the turnoff to the surfing mecca of Jeffreys Bay as you make your way to the outskirts of Port Elizabeth. The remaining time is for winding down in sublime surroundings. Spend them between the Addo National Elephant Park, where you will overnight and where you're bound to see some of the best elephant activity on offer, and Samara Game Reserve, a little more than two hours inland outside the beautiful historic Karoo town of Graaff-Reinet. Samara is a remarkable reserve that has reclaimed old farming land and been restocked with indigenous game since it was purchased. It has a standout cheetah-monitoring program and employs locals. The privacy and accommodation are as good as it gets (and don't forget the resident rhino population).

Logistics: Spend two nights in Gorah Elephant Camp in Addo, and two more nights in Samara Game Reserve.

2 Days: Johannesburg

After your Eastern Cape safari, you'll be relaxed and ready to head to Johannesburg, Africa's shopping mecca, for two final days of exploring. Visit the Maboneng precinct, see the city's exciting rejuvenation, watch some theater, and take a quad bike through Soweto—with both days accompanied by excellent food. It's a fine way to complete a fantastic trip to South Africa.

Logistics: It's a two-hour drive back to Port Elizabeth, where you board a flight to Johannesburg for two final nights. There, you can see everything on guided tours.

CAPE TOWN
AND PENINSULA

Updated by
Angus Begg
and Lee
Middleton

A favorite South African topic of debate is whether Cape Town really is part of Africa. That's how different it is, both from the rest of the country and the rest of the continent. And therein lies its attraction. South Africa's most urbane, sophisticated city sits in stark contrast to the South Africa north of the Hex River Valley. Here, the traffic lights work pretty much consistently and good restaurants are commonplace. In fact, dining establishments in the so-called Mother City always dominate the country's "best of" lists.

What also distinguishes this city is its deep sense of history. Nowhere else in the country will you find structures dating back to the 17th century. South Africa as it is known today began here. Elegant Cape Dutch buildings abut ornate Victorian structures and imposing British monuments. In the predominantly Malay Bo-Kaap neighborhood, the call to prayer echoes through cobbled streets lined with houses painted in bright pastels, and the sweet tang of Malay curry wafts through the air. Flower sellers, newspaper hawkers, and numerous markets keep street life pulsing, and every lamppost advertises another festival, concert, or cultural happening. This is a relaxed city, packed with occasions and events.

What you'll ultimately recall about this city depends on your taste. It could be the Cape Winelands over *the* mountain, the Waterfront shopping (a consistent winner, given exchange rates favoring virtually any foreign currency), or Table Mountain itself. Thoroughly imposing, presiding over the city as it does, the mountain is dramatic, with a chain of "sister" mountains leading from the Table to Cape Point (roughly 68 km/42 miles south) cascading into the sea in dramatic visual fashion. Francis Drake wasn't exaggerating when he said this was "the fairest Cape we saw in the whole circumference of the earth," and he would have little cause to change his opinion today.

A visit to Cape Town is synonymous with a visit to the peninsula south of the city, and for good reason. With pristine white-sand beaches, hundreds of mountain trails, and numerous activities from surfing to paragliding to mountain biking, the accessibility, variety, and pure beauty of the great outdoors will keep nature lovers and outdoor adventurers occupied for hours, if not days. A week exploring just the city and peninsula is barely enough.

Often likened to San Francisco, Cape Town has two things that the former doesn't: Table Mountain and Africa. The mountain, or tabletop, is vital to Cape Town's identity. It dominates the city in a way that's difficult to comprehend until you visit. In the afternoon, when creeping fingers of clouds spill over Table Mountain and reach toward the city, the whole town seems to hold its breath—because in summer it

TOP REASONS TO GO

City Sophistication. Cape Town is a cosmopolitan city with a rich heritage that's proudly on display. It might be more laid-back than Johannesburg, but it has shaken off its sleepy, parochial air and now bristles with world-class shops and restaurants and cutting-edge art and design.

Table Mountain. Fantastic Table Mountain towers over Cape Town and dominates the whole peninsula. Exploring the mountain is a must; you can either take the cable car to the top or hike up various routes. It's not a particularly difficult climb, but having an athletic frame will help you pull and scramble up the odd steep bit, and there are easy routes, too.

Nature's Playground. Capetonians are proud of their city's stylish good looks and make the most of the mountain and beaches. In summer you'll find professionals shrugging off their suits as they head for the beach after work, surfboards, picnics, and sundowner drinks in tow. In winter they bundle up against the cold and go walking, mountain biking, or running in the city's countless green spaces.

Markets Galore. Cape Town's markets are the best in the country—informal, creative, funky, and with a good selection of both tacky and splendid African curios. The Old Biscuit Mill is all about designer food, and the Oranjezicht City Farm Market is a community garden in the midst of established, well-to-do suburbs right below the mountain.

Historical Heritage. Cape Town is saturated with an extremely rich and fascinating history. At Robben Island you can stand in Nelson Mandela's old cell and learn about political and social banishment during apartheid, and the District Six Museum tells the poignant tale of the destruction of one of the country's most vibrant inner-city neighborhoods. The Castle of Good Hope—the first European building on the continent—is also a remarkable piece of history, with interiors of antique furniture and historic paintings.

brings frequent strong southeasterly winds. Meanwhile, for all of its bon-vivant European vibe, Cape Town also reflects the diversity, vitality, and spirit of Africa, with many West and Central Africans and Zimbabweans—many of them having fled from conflicts elsewhere—calling this city home.

ORIENTATION AND PLANNING

GETTING ORIENTED

Cape Town lies at the northern end of the Cape Peninsula, a 75-km (47-mile) tail of mountains that ends at the Cape of Good Hope. Drive 15 minutes out of town, and you may lose yourself in a stunning landscape of 18th-century Cape Dutch manors, historic wineries, and white-sand beaches backed by sheer mountains.

Everyone uses Table Mountain for orientation. Cape Town's aptly named heart, the City Bowl, fills the basin between the lower northern slopes of the mountain and the rim of a busy harbor. Though it's called interchangeably "City Centre" or "Cape Town Central," the City Bowl actually encompasses Cape Town Central as well as adjacent neighborhoods of Gardens and Bo-Kaap. Cape Town is compact, and neighborhood boundaries can be fluid, but navigation is generally not a problem.

Cape Town Central. Cape Town's central business district is bounded by Buitenkant Street to the east, Buitengracht Street to the west, and the Company's Garden to the south is and the Foreshore to the north. Included in this district is the standout CT International Convention Centre (CTICC), the head offices of banks and big businesses, Parliament, the central railway and bus stations, some great architecture, and a good number of tourist attractions.

> ## CAPE TOWN ADDRESSES
>
> Street signs in Cape Town alternate between English and Afrikaans. For example, *Wale* is English and *Waal* is Afrikaans, but they mean the same thing. In Afrikaans you don't put a space between the name and the street. So an address could be Orange Street or Oranjestraat. Kaapstad is Afrikaans for Cape Town. Increasingly, streets are renamed after heroes of the struggle or with African-language names.

Woodstock. Cape Town's booming creative hub, close to the city center, has good restaurants and the city's trendiest weekend market.

Bo-Kaap. Gracing the lower slopes of Signal Hill, wedged between the hill, De Waterkant, and Cape Town Central, this small City Bowl neighborhood is the historic home of the city's Muslim population and remains so to this day. Its main thoroughfare is Wale Street.

Gardens. This neighborhood is a mix of residential, entertainment, and shopping. It begins at the southern end of the Company's Garden, stretching south toward the base of Table Mountain and Lion's Head. Most shops and restaurants are centered on Kloof Street.

Tamboerskloof. A popular area beneath Signal Hill is filled with coffee shops, restaurants, and boutiques down toward Kloof Road.

Oranjezicht. Right below the Table Mountain massif, this area in the middle of the City Bowl is home to the trendy Oranjezicht community farmers' market, a few cafés, and De Waal Park.

V&A Waterfront. Once a seedy harbor, the V&A (Victoria & Alfred) Waterfront, often simply referred to as the Waterfront, is described by at least one data-capturing source as South Africa's most popular tourist destination. Nowadays, this commercial area between the bay and Table Mountain is a top spot for restaurants, bars, and upscale residential buildings. Cruises out onto Table Bay depart from here.

Green Point. The gay hot spot is home to the iconic Cape Town stadium and the neighboring Green Point Common.

Mouille Point. Cape Town's iconic lighthouse sits on the wonderful promenade lined with cafés and restaurants.

Sea Point. Lovely promenades, good restaurants, and large, grassy recreational areas make up Sea Point.

Clifton. This elite beachside residential area is fronted by granite rock formations that extend all the way to Llandudno.

Camps Bay. A wide, popular beach sits across the road from the city's trendiest café strip.

Table Mountain National Park. Running north–south through the Cape Peninsula from Cape Town, Table Mountain National Park's 220 square km (85 square miles) include Table Mountain itself, most of the high-lying land in the mountain chain that runs down the center of the peninsula from Table Mountain south, the Cape of Good Hope nature reserve at the peninsula's end, and the stunning scenery and beaches in between. The park is bordered by the Atlantic Ocean to the west and False Bay to the east.

Southern Suburbs. Southeast of the City Bowl and at the base of Table Mountain's "backside" are the mainly residential neighborhoods known collectively as the Southern Suburbs, where the fantastic Kirstenbosch National Botanical Gardens is located, along with a few other worthwhile attractions.

Cape Peninsula. The Cape Peninsula, much of which is included in Table Mountain National Park, extends for around 40 km (25 miles) from the city through to Cape Point. The peninsula's eastern border is False Bay, whose Indian Ocean waters are (relatively) warmer and calmer than those of the peninsula's wilder, emptier, and arguably more beautiful Atlantic side. A coastal road and railway line connects east-coast towns.

PLANNING

WHEN TO GO

Whatever activities you hope to accomplish in Cape Town, head up Table Mountain as soon as the wind isn't blowing. Cape Town wind is notorious, and the mountain can be shut for days on end when there are gales. Summer (October–March) is the windiest time of the year, and from December to April winds can reach 60 km (37 miles) an hour. But they will often happen in the winter months, too—just less frequently. If you're planning to visit Robben Island during peak season, it's also wise to book well in advance. One of the best months to visit is April, when the heat and wind have abated and the Cape is bathed in warm autumnal hues. Winter rains can put off visitors, but this time of the year holds its own surprises: the countryside is a brilliant green, and without fail the best sunny and temperate days come between the rainy spells. Whales are seen in False Bay in spring (late August to early September), when wildflowers are also in bloom.

EVENTS

Cape Minstrel Carnival. One of the greatest celebrations in Cape Town is the annual Cape Town Minstrel Carnival. The origins of this January festival date to the early colonial period, when this was the one day of the year that slaves were given time off. The tradition continued even after the emancipation of slaves and is the most visible reminder of a way of life that saw its finest flowering in District Six. Today thousands of wild celebrants take to the streets in vibrant costumes—complete with matching umbrellas—to sing *moppies* (pronounced a somewhat guttural *more peas*, they're vaudeville-style songs), accompanied by banjos, drums, and whistles. The celebration lasts one or two days.

Cape Town International Jazz Festival. Music, especially jazz and local African music, was an extremely potent instrument for social change during the oppressive apartheid regime. Consequently, South Africans are passionate about music, and they celebrate their love of jazz with the Cape Town International Jazz Festival, usually held in March or early April. Started in 1999, this event is arguably the best weekend of the year in Cape Town. There's an even mix of local and international stars, and past festivals have included the likes of Randy Crawford, Abdullah Ibrahim, Hugh Masekela, Ismael Lo, Earth, Wind & Fire and Ladysmith Black Mambazo. ⊕ *www.capetownjazzfest.com.*

Kirstenbosch Summer Sunset Concerts. From late November to early April, enjoy the best in South African music, from African to classical to electronica, at outdoor concerts on Sundays at Kirstenbosch Summer Sunset Concerts. It's a Cape Town summer institution, not to be missed. ⊠ *Kirstenbosch National Botanic Gardens, Rhodes Ave., Newlands* ☏ *021/799–8783* ⊕ *www.dogreatthings.co.za/music/kirstenbosch* 🎫 *R65–R140.*

MCQP (*Mother City Queer Party*). A key event on Cape Town's social calendar is December's MCQP, which started in 1993. Party animals should definitely add this to their must-do list. It's part Mardi Gras, part Gay Pride March, and one enormous fancy-dress party. Each year the party is themed, and everyone goes all out to dress up in fantastic outfits. All are welcome! ⊕ *mcqp.co.za/spacecowboys2013/home.*

GETTING HERE AND AROUND

AIR TRAVEL

Cape Town International Airport is about 19 km (12 miles) from the city center. It should take about 20 minutes to get from the airport to the city; during rush hour it can easily be double that. Private airport-transfer operators abound, and there is now public bus service to and from the airport. All major car-rental companies have counters at Cape Town International, and driving to the City Bowl or V&A Waterfront is straightforward in daylight. If your flight arrives after dark, consider prearranging transportation through your hotel. There are tourist information desks in both the domestic and international terminals. ⇨ *For information about airlines that fly to Cape Town, see Air Travel in Travel Smart.*

Contacts Cape Town International Airport ⊠ *Matroosfontein* ☏ *021/937–1200, 086/727–7888 flight information* ⊕ *www.airports.co.za.*

AIRPORT TRANSFERS

Metered taxis and shuttle services (usually minivans) are based inside the domestic baggage hall and outside the international and domestic terminals and can also be phoned for airport drop-offs. Rates vary depending on the operator, number of passengers, destination, and time of arrival. The fare for one person to the city center is R300 in a metered taxi; a group of up to four will usually pay the same rate. A surcharge of up to R50 is sometimes levied from 10 pm until early morning, and some services charge more for arrivals than for departures to cover waiting time. For single travelers, a prearranged shared shuttle is the most economical, costing about R150–R180 per person; however, there may be numerous drop-offs, so this can be slow. MyCiti, a public bus, also serves the airport, and for R90 it's the cheapest way to or from the airport and City Centre. ⚠ **Reports of overcharging are common, so discuss the fare before entering any taxi.**

Rikkis provides inexpensive, unmetered fares (R220 to City Centre, for example) from the airport. *For contact information, see Taxi Travel.*

Recommendable shared-van services include Legend Tours and Transfers or Magic Bus Airport. Citi Hopper provides both shared-van transfers and private-car transfers.

For the ultimate luxury ride you can hire a six-seat Lincoln stretch limo from Cape Limousine Services. Rates are R1,400 for the first two hours and R200 per hour thereafter (add extra for gas if you travel outside the Cape Town area).

Airport Transfers Cape Limousine Services ☎ *021/785–3100.* **Citi Hopper** ☎ *021/936–3460/1, 082/773–7678* ⊕ *www.citihopper.co.za.* **Legend Tours and Transfers** ☎ *021/704–9140* ⊕ *www.legendtours.co.za.* **Magic Bus Airport Transfers** ☎ *021/505–6300* ⊕ *www.magicbus.co.za.*

BUS TRAVEL

Intercape Mainliner is the main option for Western Cape destinations; Greyhound, Translux/City-to-City, and Baz Bus (popular with backpackers) also provide service. Common routes from Cape Town include Johannesburg and Tshwane, Springbok, Windhoek, George, Port Elizabeth, and Durban. All the main bus companies operate from the bus terminal alongside the central train station on Adderley Street, and most have their offices there. *See Bus Travel in Travel Smart for details on intercity bus companies.*

Within Cape Town, MyCiti bus service now serves the entire city, including the Cape Flats. Buses run at regular 10-minute intervals during peak period (5 am–9 am) and at 20-minute intervals for the rest of the day. The service is perfect for tourists because you can catch a bus into town—a short ride—and from there walk the entire city. Or you can catch a connecting bus almost anywhere, including Hout Bay, the Waterfront, and Blouberg Beach. Only prepaid cards are accepted for MyCiti (get these at kiosks in every station and at some retailers). Timetables are found at each stop and can be scanned for easy reference. These buses run until late in the evening and at R90 provide the cheapest way to get to and from the airport.

Contacts MyCiti ⊕ *myciti.org.za.*

CAR TRAVEL

Although many locals drive, tourists may find public transportation (MyCiti buses) or taxis a better option; save the rental car for when you are getting out of town. Cape Town's roads are excellent, but getting around can be a bit confusing. Signage is inconsistent, switching between Afrikaans and English, between different names for the same road (especially highways), and between different destinations on the same route. Sometimes the signs simply vanish. △ **Cape Town is also littered with signs indicating "Cape Town" instead of "City Centre," as well as "Kaapstad," which is Afrikaans for Cape Town.** A good one-page map is essential and available from car-rental agencies and tourism information desks. Among the hazards are pedestrians running across highways, speeding vehicles, and minibus taxis. Roadblocks for document and DWI checks are also becoming more frequent.

Parking in the city center is a nightmare. There are simply not enough parking garages, longer-stay parking spaces are scarce, and most hotels charge a small fortune for parking. There are numerous pay-and-display (i.e., put a ticket in your windshield) and pay-on-exit parking lots around the city, but parking is strictly enforced. Prices range from R6 to R12 per half hour. For central attractions like Greenmarket Square, the Company's Garden, the South African National Gallery, and the Castle of Good Hope, look for a lot around the Grand Parade on Darling Street. The Sanlam Golden Acre Parking Garage on Adderley Street offers covered parking, as does the Parkade on Strand Street, but Queen Victoria Street alongside the South African Museum (and Company's Garden) is always bound to have a few spaces.

The main arteries leading out of the city are the N1, which bypasses the city's Northern Suburbs en route to Paarl and, ultimately, Johannesburg; and the N2, which heads out past Khayelitsha and through Somerset West to the Overberg and the Garden Route before continuing on through the Eastern Cape to Durban and beyond. Branching off the N1, the N7 goes to Namibia. The M3 splits off from the N2 near Observatory, leading to the False Bay side of the peninsula via Claremont and Constantia; it's the main and quickest route to the beaches of Muizenberg, Kalk Bay, St. James, and Simon's Town. Rush hour sees bumper-to-bumper traffic on all major arteries into the city from 6 to 9, and out of the city from 4 to 6:30.

MOTORCYCLE TRAVEL

Renting a scooter or motorbike (motorcycle license and deposit required) is a good option within the city if you have a motorcycle license. Motorcycles can be rented from Moto Berlin at R1,000–R1,650 per day. Cheaper rates apply for weekly rentals.

Contacts Moto Berlin ☎ *021/421–0396, 083/377–8833* ⊕ *www.motoberlin. com.*

TAXI TRAVEL

Taxis are expensive compared with other forms of transportation but offer a quick way to get around the city center. Don't expect to see the throngs of cabs you find in London or New York, as most people in Cape Town use public transportation or their own cars. You'll be lucky to hail one on the street. Taxis rarely use roof lights to indicate availability, but if you flag down an occupied cab, the driver may radio another car for you. Your best bet is to summon a taxi by phone or head to one of the major taxi stands, such as those at Greenmarket Square or either end of Adderley Street (near the Slave Lodge and outside the train station). Expect to pay R50–R70 for a trip from the city center to the Waterfront. For lower rates at night, try prebooking the Backpacker Bus, a shuttle service on Adderley Street. In addition to the companies listed here, ask your hotel or guesthouse which company it recommends. Lodging establishments often have a relationship with particular companies and/or drivers, and this way you will be assured of safe, reliable service.

Rikkis are London taxi-style cars that provide a cheaper alternative to metered taxis. Service is door-to-door, and they operate 24 hours a day, covering the entire city and airport.

To the airport from the City Bowl will cost R220, with the cost rising the farther out you are.

Contacts Backpacker Bus ☎ 021/424–1184 ⊕ www.backpackerbus.co.za. **Excite Taxis** ☎ 021/448–4444. **Rikkis** ☎ 0861/745–547 ⊕ www.rikkis.co.za. **Unicab** ☎ 0861/710–711 ⊕ www.unicab.co.za.

TRAIN TRAVEL

Cape Town's train station is on Adderley Street, in City Centre, surrounded by lively rows of street vendors and a taxi stand. The station building received a complete revamp as part of the general ubiquitous infrastructure upgrade in 2010. The station services local, interprovincial, and the odd luxury lines (Blue Train and Rovos Rail).

Metrorail, Cape Town's commuter line, offers regular service but has issues with safety and is not recommended for most tourists.

National carrier Shosholoza Meyl runs the Trans-Karoo daily to Johannesburg and the weekly Trans-Oranjia to Durban. Shongololo Express runs multiday journey-tours, with its Good Hope train traveling from Cape Town through the Karoo and the Garden Route to Johannesburg over 16 days. And the luxurious Blue Train and Rovos Rail's *Pride of Africa* each leave weekly for Tswhane. *For more information on all these services, see Train Travel in Travel Smart.*

TUK-TUK TRAVEL

Through a municipal loophole one tuk-tuk company is now offering lifts around the city for "what you can afford." Although they are not entirely legal, tuk-tuks are generally reliable, friendly, and fun. It's run by a couple of entrepreneurial Jo'burg lads, and R25 is acceptable (if you can afford more, all the better, because this is the drivers' living).

Contacts Clarence Bros Tuk-Tuk ☎ 083/641–5453.

SAFETY

There's no reason for paranoia in Cape Town, but there are a few things to look out for. Women and couples are strongly advised not to walk in isolated places after dark. If you want to walk somewhere in the evening, make sure you do so in a large group, stay vigilant at all times, and keep flashy jewelry and expensive cameras hidden, or better yet, at the hotel, much as you would anywhere else. It's difficult for any youthful-looking tourist to pass a street corner in the city's nightlife district without being offered hard drugs or cannabis. Resist.

Street kids and roving teens are blamed for much of the petty crime in the city, but sophisticated crime syndicates are often involved, and many of Cape Town's fraudsters are smartly dressed. Windows will be smashed to snatch cell phones lying on car seats, and phones may even be pulled out of people's hands while in use, so don't talk on your cell phone while walking. Watch your pockets at busy transportation hubs and on trains. It's better to sit in a crowded car; if you suddenly find yourself alone, move to another one. Public transportation collapses after dark. Unless you're at the Waterfront or in a large group, use metered taxis.

Trendy nightlife areas like Long Street and Kloof Street (which leads on via a dogleg from Long Street), are frequented by both teens and adults. These areas are safe, but one should always be vigilant at night. The predominantly gay nightlife scene around Greenpoint has seen some ugly incidents in recent times, so make sure you know where you're going and with whom.

Despite thousands of safe visits every year, Lion's Head—the peak below Table Mountain—and the running trails around Newlands Forest have been the sites of several knife-point robberies in daylight. Just be wise and never completely off guard. The handful of incidents in recent years have happened around sunrise or sunset.

Drivers quickly discover that poor signage is a general issue in Cape Town, especially in the black townships, where most streets still have numbers rather than names and many streets are not signed at all. Carry a good map and use a GPS.

Visit township attractions only as part of an organized tour with a reputable operator.

As in other major cities, drug use is a problem in Cape Town, including both IV drugs and ingestibles. The drug of choice for children on the street is glue, and increasingly "tic" or methamphetamine. You will undoubtedly come across many people begging in Cape Town, including kids. Please do not give cash directly to children, as this often supports either a glue habit or adults lurking in the background. If you are concerned and wish to contribute, consider supporting people who sell *The Big Issue* magazine (associated with a worthy organization of the same name) or giving food instead of money.

HIV remains a problem in South Africa, so exercise appropriate caution. The sex trade carries a high risk of transmission, as does the use of IV drugs.

TOUR OPTIONS

Numerous companies offer guided tours of the city center, the peninsula, the Winelands, and any place else in the Cape (or beyond) that you might wish to visit. They differ in type of transportation used, focus, and size. For comprehensive information on touring companies, head to one of the Cape Town Tourism offices or ask for recommendations at your hotel.

2

BOAT TOURS

Boat tours are very popular, but the only ones that actually land on Robben Island are the ferries operated by the museum there.

Drumbeat Charters. Drumbeat Charters has been operating since 1989 and is based in the fishing village of Hout Bay, offering daily scenic cruises. Their big attraction is the Seals & the Shipwreck trip, where you'll visit Duiker Island, home of the Cape fur seals, and then travel farther along the Kabonkelberg Mountain range to Moari Bay to view the shipwreck of the *Bos 400,* which ran aground in 1994 during a Cape winter storm. ☎ *021/791–4441* ⊕ *www.drumbeatcharters.co.za.*

Tigger 2 Charters. This waterfront-based luxury operation offers corporate, sunset, and lunch cruises along one of the world's most dramatic and famous coastlines, including trips to Clifton 4th Beach. ☎ *021/418–0241* ⊕ *www.tigger2.co.za.*

Waterfront Boat Company. This operation seems to do everything connected to having fun on the water in Table Bay and the eastern seaboard, with trips on a range of boats, from yachts to large motor cruisers. A 1½-hour sunset cruise from the V&A Waterfront costs about R280 and includes a glass of bubbly. Cruise & Dine Packages cost R495 for dinner, R270 for lunch. Jet boat rides are R630 per hour. ☎ *021/418–3168* ⊕ *www.waterfrontboats.co.za.*

BUS TOURS

Cape Point Route. This company has been in business for a fair while, and covers the peninsula thoroughly. Cape Point Route custom-designs tours that focus on the peninsula, starting at R570 for a half-day Cape Point scheduled tour to R1,250 for a Cape Point Shipwreck & Lighthouse Tour. It's R3,195 for a Cape Peninsula helicopter tour. ☎ *021/789–0093* ⊕ *www.capepointroute.co.za.*

Cape Sidecar Adventures. Unique for Cape Town, this has seemingly captured a niche market, with vintage Chinese military motorcycles dating back to the early 1960s being used to see one of the most beautiful cities in the world. In fact the owner, who got the idea after owning one in Shangai, believes it's one of three such operations on the planet. Great for children, too, the cycles chug stylishly and safely around some of the most beautiful roads and views on the planet in their designer gear—you actually get kitted out rather stylishly. There's a nice little coffee-bar in the shop afterward that offers an awesome collection of helmets (Batman's included) for sale. It's worth noting that although this operation is entirely legal, the Harley tours in the city could be jumping through some legal loopholes. ☎ *021/434–9855, 082/308–5483 mobile* ⊕ *www.sidecars.co.za.*

City Sightseeing. The hop-on/hop-off red City Sightseeing bus is a pleasant way to familiarize yourself with Cape Town; a day ticket costs R125, and there are two routes to choose from. The Red Route runs through the city, and you can get on and off at major museums, the V&A Waterfront, Table Mountain Cableway, Two Oceans Aquarium, and other attractions. The Blue Route takes you farther afield—to Kirstenbosch National Botanic Gardens, Hout Bay, and Camps Bay, to name a few destinations. Tickets are available at the Waterfront outside the aquarium or on the bus. ⊕ *www.citysightseeing.co.za.*

Coffeebeans Routes. Coffeebeans Routes Supperclub tours pay evening visits to the homes in Lansdowne on the Cape Flats for a meal and yarn (R495) with real Capetonians. Their famous Jazz Safari (R995) takes small groups to meet key musicians of Cape Town's jazz scene in their homes for dinner, followed by a visit to nontouristy jazz clubs in the Cape Flats. If authentic is what you're looking for, this is it. These tours show Cape Town as it is, with informed guides. Whether the Revolution Route, Cape Town Cuisine Route, or World Design Capital Cape Town 2014 "Insider" tours, the experience is infused with the element of storytelling. ☎ *021/424–3572* ⊕ *www.coffeebeansroutes.com.*

Friends of Dorothy. These tours are aimed at the gay market; among the offerings are the Ruby Slipper Tour (to the Cape Peninsula), Yellow Brick Road Tour (to the Cape Winelands), and Aunty Em's Tour (a country roads tour). Small groups—maximum of seven passengers—keep the service personal. The company is gay-owned and uses the services of gay guides and drivers. ☎ *021/465–1871* ⊕ *www.friendsofdorothytours.co.za.*

Hylton Ross Tours. This fairly generic tour operator offers half-day and full-day tours of Cape Town—and pretty much the whole country—where you know what to expect. Prices typically run from R570 for a half-day trip and about R790 for a full-day tour (the smaller and more personalized the tour, the higher the price). ☎ *021/506–2575* ⊕ *www.hyltonross.co.za.*

iKapa Tours & Travel. Good references from happy clients, a prominent note about responsible tourism (for every booking over R5,000, the company has an indigenous tree planted), and an element of flexibility suggest your money will be well spent with this bunch. Among the offerings are full-day Cape Safari tours to Aquila Private Game Reserve or Inverdoorn Game Reserve, including a three-hour game drive, all meals, and Champagne. Both reserves are about a 2½-hour drive from the city. ☎ *021/506–3700* ⊕ *www.ikapa.co.za.*

WALKING TOURS

Pamphlets for a self-guided walking tour of city-center attractions can be picked up at Cape Town Tourism.

Cape Town on Foot. Owner Ursula Stevens seems to be busy, leading walks through Cape Town, around the Cape of Good Hope, and up the West Coast—all guided by the seven books she has written on the areas. So her commentary comes straight from the horse's mouth. City walking tours last about 2½ hours and cover major historical attractions, architecture, and highlights of modern-day Cape Town. Bo-Kaap tours include the Bo-Kaap Museum. ⊕ *www.wanderlust.co.za.*

VISITOR INFORMATION

From October to March, the office in City Centre is open weekdays 8–6, Saturday 8:30–2, and Sunday 9–1; from April to September, it's open weekdays 8–5:30, Saturday 8:30–1, and Sunday 9–1. The branch at the Waterfront is open daily 9–7.

Contacts Cape Town Tourism ✉ *The Pinnacle Bldg., Burg and Castle Sts., Cape Town Central* ☎ *021/487–6800, 0861/322–223 in SA only* ⊕ *www. capetown.travel.*

EXPLORING

2

Updated by
Angus Begg

Cape Town has grown as a city in a way that few others in the world have. Take a good look at the street names. Strand and Waterkant streets (meaning "beach" and "waterside," respectively) are now far from the sea. However, when they were named, they were right on the beach. An enormous program of dumping rubble into the ocean extended the city by a good few square miles (thanks to the Dutch obsession with reclaiming land from the sea). Almost all the city on the seaward side of Strand and Waterkant is part of the reclaimed area of the city known as the Foreshore. If you look at old paintings of the city, you will see that originally waves lapped at the very walls of the castle, now more than half a mile from the ocean.

CAPE TOWN CENTRAL

In Cape Town's city center, moderately sized glass-and-steel office blocks soar over street vendors selling everything from seasonal fruit and flowers to clothes and cigarettes. Sandwiched in between these modern high-rises are historic buildings dating to the 1600s. There's an impressive collection of art deco buildings, and there is always something undergoing restoration. Don't try to navigate the center of Cape Town by car. It's small enough to walk, and this way you'll be able to explore the many galleries, coffee shops, and markets that appear on every corner. If your feet have had it, the MyCiti bus works a treat if you have a card.

TIMING AND PRECAUTIONS

If you are pressed for time, you can explore the city in a day, getting the lay of the land and a feel for the people of Cape Town while visiting or skipping sights as your interests dictate. However, if you'd like to linger in various museums and galleries, you could easily fill two or three days. Start at about 9, when most workers have finished their commute, and then stop for a long, leisurely lunch, finishing the tour in the late afternoon. If you have to head out of town on either the N1 or N2, be sure to depart before 4, when rush-hour congestion takes over.

Except for the top end of Long Street and around Heritage Square where there are lots of bars and cafés, the city center is very quiet at night, and you are advised not to wander the streets after dark. The last commuters leave around 6 (note that the city center can also be deserted on weekends). The biggest threat is being mugged for your cell phone, jewelry, or money. Fortunately many of the old city buildings are being converted into upscale apartments, thus rejuvenating the city center.

Cape History at a Glance

It's said that Cape Town owes its very existence to Table Mountain. The freshwater streams running off its slopes were what first prompted early explorers to anchor here. In 1652 Jan van Riebeeck and 90 Dutch settlers established a refreshment station for ships of the Dutch East India Company (VOC) on the long voyage east. The first European toehold in South Africa, Cape Town is still called the Mother City.

Those first Dutch settlers established their own farms, and 140 years later the settlement supported a population of 20,000 whites and 25,000 slaves brought from distant lands like Java, Madagascar, and Guinea. Its strategic position on the southern edge of Africa, however, meant that the colony never enjoyed any real stability. The British occupied the Cape twice, first in 1795 and then more permanently in 1806, bringing with them additional slaves from Ceylon, India, and the Philippines. Destroyed or assimilated in this colonial expansion were the indigenous Khoekhoen (previously called Khoikhoi and Hottentots), who once herded cattle and foraged along the coast.

Diamond and gold discoveries in central and northern South Africa in the late 1800s pulled focus away from Cape Town. However, in 1910, when the Union of South Africa was created, Cape Town was named the legislative capital, and it remains so today. The diamond and gold boom fueled rapid development in Cape Town and throughout the country.

The wounds of the 20th century are due to apartheid. Although apartheid ended in the 1990s, its legacy of underdevelopment remains, and Cape Town still remains divided along racial, economic, and physical lines. As you drive into town along the N2 from the airport, you can't miss the shacks built on shifting dunes as far as the eye can see—a sobering contrast to the first-world luxury of the city center on the other side of Table Mountain.

Khayelitsha is the main "black" township, attached to which are numerous squatter camps, more politely known as informal settlements. Well over a million people live in Khayelitsha today, most of whom originated in the underdeveloped Eastern Cape province, where work is scarce and the medical and educational facilities have all but collapsed. For these reasons relatives of Khayelitsha's inhabitants arrive almost daily.

Much of South Africa's rich and fascinating history is reflected in Cape Town. Most of the sites worth seeing are packed into a small area, which means you can see a lot in just a few hours. Mandela's tiny jail cell at Robben Island has been preserved, and you can learn about his banishment there as well as about the ecological significance of the island. The District Six Museum tells the heartbreaking story of the apartheid-era demolition of one of Cape Town's most vibrant neighborhoods, and the Bo-Kaap Museum tells the story of the city's Muslim community, who settled here after the abolition of slavery. For a taste of the city's long naval history, visit Simon's Town, where you can tour a retired submarine. The Castle of Good Hope, former seat of the British and Dutch governments and still the city's military headquarters, is the oldest colonial building still standing in South Africa.

2

TOP ATTRACTIONS

Castle of Good Hope. Despite its name, the castle isn't the fairy-tale fantasy type but rather a squat fortress that hunkers down as if to avoid shellfire. Built between 1665 and 1676 by the Dutch East India Company (VOC) to replace an earthen fort constructed in 1652 by Jan van Riebeeck, the Dutch commander who settled Cape Town, it's the oldest building in the country. Its pentagonal plan, with a diamond-shape bastion at each corner, is typical of the Old Netherlands defense system adopted in the early 17th century. The design was intended to allow covering fire for every portion of the castle. As added protection, the whole fortification was surrounded by a moat, and back in the day, the sea nearly washed up against its walls. The castle served as both the VOC headquarters and the official governor's residence, and still houses the regional headquarters of the National Defence Force. Despite the bellicose origins of the castle, no shot has ever been fired from its ramparts, except ceremonially.

You can wander around on your own or join one of the highly informative guided tours at no extra cost. Also worth seeing is the excellent William Fehr Collection. Housed in the governor's residence, it consists of antiques, artifacts, and paintings of early Cape Town and South Africa. Politicians and corporations occasionally hold dinners in the grand dining room. ⌂ *1 Buitenkant St.* ☎ *021/787–1240* ⊕ *www. castleofgoodhope.co.za* ⌂ *R30* ☾ *Daily 9–3:30; tours at 11, noon, and 2.*

Company's Garden. One of Cape Town's best-kept secrets is also a great place to seek relief from a sweltering summer day if the beach is packed. These lush, landscaped gardens are all that remain of a 43-acre tract laid out by Jan van Riebeeck in April 1652 to supply fresh vegetables to ships on their way to the Dutch East Indies. By 1700 free burghers were cultivating plenty of crops on their own land, and in time the VOC vegetable patch was transformed into a botanic garden. It remains a delightful haven in the city center, graced by fountains, exotic trees, rose gardens, and a pleasant outdoor café, which was expected to be taken over in October 2014 by one of the city's most innovative restaurateurs. At the bottom of the gardens, close to Government Avenue, look for an **old well** that used to provide water for the town's residents and the garden. The old water pump, engraved with the maker's name and the date 1842, has been overtaken by an oak tree and now juts out of the tree's trunk some 6 feet above the ground. A huge **statue of Cecil Rhodes,** the Cape's prime minister in the late 19th century, looms over the path that runs through the center of the gardens. He points to the north, and an inscription reads, "your hinterland is there," a reference to Rhodes's dream of extending the British Empire from the Cape to Cairo. Continue past the pond and toward the South African Museum, outside of which the **Delville Wood Monument** honors South Africans who died in the fight for Delville Wood during the great three-day Somme offensive of 1916. A self-guided walking brochure with detailed historical information about the garden is sold at the office just outside the restaurant. ⌂ *Between Government Ave. and Queen Victoria St.* ☎ *021/426–1357* ⌂ *Free* ☾ *Summer, daily 7–7; winter, daily 7–6.*

Cape Town

Convention Center

Cruise Ship Terminal

Shimmy Beach Club

Victoria Basin

Nelson Mandela Gateway to Robben Island

San Marco Bistro

Green Point Stadium

Cape Town Railway Station

Trafalgar Place

CAPE TOWN CENTRAL

DE WATERKANT

Evangelical Lutheran Church

Oswald Pirow
Table Bay Blvd.
Hertzog Blvd.
D.F. Malan
Heerengracht
Coen Steytler
Adderley
Long
Riebeeck
Waterkant
Buitengracht
Strand
Hans Strijdom
Duncan
South Arm
South Arm
Dock
Dock
Port
Alfred
Napier
Dixon
Somerset
De Smit
Prestwich
Highfield Ter.
Western Blvd.
Main
High Level
Boundary
Vesperdene
Portswood
Breakwater Blvd.
Beach
Sir Lowry
Eastern Boulevard

← TO GREEN POINT

19
20
21
22
23
24
25

Perhaps the only really good restaurant in the immediate area, **Dias Tavern** (⊠ *15 Caledon St., District Six, Cape Town Central* ☎ *021/465–7547*) serves fantastic and filling Portuguese fare, including *trinchado* (spicy braised beef), calamari, grilled meats of all varieties, and pastas. This casual tavern setting has nonpanoramic but nice views of Table Mountain and is a favorite of office workers in the area.

District Six Museum. Housed in the Buitenkant Methodist Church, this museum preserves the memory of one of Cape Town's most vibrant multicultural neighborhoods and of the district's destruction in one of the cruelest acts of the apartheid-era Nationalist government. District Six was proclaimed a white area in 1966, and existing residents were evicted from their homes, which were razed to make way for a white suburb. The people were forced to resettle in bleak outlying areas on the Cape Flats, and by the 1970s all the buildings here, except churches and mosques, had been demolished. Huge controversy accompanied the proposed redevelopment of the area, and only a small housing component, Zonnebloem, and the campus of the Cape Technicon have been built, leaving much of the ground still bare—a grim reminder of the past. There are pockets of redevelopment and plans to bring former residents back into the area and reestablish the suburb; however, the plans are beset by in-fighting, and the old swinging District Six will never be re-created. The museum consists of street signs, photographs, life stories of the people who lived there, and a huge map, where former residents can identify the sites of their homes and record their names. This map is being used to help sort out land claims. You can arrange in advance for a two-hour walking tour of the district with a former resident for a nominal amount. ⊠ *25 Buitenkant St.* ☎ *021/466–7200* ⊕ *www.districtsix.co.za* ⌨ *R30* ☉ *Mon. 9–2, Tues.–Sat. 9–4, Sun. by appointment.*

Greenmarket Square. For more than a century this cobbled square served as a forum for public announcements, including the 1834 declaration abolishing slavery, which was read from the balcony of the Old Town House, overlooking the square. In the 19th century the square became a vegetable market as well as a popular watering hole, and you can still enjoy a drink at an open-air restaurant or hotel veranda while watching the crowds go by. Today the square has been re-cobbled, and the outdoor market sells predominantly African crafts from around the continent. It is also flanked by some of the best examples of art-deco architecture in South Africa. ⊠ *Greenmarket Sq., Burg St. between Longmarket St. and Hout St.*

Scotch Coffee House at the Ivy Garden. The Scotch Coffee House at the Ivy Garden, in the courtyard of the Old Town House, serves homemade light lunches with a South African bent (try the braised smoked snoek, a favorite local fish) and the usual teas and coffees. This leafy, green setting is a pleasant escape from the hustle and bustle of Greenmarket Square. ⊠ *Greenmarket Sq., Long Market St.* ☎ *021/423–0322.*

Old Town House. A beautiful example of urban Cape Dutch architecture, the Old Town House is now home to the extensive **Michaelis Collection.** This 17th-century collection of Dutch paintings includes evocative etchings by Rembrandt, as well as changing exhibits. ⊠ *Greenmarket Sq.* ☎ *021/481–3933* ⊕ *www.iziko.org.za/michaelis* ⊠ *R20* ⊘ *Mon.– Sat. 10–5.*

WORTH NOTING

Adderley Street. Originally named Heerengracht after a canal that once ran the length of the avenue, this street has always been Cape Town's principal thoroughfare. It was once the favored address of the city's leading families, and its oak-shaded sidewalks served as a promenade for those who wanted to see and be seen. By the mid-19th century the oaks had all been chopped down and the canal covered, as Adderley became the main commercial street. By 1908 it had become so busy that the city planners paved it with wooden blocks in an attempt to dampen the noise of countless wagons, carts, and hooves. In recent years Adderley Street has lost most of its charm. Although there are a couple of beautiful old buildings dating to the early 1900s, they are mostly crowded out by uninspiring office buildings, and the sidewalks are packed with street hawkers selling everything from fruits and vegetables to cell-phone covers and tea towels. City management is trying to halt the urban decay, however, and there's plenty of evidence of regeneration. A lot of old office buildings are now being converted to upscale apartments, and beautiful old art deco buildings are getting the spit and polish they so desperately need. ⊠ *Cape Town Central.*

Church Square. Church Square bore witness to much of Cape Town's dark history. An inconspicuous concrete plaque along Spin Street's median is all that's left of the **Slave Tree,** an enormous Canadian pine under which slaves were reportedly auctioned off. A section of the tree is on display at the District Six Museum. ⊠ *Cape Town Central.*

Church Street Arcade. The center of Cape Town's art and antiques business, this section of Church Street is a pedestrian mall filled with art galleries, antiques dealers, and small cafés. A daily antiques and flea market is held here. ⊠ *Church St., between Burg and Long Sts.*

City Hall. From a balcony in this building overlooking Darling Street, Nelson Mandela gave the historic speech on his release from prison in 1990. This attractive Edwardian building constructed in 1905 is gradually being spruced up and is still a commanding presence overlooking the Grand Parade. What was the seat of local administration is now home to the Cape Town Philharmonic Orchestra (the acoustics in the main hall are phenomenal) and a traffic department. Some of the building's stone was imported from Bath, England, and the clock is a scaled-down replica of Big Ben. From a balcony overlooking Darling Street, Nelson Mandela gave his historic speech upon his release from prison in 1990. ⊠ *Darling St.* ⊠ *Free.*

Grand Parade. Once a military parade ground, this is now just a bleak parking lot—with a statue of Edward VII serving as a parking attendant and seagull resting post. It was here that more than 100,000 of Nelson Mandela's supporters gathered on February 11, 1990, when, after

27 years in prison, he addressed an adoring crowd from the balcony at City Hall. The Grand Parade will be temporarily transformed into a fan park for the 2010 World Cup. ⊠ *Darling, Lower Plein, and Buitenkant Sts.*

Groote Kerk. Across from the slave tree on Church Square's eastern end is the entrance to the Gothic-style Groote Kerk. One of South Africa's most famous churches, the Groote Kerk (Great Church) was built in 1841 on the site of an earlier Dutch Reformed church dating from 1704. The adjoining clock tower is all that remains of that earlier building. Among the building's interesting features are the enclosed pews, each with its own

> **WHO'S THAT?**
>
> The imposing statue with his back turned toward the Slave Lodge is of Jan Smuts, a former general, prime minister, naturalist, and philosopher. He was one of the key men behind the drafting of the Covenant of the League of Nations (precursor to the United Nations). Before and after World War II, Smuts was the leader of the United Party, which believed in a unified South Africa. Had he not been defeated by the National Party in 1948, South African history would have taken a very different turn.

door—prominent families would buy these so they wouldn't have to pray with the masses. The enormous pulpit is the joint work of famous sculptor Anton Anreith and carpenter Jan Jacob Graaff. The lions supporting it are carved from local stinkwood; the upper portion is Burmese teak. The organ, with nearly 6,000 pipes, is the largest in the Southern Hemisphere. Approximately 200 people are buried beneath the Batavian soapstone floor, including eight governors. There are free guided tours on request. ⊠ *Church Sq., Parliament St.* ☎ *021/422–0569* ☜ *Free* ☉ *Weekdays 10–2; services Sun. at 10 and 7.*

Long Street. The section of Long between Orange and Strand streets is lined with magnificently restored Georgian and Victorian buildings. Wrought-iron balconies and fancy curlicues on these colorful houses evoke the French Quarter in New Orleans. In the 1960s, Long Street played host to bars, prostitutes, and sleazy hotels. Today antiques dealers, the Pan-African Market, funky clothing outlets and a plethora of cafes, bars, and restaurants make this one of the best browsing streets in the city; by night, some of its older reputation remains true. Lodgings here range from backpackers' digs to the posh Grand Daddy. At the mountain end is Long Street Baths, an indoor swimming pool and old Turkish *hammam* (steam bath). ⊠ *Long St., between Orange St. and Strand St.*

NEED A BREAK?

Portobello Café. On the other end of the spectrum, if you can't stand the idea of another heavy meal, head to funky Portobello Café, which serves fantastic vegetarian cuisine, smoothies, and fresh fruit juices that even meat-eaters will love. It closes at 5 pm. ⊠ *111 Long St.* ☎ *021/426–1418.*

Zorina's. Amid the dozens of great joints around Long and Loop streets, Zorina's is a hole-in-the-wall that's famous for great Cape Malay curries and samosas. ⊠ *172 Loop St.* ☎ *021/424–9301.*

St. George's Cathedral. This stunning cathedral was once the religious seat of one of the most recognizable faces—and voices—in the fight against apartheid, Archbishop Desmond Tutu. In his position as the first black archbishop of Cape Town (he was elected in 1986), he vociferously denounced apartheid and relentlessly pressed for a democratic government. It was from these steps that he led a demonstration of more than 30,000 people and coined the phrase the Rainbow People to describe South Africans in all their glorious diversity. Tutu, long retired, and the cathedral continue in their active monitoring role today, holding marches and the new government to account. The Anglican cathedral was designed by Sir Herbert Baker in the Gothic Revival style; construction began in 1901, using sandstone from Table Mountain. The structure contains the largest stained-glass window in the country, some beautiful examples of late-Victorian stained glass, and a 1,000-year-old Coptic cross. If you want to hear the magnificent organ, go to the choral evensong at 7 on Sunday evening. ⊠ *5 Wale St.* ☏ *021/424–7360* ▧ *Free* ⊙ *Daily 8–5; services weekdays at 7:15 am and 1:15 pm, Sat. at 8 am, Sun. at 7 am, 8 am, 10 am, and 7 pm.*

St. George's Mall. This promenade stretches from St. George's Cathedral through the city center to the financial district, which isn't that far. Shops and cafés line the mall, and street vendors hawk everything from T-shirts to African arts and crafts. Street performers and dancers gather daily to entertain crowds of locals and visitors, who rub shoulders on their way to and from work or while sightseeing. There's good food market at the Cathedral end on a Thursday afternoon. ⊠ *Between Long and Adderley Sts. from Wale St. to Prestwich St.*

Slave Lodge. Built in 1679 by the Dutch East India Company to house slaves, convicts, and lunatics, it also housed the supreme court from 1815 to 1914. The lodge now holds a museum with a sobering account of slavery in the Cape, as well as excellent and evocative temporary exhibits that tend to examine apartheid and racism. ⊠ *49 Wale St.* ☏ *021/481–3800* ⊕ *www.iziko.org.za/slavelodge* ▧ *R15* ⊙ *Weekdays 10–4:30, Sat. 10–1.*

FAMILY **South African Museum.** This museum has some excellent examples of rock art that will give you insight into the ancient Khoisan culture. The museum also has an interesting section on the fossil remains of prehistoric reptiles and other animals, and the Whale Well, where musical recitals are often held under suspended life-size casts of enormous marine mammals. Shark World thrills children with exhibits on the sharks that ply the oceans. The adjoining planetarium stages a variety of shows throughout the week, some of which are specifically designed for children as young as five. International touring photography exhibits are often on display. ⊠ *25 Queen Victoria St.* ☏ *021/481–3800* ⊕ *www. iziko.org.za/sam* ▧ *Museum R30* ⊙ *Museum daily 10–5; planetarium shows weekdays at 2 (also Tues. at 8 pm), and weekends at noon, 1, and 2:30.*

WOODSTOCK

Just a stone's throw northeast of city center, once-gritty Woodstock has been undergoing a massive regeneration in recent times and is now home to numerous galleries and restaurants, including the country's number-one-rated establishment, the Test Kitchen.

BO-KAAP

Bo-Kaap is the historic home of the city's Muslim population, brought from the East as slaves in the late 17th and early 18th century. The Auwal Mosque, the oldest mosque in South Africa, built in 1798, is also here. You'll know you're in the Bo-Kaap (Afrikaans for "on top of the Cape") when you hear the call of the muezzin from one of the many mosques in the area. You might even have to sidestep lights, cameras, and film stars, since the district is an oft-used setting for movies and magazine shoots—the brightly colored houses make a stunning backdrop. Although foreigners and locals have started buying in the area—real estate in the City Bowl is at a premium, and without gardens these properties are cheaper—it remains overtly traditional, so much so that a bar that opened up on the corner of Wale and Rose streets to attract tourists and new residents had to close because of local pressure from the Muslim community. Today the area remains strongly Muslim, and it's fascinating to wander the narrow, cobbled lanes past mosques and the largest collection of pre-1840 architecture in South Africa. The Bo-Kaap is also known as the Malay quarter, even though its inhabitants originated from all over, including the Indonesian archipelago, India, Turkey, and Madagascar. There is a Saturday morning market on Wale Street, near the corner of Rose Street.

TIMING AND PRECAUTIONS

There have been a few muggings in the Bo-Kaap, so to experience all that the area has to offer we recommend that you take a guided tour (⇨ *See Walking Tours, in Planning, at the beginning of the chapter*) or stick to Wale, Dorp, and Shortmarket streets.

TOP ATTRACTIONS

Bo-Kaap Museum. Built in the 18th century, this museum was originally the home of Abu Bakr Effendi, a well-known Turkish scholar and prominent leader in the Muslim community. He was brought here in the mid-19th century to help quell feuding between Muslim factions and is believed to have written one of the first books in Afrikaans. The house has been furnished to re-create the lifestyle of a typical Malay family in the 19th century. (Since the exhibits aren't labeled, you might do better to visit the museum as part of a guided tour of the Malay quarter.) Look for works by artist Gregoire Boonzaire, who is famous for capturing both the chaos and charm of neighborhoods such as the Bo-Kaap and District Six. ⊠ *71 Wale St.* ☎ *021/481–3938* ⊕ *www.iziko. org.za/bokaap* ⌲ *R20* ☾ *Mon.–Sat. 10–5.*

NEED A BREAK?

Noon Gun Tearoom and Restaurant. Noon Gun Tearoom and Restaurant up the *very* steep slope of Signal Hill is a good place to stop for a breather and some traditional, home-cooked Malay food. Your entertaining hostess (and TV chef) Zaine Misbach cooks up a mean curry and *biryani* (a spicy rice-based dish). And her samosas are to die for. The menu is limited, but Zaine's repertoire is anything but; she's chatty and engaging and also offers cooking lessons. ✉ *273 Longmarket St.* ☎ *0741/308–124* ⊕ *www. bokaapcookingtour.co.za/about-zainie.html.*

GARDENS

An affluent city neighborhood, Gardens is populated largely by young professionals. Gardens has numerous restaurants, cafés, hotels, and shops, as well as many beautiful homes. Main thoroughfares like Kloof Street are packed with funky boutiques and are pleasant to stroll and explore. Once the beginning of central Cape Town's residential area heading from the Company's Garden up toward Table Mountain, Gardens has increasingly merged with "town" as the number of cafés and restaurants here has grown, making it a popular place both to stay and explore, both day and night.

TIMING AND PRECAUTIONS

Unlike Cape Town Central, Gardens' commercial zone remains relatively lively into the evening. From where Kloof Street begins (at the end of Long Street) until it intersects with Camp Street, restaurants, cafés, and Cape Town's art-house cinema make the area lively and safe for walking until about 10 pm. Even after this, the main irritation for a tourist is likely only to be from beggars. In other areas take the usual precautions.

TOP ATTRACTIONS

Cape Town Holocaust Centre. The center is both a memorial to the 6 million Jews and other victims who were killed during the Holocaust and an education center whose aim is to create a caring and just society in which human rights and diversity are valued. The permanent exhibit is excellent and very moving. A multimedia display, comprising photo panels, text, film footage, and music, creates a chilling reminder of the dangers of prejudice, racism, and discrimination. The center is next to the South African Jewish Museum. ✉ *88 Hatfield St.* ☎ *021/462–5553* ⊕ *www.ctholocaust.co.za* 🎟 *Free* ⏱ *Sun.–Thurs. 10–5, Fri. 10–2.*

Mount Nelson Hotel. Government Avenue ends opposite the impressive gateway to the Mount Nelson Hotel, complete with two pith-helmeted gatekeepers. The Nellie, as it's known, was erected in 1899 to welcome the Prince of Wales on his visit to the Cape and today remains one of Cape Town's most fashionable and genteel social venues. Don't miss the legendary high tea. Served from 2:30 to 5:30, the pastry selection can tempt even the most jaded palate, and the savory treats make for a scrumptious meal. ✉ *76 Orange St.* ☎ *021/483–1000* ⊕ *www. mountnelson.co.za.*

South African Jewish Museum. Housed in the Old Synagogue—South Africa's first synagogue, built in 1863—this museum lies adjacent to the Cape Town Holocaust Centre and spans 150 years of South African Jewry. The themes of Memories (immigrant experiences), Reality (integration into South Africa), and Dreams (visions) exhibits are conveyed with high-tech multimedia and interactive displays, models, and artifacts. The complex also includes the Great Synagogue (built in 1905), an active place of worship, a computerized Discovery Center that can help you trace your family roots, a temporary gallery for changing exhibits, an auditorium, and a museum restaurant and shop. ⊠ *88 Hatfield St.* ☎ *021/465–1546* ⊕ *www.sajewishmuseum.co.za* ☞ *R40* ⊙ *Sun.–Thurs. 10–5, Fri. 10–2.*

South African National Gallery. This museum houses a good collection of 19th- and 20th-century European art, but its most interesting exhibits are the South African works, many of which reflect the country's traumatic history. The gallery owns an enormous body of work, so exhibitions change regularly, but there's always something provocative—whether it's documentary photographs or a multimedia exhibit chronicling South Africa's struggles with HIV/AIDS. The museum would like to position itself as a leader of contemporary and traditional African art. Free guided tours on Tuesday and Thursday take about an hour. ⊠ *Government Ave.* ☎ *021/481–3970* ⊕ *www.iziko.org.za/sang* ☞ *R30* ⊙ *Tues.–Sun. 10–5; tours Tues. and Thurs. at 11, noon, and 1.*

WORTH NOTING
City Bowl Market. Experience real Cape Town local life every Thursday from 5 pm in this rented church hall space. With fresh produce, a wide variety of really good food, craft beers and wines, and even clothes and jewelry on sale, this is a vibey City Bowl social gathering. ⊠ *Red Harbour Church, 14 Hope St.*

TAMBOERSKLOOF

Like Gardens, this lovely area along the lower slopes of Table Mountain, from Lion's Head toward Signal Hill and extending to Kloof Street, has grown in popularity as a place where eateries and bars frequented by the young professionals who reside here are thriving. It's also home to numerous bed-and-breakfasts and small guesthouses, most on quiet residential streets, but still within walking distance of numerous options on trendy Kloof Street.

ORANJEZICHT

The heavily residential area above Gardens and just below Table Mountain, upscale Oranjezicht is home to a few excellent B&Bs and guesthouses and is generally a quiet and tranquil place to base yourself. You'll be more likely to want wheels to get around, especially at night, but that's what taxis are for.

V&A WATERFRONT

The V&A (Victoria & Alfred) Waterfront is the culmination of a long-term project undertaken to breathe new life into the historical dockland of the city. Although some Capetonians deem the Waterfront too "mallish," it apparently remains South Africa's most popular attraction—probably because currency exchange rates overwhelmingly favor the majority of recognized foreign currencies over the rand. Expensive

2

apartments have been built at the marina, and hundreds of shops, movie theaters, restaurants, and bars share quarters in restored warehouses and dock buildings, all connected by pedestrian plazas and promenades. A major plus is that it's clean, safe, and with massive under- and over-ground parking promenades, car-free.

TIMING AND PRECAUTIONS

You could see the area's major sights in half a day, but that won't give you much time for shopping, coffee stops, or lunch, or for all that the aquarium has to offer. A more leisurely approach would be to set aside a whole day, at the end of which you could find a waterside restaurant or bar to enjoy a cold glass of wine or a cocktail. With its crowds of people, security cameras, and guards, this is one of the safest places to shop and hang out in the city. That said, you should still keep an eye on your belongings and be aware of pickpockets.

TOP ATTRACTIONS

Fodor's Choice
★
Robben Island. Made famous by its most illustrious inhabitant, Nelson Mandela, this island, whose name is Dutch for "seals," has a long and sad history. At various times a prison, leper colony, mental institution, and military base, it is finally filling a positive, enlightening, and empowering role in its latest incarnation as a museum.

Declared a World Heritage site on December 1, 1997, Robben Island has become a symbol of the triumph of the human spirit. In 1997 around 90,000 made the pilgrimage; in 2006 more than 300,000 crossed the water to see where some of the greatest South Africans spent much of their lives. Visiting the island is a sobering experience, which begins at the modern Nelson Mandela Gateway to Robben Island, an impressive embarkation center that doubles as a conference center. Interactive exhibits display historic photos of prison life. Next make the journey across the water, remembering to watch Table Mountain recede in the distance and imagine what it must have been like to have just received a 20-year jail sentence. Boats leave on the hour (every other hour in winter), and the crossing takes 30 minutes.

Tours are organized by the Robben Island Museum. (Other operators advertise Robben Island tours but just take visitors on a boat trip *around* the island.) As a result of the reconciliation process, most tour guides are former political prisoners. During the 2½-hour tour you walk through the prison and see the cells where Mandela and other leaders were imprisoned. You also tour the lime quarry, Robert Sobukwe's place of confinement, and the leper church. Due to increased demand for tickets during peak season (December and January), make bookings at least three weeks in advance. Take sunglasses and a hat in summer. ■ TIP→ **You are advised to tip your guide only if you feel that the tour has been informative.** ☒ *Nelson Mandela Gateway* ☎ *021/413–4220* ⊕ *www.robben-island.org.za* ☒ *R280* ☉ *Nov.–Apr., daily 8–3; May–Sept./Oct., daily 9–1. The last boat generally leaves the island at 6 pm in summer and 4 pm in winter. Opening times and boat departures will vary. As the phone isn't always answered and the website isn't always functioning, it can be best to get a tour operator to handle queries for you.*

FAMILY
Fodor's Choice
★

Two Oceans Aquarium. This aquarium is widely considered one of the finest in the world. Stunning displays reveal the marine life of the warm Indian Ocean and the icy Atlantic. It's a hands-on place, with a touch pool for children and opportunities for certified divers to explore the vast, five-story kelp forest or the predator tank, where you share the water with a couple of large ragged-tooth sharks (*Carcharias taurus*) and get a legal adrenaline rush (for an additional fee, of course). If you don't fancy getting wet, you can still watch the feeding in the predator tank every day at 3. But there's more to the aquarium than just snapping jaws. Look for the endangered African penguins, also known as jackass penguins because of the awkward braying noise they make; pulsating moon jellies and spider crabs; and a new frog exhibit. ⊠ *Dock Rd.* ☎ *021/418–3823* ⊕ *www.aquarium.co.za* ⊠ *R112* ۞ *Daily 9:30–6.*

WORTH NOTING

AGFA Amphitheatre. If the scattered benches looking out at the harbor activity are full, this open-air space is a good spot to eat your take-way lunch—if there's no performance on. It hosts popular outdoor space mounts performances ranging from concerts by the Cape Town Philharmonic Orchestra to gigs by jazz and rock bands and even Turkish minstrels. (Check with the Waterfront's Cape Town Tourism office for a schedule of events.) The amphitheater stands on the site where, in 1860, a teenage Prince Alfred inaugurated the construction of a breakwater to protect ships in the harbor from devastating northwesterly winds. ⊠ *Near Market Sq.* ☎ *021/408–7600 for schedule* ⊕ *www.waterfront. co.za.*

Chavonne's Cannon Battery Museum. An archaeological sight housing the remains of Cape Town's oldest cannon battery, this museum, which opened in 2008, reconstructs the outer battlements and underground rooms that formed one of the major defense outposts on the Cape. Detailed miniature replicas of the cannons and the different types of projectiles are fascinating, as are interpretative materials about the Cape's natural heritage at the time that the battery was in use. ⊠ *Clock Tower Precinct, opposite Mandela Gateway* ☎ *021/416–6230* ⊕ *www. chavonnesmuseum.co.za* ⊠ *R35* ۞ *Daily 9–4 .*

NEED A BREAK?

San Marco Bistro. San Marco Bistro offers a wide variety of options from sandwiches and salads to pasta, meat, and seafood entrées. Although it's expensive for locals, most visitors find it very affordable. There are hundreds of places to eat at the Waterfront but not many such alfresco locations that are really outdoors in such close proximity to the working harbor. It's a good place to refuel and people-watch while shopping—or waiting to tour one of the naval vessels that occasionally open their doors to the public. ⊠ *Victoria Wharf, Shop 128* ☎ *021/418–5434.*

Shimmy Beach Club. A bit of vibey Ibiza in laid-back Cape Town, this beach club is well regarded as a fun and stylish place to hang out, and it's even family-friendly, with a children's play area. You can dine in the oceanfront restaurant, spend a day on the private (man-made) beach, or swim in the pool. At night DJs come on board for an even livelier party atmosphere. Right at the harbor entrance, the club has taken trendy Cape Town by storm. On days when it's just too hot or raining, there's a covered pool and deck area. The restaurant is busy and a reservations-only spot at night. It sits in an unlikely spot, between two fish-processing warehouses, but there's no odor. Admission is free (as are children), but you are expected to buy food and drink. ⊠ *V&A Harbour, South Arm Rd.* ☎ *021/200–7778* ⊕ *www.shimmybeachclub.com* ☞ *Free* ☉ *Wed.–Fri. 11 am–2 am, Sat. 9 am–2 am, Sun. 9 am–6 pm.*

South African Maritime Centre. Inside the Union-Castle House, this museum explains the Cape's long history with the sea. Recently renovated, the center documents the history of the Union-Castle shipping line. Before World War II many English-speaking South Africans looked upon England as home, even if they had never been there. The emotional link between the two countries was symbolized most strongly by the mail steamers, carrying both mail and passengers that sailed weekly between South Africa and England. Models of ships are accompanied by memorabilia such as a collection of postcards sold from the ships between 1910 and 1960. A fascinating re-creation of Cape Town harbor as it appeared in 1885, which was built by convicts, is on permanent display, as is a chilling exhibit about the SS *Mendi*, a cargo vessel turned troopship that was carrying the South African Native Labour Contingent to help with the war effort in France. She was accidentally rammed by a British cargo ship, resulting in the deaths of 607 black troops. ⊠ *Union-Castle Bldg., Dock Rd., Quay 4* ☎ *021/405–2880* ⊕ *www. iziko.org.za/maritime* ☞ *R20* ☉ *Daily 10–5.*

GREEN POINT

Inland from the soccer stadium, this mixed residential and business area is home to numerous dining options, most of which are on Main Road (aka Somerset West) and tend to cater to locals. Numerous guesthouses and B&Bs at many price points make it a convenient base for independent travelers.

MOUILLE POINT

Just a few kilometers from the Waterfront, this lovely seafront area is mostly residential, and a convenient place to stay, though it lacks a critical mass of dining options within immediate walking distance.

SEA POINT

Defined largely by the popular pedestrian-friendly promenade that stretches from its most southern edge and carries on to Mouille Point and the Waterfront, lovely Sea Point is one of the few middle-income residential areas in Cape Town that is actually on the sea. Previously considered a dead zone dining-wise, this has changed in recent years, and the area is home to numerous inexpensive (though largely unremarkable) options, as well as a few real winners.

CLIFTON

Much of the city's most expensive housing sits above the four beaches that make up Clifton. During holidays it is almost a 24/7 madhouse, and your chances of finding parking at these times are nil. If you plan to visit the beaches in midsummer, consider renting a scooter or motorcycle instead of a car, taking a shuttle from your hotel, or going early in the morning, when people are still sleeping off their Champagne from the night before.

CAMPS BAY

Known as the beach where the beautiful people come to play, the gorgeous Camps Bay main drag (aka Victoria Road) is lined with cafés, bars, and restaurants. Most exist solely for their views—which are admittedly fantastic—but don't get your culinary hopes too high. However, for those in search of a good meal, there are a few reliable options.

TABLE MOUNTAIN NATIONAL PARK

Nowhere else in the world does an area of such spectacular beauty and rich biodiversity exist almost entirely within a metropolitan area. Large swaths of the Cape Peninsula are devoted to this spectacular 220-square-km (85-square-mile park), which is home to countless hiking trails and gorgeous beaches, as well as two world-renowned landmarks: the eponymous Table Mountain and the legendary Cape of Good Hope. Although several parts of the park are within the boundaries of Cape Town, others are in the Cape Peninsula (⇨ *See Cape Peninsula*). The park requires entrance payments only at three points: Cape of Good Hope, Boulders, and Silvermine. The rest of the park is open and free for all to enjoy.

TIMING AND PRECAUTIONS

It would be easy for nature lovers to spend days in the park. Most visitors spend a minimum of three hours to go up Table Mountain (by cable car), and another half day to visit Cape Point. For the fit, hiking up Table Mountain (and taking the cable car down) is a far more rewarding experience but requires good weather and at least half a day. To experience the wild beauty of Cape Point, a full day is recommended to visit the point (by funicular), walk to the Cape of Good Hope, and explore the gorgeous empty beaches around Olifantsbos or Platboom. Within Cape Point, the main safety issue is baboons: they are dangerous and should not be messed with. Do not feed them. Much of the park is bordered by city neighborhoods, and muggings can occur in isolated areas. Don't walk alone, and don't carry valuables if you can avoid it. Finally, when hiking on the mountain, be aware that dramatic weather changes can (and probably will) occur, so regardless of conditions when you set out, always carry extra layers of clothing, water, a hat, and sunscreen.

TOP ATTRACTIONS

Hoerikwaggo Trail. A great way to get acquainted with Table Mountain and all its moods is to hike part of the Hoerikwaggo Trail, which opened in 2006. The trail follows the spine of the mountains that run the length

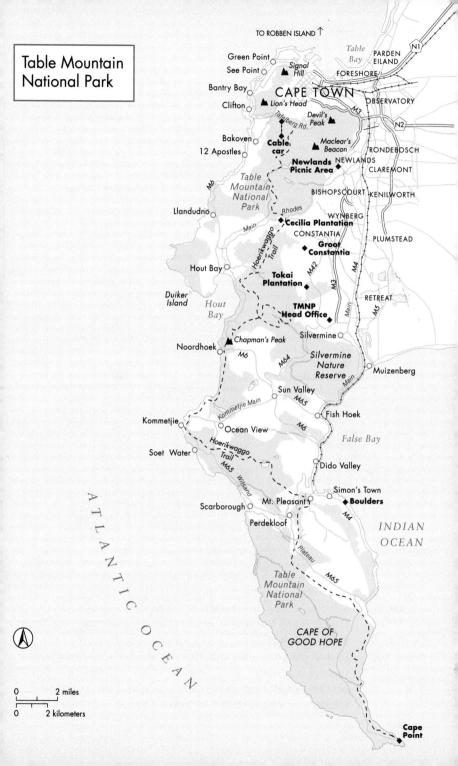

of the peninsula, linking four tented camps from the Table Mountain lower cable station all the way to the Cape Point lighthouse. The camps are located at Orangekloof, Silvermine, Slangkop, and Smitswinkel Bay. Hikes are guided and portered, but you'll have to bring your own food, which will be portered. Built on wooden platforms, the tented camps have beds, hot showers, kitchens, and *braais* (barbecues). You can opt for a single night at any of the tented camps; the adventurous can take on the whole trail (four nights). Alternately, there's the three-day "table mountain" trail aimed at international tourists, which starts at the Waterfront and ends at Kirstenbosch. It's guided, and fully catered accommodations (in cottages) are top-notch. ⊠ *Table Mountain National Park* ☎ *021/418–3803* ⊕ *www.awoltours.co.za* ✉ *R420 per person per night for Slangkop, Silvermine, and Orange Kloof; R520 per person, per night at Slangkop.*

Table Mountain. Table Mountain truly is one of southern Africa's most beautiful and impressive natural wonders. The views from its summit are awe inspiring. The mountain rises more than 3,500 feet above the city, and its distinctive flat top is visible to sailors 65 km (40 miles) out to sea. Climbing up the steplike Plattekloof Gorge—the most popular route up—will take two to three hours, depending on your fitness level. There is no water along the route; you *must* take at least 2 liters (½ gallon) of water per person. Table Mountain can be dangerous if you're not familiar with the terrain. Many paths that look like good routes down the mountain end in treacherous cliffs. ⚠ **Do not underestimate this mountain: every year local and foreign visitors to the mountain get lost, some falling off ledges, with fatal consequences.** It may be in the middle of a city, but it is not a genteel town park. Because of occasional muggings near the Rhodes Memorial (east) of the mountain, it's unwise to walk alone on that side. It's recommended that you travel in a group or, better yet, with a guide. If you want to do the climb on your own, wear sturdy shoes or hiking boots; always take warm clothes, including a windbreaker or fleece; travel with a mobile phone; and let someone know of your plans. Consult the staff at a Cape Town Tourism office for more guidelines. Another (much easier) way to reach the summit is to take the cable car, which affords fantastic views. Cable cars depart from the Lower Cable Station, which lies on the slope of Table Mountain near its western end; the station is a long way from the city on foot, and you're better off traveling by car, tuk-tuk, or taxi. ⊠ *Tokai Manor House, Tokai Rd.* ☎ *021/712–2337 main number, 021/712–0527* ⊕ *www.sanparks.org* ✉ *Free* ⊙ *Park: daily dawn–dusk. Parking lots: Oct.–Mar., daily 8–7; Apr.–Sept., daily 8–6.*

NEED A BREAK?

During the warm summer months—and on the many good winter days—Capetonians are fond of taking picnic baskets up the mountain. The best time to picnic is after 5, as some say sipping a glass of chilled Cape wine while watching the sun set from Table Mountain is one of life's great joys. The large self-service restaurant at the top of Table Mountain is called, quite simply, the **Restaurant** (☎ *021/424–8181*), and it serves good hot breakfasts, light meals, sandwiches, and local wine, and has a salad bar.

The Wilds of Table Mountain

Despite being virtually surrounded by the city, Table Mountain is a remarkably unspoiled wilderness. Most of the Cape Peninsula's 2,200 species of flora—about as many plant species as there are in all of North America and Europe combined—are found on the mountain. This includes magnificent examples of Cape Town's wild indigenous flowers known as *fynbos*, Afrikaans for "fine bush," a reference to the tiny leaves characteristic of these heathlike plants. The best time to see the mountain in bloom is between September and March, although you're sure to find flowers throughout the year.

Long gone are the days when Cape lions, zebras, and hyenas roamed the mountain, but you can still glimpse *grysbokke* (small antelopes), baboons, and the rabbitlike *dassie* (rhymes with fussy). Although these creatures, also called rock hyraxes, look like oversize guinea pigs, this is where the similarities end; the dassie's closest relative is the elephant. They congregate in large numbers near the Upper Cable Station, where they've learned to beg for food. Over the years a diet of junk food has seriously compromised their health. ■TIP→ **Do not feed the dassies, no matter how endearing they look.**

The Cocktail Bar (☎ *021/424–8181*) dishes up a spectacular view along with cocktails and bar snacks from 2 until the last cable car. As you might expect, the place has a good wine list, with local labels predominating.

Fodor's Choice ★ **Table Mountain Aerial Cableway.** This is a slick operation. Two large, wheelchair-friendly revolving cars that provide spectacular views take three to five minutes to reach the summit. The Lower Cable Station lies on the slope of Table Mountain near its western end. It's a long way from the city on foot, and you're better off traveling by car, taxi, or tuk-tuk. To get there from the City Bowl, take Buitengracht Street toward the mountain. Buitengracht turns into Kloof Nek Road, which continues all the way to a traffic circle where you turn left on Tafelberg Road. Follow signs to the Table Mountain Aerial Cableway. Taxis from the city center to the Lower Cable Station (one way) cost about R90. The scheduled MyCiti bus started covering the steep uphill from Kloof Nek to the lower cable station in July 2014.

Operating times vary from month to month according to season, daylight hours, and weather. To avoid disappointment, phone ahead for exact times. You can't prebook for the cable car, but in the ever-expanding peak season (December–April), if you arrive at 10 am you could wait for an hour. Several tour operators include a trip up the mountain in their schedules. ⊠ *Tafelberg Rd.* ☎ *021/424–8181* ⊕ *www.tablemountain.net* ⊠ *R215 round-trip, child R105 one-way* ⊗ *Hrs vary so it's best to check when you arrive, but usually daily 8:30–7:30.*

WORTH NOTING

Lion's Head and Signal Hill. The prominent peak to the right of Table Mountain is Lion's Head, a favorite hiking spot for locals. The hike takes about 1½ hours (each way), with 360-degree views of the city unfolding as you spiral up the "lion" as well as from the top. The trail is gorgeous, well marked, and on a nice day, enjoys a good flow of hikers. Though easier than hiking up Table Mountain, the last quarter will still earn you that beer or *malva* pudding (a baked sponge cake sauced with orange juice, apricot jam, and vinegar). As always, don't hike alone, and keep alert, especially as sunset approaches. For those less inclined to sweat, Signal Hill is the smaller flat-topped hill extending from the northern lower slopes of Lion's Head, also sometimes called the "Lion's Rump." Once the location for signal flags communicating weather warnings to ships visiting the bay, Signal Hill is also the home of the Noon Gun, still operated by the South African Navy and South African Astronomical Observatory. Both Lion's Head and Signal Hill are accessed by Signal Hill Road, which ends at the Signal Hill parking lot. The lot has spectacular views of Sea Point and Table Bay. Be careful around here, however, especially after hours and if it's deserted. There have been incidents of violent crime. ⊠ *Signal Hill Rd.*

Tafelberg Road. This is a very popular walking road for locals, especially when the weather is fine and windless, as it's perfectly flat with fabulous views over the City Bowl and Table Bay. The road crosses the northern side of Table Mountain before ending at Devil's Peak, providing access to the lower cable station, as well as trailheads for Platteklip Gorge (easiest ascent of Table Mountain) and Devil's Peak. After the Devil's Peak trailhead, the road is restricted to foot traffic and bicycles. As always, take the usual precautions about walking in groups and staying alert. ⊠ *Tafelberg Rd.*

SOUTHERN SUBURBS

LLANDUDNO
This strictly residential southern suburb—among the country's ritziest—has a famous eponymous beach lined with granite boulders.

HOUT BAY
About 25-minutes' drive from Cape Town Central, this once-quiet fishing village on the Atlantic coast is the gateway to Chapman's Peak Drive. Those basing themselves here will want a car to get around, but proximity to various Atlantic beaches (Hout Bay Beach itself is not great), the Constantiawine estates, the peninsula, and the city—plus relatively good-value accommodations—are the draw. The drive, which winds its way down to Nordhoek, is a must, and Hout Bay's quay-side fish-and-chips right at the farthest point of the harbor, and its all-weekend market are good value. If you're getting hungry, head to Snoekies (pronounced like cookies) right on the water, at the southern end of the little harbor. Snoek is a barracudalike fish that is eaten smoked when given its traditional Malay treatment. Try the more touristy Mariners Wharf if the former is full. Friday to Sunday sees the bustling Hout Bay market, a weekly social event for locals by night where you will also get all your original gifts for home. You'll also find craft beers, music, and good food. The market is open all day on weekends, but it gets very full.

TOP ATTRACTIONS

Chapman's Peak Drive. Rock slides and unstable cliff faces mean this fantastically scenic drive can often be closed for maintenance, as it was for the greater part of 2008–2009. Work began on the drive in 1910, when it was considered an impossibility. Charl Marais, a mining surveyor, wasn't deterred by the task and set about surveying a route by sending a worker ahead of him to chop out footholds and create rudimentary platforms for his theodolite. There are stories of him hanging on to the side of the cliff by ropes and nearly losing his life on a number of occasions. His tenacity paid off, and with the help of 700 convicts, a road was chipped and blasted out of the rock. Chapman's Peak Drive officially opened in 1922 with views rivaling those of California's Pacific Route 1 to Big Sur. When open, you can access the drive from both Noordhoek and Hout Bay. The toll-gate installed on the drive two years back has been the source of huge controversy, but you as a tourist won't notice a thing (apart from the fee). This is part of the route for the Cape Argus, the world's largest timed bicycle race, with about 35,000 entries every year from around the globe. ⊠ *Hout Bay ✛ From Hout Bay to Nordhoek* ☎ *021/791–8222* ⊕ *www.chapmanspeakdrive. co.za* ⊠ *R38 toll for cars.*

WORTH NOTING

FAMILY **World of Birds.** Here you can walk through aviaries housing 450 species of indigenous and exotic birds, including eagles, vultures, penguins, and flamingos. No cages separate you from most of the birds, so you can get some pretty good photographs; however, the big raptors are kept behind fences. The Verraux's black eagle is impressive, so be sure to stop there; it's the second-largest eagle in Africa. ⊠ *Valley Rd., Hout Bay* ☎ *021/790–2730* ⊕ *www.worldofbirds.org.za* ⊠ *R85* ☉ *Daily 9–5.*

CONSTANTIA

The most upmarket of the so-called Southern Suburbs, this primarily residential zone is home to several of the Cape's oldest wine estates, and contains a few excellent dining options as well. It's about a half-hour drive from Cape Town Central, so you'll need wheels to get around. If you don't have time for the Cape Winelands but still want to experience the Cape's stellar wines, Constantia's many excellent estates are a lovely compromise.

TOP ATTRACTIONS

Groot Constantia. The town of Constantia takes its name from the wine estate established here in 1685 by Simon van der Stel, one of the first Dutch governors of the Cape. After his death in 1712 the land was subdivided, with the heart of the estate preserved at Groot Constantia. The enormous complex enjoys the status of a national monument and is by far the most commercial and touristy of the wineries. Van der Stel's magnificent homestead, the oldest in the Cape, lies at the center of Groot Constantia. It's built in traditional Cape Dutch style, with thick, whitewashed walls, a thatch roof, small-paned windows, and ornate gables. The house is a museum furnished with exquisite period pieces. The old wine cellar sits behind the manor house. Built in 1791, it is most famous for its own ornate gable, which contains a sculpture designed by Anton Anreith. The sculpture, depicting fertility, is regarded as one of the most important in the country.

In the 19th century the sweet wines of Groot Constantia were highly regarded in Europe, but today Groot Constantia is known for its splendid red wines. The best is the excellent Bordeaux-style Gouverneurs Reserve, made mostly from Cabernet Sauvignon grapes with smaller amounts of Merlot and Cabernet Franc. The Pinotage is consistently good, too, reaching its velvety prime in about five years. The estate operates two restaurants: the elegant Jonkershuis and Simon's, which serve sophisticated meals in a spectacular setting. You can also bring your own picnic—or buy a picnic for two from Jonkershuis (R250 for two)—and relax on the lawns behind the wine cellar. ⊠ *Off Constantia Rd.* ☎ *021/794–5128 winery, 021/795–5140 museum, 021/794–6255 Jonkershuis, 021/794–1143 Simon's* ⊕ *www.grootconstantia.co.za* ⌑ *Museum R30, tastings R40, cellar tour with tastings R50* ⊗ *Museum daily 10–5. Winery May–Sept., daily 9–5; Oct.–Apr., daily 9–6. Tours 7 times per day starting at 10.*

WORTH NOTING

Buitenverwachting. Once part of Dutch governor Simon van der Stel's original Constantia farm, Buitenverwachting (which means "beyond expectation" and is roughly pronounced "Bait-in-fur-WAGH-ting") has an absolutely gorgeous setting. An oak-lined avenue leads past the Cape Dutch homestead to the modern cellar. Acres of vines spread up hillsides flanked by more towering oaks and the rocky crags of Constantiaberg Mountain. Buitenverwachting's wine is just as good as the view. The biggest seller is the slightly dry Buiten Blanc, an easy-drinking blend of a few varietals. The best red is Christine, a blend of mostly cabernet sauvignon and merlot. The winery's eponymous restaurant is one of the country's best. ⊠ *Off Klein Constantia Rd.* ☎ *021/794–5190* ⊕ *www.buitenverwachting.com* ⌑ *R40* ⊗ *Weekdays 9–5, Sat. 9–1.*

NEED A BREAK?

Buitenverwachting. Buitenverwachting serves great picnic lunches during the summer months (November–April) under the oaks on the estate's lawns. It's an idyllic setting and a most civilized way to cap a morning of wine tasting. Each picnic basket is packed with a selection of breads, chicken and other meat, pâtés, and cheeses. You can buy a bottle of estate wine as an accompaniment (they have good dry whites). The picnic costs R135 per adult, and reservations are essential. If you're looking for more formal wear, and to sit down to an excellent meal, the estate's restaurant is one of the country's best. ⊠ *Buitenverwachting Wine Estate, off Klein Constantia Rd.* ☎ *021/794–5190* ⊕ *www.buitenverwachting.com/picnic.html.*

WYNBERG

Known for its arts scene (not to mention the well-known jazz club Swingers), this southern suburb of Cape Town is a transit hub as well.

ROSEBANK

Lying largely in the shadow and protection of Table Mountain, this southern suburb is known for its leafy, affluent charm. Home to the University of Cape Town (UCT), it also boasts attractions like UCT's

Baxter Theatre *(⇨ See Nightlife and Performing Arts)*, and the Irma Stern Museum.

TOP ATTRACTIONS

Irma Stern Museum. This small but wonderful museum is dedicated to the works and art collection of Irma Stern (1894–1966), one of South Africa's greatest painters. The museum is administered by the University of Cape Town and occupies the Firs, the artist's home for 38 years. She is best known for African studies, particularly her paintings of indigenous people inspired by trips to the Congo and Zanzibar. Her collection of African artifacts, including priceless Congolese stools and carvings, is superb. ⊠ *Cecil Rd.* ☏ *021/685–5686* ⊕ *www.irmastern. co.za* ☑ *R10* ⊗ *Tues.–Sat. 10–5.*

NEWLANDS

This leafy residential suburb is famous for its many schools and as the entry for the Newlands Forest, a part of Table Mountain National Park.

TOP ATTRACTIONS

FAMILY

Fodor'sChoice
★

Kirstenbosch National Botanical Gardens. Spectacular in each season, these world-famous gardens showcase stunning South African flora in a magnificent setting, extending up the eastern slopes of Table Mountain and overlooking the sprawling city and the distant Hottentots Holland Mountains. No wonder the gardens are photographed from every angle. And now they can be seen from the Tree Canopy Walkway, opened in June. The Gardens aren't just enjoyed by out-of-town visitors; on weekends Capetonians flock here with their families to lie on the lawns and read their newspapers while the kids run riot. Walking trails meander through the gardens, and grassy banks are ideal for a picnic or afternoon nap. The plantings are limited to species indigenous to Southern Africa, including fynbos—hardy, thin-leaved plants that proliferate in the Cape. Among these are proteas, including silver trees and king proteas, ericas, and *restios* (reeds). Magnificent sculptures from Zimbabwe are displayed around the gardens, too. Garden highlights include a large cycad garden, the Bird Bath (a beautiful stone pool built around a crystal-clear spring), and the fragrance garden, which is wheelchair-friendly and has a tapping rail and Braille interpretive boards. Free 90-minute guided tours take place daily at 10 (except Sunday). Those who have difficulty walking can enjoy a comprehensive tour lasting one hour (R50, hourly 9–3) in seven-person (excluding the driver) golf carts. Another wheelchair trail leads from the main paths into the wilder section of the park, getting close to the feel of the mountain walks. Concerts featuring the best of South African entertainment—from classical music to township jazz to rock and roll—are held on summer Sundays starting an hour before sunset. But get there early, as the space fills quickly with picnicking music lovers. A visitor center by the conservatory houses a restaurant, bookstore, and coffee shop. Unfortunately, muggings have become increasingly more common in the gardens' isolated areas, and women are advised not to walk alone in the upper reaches of the park far from general activity. ⊠ *Rhodes Dr.* ☏ *021/799–8783* ⊕ *www.sanbi.org* ☑ *R50* ⊗ *Apr.–Aug., daily 8–6; Sept.–Mar., daily 8–7.*

OBSERVATORY

Popular as a residential area for nearby University of Cape Town students, this southern suburb is also home to the South Africa Astronomical Observatory, after which it is named.

RONDEBOSCH

Home to the main campus of the University of Cape Town, this suburb sits along the eastern slope of Table Mountain.

WORTH NOTING

Rhodes Memorial. Rhodes served as prime minister of the Cape from 1890 to 1896. He made his fortune in the Kimberley diamond rush, but his greatest dream was to forge a Cape–Cairo railway, a tangible symbol of British dominion in Africa. The classical-style granite memorial sits high on the slopes of Devil's Peak, on part of Rhodes's old estate, Groote Schuur. A mounted rider symbolizing energy faces north toward the continent for which Rhodes felt such passion. A bust of Rhodes dominates the temple—ironically, he's leaning on one hand as if he's about to nod off. ⊠ *Off Rhodes Dr.* ⌧ *Free.*

NEED A BREAK?

Rhodes Memorial Restaurant. The Rhodes Memorial Restaurant, tucked under towering pines behind the memorial, is a pleasant spot that serves breakfast, tea, and a light lunch. Unremarkable food, although it is under new management. ⊠ *Off Rhodes Dr.* ☎ *021/689–9151.*

TOKAI

Between Constantia and the beginning of the Cape Peninsula, this largely residential area (and effectively the southern end of the Southern Suburbs) is home to the Cape's oldest wine estate, which also hosts two excellent restaurants.

WORTH NOTING

Tokai Arboretum. This gorgeous and tranquil national forest is planted with hundreds of tree species from all over the world, including Californian redwoods and a variety of oaks. A favorite spot for picnickers and cyclists, the Arboretum also has a simple tea garden that serves hearty home-style meals and delicious cakes. On the way in to the Arboretum is a crumbling Cape Dutch manor. Built in 1795 with a facade designed by famed architect Louis Michel Thibault, the homestead, which is not open to the public, is reputedly haunted. ⊠ *Tokai Rd.* ⌧ *Free* ☉ *Daily sunrise–sunset.*

BLOUBERG

Make the 25-km (16-mile), 40-minute trip north from the city to the other side of Table Bay, and you'll be rewarded with an exceptional (and the most famous) view of Cape Town and Table Mountain as well as a good, albeit windy, beach that is known for kite surfing and also kite flying. The Kite Shop in Victoria Wharf at the V&A Waterfront has many colorful, high-tech kites for sale, and there is a kite shop in the new shopping development next to the beach. The lawns of the Blue Peter Hotel are a favorite sunset cocktail spot, especially with tired kite- and windsurfers, and the thatched restaurant Ons Huisie (an internationally recognized heritage site) is a winner for fish-and-chips and has a children's jungle gym area attached. If you want to come from the city for the sunset—possibly the best in Cape Town—leave Cape Town Central before 4 pm to avoid the horrible rush-hour traffic.

CAPE PENINSULA

The peninsula is a treat for any Cape Town visitor, and a round-trip drive that takes in both the False Bay coastline and the Atlantic Ocean is a memorable experience. Among the highlights of the False Bay coast are the quaint fishing village of Kalk Bay, and Boulders Beach; both are must-visits, the former for being an authentic, historic village right on the sea with good food and bars, and the latter for the sheer privilege of being able to walk among the threatened African (jackass) penguins that call the national park's protected beach home. Cape Point and the Cape of Good Hope nature reserve are 15 minutes farther on at the tip of the peninsula, and few fail to fall in love with the area's windswept beauty. The wilder and more rugged Atlantic coastline is one of the most stunning in the world. Highlights include a drive along the Misty Cliffs between Scarborough and Witsands, and horseback riding down Noordhoek beach. You might even consider spending a night or two in one of the many B&Bs that dot the coast, or even inside the Cape Point nature reserve at one of the cottages on Olifantsbos Beach.

TIMING AND PRECAUTIONS

Distances on the peninsula are not that great, so it's certainly possible to drive the roughly 120-km (75-mile) loop in a day, visiting a few sights of interest to you. It's equally possible, and far more rewarding, to spend three days here, either moving slowly around the peninsula and staying in a different guesthouse each night or returning to a central spot in the Southern Suburbs or town at the end of each day. Just remember, however, that during peak season (generally mid-November–mid-January) and holidays, traffic can keep you gridlocked for many frustrating hours. Although touring the peninsula poses no obvious danger, you are advised not to park or walk alone in isolated areas. And watch out for baboons at Cape Point. If you're carrying food, they invite themselves to lunch and can be highly aggressive—the result of human folly.

ATLANTIC COAST
NOORDHOEK
38 km (24 miles) southwest of Cape Town.

This popular beach community has stunning white sands that stretch all the way to Kommetjie along the aptly named Long Beach. The small bordering Noordhoek Farm Village has become a retreat for the arts-and-crafts community, with a couple of galleries and boutiques showcasing local work. Long Beach is very popular with surfers and runners, and you can walk all the way to Kommetjie. But don't walk alone or when the beach is deserted, as attacks are not uncommon. Horseback riding along the beach and through the fynbos-covered dunes is a memorable and highly worthwhile excursion.

NEED A BREAK?

Café Roux. Nestled behind Chapman's Peak—and minutes away from Noordhoek Beach—Café Roux is an unpretentious outdoor café with great homemade food and fabulous South African wines at competitive

The Cape
Peninsula

prices. You can get a taste of rural Cape Town life in "paddock" country here. ⊠ *Noordhoek Farm Village, Chapman's Peak Dr., Noordhoek* ☎ *021/789–2538.*

The Toad in the Village. The Toad in the Village, which is next to Café Roux (and has the same owners), is a country pub and restaurant with a beer garden, deck in the trees, good kids' menu, and live music in the evenings. It's a real locals place. A jungle gym for the kids sits alongside. The Toad is well known for good pub fare and an extensive range of draft beer and other beverages—try the Toad Lager, which is named after endangered Western Leopard Toad Ronald Mustafa Ponsenby McGraff. If the name sounds silly it's because it is—but it goes down very smoothly. ⊠ *Noordhoek Farm Village, Chapman's Peak Dr., Noordhoek* ☎ *021/789–2973.*

KOMMETJIE

3 km (1 mile) south of Noordhoek; 41 km (25 miles) southwest of Cape Town.

A pleasant, somewhat isolated village, Kommetjie has a scenic 45-minute walk down Long Beach that leads to the wreck of the *Kakapo*, a steamship that ran aground on her maiden voyage in 1900. This is a surfer's paradise, with some really big waves, a few gentler breaks, and for swimmers, a dangerous undertow. Because of a few muggings on Long Beach a couple of years back, people generally walk here in groups or in couples in the early mornings and at sundown.

Slangkop Point Lighthouse. If you don't have security in numbers, instead of visiting Long Beach, walk instead to the Slangkoppunt Lighthouse. At 111 feet, it's the tallest cast-iron tower on South Africa's coast and is located almost exactly midway between Robben Island and Cape Point. The lighthouse has a 5-million-candlepower light and a range of 30 nautical miles. Since the lamp was officially lit in 1919 it has been capable of producing four flashes every 30 seconds. It's one of the few lighthouses in the world still to be manned by a keeper—known these days as a "lighthouse officer." Unfortunately it's no longer famed lighthouse keeper Peter Dennett, who was known for giving great tours—he passed away in January 2012. ⊠ *Kommetjie* ☎ *021/783–1717* ☾ *Daily 10–3.*

SCARBOROUGH

9 km (5.5 miles) south of Kommetjie; 50 km (30.5 miles) southwest of Cape Town.

This tiny vacation community has one of the best beaches on the peninsula, and is populated by a disproportionate number of conservation biologists. Look no further than the setting to explain that one. From Kommetjie to Scarborough, the M65 hugs the shoreline, snaking between the mountains and the crashing surf. This part of the shore is considered unsafe for swimming, but experienced surfers, Boogie boarders, and windsurfers revel in the wind and waves, and the scenery is heart-stopping. The beach here has its own baboon troop.

FALSE BAY COAST
MUIZENBERG
30 km (19 miles) south of Cape Town.

Once a fashionable resort town, this is now one of the most cosmopolitan areas of Cape Town. Many of the beautiful art deco beachfront buildings that were fast becoming slums have been renovated into upscale apartments. New restaurants like the popular Knead, the great Sinnful ice cream shop next door, and numerous fish-and-chip shops have opened, and property prices are soaring. Muizenberg now appeals to families, beginner surfers, and stand-up paddleboarders. Surf shops offering lessons, rental boards, and wet suits line the beachfront. A dated pavilion houses a swimming pool, waterslides, toilets, changing rooms, and snack shops.

KALK BAY
30 km (19 miles) south of Cape Town.

This small, fascinating harbor, which shelters a weathered fishing fleet, takes its name from the seashells that were once baked in large kilns near the shore to produce lime (*kalk* in Afrikaans). Tiny cottages crowd the narrow, cobbled streets, which cling to the mountain. The town's funky clothing shops, galleries, antiques shops, and cozy bistros can fill a whole day of rambling. Here gnarled fisherfolk rub shoulders with artists, writers, surfers, yuppies, New Age trendies, and genteel ladies with blue hair. During whale-watching season the gentle giants rub up against the harbor wall, and if you time your visit right, you can almost touch them. You can also walk up any of the steep stairways to Boyes Drive and from there up the mountain, or relax and down a few beers in the sun at the Brass Bell while local surfers strut their stuff on Kalk Bay Reef. Other possibilities on your to-do list might include dropping your own line off the pier (fishing supplies are available from the small supermarket on the Main Road) or watching the harbor seals that loll around waiting for fishy discards when the boats come in. The lives of the fisherfolk are changing rapidly because of declining fish stocks, and many are now shorebound without an income, in part because of the controversial requirement for fishing permits.

NEED A BREAK?

Kalky's. Kalky's, right on the harbor, is a great place to get generous portions of fish-and-chips. The seagulls will fight for any of your leftover scraps, as will Robby, the resident seal. It's a great setting, and watching the waves break over the harbor wall when the sea is pounding (and you are inside) is thrilling. ⊠ *Kalk Bay Harbour, Kalk Bay* ☎ *021/788–6396.*

Olympia Café. The Olympia Café, with a menu of Mediterranean-influenced specialties, is popular and usually packed to capacity, especially on weekends. At the affiliated bakery just around the corner, you can buy take-away cappuccinos and pasties filled with springbok and sometimes even rabbit. The croissants are more bread-like than light French pastry. Grab a stool at the bar by the window and watch the ocean and passing foot-traffic on the pavement in front of you. ⊠ *134 Main Rd., Kalk Bay* ☎ *021/788–6396.*

FISH HOEK

2 km (1 mile) south of Kalk Bay; 43 km (27 miles) south of Cape Town.

Jager's Walk, from the south side of Fish Hoek Beach to Sunny Cove, is a pleasant, scenic, wheelchair-friendly pathway that meanders through the rocks, providing access to some sheltered natural rock pools that are just great for swimming. Outside of peak traffic, it takes about 40 minutes to get from Cape Town to Fish Hoek, but over Christmas and New Year's the roads get very congested, so leave early to miss the crowds.

SIMON'S TOWN

10 km (6 miles) south of Kalk Bay; 45 km (28 miles) south of Cape Town.

Picturesque Simon's Town has many lovely old buildings and possibly the peninsula's best swimming beaches at Seaforth and Boulders, a gem that is also home to a large colony of African penguins. The town has had a long association with the Royal Navy. British troops landed here in 1795 before defeating the Dutch at the Battle of Muizenberg, and the town served as a base for the Royal Navy from 1814 to 1957, when it was handed over to the South African navy. Today you are bound to see plenty of men and women decked out in crisp white uniforms.

Jubilee Square, a dockside plaza that serves as the de facto town center, is just off the main road (St. George's Road). Next to the dock wall stands a statue of Just Nuisance, a Great Dane adopted as a mascot by the Royal Navy during World War II. Just Nuisance apparently liked his pint of beer and would accompany sailors on the train into Cape Town. He had the endearing habit of leading drunken sailors—and only sailors—that he found in the city back to the station in time to catch the last train. The navy went so far as to induct him into the service as an able seaman attached to the HMS *Afrikander.* He died at the age of seven in April 1944 and was given a military funeral. Just below Jubilee Square is the popular Simon's Town Waterfront, with numerous shops and restaurants. Day cruises, deep-sea fishing trips, and kayaking trips leave from the harbor.

If you're looking for something to entertain children the area has quite a few child-friendly options, including the SAS *Assegaai,* the South African Naval Museum's submarine, which is moored in the harbor with former submariners as guides.

NEED A BREAK?

The Sweetest Thing. The Sweetest Thing serves Simon's Town's best home-made cakes, pastries, and cookies, as well as light lunch options like savory pies and quiches. It's a must-visit if you're hungry and in town during lunchtime. ⊠ *82 St. George's St., Simon's Town* ☎ *021/786–4200.*

FAMILY **Scratch Patch.** At Scratch Patch, a gemstone factory about 1 km (½ mile) north of Simon's Town, you can buy and fill a bag (you pay according to the size of the bag) with gemstones that you pick from a garden filled ankle-deep with semi-precious stones, such as tiger's eye, rose quartz, amethyst, jasper, agates, and crystals. Obviously this is a winner with children, and since 1970, when Scratch Patch opened, the owners claim it has been copied around the world. If you're lucky, you might find the rare Blue Lace Agate, which has a really interesting story linking it to mineral-rich Namibia and South Africa's little town of Springbok. Attached is Mineral World, a store that sells gemstone jewelry, which has another outlet in the V&A Waterfront in Cape Town. ☒ *Dido Valley Rd., Simon's Town* ☎ *021/786–2020* ⊕ *www.scratchpatch.co.za* ⌑ *Free; bags of gemstones R17–R95* ⊙ *Weekdays 8:30–4:45, weekends 9–5:30.*

Simon's Town Museum. The somewhat rustic Simon's Town Museum features historical exhibits of the town, including numerous photographs and memorabilia from former nonwhite residents who were removed to the townships of the Cape Flats in the 1960s. ☒ *The Residency, Court Rd., Simon's Town* ☎ *021/786–3046* ⊕ *www.simonstown.com/museum/stm.htm* ⌑ *R10* ⊙ *Weekdays 10–4, Sat. 10–1.*

South African Naval Museum. The naval museum is filled with model ships, old navigational equipment, old South African navy divers' equipment, a few real, life-size boats, and, oddly enough, a helicopter. You can also climb to the top of the building's clock tower. If you haven't been on a submarine before, a visit to the SAS *Assegaai,* moored against a pier in the harbor, is of serious interest (nice warm beanies with the sub's insignia are on sale). It's staffed by naval personnel and volunteers. ☒ *Naval Dockyard, St. George's St., Simon's Town* ☎ *021/787–4686* ⊕ *simonstown.com/navalmuseum/contact.htm* ⌑ *Free (donations accepted)* ⊙ *Daily 10–4.*

FAMILY   **Warrior Toy Museum.** Dinky Toys, boats, trains, soldiers, airplanes, some 4,000 model cars, and 500 dolls—what's not to like about this toy museum that is equally enjoyable for both kids and adults? It's packed with hundreds of models of all things locomotive: from cars to trains and tanks, these miniature vehicles date from the 1920s to the present. Some are on sale at the attached collectibles shop. ☒ *St. George's St., Simon's Town* ☎ *021/786–1395* ⌑ *Free* ⊙ *Daily 10–4.*

CAPE OF GOOD HOPE
Cape Point is 60 km (37 miles) southwest of Cape Town.

Once a nature reserve on its own, this section of Table Mountain National Park covers more than 19,000 acres. Much of the park consists of rolling hills covered with fynbos and laced with miles of walking trails, for which maps are available at the park entrance. It also has beautiful deserted beaches (you can swim at some of these beaches, but note that there are no amenities or lifeguards). Eland, baboon, ostrich, and bontebok (a colorful antelope nearly hunted to extinction in the early 20th century) are among the animals that roam the park. A paved road runs 12½ km (8 miles) to the tip of the peninsula, and a turnoff leads to the Cape of Good Hope, a rocky cape that is the southwesternmost point of the continent. A plaque marks the spot—otherwise you would never know you're standing on a site of such significance.

The park has some excellent land-based whale-watching spots. About June to November, whales return to these waters to calve. You're most likely to see the Southern Right whale in False Bay, but the occasional humpback and Bryde's whale also show up. When the water is calm, you may even be lucky enough to see a school of dolphins looping past. The Rooikrans parking lot is good for whale-watching, but there are a number of lookout points. It's just a matter of driving around until you see the characteristic spray or a shiny black fluke.

Fodor's Choice **Cape Point.** Cape Point is a dramatic knife's edge of rock that slices into
★ the Atlantic. Looking out to sea from the viewing platform, you feel you're at the tip of Africa, even though that honor officially belongs to another dramatic point at Cape Agulhas, about 160 km (100 miles) to the southeast. From Cape Point the views of False Bay and the Hottentots Holland Mountains are astonishing. The walk up to the viewing platform and the old lighthouse is very steep; a funicular makes the run every three or four minutes. Take a jacket or sweater—the wind can be fierce. It took six years, from 1913 to 1919, to build the old lighthouse, 816 feet above the high-water mark. On a clear day the old lighthouse was a great navigational mark, but when the mists rolled in it was useless, so a new and much lower lighthouse (286 feet) was built at Dias Lookout Point. The newer, revolving lighthouse, the most powerful on the South African coast, emits a group of three flashes every 30 seconds. It has prevented a number of ships from ending up on Bellows or Albatross Rock below. You can't go into the lighthouses, but the views from their bases are spectacular.

Stark reminders of the ships that didn't make it are dotted around the Cape. You'll see their rusty remains on some of the beaches. One of the more famous wrecks is the *Thomas T. Tucker,* one of hundreds of Liberty Ships produced by the United States to enable the Allies to move vast amounts of supplies during World War II. It wasn't the German U-boats patrolling the coastline that did the ship in. Rather the fog closed in, and on her maiden voyage in 1942, she ended up on Olifantsbos Point. Fortunately, all on board were saved, but the wreck soon broke up in the rough seas that pound the coast.

The mast you see on the western slopes of Cape Point near the lighthouse belongs to the Global Atmosphere Watch Station (GAW). The South African Weather Bureau, together with the Fraunhofer Institute in Garmisch, Germany, maintains a research laboratory here to monitor long-term changes in the chemistry of the earth's atmosphere, which may impact climate. This is one of 20 GAWs throughout the world, chosen because the air at Cape Point is considered particularly pure most of the time.

The large sit-down Two Oceans Restaurant has spectacular views, and the food is also good. Also here are a kiosk selling snacks and three gift shops. During peak season (December and January), visit Cape Point as early in the day as you can; otherwise you'll be swamped by horrendous numbers of tour buses and their occupants. A fun alternative is an overnight hike with comfortable basic accommodations and incredible views, booked through South African National Parks. Unfortunately the indigenous chacma baboons are increasingly under threat, and the Peninsula's population is currently estimated at only 350 to 400 individuals. Many baboons have been shot for raiding homes and stealing food. Baboon-feeding tourists are largely responsible for this serious situation. ⚠ **Be wary of baboons in the parking lot; they can be dangerous if provoked. Do not feed them.** ⊠ *Off the M65 (Plateau Rd.)* ⊕ *60 km*

(37 miles) southwest of Cape Town ☎ *021/780–9526, 021/780–9204* ⊕ *capepoint.co.za* ✉ *R60 park entrance; funicular R40* ⏲ *Apr.–Sept., daily 7–5; Oct.–Mar., daily 6–6; last exit 1 hr after closing.*

BEACHES

Updated by Angus Begg

With panoramic views of mountains tumbling to the ocean, the stunning sandy beaches of the Cape Peninsula are a major draw for Capetonians and visitors alike. Beautiful as the beaches may be, don't expect to spend hours splashing in the surf: the water around Cape Town is very, very cold (there's a slim chance you might get used to it). Beaches on the Atlantic are washed by the Benguela Current flowing up from the Antarctic, and in midsummer the water hovers around 10°C–15°C (50°F–60°F). The water on the False Bay side is usually 5°C (9°F) warmer, so if it's warmer waters you seek, head to False Bay beaches such as Muizenberg, Fish Hoek, and Boulders. Cape beaches are renowned for their clean, snow-white, powdery sand. Beachcombers will find every kind of beach to suit them, from intimate coves to sheltered bays and wild, wide beaches stretching forever. If you are looking for more tropical water temperatures, head for the warm Indian Ocean waters of KwaZulu-Natal, the Eastern Cape, or the Garden Route.

The major factor that affects any day at a Cape beach is wind. In summer howling southeasters, known collectively as the Cape Doctor, are all too common and can ruin a trip to the beach; during these gales you're better off at Clifton or Llandudno—protected by the mountain-shadow of Lion's Head—on the Atlantic side; the sheltered but very small St. James Beach, on the False Bay side; and maybe even the southern corner of False Bay's Fish Hoek Beach or one of the pools along Jager's Walk. Boulders and Seaforth are also often sheltered from southeasters.

Every False Bay community has its own beach, but most are not reviewed here. In comparison with Atlantic beaches, most of them are rather small and often crowded, sandwiched between the sea and the commuter rail line, with Fish Hoek a major exception. South of Simon's Town the beaches tend to be wilder and less developed, except for the very popular Seaforth and Millers Point beaches.

TIMING AND PRECAUTIONS

The closest beaches to town are Clifton and Camps Bay, which are just minutes away during non-rush-hour traffic. But in summer, when you can't move for traffic, getting anywhere—and especially to the beaches—can take a frustratingly long time. If you want an adventure and are eager to avoid the holiday traffic, jump on the train that runs by the False Bay beaches of Muizenberg, Fish Hoek, and Boulders. From the center of town it will take you about 40 minutes to get to Fish Hoek, and the views from the train across the bay from Muizenberg onward are absolutely spectacular.

At many beaches there may be powerful waves, a strong undertow, and dangerous riptides. The lifeguard situation is haphazard and varies according to funding and the availability of the lifeguards; the service combines voluntary and professional guards. Lifeguards work the main beaches, but only on weekends and during school breaks. Other beaches are unpatrolled. Although it's nice to stroll along a lonely beach, remember it's risky to wander off on your own in a deserted area. ⚠ **Toilet facilities at beaches are limited.**

Southeasters can also bring blue bottles—Portuguese men-of-war. As these jellyfishlike creatures can sting, you should avoid swimming at these times. (If you see them washed up on the shore, that's a good sign to stay out of the water.)

CAPE TOWN BEACHES

BLOUBERG

FAMILY
Fodor's Choice
★

Blouberg Beach. Blouberg is divided into two parts: Big Bay, which hosts surfing and windsurfing contests, and Little Bay, better suited to sunbathers, rock-pool inhabitants, and families. It can be windy here, which is great for kite flying and kite surfing. Kite surfing has become extremely popular along this side of Table Bay, and adrenaline junkies blow off work to come here and ride the waves. For safety, swim in front of the lifeguard club. **Amenities:** food and drink; lifeguards; parking; water sports. **Best for:** surfing; walking; windsurfing. ⊠ *Blouberg* ⊹ *Take the N1 north to R27 to Milnerton and Bloubergstrand. Hug road following bay.*

CLIFTON

Clifton Beach. A fantastic beach area that's almost always wind-free, this is where the in crowd comes to see and be seen. Some of the Cape's most desirable houses cling to the slopes above the beach, and elegant yachts often anchor in the calm water beyond the breakers. Granite outcroppings divide the beach into four segments, unimaginatively known as First, Second, Third, and Fourth beaches. Fourth Beach is popular with families, whereas the others support a strong social and singles' scene. Swimming is reasonably safe here, although the undertow is strong and the water, again, freezing. Lifeguards are on duty on weekends and in peak season. Clifton is also a favorite for drinks and picnics, but take care with containers, as alcohol on this beach is officially prohibited. **Amenities:** food and drink; lifeguards; parking; showers; toilets. **Best for:** partiers; sunset; walking; surfing. ⊠ *Off Victoria Rd., Clifton* Ⓜ *MyCiti bus from town. It's part of Cape Town's public transport revolution. You need to buy a card; ask at hotel. It's efficient, and generally reliable for a couple of days if you aren't driving.*

CAMPS BAY

Camps Bay Beach. The spectacular western edge of Table Mountain, known as the Twelve Apostles, provides the backdrop for this long, sandy beach that slopes gently to the very cold water from a grassy verge. Playing Frisbee or volleyball is very popular on this beach. The surf is powerful, but sunbathers can cool off in a tidal pool on the west end of the beach or under the outdoor showers. Camps Bay's über-trendy, popular bar and restaurant strip lies yards away across Victoria Road. The wind can blow hard here—or not. Inasmuch as the strip is a refreshment break for groups of cyclists training for the annual Cape Argus, movie stars, models, and the rich and famous like to stay around here. It tends toward the pretentious on weekends. **Amenities:** food and drink; parking; showers. **Best for:** partiers; surfing; walking. ⊠ *Victoria Rd., Camps Bay* Ⓜ *Hout Bay bus from OK Bazaars on Adderley St.*

BEACHES IN THE SOUTHERN SUBURBS
LLANDUDNO
Llandudno Beach. Die-hard fans return to this beach again and again, and who can blame them? Its setting, among giant boulders at the base of a mountain, is glorious, and sunsets here attract their own aficionados. The surf can be very powerful on the northern side of the beach (where you'll find all the surfers, of course), but the southern side is fine for a quick dip—and in this water that's all you'll want. Lifeguards are on duty on weekends and in season. If you come by bus, brace yourself for a long walk down (and back up) the mountain from the bus stop on the M6. Parking is a nightmare, but most hotels run shuttles in summer. There are no shops here, so take what snacks you need with you. **Amenities:** parking; showers; toilets. **Best for:** partiers; sunset; surfing; swimming; walking. ⊠ *Llandudno* ✛ *Take Llandudno exit off the M6.*

HOUT BAY
Hout Bay Beach. Cradled in a lovely bay of the same name and guarded by a 1,000-foot peak known as the Sentinel, Hout Bay is the center of Cape Town's crayfishing industry (legal and otherwise) and operates several fish-processing plants. It also has knockout views of the mountains, gentle surf, and easy access to the restaurants and bars of Mariner's Wharf. The fact that this is a working harbor, added to the raw sewage of the Inzamo Yethu informal settlement a short walk upstream, means this is unfortunately a polluted beach, however beautiful it looks. You are advised not to swim here. **Amenities:** food and drink; parking. **Best for:** solitude; walking. ⊠ *Off the M6, Hout Bay* Ⓜ *MyCiti bus from city. Ask at accommodation establishment.*

CAPE PENINSULA ATLANTIC BEACHES
KOMMETJIE
Long Beach. A vast expanse of white sand stretching 6½ km (4 miles) from the base of Chapman's Peak to Kommetjie, this is one of the wildest and least populated beaches, with fluffy white sand and dunes over which is a lagoon and private nature reserve. Because of the wind and the space, it attracts horseback riders and walkers rather than sunbathers, and the surfing is excellent. There are no lifeguards and there is no bus service, and, as at some other beaches, at the wrong times and more isolated spots, there are real safety concerns. Despite patrollers on horseback and the occasional all-terrain vehicle, crime is an issue here, and women in particular should be careful. Tourists always do best not to look like tourists. Hang out with other people, just in case, unless you're part of a group. **Amenities:** parking. **Best for:** solitude; sunset; surfing; walking. ⊠ *Off M6, Noordhoek.*

CAPE PENINSULA FALSE BAY COAST BEACHES
FISH HOEK
FAMILY **Fish Hoek Beach.** With the southern corner protected from southeasters by Elsie's Peak, this sandy beach attracts retirees and families with young kids, who appreciate the calm, clear water—it may be

the safest swimming beach in the Cape, although sharks are sighted fairly regularly in the bay between September and March (though that doesn't stop people from swimming, surfing, and Boogie boarding here); shark spotters are employed to keep an eye out. The middle and northern end of the beach are also popular with catamaran sailors and windsurfers, who often stage regattas offshore. The snorkeling is good, and it's a great beach for Boogie boarding. It's also one of the best places to see whales dur-

> ### SPOTTING SHARKS
>
> Shark spotters are employed at several of Cape Town's False Bay beaches—and on Boyes Drive looking down on the bay—to warn swimmers when great white sharks are out and about. Great whites are usually found close to the shore in the summer months (September–March), and spotters record around 170 sightings per year.

ing calving season—approximately August to November—though there have been whale sightings as early as June and as late as January. **Amenities:** food and drink; lifeguards; parking (fee); showers; toilets; water sports. **Best for:** surfing; walking; windsurfing; swimming. ⊠ *Beach Rd., Fish Hoek* ✛ *Parking is at southern end of beach.*

SIMON'S TOWN

FAMILY

Fodor's Choice

★

Boulders Beach. This series of small coves lies among giant granite boulders on the southern outskirts of Simon's Town. Part of Table Mountain National Park, the beach is best known for its resident colony of African penguins. You must stay out of the fenced-off breeding beach, but don't be surprised if a wandering bird comes waddling up to you to take a look. Penguin-viewing platforms, accessible from either the Boulders Beach or Seaforth side, provide close-up looks at these comical birds. When you've had enough penguin peering, you can stroll back to Boulders Beach for some excellent swimming in the quiet coves. This beach is great for children because it is so protected, and the sea is warm(ish) and calm. It can get crowded in summer, though, so go early. Without traffic, it takes about 45 minutes to get here from town, less from the Southern Suburbs. Priceless. ⊠ *Kleintuin Rd., Sea Forth, Simon's Town* ✛ *Follow signs from Bellvue Rd.* ☎ *021/786–2329* ⊕ *www.sanparks. org* ✉ *Adults: R45; children 2–11: R20* ☉ *Daily, Nov.–Mar. 8–7; Apr.– Aug. 8–5; Sept. and Oct. 8–6:30.*

QUICK
BITES

Boulders Beach Lodge and Restaurant. Don't be fooled by its low-key, casual atmosphere, Boulders Beach Lodge and Restaurant serves seriously good food, worth a visit even without the penguins. Sitting on the huge veranda with stunning views over False Bay, expect to enjoy spectacular and reasonably priced Pacific Rim–inspired cuisine using the freshest seafood, as well as great burgers, salads, and killer breakfasts. A tucked-away Cape Town secret. ⊠ *Boulders Beach Lodge, Simon's Town* ☎ *021/786–1758.*

MUIZENBERG

FAMILY **Muizenberg Beach.** Once the fashionable resort of South African high society, this beach is now the most cosmopolitan in Cape Town, with surfers from the townships riding the waves a happy example of the evolving new South Africa. The long, sandy beach did lose much of its glamour, but things are looking up again for this grand old lady of the city's warm-water beaches. The beach is lined with colorful bathing boxes of the type once popular at British resorts. Lifeguards are on duty, and the sea is shallow and reasonably safe. If you're keen on stretching your legs, you can walk along the beach or take the picturesque concrete path known as the Catwalk, which connects Muizenberg to St. James. **Amenities:** food and drink; lifeguards; parking; showers; toilets; water sports. **Best for:** sunrise; surfing; swimming; walking; windsurfing ⊠ *Off the M4, Muizenberg.*

> **ENDANGERED AFRICAN PENGUINS**
>
> Populations of the African penguin (*Spheniscus demersus*) have plummeted because of declining anchovy and sardine stocks, as well as predation by a growing seal population. Up to 50,000 of the birds—who call Boulders Beach and Stony Point near Betty's Bay (⇨ *Chapter 3, Western Cape*) in the Overberg home—were lost in just two years, and the current population hovers around 2,700. Penguins mate for life and have been known to return to the same nesting site for up to 15 years.

WHERE TO EAT

Updated by
Lee Middleton

Cape Town is the culinary capital of South Africa and quite possibly the continent. It certainly has the best restaurants in southern Africa. Nowhere else in the country is the populace so discerning about food, and nowhere else is there such a wide selection of high-quality restaurants. Western culinary history here dates back to the 17th century—Cape Town was founded specifically to grow food—and that heritage is reflected in the city's cuisine and the fact that a number of restaurants operate in historic town houses and 18th-century wine estates.

Cape Town dining today offers a global culinary experience, with Cape chefs showing the same enthusiasm for international food trends as their counterparts worldwide. French and Italian fare has long been available, but with Thai, Japanese, and Pan-Asian influences flooding in, accents of lemongrass, miso, and yuzu have become de rigueur in fine-dining kitchens. Middle Eastern cuisine is finally making some headway, and the Americas have also come to the fore, with plenty of burgers and ribs, and even chicken and waffles popping up on menus these days, not to mention a few South American and passable Mexican eateries. Ubiquitous pan-Asian fare is probably not as good as what you might be used to in major American cities; sushi is also easily found, though largely limited to tuna and salmon, and often prepared with lots of drizzled mayo and sauces. The locavore trend toward organic produce and healthful dishes is also gaining popularity, though attitudes toward vegetarianism in this meat-happy land remain somewhat backward.

WINE

Wine lists at many restaurants reflect the enormous expansion and resurgence of the Cape wine industry, with some establishments compiling exciting selections of lesser-known gems. More and more restaurants employ a sommelier to offer guidance on wine, but diners, even in modest establishments, can expect staff to be well-versed about both wine lists and menus. Wines are expensive in restaurants (often three times what you'd pay in a wine shop), and connoisseurs may be irritated by corkage charges (around R35), but only a handful of restaurants will refuse to open a bottle you bring.

TIMING AND WHAT TO WEAR

During summer months restaurants in trendier areas are geared up for late-night dining but will accept dinner orders from about 6. In winter locals tend to dine earlier and kitchens can often close by 9:30 if customers aren't waiting. That said, there are venues that stay open late year-round, particularly at the V&A Waterfront and the Camps Bay beachfront along the Atlantic seaboard. Other areas that are meccas for food lovers include Kloof Street and Bree Street in the City Bowl up through Gardens. Many restaurants are crowded in high season, so it's best to book in advance whenever possible; top-rated restaurants can be fully booked months in advance. With the exception of a very few high-end restaurants—where a jacket is suggested—the dress code in Cape Town is very casual.

⇨ *For more information on South Africa food, see Flavors of South Africa, in Chapter 1.*

WHAT IT COSTS IN SOUTH AFRICAN RAND				
	$	$$	$$$	$$$$
Restaurants	under R100	R100–R150	R151–R200	over R200

Restaurant prices are the average cost of a main course at dinner or, if dinner is not served, at lunch.

CAPE TOWN CENTRAL

Hardly a month goes by without a new café or restaurant opening in the city center. Many are housed in historic buildings, and most are open only for lunch and breakfast, as "town" tends to gets quiet after hours. However, the areas of Heritage Square and Long and Bree streets are an exception, and you'll find some fantastic dinner choices listed here.

$$$
ECLECTIC

✕ **Birds.** This charming and centrally located café draws diners with simple but exquisitely rendered food in a soothing setting of exposed brick and blond wood on otherwise busy Bree Street. Menus change regularly, but the chicken pie shaped like an egg is legendary, and flavorful salads like the "bird's nest" with its poached egg, broccoli, mushrooms, and toasted pine nuts leave you full but feeling healthy. Dinners are all understated extravagance with dishes like duck confit with a miso-plum glaze, or octopus with saffron potatoes, tamarind, and basil. Everything is made daily and written up on the chalkboard menu. A large selection

BEST BETS FOR CAPE TOWN DINING

With many restaurants to choose from, how will you decide where to eat? Fodor's writers and editors have selected their favorite restaurants by price, cuisine, and experience in the lists here. Fodor's Choice properties represent the "best of the best" in every price category. You can also search by neighborhood—just peruse our reviews on the following pages.

Fodor's Choice

Aubergine, $$$, p. 88
Bistro Bizerca, $$$, p. 85
Bistro 1682, $$, p. 99
5 Rooms, $$$, p. 98
The Foodbarn, $$$, p. 100
The Greenhouse, $$$$, p. 98
Hemelhuijs, $$, p. 86
La Colombe, $$$$, p. 98
Myoga, $$$, p. 99
95 Keerom, $$$, p. 86
Nobu, $$$$, p. 91
Olympia Café, $$, p. 101
The Pot Luck Club, $$$, p. 87
The Test Kitchen, $$$$, p. 87

By Price

$

Café Roux , p. 100
Giovanni's Deliworld, p. 91

$$

Food Barn & Deli, p. 100
Hemelhuijs, p. 86
Olympia Café, p. 101

$$$

Aubergine, p. 88
Birds, p. 83
Bistro Bizerca, p. 85
Catharina's, p. 99
5 Rooms, p. 98
The Foodbarn, p. 100
Myoga, p. 99
95 Keerom, p. 86
The Pot Luck Club, p. 87

$$$$

The Greenhouse, p. 98
La Colombe, p. 98
Nobu, p. 91
The Test Kitchen, p. 87

By Cuisine

SEAFOOD

The Codfather, p. 95
Harbour House, p. 101
Kyoto Sushi Garden, p. 89
Nobu, p. 91
Willoughby & Co., p. 91

By Experience

BEST BREAKFAST

Bistro 1682, p. 99
Dear Me, p. 85
Hemelhuijs, p. 86
La Petite Tarte, p. 94
Olympia Café, p. 101

BUSINESS

Aubergine, p. 88
Mondiall, p. 90
95 Keerom, p. 86
Nobu, p. 91

CHILD-FRIENDLY

Café Roux, p. 100
Empire Cafe, p. 100

Food Barn Deli, p. 100
Gold Restaurant, p. 91
Massimo's, p. 96

GREAT SEA VIEW

Azure, p. 95
Casa Labia, p. 100
Harbour House, p. 101

MOST ROMANTIC

The Greenhouse, p. 98
Harbour House, p. 101
Kyoto Sushi Garden, p. 89
Planet Restaurant, p. 88
The Roundhouse, p. 96

QUICK LUNCH

Birds Boutique Café, p. 83
Dear Me, p. 85
Food Barn Deli, p. 100
Giovanni's Deliworld, p. 91
La Boheme, p. 94
Sababa, p. 86

QUIET

Aubergine, p. 88
Bombay Brasserie, p. 85
The Greenhouse, p. 98
95 Keerom, p. 86
Planet Restaurant, p. 88

of sugar-free and wheat-free items, great coffee and teas, and amazing baked goods complete the picture. $ *Average main: R160* ✉ *127 Bree St.* ☎ *021/426–2534* ⊘ *Closed Sun. No dinner Sat.–Tues.*

$$$
FRENCH
Fodor'sChoice
★

✕**Bistro Bizerca.** With its superb cuisine and excellent service, diners adore this French bistro located in an old Cape Dutch building on Heritage Square. Using classic French techniques but drawing on local produce and adding some fusion twists, dishes like the signature raw Norwegian salmon salad with ginger, soy, and shallots are served in a warm wood-floored dining room with a vertical garden feature, as well as in a lovely outside courtyard. The culinary magic is mostly found in the form of daily specials presented chalkboard-style, including dishes like a duo of tuna with avocado wasabi-and-jalapeño dressing, or the veal tongue with Gruyère and local *waterblommetjies* (water lily). Lunch is busier than dinner, but the food is splendid every time. In the summer enjoy a tapas and drinks menu from 3 to 6 during the week in the courtyard. $ *Average main: R160* ✉ *Heritage Sq., 98 Shortmarket St.* ☎ *021/423–8888* ⊕ *www.bizerca.com* ⚏ *Reservations essential* ⊘ *Closed Sun. No lunch Sat.*

$$
INDIAN

✕**Bombay Brasserie.** Turning the old Reserve Bank Building into a scene of fantastical opulence with ornate, handblown glass chandeliers, lots of dark wood, and abundant orchids, the Taj Hotel's Indian fine-dining restaurant does not disappoint when it comes to either ambience or flavor. Choose between three- or four-course tasting menus, or order à la carte from a menu that is filled with new takes on authentic Indian classics. Dishes like apricot-and-potato "tikki" cakes with yogurt and sweet tamarind chutney will get you started, and sublime interpretations of classics like black lentils and kidney beans or spiced coconut and green mango linefish are sure to delight. Although prices are on the high end for Indian, this is not your average curry joint, and excellent service supports an overall experience, which promises to be leisurely romantic all the way. $ *Average main: R122* ✉ *Taj Cape Town, Wale St.* ☎ *021/819–2000* ⊕ *www.tajcapetown.co.za* ⚏ *Reservations essential* ⊘ *No lunch.*

$$
ECLECTIC

✕**Dear Me.** A leader in the Cape Town locavore food scene, this centrally located brasserie serves delicious fare that you don't have to feel guilty about. Start your day with anything from truffled eggs with exotic mushrooms to a tofu scramble, or homemade muesli accompanied by fresh juices, smoothies, and healthful treats like almond milk. Lunches always include great soups and salads, but also offer more decadent dishes like homemade gnocchi with Gorgonzola and walnuts or a juicy free-range beef-and-bacon cheeseburger. Dinners are available on Thursday and Friday nights only, held upstairs in the 200-year-old heritage building's romantically whimsical White Room. Tasting menus (five or eight courses) paired with wine showcase the chef's subtle and sublime take on dishes like yellowtail ceviche with chili and lime, pea-and-zuchini risotto, and poached trout. This isn't the kind of meal that you need to follow with a pizza, but it certainly won't leave you bloated. $ *Average main: R106* ✉ *165 Longmarket St.* ☎ *021/422–4920* ⊕ *www.dearme.co.za* ⚏ *Reservations essential* ⊘ *Closed weekends. No dinner Mon.–Thurs.*

$ | **✗ Dias Tavern.** This Portuguese taverna in District Six is Cape Town's
PORTUGUESE | answer to a dive-bar-meets-diner. Serving classic South African Portuguese fare—think spicy *trinchado* (braised beef), *prego* rolls (rump steak fried in wine and garlic with a fried egg), spicy peri-peri chicken livers, and grilled sardines—for lunch and dinner, Dias Tavern is something of an institution. Although there are some great views of Table Mountain, diners come here for the reasonably priced, spicy, and garlic-infused meat and seafood, the cheap drinks, and the dimly lighted atmosphere. It's a popular spot for events like bachelor's parties and big birthdays, so expect karaoke and a live band on weekend nights, when large tables can get up to rowdy fun. Service is brisk, friendly, and no-nonsense, as one would expect. ⑤ *Average main: R89* ⊠ *15 Caledon St., District Six* ☎ *021/465–7547* ⊕ *www.diastavern.co.za* ⊘ *Closed Sun.*

$$ | **✗ Hemelhuijs.** Super-stylish Hemelhuijs is both a showcase for a range
ECLECTIC | of exquisite ceramicware and fanciful lighting, and a centrally located
Fodor's Choice | restaurant serving equally fanciful and exquisite food. Though lunch
★ | prices are closer to what one would expect to pay for dinner, inventive seasonal dishes bursting with freshness like a pear-and-celeriac salad with hazelnuts and trout, or a crispy panfried veal of sublime flavor and texture, are well worth it. On one of Cape Town's few pedestrian walkways (near the footbridge crossing busy Buitengracht Street), this magical space of burnt sienna and slate, where food is served in gold-painted bowls under chandeliers hanging with beads, driftwood, and star-shape seedpods, is truly a treat. Needless to say, breakfast and brunch are also divine. ⑤ *Average main: R122* ⊠ *71 Waterkant St.* ☎ *021/418–2042* ⊕ *hemelhuijs.co.za* ⊘ *Closed Sun. No dinner.*

$$$ | **✗ 95 Keerom.** Chef-owner Giorgio Nava is so passionate about using
ITALIAN | only the finest ingredients that he catches his own fish and farms his own beef. Diners will be hard-pressed to find better Milanese cuisine. The paper-thin beef carpaccio "95" is drizzled with housemade mayonnaise and topped with fresh arugula and Parmesan shavings. When Nava manages to catch tuna, he serves it seared with cherry tomatoes, capers, and olives. The butternut-squash-filled ravioli with brown sage butter is sublime, and the soft-centered chocolate soufflé is the benchmark for every other. With its bentwood chairs, the upstairs interior is Eames-inspired; downstairs, the exposed stone reveals the building's ancient history, which began in 1682. ⑤ *Average main: R175* ⊠ *95 Keerom St.* ☎ *021/422–0765* ⊕ *www.95keerom.com* ⬦ *Reservations essential* ⊘ *Closed Sun. No lunch Sat.–Thurs.*

$ | **✗ Sababa.** This bright, all-white café on trendy Bree Street is the go-to
MIDDLE EASTERN | place for delicious, creative, and relatively healthful Middle Eastern–style fare. Hebrew slang for "awesome" or "great," Sababa is aptly named. A main table is laden with numerous salads like quinoa with roasted vegetables and cranberries, pesto potato with peas and olives, and green beans with orange and hazelnut. Both mezes, like dolmades or roast eggplant, and mains, which are slightly bigger than small plates, like butter chicken, falafel, or lamb-and-lentil biryani, are stellar. For a set price, you can load up with three or four salads and mezes, plus one main, and eat at the counter inside or a handful of tables outside, or take away. Don't forget to check out the fantastic desserts like date

balls or poppyseed cake with white chocolate ganache. Falafel dinners are served Thursday only. $ *Average main: R68* ⊠ *231 Bree St.* ☎ *021/424–7480* ⊕ *sababa.withtank.com* ☺ *Closed weekends. No dinner Fri.–Wed.*

$ ✕**Skinny Legs & All.** Serving delicious, organic fare from breakfast
CAFÉ through lunch, this unpretentious yet design-conscious café is a great addition to Cape Town's downtown food scene. Starting the day with the only muffin in town worth eating (a carrot-coconut concoction, perfectly spiced and not too sweet), breakfast also includes items like raw muesli with sheep's milk yogurt, fresh scones, and French toast with vanilla-infused compote. Lunch usually includes some kind of risotto, soup in the winter, and several salad options in the summer. Though the menu changes regularly, expect dishes like a cinnamon-spiced quinoa salad with roasted eggplant and toasted almonds, wild mushroom parcels with wild rice, or the Lumberjack sandwich of roasted chicken and avocado with homemade coriander mayo. Free Wi-Fi, plenty of reading material, and some great art on the walls complete the picture. $ *Average main: R85* ⊠ *70 Loop St., Cape Town Central* ☎ *021/423–5403* ⊕ *www.skinnylegsandall.co.za* ☺ *Closed Sun.*

WOODSTOCK

$$$ ✕**The Pot Luck Club.** A playful and inventive tapas-style venture from
ECLECTIC Cape Town star-chef Luke Dale Roberts, this hip eatery on the sixth
Fodor's Choice floor of an old silo is perfect for enjoying fine-dining nibbles set against
★ gorgeous views in a stylish yet comfortable atmosphere. The menu changes regularly, but the smoked beef fillet and truffle café au lait, and Korean fried chicken with pineapple-and-miso slaw remain favorites. Think of each plate as a half portion, and come with a crew to maximize how many you can taste. The cocktails are equally delicious, the service is friendly and efficient, and the atmosphere, with its amazing views of the harbor and mountain and funky lighting, is very relaxed. The all-you-can-drink sparkling-wine brunches (Sunday only) are also a fantastic treat. $ *Average main: R190* ⊠ *Old Biscuit Mill, 375 Albert Rd., Silo Top Floor* ☎ *021/447–0804* ⊕ *www.thepotluckclub.co.za* ⌂ *Reservations essential* ☺ *Closed Sun.*

$$$$ ✕**The Test Kitchen.** Star chef Luke Dale Roberts put South Africa on the
ECLECTIC culinary map when he opened this deceptively casual-looking eatery in
Fodor's Choice Cape Town's trendy Woodstock neighborhood in 2009. Serving vary-
★ ing tasting menus of truly mind-blowing inspiration, Roberts is working some serious foodie magic here, and you'll be lucky if you can get a table (it's typically booked four months in advance). The wonders begin with dishes like pickled fish served with carrots prepared three ways and honeycomb, a meal that brilliantly showcases Roberts' genius for texture and working sweet against savory. The journey continues with creations like a "Southern-style foie gras" of bourbon, molasses, and oak-smoked duck. Expect the unexpected (both in taste sensation and the arrival of little yummies you didn't order), and don't neglect the cocktails, which are also brilliant. The relaxed ambience created by exposed brick, funky lamps, friendly staff, and a totally open service area acts as a great foil to the cuisine coming out of this kitchen.

$ *Average main: R590* ✉ *The Old Biscuit Mill, 375 Albert Rd., Shop 104A* ☎ *021/447–2337* ⊕ *www.thetestkitchen.co.za* ⚑ *Reservations essential* ⊘ *Closed Sun. and Mon.*

GARDENS

$$$ ✕ **Aubergine.** One of Cape Town's oldest and most consistent fine-dining
EUROPEAN establishments, Aubergine has a timber-and-glass interior that matches
Fodor's Choice chef-owner Harald Bresselschmidt's classic-with-a-twist cuisine. Using
★ the freshest South African produce prepared with classical European
methods, the chef cooks with wine in mind, and Aubergine's cellar and
pairings are unsurprisingly superb. Purists who appreciate dishes that
allow natural flavors to shine will thoroughly enjoy a languorous mul-
ticourse meal. The seafood on the menu is wonderful: the octopus with
baby fennel, plum tomatoes, and eggplant in lemon-thyme crème fraiche
is divine, and the beet-cured klingklip takes this often ho-hum fish to
unexpected heights. Meanwhile, meat dishes like a Wagyu beef carpac-
cio with Jersualem artichokes are sublime. Lunch and winter specials
are more affordable ways of enjoying this fine restaurant. $ *Average
main: R195* ✉ *39 Barnet St.* ☎ *021/465–4909* ⊕ *www.aubergine.co.za*
⚑ *Reservations essential* ⊘ *Closed Sun. No lunch Mon., Tues., and Sat.*

$$$ ✕ **Planet Restaurant.** The refurbished fine-dining restaurant at the iconic
ECLECTIC Mount Nelson Hotel, the Planet occupies one of the most glamorous
rooms in the city and serves excellent fare befitting its grand location.
With a galaxy of starry lights cascading from the high-domed ceiling
and tall bay windows looking onto bucolic rose gardens, this elegant,
all-white space rarely fills to capacity, but it's a great choice for an
intimate and stylish night out. The chef makes fantastic use of local
ingredients in dishes like the springbok loin with *samp* (a staple African
grain), Jerusalem artichoke ragout, and crispy *chakalaka* (a spicy South
African relish), or the Franschhoek smoked-trout parcel with citrus and
fennel. Frequently hosting good-value "wine and dine" evenings, and
one of the few fine-dining locations serving excellent vegetarian and
even vegan tasting menus, the Planet is one of the city's most underrated upscale finds. For a bespoke culinary experience, inquire about the
Chef's Table, where the chef will create individual food-and-wine pairing menus for tables of 6 to 10. $ *Average main: R175* ✉ *Mount Nelson
Hotel, 76 Orange St.* ☎ *021/483–1000* ⊕ *www.planetbarandrestaurant.
co.za* ⊘ *Closed Sun. No lunch.*

$$ ✕ **Societi Bistro.** This much-loved neighborhood bistro offers a reliable
BISTRO and seasonally adapted menu of French- and Italian-style classics. In a
renovated 19th-century Georgian-style home just off Kloof Street, the
dining room is all exposed brick and wooden floors, with roaring fires
in the winter and a large, lovely garden in the summer. Classics like
Caesar salad, spaghetti carbonara, and mushroom risotto are all consis-
tently excellent. The roasted half chicken with crispy potatoes or sirloin
with hand-cut chips and béarnaise sauce are also winners. A small but
well-chosen wine list and perpetually convivial atmosphere add zing.
The adjacent snug bar is a great place for a predinner cocktail or post-
prandial whiskey, though be aware that smoking is allowed. $ *Average*

main: R115 ✉ *50 Orange St.* ☎ *021/424–2100* ⊕ *www.societi.co.za* ⌲ *Reservations essential* ⊘ *Closed Sun.*

TAMBOERSKLOOF

$$ ✕ **Black Sheep Restaurant.** The menu at this relatively new but instantly
ECLECTIC popular Kloof Street eatery focuses on a small regular menu of comfort fare mixed with an ever-changing array of adventurous blackboard specials. Starters like rabbit, ham, and artichoke terrine with caperberry salad, or Asian black bean beef-and-noodle broth with coriander, basil, and mint are followed by mains like five-spice Hoisin pork belly or grilled ostrich with braised red cabbage. If you've got four friends and want to book ahead, try the seven-hour pot roast larded leg of lamb in sherry and onions with boiled fingerling potatoes. Despite being spread over three levels—including a mezzanine for private parties—Black Sheep is almost always fully booked, and the mood is merry and loud. You won't leave hungry. ⑤ *Average main: R138* ✉ *104 Kloof St.* ☎ *021/426–2661* ⌲ *Reservations essential* ⊘ *Sun. No lunch Mon.*

$$ ✕ **Kloof Street House.** Set in a fanciful garden under palm trees illumi-
MEDITERRANEAN nated by strings of fairy lights, this magnificently dolled-up Victorian house on trendy Kloof Street serves a menu of Mediterranean-inspired fare with a distinctly South African twist. Expect starters like panfried Halloumi cheese with dukkah spice and honey, or baked whole Camembert with caramelized onions and cranberry jelly. The Moroccan-spiced lamb rump with tahini dressing is wonderfully flavorful, and lighter fare like the Norwegian salmon with braised fennel is perfectly cooked. Rumor has it that the house once served as a gentlemen's club, and the decor today, with its red velvet, copious candelabras, and antique lamps still channels that vibe with a wink and a nudge. Though service can sometimes be lackluster, the festive atmosphere, great cocktails, and generally tasty food make it a worthwhile stop. ⑤ *Average main: R135* ✉ *30 Kloof St.* ☎ *021/423–4413* ⊕ *www.kloofstreethouse.co.za* ⊘ *No lunch Mon.*

$$$ ✕ **Kyoto Sushi Garden.** Elegant and tranquil, this understated eatery near
JAPANESE the Kloof Street drag serves pricey but extremely well-executed Japanese fare for dinner only. Sourcing as much as possible from Japan, the owner verges on an obsession with high-quality ingredients and technique, evidenced in the lightness of the tempura and the freshness of the fish. The decor is Zen-inspired with a lot of blond wood, making for a supremely relaxing setting in which to enjoy dishes like seaweed-and-shiitake salad, crayfish miso soup, or steamed fish in a bamboo pot. What constitutes an unusually diverse range of sushi by Cape Town standards can include sea urchin, big-eye tuna, scallop, octopus, and caviar. Great cocktails, a good selection of sake and Japanese whiskey, and fine service complete the picture. ⑤ *Average main: R160* ✉ *11 Lower Kloofnek Rd.* ☎ *021/422–2001* ⊘ *No lunch.*

V&A WATERFRONT

Generally speaking, restaurants here tend to cater to tourists (i.e., they have no need to gain diners' loyalty). There are, however, some very good exceptions (though you'll pay for them), as well as plenty of cheap fast-food options.

$$$$
STEAKHOUSE

✕**Belthazar.** Boasting one of the largest selections of wines by the glass (about 100) in the land, Belthazar is also recommended for its consistently good steak and seafood. Steaks are cut and matured by an in-house butcher, and a team of sommeliers will recommend the best wine match for your meal. The springbok fillet served with a chocolate-chili sauce is a good choice. The Chicago-cut beef is a little more than a pound of on-the-bone deliciousness. The deep-fried onion blossom is a visual treat, but the creamed spinach or spiced beets are better sides. Outside seating under umbrellas (heated in winter) provides views of the bustling V&A waterfront and the harbor beyond, though it's more comfortable inside. $ *Average main: R215* ✉ *Victoria Wharf, V&A Waterfront, shop 153* ☎ *021/421–3753, 021/421–3756* ⊕ *www. belthazar.co.za* ⌕ *Reservations essential.*

$$
BELGIAN

✕**Den Anker.** Take a break from your Waterfront wanderings at this Belgian-style eatery, where you can enjoy as good a pot of mussels with frites as you're likely to find anywhere in Cape Town. With its focus on meat and seafood, expect other dishes like fillet béarnaise, rabbit simmered in Belgian beer, or Norwegian salmon in a Beurre Blanc. A wide range of imported Belgian beers is available, with six served on tap. Sitting on the pier head between the Albert Mall and the clock tower (the departure point for trips to Robben Island), this glassed-in space enjoys lovely harbor and mountain views whether you sit inside or out, and makes for great people- (or seal-) watching. $ *Average main: R140* ✉ *Alfred Mall, Pierhead* ☎ *021/419–0249* ⊕ *www.denanker.co.za.*

$$$
SEAFOOD

✕**Harbour House V&A.** Sister restaurant to the original Harbour House in Kalk Bay, the V&A location serves the same reliably fresh and tasty seafood menu from an enviable spot overlooking the harbor. As with the Kalk Bay location, the fresh fish of the day is always a good bet, and desserts are excellent. Sushi and cocktails are served upstairs, from which vantage you can also enjoy stellar views of the mountain and sunset. $ *Average main: R160* ✉ *Quay 4, V&A Waterfront* ☎ *021/418–4744* ⊕ *www.harbourhouse.co.za.*

$$
ECLECTIC

✕**Mondiall Kitchen & Bar.** Claiming a sweet spot at the V&A Waterfront with fabulous harbor and mountain views, this versatile eatery focuses on updated versions of global classics. From fish tacos to a Wagyu beef cheeseburger to salade Niçoise, dishes that you wouldn't normally expect to see on the same menu are harmonized by shared traits of freshness, flavor, and quality. With a sleek, warehouse-inspired interior and outside seating that maximizes its position overlooking both Table Mountain and the harbor, Mondiall is a highly agreeable culinary stop. Open all day, this modern brasserie is a welcome addition to the Waterfront's often ho-hum offerings. $ *Average main: R142* ✉ *Alfred Mall, V&A Waterfront* ☎ *021/418–3003* ⊕ *www.mondiall.co.za.*

2

$$$$
JAPANESE
Fodor's Choice
★

✕ **Nobu.** World-famous chef Nobuyuki "Nobu" Matsuhisa's exceptional contemporary Japanese cuisine with a South American twist may be costly by local standards, but the cost here is entirely worth it when compared with the bill at one of Nobu's sister New York or London branches. Food is the main event in this vast, modern space, in the Waterfront's One&Only resort. If your budget allows, the Omakase multicourse tasting menu is the way to go for a divine culinary experience in which the chef will surprise you with his choices for the evening. Do not miss dishes like the signature Alaskan black cod with miso. The spinach salad with dried miso and truffle oil is sublime, the kingklip tempura heavenly, and the sushi excellent, including an unusually diverse range of choices for Cape Town. There is a stellar selection of sake and, of course, excellent local wines. ⓢ *Average main: R475* ⊠ *One&Only Cape Town, Dock Rd.* ☎ *021/431–4511* ⊕ *www.oneandonlyresorts.com* ⌕ *Reservations essential* ⊗ *No lunch.*

$$
JAPANESE

✕ **Willoughby & Co.** Though unfortunately inside the mall, this buzzing hive of activity consistently churns out what many say is the city's best sushi, thus adding a certain joy to a trip to the V&A. Expect an array of fanciful and decadent signature rolls such as the creamy rock-shrimp maki (a tuna-style roll graced with large chunks of tempura fried crayfish in a spicy mayo-based sauce) and the rainbow nation roll (salmon, avocado, and tuna topped with caviar and a few squizzles of delicious sesame-oil and sweet chili sauces). The traditional sashimi is also excellent, as is the Japanese Kitchen menu. There will almost inevitably be a line during normal dinner hours; however, it goes quickly (especially if you sit at the sushi bar, which is the place to be) and you're likely to be offered free tastes of various new vintages while waiting. ⓢ *Average main: R150* ⊠ *Victoria Wharf, Shop 6132* ☎ *021/418–6115* ⊕ *www.willoughbyandco.co.za* ⌕ *Reservations not accepted.*

GREEN POINT

$
CAFÉ

✕ **Giovanni's Deliworld.** With floor-to-ceiling shelves stacked with everything delicious from French Champagne to truffle oil, Giovanni's is a great place to stock up for a gourmet picnic or enjoy a bite to eat at the counter. Fridges have fresh pasta dishes and greens, but the deli section and espresso bar are where most customers congregate. At possibly the oldest deli in the area, locals jostle for a seat with models and film-industry folk who come for the coffee and the vibe. Though a little chaotic at peak times—and to be honest, the raised counter seating is not especially comfortable—this place shouldn't be missed. There might be Italian meatballs with spaghetti or Thai plum chicken on offer. There's always a wide selection of hams and cold cuts as well as fantastic cheeses. Get anything from pumpkin-seed rolls to fresh-cut flowers and the daily newspaper. And it's just a block away from the soccer stadium and Green Point park. ⓢ *Average main: R55* ⊠ *103 Main Rd.* ☎ *021/434–6893.*

$$$$
AFRICAN
FAMILY

✕ **Gold Restaurant.** In a huge brick warehouse space decorated with Africana like giant Malian puppets, beautiful beadwork, and wooden carvings, Gold instantly prepares you for the touristy but thoroughly enjoyable meal and show to come. Your 14-course pan-African "taste

Where to Eat in Cape Town

ATLANTIC
OCEAN

Granger
Bay

Victoria
Basin

WATERFRONT

MOUILLE
POINT

GREEN
POINT

THREE
ANCHOR
BAY

Signal Hill ▲

SEA POINT

FRESNAYE

BANTRY
BAY

Lion's Head ▲

Beach
Bay
Beach
Fritz Sonnenberg
Western Blvd. M6
Wigtown
Main. M61
High Level
Springbok
Three Glengariff
Rhine
Main. M61
High Level
Marais
Beach - M6
St. John's
High Level
Kloof
Regent - M61
Beach - Beach
Des Huguenots
Fresnaye
Queens
M6
Victoria
Portswood
East Pier
Ebenezer

0   500 yards
0   500 meters

safari" may include dishes from Cape Malay curry to Moroccan tagine; the food is fine but not the sole reason you are here. Throughout the meal, performers emerge to sing, drum, and dance, and their skill makes the trip well worth while if you are looking for both food and entertainment. Service is friendly and competent, and a full vegetarian menu is also available. Although intentionally well suited for big groups, smaller tables will not feel overwhelmed or out of place. ■TIP➜ **Start your evening with the interactive Djembe drumming session, a surprisingly fun way to whet your appetite.** $ *Average main: R320* ⊠ *15 Bennett St.* ☎ *021/421–4653* ⊕ *www.goldrestaurant.co.za* ⊗ *No lunch.*

$ ✕ **La Petite Tarte.** This delightful little French-style sidewalk café in the
FRENCH charming and pedestrian-friendly De Waterkant neighborhood above Green Point serves fantastic coffees and teas, not to mention excellent breakfasts, lunches, and snacks with a focus on baked goods. Think quiches, a great croque monsieur, flourless gâteau au chocolat, fruit tartlets, and a legendary carrot, pineapple, and walnut cake. It's often full, so book ahead if possible, or come outside of typical lunch hours. $ *Average main: R70* ⊠ *Dixon St., shop 11A, De Waterkant* ☎ *021/425–9077* ⊜ *Reservations essential* ⊗ *Closed Sun. No dinner.*

SEA POINT

$$ ✕ **La Boheme Wine Bar & Bistro.** Serving hearty gourmet meals at reason-
MEDITERRANEAN able prices, this unassuming bistro and wine bar on Sea Point's Main Road is often packed, and deservedly so. The menu focuses on Mediterranean fare, including such dishes as an excellent basil-and-roasted-tomato soup, ostrich meatballs and tagliatelle in a spicy Neapolitan sauce, or sesame-crusted fish cakes with a chunky Greek salad. Choose the great-value two- or three-course prix-fixe menu, or order à la carte if you're less peckish. The restaurant's interior is comfortable, if unremarkable, but most will try to nab one of the busy outside tables (heat lamps keep things cozy in winter). With more than 60 wines by the glass, this is also a great venue in which to acquaint yourself with some new South African wines while watching the world go by. $ *Average main: R120* ⊠ *341 Main Rd.* ☎ *021/434–8797* ⊕ *www.labohemebistro. co.za* ⊜ *Reservations essential* ⊗ *Closed Sun.*

$$ ✕ **La Mouette.** La Mouette serves extremely reasonably priced, modern
MODERN FRENCH French-Mediterranean cuisine in a beautiful old Sea Point home that is all sash windows, working fireplaces, and artful wallpaper. With a choice of tasting or à la carte menus, you'll be treated to creative and mostly delicious seasonal fare such as roast chicken in butternut-squash puree with potstickers and toasted cashews, or divinely tasty wild mushrooms on artichoke brioche with a truffle-and-Parmesan sauce. The restaurant is split into several different rooms, each of which seats only about 20 people, so even the busiest nights allow for a nice lingering dinner conversation. Friendly, competent service and a beautiful garden that is very popular in the summer complete the picture. Not all courses are winners (the deconstructed Waldorf salad of celery panna cotta and raisin puree with apple granita does not come together), but at these prices, the overall experience is well worth a visit. $ *Average main:*

*R138 ⊠ 78 Regent Rd. ☎ 021/433–0856 ⊕ www.lamouette-restaurant.
co.za ⊗ Closed Mon. No lunch Tues.–Sat.*

CAMPS BAY

$$$ ✕ **Azure.** Although Azure's blue-and-white nautical-theme decor may
ECLECTIC   feel a bit outdated to some, the restaurant's jaw-dropping sea and
mountain views are reason enough to come experience the mostly
inspired menu. Signature dishes like the crayfish-and-prawn cocktail,
beef Stroganoff, and rice pudding have a classic old-school bent and
are divinely comforting. More contemporary dishes like the prawn dhal
in a coriander yogurt with pineapple salsa, or pork belly with a mirin
glaze are true winners. Though appetizers and desserts are generally
excellent, the mains can be somewhat less consistent. However, with this
level of exquisite service, fairly reasonable à la carte prices, and the truly
stunning setting, diners are in for a treat overall. Come when you can
enjoy the view, and inquire about specials like the "wine journey" or
family Sunday lunches. ■ **TIP**→ **Ask for a window table.** ⑤ *Average main:
R155 ⊠ Twelve Apostles Hotel & Spa, Victoria Rd. ☎ 021/437–9029
⊕ www.12apostleshotel.com ⌂ Reservations essential.*

$$$$ ✕ **The Codfather.** The Codfather serves an excellent array of fresh seafood
SEAFOOD   in a casual yet buzzing environment by way of a slightly unorthodox
system. Rather than ordering from a menu, you instead head to a dis-
play of fresh seafood on ice, where, with the help of your waiter, you
select everything from fish to shellfish in the quantities and style of your
choice (you're charged by weight, as in Greece). Possible selections
include calamari grilled Cajun-style; kabeljou, yellowtail, or bluenose
grilled and served with a choice of sauces; or Mozambican langous-
tines. All orders come with side dishes of stir-fried vegetables, rice, or
fries. A conveyer belt of sushi is also on offer. Although it is set back
from Camps Bay's typical sea views, diners can enjoy mountain views
from an outdoor terrace. The food here is pricey, but perfectly cooked,
always fresh, and served with a smile. ⑤ *Average main: R200 ⊠ 37
The Drive ☎ 021/438–0782, 021/438–0783 ⊕ www.codfather.co.za
⌂ Reservations essential.*

$$ ✕ **Hussar Grill.** This branch of one of the Cape's favorite steak houses
STEAKHOUSE   offers an unpretentious and friendly place to enjoy excellent and reason-
ably priced steaks and ribs in an area where restaurants tend to focus
more on views than food. A few minutes' drive away from Camps Bay's
main beach drag, the interior here is more Boston than Miami—all
leather booths and historic photographs, well suited to the carnivo-
rous feast that awaits. The gin-and-tomato soup or chicken livers with
garlic, brandy, and cream are classic starters. For the main event, the
meat-on-the-bone options are superb, and your waiter should inform
you how many days the various cuts have been aged (older = more
flavor). Game meat and burgers are also delicious, and the wine list is
impressively long. ⑤ *Average main: R125 ⊠ 108 Camps Bay Dr., shop
2 ☎ 021/438–0151 ⊕ www.hussargrill.co.za ⊗ No dinner Sun.*

TABLE MOUNTAIN NATIONAL PARK

$$$$
MODERN
EUROPEAN

✕ **The Roundhouse.** Known for its exceptional natural beauty, Cape Town is surprisingly short on restaurants with killer views: the Roundhouse is helping close that gap. Converted from its origins as an 18th-century Table Mountain–side hunting lodge, this unique fine-dining restaurant overlooking Camps Bay specializes in creative and surprising flavor combinations—think mussels with oak-smoked butter and kombu gel—served by an excellent and exceptionally suave team of waiters. The Somerset Room offers sea views, but can be noisy. The private room for up to eight guests may better suit big groups. The adjacent "Rumbullion" picnic area from which diners can enjoy breathtaking mountain and sea views serves a more casual burger and pizza style menu, and is an excellent place to while away a summer afternoon. Opening hours vary with season, so best to call and check. ⑤ *Average main: R595* ✉ *The Glen, Round House Rd.* ☎ *021/438–4347* ⊕ *www. theroundhouserestaurant.com* ✍ *Reservations essential* ۞ *Closed Mon. No dinner Sun. Rumbuillion closed May–Sept.*

HOUT BAY

$$$
ASIAN FUSION

✕ **Cheyne's.** Serving Pacific Rim cuisine from a funky little location in Hout Bay, Cheyne's is the place to go for inventive, pan-Asian small plates. The menu changes entirely each season but is generally divided into the categories of sea, land, earth, and happy endings. Plates are appetizer-size, and some winners include the chili-salt squid with shichimi spice and smoked salt; Mumbai-style chili beef with cardamom, ginger, and toasted coconut flakes; and the oddly named but insanely good deep-fried milk flavored with green chili and lemongrass. Addictive tastes, friendly service, and the graffiti-artist-meets-magazine-stylist interior have ensured that this unique and vibey joint is fully booked most weekends. ⑤ *Average main: R150* ✉ *1 Pam Arlene Pl., Main Rd.* ☎ *079/067–4919* ✍ *Reservations essential* ۞ *Closed Sun. No lunch Mon.–Wed.*

$
ITALIAN
FAMILY

✕ **Massimo's.** Having begun as a pizza joint, this casual Hout Bay eatery, which is in an old barn, now serves a range of delightfully simple Italian fare from antipasti to pastas, as well as what is still arguably Cape Town's best pizza. The "spuntini" or antipasti include classics like Italian meatballs, Caprese salad, and panfried spinach with toasted pine nuts. Pastas are great, but pizza is why you are here. The "Cacio," with Italian sausage, cacio cheese, and roasted peppers, is a favorite, but simple combos like the "Pere," with olive oil, Gorgonzola, and sliced pears, are also amazing. Warm service, an über-casual ambience, and a small play area out front make this a super family-friendly venue. ⑤ *Average main: R89* ✉ *Oakhurst Farm Park, Main Rd.* ☎ *021/790–5648* ⊕ *www.pizzaclub.co.za* ۞ *No lunch weekdays.*

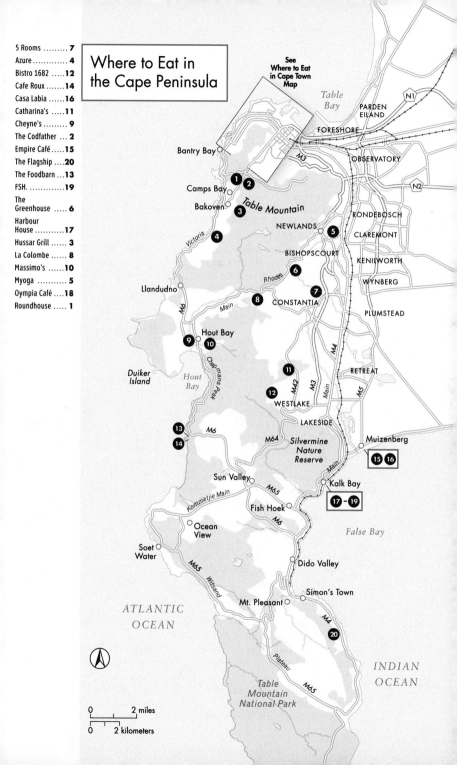

Where to Eat in the Cape Peninsula

SOUTHERN SUBURBS

CONSTANTIA

$$$
MODERN
EUROPEAN

✕ **5 Rooms.** Located in a grand old manor house, this gorgeous restaurant serves many of the usual Euro fine-dining suspects, but in a setting that is anything but predictable. A classic semicircular bar and plush lounge area meets diners upon arrival, while an upbeat but nonintrusive live band plays at the back of the room on weekends. With several dining rooms to choose from, you can select the mood, making the aptly named 5 Rooms great for groups and intimate dinners alike. All are spectacularly decorated in a grandiose, cosmopolitan style that sets the tone for a magnificent evening. Start with the crispy calamari with aioli, or oysters with grapefruit granita. For mains, expect classic meaty dishes like lamb rump with peas, mint, and ricotta, or sirloin and prawn Thermidor. Service is attentive and friendly and the food well prepared and hearty, but it's the overall experience that will have you coming back. ■ TIP→ **On a summer's day it's worth coming early for a drink at the lovely outdoor Rose Bar in the garden adjacent to the restaurant.** ⑤ *Average main: R160* ✉ *Alphen Boutique Hotel, Alphen Dr.* ☎ *021/795–6313* ⊕ *www.alphen.co.za/5rooms* ⚐ *Reservations essential* ☾ *No lunch Mon.–Sat. No dinner Sun.*

$$$$
ECLECTIC
Fodor'sChoice
★

✕ **The Greenhouse.** Wondrous culinary magic happens at this conservatory-like dining room overlooking the beautiful gardens of the Cellars-Hohenort Hotel. The cuisine is playful but high-end, where classic techniques are used on local flavors to create dishes like an ostrich fillet with celeriac mash, sour fig, kale, and sago, or a monkfish with coconut, clam, and tomato spiced with Cape Malay seasonings. An elegant room in tones of white, green, and silver, it's the kind of place where you find yourself sitting up straight and minding which fork you use. Solicitous service and an amazing wine list go without saying. ⑤ *Average main: R550* ✉ *Cellars-Hohenort Hotel, 93 Brommersvlei Rd.* ☎ *021/794–2137* ⊕ *www.collectionmcgrath.com/cellars/the-greenhouse/* ⚐ *Reservations essential* ☾ *Closed Sun. and Mon. No lunch.*

$$$$
ECLECTIC
Fodor'sChoice
★

✕ **La Colombe.** Among South Africa's most lauded fine-dining restaurants, La Colombe recently moved its award-winning French-Asian cuisine to a new location on the Silvermist organic wine estate overlooking the Constantia wine valley. Return visitors will be happy to know that favorites like the seared scallops and pork belly starter and foie-gras topped meat dishes remain, although with a slightly increased focus on the creative Asian twists: the scallops are now miso-seared, and the pork belly done Asian barbeque-style and served with a lemongrass and ginger velouté. For more traditional tastes, dishes like the aged beef in a black pepper café au lait sauce are sure to delight. The new space is both intimate and cool, the simple white-painted timber offset by charcoal finishes and black beams, all flooded with light and stunning views during the day, and elegantly refined in the evening. The lunch menu is à la carte, while dinner is a four-course affair (a gourmand tasting menu will be offered as well). However you order, consider pairing you meal with wines chosen from the excellent wine list, and conclude with one of the spectacular desserts and the chef's signature petits fours. Understated smooth service and the bucolic location will ensure that La Colombe will remain a favorite Cape Town splurge. $ *Average main: R465 Silverminst Mountain Lodge, Main Rd., Constantia Nek* ☎ *021/795–0125* ⊕ *www.lacolombe.co.za* ⟨ *Reservations essential.*

$$$ ✗ **Myoga.** This relaxed but glam eatery in the posh Vineyard Hotel
ASIAN FUSION & Spa outside Cape Town attracts well-heeled regulars, who come for chef Mike Basset's fusion flair, evidenced in dishes like the bacon-and-pea riosotto cakes, shredded spare rib soup with mushroom-soy broth, and the divine truffle-teriyaki beef fillet topped with perfectly crisped tempura vegetables. Evenings are all about the amazingly good-value seven-course tasting menu. Lunches are more casual but still boast favorite dishes like the green curry mussel chowder. High-backed sofas and black chandeliers lend a touch of Alice in Wonderland to the art-deco-meets-Japanese-nightclub-cool aesthetic. Don't neglect the fabulous wine list, which features many of the country's best. $ *Average main: R295* ⊠ *Vineyard Hotel & Spa, 60 Colinton Rd., Newlands* ☎ *021/657–4545* ⊕ *www.myoga.co.za* ⟨ *Reservations essential* ⊗ *Closed Sun. and Mon.*

TOKAI

$$ ✗ **Bistro 1682.** Named for the year the Steenberg wine estate on which it
ECLECTIC sits was established, this not-to-be-missed bistro serves dishes intended
Fodor's Choice to be paired with the estate's vintages, but it remains the opposite of
★ hoity-toity fine dining. Dishes like eggs Benedict with pork-belly bacon and rosti, or the Wagyu beef burger with foie gras are the perfect foil to a minimalist environment of bleached wood, metallic accents, and high ceilings. The outside terrace with its gorgeous mountain views is the perfect setting for brunch or lunch. Try favorites like the mushroom risotto and seared tuna with squid-ink emulsion. Or stick around until the sun drops, and indulge in a tapas menu of ginger-lime beef tataki, gnocchi carbonara, and churros and chocolate. Service stops by 8:30. This is the perfect spot to while away a beautiful Cape day. $ *Average main: R131* ⊠ *Steenberg Estate, Steenberg Rd.* ☎ *021/713–2211* ⊕ *www.steenbergfarm.com/bistro1682* ⊗ *No dinner.*

$$$ ✗ **Catharina's.** Serving excellent, unpretentious fare in an elegantly quirky
INTERNATIONAL space with lovely views across the historic Steenberg wine estate, this is a great fine-dining go-to no matter the time of day. An oak-shaded terrace overlooking manicured lawns makes for a lovely, lazy lunch spot, and the restaurant's interior with its origami swans hanging from high ceilings and huge windows is a stylishly bright space. The lunch and dinner menu features winners like the confit quail with sweetcorn puree to start, and an amazingly rich and tasty duck pappardelle or perfectly cooked Chalmar beef fillet with foie gras tortellini as mains. A Sunday lunch buffet with a South African theme and accompanying jazz quartet is a family affair, and various canapé platters are also available throughout the day, and can be taken in the plush bar and lounge area. A private dining room seats up to 24 and is a gorgeous and intimate venue for a special occasion. $ *Average main: R165* ⊠ *Steenberg Hotel, Steenberg and Tokai Rds.* ☎ *021/713–7178* ⊕ *www.steenberghotel.com.*

CAPE PENINSULA

ATLANTIC COAST
NOORDHOEK

$
CAFÉ
FAMILY

✕ Café Roux. Easy eating in a family-friendly atmosphere doesn't get much better than this. Sit outside or in, and enjoy the lively outdoorsy scene populated by Cape Peninsula nature lovers and their kids and dogs. Food is hearty and tasty, as in dishes like the fettuccine with chicken in a creamy herb sauce, seared tuna with a wasabi dressing and coriander, or a variety of burgers and wraps. Breakfast treats include everything from muesli to eggs, a grilled bacon croissant, and great smoothies. Kids have their own menu and a dedicated play area. ⑤ *Average main: R90* ⊠ *Noordhoek Farm Village, Noordhoek Main Rd., Noordhoek* ☎ *021/789–2538* ⊕ *www.caferoux.co.za* ☻ *No dinner.*

$$$
FRENCH
Fodor'sChoice
★

✕ The Foodbarn. Very probably the best restaurant on the Cape Peninsula, the aptly named Foodbarn serves French-influenced cuisine in a rustic and relaxed setting near Noordhoek Beach. Starters like a wild mushroom ravioli with ricotta and truffle cream or mussels and chorizo in a phyllo puff with smoked paprika cream set the tone for mains like a divine rack of lamb with a tomato-and-pecorino quiche. In a restored, shabby-chic barn, the venue invites you to relax and enjoy the exquisite but never pretentious fare. Well-priced tasting menus and generous winter specials make this inspired fare highly affordable. ■**TIP→ Just a stone's throw away, the laid-back Foodbarn Deli serves delicious and very reasonably priced breakfasts and lunches as well as an evening tapas menu from Tuesday to Saturday.** ⑤ *Average main: R150* ⊠ *Noordhoek Farm Village, Noordhoek Main Rd., Noordhoek* ☎ *021/789–1390* ⊕ *www. thefoodbarn.co.za* ⌑ *Reservations essential* ☻ *Call for seasonal closings.*

FALSE BAY COAST
SIMON'S TOWN

$
CAFÉ

✕ Casa Labia. Sitting atop fynbos-covered hills overlooking the magnificent surf, this excellent Italian-inspired café churns out well-priced meals, from delicious all-day breakfasts (fresh scones and poached eggs with pancetta) to homemade pastas (linguine with basil and tomato), and an excellent spinach-and-ricotta pancake with Gorgonzola. The unusually opulent setting—think gold-coffered ceilings, Venetian wallpaper, and marble fireplaces—was once the home of Count Natale Labia, South Africa's first Italian ambassador. Friendly staff encourage you to linger amid the English arts and crafts and Italian rococo mash-up, the effect of which is mellowed by a sun-filled courtyard overlooking False Bay's gorgeous blue horizon. ⑤ *Average main: R90* ⊠ *192 Main Rd., Muizenberg* ☎ *021/788–6062* ☻ *No dinner. Closed Mon.*

$
CAFÉ

✕ Empire Cafe. Overlooking Muizenberg's surfers' beach, Empire is a place to come barefoot with sand still between your toes for unexpectedly good food, though with less-than-great service. The chalkboard menu changes regularly, but the lamb rump steak is fabulous, served on sautéed spinach with chickpeas, rooibos-tea-soaked raisins, garlic butter, and eggplant, all dribbled with garlic aioli. Also delicious is the pasta carbonara. Smoothies and fresh juices are just as good, the bread baked on-site is stupendously tasty, and the coffee is great. Some will find the laid-back vibe irritating, whereas others will find it's exactly what they were looking for. ⑤ *Average main: R80* ✉ *11 York Rd., Muizenberg* ☎ *021/788–1250* ⊕ *www.empirecafe.co.za* ☾ *No dinner.*

KALK BAY

$$$$ ✕**Harbour House.** Built on the breakwater of a working harbor, the
SEAFOOD Harbor House's location is unbeatable—waves are known to crash against the huge plate-glass windows at high tide. Large, light filled, and orchid adorned, this is a beautiful space to enjoy fresh seafood. The fish of the day is usually a reliable choice: the fresh angelfish with a poached egg and Japanese mayo is excellent. Other dishes that rely more on the freshness of the seafood (oysters and calamari) than the brilliance of the chef will also surely satisfy. Accompaniments may be a disappointment, though, considering the prices, which are high by local standards (visitors enjoying good exchange rates might not even notice). However, the view really does make up for a lot. There's also a tempting dessert list. ◼ TIP➔ **If you're looking for something a bit more casual, try sister restaurants Live Bait and Polana, both just downstairs and privy to the same great view. Live Bait is also seafood focused but with lower prices, and Polana serves more Portuguese-influenced seafood and meat dishes in a hip (but smoker-friendly) setting.** ⑤ *Average main: R200* ✉ *Kalk Bay Harbour, Main Rd., Kalk Bay* ☎ *021/788–4133* ⊕ *www. harbourhousegroup.co.za* ⚓ *Reservations essential.*

$$ ✕**Olympia Café.** This tiny Kalk Bay landmark with its mismatched tables
CAFÉ and open kitchen is much beloved by locals as a super-casual destination
Fodor's Choice for consistently excellent food. The quality of the mostly Mediterranean
★ fare is high, and the servers are always sassy (some might call it something else). The chalkboard menu changes regularly, but expect dishes like seared tuna with crushed potatoes and lemon mayo, or roast duck on egg noodles teriyaki-style. Great soups—think bacon and bean or tomato and lentil—are served with legendary ciabatta. There is always a great pasta dish on offer (linguine with tuna and cherry tomatoes, anyone?), as well as creative salads. Lines are the norm at peak mealtimes and reservations are not accepted, so be prepared to wait. Meanwhile, the treats from the café's bakery around the corner are available to purchase to take home. ⑤ *Average main: R105* ✉ *134 Main Rd., Kalk Bay* ☎ *021/788–6396* ⚓ *Reservations not accepted.*

WHERE TO STAY

Updated by
Lee Middleton

Finding lodging in Cape Town can be a nightmare during peak travel season (December–January), as many of the more reasonable accommodations are booked up. It's worth traveling between April and August, if you can, to take advantage of the "secret season" discounts that are sometimes half the high-season rate. Other reduced rates can be scored by booking directly online, checking the "Best Available Rate" at large hotels, or simply asking if any specials or discounts are available. If you arrive in Cape Town without a reservation, head for any branch of the Tourism Office, which has a helpful accommodations desk.

First-time, short-term, or business visitors will want to locate themselves centrally. The historic city center is a vibrant and pedestrian-friendly place by day, but at night can feel a bit deserted and edgy, depending on where you are. Night owls may prefer to stay amid the nonstop action of Long Street or Kloof Street, or at the V&A Waterfront, with its plethora of pedestrian-friendly shopping and dining options (though be aware that locals don't consider the Waterfront the "real" Cape Town). Boutique hotels and bed-and-breakfasts in Gardens are often within walking distance of attractions and dining but will be quieter and often enjoy lovely views. Options along the Atlantic Seaboard are also close to the action and (mostly) pedestrian-friendly, with the added advantage of sea and sunset views. Staying farther out on the Cape Peninsula, whether the False Bay or Atlantic side, provides the closest thing in Cape Town to a beach-vacation atmosphere despite the cold ocean waters. The Southern Suburbs, especially around Constantia or Tokai, can make a good base from which to explore the area's wine estates as well as the peninsula, but you'll be dependent on a car for everything, and should plan on 25 to 45 minutes to get into town.

Most international flights arrive in the morning, and return flights depart in the evening. Because most hotels have an 11 am checkout and 2 pm check-in, you may find yourself with a lodging gap on travel days. All hotels will hold your luggage, and most will try to accommodate you (some of the larger hotels have lounges where you can spend the hours before your flight), but in peak season you may need to organize a backup plan. Also note that many small, luxury accommodations either do not permit children or have minimum-age restrictions. It's a good idea to inquire in advance if this will be an issue. Cape Town also follows the global trend of not smoking in public places. All hotels will have no-smoking rooms, and most are entirely smoke-free. *Hotel reviews have been shortened. For full information, visit Fodors.com.*

LODGING ALTERNATIVES

When South Africans travel, they often stay in guesthouses or B&Bs, which are numerous in Cape Town. Don't be put off by the names—choosing a B&B or guesthouse doesn't mean you'll have to eat breakfast with the family or help wash up afterward. Among them you will find some of the most elegant and professionally run establishments available, offering everything a hotel does but on a smaller, more personal scale. If you prefer a bit more anonymity or want to save money, consider renting a fully furnished apartment, especially if you're staying two or more weeks. Airbnb has listings in Cape Town, and several agencies can help you make bookings. *For agency recommendations, see Accommodations in Travel Smart.*

Cape Stay. Cape Stay offers a huge selection of accommodations to suit different needs, from very simple and affordable apartments to luxurious villas to special rates at well known hotels, covering both Cape Town and popular Western Cape destinations. $ *Rooms from: R800* ⊕ *www.capestay.co.za.*

CAPSOL Property & Tourism Solutions. CAPSOL has more than 2,000 high-quality, furnished, fully stocked villas and apartments along the Atlantic seaboard from Cape Town to Bakoven, including Clifton, Bantry Bay and Camps

Bay. $ *Rooms from: R1600* ⊠ *The Penthouse, 13 Totnes Ave., Camps Bay* ☎ *021/438–9644* ⊕ *www.capsol.co.za.*

Village & Life. Village & Life manages **De Waterkant Village,** a collection of more than 40 beautifully restored, self-catering (with cooking facilities) apartments and houses scattered around the charming, central, and gay-friendly De Waterkant area. $ *Rooms from: R1500* ⊠ *1 Loader St., Cape Town Central* ☎ *021/437–9706* ⊕ *www.villageandlife.com.*

WHAT IT COSTS IN SOUTH AFRICAN RAND			
	$	**$$**	**$$$**	**$$$$**
Hotels	under R1,500	R1,500–R2,500	R2,501–R3,500	over R3,500

Prices are the lowest price for a standard double room in high season.

CAPE TOWN CENTRAL

$ HOTEL FAMILY **Adderley Hotel.** If you're looking for an inner-city accommodation that's well priced and far away from the late-night noise of Long Street but close enough to enjoy the nightlife, the Adderley is for you. **Pros:** in the heart of historic Cape Town and a block from the Company's Garden; friendly staff; big rooms. **Cons:** the inner city can be eerily quiet at night; Wi-Fi was not free at time of writing. $ *Rooms from: R1400* ⊠ *31 Adderley St.* ☎ *021/469–1900* ⊕ *www.adderleyhotel.co.za* ⇱ *27 suites* ❍❙ *Multiple meal plans.*

$$ B&B/INN **Cape Heritage Hotel.** Built as a private home in 1771, this centrally located boutique hotel has teak-beamed ceilings, foot-wide yellow-wood floorboards, and numerous other details that recall its gracious past. **Pros:** excellent eateries in adjoining Heritage Square; free uncapped Wi-Fi in rooms and public areas; great location in Cape Town's historic district. **Cons:** bordered by one busy road; parking isn't free. $ *Rooms from: R2390* ⊠ *90 Bree St.* ☎ *021/424–4646* ⊕ *www.capeheritage.co.za* ⇱ *17 rooms* ❍❙ *Breakfast.*

$$ B&B/INN **Dutch Manor Antique Hotel.** Steeped in old-world charm, this antique hotel in the charming and centrally located Bo-Kaap is chockablock with one of the Cape's finest collections of antiques. **Pros:** the decor makes you feel as if you're sleeping in a beautiful museum; great central location; free Wi-Fi. **Cons:** parking is a two-minute walk from the entrance (though the guard will valet for you if needed); busy road across the way may be noisy; downstairs rooms a bit dark. $ *Rooms from: R1700* ⊠ *158 Buitengracht St.* ☎ *021/422–4767* ⊕ *www.dutchmanor.co.za* ⇱ *6 rooms* ❍❙ *Multiple meal plans.*

$ B&B/INN **Long Street Boutique Hotel.** The upper floors of a beautifully restored Victorian building on trendy Long Street house this incredibly good-value boutique hotel made up of 12 luxurious rooms. **Pros:** surprisingly opulent digs for the price; free unlimited Wi-Fi and a/c; in the heart of Cape Town's nightlife. **Cons:** no elevator; not a tranquil neighborhood; must pay for parking. $ *Rooms from: R950* ⊠ *230 Long St.* ☎ *021/426–4309* ⊕ *www.longstreethotel.com* ⇱ *12 rooms* ❍❙ *Breakfast.*

BEST BETS FOR CAPE TOWN LODGING

Fodor's offers a selective listing of quality lodging experiences in every price range, from the city's best budget beds to its most sophisticated luxury hotels. Here, we've compiled our top recommendations by price and experience. The very best properties—in other words, those that provide a particularly remarkable experience in their price range—are designated in the listings with the Fodor's Choice logo.

Fodor's Choice

Belmond Mount Nelson Hotel, $$$$, p. 105

Cellars-Hohenort Hotel & Spa, $$$$, p. 114

Ellerman House, $$$$, p. 111

Tinswalo Atlantic, $$$$, p. 114

Twelve Apostles, $$$$, p. 112

By Price

$

Dolphin Inn, p. 110

Monkey Valley Resort, p. 115

$$

Cape Heritage Hotel, p. 103

$$$

Radisson Blu Hotel Waterfront, p. 110

$$$$

Belmond Mount Nelson Hotel, $$$$, p. 105

Cape Grace, p. 109

Cellars-Hohenort Hotel & Spa, p. 114

The Dock House Boutique Hotel, p. 109

Ellerman House, p. 111

The Last Word Long Beach, p. 115

Steenberg Hotel, p. 114

Tinswalo Atlantic, $$$$, p. 114

Twelve Apostles, p. 112

Westin Cape Town, p. 105

By Experience

BEST FOR ROMANCE

Belmond Mount Nelson, p. 105

Cellars-Hohenort Hotel & Spa, p. 114

The Dock House Boutique Hotel, p. 109

Ellerman House, p. 111

Tintswalo Atlantic, p. 114

BEST HOTEL BARS

Alphen Boutique Hotel, p. 114

Belmond Mount Nelson Hotel, p. 105

Cape Grace, p. 109

Cape Royale Luxury Hotel & Spa, p. 110

One&Only Cape Town, p. 109

Table Bay Hotel, p. 110

BEST LOBBY

Belmond Mount Nelson, p. 105

One&Only Cape Town, p. 109

Table Bay Hotel, p. 110

Taj Cape Town, p. 105

BEST SPA

Belmond Mount Nelson Hotel, p. 105

Cape Grace, p. 109

Ellerman House, p. 111

One&Only Cape Town, p. 109

Westin Cape Town, p. 105

2

$$$$ · HOTEL — 🏨 **Taj Cape Town.** With an amazing location in the heart of historic Cape Town, the Taj sits in the grand former headquarters of the South African Reserve Bank and provides the professional and luxurious hospitality that one would expect from this brand. **Pros:** free daily walking tour; good Indian fine-dining restaurant and gorgeous Twankey bar; destination spa. **Cons:** has a bit of a business feel; breakfast not anything to write home about. ⑤ *Rooms from: R7500* ✉ *Wale St.* ☎ *021/819–2000* ⊕ *www.tajcapetown.co.za* ⮡ *176 rooms* ⑩ *Breakfast.*

$$$$ · HOTEL — 🏨 **The Westin Cape Town.** Conveniently linked to the Cape Town International Convention Centre, this sophisticated business hotel still caters to vacationers with features like an excellent spa with killer views, indoor and outdoor pools, and a stop for the water taxi that plies the canals to the V&A Waterfront. **Pros:** stellar views over the harbor and Signal Hill on one side and city and Table Mountain on the other from the top-floor restaurant; fantastic spa, gym, and infinity pool; excellent and varied conference and business facilities. **Cons:** busy corporate hotel; not much within immediate walking distance in this part of the city, referred to as the Foreshore. ⑤ *Rooms from: R6300* ✉ *Convention Sq., 1 Lower Long St.* ☎ *021/412–9999* ⊕ *www.westincapetown.com* ⮡ *451 rooms, 32 suites* ⑩ *Breakfast.*

GARDENS

$$$$ · HOTEL · **Fodor'sChoice** · ★ — 🏨 **Belmond Mount Nelson Hotel.** This distinctive pink landmark has been the grande dame of Cape Town since it opened its doors in 1899 to accommodate passengers just off the Union-Castle steamships. **Pros:** aesthetically, this is the real colonial deal; guests include movie stars and diplomats; excellent restaurant. **Cons:** breakfast restaurant Oasis lacks the charm of the rest of the hotel. ⑤ *Rooms from: R7565* ✉ *76 Orange St.* ☎ *021/483–1000* ⊕ *www.belmond.com/mount-nelson-hotel-cape-town/* ⮡ *133 rooms, 65 suites* ⑩ *Breakfast.*

$$$ · B&B/INN — 🏨 **Cape Cadogan Boutique Hotel.** This lovely and well-located Georgian and Victorian boutique hotel dates back to the beginning of the 19th century. **Pros:** free shuttle to the Waterfront; free Wi-Fi; apartments available for those who want to self-cater. **Cons:** traffic noise (hooting minibus taxis at nearby intersection); rooms can be quite uneven in size and design; breakfast mediocre. ⑤ *Rooms from: R2760* ✉ *5 Upper Union St.* ☎ *021/480–8080* ⊕ *www.capecadogan.co.za* ⮡ *7 rooms, 7 luxury suites, 1 superior* ⑩ *Breakfast.*

$$$$ · B&B/INN — 🏨 **Kensington Place.** A beautiful garden entrance leads you into this stylish and luxurious boutique guesthouse that feels like a little piece of heaven. **Pros:** great views of Cape Town and Table Mountain; all meals available from kitchen; free Wi-Fi. **Cons:** not within walking distance of town; no kids under 12. ⑤ *Rooms from: R3553* ✉ *38 Kensington Crescent, Higgovale* ☎ *021/424–4744* ⊕ *www.kensingtonplace.co.za* ⮡ *8 rooms* ⑩ *Breakfast.*

$$ · HOTEL — 🏨 **Protea Fire & Ice.** Initially built as a highly themed hotel—interior elements like elevators kitted out as a shark cage underwater or a Table Mountain cable car mid-journey, and a "climbing wall" still exist—this place will appeal to those who value a vibey social atmosphere and proximity to Cape Town's nightlife. **Pros:** proximity to restaurants and

Where to Stay in
Cape Town

ATLANTIC
OCEAN

Granger
Bay

Victoria
Basin

East Pier

1

2

WATERFRONT

4

5

MOUILLE
POINT

Beach

3

Portswood

6

Fritz Sonnenberg

Ebenezer

Beach

Bay

8

GREEN
POINT

9

10

Western Blvd. M6

Wigtown

11

Main M61

High Level

Springbok

Three Glen

THREE
ANCHOR
BAY

Gartir

20

Signal Hill

Rhine

High Level

Main M61

Marais

Beach - M6

21

SEA POINT

St. John's

High Level

Regent - M61

Kloof

Des Huguenots

Fresnaye

Beach

Beach

FRESNAYE

Queens

M6

BANTRY
BAY

Victoria

32

0   500 yards

0   500 meters

Lion's Head

other activities on foot; brilliant views of Table Mountain from rooms above the fifth floor; daily "experience" boards to keep guests abreast of what's hot in the city. **Cons:** some will be irritated by the zany decoration that remains; rooms are small. ⑤ *Rooms from: R2025* ⊠ *New Church and Victoria Sts.* ☎ *021/430–5300* ⊕ *www.proteahotels.com* ⤴ *189 rooms, 12 executive suites* ⑩ *Breakfast.*

$$
B&B/INN

Welgelegen Boutique Hotel. In Afrikaans, *welgelegen* means "well situated," and this classy boutique hotel in two beautifully restored Victorian mansions is just that: nestled under Table Mountain in a quiet street just minutes away from city attractions. **Pros:** great staff make guests feel like part of the family; walking distance to Kloof street cafés; free unlimited Wi-Fi. **Cons:** as it's an old building, the occasional creaky floorboard is to be expected. ⑤ *Rooms from: R2175* ⊠ *6 Stephen St.* ☎ *021/426–2373, 021/426–2374* ⊕ *www.welgelegen.co.za* ⤴ *13 rooms, 1 cottage* ⑩ *Breakfast.*

TAMBOERSKLOOF

$$
HOTEL

Cape Milner Hotel. The only midsize hotel in the lovely Tamboerskloof area, the clean and comfortable Milner makes a convenient location from which to explore trendy nearby Kloof Street and beyond. **Pros:** great location minutes from city; good dining options within walking distance; near Table Mountain. **Cons:** one-way roads make it tricky to access; overlooks a road that's busy at peak times; Table Mountain views from rooms that have them are partially obscured by strange window awnings. ⑤ *Rooms from: R2380* ⊠ *2A Milner Rd.* ☎ *021/426–1101* ⊕ *www.capemilner.com* ⤴ *55 rooms; 2 suites* ⑩ *Breakfast.*

$$
B&B/INN

Derwent House. This beautiful old house in a fantastic and very central Tamboerskloof location makes for a stylish and convenient base while exploring Cape Town. **Pros:** super-convenient location to Kloof Street eateries and attractions; family room with kitchenette option; great breakfast. **Cons:** some rooms a bit small; can hear creaks and noises on occasion; most rooms lack views. ⑤ *Rooms from: R1850* ⊠ *14 Derwent Rd.* ☎ *021/422–2763* ⊕ *www.derwenthouse.co.za* ⤴ *9 rooms, 1 suite, 1 apartment* ⑩ *Breakfast.*

$
B&B/INN

La Villa Belle Ombre. Located in a restored 1870 Cape Victorian mansion in lovely, quiet Tamboerskloof, this B&B is within walking distance of trendy Kloof Street and a five-minute drive from Table Mountain. **Pros:** excellent value for money; good breakfast included in the rates; free Wi-Fi. **Cons:** insufficient closet space in some bedrooms. ⑤ *Rooms from: R1020* ⊠ *16 Belle Ombre Rd.* ☎ *021/424–2727* ⊕ *www.villabelleombre.com* ⤴ *6 rooms, 1 apartment* ⑩ *Breakfast.*

ORANJEZICHT

$
B&B/INN

Cactusberry Lodge. This great-value guesthouse in an appealing shade of cinnamon terra cotta (a.k.a. cactusberry) is in a quiet neighborhood that is still within walking distance of some attractions and restaurants. **Pros:** personalized concierge service from the owner; homey, friendly place to meet other travelers; great breakfast. **Cons:** rooms on the small side; creaky floors if downstairs; no TV in rooms. ⑤ *Rooms from:*

R1200 ✉ *30 Breda St.* ☎ *021/461–9787* ⊕ *www.cactusberrylodge.com* ↩ *6 rooms* ⦿ *Breakfast.*

$$$$ ⌂ **Manna Bay.** On the slopes of Table Mountain with stupendous views
HOTEL overlooking the whole of Cape Town, this luxurious new boutique hotel is all tranquil privacy and bold designer style. **Pros:** amazing views and style; attentive service; great food. **Cons:** set back from the city, so you'll need a car to go anywhere; only two rooms have a private bath. Ⓢ *Rooms from: R5000* ✉ *8 Bridle Rd.* ☎ *021/461–1094* ⊕ *www. mannabay.com* ↩ *8 rooms (2 with bath)* ⦿ *Breakfast.*

$$ ⌂ **The Three.** On a quiet street in leafy Oranjezicht, this midsize bou-
HOTEL tique hotel has spacious, contemporary rooms laid out on two floors around a lovely courtyard in a beautifully restored old building. **Pros:** good eco principles in place; private shuttle service that costs the same as a local taxi but lets you know the driver; friendly, helpful staff. **Cons:** Nespresso coffee in room not free; no real views from rooms and they also lack outward-facing windows that can open, so if you want fresh air, you are somewhat exposed to passersby in courtyard. Ⓢ *Rooms from: R2300* ✉ *3 Flower St.* ☎ *083/672–5363, 086/637–2596* ⊕ *www. thethree.co.za* ↩ *14 rooms, 1 suite* ⦿ *Breakfast.*

V&A WATERFRONT

$$$$ ⌂ **Cape Grace.** Enjoying a stellar location in the working harbor section
HOTEL of the Waterfront—and rightfully renowned for its excellent service—
FAMILY the Cape Grace is popular with American celebrities, including the likes of Bill and Hillary Clinton. **Pros:** mountain or harbor views from all rooms; excellent, personalized service; particularly family-friendly for such a posh hotel; free shuttle within 10-km (6-mile) radius. **Cons:** unconventional decor may not suit all tastes; some rooms a bit dark. Ⓢ *Rooms from: R7372* ✉ *West Quay Rd.* ☎ *021/410–7100* ⊕ *www. capegrace.com* ↩ *120 rooms* ⦿ *Breakfast.*

$$$$ ⌂ **The Dock House Boutique Hotel.** Victorian splendor meets modern glam
HOTEL at this stunning boutique hotel perched over Cape Town's trendy and ever-popular V&A Waterfront. **Pros:** the hotel's elegant interior has been featured in decor magazines; close to activities, dining, and shopping; excellent room service. **Cons:** guests have to walk outside to reach the gym and spa; those wishing to socialize with other guests should look elsewhere. Ⓢ *Rooms from: R6830* ✉ *Portswood Close, Portswood Ridge* ☎ *021/421–9334* ⊕ *www.dockhouse.co.za* ↩ *5 rooms; 1 suite; 2 villas* ⦿ *Breakfast.*

$$$$ ⌂ **One&Only Cape Town.** In the spirit of founding investor Sol Kerzner's
RESORT "go big or go home" philosophy, the One&Only Cape Town is a splen-
FAMILY did tribute to excess with its four-story glass window views onto Table Mountain from the aptly named Vista Bar and decadent island spa surrounded by a moat. **Pros:** conveniently located in the heart of the Watefront; oceans of space and great views from all rooms; excellent personalized service; great kids' programs. **Cons:** Marina Rise guests must walk through the lounge in their swimsuit/robe to reach the pool or spa; lacks the intimacy of a smaller hotel. Ⓢ *Rooms from: R7215* ✉ *Dock Rd.* ☎ *021/431–5888* ⊕ *www.oneandonlyresorts.com* ↩ *131 rooms* ⦿ *Breakfast.*

$$$$ ⊞ **Radisson Blu Hotel Waterfront.** When it comes to great locations, this
HOTEL   hotel is one of Cape Town's front-runners, perched on the edge of the
Atlantic Ocean. **Pros:** sound of the water crashing against the breakwater; free shuttle to the Waterfront; proximity to Cape Town's popular
seafront pedestrian promenade. **Cons:** rooms without views and/or not
yet updated don't warrant the cost; has the impersonal feel of a big
hotel. Ⓢ *Rooms from: R5000* ✉ *Beach Rd.* ☎ *021/441–3000* ⊕ *www.
radissonblu.com* ⬅ *177 rooms* ⍩⃝l *Breakfast.*

$$$$ ⊞ **Table Bay Hotel.** This glitzy hotel sits in a prime spot at the tip of the
HOTEL   V&A Waterfront, enjoying fabulous views from all sides. **Pros:** attentive service despite being a large hotel; all rooms have sea/harbor or
mountain views. **Cons:** shallow pool and moldy steam room; breakfast quality doesn't quite meet expectations based on its grand presentation. Ⓢ *Rooms from: R5615* ✉ *Quay 6* ☎ *021/406–5000* ⊕ *www.
suninternational.com* ⬅ *311 rooms, 18 suites* ⍩⃝l *Breakfast.*

$$$$ ⊞ **Victoria & Alfred Hotel.** This upscale hotel in a converted warehouse
HOTEL   is smack in the middle of the Waterfront and surrounded by shops,
bars, and restaurants. **Pros:** best value at the Waterfront; excellent
breakfasts include healthy and diabetic options; great service from restaurant and hotel staff. **Cons:** there's a drawbridge nearby that seafar-
ers have to alert with a whistle; buskers in the piazza are loud; pool
and gym an effort to find. Ⓢ *Rooms from: R4050* ✉ *On Waterfront
Pierhead* ☎ *021/419–6677* ⊕ *www.newmarkhotels.com* ⬅ *94 rooms*
⍩⃝l *Breakfast.*

MOUILLE POINT

$ ⊞ **Dolphin Inn.** An excellent value-for-money location on Mouille Point's
B&B/INN   sought-after strip, this simple inn's rooms are basic but neat and comfortable, a few even enjoying sea views. **Pros:** great location; good value
for money; free Wi-Fi. **Cons:** basic amenities might leave you wanting
more; sea-facing rooms are noisy, located by the entrance/over the road;
restaurant serves breakfast only. Ⓢ *Rooms from: R1350* ✉ *75 Beach Rd.*
☎ *021/434–3175* ⊕ *www.dolphin-inn.co.za* ⬅ *8 rooms* ⍩⃝l *Breakfast.*

$$ ⊞ **La Splendida Luxury Suites.** This chic art deco–style hotel enjoys a
HOTEL   great location across from the popular seafront promenade and is a
15-minute walk from the V&A Waterfront. **Pros:** expansive views from
sea-facing rooms; very reasonably priced for location and room size;
friendly staff. **Cons:** security is a bit lax, as restaurant patrons can access
hotel elevators; attention to detail not always there in service. Ⓢ *Rooms
from: R1600* ✉ *121 Beach Rd.* ☎ *021/439–5119* ⊕ *www.lasplendida.
co.za* ⬅ *24 suites* ⍩⃝l *Breakfast.*

GREEN POINT

$$$ ⊞ **Cape Royale Luxury Hotel & Spa.** Just a stone's throw from the Green
HOTEL   Point stadium and the V&A Waterfront—and surrounded by restau-
rants and public transportation—the Cape Royale offers spacious
apartment-style accommodations that make a great base for longer-
term travelers. **Pros:** roomy, well-designed suites at competitive prices;
great location; Sky Bar and Equinox Spa. **Cons:** only 1GB free Wi-Fi per

three days; on-site restaurant keeps closing and reopening as something new. ⑤ *Rooms from: R3500* ✉ *47 Main Rd.* ☎ *021/430–0500* ⊕ *www. caperoyale.co.za* ⤴ *32 1-bedroom suites, 45 2-bedroom suites, 4 3-bedroom suites, 2 villas* ❣️ *Multiple meal plans.*

$$ **Dysart Boutique Hotel.** This small and elegant boutique hotel in Green

HOTEL Point is perfect for style mavens and art lovers seeking a quiet stay in a convenient location. **Pros:** tasteful, arty decor; nice views from pool/ common areas; owner managed. **Cons:** located between Green Point and Sea Point, it's a (little) bit of a walk to restaurants. ⑤ *Rooms from: R2400* ✉ *17 Dysart Rd.* ☎ *021/439–2832* ⊕ *www.dysart.de* ⤴ *8 rooms* ❣️ *Breakfast.*

SEA POINT

$$ **Blackheath Lodge.** Conveniently located on a quiet street in upper

B&B/INN Sea Point, this small, stylish Victorian-era hotel with great concierge-level owner-rendered service is an extremely good value. **Pros:** excellent service; 24-hour minibar; nice location. **Cons:** no bathtubs in rooms; no gym. ⑤ *Rooms from: R1950* ✉ *Blackheath Rd.* ☎ *021/439–2541* ⊕ *www.blackheathlodge.com* ⤴ *15 rooms* ❣️ *Breakfast.*

$$$$ **Ellerman House.** Built in 1906 for shipping magnate Sir John Ellerman,

HOTEL what may be Cape Town's finest hotel sits high on a hill up from Sea

Fodor'sChoice Point in Bantry Bay, graced with stupendous views of the sea, and an

★ art collection that puts the National Gallery to shame. **Pros:** stunning national art collection; free transfers within 15km; hand-finished laundry packed in tissue paper; free, fully stocked guest pantry. **Cons:** Kloof Road is busy; often booked a year in advance. ⑤ *Rooms from: R10000* ✉ *180 Kloof Rd., Bantry Bay* ☎ *021/430–3200* ⊕ *www.ellerman.co.za* ⤴ *11 rooms, 2 suites, 2 villas* ❣️ *Breakfast.*

$$ **Glen Boutique Hotel.** This midsize boutique hotel on a quiet street in

HOTEL Sea Point exudes a playful, Ibiza-inspired energy with its mix of modern style—think orchids and stylish men's shirts for sale—and a bright Greek Isle palette of white and turquoise. **Pros:** great dual pool area with seaside vibey atmosphere; very close to Sea Point promenade; full-service restaurant. **Cons:** a bit clubby for some tastes. ⑤ *Rooms from: R1950* ✉ *3 The Glen* ☎ *021/439–0086* ⊕ *www.glenhotel.co.za* ⤴ *24 rooms* ❣️ *Breakfast.*

CAMPS BAY

$ **The Bay Atlantic Guesthouse.** This unpretentious, value-oriented guest-

B&B/INN house is extremely well located a couple of blocks from Camps Bay's lively main drag. **Pros:** great location and views for money; friendly, homey space. **Cons:** decor is old-fashioned; rooms without views are underwhelming. ⑤ *Rooms from: R1400* ✉ *3 Berkley Rd.* ☎ *021/438–4341* ⊕ *www.thebayatlantic.com* ⤴ *7 rooms* ❣️ *Breakfast.*

$$$$ **The Bay Hotel.** The only large hotel in Camps Bay, this luxurious yet

HOTEL relaxed property sits across the street from a white-sand beach and is backed by the towering cliffs of the Twelve Apostles. **Pros:** popular beach across the way; at the epicenter of high-season social life. **Cons:** road between hotel and beach is often busy and sometimes gridlocked;

unpleasant when the southeaster wind blows hard; Wi-Fi free only up to 250 MB/day. *⑤ Rooms from: R4680 ⊠ 69 Victoria Rd. ☎ 021/430–4444 ⊕ www.thebayhotel.com ➾ 78 rooms ⍥ Breakfast.*

$$ ⚟ **Boutique @10.** Up against the mountainside right in the middle of
B&B/INN Camps Bay, this small, intimate guesthouse enjoys stunning views over the popular seaside neighborhood below and across the ocean beyond. **Pros:** amazing views; owner-managed; nice touches like complimentary wine tastings. **Cons:** no fridges in rooms (except one); decor in some rooms tending toward a 1970s vibe, in need of small updates; lots of stairs. *⑤ Rooms from: R2195 ⊠ 10 Medburn Rd. ☎ 021/438–1234 ⊕ www.boutique10.co.za ➾ 4 rooms ⍥ Breakfast.*

$$$$ ⚟ **Pod.** This sexy designer boutique hotel enjoys a great location on a
HOTEL quiet corner just a block from Camps Bay's main drag. **Pros:** excellent breakfast; spa with shower for use by late check-outs; eco-friendly additions like door sensor to switch a/c off and tree planting for guests of three nights or more. **Cons:** classic rooms are small; no on-site restaurant after breakfast. *⑤ Rooms from: R5150 ⊠ 3 Argyle Rd. ☎ 021/438–8550 ⊕ www.pod.co.za ➾ 17 rooms ⍥ Breakfast.*

$$$$ ⚟ **Twelve Apostles Hotel & Spa.** If you fancy taking a helicopter to the
HOTEL airport or lazing in a bubble bath while looking out floor-to-ceiling
Fodor's Choice windows at sea and mountains, then this award-winning, luxurious
★ hotel and spa may be for you. **Pros:** wonderfully attentive staff; Table Mountain is your back garden; sports buddy program provides a companion for runs or mountain biking in surrounding area. **Cons:** overlooks a road that gets busy; nearest off-site restaurant is at least 10 minutes by car; views from some rooms partially blocked by overhanging beam. *⑤ Rooms from: R5685 ⊠ Victoria Rd. ☎ 021/437–9000 ⊕ www.12apostleshotel.com ➾ 55 rooms, 15 suites ⍥ Breakfast.*

SOUTHERN SUBURBS

HOUT BAY

$$ ⚟ **Cube Guest House.** This stylish, modern guesthouse high on a hill in res-
B&B/INN idential Hout Bay enjoys stunning bay and mountain views and makes the perfect pampered base from which to explore all the Cape's offerings. **Pros:** great service; no end-time for breakfast; free unlimited Wi-Fi. **Cons:** not kid-friendly; all rooms accessed by stairs; you'll need a car for most activities. *⑤ Rooms from: R1800 ⊠ 20 Luisa Way ☎ 072/053–5038 ⊕ www.cube-guesthouse.com ➾ 5 rooms ⍥ Breakfast.*

$$ ⚟ **Hout Bay Hideaway.** Tranquil and intimate with only four rooms, this
B&B/INN owner-managed guesthouse tucked away in a lush neighborhood setting is perfect for those seeking peace and quiet. **Pros:** free unlimited Wi-Fi; wood-burning fires and underfloor heating; barbecue grills for guests. **Cons:** smokers aren't welcome; you'll want to have a car for most activities. *⑤ Rooms from: R1650 ⊠ 37 Skaife St. ☎ 021/790–8040 ⊕ www.houtbay-hideaway.com ➾ 3 suites, 1 apartment ⍥ Breakfast.*

$$$$ ⚟ **Hout Bay Manor.** Situated in the heart of Hout Bay's shops and res-
HOTEL taurants, this classic Cape Dutch edifice decorated in a playful funky
FAMILY African style has been a working hotel since 1871. **Pros:** friendly service; child-friendly offerings; convenient location. **Cons:** no gym; no views of either mountain or sea from the rooms. *⑤ Rooms from: R3905 ⊠ Off*

Where to Stay in the Cape Peninsula

See
Where to Stay
in Cape Town
Map

*Table
Bay*

PARDEN
EILAND

N1

FORESHORE

OBSERVATORY

M3

N2

Bantry Bay

❶

❷

Camps Bay

Table Mountain

3 4

Bakoven

RONDEBOSCH

NEWLANDS

❻

CLAREMONT

❺

Victoria

KENILWORTH

BISHOPSCOURT

WYNBERG

Rhodes

❼

❽

❾

CONSTANTIA

PLUMSTEAD

Llandudno

Main

M6

10 – 12

Hout Bay

M4

*Duiker
Island*

*Hout
Bay*

Chapmans Peak

❶❸

WESTLAKE

M42

M3

Main

M5

RETREAT

❶❹

LAKESIDE

M6

*Silvermine
Nature
Reserve*

Muizenberg

❶❺

M64

❶❼

Sun Valley

Kalk Bay

❶❽

❶❻

Kommetjie Main

M65

❶❾

Fish Hoek

*Ocean
View*

M6

False Bay

*Soet
Water*

❷⓿

Dido Valley

M65

Witsand

❷❶

Simon's Town

*ATLANTIC
OCEAN*

Mt. Pleasant

M4

*INDIAN
OCEAN*

Plateau

M65

*Table
Mountain
National Park*

0   2 miles

0   2 kilometers

Main Rd., Baviaanskloof ☎ *021/790–0116* ⊕ *www.houtbaymanor. co.za* ☞ *16 rooms* ﴾○﴿ *Breakfast.*

$$$$
RESORT
Fodor's Choice
★

☒ **Tintswalo Atlantic.** Visitors attracted to the Cape Peninsula for its natural grandeur will think they've died and gone to heaven when arriving at this discreetly luxurious boutique hotel. **Pros:** unique mind-blowing location; stupendous breakfast; gorgeous beach chic decor. **Cons:** must drive to all activities and sights; ⑤ *Rooms from: R8520* ☒ *Chapman's Peak Dr., Km 2* ☎ *021/201–0025* ⊕ *www.tintswalo.com* ☞ *10 island suites, 1 presidential suite* ﴾○﴿ *Some meals.*

CONSTANTIA

$$$$
HOTEL

☒ **Alphen Boutique Hotel.** Situated on 11 acres of gardens in leafy Constantia, this glamorous and avant-garde boutique hotel was originally an 18th-century Cape Dutch manor house and working farm. **Pros:** beautiful setting and landscaped gardens; great pool even though it's unheated. **Cons:** no gym; no elevator. ⑤ *Rooms from: R3600* ☒ *Alphen Dr.* ☎ *021/795–6300* ⊕ *www.alphen.co.za* ☞ *19 rooms* ﴾○﴿ *Breakfast.*

$$$$
HOTEL
Fodor's Choice
★

☒ **Cellars-Hohenort Hotel & Spa.** With acres of gardens and spectacular views across the Constantia Valley, this idyllic getaway makes the world beyond disappear. **Pros:** exquisite gardens; two pools (one for children); fantastic breakfast in lovely Conservatory Restaurant. **Cons:** need a car to get around; more modern rooms are less spectacular; a lot of stairs to access best rooms. ⑤ *Rooms from: R5000* ☒ *93 Brommersvlei Rd.* ☎ *021/794–2137* ⊕ *www.cellars-hohenort.com* ☞ *52 rooms, 1 suite* ﴾○﴿ *Breakfast.*

$$$$
HOTEL

☒ **The Last Word Constantia.** Nestled in the exclusive suburb of Bishopscourt, this peaceful boutique hotel with unrivaled views over Kirstenbosch and Table Mountain is a good combination of elegance and homey intimacy. **Pros:** mountain views from rooms; beautiful gardens and lovely heated pool; peace and quiet. **Cons:** no dining options on foot; a car is needed to do anything; no gym. ⑤ *Rooms from: R5225* ☒ *Spaanschemat River Rd.* ☎ *021/794–6561* ⊕ *www.thelastword.co.za* ☞ *4 rooms, 5 suites* ﴾○﴿ *Breakfast.*

TOKAI

$$$$
HOTEL

☒ **Steenberg Hotel.** Located on the Cape's oldest—and still working—wine estate, this intimate luxury hotel is surrounded by manicured gardens, vineyards, and a championship 18-hole golf course. **Pros:** tranquillity; good location between the Constantia Winelands and the Cape Peninsula; free shuttle twice a day to the V&A Waterfront in Cape Town. **Cons:** a bit far from Cape Town's main attractions for first-time visitors; entry-level rooms a bit small. ⑤ *Rooms from: R4400* ☒ *Steenberg Rd.* ☎ *021/713–2222* ⊕ *www.steenbergfarm.com* ☞ *24 rooms* ﴾○﴿ *Breakfast.*

CAPE PENINSULA

The gorgeous but wild Atlantic side of the Cape Peninsula is primarily residential where there is any development. Most accommodation this side is in the form of self-catering vacation homes, but there are also a few lovely B&Bs and guesthouses. You'll need a car to go anywhere. The eastern or False Bay side of the Cape Peninsula includes the popular seaside villages of Muizenberg, St James, Kalk Bay, and Simon's Town. It's a lovely base for nature lovers or those seeking more of a beach-vacation vibe, and some of the Cape's most popular swimming and surfing beaches are found here, along with some clusters of charming shops and restaurants, and plenty of hiking opportunities. The train connects you to the city, but for full-on exploration, a car is still the easiest option.

ATLANTIC COAST
NOORHOEK

$
RESORT
FAMILY
🏠 **Monkey Valley Resort.** This secluded and charming resort on the peninsula is great for families, as well as popular for small conferences and events. **Pros:** expansive views of sea and mountains; direct beach access; great low-season specials. **Cons:** no a/c; thatched roof invites insects; other than beach, not much available on foot. $ *Rooms from: R1340* ✉ *Mountain Rd.* ☎ *021/789–8000* ⊕ *www.monkeyvalleyresort. com* ⇌ *24 rooms, 15 cottages* ⧉ *Breakfast.*

KOMMETJIE

$$$$
HOTEL
🏠 **The Last Word Long Beach.** Superbly spacious rooms in an elegant beach-house theme all have balconies with sea views making the most of the fact that you are, after all, on the beach. **Pros:** complimentary minibar and snacks; free Wi-Fi; staff make you feel like they are there to serve only you. **Cons:** need a car to get around; poor mobile phone reception in lower-level rooms. $ *Rooms from: R5225* ✉ *1 Kirsten Ave., Kommetjie* ☎ *021/794–6561* ⊕ *www.thelastword.co.za* ⇌ *6 rooms* ⧉ *Breakfast.*

FALSE BAY COAST
KALK BAY

$
B&B/INN
🏠 **Chartfield Inn.** This surprisingly stylish and great-value guesthouse is within walking distance of all the bohemian pleasures in the charming fishing village of Kalk Bay. **Pros:** great value for the location; within walking distance of numerous restaurants and the train. **Cons:** no parking; lots of stairs (some very steep). $ *Rooms from: R900* ✉ *30 Gatesville Rd.* ☎ *021/788–3793* ⊕ *www.chartfield.co.za* ⇌ *16 rooms, 1 apartment* ⧉ *Breakfast.*

$
B&B/INN
🏠 **Inn at Castle Hill.** This reasonably priced inn in an Edwardian villa is a pleasant stroll away from charming Kalk Bay's numerous restaurants, antiques shops, and seaside. **Pros:** good value at a great location; free bicycles for guest use; friendly management. **Cons:** location on top of a steep hill; limited on-site parking; two rooms do not have bathrooms. $ *Rooms from: R800* ✉ *37 Gatesville Rd.* ☎ *021/788–2554* ⊕ *www. innatcastlehill.co.za* ⇌ *5 rooms (2 with shared bath)* ⧉ *No meals.*

ST JAMES

$$$
RENTAL
🏠 **St. James Seaforth.** For a luxurious and private seaside retreat, a room in this casually elegant seaside retreat—or even better, the whole house—is just the ticket. **Pros:** lots of perks like inclusive beverages; intimacy and privacy; great views. **Cons:** noise from the road out front can be irritating; not all rooms are equally stunning. $ *Rooms from: R3400* ✉ *Main Rd., St. James, Peninsula False Bay* ☎ *021/788–4543* ⊕ *www.stjamesguesthouses.com* ⇌ *3 rooms* ⧉ *Multiple meal plans.*

SIMON'S TOWN

$
B&B/INN

Simon's Town Guest House. This clean and contemporary African-themed guesthouse is in a residential area about 3 km (2 miles) outside of Simon's Town and enjoys absolutely magnificent views over False Bay. **Pros:** delicious full English and continental breakfast; amazing views; friendly staff. **Cons:** not within walking distance of anything; breakfast ends at 9:30. $ *Rooms from: R1300* ⌧ *20 Bennett Close* ☎ *021/786–5552* ⊕ *www.simonstownguesthouse.co.za* ⇌ *5 rooms* ☉ *Breakfast.*

$$
HOTEL

Simon's Town Quayside Hotel. On Jubilee Square, part of the Simon's Town Waterfront, this hotel is right in the action and has wonderful views over Simon's Town Bay, the harbor, and the yacht club. **Pros:** great location at Jubilee Square, the town's epicenter; great views of fishing boats and naval fleet from sea-facing bedrooms. **Cons:** no nightlife in Simon's Town; mountain view rooms look over Main Road, which can be noisy. $ *Rooms from: R1790* ⌧ *Jubilee Sq., St. Georges St.* ☎ *021/786–3838* ⊕ *www.quaysidehotel.co.za* ⇌ *26 rooms* ☉ *Breakfast.*

NIGHTLIFE AND PERFORMING ARTS

NIGHTLIFE

Updated by
Angus Begg

There's plenty to do in Cape Town after dark. The city's nightlife is concentrated in a number of areas, so you can explore a different one each night or move from one hub to another. Walking, however, isn't always advisable, as some parts of the city are completely deserted and unsafe. Women who are not street savvy should not walk alone or in pairs at night.

NIGHTLIFE AREAS

One of the safer places after dark is the V&A Waterfront, where you can choose from movies, restaurants, bars, and pubs and walk between them quite happily, as there are plenty of security guards and other people walking around. The top end of Long Street is probably the city's best-known young nightlife area. Here you'll find several blocks of bars, restaurants, and backpacker lodges that are open late. The area bounded by Loop, Long, Wale, and Orange streets is the best place to get a feeling for Cape Town's always-changing nightclub scene, but the district known as the Fringe—around Roeland, Harrington, and de Villiers streets—is increasingly where the younger set hang out (clubbers at the latter). De Waterkant in Green Point is also very busy at night and is home to many of Cape Town's gay venues; if you're in the area, you can take in the Green Point strip, where restaurants and bars open out onto the streets. On weekends these bars are packed, and you'll get a good idea of how Capetonians let down their hair. Heritage Square, in Cape Town Central, hosts an ever-changing mix of bars and restaurants generally catering to a more discerning (think wine bars and microbrewery) crowd. Mouille Point's Platinum Mile and Granger Bay are excellent for evening cocktails, though they're not late-night spots. The views over the Atlantic and onto Robben Island are breathtaking, and this is where the ultracool set hangs out after a hard day at the beach or gym. Be prepared to line up to get in to places, especially on a Friday night.

PUBLICATIONS

The weekly entertainment roundup for Cape Town is called *48 Hours* and is available all over town. The "Top of the Times" in Friday's *Cape Times*, along with the *Argus* newspaper's "Tonight" section provide informed, opinionated, and up-to-date information. The latter gives you a complete daily listing of what's on, plus contact numbers.

Cape Town is a very gay-friendly city. Geared toward gay and lesbian travelers, *Gay Net Cape Town* (⊕ *www.gaynetcapetown.co.za*) provides information on events and venues in Cape Town.

CAPE TOWN CENTRAL

BARS AND PUBS

Caveau Wine Bar & Deli. Caveau Wine Bar & Deli is a hip yet unpretentious wine bar where you can sample a dizzying array of fabulous local wines by the glass while munching on excellent tapas or entrées. Extra seating is available in an inner courtyard. ⊠ *Heritage Sq., 92 Bree St.* ☎ *021/422–1367.*

The Orphanage. This new and happening upmarket contemporary cocktail bar is downtown on Bree Street. It's a great spot for a well-composed drink. ⊠ *227 Bree St.* ☎ *021/424–2004.*

The Perseverance. Cape Town's oldest pub is traditional and recommendable, with good food and pizza, craft beers, and even an inviting outdoor area. Plus, you'll find plenty of TV screens to watch football. ⊠ *83 Buitenkant St.* ☎ *021/461–2440* ⊕ *www.perseverancetavern.co.za.*

CAFÉS

Truth. This great spot captures the happening atmosphere in Cape Town's creative Fringe, in District Six. With steam-punk design, a coffee shop, bar, and live music on most nights, the fun usually spills out onto the pavement. It's open from 7 am to 6 pm weekdays (till late on Friday), and from 8 am to late on Saturday. ⊠ *36 Buitenkant St.* ☎ *021/200–0440* ⊕ *www.truthcoffee.com.*

LIVE MUSIC

The Assembly. The Assembly is one of Cape Town's best and hottest live-music venues, featuring everything from South African indie-rock to Afro-Brazilian electronica. The crowd is typically pretty young, with plenty of guests in their late teens. ⊠ *161 Harrington St., District Six* ☎ *021/465–7286* ⊕ *www.theassembly.co.za.*

Mama Africa. Among the clubs with live African music, a good spot is Mama Africa. It has a live marimba band Monday through Saturday, as well as authentic African food, music, and pulse. ⊠ *178 Long St.* ☎ *021/426–1017.*

V&A WATERFRONT

BARS AND PUBS

Bascule Whisky Bar and Wine Cellar. Built right on the water's edge adjacent to the yacht marina, Bascule Whisky Bar and Wine Cellar is a fancy watering hole for well-heeled, cigar-puffing locals. Its 450 whiskies are reputed to be the biggest selection in the Southern Hemisphere. ⊠ *Cape Grace Hotel, West Quay Rd.* ☎ *021/410–7238.*

CAFÉS

Grand Café & Beach. In a restored warehouse, this trendy operation has made good use of what was once a derelict piece of land between the V&A Waterfront and some other harborside development. It's now a place for locals to be seen, with a private beach, bars, and very comfortable covered seating scattered around Granger Bay Road. It's essentially an extension of the Waterfront and faces Table Bay with the Green Point Stadium, Signal Hill, and Table Mountain as pleasant backdrops. The first Grand Café is in Camps Bay, but it does not have nearly as much to distinguish itself from the people-watching cafés on the main road there. ⊠ *Granger Bay Rd., off Beach Rd.* ☎ *021/425–0551* ⊕ *www. grandafrica.com/GrandCafeandBeachCapeTown.aspx.*

LIVE MUSIC

Green Dolphin Jazz Restaurant. On any old night, the Green Dolphin Jazz Restaurant attracts some of the best mainstream jazz musicians in the country, as well as a few from overseas. The cover charge is R30–R35. It's open nightly from 8:15 pm to midnight. ⊠ *Alfred Mall* ☎ *021/421–7471.*

MOUILLE POINT

BARS AND PUBS

Wakame. For a fab evening on Mouille Point's Platinum Mile, plan to have drinks at Wakame and then head to the downstairs restaurant for sushi and champagne. You'll have great views of the Atlantic and Robben Island. Barefoot glam if you wish. ⊠ *Beach Rd. and Surrey Pl., 1st fl.* ☎ *021/433–2377* ⊕ *www.wakame.co.za.*

LIVE MUSIC

Swingers. It's a tradition for jazz festival performers to play the Monday night jam at Swingers, a well-known but out-of-the-way jazz club in Wynberg. Dance music is played Friday and Saturday, but Monday (no cover charge) is the night for jazz aficionados. There's also a full restaurant serving traditional Cape curries, seafood, and steaks. ⊠ *1 Wetwyn Rd.* ✢ *Near Wetton station* ☎ *021/762–2443.*

KALK BAY

BARS AND PUBS

Polana. Out of town in the quaint fishing village of Kalk Bay, Polana has jaw-dropping views across the bay. You can see all the way to Cape Hangklip, and when the weather is good the open windows allow sea breezes to further cool a glass of South Africa's best. There's live music and DJs on Friday and Sunday. ⊠ *Kalk Bay Harbour, Main Rd.* ☎ *021/788–7162.*

PERFORMING ARTS

Tickets for almost every cultural and sporting event in the country (including movies) can be purchased through Computicket.

Contacts Computicket ☎ *0861/915–8000* ⊕ *www.computicket.co.za.*

FILM

The Waterfront and Cavendish Mall both have movie houses: respectively, the NuMetro, which plays mainstream fare, and the Cinema Nouveau theater, which concentrates on foreign and art films. Check newspaper listings for what's playing.

Labia. The Labia is a local gem—an independent art house and Cape Town institution that screens good-quality mainstream and alternative films. There are four screens at the Labia on Orange and two at the Labia on Kloof, just up the road. A small coffee bar serves snacks and wine at both venues. ⊠ *68 Orange St., Gardens* ☎ *021/424–5927* ⊕ *www.labia.co.za.*

THEATER

Baxter Theatre Complex. The Baxter Theatre Complex, part of the University of Cape Town, hosts a range of productions from serious drama to satirical comedies, as well as some rather experimental stuff. The complex includes a 666-seat theater, a concert hall, a smaller studio, and a restaurant and bar. ⊠ *Main Rd., Rondebosch* ☎ *021/685–7880* ⊕ *www.baxter.co.za.*

Fugard Theater. This theater is named after legendary and internationally renowned playwright Athol Fugard, who was at the heart of the protest theater movement in 1980s apartheid South Africa. Anything cutting edge and politically relevant arrives at the Fugard, with the timeless *Rocky Horror Picture Show* starting its second season here in August 2014. It's on the edge of the historical and oh-so politically relevant District Six area—today Cape Town's creative Fringe Festival. ⊠ *Caledon and Lower Buitenkant Sts., Cape Town Central* ☎ *021/461–4554.*

Maynardville Open-Air Theatre. During the summer, when the weather's good, Cape Town has its own version of New York City's Central Park's Shakespeare in the Park at the excellent Maynardville Open-Air Theatre. Theatergoers often bring a picnic supper to enjoy before the show. ⊠ *Wolfe and Church Sts., Wynberg* ☎ *021/421–7695* ⊕ *www. maynardville.co.za/pages/index.php.*

Theatre on the Bay. The most current local and international productions are put on here. One of South Africa's best theaters, it was started and is still run by renowned local impresario Bobby Heaney. The location across the road from Camps Bay is great. Ruby Wax loved performing here so much that she bought a house down the road. ⊠ *1A Link St., Camps Bay* ☎ *021/438–3301* ⊕ *www.theatreonthebay.co.za.*

SPORTS AND THE OUTDOORS

Updated by
Angus Begg

Cape Town is the adventure capital of the universe. Whatever you want to do—dive, paddle, fly, jump, run, slide, fin, walk, or clamber—this is the city to do it in and somebody will help you do it.

For spectator sports, it's easy to get tickets for ordinary club matches and interprovincial games. Getting tickets to an international test match is more of a challenge; however, there's always somebody selling tickets—at a price, of course.

BIKING

Baz Bus. Baz Bus tours the south peninsula with a trailer full of bikes. You cycle the fun parts and sit in the bus for the rest. It costs about R540 for the whole day. ☎ *021/439–2323* ⊕ *www.bazbus.com*.

Downhill Adventures. Downhill Adventures offers great cycling trips around the peninsula. You can opt for a full day at the nature reserve at Cape Point, including a picnic lunch, or a leisurely cycle through the Constantia Winelands, stopping for wine tasting along the way. The company can also arrange mountain-bike tours, or you can simply rent a bike. Their range of combination tours includes a Cape Point & Winelands Biking Tour, a Table Mountain Bike & Abseil Combo, or even a Sandboard & Tandem Skydive Combo. The company also arranges shark-cage dives. ☎ *021/422–0388, 021/422–1580* ⊕ *www. downhilladventures.com* ✉ *Rentals from R200; tours from R895*.

BIRD-WATCHING

Brians-Birding. Specialized birding walks can be organized through Brians-Birding, which offers full-day birding walks with a max of about five people. Brian Vanderwalt is one of only two birders in the Western Cape who has spotted more than 200 birds in 24 hours for three years running in the annual Big Birding Day competition. In short, he knows his stuff. ☎ *021/919–2192* ⊕ *www.brians-birding.co.za* ✉ *From R2,500*.

CLIMBING

Cape Town has hundreds of bolted sport routes around the city and peninsula, ranging from an easy 10 to a hectic 30. (To give you some idea of difficulty, a route rated a 10 in South Africa would be equivalent to a 5.5 climb in the United States. A 20 climb would register around 5.10c, and the hardest you'll find in South Africa is probably a 34, which American climbers would know as a 5.14b. The toughest climb up Table Mountain rates about 32, which is a 5.14a.) Both Table Mountain sandstone and Cape granite are excellent hard rocks. There are route guides to all the major climbs and a number of climbing schools in Cape Town. A few favorite climbs include Table Mountain (from various angles), Lion's Head, Du Toit's Kloof, and Muizenberg Peak. ⇨ *For more information, see Hiking and Canyoning, below.*

High Adventure. High Adventure specializes in climbing in the Cape Town area but also organizes trips farther afield that can be anything from short two- to four-hour hikes, to half-day outings or full-day trips. A minimum group is two clients; there's a singles supplement of 80% for a solo traveler. ☎ *021/689–1234* ⊕ *www.highadventure.co.za* ✉ *From R480*.

FISHING

Hooked on Africa. Based in Hout Bay Harbour, this operation is in one of the richest fishing grounds left in the world today. If you're keen to take to the open ocean for some deep-sea fishing, you'll have plenty of choices, as South Africa has excellent game fish, such as dorado, yellowfin tuna, and broadbill swordfish. The company offers private, full-boat charters of a 32-foot catamaran for a full day of deep-sea fishing. Call to inquire about current rates and to see if there are any organized trips you could join in lieu of a full-boat charter. ☎ *021/790–5332* ⊕ *www. hookedonafrica.co.za* ✉ *From R10,000.*

Inkwazi Fly-Fishing Safaris. In the mountains, just an hour or so away from Cape Town, you'll encounter wild and wily fish in wild and wonderful rivers. The season runs September–May and Inkwazi Fly-Fishing Safaris offers escorted tours, all the equipment you'll need, and plenty of good advice. Regulations allow them to guide no more than two anglers, and trips are frequently just one person. ☎ *083/626–0467* ⊕ *www.inkwaziflyfishing.co.za.*

GOLF

Most golf clubs in the Cape accept visitors, but prior booking is essential. Expect to pay R250–R400 for 18 holes and R200–R350 to rent golf clubs. You can also rent golf carts for around R200, but you are encouraged to employ a caddie instead, as this offers valuable employment to local communities. Expect to pay around R150 plus a tip of 10%–20% for good service. Exclusive golf courses can cost even more.

Royal Cape Golf Club. Founded in 1885, Royal Cape Golf Club is the oldest course in Africa and has hosted the South African Open many times. Although the course is on flat terrain, the playing of Royal Cape is subject to three of nature's beguiling offerings: a near constant wind to challenge you, sweeping mountain views to charm you, and water features to ensnare you. It's tree lined with narrow fairways and subtle United States Golf Association-spec-built greens. The 14th hole is rated by the *Compleat Golfer* as the best 14th hole in the country—par is gold on this long left-to-right dogleg par four, even for the low handicapper. This is one of the best and most challenging courses to play both in the Western Cape and the country. ✉ *Royal Cape Golf Club, 174 Ottery Rd., Wynberg* ☎ *021/761–6551* ⊕ *www.royalcapegolf.co.za* ✉ *R500 for 18 holes* ⅃ *Par 72.*

Steenberg Golf Estate. The challenging and scenic Steenberg Golf Estate is the most exclusive and expensive course on the peninsula; the golf course is rated as one of the top three courses to visit in South Africa. Dress codes are strictly enforced here. Great Sauvignon Blanc is produced at the estate, and it has a profound history, having been a land grant by the first governor of the Cape in the late 17th century to Catherina Ras, one of the country's first female landowners. ✉ *Steenberg Golf Estate, 10978 Tokai Rd.* ☎ *021/715–0227* ⊕ *www.steenberggolfclub. co.za* ✉ *R1065 for 18 holes* ⅃ *18 holes, 8700 yards, par 72.*

HIKING AND CANYONING

Cape Town and the surrounding areas offer some of the finest hiking in the world. Kloofing, known as canyoning in the United States, is the practice of following a mountain stream through its gorge, canyon, or kloof by swimming, rock hopping, and jumping over waterfalls or cliffs into deep pools, so it's definitely a bit more than simple hiking. There are some exceptional kloofing venues in the Cape. ⇨ *For more information on the Hoerikwaggo Trail, see Table Mountain, above.*

Active Africa. This company is busy in Rwanda, Tanzania, and Namibia, but walking tours of four days and longer outside Cape Town can also be arranged. Their main Cape Town offering is a combination tour, customized to include a variety of different activities such as kayaking, rock climbing, canyoneering, and rappelling. ☎ 021/788–6083 ⊕ www. active-africa.com ✉ From R3,909.

Mother City Hikers. Originally from Chicago, Lauren Medcalf came to Cape Town on an extended vacatin in 2006 and has never left. With Table Mountain standing tall over the city and surrounded by the southern oceans, it has become her home away from home. Mother City Hikers uses qualified and accredited mountain guides, who have fulfilled the requirements for Adventure Guiding/Mountaineering and are also qualified to offer mountain walking and overnight trips. All guides are also certified in first aid and CPR with the National First Aid Academy in South Africa. Prices include pickup at your hotel and transportation to the hiking site. ☎ 072/530–3464 ⊕ mothercityhikers. co.za ✉ From R500.

RidgwayRamblers. Binny Ridgway is one of the most experienced Table Mountain guides. If you want to get the most out of this iconic rock, it's best to learn a little about the area and its flora and fauna while getting some exercise and not having to think too hard for yourself. Hikes may go from Skeleton Gorge to Maclears Beacon (on the mountain) or to the Twelve Apostles (above Camps Bay). His prices get you a packed lunch and complimentary transportation to and from the hike. ☎ 082/522–6056 ⊕ www.ridgwayramblers.co.za ✉ From R750.

Table Mountain Walks. Table Mountain Walks offers various hikes, including options at Table Mountain and Silvermine Nature Reserve, with a well-informed guide. Owner Margaret" is a veteran hiker with experience on all the continental "biggies." ☎ 021/715–6136 ⊕ www. tablemountainwalks.co.za ✉ From R550.

HORSEBACK RIDING

Cantering down one of the Cape's long white-sand beaches or riding through the fynbos-covered dunes at sunset is a unique and tranquil pleasure, and Noordhoek is the place to do it, whatever your level.

Sleepy Hollow Horse Riding. Sleepy Hollows Horse Riding has three guided rides a day. A two-hour ride goes mostly at a walking pace. But the company also has some specialized offerings and has experience with riders with disabilities. ⊠ Sleepy Holly La., Noordhoek ☎ 021/789–2341 ⊕ www.sleepyhollowhorseriding.co.za ✉ From R460.

KAYAKING

Coastal Kayak Trails. You don't have to be a pro to discover Cape Town by kayak. Coastal Kayak Trails has regular sunset and sunrise paddles off Sea Point. The two-hour paddles are reasonably priced and popular. ☎ 021/439–1134, 083/346–1146 ⊕ www.kayak.co.za ✉ From R300.

Real Cape Adventures. Real Cape Adventures offers regular scenic paddles off Hout Bay and from Simon's Town around to Boulders. Trips can last anywhere from two hours to a half-day. You'll need to make provision in your planning for traveling to and from the point of departure, and add an hour for getting ready and for kayak and safety instructions, as well as for ending the trip, packing up, and getting dressed. They also offer tailor-made sea kayak overnight trips on request. Accommodation, transport, and meals can be included in the packages. ☎ *021/790–5611* ⊕ *www.seakayak.co.za* ✉ *From R250.*

PARAGLIDING AND SKYDIVING

Para-pax Tandem Paragliding. Para-pax Tandem Paragliding will take you flying off landmarks such as Lion's Head, Signal Hill, and Table Mountain, depending on the wind and weather conditions. The company claims to be the original tandem paragliding operation in Africa. With some 13,000 flights under their belt, they have earned their reputation. They have a wide range of operational centers, from the paragliding mecca of Porterville to Wilderness, Hermanus, and Franschhoek. ☎ *082/881–4724* ⊕ *www.parapax.com* ✉ *From R1150.*

Skydive Cape Town. You can do a tandem sky dive (no experience necessary) and have a video taken of you hurtling earthward with Table Mountain in the background with Skydive Cape Town—in business since 2002. On a tandem jump, you are strapped to an instructor with a special harness that's attached to a specially designed parachute large enough to support both of you. After only 15 minutes of ground briefing you will enjoy a spectacular 20-minute aircraft ride, with views of the West Coast, Cape Town, Robben Island, and Table Mountain before making the jump. ☎ *082/800–6290* ⊕ *www.skydivecapetown. za.net* ✉ *From R1,900.*

RAPPELLING

Abseil Africa. Abseil Africa offers a 350-foot abseil (rappel) off the top of Table Mountain. Another excursion takes you over a waterfall in the Helderberg Mountains, an hour's drive away. Tours include both transportation and lunch. This is a good operation that's been around a long time. ☎ *021/424–4760* ⊕ *www.abseilafrica.co.za* ✉ *From R700.*

SCUBA DIVING

The diving around the Cape is excellent, with kelp forests, cold-water corals, very brightly colored reef life, and numerous wrecks. An unusual experience is a dive in the Two Oceans Aquarium. CMSA, NAUI, and PADI dive courses are offered by local operators; open-water certification courses begin at about R2,800 (all-inclusive).

Orca Industries. Orca offers dive courses, from beginners to specialist wreck divers. A PADI open-water certification takes a week and includes all dives, lectures, course materials, registration, and gear rental. ☎ *021/671–9673* ⊕ *www.orca-industries.co.za* ✉ *From R3,500.*

Scuba Shack. The friendly Scuba Shack is based out of Muizenberg and can organize dives around the peninsula—both the Atlantic and the warmer False Bay, with Simon's Town as the meeting point. Options include diving with cow sharks, traveling through kelp forests, and snorkeling with seals. It's a refreshing experience—and not just the water temperature—but so very different from the more typical vacation diving world of subtropical corals. ☎ *072/603–8630* ⊕ *www. scubashack.co.za* ✉ *From R1,300.*

SHARK DIVING

Seeing great white sharks hunting seals around False Bay's Seal Island is one of the most exhilarating natural displays you're likely to witness. And if witnessing it all from a boat is not thrill enough, you can get in the water (in a cage).

Apex Predators. Run by marine biologists, Apex Predators operates small-group trips from Simon's Town during season (February–September). If the great whites aren't around, try the Ocean Predator Trip, in which you cage dive with makos and blues. Co-founder Chris Fallows is a local legend in the shark photography and observation world, and the go-to guy for many international broadcasters. ⊠ *Quayside Bldg., Main Rd., shop 3, Simon's Town* ☎ *079/051–8558, 021/786–5717* ⊕ *www. apexpredators.com.*

SURFING

Cape Town has some great but cold surf, and conditions can be complicated by the winds. Though it's no J-Bay (Jeffreys Bay), Cape Town still has some killer spots, Bloubergstrand (beach) being host to regular international events.

FAMILY **Gary's Surf School.** Gary's Surf School offers surfing lessons to youngsters and the young at heart in the relatively warm and gentle waters at Muizenberg. You can also rent boards and wet suits. A basic two-hour lesson includes an hour of instruction and an hour of practice. You do need to be aware, however, that you'll be sharing the ocean with plenty of sharks, as you would around the world, though the company has never had an incident. ⊠ *Balmoral Bldg., 34 Beach Rd., Muizenberg* ☎ *021/788–9839* ⊕ *www.garysurf.com* ⊠ *From R350.*

SHOPPING AND SPAS

Updated by
Angus Begg

When it comes to shopping, Cape Town has something for everyone—from sophisticated malls to trendy markets. Although African art and curios are obvious choices (and you will find some gems), South Africans have woken up to their own sense of style and creativity, and the results are fantastic and as diverse as the people who make up this rainbow nation. So in a morning you could bag some sophisticated tableware from Carrol Boyes, a funky wire-art object from a street vendor, and a beautifully designed handbag made by HIV-positive women working as part of a community development program.

Cape Town has great malls selling well-known international brands. The V&A Waterfront is an excellent place to start by virtue of its location at the harbor. Cavendish Square in Claremont and Canal Walk at Century City are also vast, the latter on the N1 heading out of town toward Paarl. But you could be anywhere in the world. Gardens Centre in the suburb of Gardens is small and manageable, offering a good selection of stores (Germans love it for the German deli). It's beyond the malls that you can get a richer shopping experience, one that will give you greater insight into the soul of the city and its people.

Shopping malls usually have extended shopping hours beyond the normal 9–5 on weekdays and 9–1 on Saturday. Most shops outside of malls (except for small grocery stores) are closed on Sunday.

CAPE TOWN CENTRAL

ARTS AND CRAFTS

A number of stores in Cape Town sell African art and crafts, much of which comes from Zululand or neighboring countries. Street vendors, particularly on St. George's Mall and Greenmarket Square, often sell the same curios for half the price. Pick up the excellent "Not the Official Arts + Crafts Map" and "Cape Town Design Route" brochures available at Cape Town Tourism for listings of excellent and cutting-edge galleries, boutiques, and designers.

African Image. Look here for contemporary African art and township crafts, colorful cloth from Nigeria and Ghana, plus West African masks, Malian blankets, and beaded designs from southern African tribes. Local and international collectors, as well as local institutions such as the South African National Gallery and the Standard Bank Collection of African Art, buy goods here. It's a top-notch place offering fair-trade pricing. ⊠ *Burg and Church Sts.* ☎ *021/423–8385* ⊕ *www. african-image.co.za.*

Pan-African Market. You'll see some glorious cultural contradictions here. The lobby of this building is a gem of Victorian tiling, and the first and second floors are a beehive of traders in new and old folk art, with representatives from most locales in West, sub-Saharan, and southern Africa. Once you've ordered your custom-tailored garment and finally chosen your mask from among the many thousands, enjoy a coffee or a Swahili-infused lunch on the oh-so-quaint first-floor terrace. Bargaining is welcomed. ⊠ *76 Long St.* ☎ *021/426–4478.*

Streetwires. There must be some budding engineers among these artists. You'll see streetwire art everywhere in Cape Town, but this shop is a trove of the form, which uses a combination of wire, beads, and other recycled materials to create bowls, lights, mobiles, and expressive sculptures. You might even want to buy a working wire radio. ⊠ *77 Shortmarket St.* ☎ *021/426–2475* ⊕ *www.streetwires.co.za.*

BOOKS AND MUSIC

African Music Store. The people who work here are passionate about African music and eager to pass on their love to anybody who lends them half an ear. You could easily spend a couple of hours listening to any and everything in the store. With a listening booth to sample any CD in the shop, you're bound to find something here that captures the heart of the country for you. ⊠ *134 Long St.* ☎ *021/426–0857.*

The Book Lounge. Cape Town's best independent bookstore has a fantastic selection of titles, with many classics and contemporary must-haves on all things African. It also frequently hosts readings and book launches and has a nice café downstairs where you can enjoy a cappuccino while browsing. ⊠ *71 Roeland St.* ☎ *021/423–5739* ⊕ *www. booklounge.co.za.*

MARKETS

Greenmarket Square. You can get good buys on clothing, T-shirts, and locally made leather shoes and sandals, and you can find a plethora of African jewelry, art, and fabrics here, too. It's one of the best places in town to purchase gifts, but it's lively and fun whether or not you buy anything. More than half the stalls are owned by people not from South Africa. Here you'll find political and economic refugees from Ethiopia, Eritrea, Zimbabwe, and the Democratic Republic of Congo trying to eke out a living. Bargain, but do so with a conscience. ⊠ *Longmarket, Burg, and Shortmarket Sts.* ⊘ *Mon.–Sat. 9–4:30.*

WOODSTOCK

MARKETS

Woodstock Neighbour Goods Market. Also known as the Old Biscuit Mill market, Woodstock is aimed at Cape Town's hip, organic types on their Vespas looking for artisan breads, pesto, home-cured olives, and produce imported from France. It gets frantically busy, which indicates just how popular it is, but if you want to rub shoulders with trendy design types and eat fabulous artisanal everything, this is the place to be. One of the stalls sells seared-tuna sandwiches and salads; it's worth standing in line. When you're done browsing at the market, head to some of the great stores in the same complex. Get there before 9:30 or be crushed by the crowds. ⊠ *373–375 Albert Rd.(Lower Main Rd.)* ⊘ *Sat. 9–3.*

V&A WATERFRONT

BOOKS AND MUSIC

Exclusive Books Waterfront. This is the biggest chain of bookstores in the country. It carries a wide selection of local and international periodicals and coffee-table books on Africa, and all the best sellers making literary waves around the world. You'll find branches nationally, at all the big malls and the airports, with branches in Cape Town's Southern Suburbs and in the city. ⊠ *Victoria Wharf, shop 6160* ⊕ *www. exclusivebooks.com.*

MARKETS

V&A Craft Market. This indoor market contains an assortment of handcrafted jewelry, rugs, glass, pottery, and leather sandals, the majority of which are made in South Africa. There's also a wellness center where you can have a shiatsu massage or some reflexology to pep you up if you're shopped out. ⊠ *Dock Rd., next to Aquarium* ☎ *021/408–7842* ⊘ *Daily 9–9.*

WINE

Most Capetonians wouldn't dream of having supper without a glass of wine, and most supermarket chains carry a good range of affordable local labels. A visit to Cape Town isn't complete until you've tasted and bought some of the wine the area is famous for. Your best bet is to buy directly from the vineyards, although given bulk-purchase deals with large retailers, it won't necessarily be cheaper. But if you don't manage to get out to the Winelands, head to one of the area stores that can fix you up with local or international wines. ⇨ *For information on how to ship wine to the U.S., see Chapter 3, The Western Cape.*

Vaughan Johnson Wine & Cigar Shop. This wine shop has a terrific selection and staff members who know their stuff. It has specially designed boxes to take a few cases home with you. And who could blame you? ⊠ *Dock Rd.* ☎ *021/419–2121* ⊕ *www.vaughanjohnson.co.za.*

CAPE QUARTER
ARTS AND CRAFTS

Africa Nova. If you aren't crazy about traditional African artifacts, you might want to visit this store, which stocks contemporary African art that's quirky and interesting. Original African art is showcased for those looking for one-of-a-kind pieces. Come Christmastime, the store is transformed with beaded African Christmas decorations: gorgeous stars, divine angels, and brilliant nativity animals. Even if you aren't buying, it's worth visiting for the display. ⊠ *Cape Quarter, 72 Waterkant St.* ☎ *021/425–5123* ⊕ *www.africanova.co.za.*

ORANJEZICHT
MARKETS

Oranjezicht City Farm. This has to be the most beautiful setting in the world for a fresh produce and food market—on the slopes of Table Mountain in the gorgeous suburb of Oranjezicht, with the harbor and city down below. Some of the veggies are grown just next door, on an old bowling green dug up and replanted in 2012. There's also a children's playground, a 300-year-old slave bell, and an old barn on the same site, which is also known as Homestead Park. The Oranjezicht City Farm market is a not-for-profit project celebrating local food, culture, and community through urban farming in Cape Town. ⊠ *Sidmouth Ave. and Upper Orange St.* ☎ *083/628–3426* ⊕ *www.ozcf.co.za* ☉ *Farm Mon.–Sat. 8–4, market Sat. 9–2.*

HOUT BAY
MARKETS

Hout Bay Harbour Market. Food, drink, clothing, crafts, and even good-quality live music performances: this is a great all-weekend shopping and chill spot—by day or night—in the Hout Bay Harbour area. ⊠ *31 Harbour Rd.* ☎ *082/570–5997* ⊕ *www.bayharbour.co.za* ☉ *Fri. 5–9 pm, weekends 9:30–4.*

OBSERVATORY
ARTS AND CRAFTS

Mnandi Textiles. Here you'll find a range of African fabrics, including traditional West African prints and Dutch wax prints. The store sells ready-made African clothing for adults and children, and you can also have garments made to order. ⊠ *90 Station Rd.* ☎ *021/447–6814.*

SPAS

CAPE TOWN CENTRAL

Westin Heavenly Spa. Breathtaking 360-degree views and ambrosial aromas (courtesy of Africology and Dermalogica products) greet you at this large, streamlined 19th-floor spa. On arrival, you're offered use of the infinity lap pool and sauna—both with stunning city and mountain views—and steam room. These facilities are all coed, but well worth scheduling in an extra hour or so to enjoy while you're here. Signature treatments like the African Breeze 90-minute massage using marula oil blended with African shea butter, or the Classic Dermalogica facial are pure indulgence. Don't miss a post-treatment lie-down in the heated water beds. ⊠ *The Westin Cape Town, Convention Sq., Lower Long St., 19th fl.* ☎ *021/412–8200* ⊕ *www.westincapetown.com* ⊘ *Treatments daily 9–5; sauna/gym facilities daily 6 am–10 pm.*

V&A WATERFRONT

Spa at Cape Grace. Impeccable service and professionalism are the hallmarks of this intimate spa in the Cape Grace, whose paprika-and-saffron-hued spice-route motif is vibrant yet elegant. It's widely considered one of the top spas in South Africa. Drawing on Khoi-San healing customs, Kalahari treatments use a signature range of products from the Namibian desert, and other facial therapies and body treatments employ either the Comfort Zone or QMS ranges. The relaxation and hot spa area facilities (sauna, steam room, rain showers) are coed and on the small side, but enjoy lovely views of Table Mountain. ⊠ *Cape Grace, West Quay Rd.* ☎ *021/410–7140* ⊕ *www.capegrace.com.*

GARDENS

Librisa. An oasis of elegant calm in the Belmond Mount Nelson Hotel's bucolic English gardens, this spa has a glassed-in relaxation room with stunning views of Lion's Head. Many treatments feature local ingredients like *marula* (a fruit) and South African geranium. The therapeutic massage relieves travel stress, and the decadent Rekindle Spa Experience combines an aromatic massage and facial followed by the hotel's legendary afternoon tea. Teen and kids' treatments are available, and you are welcome to use the hotel's family pool. ⊠ *Belmond Mount Nelson Hotel, 76 Orange St.* ☎ *021/483–1550* ⊕ *www.mountnelson. co.za* ⊘ *Daily 9–7.*

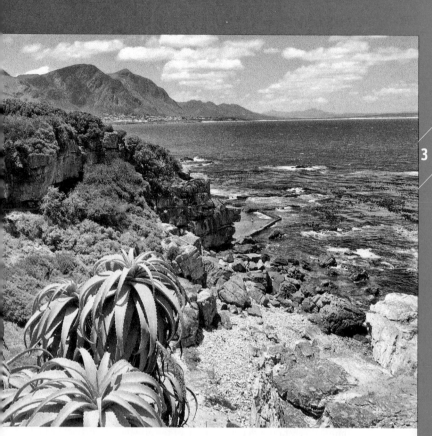

THE WESTERN CAPE

Including the Cape Winelands

Updated by
Karena du
Plessis

Anchored by Cape Town in the southwest, the Western Cape is an alluring province, a sweep of endless mountain ranges, empty beaches, and European history dating back more than three centuries. The cultures of the indigenous Khoekhoen and San people—the first inhabitants of this enormous area—also contribute to the region's richness. You can reach most of the province's highlights in less than two hours from Cape Town, making the city an ideal base from which to explore.

The historic Winelands, in the city's backyard, produce fine wine amid the exquisite beauty of rocky mountains, serried vines, and elegant Cape Dutch estates. Here farms have been handed down from one generation to another for centuries, and old-name families like the Cloetes and Myburghs have become part of the fabric of the region. Even first-time visitors may notice subtle differences between these Cape Afrikaners and their more conservative cousins in the hinterland. For the most part they are descendants of the landed gentry and educated classes who stayed in the Cape after the British takeover in 1806 and the emancipation of the slaves in 1834.

The region they stayed behind in was one truly blessed by nature. Wild-flowers are one extraordinary element of this natural bounty. The Western Cape is famous for its fynbos (pronounced *fane*-boss), the hardy, thin-leaf vegetation that gives much of the province its distinctive look. Fynbos composes a major part of the Cape floral kingdom, the smallest and richest of the world's six floral kingdoms. More than 8,500 plant species are found in the province, of which 5,000 grow nowhere else on earth. The region is dotted with nature reserves where you can hike through this profusion of flora, admiring the majesty of the king protea or the shimmering leaves of the silver tree. When the wind blows and mist trails across the mountainsides, the fynbos-covered landscape takes on the look of a Scottish heath.

Not surprisingly, people have taken full advantage of the Cape's natural bonanza. In the Overberg and along the West Coast, rolling wheat fields extend to the horizon, while farther inland jagged mountain ranges hide fertile valleys of apple orchards, orange groves, and vineyards. At sea, hardy fisherfolk battle icy swells to harvest succulent crayfish (similar to lobster), delicate *perlemoen* (abalone), and line fish, such as the delicious *kabeljou*. Each June–November hundreds of whales return to the Cape shores to calve, and the stretch of coastline that includes Hermanus, now referred to as the Whale Coast, becomes one of the best places for land-based whale-watching in the world.

For untold centuries this fertile region supported the Khoekhoen (Khoikhoi) and San (Bushmen), indigenous peoples who lived off the land as pastoralists and hunter-gatherers. With the arrival of European settlers, however, they were chased off, killed, or enslaved. In the remote recesses of the Cederberg mountains and along the West Coast you can still see the fading rock paintings left by the San, whose few remaining clans have long since retreated into the Kalahari Desert. The population of the Western Cape today is largely "coloured," a term used to describe South Africans of mixed race and descendants of imported slaves, the San, the Khoekhoen, and European settlers (⇨ "A Note on the Term 'Coloured'" box, below).

3

ORIENTATION AND PLANNING

GETTING ORIENTED

The Cape Winelands, 45 minutes east of Cape Town, is the Napa Valley of southern Africa. The region boasts some of South Africa's best restaurants and hotels, not to mention incredible wine. Running in a broad band from northeast to southeast is the beautiful Breede River valley, home to farms, vineyards, and orchards.

East of the Cape Winelands and bordering the Atlantic Ocean, the Overberg is home to the small towns and villages of Gordon's Bay, Betty's Bay, Kleinmond, Hermanus, Stanford, and Gansbaai. Inland, Overberg villages of Elgin, Greyton, Swellendam, and Elim embody a bygone age.

Heading north out of Cape Town is the drier, more windswept West Coast. Small fishing villages hunker down next to the sea and offer visitors plenty of space to roam.

The Cape Winelands. This area fans out around three historic towns and their valleys. Founded in 1685, Stellenbosch's oak-lined streets, historic architecture, good restaurants, interesting galleries and shops, and vibrant university community make it an ideal base for wine travel. Franschhoek, enclosed by towering mountains, is the original home of the Cape's French Huguenots, whose descendants have made a conscious effort to reassert their French heritage. Paarl lies beneath huge granite domes, its main street running 11 km (7 miles) along the Berg River past some of the country's most elegant historical monuments.

Breede River Valley. Farms, vineyards, and orchards make up most of the Breede River valley. (So it should come as no surprise that one of the towns in the area is called Ceres, after the Roman goddess of agriculture.) Small-town hospitality, striking mountains, and wide-open spaces are hallmarks of this area. In summer the heat can be overwhelming, and in winter the mountain peaks are often covered with snow.

The Overberg. The genteel atmosphere of the southwestern Cape fades quickly the farther from Cape Town you go. The Overberg, separated from the city by the Hottentots Holland Mountains, presides over the rocky headland of Cape Agulhas, where the Indian and Atlantic oceans meet (officially) at the southernmost tip of the continent. Unspoiled

TOP REASONS TO GO

Land of Divine Wine. Few places in the world can match the drama of the Cape Winelands, where mountains rise above vine-covered valleys and 300-year-old homesteads. Against this stunning backdrop you can visit scores of wineries, tour their cellars, relax under old oaks with a picnic basket, and dine at the many excellent restaurants in the area. You'll be hard-pressed to decide which wines to take home with you.

Whale of a Time. Come spring, when the winter rains are no longer lashing the Cape, the icy seas teem with Southern Right whales, which come here to calve. Towns like Hermanus offer some of the best land-based whale-watching in the world, and you can also take a boat trip out to see these gentle giants. If it's adrenaline you're after, head to Gansbaai, where you can go diving amid great white sharks.

Flower Power. In summer, when the temperatures soar and the land is dusty, parched, and brown, it's hard to imagine the transformation that takes place each spring when millions of flowers carpet the West Coast hills. It's a photographer's dream, with the blue ocean in the background and swaths of yellow, white, and orange daisies.

Fabulous Food. South African food has come into its own. Boring *boerekos* (directly translated as "farmer's food"), characterized by meat and overcooked vegetables, has given way to an explosion of great cuisine. A new generation of chefs is making the most of the area's fabulous fresh produce, and restaurants in Franschhoek and Stellenbosch regularly get voted among the world's best.

The Great Outdoors. The Western Cape's real charm lies outdoors. Erinvale and the Arabella Western Cape Hotel & Spa, near Kleinmond, have some of the most spectacular golf courses in the world. In the Cederberg you can hike for days and explore ancient rock formations while learning about the leopard-conservation programs. You can also ride horses through the vineyards of the Cape Winelands or go boating in the Klein River lagoon near Hermanus.

beaches, coastal mountains, and small towns are the lure of this remote area.

West Coast. North of Cape Town on the West Coast, civilization drops away altogether, save for a few lonely fishing villages and mining towns. Each spring, though, the entire region explodes in a spectacular wildflower display that slowly spreads inland to the desiccated Namaqualand and the Cederberg mountains. For nature lovers, the West Coast provides some unique opportunities, including birding at West Coast National Park at the Langebaan Lagoon and hiking or rock climbing in the remote wilderness areas of the Cederberg.

PLANNING

Many people come to the Western Cape after getting a big-game fix in Kruger. Although it's possible to explore Cape Town and the Cape Winelands in three or four days—the area is compact enough to allow it—you need six or seven to do it justice. You can get a good sense of either the Overberg or the West Coast on a three- or four-day jaunt, but set aside a week if you plan to tackle more than one or two of the regions in this chapter.

WHEN TO GO

Summer (late November–January) is high season in the Western Cape, and during that time you will seldom visit major places of interest without encountering busloads of fellow visitors. The weather is warm and dry, and although strong southeasterly winds can be a nuisance, they do keep the temperature bearable. ■ TIP➜ The UV index in the Western Cape is exceptionally high in summer, so if you do plan to visit then, make sure you take precautions to avoid severe sunburn. If soaking up the sun is not of primary importance and you prefer to tour during quieter times, spring (September and October) and autumn–early winter (late March through May) are ideal. The weather is milder, and the lines are shorter. Spring also brings Southern Right whales close to the shores of the Western Cape to calve, and late August–October are the months to see the wildflowers explode across the West Coast. If the Cape Winelands are high on your list of must-dos, remember that the busiest time in the vineyards and cellars is January–April, when they begin harvesting and wine making.

GETTING HERE AND AROUND

The best way to explore the Western Cape is to rent a car and take to the roads. You need to be flexible to enjoy all this region has to offer, and public transportation is too limited. Navigating your way around is not difficult. There are three main routes out of the city: the N1, N2, and N7. The N1 and N2 take you to the Cape Winelands of Stellenbosch, Franschhoek, and Paarl, and the N7 heads up the West Coast. To reach the Overberg, take the N2 out of town and head up over Sir Lowry's Pass. ■ TIP➜ Getting lost after taking a wrong turn can take you into unsafe areas, so plan your route before setting out and use GPS.

PLANNING YOUR TIME

3 Days: You could devote a couple of days to touring the wineries, spending perhaps one day visiting Stellenbosch-area wineries such as Simonsig and Villiera, and another day around Franschhoek or Paarl. Consider breaking up your wine touring with horseback riding at one of the vineyards and a night in Franschhoek. A third day could be devoted to a long, scenic route back to Cape Town after lunch at one of Franschhoek's many good restaurants. Another option is to spend the first day wine tasting, and then drive over Sir Lowry's Pass through Elgin and on to Greyton, where you can wander around the village and visit the Moravian Mission complex in Genadendal. The last morning of your stay could be spent in Greyton before you head back to Cape Town via coastal Clarence Drive, which passes Kleinmond, Betty's Bay, Pringle Bay, and Gordon's Bay.

5 Days: With five days, you can work in time to see the Cape Winelands as well as Clanwilliam, at the edge of the Cederberg. (The drive to the Clanwilliam area will take you through the Swartland and the beginning of the wildflower route, which is best in spring.) If nature beckons, head into the Cederberg, where you can easily spend two nights in some of the country's most spectacular scenery. You can hike, swim in crystal-clear rock pools, and admire ancient San rock art. You could also combine a trip to the Cape Winelands or Cederberg with a visit to the coast's Langebaan and West Coast National Park, where the birding is exceptional.

7 Days: A week would allow you to comfortably visit the Cape Winelands, Cederberg, and the coast. You could spend a few days in the Cederberg and then head through Riebeek Kasteel and Wellington and on to the Cape Winelands towns of Paarl, Stellenbosch, and Franschhoek, where you can linger for the next two or three days. You could easily spend your last days in the beautiful Franschhoek valley. Or you could take a scenic back route on the R45 and then the R321 into the Overberg. You could spend a couple of days exploring the coast, overnighting in Hermanus or Arniston. If it's winter, watch whales, and if you're not sick of wine by this point, sample some of the Overberg wines. Drive back to Cape Town via the spectacular coastal road of Clarence Drive.

HEALTH AND SAFETY

If you plan to go hiking in the mountains, come prepared with the right clothing and the correct attitude—each year tourists get lost in the mountains. Cape weather is notoriously changeable, so you need something warm and preferably waterproof. Take at least two liters of water per person and something to eat. If possible, hike with somebody who knows the area well, but if you're walking alone, be sure to take a cell phone and program in some emergency numbers (but be aware that cell phones won't work in all areas). Let somebody know of your route and when you expect to return, and don't stray from the paths if the mist closes in.

HOTELS

The Cape Winelands are sufficiently compact that you can make one hotel your touring base. Stellenbosch and Paarl, situated close to dozens of wineries and restaurants as well as the major highways to Cape Town, offer the most flexibility. Here bed-and-breakfasts and self-catering (with cooking facilities) options are often less expensive than hotels and provide a better taste of life in the country. Franschhoek is comparatively isolated, which many visitors consider a blessing. The West Coast, the Cederberg, and the Overberg are much more spread out, so you'll want to stay in one place for a day or two and then move on. During the peak season of December–January, book well in advance and be prepared for mandatory two-night stays on weekends. Although the winter months of June–September are usually a lot quieter and bring negotiable rates, seaside towns get really busy (and booked up) when the whales arrive to calve. The same is true up the West Coast during flower season. *Hotel reviews have been shortened. For full information, visit Fodors.com.*

RESTAURANTS

The dining scene ranges from fine South African cuisine complete with silver service to local, laid-back, country-style cooking. Franschhoek restaurants attract some of the country's most innovative chefs, who

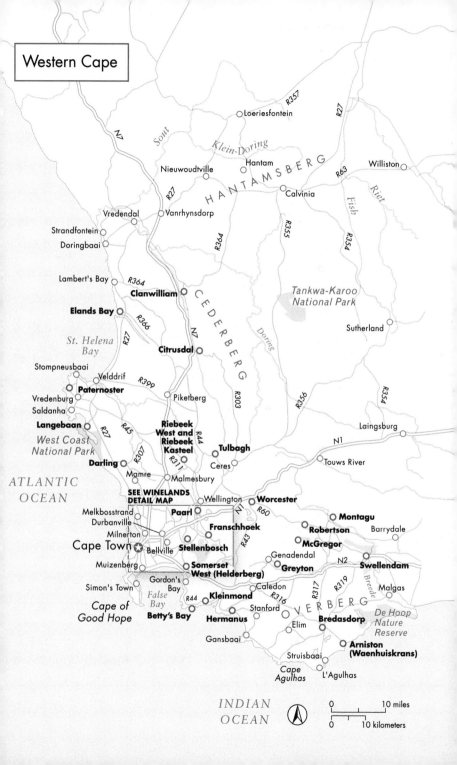

Western Cape

Loeriesfontein

R357

R27

Klein-Doring

Sout

N7

Nieuwoudtville

Hantam

HANTAMSBERG

Williston

R63

Calvinia

R27

Vredendal

Vanrhynsdorp

R355

Fish

Riet

R354

Strandfontein

Doringbaai

R364

Tankwa-Karoo
National Park

Lambert's Bay

R364

Clanwilliam

C

Sutherland

Elands Bay

R366

R27

E

D

St. Helena
Bay

Citrusdal

E

R

Doring

N7

Stompneusbaai

Veldhdrif

R399

B

R356

R354

Laingsburg

Vredenburg

Paternoster

Piketberg

E

Saldanha

R303

N1

Langebaan

R27

R45

**Riebeek
West and
Riebeek
Kasteel**

R44

G

Touws River

West Coast
National Park

R307

R311

Tulbagh

Ceres

Darling

Mamre

Malmesbury

ATLANTIC
OCEAN

**SEE WINELANDS
DETAIL MAP**

Wellington

Paarl

Worcester

N1

R60

Montagu

Melkbosstrand

Franschhoek

Robertson

Barrydale

Durbanville

Milnerton

R43

McGregor

Cape Town

Bellville

Stellenbosch

Genadendal

N2

Swellendam

Muizenberg

**Somerset
West (Helderberg)**

Greyton

Simon's Town

Gordon's
Bay

Caledon

Malgas

Cape of
Good Hope

False
Bay

Kleinmond

R44

Stanford

R316

R317

R319

VERBERG

Breede

De Hoop
Nature
Reserve

Betty's Bay

Hermanus

Elim

Bredasdorp

Gansbaai

**Arniston
(Waenhuiskrans)**

Struisbaai

Cape
Agulhas

L'Agulhas

INDIAN
OCEAN

0   10 miles

0   10 kilometers

aren't afraid to experiment with unusual ingredients or food-and-wine combinations, and offer up a very sophisticated dining experience in a gorgeous setting. West Coast fare is not as urban as what you find in the Cape Winelands, and coastal towns usually concentrate on seafood, often served in open-air restaurants. Farther inland the cuisine tends to be less trendy and the portions more generous. Be sure to try some Cape Malay cuisine, characterized by mild, slightly sweet curries and aromatic spices. The only places you're likely to be disappointed in the food are in smaller agricultural towns in the Overberg or up the West Coast, where overcooked veggies and an uninspiring and indistinguishable roast are still the norm. But this is changing from month to month as weary city slickers head out of town to open lovely restaurants serving high-quality food.

Country restaurants tend to serve lunch from noon and dinner from 6, and do not cater to late diners except on weekends. Because these areas rely heavily on tourists and local day-trippers, most restaurants in the Cape Winelands and seaside towns are open on weekends, especially for leisurely Sunday lunches, but may catch their breath on Sunday evenings or quieter Mondays. Dress codes vary as much as the dining experiences. Casual wear is acceptable during the day and at most restaurants in the evening. On the coast people pull shorts and T-shirts over their swimsuits before tucking into a plate of calamari and chips (fries), but some Winelands restaurants like their patrons to look as good as the cuisine they deliver. Even so, a nice pair of jeans or pants and a good shirt are usually enough; jackets and ties are rarely expected. If there's someplace you really want to eat, reserve ahead. In December and January, popular restaurants book up quickly, and reservations are advised at least a day or two in advance.

WHAT IT COSTS IN SOUTH AFRICAN RAND			
$	**$$**	**$$$**	**$$$$**
Restaurants	under R100	R100–R150	R151–R200	over R200
Hotels	under R1,500	R1,500–R2,500	R2,501–R3,500	over R3,500

Restaurant prices are the average cost of a main course at dinner or, if dinner is not served, at lunch. Hotel prices are the lowest cost of a standard double room in high season.

VISITOR INFORMATION
You can get almost all the information you need about the Western Cape and Winelands from the very organized Cape Town Tourism offices. *See ⇨ Visitor Information in Cape Town.*

THE CAPE WINELANDS

Frank Prial, wine critic for the *New York Times,* wrote that he harbored "a nagging suspicion that great wines must be made in spectacular surroundings." If that's true, then the Cape Winelands are perfectly poised to produce fantastic wines, because the setting of dramatic mountains and lush valleys is absolutely stunning.

CLOSE UP

A Note on the Term "Coloured"

South Africa has come a long way since the first democratic elections in 1994. Parts of the country are, in fact, just about unrecognizable. What hasn't changed, however, is the enormous complexity surrounding language, race classification, and cultural identity. Whereas for many Americans the term *colored* is offensive, in South Africa the term (spelled *coloured*) is not considered offensive and is widely used to describe South Africans of mixed race, often descended from imported slaves, the San, the Khoekhoen, and European settlers. Over the years the term *coloured* has lost its pejorative connotations. Coloureds don't regard themselves as black Africans, and culturally they are extremely different. What is especially confusing to people just passing through South Africa is that many coloureds share so much in common with Afrikaners and are united in their love for and use of Afrikaans.

3

Although the Cape Winelands region is largely thought of as the wine centers of Stellenbosch, Franschhoek, and Paarl, today these areas make up only about 33% of all the land in the Cape under vine. This wine-growing region is now so vast, you can trek to the fringes of the Karoo Desert, in the northeast, and still find a grape. There are around 18 wine routes in the Western Cape, ranging from the Olifants River, in the north, to the coastal mountains of the Overberg and beyond. There's also a well-established Winelands brandy route, and an annual port festival is held in Calitzdorp, in the Little Karoo.

The secret to touring the Cape Winelands is not to hurry. Dally over lunch on a vine-shaded veranda at a 300-year-old estate, enjoy an afternoon nap under a spreading oak, or sip wine while savoring the impossible views. Of the scores of wineries and estates in the Cape Winelands, the ones listed here are chosen for their great wine, their beauty, or their historic significance. It would be a mistake to try to cover them all in less than a week. You have nothing to gain from hightailing it around the Cape Winelands other than a headache. If your interest is more aesthetic and cultural than wine driven, you would do well to focus on the historic estates of Stellenbosch and Franschhoek. Most Paarl wineries stand out more for the quality of their wine than for their beauty.

GETTING HERE AND AROUND

Driving yourself is undoubtedly the best way to appreciate the area. Each wine route is clearly marked with attractive road signs, and there are complimentary maps available at the tourism bureaus and at most wine farms. Roads in the area are good, and even the dirt roads leading up to a couple of the farms are nothing to worry about.

The best way to get to the Cape Winelands is to take the N2 out of Cape Town and then the R310 to Stellenbosch. Outside of rush hour, this will take you around 45 minutes. Expect some delays during the harvest months (generally late January–late March), when tractors ferry grapes from farms to cellars on the narrower secondary roads. On your way back to Cape Town, stick to the R310 and the N2. Avoid taking

the M12, as it gets very confusing, and you'll end up in suburbs that aren't on tourist maps.

The major car-rental agencies have offices in the smaller towns, but it's best to deal with the Cape Town offices. Besides, you'll probably want to pick up a car at the airport. Since driving yourself around limits the amount of wine you can taste, unless you have a designated driver, it's best to join a tour, take a taxi, or—do it in style—rent a limo from Cape Limousine Services. Limos cost about R1,500 for the first hour and R600 per hour thereafter, so they're relatively cost-effective if you have a group of four or five.

Paarl Radio Taxis will transport up to three people at about R10 per kilometer (half mile). Waiting time is around R60 per hour. Larger groups can arrange transportation by minibus. Daksi Cab, based in Stellenbosch, works on a trip rate rather than a per-kilometer basis. A trip to a local restaurant costs around R90 regardless of the number of people. Daksi also provides shuttle service to the airport.

There's no regular bus service to the Cape Winelands suitable for tourists. If you are based in Stellenbosch, however, and don't want to drive to the wineries, you can make use of the Vine Hopper, a minibus that follows a fixed route to six wine farms. Tickets cost around R240 for a one-day ticket and R420 for a two-day ticket, and you'll be given a timetable so that you can get on and off as you please.

We do not recommend Cape Metro trains to Stellenbosch and Paarl because of an increase in violent muggings.

Contacts **Cape Limousine Services** ⊠ *Capri Village, 20 Tobago Way, Sunnydale, Fish Hoek* ☎ *021/785–3100.* **Daksi Cab** ☎ *084/400–4480* ⊕ *www.daksicab.co.za.* **Paarl Radio Taxis** ☎ *021/872–5671.* **Vine Hopper** ⊠ *Black Horse Centre, Dorp St. and Mark Rd., Stellenbosch* ☎ *021/882–8112* ⊕ *www.vinehopper.co.za.*

SAFETY AND PRECAUTIONS

If you spend a day out in the Cape Winelands and return at dusk or after dark, be on the lookout for pedestrians, especially on weekends, when people are likely to have been drinking. There is, unfortunately, a high incidence of pedestrian-related accidents on these roads. Also be sure to designate a driver to avoid the risks associated with drinking and driving. ■TIP→ **Under no circumstances do you want to spend even a night in a South African jail. If you are stopped by traffic police, they may well try to solicit a bribe. Do not offer a bribe.**

TOURS

Most tours of the Cape Winelands are operated by companies based in Cape Town; most have half- or full-day tours, but they vary by company and might include a cheese tasting or cellar tour in addition to wine tasting. Expect to pay around R580 for a half day and R800 for a full day, including all tasting fees. Though you stop for lunch, it is not included in the cost.

African Eagle Day Tours. Great half- and full-day Winelands tours are offered by African Eagle. On the full-day tour (about R810), you"ll be whisked through Stellenbosch, Paarl, and Franschhoek. In Stellenbosch there's a walking tour of the town, followed by a cellar tour and cheese and wine tasting at a local wine estate. In Paarl you'll take a drive around before visiting a wine estate, and you will also see Nelson Mandela's former prison (Victor Verster Prison). Then it's on to Franschhoek, where you can visit the Huguenot memorial and do some (more) wine tasting before journeying over the Helshoogte Pass. The half-day tour—you can choose morning or afternoon—is all about Stellenbosch: you'll see the sights, take a cellar tour, do some cheese and wine tasting, and even experience a biltong and wine pairing. This tour costs R585. ✉ *4 Malta Rd., Salt River, Cape Town* ☎ *021/464–4266* ✒ *daytours@aecpt.co.za* ⊕ *www.daytours.co.za* ✇ *From R585.*

Amber Wine Tours. Lesley Cox from Amber Wine Tours is wildly enthusiastic about Cape wines and knows many of the Cape winemakers and wine-farm owners. Lesley prefers visiting boutique farms not on the tourist map, but she'll tailor tours to your tastes. So if you want to sample only Sauvignon Blancs, for instance, she'll know just where to take you. If you're not crazy about wine but want to tour the Winelands, Lesley can tell you about Cape Dutch architecture and the history of the area. ✉ *44 Hastings St., Tamboerskloof, Cape Town* ☎ *083/448–7016* ⊕ *www.ambertours.co.za* ✇ *From R1,400.*

Cape Fusion Tours. Foodie Pam McOnie from Cape Fusion Tours is a breath of fresh air and has an eye for the quirky. She focuses on small to medium wine farms and will really tailor your trip to incorporate the things you love. She can make plenty of suggestions, too, and has the inside scoop on what's new in Cape Town and the Winelands' food-and-wine world. ✉ *Cape Town* ☎ *021/461–2437, 083/235–9777* ⊕ *www.capefusiontours.com.*

Easy Rider Wine Tours. This outfitter has a great all-day tour that's very reasonably priced—around R500, including all fees and even lunch. You get picked up around Stellenbosch about 10:30 for a visit to four estates in the three regions, including Fairview, Simonsig, and Boschendal. The day starts with a cellar tour at Simonsig Wine Farm, and then it's on to Fairview for some cheese tasting. Next you'll stop for lunch in Franschhoek—vegetarians are catered for, too—where you can expect a variety of tasty dishes, from salads and burgers to savory pancakes and pasta. After lunch you'll visit Dieu Donne and Boschendal for some more wine tasting. ✉ *12 Market St., Stellenbosch* ☎ *021/886–4651* ⊕ *www.winetour.co.za* ✇ *From R500.*

Gourmet Wine Tours. This is an excellent choice for individuals or small groups wanting a tour of the greater Winelands area, including Constantia, Durbanville, Elgin, Franschhoek, Paarl, Somerset West, Stellenbosch, and Hermanus. The mountain and coastal views are reason enough to take a tour, and each of these towns has unique wines to offer. Tour operator Steven is well informed and great at selecting the right wine and restaurant. He's happy to tailor the itinerary to suit your personal tastes. Expect to pay around R2,000 for the first person and R1,000 per additional person per day for a personalized tour. ✉ *11 Peninsula Rd., Cape Town* ☎ *021/705–4317, 083/299–3581* ⊕ *www. gourmetwinetours.co.za* ✇ *From R1,400.*

Hylton Ross Tours. A full-day Winelands tour with Hylton Ross starts with a morning in Paarl at Anura Wine Estate before moving on to Franschhoek via the Victor Verster Prison, where Nelson Mandela was incarcerated. In Franschhoek you'll have a second wine tasting of the day and lunch (not included) before heading to Stellenbosch. A full-day tour costs around R880 per person; a half-day tour is R640 per person. ⊠ *2 Wessex Rd., Paarden Eiland, Cape Town* ☎ *021/506–2575* ⊕ *www. hyltonross.co.za* ✉ *From R640.*

iKapa Tours & Travel. The itinerary for a full-day Winelands tour includes wine tasting and cellar tours in Paarl, Stellenbosch, and Franschhoek. The day starts with cheese and wine tasting at Anura Wine Estate in Paarl before a quick photo op at the prison where Nelson Mandela was incarcerated at the time of his release in 1990. Then it's on to Franschhoek for lunch and wine tasting, followed by a drive over the majestic Helshoogte Pass. If there's time, you'll end the day with a final wine tasting before heading back to Cape Town. ⊠ *94 Voortrekker Rd., Salt River, Cape Town* ☎ *021/506–3700* ⊕ *www.ikapa.co.za* ✉ *From R915.*

Springbok Atlas. This tour outfitter offers full-day tours of the Winelands that include Paarl, Franschhoek, and Stellenbosch and cost around R700 per person, excluding lunch. A three-hour afternoon tour includes wine tasting at one or two estates in Stellenbosch and costs R580 per person. ⊠ *179 Albert Rd., Woodstock, Cape Town* ☎ *021/460–4700* ⊕ *www.springbokatlas.com* ✉ *From R580.*

Vineyard Ventures. For those serious about wine, Vineyard Ventures is the best of the Winelands tour companies. Sisters Gillian Stoltzman and Glen Christie are knowledgeable and passionate about wine and will tailor tours to your interests. The cost ranges from around R1,600 per person and includes all tastings, museum entries, and a fabulous lunch (with wine, of course). One to four people pay around R3,600 for a car and driver all inclusive. The rates come down as the number of people increases, so it's good to team up with another couple for a great day out. ⊠ *5 Hanover Rd., Sea Point, Cape Town* ☎ *021/434–8888, 082/920–2825* ⊕ *www.vineyardventures.co.za* ✉ *From R1,600.*

Wellington Wine Walk. A great way to combine wine tasting with exercise, this three- or four-day walking tour leads you from one upscale guesthouse to the next through vineyards and indigenous fynbos in the picturesque Wellington Valley. Your guides and hosts know all there is to know about the history and culture of the area, as well as the wines. They're also passionate about good food, and each day you'll have a picnic lunch and a gourmet dinner paired with the appropriate wines. The walking isn't tough, but you cover around 18 km (11 miles) each day. Your luggage is transferred for you from place to place, so all you have to carry is a light day pack. The best times to go are in autumn (April and May) and then again in spring (October and November) before the temperatures soar. ⊠ *Wellington* ☎ *083/313–8383* ⊕ *www. winewalk.co.za* ✉ *From R5,465.*

Windward Charters. Take a tour of the premier wine-producing regions of Paarl, Franschhoek, and Stellenbosch with Windward Charters. The full-day tour includes cheese and wine tasting, a stop at the historical

South African Wine

The South African wine industry is booming. Buried by sanctions during apartheid, South African wines were largely unknown internationally. But today there's enormous interest in South African reds *and* whites. Although South Africa has a reputation for delivering good quality at the bottom end of the market, more and more ultrapremium wines are emerging. Good-quality wines at varied prices are readily available—even in supermarkets.

Currently white wine production outstrips red, but the quality continually improves for both, and they regularly win international awards. Particularly notable is Pinotage, South Africa's own grape variety, a cross between Pinot Noir and Cinsaut (formerly Hermitage). Chenin Blanc is the country's most widely planted variety and is used in everything from blends to bubbly (known in South Africa as Méthode Cap Classique).

The industry is transforming itself slowly. The illegal *dop* (drink) or tot system, in which farmers pay some of laborers' wages in wine, is finally on its way out, and there's a concerted effort among producers to uplift their laborers' quality of life. Many international companies refuse to import wine from farms that don't secure their workers' rights, and many farms are working at black empowerment. Tukulu, Riebeek Cellars, Thandi Wines, Ses'Fikile (which translated means "we have arrived"), M'hudi, and Freedom Road are just some of the pioneers. Three farms that deserve a special mention when it comes to transformation are Bosman Family Vineyard (Wellington), Solms-Delta wine estate (Franschhoek), and Van Loveren Family Cellar (Robertson). Tragically, South Africa has one of the highest incidences of fetal alcohol syndrome, a legacy left over from the dop system.

If you're serious about wine, arm yourself with *John Platter's Wine Guide* or visit ⊕ *www.winemag.co.za* (the new digital form of *Wine* magazine), featuring local wineries. For an in-depth read and fantastic photos, pick up *Wines and Vineyards of South Africa* by Wendy Torein or *New World of Wine from the Cape of Good Hope: The Definitive Guide to the South African Wine Industry* by Phyllis Hands, David Hughes, and Keith Phillips. *Wines of the New South Africa: Tradition and Revolution* by Tim James is also recommended reading.

Taal Monument, a tour of the town of Stellenbosch, and a visit to some of the local shops and markets. The half-day version is a trip to Stellenbosch, either in the morning or afternoon, with a tour of the town, wine tasting, and a cellar tour. ⊠ *277 Koeberg Rd., Cape Town* ☎ *021/510–0961* ⊕ *www.windward.co.za* ✉ *From R515.*

SOMERSET WEST (HELDERBERG)

45 km (28 miles) southeast of Cape Town on the N2.

Somerset West, nestled at the foot of the Helderberg Mountains, is just 30 minutes from the center of Cape Town and close to Gordon's Bay and the Strand beaches. Once an important farming town, its former dairy fields are now covered with dreary town houses and faux Tuscan villas. But a few historic estates still remain and are worth visiting.

Just before you reach the center of town you'll see the turnoff to Lourensford Road, which runs 3 km (2 miles) to Vergelegen and Morgenster. If you're keen to stretch your legs, the Helderberg Nature Reserve overlooks the beautiful False Bay and is home to plenty of fauna and flora.

GETTING HERE AND AROUND

Somerset West is 30 minutes southeast of Cape Town on the N2 and 20 minutes from the airport. Public transport in these outlying towns leaves a lot to be desired. Your best bet is to rent a car and invest in a good map or GPS. Don't be tempted to catch trains out to the Cape Winelands after dark—you run the risk of being mugged.

VISITOR INFORMATION

Contacts Cape Town Tourism–Helderberg Branch ⊠ *186 Main Rd.* ☎ *021/840–1400* ⊕ *www.capetown.travel* ⊗ *Weekdays 9–5, weekends 9–1.*

EXPLORING

Morgenster. A leading producer of excellent extra-virgin olive oils and wines is the historic estate Morgenster (Morning Star), which is part of Cape Governor Simon van der Stel's original 17th-century farm. In the mid-1990s the estate was restored to its original splendor, and thousands of olive trees were imported from Italy and planted. It is now producing some of the best oils in the country and internationally. Seventeen different olive cultivars on the farm have been carefully selected from all the regions in Italy; these are pressed and stored individually before they're blended. For R20 you can taste the olives, the oil, balsamic vinegar, and the delicious olive paste. It's also worth lingering in the beautiful wine-tasting room, which was designed by acclaimed South African architect Revel Fox. To avoid disappointment, phone a day ahead if you're traveling in a group bigger than six. ⊠ *Vergelegen Ave., off Lourensford Rd.* ☎ *021/852–1738* ⊕ *www.morgenster.co.za* 🍽 *Olive tasting R20, wine tasting R25–R45* ⊗ *Daily 10–5.*

Rust en Vrede. Nestled against the base of Helderberg Mountain and shaded by giant oaks, the peaceful Rust en Vrede winery looks over steep slopes of vines and roses. This comparatively small estate specializes entirely in red wine and produces some of the very best in South Africa. In fact, Nelson Mandela chose this wine to be served at state functions when he was president. Rust en Vrede Estate is the flagship wine, a blend of predominantly Cabernet Sauvignon, Shiraz, and around 10% Merlot grapes. The 2011 vintage is the current hot seller; its lush flavors are testimony to the hot Stellenbosch summers that give the fruit their flavor. Enjoy it now, but you can also put it away to mature in the bottle for another 10 years or more. Another weighty wine is the 1694 Classification (named after the year the farm was established). Look out for raspberry, cedar, and pencil shavings on your palate and nose. ⊠ *Annandale Rd., off R44, between Somerset West and Stellenbosch* ☎ *021/881–3881* ⊕ *www.rustenvrede.com* 🍽 *Tastings R30–R70* ⊗ *Mon.–Sat. 9–5.*

Fodor's Choice
★

Vergelegen. Established in 1700 by Willem Adriaan van der Stel, who succeeded his father as governor of the Cape, this traditional Cape Dutch homestead, with thatch roof and gables, looks like something out of a fairy tale. An octagonal walled garden aflame with flowers surrounds it, and huge camphor trees, planted almost 300 years ago, stand as gnarled sentinels. These trees were declared a National Monument in the 1940s, and you can picnic under them during the summer months. The homestead is now a museum and is furnished in period style. Other historic buildings include a magnificent library and the old stables, which is now the Stables Restaurant, where you can have breakfast and lunch while looking onto the magnificent Hottentots Holland Mountains. Behind the house is the farm's signature restaurant, Camphors at Vergelegen.

Vergelegen wines rake in the accolades year after year, and there's no award that they haven't won—usually more than once. Vergelegen's flagship wines include the Vergelegen V (a full-bodied Cabernet Sauvignon), and the Vergelegen GVB Red, a Bordeaux blend of Cabernet Sauvignon, Merlot, and Cabernet Franc. If you prefer white wine for summer drinking, the Vergelegen GVB White is a Sauvignon-Semillon blend. Reservations are essential for the wine tours, but no children are allowed. There are also 70 steep stairs up and down into the state-of-the-art cellar, so you need to be able to manage these. Cellar tours last an hour. Apart from their award-winning wine, the farm is keen to show off all they have achieved, and they host a number of other farm tours. Look out for the sunset vineyard tour, an environmental tour, and a winter weekend celebrating the magnificent camellias that brighten the immaculate gardens. There's a lovely children's play area, including a shallow riverbed complete with a pebbled path that will keep children happy for hours. ✉ *Lourensford Rd.* ☎ *021/847–1334/7* ⊕ *www.vergelegen.co.za* ✉ *Homestead and museum R10, tastings R30* ☉ *Daily 9:30–4:30. Cellar tours 11:30 am and 3 pm.*

OFF THE BEATEN PATH

Mooiberge Farm Stall. You can't drive down the R44 between Somerset West and Stellenbosch without noticing the remarkable scarecrows at Mooiberge Farm Stall. They're riding bicycles, driving tractors, and working in the strawberry fields, where you can spend a morning picking the luscious red fruit. The strawberry season varies from one year to the next but usually begins in October and runs to January. You pay for what you pick, and you can also buy jams, dried fruit, and other refreshments at the farm stall. Look out for the interesting display of old farm implements at the side of the building. ✉ *R44, between Somerset West and Stellenbosch* ☎ *021/881–3222* ✉ *Free* ☉ *Daily 8:30–6; picking daily 9:30–4:30 during strawberry season.*

WHERE TO EAT

$$$$
INTERNATIONAL

✕ **Camphors at Vergelegen.** In summer you need to reserve a table weeks in advance at this idyllic restaurant on the Vergelegen Estate. In pleasant weather ask for a table on the terrace, shaded by liquidambar trees. With a big emphasis on fresh, free-range, ethically farmed produce, the innovative menu serves starters such as fried Saldanha oysters served with smoked avocado, elderflower yogurt, and pickled cucumber; or bone marrow and mussels with chard, seaweed, and lime marmalade.

Cape Dutch Architecture

As you travel around the region, the most visible emblems of settler culture you'll encounter are the Cape Dutch–style houses. Here 18th- and 19th-century manor houses share certain characteristics: thick, white-washed walls, thatch roofs curving around elegant gables, and small-pane windows framed by wooden shutters. It's a classic look—a uniquely Cape look—ideally suited to a land that is hot in summer and cold in winter. The Cape Dutch style developed in the 18th century from traditional long houses: simple rectangular sheds capped by thatch. As farmers became more prosperous, they added the ornate gables and other features. Several estates, most notably Vergelegen (near Somerset West) and Boschendal (on the Franschhoek wine route), have opened their manor houses as museums. The Oude Drostdy Museum just outside of Tulbagh is another fine example of classic Cape Dutch architecture.

Main courses include Karoo lamb and sweetbreads, or an interesting vegetarian option of goat butter, cauliflower, and porcini *arancini* (Italian rice balls). A five-course tasting menu (around R585 per person) takes the agony out of having to decide. Even better, the tasting menu with wine pairing includes sublime Vergelegen wines (around R795 per person). The menu changes regularly, depending on what produce is available. If you can't get a reservation, head to the estate's Stables at Vergelegen for simpler—but equally delicious—food. $ *Average main: R600* ⊠ *Vergelegen Estate, Lourensford Rd.* ☎ *021/847–1346* ⊕ *www. vergelegen.co.za* ⌂ *Reservations essential* ⋒ *Jacket required* ⊘ *No lunch Mon. and Tues. No dinner Sun.–Thurs.*

$$ **✕ 96 Winery Road.** This relaxed venue is always buzzing with folk from
INTERNATIONAL the wine industry, regulars, and upcountry visitors. Inside, burgundy walls are cozy for winter, and outside terrace seating offers soothing mountain views during summer. The menu changes regularly but tempts with such fresh and flavorful first courses as prawn tempura and salmon and line-fish sashimi. Steak lovers are treated well here; dry-aged cuts of prime beef are grilled and teamed with a variety of sauces. Vegetarians will find good choices, too, such as a salad of organic mixed leaves with grilled vegetables, feta, olives, Parmesan cheese, and toasted pine nuts. A good cheese board makes a savory—and, many think, superior—option to rich desserts. The selection of wine is also impressive: the restaurant regularly wins the Wine Spectator Grand Award for its comprehensive and innovative wine list. $ *Average main: R125* ⊠ *Zandberg Farm, Winery Rd., between Somerset West and Stellenbosch* ☎ *021/842–2020* ⊕ *www.96wineryroad.co.za* ⌂ *Reservations essential* ⊘ *No dinner Sun.*

WHERE TO STAY

$$$$ ⊞ **Majeka House.** This complex of bright white buildings nestled in gar-
HOTEL dens overflowing with roses, lavender, frangipani, and jasmine in an upmarket residential corner of Somerset West is a perfect oasis and a great base for exploration. **Pros:** fantastic and convenient location;

outstanding restaurant; the main pool is heated and big enough to enjoy a proper swim. **Cons:** you will need a car to explore the area. $ *Rooms from: R3000* ✉ *26–32 Houtkapper St., Paradyskloof* ☎ *021/880–1549* ⊕ *www.majekahouse.co.za* ⇨ *23 rooms* ⦿ *Multiple meal plans.*

$$
B&B/INN
🖼 **Willowbrook Lodge.** Hidden among beautiful gardens that extend down to the Lourens River, this peaceful lodge makes a good base for exploring the entire southwestern Cape, including the peninsula, the Winelands, and the Overberg. **Pros:** close to top golf courses, beautiful beaches, and the Cape Winelands; away from the hustle of Cape Town. **Cons:** very few rooms available; only one restaurant on-site. $ *Rooms from: R2000* ✉ *Morgenster Ave.* ☎ *021/851–3759* ⊕ *www.willowbrook.co.za* ⇨ *15 rooms, 1 suite* ⦿ *Breakfast.*

SPORTS AND THE OUTDOORS

Erinvale Golf Club. The Gary Player–designed Erinvale Golf Club is beautifully nestled beneath the Hottentots Holland Mountains. This world-renowned course hosted the 1996 World Cup of Golf, and, not surprisingly, the facilities are top-notch. Nonmembers can play on visitors' days: Monday, Wednesday, Friday, and Sunday. ✉ *Lourensford Rd.* ☎ *021/847–1144* ⊕ *www.erinvalegolfclub.com* ⳾ *18 holes, 6782 yards, par 72.* 🖾 *R950.*

Somerset West Golf Club. Set against the Helderberg Mountains, Somerset West Golf Club has breathtaking views. This parkland course is easy, with plenty of leeway for errant tee shots, except when the wind blows. Look out for the resident white squirrels at the first nine holes. ✉ *Rue de Jacqueline Ave.* ☎ *021/852–2925* ⊕ *www.somersetwestgolfclub.co.za* ⳾ *18 holes, 6498 yards, par 72.* 🖾 *R350.*

STELLENBOSCH

15 km (9½ miles) north of Somerset West.

You could easily while away a week in this small, sophisticated, beautiful, and absolutely delightful town. South Africa's second-oldest municipality, after Cape Town, Stellenbosch actually *feels* old, unlike so many other historic towns. Wandering the oak-shaded streets, which still have open irrigation furrows (known as the *lei water,* pronounced lay *vaa*-ter), you'll see some of the finest examples of Cape Dutch, Georgian, Victorian, and Regency architecture in the country. The town was founded in 1679 by Simon van der Stel, first governor of the Cape, who recognized the agricultural potential of this fertile valley. Wheat was the major crop grown by the early settlers, but vineyards now blanket the surrounding hills. Stellenbosch is considered the center of the Cape Winelands, and many of the older and more established wineries are nearby. Wine routes fan out like spokes of a wheel, making excellent day trips if you're staying in town. The town is also home to the University of Stellenbosch, the country's first and most prestigious Afrikaner university.

GETTING HERE AND AROUND

The best way to explore this area is by renting a car. Expect to pay around R170 for an entry-level car per day and up to R700 for a Mercedes C Class. Avoid public transportation.

TOURS

The historic area of Stellenbosch is so pretty and compact that it's a pity just to drive through. Pull on your walking shoes and stride out with Stellenbosch on Foot for their 1½-hour walking tour.

Stellenbosch on Foot. Take a walking tour with Sandra Krige from Stellenbosch on Foot. Tours last around 1½ hours and take in all the well-known sights. Sandra is a mine of information about the town and even offers an evening ghost tour. Expect to pay around R100 per person if there are two of you for the evening tour. If you're alone, you'll pay around R170. ⊠ *36 Market St.* ☎ *021/887–9150, 083/218–1310* ⌨ *From R100.*

VISITOR INFORMATION

Contacts **Stellenbosch Tourism and Information Bureau** ⊠ *36 Market St.* ☎ *021/883–3584* ⊕ *www.stellenbosch.travel* ☉ *Summer, daily 8–5; winter, weekdays 9–5, Sat. 9–2, Sun. 9–1.*

EXPLORING

Start your tour of the town at the corner of Dorp Street and the R44, where you first enter Stellenbosch. Look for street names written in yellow on curbs; they're easy to miss, so remember to look down and not up.

Architecture buffs will be happy to know that there are still examples of 19th-century Stellenbosch design around. To check them out, turn left off Market Street onto Herte Street. (Market is Mark in Afrikaans; some maps use the names interchangeably, which can be confusing.) The whitewashed cottages along this street were built by and for freed slaves after the Emancipation Act of 1834. Although they are no longer thatch, the houses on the left-hand side of the road are still evocative of this era.

TOP ATTRACTIONS

Dorp Street. Stellenbosch's most historic avenue is oak-lined Dorp Street. Almost the entire street is a national monument, flanked by lovely restored homes from every period of the town's history. ⊠ *Dorp St. and Papegaai Rd.*

Oom Samie Se Winkel. Redolent of tobacco, dried fish, and spices, this 19th-century-style general store is one of Stellenbosch's most popular landmarks. In addition to the usual Cape kitsch, Oom Samie sells some genuine South African produce, including *witblitz* and *mampoer,* both Afrikaner versions of moonshine. The shop has a restaurant, too. ⊠ *84 Dorp St.* ☎ *021/887–0797* ☉ *Daily 8:30–5.*

WORTH NOTING

Die Braak. Some of Stellenbosch's most historic buildings face the Braak, the grassy town square, which is a national monument. **St. Mary's Church** stands at the far end of the Braak. Built in 1852 as an Anglican church, it reflects the growing influence of the English in Stellenbosch. Across Bloem Street from St. Mary's is the **Burgher House,** built in

Sip and Spoeg Like an Expert

South Africa currently has more growing areas than ever that yield a huge selection of very different wines. One of the best ways to find your way around the enormous selection is to visit ⊕ www.winemag.co.za (formally Wine magazine), devoted to the subject. Wine prices ex-cellar are significantly cheaper than most retail outlets, so if you're looking for a bargain, buy directly from the farm.

AH, BUT YOUR LAND IS BEAUTIFUL

When it comes to South African terroir, think sun, sea, and soil. Whereas Northern Hemisphere farmers work hard to get as much sunlight onto their grapes as possible, local viticulturists have to deal with soaring summer temperatures (this is why the cooling influence of the two oceans is so welcome). South Africa also has some of the world's oldest soil, and there's a mineral element to its wines, a quality that's most prominent in the top-end Sauvignon Blancs like those produced by Cape Point Vineyards, Steenberg, Thelema, Diemersdal, Groote Post, Cederberg, and Springfield.

YOU CAN'T LEAVE WITHOUT TRYING PINOTAGE

In 1920s, a professor at Stellenbosch University decided to create a truly South African varietal. He crossed Pinot Noir (a tricky grape to grow) with Cinsaut (a vigorous and very hardy grape)—he liked the idea of combining a drama queen with a pragmatic, no-nonsense type—and came up with Pinotage. Though it's had its ups and downs, including being accused by everyone from critics to connoisseurs of being bitter and rubbery, strides are being made

to express the grape's character. One example is the coffee Pinotage. It's been on the market for just a few years and is hugely popular because it's a ballsy, bold wine. There's a distinct mocha flavor to it that's a combination of the soil and the wine-making technique. A good example of this is the Diemersfontein Carpe Diem Pinotage. Other Pinotages to keep an eye out for: Stellenzicht Golden Triangle Pinotage, Spier Private Collection Pinotage, and Kanonkop Pinotage. Former Kanonkop cellar master Beyers Truter is known as the Pinotage King in South Africa; be sure to try Beyerskloof Pinotage.

HUNDREDS AND THOUSANDS TO CHOOSE FROM

Wines that have helped put South Africa on the map include Chenin Blanc, Sauvignon Blanc, and Bordeaux-style red blends of Cabernet Sauvignon, Merlot, and Cabernet Franc. South African red blends have done well at international competitions, and the quality rivals some of the world's best producers. Until recently, Chenin Blanc was something of a Cinderella varietal. It accounts for the bulk of South African white wine plantings but, because of its versatility, was largely overlooked. Luckily, this has shifted, and there are now more than 100 Chenin Blancs out there demanding attention and commanding top prices.

■ Good Sauvignon Blancs: Alexanderfontein Sauvignon Blanc, Springfield Estate Life from Stone Sauvignon Blanc, and Cape Point Vineyards Sauvignon Blanc.

■ Great red blends: Stellenrust Timeless, Rustenberg John X Merriman, and Kanonkop Paul Sauer.

■ Great Chenin Blancs: Kleine Zalze Chenin Blanc, Rudera Robusto Chenin Blanc, and Ken Forrester FMC Chenin Blanc.

A ROSÉ BY ANY OTHER NAME
Though it legally can't be called Champagne, Méthode Cap Classique, South Africa's version of the bubbly, is made in exactly the same way. You'd be unwise to pass on an offer of Graham Beck Cuvée Clive or Villiera Brut Tradition.

NAME-DROPPING
There are some iconic South African wines you really should try before you leave the country. Of course, the list of such wines varies depending on whom you talk to, but keep an eye out for these:

■ Boekenhoutskloof Cabernet Sauvignon

■ Boplaas Vintage Reserve Port

■ Cape Point Isliedh

■ De Toren Fusion V

■ Hamilton Russell Chardonnay and Pinot Noir

■ Jordan Chardonnay

■ Kanonkop Pinotage or Paul Sauer

■ Klein Constantia Vin de Constance

■ Meerlust Rubicon

■ Springfield Méthode Ancienne Cabernet Sauvignon

■ Steenberg Sauvignon Blanc Reserve

■ Vergelegen V

Potential future icons include Columella and Palladius, both made by Eben Sadie, and Raats Family Vineyard Cabernet Franc.

TO SHIP OR NOT TO SHIP
You're bound to want to take some great South African wine home with you, but it's not as easy as cramming your hand luggage with your favorite tipple. Travelers to the United States can take only two bottles on board. Any more than that and it will need to be shipped to you by an agent. Each person is allowed two cases (or 24 bottles), but some states won't allow you to import a single bottle without an importer's license. Expect to pay between R1,200 and R3,000 per case (East Coast destinations are usually cheaper than those on the West Coast) and that it will take anywhere from 6 to 18 days to reach you. Alternately, when you're wine tasting, ask the estate if they distribute in the United States, as you might find a local agent closer to home. The Vineyard Connection (⊕ *www.vineyardconnection.co.za*) is just one of the agents who can help you get your favorite bottle delivered to your door.

1797. Today it houses the offices of Historical Homes in South Africa. At the southern end of the Braak is the **Rhenish Mission Church**, erected by the Missionary Society of Stellenbosch in 1823 as a training school for slaves and blacks. ⊠ *Bordered by Bloem, Alexander, and Bird Sts.*

La Gratitude. This early 18th-century Dorp Street home was built in traditional Cape Dutch town-house style. The all-seeing eye of God molded on its gable was designed as a talisman to watch over the owner's property and keep him and his family safe from harm. ⊠ *95 Dorp St.*

Oude Werf. Possibly the country's oldest boardinghouse and now a welcoming guesthouse, Oude Werf (formally d'Ouwe Werf) first took in paying guests in 1802. To get here from Dorp Street, turn onto Andringa Street and then right onto Church (aka Kerk) Street; Oude Werf will be on your left. ⊠ *30 Church St.* ☎ *021/887–4608* ⊕ *www. oudewerfhotel.co.za.*

Rhenish Complex. One of the most impressive restoration projects ever undertaken in South Africa and a good example of what early Stellenbosch must have been like, this complex consists of an art center, which melds elements of English and Cape architecture; and a two-story building that is typically English. The complex is just east of the Tourism and Information Bureau on Market Street, on your left, facing a large lawn. The **Toy and Miniature Museum** (R20, ☎ 079/981–7067) houses a collection of scale dollhouses and antique toys, as well as a miniature model of the famous Blue Train. ⊠ *Bordered by Herte, Market, Bloem, and Dorp Sts.* ☾ *Museum weekdays 9–5, Sat. 9–2, alternate Sun. 9–1*

Stellenbosch Museum. This museum comprises four dwellings scattered within a two-block radius. Dating from different periods in Stellenbosch's history, the houses have been furnished to reflect changing lifestyles and tastes. The oldest is the very basic Schreuderhuis, built in 1709. The others date from 1789, 1803, and 1850. ⊠ *18 Ryneveld St., at Church St.* ☎ *021/887–2948* ⊕ *www.stelmus.co.za* ⊠ *R20* ☾ *May– Aug., Mon.–Sat. 9–4:30, Sun. 10–1; Sept.–Apr., Mon.–Sat. 9–4:30, Sun. 10–4.*

V.O.C. Arsenal. Next to the Burgher House, just across from the Braak on a traffic island in Market Street, stands the V.O.C. Arsenal, often called the **V.O.C. Kruithuis** (*kruithuis* means "powder house"). It took 91 years for the political council to decide that Stellenbosch needed its own magazine, and just six months in 1777 to complete the structure. Today the arsenal contains a wide selection of guns, gunpowder holders, and cannons. If the arsenal is closed, call or pop into the Toy and Miniature Museum (⇨ *Rhenish Complex)* and someone will open it up for you. ⊠ *Market St.* ☎ *021/886–4153* ⊠ *By donation* ☾ *Weekdays 9–4:30.*

Voorgelegen. This 19th-century home and the houses on either side of it form one of the best-preserved Georgian buildings in town. ⊠ *116 Dorp St.*

Stellenbosch Wine Route

ALONG R310

West of Stellenbosch, the R310 (also known locally as Baden Powell Drive) forks to the left, but go straight on the M12 (also known as Polkadraai Road); Asara is first up on your right, followed by **Neethlingshof.** Turn right on Stellenbosch Kloof Road, where **Overgaauw** is a Merlot mainstay. Follow the winding road through pretty vineyards; at the end is **Jordan,** known for its excellent Chardonnay. Double back to Stellenbosch, and at the set of traffic lights, take the R310 to your right to the touristy but fun **Spier.** Next up this road is **Meerlust,** with its submerged windmill.

If you drive east on the R310 from Stellenbosch, detour up the Idasvallei Road and follow a narrow lane through cattle pastures and oak groves to **Rustenberg,** which focuses on reds. Then it's up and over the scenic Helshoogte Pass to **Thelema Mountain Vineyards,** which has knockout reds and whites. Its neighbor, **Tokara,** is a great lunch spot, and **Delaire Graff Estate,** over the road, has breathtaking views and an upmarket wine-tasting lounge.

ALONG R44

Some important wineries are on the R44 north of Stellenbosch. At **Morgenhof** you can sip Chardonnay and Pinotage and linger for lunch. About 3 km (2 miles) farther along on the R44, turn right on Knorhoek Road to reach low-frills **Muratie,** with some good reds. Back on the R44, travel a short way and then turn left on Kromme Rhee Road to visit **Simonsig,** home to wonderful bubbly. On the R44 once more, continue to **Kanonkop,** which has won numerous awards, and **Warwick,** with great red blends and lots of place to picnic. Carry on to Klapmuts and take the Simondium Road to the right to get to Babylonstoren, not to be missed for its gardens and interesting restaurant.

ALONG R304

This road shoots northwest from Stellenbosch past several wine farms. Stop at **Mulderbosch** for its excellent white wines (and great pizzas). Cross over Kromme Rhee Road and on to **Villiera,** known for sparkling wine and lush Sauvignon Blanc.

WINERIES

Many wine estates are wheelchair friendly, and you'll be able to access the tasting rooms without a problem. But some don't have restroom facilities for those using wheelchairs. You might want to phone ahead so you know what to expect.

TOP ATTRACTIONS

Fodor's Choice
★

Kanonkop. In the days when ships of the Dutch East India Company used Cape Town as a refreshment station on their way to the East, a ship would fire a cannon as it entered the harbor to let farmers know provisions were needed, and a set of relay cannons, all set on hilltops, would carry the message far inland. One such cannon was on this farm, which was then called Kanonkop, Afrikaans for Cannon Hill. The beauty of Kanonkop today is not in its history or its buildings but in its wine. Winemaker Abrie Beeslaar has taken over from the legendary Beyers Truter (a very hard act to follow), but Kanonkop continues to reel in numerous awards and accolades. Paul Sauer, a blend of about 70% Cabernet Sauvignon and 15% each Merlot and Cabernet Franc, rakes in awards both in South Africa and internationally year after year. Bow before the Kanonkop Black Label Pinotage. It's an iconic wine that is produced only in small quantities (fewer than 2,000 bottles a year) and is sold only from the farm. It recently scored 97 points out of 100 at an international tasting. There are no guided cellar tours, but during harvest you can do a walkabout in the cellar to see all the action. An added attraction to this farm is the art gallery that features art from around 50 leading South African artists. It's a wonderful selection of the really modern to totally traditional and gives good insight into the artist soul of the nation. ✉ *R44, between Paarl and Stellenbosch* ☎ *021/884–4656* ⊕ *www.kanonkop.co.za* 🍷 *Tastings R10* ☯ *Weekdays 9–5, Sat. 9–2.*

Meerlust. A visit to Meerlust, probably South Africa's most celebrated estate, provides an introduction to Cape history. In the same family for generations, the wine farm was bought by Johannes Albertus Myburgh in 1757. When Nicolaas Myburgh, eighth-generation Myburgh and father of Hannes (the current owner), took over the reins in 1959, he began restoring the farm's Cape Dutch buildings. The entire complex was declared a national monument in 1987. But Nico Myburgh did more than just renovate. He took a fresh look at red wines and broke with tradition by deciding to make a red blend. In the '70s, conventional wisdom had it that Cabernet Sauvignon was king, but Nico went against the grain and opted for a Bordeaux-style blend, planting both Merlot and Cabernet Franc. The first wine, made in 1980 and released in 1983, was named Rubicon (an allusion to Julius Caesar) to symbolize the crossing of a significant barrier. Rubicon garners awards year after year and is rated as an international best seller. The estate makes only one white, a delicious, full-bodied Chardonnay. If a vintage of any of their grapes isn't good enough to bottle, they don't bother, so you can be assured of outstanding quality. Scoop up a bottle of the Rubicon 2009. Meerlust's other wines—Chardonnay 2012, Pinot Noir 2012, and Merlot 2012—are also notably good. ✉ *Off R310* ☎ *021/843–3587* ⊕ *www.meerlust.co.za* 🍷 *Tastings R30* ☯ *Weekdays 9–5, Sat. 10–2.*

Thelema Mountain Vineyards. On the slopes of the Simonsberg, just off the Helshoogte Pass, this is an excellent example of the exciting developments in the Cape Winelands since the early 1980s, when farmers began to eye land that hadn't traditionally been earmarked for wine farming. When Gyles and Barbara Webb started the farm in 1983, there was nothing here but very good soil and old fruit trees. It's a testament to their efforts that the winery has regularly won prizes for both its reds and whites ever since. To cap it all off, the view of the Groot Drakenstein Mountains from the tasting room is unforgettable. Ever the pioneers, the Webbs have also bought Sutherland, an old fruit farm (not open to the public) in the Elgin area, an exciting new wine-growing region at the top of Sir Lowry's Pass. The Sutherland vineyard sits in the middle of the Kogelberg Biosphere, where many rare and endangered species of protea can be found. The Sutherland wines, which can be tasted at Thelema, are wonderfully fragrant; look out for the Pinot Noir and Chardonnay. The Mint Cabernet Sauvignon is Thelema's flagship red wine, exhibiting light mint and herbal flavors. The locals' favorite, however, is Ed's Reserve, a single-vineyard Chardonnay named after the farm's matriarch, the late, legendary Edna McLean, Barbara's mother; she originally bought the Thelema farm, was a stalwart in the tasting room, and received all the farm's visitors. ⊠ *Off R310, between Stellenbosch and Franschhoek* ☎ *021/885–1924* ⊕ *www.thelema.co.za* ☜ *Tastings R25* ⊘ *Weekdays 9–5, Sat. 10–3.*

FAMILY

Fodor'sChoice

★

Tokara. Perched on the crest of the Helshoogte Pass between Stellenbosch and Franschhoek, Tokara is the brainchild of banker G. T. Ferreira. For a city slicker with lots of money, he's done everything right by employing an excellent winemaker in the super-sexy Miles Mossop and paying careful attention to the quality of his vines. From the start, Tokara has scooped up awards; its Chardonnay was recently voted one of the top 10 wines from around the world at the Chardonnay-du-Monde Awards. The flagship red, a blend of Cabernet Sauvignon, Merlot, Petit Verdot, and Malbec, is well worth taking home. Be on the lookout for the farm's limited release Pinotage 2012. A fire destroyed a chunk of the farm's vineyards a few years ago, and only 1,400 bottles of Pinotage were produced, so this is bound to be a hot collector's item. Tokara also has farms in the cooler Elgin and Hemel-en-Aarde regions, which means it can produce a stunning white wine blend (Sauvignon Blanc and Semillon) with plenty of complexity. The farm also produces its own premium olive oil, which you can buy from the Olive Shed. The restaurant is a foodie's delight, and the Delicatessen is a perfect venue for a breakfast or light lunch. Kids love the free-form jungle gym—as good-looking as any contemporary sculpture—and the weaver's nest they can climb into that hangs in a huge oak; the nest is the creation of visionary South African artist Porky Hefer. ⊠ *Off R310, between Stellenbosch and Franschhoek* ☎ *021/808–5900, 021/808–5959 restaurant* ⊕ *www.tokara.com* ☜ *Tastings free* ⊘ *Weekdays 9–5, weekends 10–3.*

WORTH NOTING

Delaire Graff Estate. This has to be one of the most spectacular settings of any winery in the country. Sit on the terrace of the tasting room or restaurant and look past a screen of pin oaks to the valley below and the majestic crags of the Groot Drakenstein and Simonsberg Mountains. It's an ideal place to stop for lunch, and you'll need at least three hours to do your meal and the wines justice. The wine lounge has an upmarket, clubby feel, and the staff are slick and on top of their game. So are the crew in the vineyard and cellar. Within just three years the estate has gone from so-so to stellar, and now it's regarded as one of the country's top 10 wine producers. Although the Botmaskop Red Blend is the farm's flagship wine, do try the Cabernet Franc Rose. It's a new release and a lovely take on a varietal that usually gets added to the Bordeaux Blend. The Coastal Cuvée Sauvignon Blanc is exceptional and is reeling in the awards. The Chardonnay is very elegant with fresh lime and creamy butterscotch flavors. ⊠ *Helshoogte Pass Rd., between Stellenbosch and Franschhoek* ☎ *021/885–8160* ⊕ *www.delaire.co.za* ☜ *Tastings R25 for 5 wines plus canapés; food and wine pairing R150* ⊘ *Mon.–Sat. 10–5, Sun. 9:30–4:30.*

Jordan. At the end of Stellenbosch Kloof Road, this meticulous winery, flanked by the Bottelary hills, overlooks rolling vineyards and jagged mountains. Husband-and-wife team Gary and Kathy Jordan studied at the University of California at Davis and worked at California's Iron Horse Winery. The family made its fortune producing practical shoes, and although it produced its first vintage only in 1992, it has already established a formidable reputation. The Sauvignon Blanc, with refreshing hints of asparagus, makes for good summer drinking; the multi-award-winning, dense but fruity Chardonnay is extremely popular and has regulars stocking up on cases at a time. The 2013 Chardonnay won the Decanter wine of the year award. The Sauvignon Blanc and Chardonnay are combined in the versatile, flavorful, and well-priced Chameleon dry white. Another wine to try is the Cobblers Hill Bordeaux blend. The wine estate has an excellent restaurant on-site, as well as a bakery where you can have breakfast or a light lunch. Cellar tours are available by appointment; book at least a day ahead. ⊠ *Stellenbosch Kloof Rd.* ☎ *021/881–3441 cellar, 021/881–3612 restaurant, 021/881–3004 bakery* ⊕ *www.jordanwines.com* ☞ *Tastings R35* ☉ *Daily 9:30–4:30.*

Morgenhof Wine Estate. This beautiful Cape Dutch estate, with a history stretching back 300 years, lies in the lee of a steep hill covered with vines and pine trees. In 1993 Morgenhof was acquired by Anne Cointreau of Cognac, France, who spared no expense in making this a showpiece estate with a lovely rose garden on top of the working underground cellar. The estate has a talented winemaker, Andries de Klerk, and some distinguished wines. The Morgenhof Estate Blend 2005 is a complex wine made from a blend of Cabernet Sauvignon, Merlot, Malbec, and Cabernet Franc. Look out for black cherries, prunes, hints of chocolate, and spice on your palate. On a hot summer's day (and the temperatures can soar in Stellenbosch) try the 2013 Chardonnay with fresh pear, passion fruit, and pineapple flavors. Morgenhof is an excellent place to stop for lunch while you watch the peacocks roaming around. There's also a coffee shop if you want a snack before heading off to the next farm. Tour reservations are advisable in summer. ⊠ *R44, between Paarl and Stellenbosch* ☎ *021/889–5510* ⊕ *www.morgenhof.com* ☞ *Tastings R25* ☉ *Weekdays 8:30–5, weekends 10–3.*

FAMILY **Mulderbosch Vineyards.** Nobody likes change, and the wine industry—steeped in tradition—was twitchy when Mulderbosch was sold in 2011 to an overseas investor and the extremely talented winemaker Mike Dobrovic moved on. However, Mulderbosch fans can rest easy. The new team has revised the wines and is producing some stunners. Do try the Single Vineyard Chenin Blanc series; these wines capture all that's good about the underrated Chenin varietal. Look for mango, pineapple, and citrus flavors with crisp acidity, perfect for summer drinking. The Chardonnay is winning awards and is about as good as it gets. A huge portion of the farm has been left to indigenous vegetation and wildlife, and they're attempting to restore endangered renosterveld and fynbos. There's a lovely children's play area and a restaurant in the tasting room with great views. ⊠ *M12, Polkadraai Rd.* ☎ *021/881–8140* ⊕ *www.mulderbosch.co.za* ☞ *R50* ☉ *Tues.–Sun. 10–6.*

Muratie. Ancient oaks and a cellar that truly seems to be more concerned with the business of producing wine than with decor make this a refreshing change from the "prettier" wineries. It's a small estate, specializing in rich, earthy reds and full-bodied dessert wines. Muratie's port is an old favorite in the Cape, and the well-balanced amber is a fortified dessert wine of note, with pleasing citrus overtones to counter the sweetness. The cellar produces some fine red wines. Worth looking out for are the Pinot Noirs, from some of the oldest vines of this cultivar in the Cape. The farm's flagship wine is the Ansela van der Caab, a red blend of Cabernet Sauvignon, Cabernet Franc, and Merlot, named after the freed slave who married the first owner of the farm, Laurens Campher, and helped set up the vineyards in the early 1700s. The Ronnie Melck Shiraz also comes highly recommended. Cellar tours by appointment only. ☒ *Knorhoek Rd., off the R44, between Stellenbosch and Paarl* ☎ *021/865–2330* ⊕ *www.muratie.co.za* ☒ *Tastings R30* ☉ *Daily 10–5.*

FAMILY **Neethlingshof.** A long avenue of pines leads to this lovely estate, which traces its origins to 1692. The magnificent 1814 Cape Dutch manor house looks out across formal rose gardens to the Stellenbosch Valley and the Hottentots Holland Mountains. There's even a large play area, complete with jungle gyms, for kids. The Gewürztraminer is an off-dry, very elegant wine with rose-petal and spice aromas, and the Maria Noble Late Harvest (named after the feisty woman who built the manor house, now the restaurant) is one of the best of its kind, having scooped up almost every local award since 1990. The farm's Owl Post Pinotage is a single-vineyard wine matured in Hungarian oak, which makes it a funkier take on an old South African favorite. Look out for mocha, chocolate, and licorice flavors. Try the food-and-wine parings, which include five bite-size tastes of food paired with the estate wines. On Wednesday evenings in summer enjoy live music, food, and wine as the sun sets. ☒ *Neethlingshof Estate, 7599 Polkadraai Rd.(M12)* ☎ *021/883–8988* ⊕ *www.neethlingshof.co.za* ☒ *Tastings R35, food and wine pairings R65, cellar tours R20* ☉ *Weekdays 9–5, weekends 10–4 (may stay open about 2 hrs later Dec. and Jan.); cellar tours by appointment.*

Overgaauw. Among the established estates on Stellenbosch Kloof Road, Overgaauw definitely deserves a visit. You can admire the pretty Victorian tasting room while exploring the range of big red wines. David van Velden took over as winemaker in 2007; he's the fourth-generation winemaker on the farm. Tradition hasn't stood in the way of innovation, however. In 1982 Overgaauw was the first South African estate to make a Merlot, but it also experiments with other varietals, and you should too. Try the Cape Vintage Port made with Portuguese varietals such as *touriga, tintas, souzao,* and *cornifesto.* Confused? Don't be. The result is a wonderful richly balanced blend. The Tria Corda sells out faster than it can be released. The spicy, fruity Sylvaner is named for a grape of the same name. To date, Overgaauw is the only Cape estate to grow this varietal, which comes from the Alsace region of France, so it's definitely worth exploring. ☒ *Stellenbosch Kloof Rd., Vlottenburg*

☎ *021/881–3815* ⊕ *www.overgaauw.co.za* ✉ *Tastings R20* ⊙ *Weekdays 8:30–5, Sat. 10–12:30.*

Rustenberg. This estate may date back to 1682, but it's been brought thoroughly up-to-date with a state-of-the art winery and underground vaulted maturation rooms. It is known for red wine, particularly its 100% Cabernet Peter Barlow (named after the present owner's father), which is made from grapes from one lovely, well-tended vineyard. The Five Soldiers Chardonnay is delicious and also made from a single vineyard, which gives it its unique character; it's named for the five tall pine trees that stand guard on top of the hill above the Chardonnay grapes. The farm uses screw caps on about half of its wines for quality and environmental reasons. Make time to explore the estate's beautiful gardens and labyrinth. These are open year-round but are best in summer. The lovely manor house gardens are open to the public only once a year, alas. ✉ *Off R310 (Rustenberg Rd.), Ida's Valley* ☎ *021/809–1200* ⊕ *www.rustenberg.co.za* ✉ *Tastings R25* ⊙ *Weekdays 9–4:30, Sat. 10–4, Sun. 10–3.*

FAMILY **Simonsig.** Sitting in a sea of vines is this estate with tremendous views back toward Stellenbosch and the mountains. Simonsig has more than a dozen white and red wines of impressive range, both in terms of taste and price. But quantity certainly doesn't mean that it has compromised on quality. This family-run farm produces exciting and consistent wines. Kaapse Vonkel was South Africa's first Méthode Cap Classique, and since 1971 this classic blend of Chardonnay, Pinot Noir, and a touch of Pinot Meunier has been among the best. The 2010 Tiara is a great Bordeaux blend. The Pinotage demonstrates how well this varietal fares with no wood aging, but the Red Hill Pinotage, from old bush vines, shows just how much good oaking can improve it. This is a good place for kids, with a small playground, a labyrinth that takes about 10 minutes to walk through, and a small vineyard of all the grape varietals; here you can see which grape is used for the different wines and taste grapes directly from the vine. The glam Cuvee restaurant, with its dark walls and Persian carpets, has a seasonal menu of South African dishes with French influences. Phone and ask about the Méthode Cap Classique and cake pairings. Cellar tours are free for groups of 10 people or more. ✉ *Kromme Rhee Rd., Koelenhof* ☎ *021/888–4900* ⊕ *www.simonsig.co.za* ✉ *Tastings R30, R45 including sabrage; cellar tour R25* ⊙ *Weekdays 8:30–5, Sat. 8:30–4, Sun 10–3 (summer) and 11–3 (winter); cellar tours weekdays at 11 or by appointment.*

FAMILY **Spier.** Spier has undergone some serious restructuring and ditched some of its touristy trappings, which is probably a good thing; you can spend a very happy day here. This is one of the oldest farms in the area, established in 1692 on the banks of the Eerste Rivier. The farm produces excellent wines, which go from strength to strength. The latest flagship wine is the Frans K. Smit 2008, named after its winemaker. Also try the 21 Gables Chenin Blanc—the 2013 looks set to be a winner. The 2012 Pinotage in the 21 Gables range is also excellent. The farm's owners value biodiversity and arts and culture: their enormous art collection is open to the public, and their farm-grown produce is used in the restaurant, Eight, and the deli. You can also order a picnic and enjoy it on the banks of the river. Visit Eagle Encounters, an on-site rehabilitation center for raptors—your kids will never want to leave. ✉ R310 (Lyne-doch Rd.) ☎ 021/809–1100 ⊕ www.spier.co.za ✆ Tastings R35–R90 ⊗ Daily 9–5, tasting 10–4:30.

Villiera. Since it started wine making in 1984, the Grier family has notched numerous successes. As John Platter, one of South Africa's foremost wine writers, says, "Other winemakers might jog or work out in the gym; Jeff Grier gets all the exercise he needs stepping up to the podium for wine industry awards." The farm is famous for its range of Méthode Cap Classique sparkling wines. Try the Brut Natural, which is 100% Chardonnay and made using wild yeast. It has no added sulfur and no added sugar, making it the perfect bubbly—delicious and good for you. The creamy Monro Brut made of Chardonnay and Pinot Noir is a multiple award winner. The barrel-fermented Chenin Blanc is also very popular. Registered as a biodiversity farm, the winery produces chemical-free wines as much as possible; they use ducks to help control the snails and work to attract raptors to scare off the smaller birds that feast on the ripening grapes. You can combine a wine tasting with a drive through the 545-acre wildlife sanctuary (2 hrs, R150), where you'll see eland, gemsbok, giraffe, bush pig, and other wild animals. Booking is essential. ✉ R101 and R304 (Old Paarl and Stellenbosch Rds.), Koelenhof ☎ 021/865–2002, 021/865–2003 ⊕ www.villiera.com ✆ Tastings R20 ⊗ Weekdays 8:30–5, Sat. 8:30–3; wildlife sanctuary weekdays 9–3, Sat. 9–1.

Warwick. This Ratcliffe-family-run farm is all business. Norma Ratcliffe, the grande dame of the estate, spent a couple of vintages in France perfecting traditional techniques, which have influenced Warwick's reds. The first female winemaker in South Africa, Norma pioneered the way for a new breed of young women who are now making their mark in the industry. Trilogy is a stylish and complex red made predominantly from Cabernet Sauvignon, with about 20% Merlot and 30% Cabernet Franc. The 2004 Trilogy was voted one of the top five wines in the world by *Wine Spectator*—no mean feat! The 2010 vintage was also voted best wine on show and was awarded five stars, the highest rating any wine can receive. Another great red, the Three Cape Ladies, was named after the indomitable Ratcliffe women. It's been described as a "feminine" blend of Cabernet Sauvignon, Cabernet Franc, and Pinotage. Their Cabernet Franc is undoubtedly one of the best wines made from this varietal in the Winelands. Cellar tours on request. ■TIP➔ On the hour-long Big 5 Vineyard tour (R50), the grape varietals are compared to South Africa's famous Big Five wild animals; afterward you can relax with a farm picnic (R350) on the lawn or in one of the picnic pods. ✉ R44, between Stellenbosch and Klapmuts, Elsenburg ☎ 021/884–4410 ⊕ www.warwickwine.com ✆ Tastings R25 ⊗ Daily 9–5.

WHERE TO EAT

$$ ╳ **Bodega.** On the huge veranda of a historic barn, a languid air of
ECLECTIC well-fed ease wafts around Bodega. Happy children run around on the lawn against the backdrop of jagged mountains, and the vibe is casual all the way. An enormous blackboard announces the tapas options: lovely bite sizes of mussels, hake, *nasi goreng* (Indonesian fried rice),

and meatballs are just some of the options. Alternately choose from the menu; the daily line fish is succulent and well dressed, the pastas are perfectly flavored, and the beef fillet is a dream. Desserts are fantastic, so save space. In summer, Sunday lunch should be booked a week in advance; the rest of the week can be calmer. Come early, as the restaurant closes at 5 pm. $ *Average main: R140* ⊠ *Blaauwklippen Rd.* ☎ *021/880–0557* ⊕ *www.dornier. co.za* ⚱ *Reservations essential* ⊘ *No lunch Mon. and Tues. No dinner.*

> **TASTING TIP**
>
> One of the funny things about small, family-owned farms is that they won't charge you for a tasting if they don't feel like it. But it's at the owners' discretion, and it all depends on whether they wake up in a good or a bad mood. If they like you, you could end up with a tasting, tour, and lunch at their home. So be at your best and most charming. But don't tell them we told you.

$$$$
ECLECTIC ✕**Overture.** At the end of Annandale Road, Hidden Valley Estate perches on a mountain ridge, flanked by the splendor of fynbos-covered hills and a silvery grove of olive trees. The estate's spectacular upscale restaurant has a constantly changing menu of seasonal ingredients that manifests a pure love of food, further evidenced in the presence of the head chef and owner, who comes to chat with diners in between plating dishes like yellowtail tartare with Asian flavors, avocado puree, sago chips, and sesame, or entrecôte with parsnip puree, mushrooms, and Jerusalem artichokes. Expect extremely good value for this level of cuisine; the menu can be ordered à la carte or you can choose the three-course (R355) or five-course menu (R540). The food comes paired with excellent wines from the estate and beyond. Service is friendly, competent, and unobtrusive—that is to say, just right. Little wonder this restaurant wins regular awards; book at least a month in advance during summer. $ *Average main: R355* ⊠ *Hidden Valley Wines, Annandale Rd.* ☎ *021/880–2721* ⊕ *www.dineatoverture.co.za* ⚱ *Reservations essential* ⊘ *Closed Mon. and Tues. No dinner Wed. or Sun.*

$$
ECLECTIC ✕**Pomegranate.** The busy road and the swaths of invasive nonnative trees that have to be chopped down give absolutely no indication of the gem that lies beyond the entrance to Vergenoegd wine farm. Pomegranate chef Mike Israel is known for his fresh, contemporary cuisine, but you'll be hard-pressed to concentrate on the menu—the views are fantastic and the historic manor house has been wonderfully restored. Luckily, the menu is dead simple. Mike has gone for the less-is-more approach and simply lists fish, lamb, game, poultry, and vegetarian. This gives him plenty of scope to play with the fresh ingredients he has available. You could start with the famous Pomegranate tomato tart or opt for the beetroot carpaccio starter with goat cheese. There are field mushrooms served with rosemary and Gorgonzola in a poppy-seed crepe. Mains come with Mike's classic, flavor-filled sauces. The wine list is clever and has an excellent selection of good wines divided into three price categories, the cheapest cheekily referred to as Bank Manager's Choice. $ *Average main: R145* ⊠ *Vergenoegd Wine Estate, Baden Powell Dr. (R310), off the N2* ☎ *021/843–3248* ⊕ *www.vergenoegd.co.za*

Reservations essential ☾ *No lunch Mon. No dinner in winter; no dinner in summer Sat.–Mon.*

$$$$
ECLECTIC
Fodor'sChoice
★

✕**Rust en Vrede.** When you arrive at this gorgeous old Dutch farmhouse, a staff member greets you outside the door, suggesting a predinner drink on the rose-trellised terrace: the perfect introduction to your evening at one of South Africa's top-ranked restaurants. A dining room of exposed yellowwood beams, plush chairs, photos of the estate owner and company, and a scarlet-and-cream color scheme create a warm and elegant atmosphere with a masculine no-nonsense element. A four- (R550) or six-course tasting menu (R680) keeps things deceptively simple with complex flavors like the sublime *ajo blanco* (white gazpacho) soup with white peach, Champagne jelly, and fresh honeycomb as well as the roasted baby chicken with curried mango and coriander. Service is exquisite all the way. An incredibly knowledgeable sommelier, wine pairing options, and surprisingly reasonably priced wine list complete the picture. ■TIP➔ For a real splurge, opt for the Estate Experience (R2,000): four to five hours of culinary surprise. They won't tell you what's on the menu, but you won't be disappointed. Ⓢ *Average main: R550* ✉ *Annandale Rd.* ☎ *021/881–3757* ⊕ *www.rustenvrede.com* ✍ *Reservations essential* 🏛 *Jacket required* ☾ *No lunch. No dinner Sun. and Mon.*

$$$
ECLECTIC
FAMILY
Fodor'sChoice
★

✕**Terroir.** The setting on a golf estate and wine farm is pretty, but it's the excellent food and service that really stand out here. Chef Michael Broughton does his best to honor the concept of *terroir* (from the French *terre* for "earth") and get as many ingredients from the surrounding area as possible. The menu changes regularly to make use of the fresh produce, so be prepared to try something new each visit. The prawn risotto, however, is a regular—you'll want to clean your plate of every trace of the lovely, creamy sauce américaine that it comes in. Main courses might include braised pork belly with ginger, juniper, and soy on smoked mashed potatoes with braising juices and cabbage puree. Try the heart-stopping Black Forest dessert with kirsch ice cream. There's a jungle gym for small foodies (but, interestingly, no separate menu). The wine list is small but includes several wines by the glass; try the barrel-fermented Chenin Blanc, one of the estate's best-kept secrets. To avoid disappointment, be sure to book well in advance. Ⓢ *Average main: R190* ✉ *Kleine Zalze Residential Golf Estate, Strand Rd. (R44), between Somerset West and Stellenbosch* ☎ *021/880–8167* ⊕ *www.kleinezalze.com* ✍ *Reservations essential* ☾ *No dinner Sun.*

$$$
ECLECTIC
Fodor'sChoice
★

✕**Tokara.** At the top of the Helshoogte Pass with absolutely amazing views of the valley and mountains, Tokara is a Winelands must-do. Chef Richard Carstens is known for innovation and playful twists. His adventurous menu changes seasonally but could include such starters as broccoli with a Gruyère custard, marinated mushrooms, and pine nuts with a teriyaki brown butter or roasted cob with crisp calamari, prawns, and squid-ink brioche served with a garlic-and-lemon cream. For mains there are some unusual combinations that work brilliantly. Try the panfried springbok with cauliflower puree, brandy prunes, and sauce miroir (a deglazed, reduced gravy made with pan juices). End with the chef's famous Gorgonzola ice cream served with red-wine beets, walnut, mint, and honeycomb. Children are welcomed with their own version of fish-and-chips or steak and fries. ■TIP➔ In season you need to book at least a week in advance; ask for a window table. $ *Average main: R170* ✉ *Helshoogte Pass Rd.* ☎ *021/885–2550* ⊕ *www.tokara.co.za* ⚲ *Reservations essential* ⊘ *Closed Mon. No dinner Sun.*

WHERE TO STAY

$$$ ☷ **Asara Wine Estate & Hotel.** This hotel on the outskirts of Stellenbosch

HOTEL   might not have the most breathtaking setting that the Winelands has to offer, but what it lacks in location it more than makes up for in luxury and attention to detail. **Pros:** easy access to both Cape Town and the Winelands; highly rated wines produced on the estate. **Cons:** not far from the Stellenbosch municipal garbage dump; lacks the gracious charm of some historic wine farms; you'll need a deep pocket. $ *Rooms from: R3500* ✉ *Polkadraai Rd. (M12), Vlottenburg* ☎ *021/888–8000* ⊕ *www.asara.co.za* ⌨ *36 rooms* ❏ *Breakfast.*

$$$$ ☷ **Delaire Graff Estate Lodges.** At the top of the Helshoogte mountain

HOTEL   pass and looking onto two surrounding mountain ranges, Delaire Graff

Fodor's Choice   enjoys one of the wine country's most dramatic locations. **Pros:** stunning

★   natural setting; lodge guests enjoy free tastings and shuttles into Stellenbsoch; staff accounts for personal preferences from pillows to newspapers. **Cons:** this level of luxury doesn't come cheap. $ *Rooms from: R11000* ✉ *Helshoogte Pass Rd., between Stellenbosch and Franschhoek* ☎ *021/885–8160* ⊕ *www.delaire.co.za* ⌨ *10 suites* ❏ *Breakfast.*

$$$ ☷ **Lanzerac Manor.** The sense of history is almost tangible at this large

HOTEL   working wine estate dating from 1692. **Pros:** winery on-site; stunning location with views of the Helderberg Mountains; distinguished example of Cape Dutch architecture; wheelchair-friendly. **Cons:** not within walking distance of Stellenbosch; quiet and peaceful, so won't suit you if you're looking for a vibe. $ *Rooms from: R3000* ✉ *Jonkershoek Valley, Lanzerac Rd., 1 km (½ mile) from Stellenbosch* ☎ *021/887–1132* ⊕ *www.lanzerac.co.za* ⌨ *41 rooms, 7 suites* ❏ *Breakfast.*

$$$ ☷ **Oude Werf Hotel.** A national monument, this attractive 1802 inn is

B&B/INN   thought to be the oldest in South Africa. **Pros:** perfect location in the heart of Stellenbosch; landmark in-house restaurant; two family-size, self-catering houses available; heated outdoor swimming pool. **Cons:** can get a bit noisy in the center of town; some rooms are dark. $ *Rooms from: R2500* ✉ *30 Church St.* ☎ *021/887–4608* ⊕ *www.oudewerfhotel. co.za* ⌨ *44 rooms, 5 apartments* ❏ *Breakfast.*

$$ ☷ **Spier Hotel.** The innovative design of these two-story buildings

HOTEL   grouped around six courtyards, each with its own pool and leisure

FAMILY   area, makes this complex feel like a Mediterranean village, albeit a very luxurious one. **Pros:** plenty of entertainment on hand; perfect for the whole family; very accessible and close to the N2. **Cons:** can get busy in peak season; you'll have to share the wine farm with day visitors. $ *Rooms from: R2100* ✉ *Spier Estate, Lynedoch Rd.* ☎ *021/809–1100* ⊕ *www.spier.co.za* ⌨ *153 rooms, 5 suites* ❏ *Breakfast.*

$ ☷ **Stumble Inn Backpackers Lodge.** Stellenbosch's original backpack-

B&B/INN   ers' lodging, within easy walking distance of most major town sights, is a great place to stay if you're traveling on a limited budget. **Pros:** central location in town; helpful staff; camping site in the gardens. **Cons:** bunk beds (need we say more?); shared bathroom facilities.

$ *Rooms from: R370* ⊠ *12 Market St.* ☎ *021/887–4049* ⊕ *www.stumbleinnbackpackers.co.za* ⇆ *7 rooms, 5 dormitories* ⦿ *No meals.*

NIGHTLIFE AND PERFORMING ARTS

NIGHTLIFE

Wijnhuis. Take a stroll into the Church Street part of town, where shops stay open late and bars and cafés spill onto the streets. A good place to start, the Wijnhuis quickly fills up with trendy locals wanting to unwind. ⊠ *Church and Andringa Sts.* ☎ *021/887–5844* ⊕ *www.wijnhuis.co.za.*

PERFORMING ARTS

For tickets to most events in South Africa, contact **Computicket** (☎ *083/915–8000* ⊕ *www.computicket.co.za*).

Oude Libertas Amphitheatre. Each summer, performances ranging from African jazz to opera to ballet are staged at the Oude Libertas Amphitheatre, a delightful open-air venue across from and run and owned by Distell, a South African liquor company. Book tickets online through Computicket. ⊠ *Corner of Adam Tas St. and Oude Libertas Rd.* ☎ *021/809–7473* ⊕ *www.oudelibertas.co.za.*

SPORTS AND THE OUTDOORS

GOLF

Stellenbosch Golf Club. One of the oldest in South Africa, this golf course has hosted numerous prestigious tournaments, including the South African Open and South African Masters. Tree-lined fairways here will pose a problem if you don't hit the ball straight. ⊠ *R44 (Strand Rd.)* ☎ *021/880–0103* ⊕ *www.stellenboschgolfclub.com* ⚑ *18 holes, 6408 yards, par 72.* 🏌 *R650.*

EN ROUTE From Thelema the **R310** runs down into the fruit orchards and vines that mark the beginning of the Franschhoek Valley. The R310 dead-ends at the R45. To the left is Paarl, to the right Franschhoek. When you head up the R310 from Franschhoek back to Stellenbosch, keep a look out for the "angel" etched onto the mountain in among the vines. Well-known land artist Strijdom van der Merwe was asked to help create the Bartinney Wine Estate's winged figure of Élevage in the landscape. Élevage is a French wine-making term that describes the art of liberating grapes to reveal their true characteristics. The image was created by planting endemic fynbos among the new Chardonnay vines.

FRANSCHHOEK

22 km (14 miles) northeast of Stellenbosch.

Franschhoek (French Corner) takes its name from its first white settlers, French Huguenots who fled to the Cape to escape Catholic persecution in France in the late 1600s. By the early 18th century about 200 Huguenots had settled in the Cape; today their descendants—with names like de Villiers, Malan, and Joubert—number in the tens of thousands. With their experience in French vineyards, the early Huguenots were instrumental in nurturing a wine-making culture in South Africa.

Franschhoek is the most spectacular of the three wine centers: a long valley encircled by towering mountain ranges and fed by a single road that runs through town. As spectacular as the valley is today, it must have been even more so in the 17th century, when it teemed with game. In calving season herds of elephants would migrate to the valley via the precipitous Franschhoek Mountains. The last wild elephant in the valley died in the 1930s. Some leopards still survive high in the mountains, but you won't see them.

What you will see today is an increasingly upscale village with beautifully renovated cottages and gorgeous gardens. Although it can get very busy during the summer season, you will always be able to find a quiet spot with a view of the mountains, roses, and swaths of lavender, which do well here. Franschhoek has developed into a culinary mecca, with some of the country's best restaurants and cafés lining the pretty main street. In May the fabulous Franschhoek Literary Festival (⊕ *www.flf.co.za*) features local and international writers. Bastille Day (⊕ *www.franschhoek.co.za/bastille.html*) is a huge draw, when the town is decked out in red, white, and blue, and events commemorate the town's French history. The town is more touristy than agrarian, although you will see the occasional wine farmer steaming into town with his dogs on the back of his *bakkie* (pickup truck), looking for tractor tires or other essentials. It's a great place for lunch or for a couple of days, as there are excellent small hotels and guesthouses to choose from.

GETTING HERE AND AROUND
The best way to explore this area is by renting a car and braving the Cape's highways and byways. Be aware that drunken walking is a real hazard in wine-growing areas, and you need to keep a sharp eye out for staggering pedestrians, especially over the weekends.

VISITOR INFORMATION
Contacts Franschhoek Vallée Tourisme ⊠ *62 Huguenot Rd.* ☎ *021/876–3603* ⊕ www.franschhoek.org.za ☉ *Oct.–Apr., weekdays 8–6, Sat. 9–6, Sun. 9–4; May–Sept., weekdays 8–5, Sat. 9–5, Sun. 9–4.*

EXPLORING
Huguenot Memorial Museum. To trace the history of the Huguenot community here, visit the Huguenot Memorial Museum. Its main building is modeled after the Saasveld house, built in 1791 by renowned Cape architect Louis Thibault in Cape Town. Wall displays profile some of the early Huguenot families. Exhibits also focus on other aspects of the region's history, such as the development of Cape Dutch architecture and the relationship of the Huguenots with the Dutch East India Company. Displays in the annex cover the culture and life of the Khoekhoen, or Khoikhoi, once derogatorily known as Hottentots, as well as the role of slaves and local laborers in the development of the Franschhoek Valley. A restaurant serves simple meals. Be sure to visit the adjacent Huguenot Museum gardens and the graveyard next to the monument. The graves date back 300 years; note that most are marked with simple, rectangular headstones or the obelisk, pointing toward heaven, rather than the symbol associated with the church the Huguenots were so desperate to escape. ⊠ *Lambrecht St.* ☎ *021/876–2532* ▨ *R10* ☉ *Mon.–Sat. 9–5, Sun. 2–5.*

CLOSE UP

Franschhoek Wine Route

ALONG R310

The drive out of Stellenbosch up the Helshoogte Pass is spectacular. In winter you'll more than likely find snow on the mountain peaks; in summer, once you top the pass you enter a verdant valley of fruit trees and ordered vineyards.

Then head to **Boschendal,** one of the oldest and most established estates in the country.

ALONG R45

There are well more than 40 estates to choose from here, and there's something for everyone—from enormous farms covering hundreds of acres to smaller, boutique vineyards producing just a few hundred bottles each year. If you turn right on R45 from the R310, **L'Ormarins** is one of the first wine farms you'll come to (off the R45 through a tunnel of trees). It's a well-established estate that's undergone some massive changes since the founder, Anthonij Rupert, died in 2001. Just outside town, **La Motte** is a sister farm to L'Ormarins. Closer to town the estates come thick and fast. Amid this flurry—Môreson (up the aptly named Happy Valley Road), Rickety Bridge, Agusta, Chamonix, and Dieu Donne—is **Mont Rochelle,** a relatively small producer of lovely wine and home to a boutique hotel. Outside town and up the Franschhoek Pass toward Villiersdorp, the fabulous **Cabrière,** at Haute Cabrière, is built into the mountain. **La Petite Ferme** is worth phoning ahead for (you can't just pop in).

If you turn left on the R45 from the R310, you'll find more outstanding wine farms, including **Plaisir de Merle,** which makes a distinctive Cabernet and Sauvignon Blanc.

Huguenot Monument. At the end of the main road through Franschhoek is the Huguenot Monument, built in 1948 to commemorate the contribution of the Huguenots to South Africa's development. The three arches symbolize the Holy Trinity, the sun and cross reference the Huguenots' emblem, and the female figure in front represents Freedom of Conscience. ✉ *Lambrecht and Huguenot Sts.*

WINERIES

It should come as no surprise that the Franschhoek Valley produces excellent wines. After all, the original French settlers brought with them an extensive and intimate understanding of viticulture. Some of the country's oldest estates nestle at the base of the spectacular Groot Drakenstein Mountains, and the wine farmers here are constantly trying to top themselves.

TOP ATTRACTIONS

Boschendal. With a history that dates back three centuries, this lovely estate is one of the Cape's major attractions. You can easily spend half a day here, and recent renovations have added polish to an already premier estate. Cradled between the Simonsberg and Groot Drakenstein Mountains at the base of Helshoogte Pass, the farm—formerly called Bossendaal—was originally granted to Jean le Long, one of the first French Huguenot settlers in the late 17th century. Boschendal runs one of the most pleasant wine tastings in the region: you can sit inside at the Taphuis, a Cape Dutch *langhuis* (longhouse), or outside at wrought-iron tables under a spreading oak. In 1981 Boschendal was the first to pioneer a Blanc de Noir, a pink wine made in a white-wine style from black grapes. The Boschendal Blanc de Noir remains one of the best-selling wines of this style. Of the farm's extensive range of wines, a recent addition is the Cecil John range named after Cecil John Rhodes, the late-19th-century Cape prime minister who owned Rhodes Fruit Farms, of which Boschendal was once a part. There is one premier wine under this label, an impressive Shiraz. From the Taphuis it's a two-minute drive through vines and fruit trees to the main estate complex. The recently renovated Boschendal Restaurant serves a buffet of Cape specialties, and Le Pique Nique (October–May) provides picnic baskets that you can enjoy on the lawns; reservations are essential for both. Hour-long vineyard tours and tours of the manor house are available; be sure to book ahead. ⊠ *R310, between Franschhoek and Stellenbosch, Groot Drakenstein* ☎ *021/870–4200, 021/870–4211 for winery, 021/870–4272 for restaurants* ⊕ *www.boschendal.co.za* ⊡ *Tastings R35–R65* ⊙ *Oct.–Apr., daily 9:30–5:30; May–Sept., daily 9:30–4:30.*

L'Ormarins. Dating from 1811, the archetypal Cape Dutch manor house is festooned with flowers and framed by majestic peaks, but instead of remaining in the past, this winery has embraced the future and pumped serious money into a major revamp. L'Ormarins is the main estate and part of the Rupert empire, but there are five labels produced by their various farms dotted around the Western Cape. The wines include the premium Anthonij Rupert range, the L'Ormarins label, Terra Del Capo, Cape of Good Hope, and Protea range. The farm has three state-of-the-art cellars and two tasting rooms. At the Anthonij Rupert Tasting Room, in the manor house, you can try the Cape of Good Hope and Anthonij Rupert wine ranges. High tea is served here in the afternoon. You can try the other ranges at the Terra Del Capo Tasting Room. There's an antipasto bar below the tasting room, where you can enjoy tasty tapas. Chat with the winemakers, and they'll tell you that the farm has introduced revolutionary farming practices, from transporting the grapes to the cellar in cool trucks to hand-sorting and hand-stemming. The results are impressive, and you're likely to find something to suit your taste and pocket. The AR Merlot is exceptional: look out for mulberries, blackberries, and hints of fynbos along with fruitcake and cloves. The TDC Sangiovese is a brilliant, light drinking wine, and the Pinot Grigio is always a pleasure. ■ **TIP→ Visit the estate's Franschhoek Motor Museum, home to more than 80 cars of varying ages in mint condition.** ⊠ *R45(Franschhoek Rd.), Groot Drakenstein* ☎ *021/874–9000* ⊕ *www.rupertwines.com* ⊡ *Tastings R15–R60, Motor Museum R60* ⊙ *Weekdays 9–5, weekends 10–5. Anthonij Rupert Tasting Room closed Sun.*

WORTH NOTING

FAMILY **Allée Bleue.** Set against the dramatic Drakenstein Mountains with lavender fields and meadows, Allée Bleue is one of the oldest wine farms in the Cape. This picturesque estate is well known for its fresh and fruity white wines and well-matured, spicy reds. You can taste their award-winning wines on the tree-shaded terrace overlooking the vineyards, or by an open fire in the tasting room. Bistro Allée Bleue (R90) offers breakfast and light lunches, or you can create your own picnic basket from a selection of salads, homemade ciabatta sandwiches, quiches, cheeses, and desserts. There's even a kids' picnic menu, and a jungle gym, trampoline, and jumping castle to keep the little ones occupied. The estate cultivates their own herbs, and you can join an Herb Tour, including a three-course herb-inspired lunch, every Friday (R185 per person). Look out for the pop-up restaurant, which is open some months; here you can select your own herbs to personalize your pizza or pasta. ⊠ *Intersection of R45 and R310, Groot Drakenstein* ☎ *021/874–1021* ⊕ *www. alleebleue.co.za* 🍽 *Tastings R25* ☉ *Weekdays 9–5, weekends 10–5.*

Haute Cabrière. Built in 1994 on the lower slopes of the Franschhoek Mountains, Haute Cabrière is the brainchild of Achim von Arnim, one of the Cape's most colorful winemakers. To avoid scarring the mountain, the complex, which includes the fine Haute Cabrière restaurant and terrace, hunkers into the hillside. There are two Cap Classique sparkling wines under the Pierre Jordan label, and four Haute Cabrière wines. The fruity, mouth-filling unwooded Pinot Noir is consistently one of the best. Also delicious is the Chardonnay–Pinot Noir blend, an ideal, extremely quaffable wine to enjoy at lunchtime. Take a Saturday-morning cellar tour with von Arnim or his son, Takuan, and watch him perform his trademark display of *sabrage*—the dramatic decapitation of a bottle of bubbly with a saber. ⊠ *R45(Franschhoek Pass Rd.)* ☎ *021/876–8500* ⊕ *www.cabriere.co.za* 🍽 *Tastings R20–R60, cellar tours R60* ☉ *Weekdays 9–5, Sat. 10–4, Sun. 11–4.*

La Motte Estate. This estate is owned by a branch of the same Rupert family that owns L'Ormarins, and is a partner in Rupert & Rothschild, a vineyard closer to Paarl. There's a lot happening at this farm: do a sustainability walk through the vineyards and vegetables, which are grown as organically as possible; explore the hiking trail; and take a history tour. And then there's great wine tasting, food-and-wine pairings, and high tea; the Pierneef restaurant on the estate is regularly voted one of the country's top 10. Hanneli Rupert-Koegelenberg is among South Africa's leading mezzo-sopranos, and the estate also hosts elegant music recitals. The farm also has a wonderful collection of Jacob Hendrik Pierneef's art; view his iconic landscapes in the gallery. But don't get too sidetracked—the wine is excellent as well. The Pierneef Collection is the farm's premium range, and the Shiraz-Viognier blend is being snapped up for its whiffs of dark chocolate, smoked beef, black cherry, and blackberry. The estate's organically grown Sauvignon Blanc is also outstanding. ⊠ *R45 (Huguenot Rd.)* ☎ *021/876–3119* ⊕ *www.la-motte. com* 🍽 *Tastings R50, cellar tour and tasting R70* ☉ *Mon.–Sat. 9–4:30.*

La Petite Ferme. You'll have to phone ahead to arrange a tasting here, but it's worth it, because then you'll know what to have with your lunch if you decide to dine here. True to its name, this is a small, family-run estate producing just enough wine for the restaurant and to keep its faithful customers happy. Try the full-bodied, barrel-fermented Chardonnay 2013 or the Merlot, which scoops awards year after year. The Verdict 2012, a Bordeaux-style blend, is now available and the jury is clear about this wine. ⊠ *R45(Franschhoek Pass Rd.)* ☎ *021/876–3016/8*

3

⊕ *www.lapetiteferme.co.za* ☉ *Sales daily noon–4; tastings and tours by appointment at 11.*

Mont Rochelle. This picture-pretty estate has one of the best views in the valley. Mont Rochelle, recently purchased by Sir Richard Branson, boasts more than 90 acres of vineyard, and the wines produced here are excellent. If the sun is shining, consider a picnic at the vineyards. You can order wine to accompany your picnic, or visit the tasting center and sample a variety of Mont Rochelle wines—try the Artemis 2008 and the signature Miko Chardonnay. If you have the time, take a tour of the 150-year-old cellar, which was originally a fruit-packing shed. For relaxed and formal dining, the hotel has two restaurants: the Country Kitchen, which is the perfect place for a light lunch or relaxed dinner, and Miko, a contemporary gourmet restaurant, where you can enjoy a cocktail at sunset or an intimate meal. ⊠ *Dassenberg Rd.* ☎ *011/325–4405* ⊕ *www.montrochelle.co.za* ✉ *Tastings R20–R40, cellar tours free* ☉ *Tastings daily from 11; cellar tours weekdays at 11.*

Plaisir de Merle. The name means "Pleasure of the Blackbird" and has its origins with the original French owners of the farm. This huge estate is the showpiece of Distell, a big wine and spirit producer. With its innovative architecture and conservation area, it truly feels different from the ubiquitous oak-and-gable wineries that you see all over the Cape. But forget all the frills—it really is about the wine. Don't miss the full-bodied barrel-fermented Chardonnay, which spends nine months in the barrel developing its lovely rich and layered flavor. The farm's flagship wine is the Grand Plaisir, a complex Bordeaux blend; the 2008 vintage is currently available. When tasting, look out for flavors of sweet ripe plums, oak with hints of tobacco, vanilla, and cedar. ⊠ *R45, Simondium* ☎ *021/874–1071, 021/874–1072* ⊕ *www.plaisirdemerle.co.za* ✉ *Nibbling tasting (nuts and biltong) R50, cellar tour with tastings R120* ☉ *Apr.–Oct., weekdays 9–5, Sat. 10–2; Nov.–Mar., weekdays 9–5, Sat. 10–4; cellar tours by appointment.*

Solms-Delta. In 2002 neuroscience professor Mark Solms took charge of Delta wine estate and set about altering wine-making traditions in the region; the grapes grown at Solms-Delta are French, but the technique used is from ancient Greece. This process is called desiccation: grapes are clamped on the vine, cutting off the flow of nutrients, leading to dehydrated fruit with intense flavor. The estate produces two ranges. In the Solms-Delta range, try the Gemoedsrus 2009, a desiccated Shiraz wine fortified with grappa. In the Solms-Astor range you'll find reasonably priced, unusual blends; try the Langarm, an innovative red blend of Pinotage and southern European varietals. On the farm you can also visit the Museum van de Caab, where you'll learn the story of the farm and the fascinating history of the Cape. Produce from the estate's 5-acre garden of *veldkos* (indigenous edible plants) is used in Fyndraai Restaurant, which serves traditional Cape cuisine with strong European and Cape Malay influences. If you'd prefer an informal lunch, you can opt to picnic on the grounds. ⊠ *Delta Rd., off the R45* ☎ *021/874–3937* ⊕ *www.solms-delta.co.za* ✉ *Tastings R20–R30* ☉ *Daily 9–5.*

3

WHERE TO EAT

$$$$
SOUTH AFRICAN

✕**Boschendal Restaurant.** Reserve well in advance for the buffet lunch here at one of the Cape's most beautiful and historic wineries. A wide selection of soups, quiches, and pâtés prefaces a bewildering array of cold and hot main dishes, including pickled fish, roasts, and imaginative salads; traditional Cape dishes are well prepared. End with an excellent sampling of South African cheeses and preserves or a quintessentially Cape dessert such as malva pudding. Unobtrusive, professional, but friendly service complements the bounty, priced at R260 a head. $ *Average main: R260* ✉ *R310, between Franschhoek and Stellenbosch, Groot Drakenstein* ☎ *021/870–4272, 021/870–4273, 021/870–4274, 021/870–4275* ⌂ *Reservations essential* ☾ *No dinner.*

$$$
ECLECTIC
FAMILY

✕**Bread & Wine Vineyard Restaurant.** This rustic restaurant on Môreson Farm has won numerous accolades for its food and is a great place to stop for lunch on the Wine Tram route. Owner Neil Jewell, "the Charcuterie Guru," is the man behind the food, and he has stuck to local, seasonal produce. The menu changes often, and on a whim, but you can expect dishes like mussels in a creamy sauce and herb risotto with whipped *boerenkaas* cheese. There's an interesting selection of side dishes, including *dauphinoise* potatoes and root vegetables braised in beer. The dessert menu is full of rich, decadent sweets, from truffles and nougat to soufflés and pana cotta. The restaurant is child-friendly, with an indoor play area complete with books and toys and a garden outside. After lunch, you can stock up on homemade preserves, bread, and charcuterie, including bacon and "lamb ham" at the Farm Grocer. If you like, you can also try a bread-, wine-, or charcuterie-making course on the farm. $ *Average main: R170* ✉ *Môreson Farm, Happy Valley Rd.* ☎ *021/876–3692* ⊕ *www.moreson.co.za* ☾ *No dinner.*

$$
ECLECTIC

✕**Café des Arts.** When Topsi Venter, doyenne of the Cape culinary scene, decided to hang up her apron and retire, it seemed appropriate that one of her former students, Chris Hoffman, should take over her popular restaurant. Chris peeled his first potato while apprenticed to Topsi and then went on to work at other restaurants. He has carried on with Topsi's tradition of delicious no-fuss food in a town in love with fine dining and foodie fuss. The blackboard menu changes regularly, and the food is rustic and hearty. Look out for slow-roasted duck served with stir-fried couscous and a spicy apricot sauce, or mushroom, basil, chili, and lemon pasta. Malva pudding (a South African traditional baked sticky pudding) is an all-time favorite and served with a delicate crème anglaise. In this valley of wonderful wines it's great to be able to BYOB, but they also have a small wine menu. $ *Average main: R125* ✉ *7 Reservoir West St.* ☎ *021/876–2952* ⊕ *www.cafedesarts. co.za* ⌂ *Reservations essential.*

$$$$
ECLECTIC
Fodor's Choice
★

✕**Haute Cabrière.** Try to reserve a window table for views across the vine-clad valley at this restaurant atop a working winery built into the mountainside. The mix-and-match menu is intended to complement the estate wines maturing in the cellar beneath you; the flavors are complex—these aren't the kind of dishes you could easily whip up at home. Selections might include a sweet potato soup with a chakalaka (spicy relish) and sweet potato foam, or smoked-cheese-and-tomato risoto with a nasturtium pesto; the roasted prawn broth is a popular favorite. A lot of the produce is grown on the farm or locally, and the aim is to get you to try different flavors with the wines to see which taste combinations appeal to you most. Regulars come back for the organic, sugar-cured fillet served with crispy sweetbreads. You can opt for the chef's recommended tasting menu—six delicious courses for R650, including wine—one of three different tasting menus on offer. In summer from October they have music and tapas on the terrace from 3 to 7. $ *Average main: R650* ⊠ *Franschhoek Pass Rd. (R45)* ☎ *021/876–3688* ⊕ *www.cabriere.co.za* ⌖ *Reservations essential* ⊘ *Closed Mon. Oct.–Apr., no dinner Sun. May–Sept., no dinner Sun.–Thurs.*

$$$

INTERNATIONAL

✕ **Miko.** Named after Mont Rochelle's previous owner, Miko Rwayitare, Miko is a contemporary fine-dining restaurant with seating indoors and out. The terrace offers spectacular views of the Franschhoek valley and mountains and has quirky touches such as chairs covered in faux grass with beaded sheep grazing among them. The menu consists of dishes cooked with local, seasonal produce, and the cuisine is international with South African influences. Dinner could begin with scallops served with a puree of guava, peas, a vanilla foam, and micro-greens. For mains there's an array of delicious meat dishes—from springbok and lamb loin to beef fillet and Cape Malay chicken—as well as line-fish options and vegetarian dishes. Round off the meal with a citrus soufflé with orange-and-marmalade ice cream, crème brûlée with fresh strawberries, or parfait made with pineapple, coconut, peanut butter, and nut brittle. $ *Average main: R195* ⊠ *Dassenberg Rd.* ☎ *011/325–4405* ⊕ *www.montrochelle.co.za* ⊘ *No dinner Sun.*

$$$$

ECLECTIC

✕ **The Restaurant at Grande Provence.** The chic and industrial decor of the Restaurant at Grande Provence is a bold contrast to the old-world charm of whitewashed Huguenot architecture: high-back white leather chairs, blue-gray walls, steel doors that open onto a sculpture garden, and skylights make for a striking setting at this restaurant. The food is superb, and the level of service is exceptional. If you're unsure about what to eat, just ask your waiter to send through their best, which they will do with great pleasure. Lunch and dinner are formal, three-course affairs, so make sure you have time to linger. Starters include a burrata salad made up of rosemary and Parmesan shortbread, purple basil pesto, and rosa tomato emulsion. Mains include acorn-smoked pressed pork belly, bacon-wrapped scallops, horseradish potato, pork cheek Boudin Blanc, spiced apple and beetroot gel, and apple essence served in a pipette for you to drizzle on your food. An amuse-bouche kicks off the meal, and between courses there are palate cleansers. The honey bavarois is a lovely way to end the meal. Each dish is paired with the estate wines, and the unobtrusive but eagle-eyed waiters make sure your glass is never empty. $ *Average main: R495* ⊠ *Grande Provence, off R45* ☎ *021/876–8600* ⊕ *www.grandeprovence.co.za.*

$$$

ECLECTIC

✕ **Reuben's.** Everybody loves à success story, and Reuben Riffel has hit the jackpot: a string of restaurants in desirable South African destinations, all born of this one. Reuben cooks food he would like to eat, and so, it seems, would everyone else. For starters consider the chili-salted squid with *nuac cham* (Vietnamese dipping sauce), fragrant salad, and lime mayo, or spicy beef tartare, crispy fried egg yolk, parsley-caper salsa, and grana padano herb salad. Mains include grilled miso-marinated quail served with a spiced citrus sauce, beetroot discs, cumin-carrot puree, and potato gratin. The decor is minimalist but welcoming, with a roaring fire in winter, and service is impeccable and well informed. Have a drink at the trendy bar, made from an airplane wing. $ *Average main: R165* ✉ *19 Huguenot Rd.* ☎ *021/876–3772* ⊕ *www.reubens.co.za* ✍ *Reservations essential.*

$$$$
CONTEMPORARY
Fodor's Choice
★

✕ **The Tasting Room.** You can't go anywhere in Franschhoek without somebody mentioning Margot Janse, Africa's only female Grand Chef and the culinary genius behind Le Quartier Francais's signature restaurant, the Tasting Room. Set aside 3½ hours to enjoy an eight-course "surprise" menu. Janse is passionate about using local ingredients, like *amasi* (sour milk), baobab (pod from a tree), buchu (an indigenous herb), and maize (corn). You might be served cornbread with caramelized brown butter baked in a tin can; a salad of local foraged greens; lamb cheek and tongue with eggplant and black garlic; or quail with amasi, sweet corn, and granola. The decor is designed to complement the cuisine; tables are simply decorated and unadorned, with custom-made crockery. You can expect to pay R850 for the meal alone, and an extra R450 for the tasting menu paired with local wines. Booking is essential, and so is an open mind. $ *Average main: R850* ✉ *Le Quartier Francais, Berg and Wilhelmina Sts.* ☎ *021/876–2151* ⊕ *www.lqf.co.za* ✍ *Reservations essential* ☉ *Closed Sun. and Mon. No lunch.*

WHERE TO STAY

$$$$
B&B/INN

🛏 **Holden Manz.** Guests visiting this house originally built as the private home of owners Holden and Migo Manz will certainly feel as if they are visiting a friend; the 74-acre estate is just outside town, close enough to go to dinner but far enough away to feel as if you've escaped. **Pros:** on-site spa is a divine addition to your escape; private balconies are a great place to sip your morning coffee; 74 acres to stretch your legs. **Cons:** the location outside town may be inconvenient if you don't have a car. $ *Rooms from: R4000* ✉ *Green Valley Rd.* ☎ *021/876–2738* ⊕ *www.holdenmanz.com* 🛏 *5 rooms* ⍩ *Breakfast.*

$
B&B/INN

🛏 **Le Ballon Rouge.** If you fancy being in the heart of the village, Le Ballon Rouge makes a good base: here you're just a five-minute walk from galleries, restaurants, and the general buzz. **Pros:** central location; personal and attentive service; airport shuttle can be arranged. **Cons:** few rooms available; children under 12 not allowed. $ *Rooms from: R1100* ✉ *7 Reservoir St.* ☎ *021/876–2651* ⊕ *www.ballonrouge.co.za* 🛏 *8 rooms, 2 suites* ⍩ *Breakfast.*

$$$$
HOTEL
FAMILY
Fodor's Choice
★

🛏 **Le Quartier Français.** Part of the Relais & Châteaux group, this classy guesthouse exuding privacy and peace is a Winelands favorite: rooms in two-story whitewashed cottages face a pool deck and central garden exploding with flowers. **Pros:** many children's activities in the area; an in-house treatment room; screening room for moviegoers; cooking classes with Margot Janse. **Cons:** pricey; home will seem very dull; the food is so good, you might leave a few pounds heavier. $ *Rooms from: R5300* ✉ *Berg and Wilhelmina Sts.* ☎ *021/876–2151* ⊕ *www.lqf.co.za* 🛏 *13 rooms, 8 suites* ⍩ *Breakfast.*

$$$$
B&B/INN

☒ **The Owner's Cottage.** You know you're in good company at the Owner's Cottage on Grande Provence wine estate when the visitors' book includes Jude Law and British royals Sophie and Prince Edward. **Pros:** to the manor born—you'll be made to feel right at home; close to Franschhoek action but far enough to escape; lovely pool. **Cons:** some people don't like the smell of thatch; unless you rent the whole house, you'll have to share it with other guests. ⑤ *Rooms from: R6000* ☒ *Grand Provence, off R45* ☎ *021/876–8600* ⊕ *www.grandeprovence.co.za* ↩ *5 rooms* ⎮◯⎮ *Breakfast.*

$$
B&B/INN

☒ **Résidence Klein Oliphants Hoek.** Originally built as the home of a British missionary, this lovingly restored guesthouse also once served as a school before becoming a hotel with rooms decorated with rich fabrics and luxurious finishes. **Pros:** intimate setting with peaceful surroundings; a couple of the rooms have private splash pools. **Cons:** the upstairs loft room has a sloping ceiling (so watch out if you're tall); those with allergies should know they have cats. ⑤ *Rooms from: R2300* ☒ *14 Akademie St.* ☎ *021/876–2566* ⊕ *www.kleinoliphantshoek.co.za* ↩ *8 rooms* ⎮◯⎮ *Breakfast.*

PAARL

21 km (13 miles) northwest of Franschhoek.

Paarl takes its name from the granite domes of Paarl Mountain, which looms above the town—*paarl* is Dutch for "pearl." The first farmers settled here in 1687, two years after the founding of Stellenbosch. The town has its fair share of historic homes and estates, but it lacks the charm of its distinguished neighbor simply because it's so spread out. Main Street, the town's oak-lined thoroughfare, extends some 11 km (7 miles) along the western bank of the Berg River. You can gain a good sense of the town's history on a drive along this lovely street.

GETTING HERE AND AROUND

As in the rest of the area, driving yourself is your best option in and around Paarl. Estates are spread so there is distance between them, and to really get the best out of the area you do need your own wheels.

VISITOR INFORMATION

Contacts Paarl Tourism Bureau ☒ *216 Main St.* ☎ *021/872–4842, 021/872–6737* ⊕ *www.paarlonline.com* ⊙ *Weekdays 8:30–5, weekends 10–1.*

EXPLORING

Most visitors to Paarl drive down the town's main street, take in the historic buildings, and then head off to the Cape Winelands, golf estates, and restaurants. If you have the time, check out the Afrikaanse Taalmonument (Afrikaans Language Monument) and Jan Phillips Mountain Drive. For some excellent examples of Cape Dutch, Georgian, and Victorian homes, head to Zeederberg Square, a grassy park on Main Street just past the Paarl Tourism Bureau.

Afrikaanse Taalmonument (*Afrikaans Language Monument*). Like the Voortrekker Monument in Pretoria, the concrete Afrikaanse Taalmonument, set high on a hill overlooking Paarl, holds a special place in the hearts of Afrikaners, who struggled for years to gain acceptance for their language alongside English. The rising curve of the main pillar is supposed to represent the growth and potential of Afrikaans. When it was erected in 1973, the monument was as much a gesture of political victory as a paean to the Afrikaans language. Ironically, it may become the language's memorial. Under the new South Africa, Afrikaans has become just one of 11 official languages and is gradually losing its dominance, although attempts are being made to ensure that the rich culture isn't lost. The view from the top of the hill is incredible, taking in Table Mountain, False Bay, Paarl Valley, and the various mountain ranges of the Winelands. ■ TIP→ You can buy a picnic basket at the monument's restaurant and find a pretty spot to enjoy the wonderful view; a basket costs around R210 for two people and is crammed with cold meats, salad, cheese, breads, fresh fruit, and something sweet. A short, paved walking trail leads around the hillside past impressive fynbos specimens, particularly proteas. After the N1 bridge, a sign on your right points the way to the monument. ⊠ *Afrikaanse Taalmonument Rd.* ☎ *021/863–0543* ☒ *R20* ⊘ *Daily 8–5 (monument sometimes stays open later in summer, but this varies).*

Bain's Kloof Pass Road. The Bain's Kloof Pass Road, built by engineer Andrew Geddes Bain and opened in 1853, links Wellington to Ceres and Worcester. The road (an extension of the R303 from Paarl through Wellington) winds north from Wellington, through the Hawekwa Mountains, revealing breathtaking views across the valley below. On a clear day you can see as far as the coast. The road has a good tar surface, but unlike many Western Cape passes, Bain's Kloof has not been widened much since it was built, so take your time and enjoy the views. There are places where you can park and walk down to lovely, refreshing mountain pools—great on a hot summer's day.

Jan Phillips Mountain Drive. Halfway down the hill from the Afrikaans Language Monument is a turnoff onto a dirt road and a sign for the Paarl Mountain Nature Reserve. The dirt road is Jan Phillips Mountain Drive, which runs 11 km (7 miles) along the mountainside, offering tremendous views over the valley. Along the way it passes the **Mill Water Wildflower Garden** and the starting points for several trails, including hikes up to the great granite domes of Paarl Mountain. The dirt road rejoins Main Street at the far end of Paarl.

WINERIES

TOP ATTRACTIONS

Avondale Wine. Although the farm was established as early as 1693, current owners Johnny and Ginny Grieve have done some serious reorganizing in the vineyards and built a state-of-the-art cellar, which is dug into a dry riverbed. Avondale started producing wines only in 1999, making it one of the newer kids on the block. No matter. The winery hit the ground running, and its wines win one award after another. The reds are especially good, and the intense Paarl summers result in full-bodied grapes that deliver knockout flavors. Be sure to try the Armilla Blanc de Blanc 2009, a rich wine with a balance of hazelnut bread, fresh quince, and gardenia flavors. The Grieves are also farming as biodynamically as possible, and Avondale is now registered as biodiversity-compliant by South African authorities. Great care is taken to maintain

Paarl Wine Route

Wineries here are spread far apart, so you might want to select only a couple or take a whole day to taste at leisure. Start in Paarl, home to the impressive **KWV**, with cellars covering 55 acres and a wide selection of wines.

Along R301/303. On its way to Franschhoek, the R301/303 runs past **Avondale Wine**, a relatively new farm with a state-of-the-art cellar, a gorgeous rose garden, and excellent wines.

Between R44 and R45. On your way from Franschhoek to Paarl, take a quick detour down the Simondium Road to **Backsberg** and, a bit farther, **Glen Carlou**. Backsberg has more going on than Glen Carlou, but they both have wines that are worth tasting and buying. Be sure to make time to visit Babylonstoren, just

beyond Glen Carlou, where you could easily spend a day. Continue on, and turn right on the R44. At a four-way stop, turn right onto the R101 and cross over the N1. Follow the goat signs to Suid-Agter-Paarl Road and Fairview.

Along Suid-Agter-Paarl and Noord-Agter-Paarl roads. Fairview is as famous for its goats and cheese as it is for its wines. Leave yourself plenty of time here. From Fairview, turn right onto the Suid-Agter-Paarl Road and make your way to **Landskroon,** known for full-bodied reds. Turn right on the R44 and, after about 10 km (6 miles), right onto the WR8 (Noord-Agter-Paarl Road), and then right again to **Rhebokskloof Private Cellar.** If you continue on the R44 toward Wellington, you'll pass Nelson Wine Estate (a.k.a. Nelson's Creek) on your left.

top-quality soil, and no pesticides or herbicides are used. If you're interested in the wine-making process, book an Eco Tour (R200) and visit Avondale's state-of-the-art gravity-flow cellar, constructed three stories underground. Many farms have absent owners, but the Grieve family takes a hands-on approach here. The casually dressed guy behind the wine-tasting counter is, in all likelihood, the owner. ✉ *Lustigan Rd., off R301* ☎ *021/863–1976* ⊕ *www.avondalewine.co.za* 🍷 *Tastings R50* ☉ *Mon.–Sat. 10–4, cellar tours by appointment.*

FAMILY **Fairview.** This is one of the few wineries that is good for families. Children get a kick out of seeing peacocks roaming the grounds and goats clambering up a spiral staircase into a goat tower. In fact, Fairview produces a superb line of goat cheeses and olive oil, all of which you can taste. But don't let Fairview's sideshows color your judgment about the wines. Charles Back, a member of the family that runs Backsberg, is one of the most successful and innovative winemakers in the Cape, and the estate's wines are top-drawer and often surprising. Back doesn't stick to the tried-and-true Cape varietals. The 2009 Pinotage is excellent, as is the 2013 La Beryl Blanc. The winery also makes creative use of the farm's many Rhône varieties. Perhaps it's just because the pun was irresistible, but (as claimed by the label) goats are sent into the vineyard to personally select grapes for the Goats-do-Roam, which is indeed like a young Côtes du Rhône (infuriating French winemakers). The cheese at Fairview is not to be missed. Visit the Vineyard Cheesery, the first carbon-neutral cheesery on the African continent, and taste the Roydon Camembert. If you care to linger, you can have a light meal and freshly baked bread at the Goatshed restaurant for around R80. ⊠ *WR3, off R101 (Suid-Agter-Paarl Rd.)* ☎ *021/863–2450* ⊕ *www.fairview.co.za* 🖫 *Wine and cheese tastings R25, cheese tastings R12* ⊙ *Daily 9–5.*

Spice Route. Charles Back, the owner of Fairview, has bought the estate two farms down from him in Paarl. The Spice Route produces deep-flavored wines, using mostly bush vines (untrellised vines). This practice, which is uncommon outside of South Africa, leads to fruit with great flavor intensity but lower volumes. Try the maiden vintage Grenache 2012, which has been recognized as one of the Top 100 South African Wines for 2014. The farm's flagship wine, Malabar, is produced in a separate cellar where the fruit is sorted by hand to ensure top quality. There is good reason to spend an entire day on the estate: artisan shops include Charles Bosman's charcuterie meat shop; DV Chocolates, where you can taste chocolates from six different regions of the world; and the Cape Brewing Company, which offers craft beer tasting. At the Grapperia, you can taste grappa and schnapps made on-site with pizzas and charcuterie. The Spice Route Restaurant is a great place to enjoy the estate wines with a gourmet lunch. The cuisine is traditional, with spice route influences from Europe to Asia. ⊠ *Suider-Agter-Paarl Rd., off the R44* ☎ *021/863–5200* ⊕ *www.spiceroutewines.co.za* 🖫 *Tastings R25* ⊙ *Daily 9–5.*

WORTH NOTING

FAMILY **Backsberg.** Framed by the mountains of the Simonsberg, this lovely estate is run by the Back family, well known for producing great wines of good value. Backsberg has a comprehensive range of red and white wines and a very fine brandy made from Chenin Blanc. Among the wines to look out for are Backsberg Family Reserve White 2009 and the Backsberg Family Reserve Red 2008. It also produces five kosher wines that are palatable: an unwooded Chardonnay, a Merlot, a Kiddush, a sparking MCC Brut, and a Pinotage. The restaurant does a lamb spit every lunch, so you can taste some excellent wines before digging in to a typical South African meal. The estate has self-guided cellar tours. Concerned about climate change and the environment, the Back family has put measures in place to reduce the farm's carbon footprint. They've done a good job, and Backsberg is the first carbon-neutral wine estate in South Africa. Here's hoping others will soon follow suit. ⊠ *WR1 (Simondium Rd.), between R44 and R45* ☎ *021/875–5141* ⊕ *www.backsberg.co.za* 🖫 *Tastings R15, cellar tours by appointment* ⊙ *Weekdays 8–5, Sat. 9:30–4:30, Sun. 10:30–4:30.*

Bovlei Winery. Driving down Bain's Kloof Road, as you approach the initial slopes of Bain's Kloof, look out for the Bovlei Winery, on the right. Constructed in 1907 in traditional style, the building itself is not noteworthy, but it has a vast picture window offering a stupendous view of the undulating vineyards beyond. This winery celebrated its centennial in 2007, and its wines just keep getting better. Be sure to try the Centennial range Shiraz-mourvèdre blend, which promises great things. With plenty of well-priced, good-quality wines to choose from, you likely won't go away empty-handed. ✉ *Bain's Kloof Rd., Wellington* ☎ *021/873–1567* ⊕ *www.wellingtonwines.com* 🍷 *Tastings free* ⊗ *Weekdays 9–5, Sat. 9–1.*

Glen Carlou. What comes out of Glen Carlou is rather special. The Quartzstone Chardonnay 2010 is exceptional, "The Welder" dessert wine is excellent, and the Gravel Quarry Cabernet 2006 is also remarkable. A unique feature of the estate is the Zen Fynbos Garden, a great place to relax after you've stocked up on some seriously good wines. You can always enjoy a meal at the restaurant; expect to pay around R260 for two courses. The citrus-glazed line fish is lovely in summer, and the lamb rump and beef sirloin are perfect for when the rain is pelting down outside. ✉ *WR1 (Simondium Rd.), between R44 and R45, Klapmuts* ☎ *021/875–5528* ⊕ *www.glencarlou.co.za* 🍷 *Tastings R15* ⊗ *Weekdays 8:30–5, weekends 10–3.*

KWV. Short for Ko-operatieve Wijnbouwers Vereniging (Cooperative Winegrowers' Association), KWV regulated and controlled the Cape wine industry for decades. This is no longer the case, and KWV is seeking to redefine itself as a top wine and spirit producer. KWV has won numerous awards, including Best Producer at Veritas for three years in a row. They also make some of the finest spirits, with KWV 12-year Barrel Select Brandy winning the title of Worldwide Best Brandy at the International Wine & Spirit Competition in both 2013 and 2014. KWV produces an enormous selection of excellent wines, and its cellars are some of the largest in the world, covering around 55 acres. Cellar tours here are very popular; among the highlights is the famous Cathedral Cellar, with a barrel-vaulted ceiling and giant vats carved with scenes from the history of Cape wine making. In an adjoining cellar you can see the five largest vats in the world under one roof. The tour begins with a short audiovisual presentation and ends with a tasting of some of KWV's products. ✉ *André du Toit Bldg., Kohler St.* ☎ *021/807–3911* ⊕ *www.kwv.co.za* 🍷 *Tastings, pairings, and cellar tours R25–R65* ⊗ *Mon.–Sat. 9–4:30, Sun. 10-4; English tours Mon.–Sat. at 10, 10:30, and 2:15, Sun. at 11.*

Landskroon. With a name meaning "crown of the land" in Afrikaans, this venerable estate, run by the ninth generation of the de Villiers family, produces a lovely Cabernet Sauvignon—with hints of spice and oak—that's up there with the best. Look out for the Paul de Villiers Wine Range. In particular, the 2010 Paul de Villiers Shiraz is deliciously fruity. For a little something to sip after a long, leisurely dinner, try the Port 2011—a dark, fortified wine with aromas of black prunes and tobacco. ✉ *Suid-Agter-Paarl Rd., off R44, Suider Paarl* ☎ *021/863–1039* ⊕ *www.landskroonwines.com* 🍷 *Tastings free* ⊗ *Weekdays 8–5, Sat. 9:30–1.*

Nabygelegen. Before you head up the spectacular Bain's Kloof Pass, do a quick detour to a quieter corner of the busy winelands. Situated in the heart of the Bovlei upper valley outside Wellington, Nabygelegen is known for its handcrafted wines. Their motto is "good wine takes time," and they are dedicated to producing top-quality wine with concentrated flavors. Try the Seventeen Twelve 2009, with richness of black currant and plum overlaid with smokey tannins, and the Scaramanga 2013, which has aromas of leather, black currant, and pepper. Nabygelegen's Chenin Blanc 2008 and Snow Mountain Pinot Noir 2009 were served at Queen Elizabeth II's 60th jubilee lunch, earning the winery international acclaim. The tasting room, in the old forge—remember this would have been the old wagon route out of Cape Town—offers pairings of wine and light meals, as well as coffee and cakes. ⊠ *Bovlei Division Rd., Wellington* ☎ *021/873–7534* ⊕ *www.nabygelegen.co.za* 🖾 *Tastings R10; cellar tours by appointment only* ☽ *Weekdays 10–5, Sat. 10–1.*

Rhebokskloof Private Cellar. This winery sits at the head of a shallow valley, backed by hillsides covered with vines and fynbos. It's a lovely place for lunch on a sunny day, and you can also take horseback rides through the vineyards. The Victorian Restaurant serves à la carte meals and teas on an oak-shaded terrace overlooking the gardens and mountains; in inclement weather meals are served in the Cape Dutch Restaurant, which also has a child-friendly Sunday buffet lunch. You can also order a picnic basket for two, brimming with fresh baguettes, cold meats, delicious cheeses, dips, *koeksisters* (doughnuts), and milk tart, for around R295. The Estate Chardonnay 2012 is wonderfully fresh, with a lovely balance of citrus flavors and toasty overtones. Also try the 2010 Estate Mourvèdre, a Grenache and Shiraz blend. It's a spicy wine with layers of dark fruit and savory aromas. ⊠ *WR8, Agter Paarl* ☎ *021/869–8386* ⊕ *www.rhebokskloof.co.za* 🖾 *Tastings R15, cheese and wine tastings R55, food and wine tastings R95* ☽ *Weekdays 9–5, weekends 10–3.*

WHERE TO EAT

$$$
ECLECTIC
Fodor's Choice
★

✕ **Babel.** Set on the grounds of one of the Cape's oldest Dutch farms, Babel and the Babylonstoren boutique hotel are a vision in white surrounded by lush fruit and vegetable gardens with a gorgeous backdrop of mountain views. Everything about this farm is stylish: the restaurant is in a converted cow shed, and no expense has been spared in the creation of this spectacular venue. Aiming to use as much of its own produce as possible, Babel's menu includes inventive categories; for example, the salad menu is defined by colors. The Red Salad features warm pickled beetroot, salmon gravlax, blood orange, pomegranate, and pink oyster mushrooms. Green is made from braised bok choy hearts, kiwi, fennel, and white oyster mushrooms drizzled with a blue cheese dressing. Scrumptious main courses include grilled almond-crusted line fish, and lamb cutlets with a roasted garlic sauce. Expect bold flavors and unusual combinations like poached guava with beetroot crumble, or baked Brie with olive tapenade and strawberry crisps for dessert. Ⓢ *Average main: R190* ⊠ *Klapmuts Rd.* ☎ *021/863–3852* ⊕ *www.babylonstoren.com* ⌂ *Reservations essential* ☽ *No lunch Mon. and Tues. No dinner Sun.–Thurs.*

$$$$
ECLECTIC
Fodor's Choice
★

✕ **Bosman's.** Set amid the heady opulence of the Grande Roche hotel, this elegant restaurant ranks as one of the country's finest. The level of service is extraordinary, commensurate with that of the finest European restaurants. Michelin-trained executive chef Roland Gorgosilich gives classic international cuisine an innovative spin. Once you overcome the hurdle of which menu to choose—tasting (six to eight dishes), three- or four-course set menu, or à la carte—you start with a complimentary amuse-bouche. A first course of low-roasted baby beets with goat cheese, rye bread crackers, and herb salad could precede a main course of oven-roasted beef fillet with baby cabbage, pearl onions, mashed potato, and oxtail nuggets. The dessert menu is confidently concise; expect a lavish panna cotta, parfait, or cheesecake with opulent trimmings. If you're looking to go big, try the four-course set menu, with sorbet, for R520. Oenophiles will delight in the restaurant's wine list, which runs over many pages and has garnered awards of its own. $ *Average main: R225* ⊠ *Grande Roche, Plantasie St.* ☎ *021/863–5100* ⊕ *www.granderoche.com.*

$$ ✕ **Harvest.** La Borie Wine Estate is nestled in the Paarl valley, with Paarl
SOUTH AFRICAN rock as its backdrop. Harvest, the on-site restaurant, offers elegant,
FAMILY relaxed dining for the whole family. You know you're in luck when you go to a restaurant headed up by Matthew Gordon, a fine chef who knows the business inside out. Enjoy an eclectic mix of South African cuisine on the oak-shaded terrace. Ingredients are sourced locally or grown in the restaurant's own garden. Look for free-range organic lamb, mussels, and fresh line fish. The menu also features scrumptious vegetarian options such as grilled large black mushrooms with a parsley crust and brown herb butter. The wine list includes wines from La Borie's own cellars and from KWV Wine Estate. Harvest is the winner of a Klink Award for best restaurant on a wine farm and has been voted among the top-10 most child-friendly restaurants, with a fabulous kids' menu that manages to avoid the tedious and overprocessed options so many other restaurants dish up. $ *Average main: R120* ⊠ *La Borie Wine Estate, Taillefert St., Paarl North* ☎ *021/807–3095* ⊕ *www. harvestatlaborie.co.za.*

$$ ✕ **Marc's Mediterranean Cuisine & Garden.** Chef-owner Marc Friederich is
MEDITERRANEAN a foodie with an instinctive feel for what will work. And work his res-
FAMILY taurant does: it's consistently full, consistently interesting, and always a pleasure to eat in. What to choose? There's a Lebanese mezze for starters made up of mouthwatering dips, dolmades, falafel, and warm pitas for scooping, or you could opt for Marc's fish soup with a dash of ouzo and aioli crostini. For entrées there's organic beef, paella, or free-range duck breast with a fruity salsa. Children are also well looked after—there's spaghetti with tomato sauce, a choice of burgers with fries, and vanilla ice cream and chocolate sauce as part of the deal for a very reasonable R50. Marc also serves as sommelier, so the wine list is comprehensive and he can help you with food-and-wine pairings. $ *Average main: R150* ⊠ *129 Main St.* ☎ *021/863–3980* ⊕ *www. marcsrestaurant.co.za* ⊙ *Closed Sun. and Mon.*

$$ ✕ **Terra Mare.** Owner-run Terra Mare has become a favorite with locals
ECLECTIC and tourists alike, offering not just great food, but a wonderful dining experience in a friendly and laid-back setting. Enjoy freshly prepared meals and affordable wine on the terrace overlooking the Paarl vineyards, or have a drink in the cozy dining room. The owners, Swiss-born Olivier, and Delenia, a local of Italian heritage, have fused their diverse cultural backgrounds to produce opulent food with French, Italian, Afrikaans, and German influences. Olivier and Delenia are hands-on

and have created a warm and inviting space; customers become regulars and soon become friends. As for the food, the kudu fillet and steak tartare are favorites, as is the three-mushroom risotto. For dessert how does limoncello sorbet or tiramisu sound? A good selection of wines, not limited to wines from the Paarl area, is available. ⑤ *Average main: R120* ✉ *90A Main St.* ☎ *021/863–4805* ⊘ *Closed Sun.*

WHERE TO STAY

$$$$
HOTEL
Fodor'sChoice
★
🏨 **Babylonstoren.** Set on a 500-acre working farm that is one of the Cape's oldest, Babylonstoren is a bucolic vision in white. **Pros:** option to harvest your own organic produce and enlist the help of a chef to prepare; five additional rooms in the 17th-century manor house; 8 acres of organic landscaped gardens to wander. **Cons:** in-cottage book selection dominated by Afrikaans titles. ⑤ *Rooms from: R4900* ✉ *45 Klapmuts Rd., Klapmuts* ☎ *021/863–3852* ⊕ *www.babylonstoren.com* 🛏 *6 suites, 7 cottages* ⦿| *Breakfast.*

$$$$
B&B/INN
Fodor'sChoice
★
🏨 **Bartholomeus Klip Farmhouse.** This Victorian guesthouse on a nature reserve and working farm offers luxurious accommodations and excellent food in the middle of 9,900 acres of rare renosterveld scrubland, home to the endangered geometric tortoise. **Pros:** separate house available for self-catering families; very tranquil setting close to wine farms and small towns; gobs of wildlife. **Cons:** may be a bit intimate for some, as all the rooms are in the manor house; this part of the Western Cape can get unbearably hot in summer. ⑤ *Rooms from: R6630* ✉ *Off the R44, near Bo-Hermon* ☎ *082/829–4131, 022/448–1820* ⊕ *www. bartholomeus.co.za* 🛏 *4 rooms, 1 suite, 1 self-catering house* ⊘ *Closed July* ⦿| *Multiple meal plans.*

$
B&B/INN
🏨 **De Leeuwenhof Estate.** Situated on 30 acres of farmland in the Klein Drakenstein area, De Leeuwenhof Estate promises a tranquil and intimate stay. **Pros:** exceptional service with a personal touch; a/c in all rooms. **Cons:** TV reception is poor in some rooms; children over the age of 2 are charged as adults. ⑤ *Rooms from: R1450* ✉ *Sonstraal Rd.* ☎ *021/862–1384* ⊕ *www.deleeuwenhof.co.za* 🛏 *10 rooms, 2 apartments, 4 cottages* ⦿| *Breakfast.*

$$
B&B/INN
🏨 **Diemersfontein Wine & Country Estate.** Built in the 19th century, this historic farmstead is set in a lush garden with rolling lawns and abundant roses and azalea bushes. **Pros:** lots to do, including fishing, horseback riding, wine tasting; lovely gardens; airport shuttle can be arranged. **Cons:** frequently used as wedding and conference venue so can get quite busy. ⑤ *Rooms from: R1500* ✉ *Jan van Riebeek Dr. (R301), Wellington* ☎ *021/873–2671 lodging, 021/864–5060 restaurant, 021/864–5050 winery* ⊕ *www.diemersfontein.co.za* 🛏 *30 rooms* ⦿| *Breakfast.*

$$$$
HOTEL
Fodor'sChoice
★
🏨 **Grande Roche.** Part of the Small Luxury Hotels of the World Collection, this establishment can stake a claim to being one of the best hotels in South Africa. **Pros:** estate declared a national monument in 1993; award-winning cuisine. **Cons:** not within easy walking distance of town; rarified atmosphere doesn't suit everybody. ⑤ *Rooms from: R5130* ✉ *Plantasie St.* ☎ *021/863–5100* ⊕ *www.granderoche.com* 🛏 *28 suites* ⦿| *Breakfast.*

$
B&B/INN
🏨 **Lemoenkloof Guest House.** This Victorian guesthouse on the Paarl Wine Route is run by owners Dion and Hanlie Naude, who are prepared

3

to go the extra mile to make your stay a happy one. **Pros:** walk-in guests are welcome until 11 pm; very reasonable rates and weekend specials; 10-minute drive from Pearl Valley and Boschenmeer golf courses. **Cons:** no room service. ⑤ *Rooms from: R700* ⊠ *396A Main St.* ☎ *021/872–7520, 021/872–3782* ⊕ *www.lemoenkloof.co.za* ⋐ *30 rooms* ⦿ *Breakfast.*

SPORTS AND THE OUTDOORS

BALLOONING

Wineland Ballooning. This company makes one-hour flights over the Winelands every morning from about November through April, weather permitting. The balloon holds a maximum of five passengers, and the trip costs about R3,600 per person. After the flight there's a champagne breakfast at the Grand Roche. ☎ *021/863–3192, 083/983–4687* ⊕ *www.kapinfo.com.*

GOLF

Boschenmeer Golf Club. This picturesque 18-hole golf course has stunning mountain views. The course is covered with trees and dotted with water hazards. Boschenmeer's Ben Fouchee was named PGA Teacher of the Year in South Africa in 2013. ⊠ *848 Wemmershoek Rd.* ☎ *021/863–1140, 021/863–2828 pro shop* ⊕ *www.boschenmeergolf.co.za* ⌇ *18 holes, 6368 yards, par 72.* ⌸ *R520.*

Pearl Valley Signature Golf Estate & Spa. In a breathtaking setting in the valley, the course, designed by Jack Nicklaus, has golfers in rapture. After your game you can relax at the great clubhouse, pool, or wellness center (which is also nice if some members of your party want to play while others want a bit of pampering). ⊠ *R301* ☎ *021/867–8000* ⊕ *pearlvalley.co.za* ⌇ *18 holes, 6654 yards, par 72.* ⌸ *R795.*

HORSEBACK RIDING

Wine Valley Horse Trails. Michelle Mazurkiewicz guides scenic rides around the Rhebokskloof vineyards or up into the surrounding Paarl Mountain Nature Reserve. If horses aren't your thing, you can have fun on an all-terrain vehicle. It costs R400 for one hour on a horse or all-terrain vehicle. A two-hour ride will cost you R650, and half-day wine tasting on horseback costs R950. ⊠ *Rhebokskloof wine farm, WR8, off the R44* ☎ *083/226–8735, 021/869–8687* ⊕ *www.horsetrails-sa.co.za.*

BREEDE RIVER VALLEY

The upper and central part of the catchment of the Breede River extends over a large area. It's a beautiful part of the country, with a combination of fantastic mountain scenery, fabulous fynbos, pretty, bucolic farmlands, and small towns. A short drive over any one of the scenic mountain passes is sure to bring you into a secluded valley resplendent with the greens of spring, the grape-laden vines of summer, the myriad colors of autumn, or the snowcapped peaks and crisp misty mornings of winter.

A natural climatic combination of comparatively mild but wet winters followed by long, warm summers makes this area perfectly suited for the cultivation of deciduous fruit, especially viticulture. In the summer the intense sunshine allows the wine and table grapes to develop rich ruby colors. Virtually deprived of rain in summer, the vines nurture their precious crop, irrigated from the meandering Breede River and the huge Brandvlei dam, near Worcester.

GETTING HERE AND AROUND

Driving is definitely the way to go when exploring the Breede River valley, as it will give you the flexibility you need to discover interesting back roads or to linger at a lovely lunch spot. The roads in the Western Cape are generally good. Although you might have to navigate some dirt roads, they tend to be graded regularly and are in fine condition.

The major car-rental agencies have offices in some of the smaller towns, but it's best to deal with the Cape Town offices. An alternative is to pick up a car in Stellenbosch. ⇨ *For car-rental agencies, see the Cape Winelands, above.*

The best way to get to this area is to take the N1 from Cape Town past Paarl. You can either go through the Huguenot toll tunnel (around R29 per vehicle) or over the spectacular Bain's Kloof mountain pass to Worcester. From there take the R60 to Robertson and Montagu.

Greyhound, Intercape Mainliner, and Translux provide daily bus service throughout most of the Western Cape, stopping at bigger towns such as Worcester and Robertson on their way upcountry. Although each company's timetable varies, most have approximately four trips a day from Cape Town. From Cape Town it takes about 1½ hours to Worcester and about 2 hours to Robertson. A one-way trip to Worcester costs around R325, and the drop-off spot is a service station on the side of the N1. It is a little way out of town, but shuttle buses will take you into town for a small fee. ⇨ *For detailed information about traveling by bus, see Bus Travel in Travel Smart.*

TOURS

Instead of big tour companies, there are a couple of individual guides operating in Breede River towns. Because the guides are usually from the area, they provide rare insights about the towns. Your best bet is to ask at local tourism offices for names and numbers. If you wish to hike in the Montagu Mountain Reserve, where trails are not well marked, go with someone familiar with the area; ask at the local tourism office for names of people to hike with. There's a strenuous hike of just over 15 km (9 miles) and an easier one of just over 11 km (7 miles). Best times to go are in spring or autumn, as it can get very hot in summer.

TULBAGH

60 km (37 miles) north of Paarl.

Founded in 1743, the town of Tulbagh is nestled in a secluded valley bound by the Witzenberg and Groot Winterhoek mountains. A devastating earthquake in September 1969 shook the city and destroyed many of the original facades of the historic town. After this disaster, well-known South African architect Gawie Fagan—together with his wife, Gwen—helped rebuild the buildings in the style of an 1860s hamlet, and the result is a photographer's paradise. The 32 buildings that make up Church Street were all declared national monuments and constitute the largest concentration of national monuments in one street in South Africa. It's not all white gables and brass doorknobs, however. The workaday side of town is quite dreary, and unemployment is rife.

GETTING HERE AND AROUND

You won't be able to experience the beauty of this area unless you can explore on your own terms, so be sure to rent a car. If you want to travel on the back routes, do some asking around first—you might need a 4x4 in winter after heavy rains, when the gravel roads become very slippery.

VISITOR INFORMATION

Contacts Tulbagh Tourism ⊠ *4 Church St.* ☎ *023/230–1375* ⊕ *www. tulbaghtourism.co.za* ⊙ *Weekdays 9–5, weekends 10–3.*

EXPLORING

Church Street. Much of the town is unlovely, having simply been rebuilt, often prefab style, on old foundations, but the real attraction of Tulbagh is Church Street, parallel to the main Van der Stel Street, where each of the 32 buildings was restored to its original form and subsequently declared a national monument.

Oude Drostdy Museum. Around 4 km (2.5 miles) out of town, set on high ground commensurate with its status, is the majestic Oude Drostdy Museum. Built by architect Louis Thibault in 1804, the structure was badly damaged by fire in 1934 and later by the 1969 quake, but it has been carefully restored and is a fine example of neoclassical architecture. The building now houses an impressive collection of antique furniture and artifacts. Look for the gramophone collection and the Dutch grandfather clock that has a picture of Amsterdam harbor painted on its face. As the original magistrate's house, the Drostdy had a cellar that served as the local jail; it's now used by Drostdy-Hof as a wine cellar. Linger and taste some of their flavorful and fruity wines. ⊠ *Winterhoek Rd.* ☎ *023/230–0203* 🎟 *Museum R10, museum and wine tasting R20* ⊙ *Weekdays 10–5, Sat. 10–2.*

Oude Kerk (*Old Church*). The Oude Kerk museum stands at the entrance to Church Street and is the logical departure point for a self-guided tour of the area, which is well marked. The church has been extensively restored and has an interesting collection of artifacts from the area, including carvings made by Boer prisoners of war. A ticket includes admission to another two buildings on Church Street, which operate as annexes of the main museum. These show a practical history of events before, during, and after the quake. The buildings have been painstakingly reconstructed. ⊠ *21 Church St.* ☎ *023/230–1041* 🎟 *R15* ⊙ *Weekdays 9–5, Sat. 10–3, Sun. 11–3.*

Twee Jonge Gezellen. If you stand in front of the church on Van der Stel Street, you will see a wine barrel indicating the road to Twee Jonge Gezellen estate, which is about 8 km (5 miles) from town. The House of Krone at Twee Jonge Gezellen specializes in the production of MCC sparkling wine. One of the finest and oldest wineries in the area, it's best known for its fantastic Cap Classique—Krone Borealis Brut. But many Capetonians are more familiar with the tried and trusted TJ39, an easily drinkable, well-priced blend of *weisser* (white) Riesling, Chardonnay,

Chenin Blanc, and Sauvignon Blanc that has been making a regular appearance on local tables for years. The Krone Engeltjipipi (referring to—er—a certain body waste of little angels) is a blend made from grapes naturally infected with botrytis (a type of fungus) and considered a gift from the cherubs. The grapes are harvested by hand over a number of nights at the end of the season. ☒ *Twee Jonge Gezellen Rd.* ☎ *023/230–0680* ⊕ *www.houseofkrone.co.za* 🖙 *Tastings free* ☾ *Weekdays 10–4, Sat. 10–2.*

Waverley Hills Estate. If you're looking for a day trip, Waverley Hills Estate is a 20-minute drive from Tulbagh. This 320-acre estate is known for its organic wines with robust fynbos characteristics. As you drive onto the farm, keep a lookout for the ducks that do "snail patrol" through the vineyards. Waverley Hills also produces a range of organic olive products, which can be sampled in the tasting room. The restaurant, with panoramic views of the valley, serves South African–inspired cuisine such as smoked snoek pâté, olive tapenade, black mussels, and pork belly with sweet chili jam. They also offer chicken, hot dogs, and pizza for the little ones. A five-course organic food-and-wine pairing experience costs about R300 per person for either lunch or dinner (reservations essential). The restaurant is open for breakfast, lunch, and dinner (twice a week), and picnic baskets can be ordered in advance. Given the dining options on-site, this makes for a great day. ☒ *Off the R46, between Tulbagh and Ceres, Wolseley* ☎ *023/231–0002* ⊕ *www. waverleyhills.co.za* ☾ *Closed Mon. No dinner Sat.–Tues. and Thurs.*

WHERE TO EAT

$ × **Olive Terrace Bistro.** At the Tulbagh Hotel, the Olive Terrace Bistro
SOUTH AFRICAN serves local wines and tasty food on a pretty terrace, shaded by a white karee tree for warm summer days, and in a cozy indoor dining area with a view of the snow-covered mountains. The à la carte menu features South African dishes made with locally sourced fresh produce. Breads, jams, and chutneys are homemade, and all eggs are free-range. Try the springbok carpaccio on scrambled eggs for breakfast; a hummus, sun-dried tomato, and goat cheese wrap for lunch; and the game fillet with red-wine-and-cranberry reduction for dinner. Vegetarian options include veggie burgers, vegetarian chow mein, and vegan bobotie; there is also a children's menu. ⑤ *Average main: R80* ☒ *Tulbagh Hotel, 22 Van der Stel St.* ☎ *023/230–0071* ⊕ *www.tulbaghhotel.co.za/restaurant.*

$$ × **Readers.** The historic residence of the former church reader (lay-
ECLECTIC person trained to preach and lead worship) makes a cozy setting for this restaurant with consistently high-quality food and service. Carol Collins's innovative fare offers sophisticated contrasts, although she keeps presentation simple and appetizing. Her small seasonal menu changes daily. Dinner could start with a deep-fried whole onion with sweet chili sauce, or kudu carpaccio with fresh asparagus and hollandaise sauce. If the delicious wildebeest with gooseberry and amarula sauce is on the menu, do not miss out! The flavors of the popular ice-cream trio change often, but you can expect coconut and sesame or ginger and rooibos tea, or even curry and balsamic vinegar flavors. The carefully chosen and well-priced wine list reflects regional labels. ⑤ *Average main: R105* ☒ *12 Church St.* ☎ *023/230–0087, 082/894–0932*

⊕ *www.readersrestaurant.co.za* ⊗ *Wed.–Mon. 9 am–9:30 pm* ⊗ *Closed Tues. Closed Aug.*

WHERE TO STAY

$$
B&B/INN

🔲 **Rijk's Country House.** This top-notch lodge is on the outskirts of the village, on a ridge overlooking a lake where you can enjoy sweeping views of the surrounding mountains. **Pros:** tranquil and remote location; fine dining on your doorstep; you can participate in night harvesting during summer. **Cons:** quite far from bigger towns; pool, dam, and river not fenced, so kids need to be water safe. ⑤ *Rooms from: R1600* ⊠ *Van Der Stel Extension, Winterhoek Rd.* ☎ *023/230–1006* ⊕ *www. rijkscountryhouse.co.za* ⊅ *12 suites, 3 cottages* ◯| *Breakfast.*

$
B&B/INN

🔲 **Tulbagh Country Guest House.** This 200-year-old manor house, on historic Church Street, offers authentic Cape Dutch living with modern amenities. **Pros:** in the heart of Tulbagh; stunning manor house; swimming pool. **Cons:** the guesthouse is small, so you will be aware of other guests. ⑤ *Rooms from: R1100* ⊠ *24 Church St.* ☎ *023/230–1171* ⊕ *www.cdq.co.za* ⊅ *6 rooms* ◯| *Breakfast.*

WORCESTER

45 km (28 miles) southeast of Tulbagh; 50 km (31 miles) east of Paarl.

You're unlikely to linger in Worcester, by far the largest town in the Breede River valley. It's often termed the region's capital by locals, and with good cause. Much of the town's burgeoning commerce and industry is connected to agriculture—viticulture, in particular. But the town itself is unexciting and serves as a pit stop for prettier inland destinations. Pause to visit the Karoo National Botanical Garden or pop in at the Worcester Museum.

GETTING HERE AND AROUND

Worcester is east of Paarl on the N1, on the other side of the du Toits Kloof Pass or tunnel, an 80-minute drive from Cape Town. Renting a car is the only way to get around.

VISITOR INFORMATION

Contacts Worcester Tourism Bureau ⊠ *23 Baring St.* ☎ *023/348–2795* ⊕ *www.worcester.org.za* ⊗ *Weekdays 7:45–4:30.*

EXPLORING

Karoo National Botanical Garden. With several hundred species of indigenous flora, including succulents, aloes, and trees, the Karoo National Botanical Garden has been billed as one of the most important such collections in the world. The Braille Garden is geared toward the visually impaired. If you phone ahead, you can arrange to watch a slide show and take a guided walk through the gardens and the collection houses for around R85 per person. Unfortunately, they won't do the tour unless there are at least seven people. The garden lies on the opposite side of the N1 highway from the town of Worcester but is easy to find if you follow the signs eastward from the last set of traffic lights on High Street. Follow the road from the entrance to the garden to the main parking area, the starting point of three clearly marked walks. ⊠ *Roux Rd.* ☎ *023/347–0785* ⊠ *Aug.–Oct. R14, Nov.–July free* ⊗ *Daily 7–6.*

FAMILY **Worcester Museum.** A welcome change from dusty artifacts in glass cases, this fascinating museum is actually a collection of original buildings from the area that have been re-erected around a working farmyard. After a narrated slide show, venture into the farmyard and watch the museum staff, intent on keeping traditional skills alive, as they bake bread, twist tobacco, make horseshoes in a smithy, and distill *witblits* (directly translated it means "white lightning" because of the astonishing effect it has on you). The museum also has a shop where you can buy produce from the farmyard. They run bread-baking demonstrations, and you can do some coffee and witblits tastings as well. Considering that some witblits has an alcohol content of almost 80%, you might want to do that tasting first and then sober up with the coffee afterward. ✉ *Kleinplasie Agricultural Showgrounds, Traub St.* ☎ *023/342–2226* ⊕ *www.worcestermuseum.org.za* 🎫 *R15* ⏱ *Weekdays 9–4:30, Sat. 8–1.*

SPORTS AND THE OUTDOORS
RAFTING AND CANOEING
The Breede River has tiny rapids near Worcester, where it twists and turns between clumps of *palmiet* (river reeds) and overgrown banks.

River Rafters. Using two-person inflatables, River Rafters offers a one-day trip for R655 (R545 for children under 18). If you want to do more than just float down the river, they can add in some wine tasting with wines from the valley and mountain biking for an extra fee. ☎ *021/975–9727* ⊕ *www.riverrafters.co.za.*

Wildthing Adventures. Now part of the well-established Felix Unite river-rafting company, Wildthing Adventures runs river trips down the Breede. Enjoy a two-night stay at bungalows near the river and head out each day to negotiate some rapids or drift lazily along, depending on the water levels. An all-inclusive two-day trip will cost around R1,500 (R900 for children under 12). Check their website, as prices change regularly. ☎ *087/354–0578* ⊕ *www.wildthing.co.za.*

ROBERTSON

48 km (30 miles) southeast of Worcester.

Robertson was founded primarily to service the surrounding farms, and it retains its agricultural and industrial character. The town largely lives up to its mantra of "small town, big heart"—the townsfolk are welcoming and friendly, which makes up for the lack of action. Some effort has been made to beautify the town with tree-lined roads, and the town comes alive each year during two festivals: the Wacky Wine Weekend (⊕ *www.wackywineweekend.com*) in June and the Robertson Slow festival in August, which will also give you an insight into farming life. If, however, you're on your way to McGregor or Montagu, don't be in too much of a rush. There are some excellent—and underrated—wine farms in the area.

GETTING HERE AND AROUND
Robertson is less than a 30-minute drive from Worcester. Renting a car is the only way to get around in a reasonable amount of time.

VISITOR INFORMATION

Contacts Robertson Tourism Bureau ⊠ *2 Reitz St.* ☎ *023/626–4437* ⊕ *www.robertsonr62.com* ⊗ *Weekdays 8–5, Sat. 9–2, Sun. 10–2.*

EXPLORING

Graham Beck Wines. Who needs French Champagne when you have top-class South African MCC at very affordable prices? The Robertson cellar of Graham Beck Wines, on the road between Worcester and Robertson, produces some very sophisticated wines, and winemaker Pieter Ferreira is known as Mr. Bubbles for his wonderful sparkling wines. The iconic Cap Classique flagship, Cuvée Clive, is produced with Chardonnay grapes from the Robertson estate and with Pinot Noir fruit from the Graham Beck Stellenbosch estate. It is the undisputed favorite in the Cap Classique range. The Rhona Muscadel (named after Graham Beck's wife) has won numerous John Platter Wine Guide awards. It's a lightly perfumed wine with delicious honey undertones and great aging potential. When it comes to reds, don't miss out on the Ridge Syrah, perfect with flavorsome meaty dishes. You can taste a couple of wines for free, or pay to taste specific labels. The other wine farm in the Graham Beck stable is the super-stylish Steenberg estate in Constantia, Cape Town. ⊠ *R60, about 10 km (6 miles) northwest of Robertson* ☎ *023/626–1214* ⊕ *www.grahambeckwines.com* ⊠ *Tastings free–R75* ⊗ *Weekdays 9–5, weekends 10–4, cellar tours by appointment.*

Rooiberg Winery. Capetonians in the know have long considered Rooiberg Winery, between Worcester and Robertson, one of the best value-for-the-money wineries in the area. The red Muscadel is reputedly one of the best in the world, and the Rooiberg port, Shiraz, and Merlot are all award winners for good reason. ■**TIP→ The Bodega de Vinho deli serves light lunches and delectable pastries, making this a good place to stop for something to eat.** ⊠ *R60, about 10 km (6 miles) northwest of Robertson* ☎ *023/626–1663* ⊕ *www.rooiberg.co.za* ⊠ *Tastings free* ⊗ *Weekdays 9–5:30, Sat. 9–4.*

Springfield Estate. Abrie Bruwer, winemaker and viticulturist at Springfield Estate, has a fan club, and for good reason. Quality is assured, and if the wine doesn't meet Bruwer's stringent standards, it isn't released. Although the Cabernet has its loyal following, this innovative estate is best known for its unusual approach to white wines, especially Chardonnay. The Méthode Ancienne Chardonnay 2009 is made in the original Burgundy style, a technique that uses wild yeast and no fining/filtration. It has tropical fruit flavors, layered with lime and cream. The creamy Wild Yeast Chardonnay 2011, with its all-natural fermentation, is an unwooded version of the above and comes highly recommended. Another great white is the 2013 Special Cuvée. It originates from the estate's prime Sauvignon Blanc vineyard and has notes of passion fruit and nettle. ⊠ *R317, to Bonnievale* ☎ *023/626–3661* ⊕ *www.springfieldestate.com* ⊠ *Tastings free* ⊗ *Weekdays 8–5, Sat. 9–4; tours by appointment.*

FAMILY **Van Loveren Winery.** This winery between Robertson and Bonnievale produces around 40 wines, so there's something to suit everybody's palate. The 2011 Van Loveren Blanc de Noir Red Muscadel Blush and 2011

Van Loveren Neil's Pick Colombar have both won Veritas awards. In addition to sampling the extensive wines, be sure to visit the unusual grounds of this family-owned and family-run farm. An established garden of indigenous and exotic plants and trees surrounds a water fountain that supplies the entire farm. Weather permitting, instead of visiting the usual tasting room, sit out under the trees and have the various wines brought to you. It's very relaxed and friendly, and you may feel like part of the family before you know it. The tasting room offers seven different tastings, including cheese and wine, chocolate and wine, and charcuterie and wine. There are even nonalcoholic tastings and a pairing for kids. As a broad-based black economic empowerment (BBBEE) deal, De Goree farm, which is 52% worker owned, signed a long-term grape-supply contract with Van Loveren Private Cellar. The farm has been profitable ever since, and Van Loveren Winery takes great pride in their involvement in this project. ⌧ *Off R317* ✛ *15 km (9 miles) southeast of Robertson* ☎ *023/615–1505* ⊕ *www.vanloveren.co.za* ✉ *Tastings free–R75* ☉ *Weekdays 8:30–5, Sat. 9:30–3:30, Sun. 11–2:30.*

WHERE TO EAT

$$ ╳ **Fraai Uitzicht.** In a deeply rural setting between Robertson and Ashton,
ECLECTIC this 200-year-old fruit and wine farm is home to a rustic restaurant where the menu consists of country-style cuisine made with seasonal vegetables and fresh herbs from the garden. You might start with a sage risotto with crispy parma ham or lightly smoked springbok carpaccio dressed with lemon juice and olive oil. Main courses might include seared salmon trout fillet with Asian-inspired flavors of soy, ginger, and sesame, served with jasmine rice. Desserts are as admirable, their sauces as stellar as those of the savory variety. Try the "dream of Africa," a freshly baked fondant of Belgian chocolate served with vanilla yogurt cream and Merlot syrup. The wine list does not disappoint, presenting a selection of the Robertson Valley's best, augmented with French Champagne. Plan ahead, as open hours are limited. ⑤ *Average main: R125* ⌧ *Off the R60, Klaas Voogds East* ☎ *023/626–6156* ⊕ *www. fraaiuitzicht.com* ⌲ *Reservations essential* ☉ *Closed to nonguests May–Sept. No lunch Mon.–Sat. No dinner Mon. and Tues.*

EN ROUTE On the R60 out of Robertson you can either take the clearly marked turnoff to McGregor, which snakes between vineyards and farms—a picture of bucolic charm—or continue on toward Montagu on the R62. Before reaching the latter, you'll pass through the unlovely agricultural town of Ashton. Keep left (don't turn off to Swellendam), and enter the short but spectacular **Cogman's Kloof Pass.** On either side of the pass, which runs in a river gorge, you can see the magnificent fold mountains, which are ultimately the source for Montagu's hot springs.

MCGREGOR

20 km (12 miles) south of Robertson.

Saved from development as a result of a planned mountain pass that never materialized, McGregor is the epitome of the sleepy country hollow, tucked away between the mountains, and is one of the best-preserved examples of a 19th-century Cape village. As you approach

McGregor from Robertson, farmsteads give way to small cottages with distinctive red-painted doors and window frames. McGregor Wines, on the left, heralds your entry into the town with its thatch cottages in vernacular architecture.

McGregor has become popular with artists who have settled here permanently and with busy executives from Cape Town intent on getting away from it all. Frankly, this is an ideal place to do absolutely nothing, but you can take a leisurely stroll through the fynbos, watch birds from one of several blinds on the Heron Walk, or follow one of the hiking or mountain-bike trails if you are feeling more energetic. There is a great hiking trail across the Riviersonderend Mountains to Greyton.

GETTING HERE AND AROUND
McGregor is a 10- to 15-minute drive from Robertson.

EXPLORING

FAMILY   **Esletjiesrus Donkey Sanctuary.** About 15 km (9½ miles) outside Robertson on the road to the village of McGregor, Esletjiesrus Donkey Sanctuary provides a place of safety for neglected and abused donkeys and is a great place to visit with kids. They can meet the residents while you relax at the restaurant, which serves teas and light lunches. ⊠ *Main Rd.* ☎ *023/625–1593* ⊕ *www.donkeysanctuary.co.za* ☉ *Thurs.–Sun. 10–4.*

McGregor Wines. An unpretentious and popular attraction, McGregor Wines makes surprisingly inexpensive wines, considering their quality. Try the 2014 unwooded Chardonnay; previous vintages won Veritas Gold awards, and this one is also a cracker. Their fortified wines are perfect for sipping near a log fire in winter. The white Muscadel and the Cape ruby port are very different, but both are delicious. The off-dry Colombar gets rave reviews year after year. ⊠ *Main Rd.* ☎ *023/625–1741* ⊕ *www.mcgregorwinery.co.za* ☒ *Tastings free* ☉ *Weekdays 8–5, Sat. 9–1; cellar tours by appointment.*

WHERE TO STAY

$ ⊞ **Green Gables Country Inn.** In the manor house that used to serve the
B&B/INN   mill, Green Gables is a good place to escape; it's a family-run affair, and the Meyers are proud of their hospitality and food. **Pros:** amazing setting; good food; you'll soon feel part of the village; pool. **Cons:** limited accommodation; not the place if you're wanting anonymity. ⑤ *Rooms from: R800* ⊠ *Smith and Mill Sts.* ☎ *023/625–1626* ⊕ *www.greengablescountryinn.co.za* ☞ *8 rooms* ▭ *No credit cards* ⑪ *Breakfast.*

SPORTS AND THE OUTDOORS

HIKING

Vrolijkheid Nature Reserve. The 19-km (12-mile) Rooikat Trail through the Vrolijkheid Nature Reserve takes about eight hours to complete. It's a strenuous, circular route winding up into the Eldandsberg Mountains, and an early start is recommended. There are two self-catering cottages available for overnight visitors. They each accommodate a maximum of four people and are fully equipped. The cottages cost around R650 per night in low season and around R870 during high season. There is also basic self-catering accommodation at the reserve—eight *rondavels* (simple round huts) sleep four people each. There's a shared ablution block with showers and toilets. You need to get a permit (around R40 per adult and R20 per child under 12 years) at the entrance of the reserve. It's based on the honor system, and you put your money in a box on entry. If you don't want to hike, there are two bird blinds and a mountain-bike trail. ⊠ *5 km (3 miles) outside McGregor* ☏ *023/625–1621.*

MONTAGU

29 km (18 miles) northeast of Robertson.

Montagu bills itself as "the Gateway to the Little Karoo," and its picturesque streets lined with Cape Victorian architecture lend this some credence. Today the town's main attraction is its natural hot springs, and many of the Victorian houses have been transformed into B&Bs and guesthouses. You know you're in a special place when farmers drop off their produce at the Honesty Shop (an unmanned shop that operates on the honor system) and buyers leave money for what they owe.

There are a number of resorts where you can stay and "partake of the waters."

GETTING HERE AND AROUND
Montagu is a 20-minute drive from Robertson.

VISITOR INFORMATION
Contacts Montagu/Ashton Tourism Bureau ⊠ *24 Bath St.* ☏ *023/614–2471* ⊕ *www.montagu-ashton.info* ⊗ *Weekdays 8–6, Sat. 9–5, Sun. 9:30-5.*

EXPLORING
FAMILY **Avalon Springs.** Popular Avalon Springs, the only resort open to day visitors, is not the most stylish, and the architecture leaves a lot to be desired. But if you look beyond this and the numerous signs carrying stern warnings and instructions, you'll get good insight into South African life and culture, as people float and splash around in the various pools. If you're not staying at the resort, you can rent bikes from the village (at around R25 an hour) and cycle to the springs, where you can spend a few hours before heading home again. ⊠ *Uitvlucht St., 3 km (2 miles) outside Montagu* ☏ *023/614–1150* ⊕ *www.avalonsprings.co.za* ⊠ *Weekdays R40, weekends R50* ⊗ *Daily 8 am–10 pm.*

FAMILY **Langeberg Tractor Ride.** The popular three-hour Langeberg Tractor Ride takes you to the summit of the Langeberg (Long Mountain) and back. The tractor winds up some tortuously twisted paths, revealing magnificent views of the area's peaks and valleys. After a short stop at the summit, a similarly harrowing descent follows, but you won't be disappointed by the views or the driver's chirpy banter. If you're here in spring or summer when the flowers are in bloom, you might even get to pick some gorgeous proteas on the way down. Following your trip, you can enjoy a delicious lunch of *potjiekos* (traditional stew cooked over a fire in a single cast-iron pot). Reservations are essential. ⊠ *Protea Farm, R318* ☏ *023/614–2471* ⊠ *R220 for tractor ride and lunch* ⊗ *Wed. and Sat. at 10 and 2.*

WHERE TO STAY

$ 🖼 **7 Church Street.** In the heart of the village sits this guesthouse in a lov-
B&B/INN   ingly restored Victorian home; each room is individually and stylishly
decorated with hand-embroidered cotton percale linens. **Pros:** peaceful
and secluded location; within easy walking distance of the hot springs.
Cons: young kids "by appointment only"; may be too quiet for some.
⑤ *Rooms from: R1200* ✉ *7 Church St.* ☎ *023/614–1186, 084/507–*
8941 ⊕ *www.7churchstreet.co.za* ⤶ *5 suites* ⦿| *Breakfast.*

$$ 🖼 **Montagu Country Hotel.** This salmon-color hotel was built in Victorian
HOTEL   times but was extensively remodeled in the early 1930s; the present
owner, Gert Lubbe, highlights its many art deco features and collects
furniture and artifacts from this era to complement the interior. **Pros:**
on-site spa and restaurant; centrally located; spacious luxury rooms.
Cons: Sundays very quiet generally; avoid if you're not a fan of art deco.
⑤ *Rooms from: R1600* ✉ *27 Bath St.* ☎ *023/614–3125, 082/899–3670*
⊕ *www.montagucountryhotel.co.za* ⤶ *34 rooms* ⦿| *Breakfast.*

THE OVERBERG

Overberg, Afrikaans for "over the mountains," is an apt name for this
remote but beautiful region at the bottom of the continent, separated
from the rest of the Cape by mountains. Before 19th-century engineers
blasted a route over the Hottentots Holland mountain range, the Over-
berg developed in comparative isolation. To this day it possesses a wild
emptiness far removed from the settled valleys of the Cape Winelands.

It's a land of immense contrasts, and if you're planning a trip along the
Garden Route, you would be well advised to add the Overberg to your
itinerary. The coastal drive from Gordon's Bay to Hermanus unfolds
a panorama of deserted beaches, pounding surf, and fractured granite
mountains. Once you pass Hermanus and head out onto the windswept
plains leading to Cape Agulhas, you have to search harder for the Over-
berg's riches. Towns are few and far between, and the countryside is an
expanse of wheat fields, sheep pastures, and creaking windmills. The
occasional reward of the drive is a coastline of sublime beauty. Dunes
and unspoiled beaches extend for miles. Currently no roads run parallel
to the ocean along this stretch, and you must repeatedly divert inland
before heading to another part of the coast.

Unfortunately, the ocean's bounty has been the undoing of communi-
ties along this coastline. Perlemoen (abalone) poaching is an enormous
problem. These sea mollusks are being illegally poached faster than
they can reproduce and are then shipped to the East, where they are
considered a powerful aphrodisiac. Violent Western Cape gangs are
involved in perlemoen trafficking, and children as young as 11 are used
as runners in exchange for drugs.

Naturally, the coast also has plenty of good on tap. Hermanus is one
of the best places in South Africa for land-based whale-watching dur-
ing the annual migration of Southern Right whales between June and
November. Spring is also the best time to see the Overberg's wildflow-
ers, although the region's profusion of coastal and montane fynbos is

beautiful year-round. The raw, rugged beauty of Africa's southernmost coastline can be found at De Hoop Nature Reserve. The Whale Trail, a five-day hike mapped out through De Hoop, might just oust the Garden Route's Otter Trail as South Africa's most popular. In fact, walking is one of the Overberg's major attractions, and almost every town and nature reserve offers a host of trails.

The upper part of the Overberg, north of the N2 highway, is more like the Cape Winelands, with 18th- and 19th-century towns sheltered in the lee of rocky mountains. Here the draws are apple orchards, inns, and hiking trails that wind through the mountains. The historic towns of Swellendam and Greyton are good places to spend a night before moving on to your next destination. Stanford, a tiny hamlet just outside of Hermanus, is also a lovely place to stay if you want to avoid the crowds that clog the streets of Hermanus on holidays.

3

Touring the whole area would take three to four days, but you could easily spend a week in the Overberg. For a shorter trip, focus on the splendors of the coastal route from Gordon's Bay to Hermanus, and then head north toward Greyton and Swellendam.

GETTING HERE AND AROUND
Driving yourself is undoubtedly the best way to appreciate this lovely and diverse area. The roads here are generally good. They are sign-posted, and major routes are paved. For the most part, you'll come across gravel roads only around Elim and Napier and from Swellendam to Malgas, and they may be a bit rutted and bumpy. A two-wheel-drive vehicle is fine, but take it easy if it's been raining, as gravel roads can get slippery. You'll need a 4x4 only if you're planning to tackle some of the more remote back roads or want to do a 4x4 route.

The major car-rental agencies have offices in the bigger towns, such as Hermanus and Swellendam. However, it's best to deal with the Cape Town offices; you'll probably want to pick up a car at the airport anyway. ⇨ *For car-rental agencies, see the Cape Winelands.*

The Overberg stretches over an enormous area, so you need to decide where you're heading before planning your route. If you want to enjoy the beauty of the coast, then take the N2 from Cape Town, but, instead of heading up Sir Lowry's Pass, turn off to Gordon's Bay and follow the R44, also known as Clarence Drive, along the scenic route. Just after Kleinmond the road becomes the R41 and turns inland to bypass the Bot River lagoon. It becomes the R43 as it makes its way toward Hermanus. If you want to explore inland, however, take the N2 over Sir Lowry's Pass and past Caledon and Swellendam. To get to the pretty hamlet of Greyton, take the R406 to your left just before Caledon.

Intercape Mainliner, Greyhound, and Translux have daily bus service throughout most of the Western Cape, especially to the bigger towns on the N2. Swellendam is a major hub and a good transit point, but to enjoy smaller towns such as Greyton or those along the coast, you'll need your own transportation. ⇨ *For more information about traveling by bus, see Bus Travel in Travel Smart.*

SAFETY AND PRECAUTIONS

Keep in mind that on Sunday afternoons and in early evenings traffic returning to the city via Sir Lowry's Pass can be very congested. Expect delays as you enter Somerset West, and be very careful if it is misty (which it often is on the pass), as this stretch of road sees numerous accidents each year. Leaving Cape Town on a Friday afternoon can also take time, so try to leave by lunchtime to avoid traffic jams.

TOURS

A number of individuals and small companies offer customized tours. A day trip, which should cost R1,850 per person per day (excluding transport, accommodation, and meals), could involve an excursion to De Hoop Nature Reserve, with plenty of time to admire the birds, fynbos, and whales; a ride on the ferry at Malgas; and time at Bontebok National Park. Or, you could start in Swellendam and then head over picturesque Tradouw Pass through the spectacular Cape Fold Mountains to Barrydale, where you could do some wine tasting before heading on to Robertson. Other tours concentrate on the historic fishing village of Arniston (Waenhuiskrans), Bredasdorp, and Elim.

Louis Willemse. Ex-pilot and navy man Louis Willemse is an experienced and accredited nature and culture guide, who can offer you a varied day tour. Louis's passion, apart from the Overberg, is Namaqualand and the Richtersveld— not just in the flower season but all year round. He can tell you all about the survival strategies of the desert flora and fauna, the geology of the area, and the night skies. If he can't help you out, he'll refer you to other specialists in the area. ☎ 028/423–3317 ✎ louisfieldguide@kingsley.co.za.

Stephen Smuts. A distant relative of the famous South African prime minister General Jan Smuts, Stephen Smuts is passionate about fynbos and will be able to give you an insiders' guide to the amazing flora of the area. He owns a private nature reserve, and you can organize a day walk with him as well. ☎ 028/423–3049, 076/972–0450.

Wilson Salukazana. A former Hermanus whale crier, Wilson Salukazana now conducts whale-watching boat tours. His experience as whale crier—one who stands watch and raises the alarm when whales are in sight—means he can spot a Southern Right whale from miles away. Expect to pay R650 per person. When the whales aren't blowing in the bay, he conducts township tours. On a guided walk through the nearby township of Zwelihle, you learn a bit about the settlement's history, visit missionary churches, see handmade crafts, and hear gospel singing. The tour is an hour and a half and costs R350 per person. ✉ Hermanus ☎ 073/214–6949, 084/509–6044 ✎ ubuntutours@telkomsa.net.

Contacts Overberg Tourism ✉ 22 Plein St., Caledon ☎ 028/214–3370 ⊕ www.overberg.co.za.

EN ROUTE Gordon's Bay, 70 km (43½ miles) southeast of Cape Town, is built on the steep mountain slopes of the Hottentots Holland Mountains overlooking the vast expanse of False Bay. You can often see whales and their calves in the bay in October and November. This is a good point to start on the fantastic coastal route known as **Clarence Drive** (R44), one of the country's most scenic drives, particularly if you take the time to follow some of the dirt roads leading down to the sea from the highway. There are numerous paths down to the seashore from the road between Gordon's Bay and Rooiels. It's worth walking down to watch the waves pounding the rocky coast, but take care. If there are no other people around and the waves are quite big, stay a few yards back from the water, as this section of coast is notorious for rogue waves in certain swell and wind conditions. Note the many crosses on the side of the road—each one denotes somebody who has been swept off the rocks and drowned at sea.

The road passes the tiny settlement of **Rooiels** (pronounced *roy*-else), then cuts inland for a couple of miles. A turnoff leads to **Pringle Bay,** a collection of vacation homes sprinkled across the fynbos. The village has little to offer other than a beautiful wide beach (check out the sign warning of quicksand). If you continue through Pringle Bay, the tar road soon gives way to a gravel road, now closed by shifting sand dunes, that used to lead to Betty's Bay (you now have to backtrack and take the inland route to get to Betty's Bay).

BETTY'S BAY

30 km (19 miles) southeast of Gordon's Bay.

Betty's Bay, or Betty's, as the hamlet is fondly known, is worth visiting for its penguins and botanical garden. The village is made up of retirees and weekenders wanting to escape the city hustle. The scenery is wild and untamed and the settlement unfussy, but don't go unless you're happy to hunker down inside when the summer wind is howling or when the winter rains set in.

If you're in the area, the colony of African penguins at Stony Point is definitely worth exploring. They are one of only two mainland colonies in southern Africa (the other is at Boulders Beach on the Cape Peninsula, where it is much easier to see them). The Stony Point colony lies about 600 yards from the parking area along a rocky coastal path. Along the way you pass the concrete remains of tank stands, reminders of the days when Betty's Bay was a big whaling station. The African penguin is endangered, so the colony has been fenced off for protection, but this still doesn't stop leopards from making forays into the colony.

To get to the penguins from Pringle Bay, return to Clarence Drive (the R44) and continue 2 km (1¾ miles) to the turnoff to Stony Point, on the edge of Betty's Bay. Follow Porter Drive for 2¼ km (1¾ miles) until you reach a sign marked "mooi hawens" and a smaller sign depicting a penguin.

GETTING HERE AND AROUND

Head out of Cape Town on the N2 toward Somerset West. Once you've made your way through the town (the traffic can be torturous on a Friday afternoon), take the R44 turnoff to Gordon's Bay. From there the road hugs the coast. It takes 45 minutes from Cape Town to Gordon's Bay if there are no traffic jams and then about 30 minutes to Betty's Bay, but this will vary depending on the traffic and weather—and how often you stop to admire the view.

VISITOR INFORMATION

The Hangklip-Kleinmond Tourism Bureau has information on Betty's Bay.

Contacts Hangklip–Kleinmond Tourism Bureau ⊠ *Protea Centre, Main Rd., shop 1, Kleinmond* ☎ *028/271–5657* ⊕ *www.kleinmondtourism.co.za* ⊙ *Weekdays 8:30–5, Sat. 9–2, Sun. 10–2.*

EXPLORING

Harold Porter National Botanical Garden. This 440-acre nature reserve is in the heart of the coastal fynbos, where the Cape floral kingdom is at its richest. The profusion of plants supports 96 species of birds and a wide range of small mammals, including large troops of chacma baboons. You couldn't ask for a more fantastic setting, cradled between the Atlantic and the towering peaks of the 3,000-foot Kogelberg Range. Walking trails wind through the reserve and into the mountains via Disa and Leopard's kloofs, which echo with the sound of waterfalls. Back at the main buildings, a pleasant restaurant serves light meals and teas. Book ahead for a volunteer guide to take you around the gardens, for which a donation is welcome. To get to the garden from the penguin colony, return to Porter Drive and turn right to rejoin the R44. Drive another 2 km (1 mile) to get here. ⊠ *Clarence Dr. and Broadwith Ave.* ☎ *028/272–9311* ⊕ *www.sanbi.org/gardens/harold-porter* ⊠ *R20* ⊙ *Weekdays 8–4:30, weekends 8–5.*

WHERE TO EAT

$$ ✕ **Hook, Line and Sinker.** Owners Jacqi and Stefan Kruger can be a bit
SEAFOOD　gruff, though they're well-meaning. Only the most obedient diners will escape unscathed, but the trial, like all heroes' journeys, makes survival and the meal that much sweeter. Expect fish—which is fresher than you'll find just about anywhere else—prepared simply, usually with salsa verde or a bourbon-and-mustard sauce. The dishes, all cooked on a wood fire, come only with fries. Start with either the rich and fragrant crab bisque or mussels in a tomato-based sauce. Beer-battered hake and chips is served for lunch Tuesday through Saturday. The restaurant is small, the waiting list long. ⑤ *Average main: R100* ⊠ *382 Crescent Rd., Pringle Bay* ☎ *028/273–8688* ⚑ *Reservations essential.*

WHERE TO STAY

$$ 🏨 **Moonstruck on Pringle Bay.** About 60 km (37 miles) from Hermanus,
B&B/INN　Pringle Bay is a great place to be if you want to escape the Hermanus holiday crush, and situated within 1,600 feet of sandy beach, this modern, four-star guesthouse has spectacular sea and mountain views and is an excellent location for whale-watching. **Pros:** stunning views; close to restaurants; near the beach. **Cons:** the guesthouse is small, so you'll be aware of other guests. ⑤ *Rooms from: R1850* ⊠ *264 Hangklip Rd., Pringle Bay* ☎ *028/273–8162* ⊕ *www.moonstruck.co.za* ⚐ *4 rooms* ⑩ *Breakfast.*

KLEINMOND

25 km (15½ miles) southeast of Gordon's Bay.

The sleepy coastal town of Kleinmond (Small Mouth) presides over a magnificent stretch of shoreline, backed by the mountains of the Palmietberg. It's a favorite among retirees, but more and more city-weary folks are moving here preretirement as well. A harbor development near the old slipway is bustling with restaurants and shops.

GETTING HERE AND AROUND
Kleinmond is about 45 minutes from Gordon's Bay, depending on the weather and traffic on the R44.

VISITOR INFORMATION
Contacts **Hangklip–Kleinmond Tourism Bureau** ✉ *14 Harbour Rd.* ☎ *028/271–5657* ⊕ *www.kleinmondtourism.co.za* ⊘ *Weekdays 8:30–5, Sat. 9–2, Sun. 10–2.*

EXPLORING
Beaumont Wines. The R44 becomes the R41 and cuts inland around the Bot River lagoon. About 10 km (6 miles) past Kleinmond is the junction with the R43. Hermanus is to the right, but take a quick detour to the left through the sleepy town of Bot River to the big, old white gates of Beaumont Wines. This is a fabulous family-run winery. It's just sufficiently scruffy to create an ambience of age and country charm without actually being untidy. But, charm aside, it's the wine you come here for, and it really is worth the detour. Beaumont produces a range of dependable, notable wines, like the juicy Pinotage and the first mourvèdre to be bottled in South Africa. ✉ *Compagnes Drift Farm, R43, Bot River* ☎ *028/284–9194* ⊕ *www.beaumont.co.za* ✉ *Tastings R25* ⊘ *Weekdays 9–4, Sat. 10–3.*

NEED A BREAK?

The Shellfish Bar. This is one of the places where you can try abalone quite legally. At the big abalone factory the mollusks are cultivated, harvested, and packaged for local restaurants and overseas markets. The restaurant has a full sushi menu with everything from salmon and tuna to crab and eel. The fresh oysters and crayfish are sensational, but if you don't like seafood, expect to go hungry. The bar doesn't hold a liquor license, so bring your own alcohol. ✉ *35 Harbour Rd.* ☎ *082/043-7913* ⊘ *No dinner Sun.-Tues.*

Gabriëlskloof. As you're heading out of the confines of the city and inland to explore the Overberg or Garden Route, be sure to stop at the impressive Gabriëlskloof, 10 km (6 miles) outside Bot Rivier on the right as you're driving up the N2. Try the Decanter award-winning Gabriëlskloof Shiraz 2010 and Five Archers 2009. You can taste the estate wines in front of a log fire in the tasting room or in the garden. You can also sample the estate's extra virgin olive oil, and olive products can be purchased from the deli. The Gabriëlskloof restaurant (R110) is a great place to stop for lunch if you're in the area. The menu changes regularly, but the food is always no-fuss homecooked fare made with fresh local Overberg farm produce. If you visit Gabriëlskloof in

December, aim for the weekend they host an evening market with 30 local produce and crafts stalls. ⊠ *Bot River* ☎ *028/284–9865* ⊕ *www. gabrielskloof.co.za* 🍷 *Tastings R30, cellar tours by appointment only* ⊙ *Weekdays 9–5, Sat. 11–3.*

Kogelberg Nature Reserve. Close to town, on the Cape Town side and clearly marked with signs from the main street, is the Kogelberg Nature Reserve, a 66,000-acre area of fynbos that extends from the mountains almost to the sea and includes most of the course of the Palmiet River. Declared a UNESCO World Heritage Site in the 1990s, it has fauna and flora found nowhere else in the world. Take one of the well-marked nature walks through the reserve and you are sure to see some of the area's magnificent flora and birdlife. ■**TIP→ One of the best-kept secrets of this nature reserve are the five Oudebosch eco-cabins, which sleep four people each.** ☎ *028/271–5138* ⊕ *www.capenature.co.za* 🍷 *R40* ⊙ *Daily 7:30–4.*

■ NEED A BREAK? **The Milkwood. Overlooking the lagoon in Onrus, the Milkwood is a great place for a languid lunch. You can sit on the deck after a quick dip and eat some fresh fish (what kind of fish depends on the day's catch), grilled and served with a lemon or garlic-butter sauce.** ⊠ *95 Atlantic Dr., Onrus* ☎ *028/316–1516.*

Onrus. Head back toward Kleinmond, continuing on the R43 toward Hermanus and across the Bot River. The R43 swings eastward around the mountains, past the not particularly attractive fishing village of Hawston, one of the Overstrand communities hardest hit by abalone poaching and drug peddling, and the small artists' colony of Onrus. The Onrus lagoon is a great swimming spot for children; the water is always a couple of degrees warmer than the sea and is safe for the newly waterborne. ⊠ *Onrus.*

Sandown Bay. About 10 km (6 miles) of sandy beach fringes the impressive Sandown Bay, at the eastern edge of town. Much of the beach is nothing more than a sandbar, separating the Atlantic from the huge lagoon formed by the Bot River. Swift currents make swimming risky, although there is a sheltered corner near the rocks close to the old Beach House hotel, which burned down in 2006. Keep an eye out for the famous Bot River horses that live on *vlei* (pronounced flay), or marsh. There are lots of theories about just how the horses got here. One has it that they were turned loose during the Boer War to save them from being killed and ended up on the vlei for safety. DNA tests show that these horses are descendants of the Kaapse Waperd (Cape wagon horse), a sturdy breed used to help settle the wild regions of the Overberg. **Amenities:** food and drink; parking (fee); showers; toilets; water sports. **Best for:** solitude; swimming; walking. ⊠ *Beach Rd.* 🚗 *R10 parking.*

WHERE TO STAY

$$$ 🏨 **The Arabella Western Cape Hotel & Spa.** Gone are the days when heading
HOTEL out into the country meant staying in pokey hotels with dodgy beds: the
FAMILY Arabella Western Cape Hotel & Spa is luxurious lodging in the most
Fodor'sChoice amazing setting—on the edge of the Bot River lagoon. **Pros:** plenty of
★ activities to keep both adults and children entertained; world-rated

golf course. **Cons:** windy during summer months. $ *Rooms from: R2660* ✉ *Arabella Country Estate, R44* ☎ *028/284–0000* ⊕ *www. arabellacountryestate.co.za* ➷ *145 rooms* ‖O‖ *Breakfast.*

SPORTS AND THE OUTDOORS

GOLF

Arabella Golf Club. The setting of the Arabella Golf Club is so beautiful that you'd do well to take time to admire the views at the 8th hole, with the lagoon, the mountains, and the sea in the distance. This is Ernie Els's favorite spot and the most photographed hole on the course. Don't lose your head to the views—the course is fairly challenging. It's also expensive. ✉ *R43* ☎ *028/284–0000* ⊕ *www.arabellacountryestate. co.za/arabella-golf-course* ⚑ *18 holes, 6651 yards, par 72.* ☎ *R690* ⊙ *Daily 7–6.*

RAFTING

The Palmiet River is a low-volume, technical white-water river of about Grade III.

Gravity Adventures. The Palmiet River, which runs through the Kogelberg Nature Reserve, is perfect for white-water adventures. In high water in summer and winter, Gravity Adventures offers rafting trips in two- or four-seater inflatable rafts. In low water it does the same trip but on specially designed one-person inflatable crafts called "geckos." A full-day rafting trip (including a light breakfast and lunch) costs R695. Tubing costs R475 for a full day; you can order lunch for an extra R65 or bring your own. Remember to take along plenty of sun protection. ✉ *21 Selous Rd., Claremont, Cape Town* ☎ *021/683–3698, 082/574–9901* ⊕ *www.gravity.co.za.*

SA Forest Adventures. Tubing and river rafting trips down the Palmiet River are offered by SA Forest Adventures in Kleinmond. Expect to pay around R550 for a half day of fun and heart-stopping action. If this isn't enough, ask about their sand-boarding trips, where you get to ski down sand dunes that overlook Betty's Bay and the Atlantic Ocean. ✉ *Harbour Rd., Unit B1* ☎ *083/517–3635* ⊕ *saforestadventures.co.za.*

HERMANUS

34 km (21 miles) southeast of Kleinmond.

Pristine beaches extend as far as the eye can see, and the Kleinriviersberg provides a breathtaking backdrop to this popular resort, the Overberg's major coastal town. Restaurants and shops line the streets, and Grotto Beach was awarded Blue Flag status (an international symbol of high environmental standards as well as good sanitary and safety facilities) in 2003 and is still going strong. Though the town has lost much of its original charm—thanks to the crowds and fast-food joints—it is still most definitely worth a visit. If you're in Hermanus for the weekend, visit the Saturday morning organic farmers' market to get a real feel for the area.

GETTING HERE AND AROUND

Hermanus is about a 40-minute drive from Kleinmond on the R41 and the R43. In summer expect delays, as the traffic into town is often gridlocked.

VISITOR INFORMATION

Contacts Hermanus Tourism Bureau ✉ *Lord Robert and Mitchell Sts.* ☎ *028/312-2629* ⊕ *www.hermanus. co.za* ⊙ *Summer weekdays 8–6, Sat. 9–5, Sun. 11–3; winter Mon.–Sat. 9–5,*

EXPLORING

Hermanus sits atop a long line of cliffs, which makes it one of the best places in South Africa for land-based whale-watching. The town is packed during the Whale Festival in late September as well as over Christmas vacation. The 11-km (7-mile) Cliff Walk allows watchers to follow the whales, which often come within 100 feet of the cliffs as they move along the coastline. Keep an ear and an eye out for the whale crier, who makes his rounds during the season. Using horns made from dried kelp, he produces a long note to indicate where you can find him on the harbor wall. Once you've located him, he will tell you where to catch the best sighting of these mighty giants of the deep.

> ## WONDER OF WHALES
>
> Whale sightings off South African shores weren't always so frequent, but each year it seems whales are arriving earlier and leaving later. In the 1960s, whale populations, especially Southern Right whales, showed an increase around the coast. The population was probably around 1,000 in the '80s, and in 1984 the Dolphin Action and Protection Group, an organization campaigning to stop whaling, finally won year-round protection for the creatures. Today, around 4,000 Southern Right whales call SA waters home.

Bouchard Finlayson. West of town off the R43, the R320 (Hemel-en-Aarde Valley Road) leads through the vineyards and orchards of the scenic Hemel-en-Aarde Valley and over Shaw's Pass to Caledon. A bit past Hamilton Russell Vineyards and with only 44 acres under vine, Bouchard Finlayson nevertheless thrills critics and wine lovers year after year. Winemaker Peter Finlayson makes good use of the cool sea breeze and unique terroir of the estate to create some fantastic deep-south wines. Finlayson, who has a great voice, maintains that Pinot Noir "is like opera. When it's great, it is pure seduction, almost hedonistic. There is no middle road." You might wish to lay down a few bottles of the much-lauded Tête de Cuvée Galpin Peak Pinot Noir, a velvety and fruity wine. The 2012 vintage is exceptional. ✉ *Off Hemel-en-Aarde Valley Rd. (R320)* ☎ *028/312-3515* ⊕ *www.bouchardfinlayson.co.za* 🔖 *Tastings free* ⊙ *Weekdays 8–5, Sat. 10–1.*

Hamilton Russell Vineyards. A short way down the R320 (Hemel-en-Aarde Valley Road) in a thatch building overlooking a small dam, Hamilton Russell Vineyards produces only two varietals: the temperamental Pinot Noir and Chardonnay. Their wines are regarded as some of the best in the world. The Chardonnay, with lovely pear aromas and flavors, won the Chardonnay category at the 2014 South African Wine Index Awards. The Pinot Noir, great for pairing with veal, pork, and gamey meats, was also a winner at the 2014 SAWi Awards.

The farm doesn't do official picnics, but they don't mind you bringing your own nibbles and enjoying the remarkable setting; there's a lawn outside the tasting room where you can spread your blanket. ⊠ *Off Hemel-en-Aarde Valley Rd. (R320), Walker Bay* ☎ *028/312–3595* ⊕ *www.hamiltonrussellvineyards.co.za* 🍴 *Tastings free* ☉ *Weekdays 9–5, Sat. 9–1.*

FAMILY **Old Harbour Museum.** Originally, Hermanus was a simple fishing village. Its Old Harbour, built in 1904 and the oldest original harbor in South Africa that is still intact, has been declared a national monument. The Old Harbour Museum bears testimony to the town's maritime past. A small building at the old stone fishing basin displays a couple of the horrific harpoons used to lance whales and sharks, as well as some interesting whale bones. There are also exhibits on fishing techniques, local marine life, and angling records. The white building next to the harbor parking lot on Market Square is **De Wet's Huis,** which houses the Old Harbour Museum Photographic Exhibition. Here are photos of old Hermanus and of many of the town's fishermen proudly displaying their catches of fish, sharks, and dolphins—yes, dolphins. The museum's third component is the **Whale House,** with an interactive display. Although the exhibit is still only 75% complete, the touch screens, submarine, and skeleton of a whale make it a great place for kids. A whale movie runs twice a day, at 10 am and 3 pm. A crafts market every weekend outside De Wet's Huis is fun for browsing. ⊠ *Old Harbour, Marine Dr.* ☎ *028/312–1475* ⊕ *www.old-harbour-museum. co.za* 🍴 *R20* ☉ *Mon.–Sat. 9–4:30, Sun. noon–4.*

Rotary Way. On the outskirts of town a pair of white gateposts set well back from the R43 signal the start of Rotary Way. This scenic drive climbs along the spine of the mountains above Hermanus, with incredible views of the town, Walker Bay, and the Hemel-en-Aarde (Heaven and Earth) Valley, as well as some of the area's beautiful fynbos. It's a highlight of a trip to Hermanus and shouldn't be missed. The entire mountainside is laced with wonderful walking trails, and many of the scenic lookouts have benches.

WHERE TO EAT

$$ ✕**Burgundy.** In one of the village's original stone-and-clay fisherfolk cot-
SEAFOOD tages, the cozy Burgundy is one of Hermanus's oldest and best-loved restaurants. Not surprisingly, there's plenty of seafood to be had on the extensive menu, from prawns to line fish. Start with the delicate west coast mussels, steamed with Sauvignon Blanc, before you move on to succulent tiger prawns with basmati rice pilaf or the fantastically fresh line fish served with passion-fruit hollandaise, seasonal vegetables, and crushed potatoes. The menu also includes a large choice of meat dishes, ranging from chicken to ostrich, and there's a good vegetarian selection—something of a novelty in smaller towns. Then there's the delicious apple tarte tartin and malva pudding—a South African favorite. ⑤ *Average main: R130* ⊠ *Marine Dr.* ☎ *028/312–2800* ⊕ *www. burgundyrestaurant.co.za.*

$$ ✕**Heaven.** If you're keen to escape the crush in Hermanus, head to
ECLECTIC Heaven, situated on Newton Johnson Family Vineyards. It's up the picturesque Hemel-en-Aarde Valley Road, where vines and fynbos cover

the slopes and where you may wish you owned a country home. The view is wonderful, the service is attentive, and there's a good selection of local wines. The menu, which changes often, always emphasizes the best seasonal produce. Starters could include hot-smoked yellowtail and slow-braised beef tongue. Mains, served with hand-cut chips or a green salad with mature Gruyère, include winter root vegetables with cheese and hazelnuts, cashew-crusted hake, and pork loin with braised lentils. The restaurant is big on foraging. Michelin-star chef Eric Bulpitt heads the team and sends them out into the garden for fresh herbs and the fields for wild greens and *waterblommetjies* (literally translated from Afrikaans, this means "water flowers"). ⑤ *Average main: R150* ⊠ *Newton Johnson Family Vineyards, Hemel-en-Aarde Valley Rd. (R320)* ☎ *021/200–2148* ⊕ *www.newtonjohnson.com* ⊗ *Closed Sun. No dinner Mon.–Thurs. No lunch Sat.*

$$　✕ **La Pentola.** With a panoramic view of Walker Bay, La Pentola special-
ECLECTIC　izes in international cuisine with South African flavors. Drawing on French, Italian, and Mediterranean influences, executive chef Shane Sauvage uses the best local ingredients to create delectable dishes. The extensive menu includes fresh seafood, duck, ostrich, prime cuts of beef, pastas, salads, and exotic game dishes. For starters order one of the house specialties: basil and pork livers or Spanish snails wrapped in bacon and steamed in Chardonnay. Entrees include line fish basted in butter and cooked with red onion and tomato, and beef fillet served with a KWV brandy, dijon mustard, and cream sauce. If you're in the mood for something exotic, try the warthog loin fried with butter, brandy, honey, and mustard, or cubed crocodile tail and curry sauce in pastry. Wine connoisseurs will be delighted with the award-winning wine list, which is as varied as the menu. ⑤ *Average main: R135* ⊠ *Ocean View, 87 Marine Dr., shop 4* ☎ *022/313–1685* ⊕ *hermanus. lapentola.co.za.*

$$　✕ **Mariana's.** Mariana and Peter Esterhuizen started out selling organic
ECLECTIC　vegetables at the Hermanus farmers' market before converting a house in the little village of Stanford, just 10 minutes away, into a restaurant. Capetonians regularly make the trip here for the excellent food, local wines, relaxed setting, friendly hosts, and seasonal organic produce grown behind the restaurant. The produce from the garden dictates the menu, and ingredients are sourced from local producers. The food leans toward a Mediterranean style with a strong element of Cape cooking present in most dishes. The Gruyère soufflé is a sublimely light, cheesy concoction served in a pool of tomato cream. Starters like springbok rillettes and fresh broad-bean salad are served in season, and main courses such as the confit duck with preserved clementine and slow-cooked falling-off-the-bone shoulder of Overberg lamb have a firm following. Last orders are taken at 1:30 pm, so don't be late. ⑤ *Average main: R120* ⊠ *12 du Toit St., Stanford* ☎ *028/341–0272* ⚠ *Reservations essential* ⊟ *No credit cards* ⊗ *Closed Mon.–Wed. No dinner.*

$$　✕ **Mogg's Country Cookhouse.** Don't be put off by the bumpy dirt road
ECLECTIC　heading up the Hemel-en-Aarde Valley. This restaurant on a fruit farm at the top of the valley is worth any amount of dust and corrugations. The converted laborer's cottage is as pretty as a picture in a

tumbledown, overgrown kind of way, and the food is excellent in a relaxed and friendly setting. The seasonal menu is scribbled on a chalk-board. For starters you could expect caramelized pear, Gorgonzola, avocado, and walnut salad, or smoked trout and sautéed prawns in a phyllo pastry basket with lime-wasabi vinaigrette. Main courses might include Moroccan-style slow-roasted lamb on potato mash with a cool yogurt dressing, or battered pork medallions with a mustard sauce and a warm green bean, olive, and potato salad. For dessert, homemade vanilla or coffee ice cream is served with a hot chocolate sauce. You're welcome to bring your own wine, and they don't charge corkage. $ *Average main: R100* ⊠ *Nuwe Pos Farm, off Hemel-en-Aarde Valley Rd. (R320)* ☎ *076/314–0671* ⊕ *www.moggscookhouse.com* ⬟ *Reservations essential* ⊘ *Closed Mon. and Tues. No dinner.*

WHERE TO STAY

If you want to avoid the crowds of Hermanus, consider lodging in the nearby tiny hamlet of Stanford.

$
B&B/INN
Auberge Burgundy Guesthouse. If you want to be in the center of the village, this stylish guesthouse is an excellent choice; you're a stone's throw from the famous whale-watching cliffs and the market, and three minutes from the Old Harbour Museum. **Pros:** close proximity to everything Hermanus has to offer; very friendly staff; less than 200 feet from the sea. **Cons:** some suites facing the street are noisy; no children under 12 (exceptions made during winter months). $ *Rooms from: R1360* ⊠ *16 Harbour Rd.* ☎ *028/313–1201* ⊕ *www.auberge.co.za* ⬟ *19 rooms* ⦿*l Breakfast.*

$$
B&B/INN
Blue Gum Country Estate. Husband-and-wife team Anton and Tarryn de Kock run a top-notch establishment on the banks of the Klein River just 10 minutes from Stanford and 30 minutes from Hermanus. **Pros:** brilliant base from which to explore the area; feels like home away from home with added luxury. **Cons:** you'll need to drive a distance to get to the busier areas; pitiful nightlife in Stanford. $ *Rooms from: R2400* ⊠ *Off R326, Stanford* ☎ *028/341–0116* ⊕ *www.bluegum.co.za* ⬟ *12 rooms* ⦿*l Breakfast.*

$$$$
RESORT
FAMILY
Fodor'sChoice
★
Grootbos Private Nature Reserve. Only a 30-minute drive from Hermanus and two hours from Cape Town, this private nature reserve is on 2,500 acres of Western Cape landscape overlooking Walker Bay. **Pros:** certified green property; secluded natural surroundings; whale-watching. **Cons:** confining for longer stays; expensive. $ *Rooms from: R6000* ⊠ *Gansbaai* ☎ *028/384–8000, 028/384–8053* ⊕ *www.grootbos. com* ⬟ *23 suites* ⦿*l Some meals.*

$$$$
HOTEL
FAMILY
Fodor'sChoice
★
The Marine. The Marine is one of the Southern Hemisphere's most spectacular seaside properties, with an incomparable cliff-top setting and sumptuously decorated rooms. **Pros:** wonderful views of the ocean; old-world service excellence and attention to detail. **Cons:** you'll need a tony wardrobe to blend in; not a super-relaxed environment. $ *Rooms from: R6500* ⊠ *Marine Dr.* ☎ *021/794–5535* ⊕ *www. collectionmcgrath.com/marine* ⬟ *40 rooms* ⦿*l Breakfast.*

$
B&B/INN
Whale Cottage, Hermanus. Decorated in restful shades of blue and white, this is a great base from which to take long whale-watching walks. **Pros:** swimming beach within walking distance; children welcome. **Cons:**

Southern Rights make a lot of noise when they're having a whale of a time; only three rooms are sea facing, so book early if you want to see the whales. $ *Rooms from: R1100* ⊠ *38 Westcliff Dr.* ☎ *021/433–2100* ⊕ *www.whalecottage.com* ➥ *6 rooms* ⦿ *Breakfast.*

$ ⬚ **Windsor.** If you come to Hermanus anytime from July to Novem-
HOTEL ber, consider staying at this hotel in the heart of town. **Pros:** world-class views of Walker Bay; in the heart of Hermanus; reasonable rates. **Cons:** tired decor needs a revamp; no pool. $ *Rooms from: R950* ⊠ *49 Marine Dr.* ☎ *028/312–3727* ⊕ *www.windsorhotel.co.za* ➥ *60 rooms* ⦿ *Breakfast.*

SPORTS AND THE OUTDOORS

East of Hermanus the R43 hugs the strip of land between the mountains and the Klein River lagoon. The lagoon is popular with water-skiers, boaters, and anglers.

KAYAKING

Walker Bay Adventures. For a really fun outing, join a gentle paddling excursion from the Old Harbour operated by Walker Bay Adventures. You paddle in safe, stable double sea kayaks accompanied by a guide, and will pay around R350 for a two-hour trip. Children 10 and older are welcome to join. From July to December, Walker Bay is a whale sanctuary, and this is the only company with a permit to operate here. ⊠ *Old Harbour, off Marine Dr.* ☎ *082/739–0159* ⊕ *www.walkerbayadventures.co.za.*

WHALE-WATCHING AND SHARK DIVING

Dyer Island Cruises. This company, which strives to create awareness about conservation, is a good bet for whale-watching, and the guides are full of information. You're likely to see some of the Marine Big Five—whales, dolphins, penguins, seals, and sharks—on the guided boat trip. Expect to pay R900 per adult. Transfers to and from Cape Town can be arranged. ⊠ *5 Geelbek St., Kleinmond* ☎ *082/801–8014* ⊕ *www.dyer-island-cruises.co.za.*

White Shark Diving Company. Shark diving is extremely popular (even Brad Pitt took the plunge), and Gansbaai has a number of operators working from the small harbor, including White Shark Diving Company. A 4½-hour trip (with plenty of adrenaline) costs around R1,350, including breakfast, snacks on the boat, and a light lunch after the trip. If you don't want to take the plunge—which you do in a cage, to keep you safe from the sharks—you can just stay in the boat and watch the sharks from the deck. ⊠ *Kleinbaai Harbour, 9 Kus Dr., Gansbaai* ☎ *082/559–6858* ⊕ *www.sharkcagediving.co.za.*

SHOPPING

Wine Village. This shop carries a good selection of South African wines, including wines from neighboring vineyards Hamilton Russell and Bouchard Finlayson as well as Southern Right. ⊠ *R43 and R320* ☎ *028/316–3988* ⊕ *www.wine-village.co.za.*

BREDASDORP

89 km (55 miles) east of Hermanus; 60 km (37 miles) east of Stanford.

This sleepy agricultural town has a certain charm, as long as you don't catch it on a Sunday afternoon, when everything's closed and an air of ennui pervades the brassy, windswept streets. Each spring, however, the usual lethargic atmosphere is abandoned, and a radical sense of purpose takes its place when Bredasdorp hosts the Foot of Africa Marathon. Don't be lulled by the small-town country setting into thinking that this race is a breeze; word has it that the undulating landscape has the fittest athletes doubting their perseverance.

GETTING HERE AND AROUND

Travel time from Hermanus is around 45 minutes and from Stanford 30 minutes. From Hermanus you travel on the R43 to Stanford; then you take the R326 and then the R316. The route is well signposted.

VISITOR INFORMATION

The Cape Agulhas Tourism Bureau has two offices with information for Bredasdorp.

Contacts Cape Agulhas Tourism Bureau ✉ *22 Long St.* ☎ *028/424–2584* ⊕ *www.discovercapeagulhas.co.za* ⊙ *Weekdays 9–5, Sat. 9–12:30.*

EXPLORING

Bredasdorp Shipwreck Museum. Housed in a converted church and rectory, the Bredasdorp Shipwreck Museum has an extensive collection of objects salvaged from the hundreds of ships that have gone down in the stormy waters off the Cape. In addition to the usual cannons and figureheads, the museum displays a surprising array of undamaged household articles rescued from the sea, including entire dining-room sets, sideboards, china, and phonographs. Be sure to visit the buildings out back, which contain old wagons and the first fire engines used in South Africa. ✉ *6 Independent St.* ☎ *028/424–1240* ⊕ *www.westerncape.gov.za/facility/shipwreck-museum* 🎟 *R40* ⊙ *Weekdays 9–5, Sat. 10–4, Sun. 11–4.*

De Hoop Nature Reserve. This huge conservation area covering 88,900 acres of isolated coastal terrain as well as a marine reserve extending 5 km (3 miles) out to sea is a World Heritage Site and well deserving of this status. Massive white-sand dunes, mountains, and rare lowland fynbos are home to eland, bontebok, and Cape mountain zebra, as well as more than 250 bird species. Though the reserve is only three hours from Cape Town, it feels a lifetime away. Access is via the dirt road between Bredasdorp and Malgas. This is a fantastic place to watch whales from the shore—not quite as easy as in Hermanus but much less crowded. You can also hike the enormously popular **Whale Trail,** which runs through this reserve. A shuttle service takes your bags to each new stop, so all you have to carry is a small day pack and some water between overnight stops. You need to book up to a year in advance to enjoy the Whale Trail, or you might get lucky and snag a last-minute cancellation. In fact, this hike is now so popular that it's beginning to appear in online auctions. Self-catering cottages sleep up to four people and range from basic to fully equipped. The trail costs R950 per person, but there's a minimum of six people each time, so you'll have to drum up other happy hikers. You can still enjoy De Hoop without doing the Whale Trail; they have lovely accommodation ranging from camping to luxurious rooms in the old manor house. ☎ 028/542–1253 ⊕ *www. capenature.org.za* ⊗ *Mon.–Thurs. and weekends 7–6, Fri. 7–7.*

OFF THE BEATEN PATH

Elim. Little has changed in the last hundred years in the Moravian mission village Elim, founded in 1824. Simple whitewashed cottages line the few streets, and the settlement's coloured residents all belong to the Moravian Church (⇨ *"A Note on the Term 'Coloured'"* box). At the Sunday 10 am church service, which you're welcome to attend, just about the whole town turns out in their Sunday best, and voices soar in the white church at the top of the main street. The whole village has been declared a national monument, and it's the only town in the country that has a monument dedicated to the freeing of the slaves in 1838. It's also home to the country's oldest working clock and biggest wooden waterwheel. Elim is 36 km (22 miles) west of Bredasdorp and accessible only by dirt road. The easiest access is via the R317, off the R319 between Cape Agulhas and Bredasdorp.

Malgas. Past De Hoop Nature Reserve on the dirt road from Bredasdorp is the small hamlet of Malgas, a major port in the 19th century before the mouth of the Breede River silted up. In addition to a tiny village, you will find the last hand-drawn car ferry in the country (R42 round-trip). It's fascinating to watch the technique, as the ferry operators "walk" the ferry across the river on a huge cable, leaning into their harnesses.

OFF THE BEATEN PATH

Cape Agulhas. From Bredasdorp it's just 41 km (25½ miles) through rolling farmland to the tip of the African continent. Although this cape is not nearly as spectacular as Cape Point, it's a wild and lonely place—rather fitting for the end of a wild and wonderful continent. For R22, you can climb the Cape Agulhas lighthouse tower from 9 to 5 daily. ✉ *Lighthouse St., Cape Agulhas.*

ARNISTON (WAENHUISKRANS)

25 km (15½ miles) southeast of Bredasdorp.

Although its official name is Waenhuiskrans, and that's what you'll see on maps, this lovely, isolated vacation village is almost always called Arniston—after a British ship of that name that was wrecked on the nearby reef in 1815. Beautiful beaches, water that assumes Caribbean shades of blue, and mile after mile of towering white dunes attract anglers and vacationers alike. Only the frequent southeasters that blow off the sea and the chilly water are likely to put a damper on your enjoyment.

For 200 years a community of local fisherfolk has eked out a living here, setting sail each day in small fishing boats. Today their village, **Kassiesbaai** (translation: "suitcase bay," supposedly for all the suitcases that washed ashore from the frequent shipwrecks), is a national monument. It's fascinating wandering around the thatch cottages of this still-vibrant community, although declining fish stocks have left many families vulnerable. Perlemoen poaching is also a problem here. The adjacent village of Arniston has expanded enormously in the last two decades, thanks to the construction of vacation homes. Unfortunately, not all of the new architecture blends well with the whitewashed simplicity of the original cottages.

Waenhuiskrans is Afrikaans for "wagon-house cliff," a name derived from the vast cave 2 km (1 mile) south of town that is theoretically large enough to house several wagons and their spans of oxen. Signs point the way over the dunes to the cave, which is accessible only at low tide. You need shoes to protect your feet from the sharp rocks, and you should wear something you don't mind getting wet. It's definitely worth the trouble, however, to stand in the enormous cave looking out to sea.

GETTING HERE AND AROUND

It'll take drivers about 20–30 minutes to get here from Bredasdorp. Don't bother with public transport. Rent a car and you'll have the freedom to explore this vast area.

VISITOR INFORMATION

The Cape Agulhas Tourism Bureau has information for Arniston.

Contacts Two Oceans Visitor Info Centre ⊠ *Lighthouse, Bredasdorp* ☎ *028/435–7185* ⊕ *www.discovercapeagulhas.co.za* ⊗ *Daily 9–5.*

WHERE TO STAY

$$
HOTEL
FAMILY

⌂ **Arniston Spa Hotel.** You could easily spend a week here and still need to be dragged away: the setting, a crescent of white dunes, has a lot to do with Arniston's appeal, but the hotel also strikes a fine balance between elegance and beach-vacation comfort. **Pros:** great views of the beach; located on a beach safe for children. **Cons:** windy in summer; a bit noisy during high season. ⑤ *Rooms from: R1880* ⊠ *Beach Rd.* ☎ *028/445–9000* ⊕ *www.arnistonhotel.com* ⇆ *67 rooms* |◎| *Breakfast.*

SWELLENDAM

72 km (45 miles) north of Arniston (Waenhuiskrans).

Beautiful Swellendam lies in the shadow of the imposing Langeberg Range. in 1745, it is the third-oldest town in South Africa, and many of its historic buildings have been elegantly restored. Even on a casual drive along the main street you'll see a number of lovely Cape Dutch homes, with their traditional whitewashed walls, gables, and thatch roofs.

GETTING HERE AND AROUND

Swellendam is about an hour's drive from Arniston. Rent a car to get around.

VISITOR INFORMATION

Contacts Swellendam Tourism Bureau ⊠ *22 Swellengrebel St.* ☎ *028/514–2770* ⊕ *www.swellendamtourism.co.za* ⊗ *Weekdays 9–5, weekends 9–2.*

EXPLORING

Bontebok National Park. Covering just 6,880 acres of coastal fynbos, Bontebok National Park is one of the smallest of South Africa's national parks. Don't expect to see big game here—the park contains no elephants, lions, or rhinos. What you will see are bontebok, graceful white-face antelope nearly exterminated by hunters in the early 20th century, as well as red hartebeest, Cape grysbok, steenbok, duiker, and the endangered Cape mountain zebra. There is simple, self-catering accommodation in the reserve, as well as camping facilities. ⊠ *Off the N2, 5 km (3 miles) from Swellendam* ☎ *028/514–2735* ⊕ *www. sanparks.org* ⊠ *R80* ⊙ *Daily 10–6.*

Drostdy Museum. The centerpiece of the town's historical past is the Drostdy Museum, a collection of buildings dating from the town's earliest days. The Drostdy was built in 1747 by the Dutch East India Company to serve as the residence of the *landdrost,* the magistrate who presided over the district. The building is furnished in a style that was common in the mid-19th century. A path leads through the Drostdy herb gardens to Mayville, an 1855 middle-class home that blends elements of Cape Dutch and Cape Georgian architecture. Across Swellengrebel Street stand the old jail and the Ambagswerf, an outdoor exhibit of tools used by the town's blacksmiths, wainwrights, coopers, and tanners. ⊠ *18 Swellengrebel St.* ☎ *028/514–1138* ⊕ *www.drostdy.com* ⊠ *R25* ⊙ *Weekdays 9–4, weekends 10–3.*

Dutch Reformed Church. Swellendam's Dutch Reformed Church is an imposing white edifice built in 1911 in an eclectic style. The gables are baroque, the windows Gothic, the cupola vaguely Eastern, and the steeple extravagant. Surprisingly, all the elements work together wonderfully. Inside is an interesting tiered amphitheater with banks of curving wood pews facing the pulpit and organ. ⊠ *7 Voortrek St.* ☎ *028/514–1225* ⊠ *R5; services free* ⊙ *Mon.–Wed., Fri., and Sat. 8–4; services (in Afrikaans) Sun. at 9:30.*

Marloth Nature Reserve. If you'd like to stretch your legs, take a hike in the Marloth Nature Reserve in the Langeberg above town. Five easy walks, ranging from one to four hours, explore some of the mountain gorges. An office at the entrance to the reserve has trail maps and hiking information. If you're doing a day walk, park outside the entrance boom. Although you can stay in the reserve until sunset, the gates close at the time advertised. ⊹ *1½ km (1 mile) from Voortrek St. on Andrew White St. to golf course, and follow signs* ☎ *028/514–1410* ⊕ *www. capenature.co.za* ⊠ *R40* ⊙ *Weekdays 7–7.*

WHERE TO STAY

$
RENTAL
FAMILY
🏠 **A Hilltop Country Retreat.** Set in the foothills of the Langeberg Mountains, A Hilltop Retreat offers spacious and luxurious self-catering accommodation. **Pros:** beautiful setting; children of all ages are welcome. **Cons:** no oven in the kitchenette; rooms are close together. Ⓢ *Rooms from: R1000* ⊠ *7 Bergsig Ave.* ☎ *028/514–2294* ⊕ *www. ahilltop.co.za* ⤜ *4 rooms, 2 suites* ⊙| *No meals.*

$$
B&B/INN
🏠 **Augusta de Mist.** This elegant Cape Dutch homestead, established in 1802, now serves as a comfortable retreat on 3½ acres of fynbos; the house still has original reed and mud ceilings, yellowwood shutters, and authentic metalwork. **Pros:** quiet, peaceful setting; highly acclaimed restaurant. **Cons:** no children under 14. Ⓢ *Rooms from: R1670* ⊠ *3 Human St.* ☎ *028/514–2425* ⊕ *www.augustademist.com* ⤜ *6 suites* ⊙| *Breakfast.*

$$ **De Kloof Luxury Estate.** Situated in manicured gardens with breathtak-
HOTEL ing scenery, De Kloof Luxury Estate is a chic, upmarket boutique hotel that offers five-star accommodation in one of the oldest Cape Dutch manors in Swellendam. **Pros:** set in manicured gardens; swimming pool; family suite available. **Cons:** prior approval is needed for children under 8. $ *Rooms from: R2100* ⊠ *8 Weltevrede St.* ☎ *028/514–1303* ⊕ *www. dekloof.co.za* 🛏 *8 suites* ⏎ *Multiple meal plans.*

$$ **Schoone Oordt.** The ultimate luxury getaway, this renovated Victorian
HOTEL manor house, with original ceilings, wooden floors, and antique furnishings, boasts five-star accommodation. **Pros:** lush gardens with a swimming pool; the staff are happy to cater to special dietary requirements. **Cons:** not all rooms are in the beautiful main house. $ *Rooms from: R2250* ⊠ *1 Swellengrebel St.* ☎ *028/514–1248* ⊕ *www.schooneoordt. co.za* 🛏 *8 rooms, 1 suite, 1 cottage* ⏎ *Breakfast.*

SPORTS AND THE OUTDOORS
HORSEBACK RIDING
Two Feathers Horse Trails. You can take just a little trot or a longer excursion through the Marloth Nature Reserve on horseback with Two Feathers Horse Trails. Expect to pay around R300 for a 1½-hour excursion. Full-day rides can be arranged on request and include a picnic lunch. ⊠ *5 Liechtenstein St.* ☎ *082/494–8279* ⊕ *www. swellendambackpackers.co.za.*

EN ROUTE From Swellendam return to the N2 and turn right toward Cape Town. The road sweeps through rich, rolling cropland that extends to the base of the Langeberg. In the town of Riviersonderend (pronounced riff-*ear*-son-der-ent), stop at the excellent Ou Meul Bakkery (Old Mill Bakery) in Riversonderend to stock up on succulent pies, rusks (dry biscuits), and home produce. A few kilometers on, turn right onto the R406, a good gravel road that leads to the village of Greyton, in the lee of the Riviersonderend Mountains.

GREYTON

32 km (20 miles) west of Swellendam.

The charming village of Greyton, filled with white thatch cottages and quiet lanes, is a popular weekend retreat for Capetonians as well as a permanent home for many retirees. The village offers almost nothing in the way of traditional sights, but it's a relaxing place to stop for a meal or a night, and a great base for walks into the surrounding mountains. There are plenty of small B&Bs and guesthouses to stay in, but no large hotels.

GETTING HERE AND AROUND
If you're driving from Swellendam, take the N2 west. Expect the trip to take an hour to an hour and a half.

VISITOR INFORMATION
Contacts Greyton Tourism Bureau ⊠ *29 Main Rd.* ☎ *028/254-9564, 028/254-9414* ⊕ *www.greytontourism.com* ⏱ *Weekdays 8-1 and 2-5, Sat. 9-2.*

EXPLORING

Genadendal (*Valley of Grace*). The neighboring village to Greyton is Genadendal, a Moravian mission station founded in 1737 to educate the Khoekhoen and convert them to Christianity. Seeing this impoverished hamlet today, it's difficult to comprehend the major role the mission played in the early history of South Africa. In the late 18th century it was the second-largest settlement after Cape Town, and its Khoekhoen craftspeople produced the finest silver cutlery and woodwork in the country. Some of the first written works in Afrikaans were printed here, and the coloured community (⇨ "*A Note on the Term 'Coloured'*" box) greatly influenced the development of Afrikaans as it is heard today. None of this went down well with the white government of the time. By 1909 new legislation prohibited coloured ownership of land, and in 1926 the Department of Public Education closed the settlement's teachers' training college, arguing that coloureds were better employed on neighboring farms. In 1980 all the buildings on Church Square were declared national monuments (it's considered the country's most authentic church square), but despite a number of community-based projects, Genadendal has endured a long slide into obscurity and remains impoverished. In 1995, then president Nelson Mandela renamed his official residence Genadendal. You can walk the streets and tour the historic buildings facing Church Square. Ask at the Genadendal Mission Museum for somebody to show you around or phone ahead for a guided tour. With luck you'll meet up with Samuel Baatjes, a fourth-generation Genadendal resident. Tours last as long as you would like them to and depend on your level of interest. ⊠ *Genadendal* ☎ *028/251–8582* ⊕ *www.viewoverberg.com/Genadendal.asp.*

Genadendal Mission Museum. Of particular note in Genadendal is the Genadendal Mission Museum, spread through 15 rooms in three buildings. The museum collection, the only one in South Africa to be named a National Cultural Treasure, includes unique household implements, books, tools, and musical instruments, among them the country's oldest pipe organ, which arrived in the village in 1832. Wall displays examine mission life in the Cape in the 18th and 19th centuries, focusing on the early missionaries' work with the Khoekhoen. ⊠ *Church Sq., Genadendal* ☎ *028/251–8582* ⊕ *www.museumsonline.co.za* ▭ *R10* ☉ *Mon.–Thurs. 9–5, Fri. 9–3:30, Sat 10–2* ☉ *Closed Sun.*

SPORTS AND THE OUTDOORS

HIKING

Boesmanskloof Trail. In addition to day hikes and short walks, you can take the 32-km (20-mile) Boesmanskloof Trail through the Riviersonderend Mountains between Greyton and the exquisite hamlet of McGregor. In the good old days, youngsters used to walk from Greyton to McGregor for an energetic game of tennis before walking home again the same evening. Hikers often book the following night's accommodation at a local B&B and have a good meal and a good night's sleep before heading home. In McGregor the trailhead is about 14 km (8½ miles) away from the town, but most guesthouses will have someone pick you up and drop you off. Note that cell-phone coverage is sporadic on the trail. You do need a permit to do the hike; buy one from the

Greyton Tourism Bureau. Take water and adequate protective clothing, as the weather can change quickly. A great place to stay if you're walking from Greyton to McGregor is the Eagle's Nest guesthouse (⊕ *www.boesmanskloofmcgregor.com*), perched right at the top of the mountain; the views are spectacular and the beds comfortable. Simpler accommodation, in hiking huts on a private farm (R130 per person with bedding), can be booked through **Barry Oosthuizen** (023/625–1794 or 072/240–0498), who will also buy groceries and leave them at the hut before you arrive. He can also arrange for your permit for the full hiking route, for R80.

EN ROUTE

To head back toward Cape Town, follow the R406 to the N2. After the town of Bot River, the road leaves the wheat fields and climbs into the mountains. It's lovely country, full of rock and pine forest interspersed with orchards. **Sir Lowry's Pass** serves as the gateway to Cape Town and the Cape Winelands, a magnificent breach in the mountains that opens to reveal the curving expanse of False Bay, the long ridge of the peninsula, and, in the distance, Table Mountain.

WEST COAST

The West Coast is an acquired taste. It's dry and bleak, and other than the ubiquitous exotic gum trees, nothing grows higher than your knees. But it's a wild and wonderful place. An icy sea pounds long, deserted beaches or rocky headlands, and the sky stretches for miles.

Historically, this area has been populated by hardy fisherfolk and tough, grizzled farmers. Over the years they have worked out a balance with the extreme elements—responding with a stoic minimalism that is obvious in the building styles, the cuisine, and the language.

Unfortunately, minimalism became fashionable, and urban refugees started settling on the West Coast. The first lot wasn't bad—they bought tattered old houses and renovated them just enough to make them livable. Then came those who insisted on building replicas of their suburban homes at the coast. And then—worst of all—came the developers. They bought up huge tracts of land and cut them into tiny little plots, popping horrid little houses onto them. Or perhaps they'd turn a whole bay into a pseudo-Greek village. As a result, the austere aesthetic that makes the West Coast so special is fast disappearing. But it's not gone—at least not yet.

Just inland from the West Coast is the Swartland (Black Ground, a reference to the fertile soil that supports a flourishing wheat and wine industry). Rolling wheat fields extend as far as the eye can see to mountains on either side. In summer the heat is relentless, and there's a sea of golden-brown grain, but in winter the landscape is a shimmery green, and when there's snow on the mountains, it's as pretty as can be. The Swartland includes Piketberg, Malmesbury, Darling (also considered part of the West Coast), and the twin towns of Riebeek West and Riebeek Kasteel.

To the north, the Cederberg is an absolutely beautiful and rugged range of mountains, most of which is a designated wilderness area. In South

Africa that means you may hike there with a permit, but there are no laid-out trails and no accommodations or facilities of any kind. Fantastic rock formations, myriad flowering plants, delicate rock art, and crystal-clear streams with tinkling waterfalls and deep pools make this a veritable hiker's paradise.

A loop around the West Coast, Swartland, and the Cederberg, starting from Cape Town, will take a minimum of three days, but the distances are long, so plan to spend more time here if you can.

GETTING HERE AND AROUND
The roads up the West Coast are generally good, but some dirt roads are rutted and bumpy. If you plan to head into the Cederberg mountains rather than just sticking to the small towns, consider renting a 4x4, especially in winter, when roads become muddy and you run a small risk of being snowed in.

The major car-rental agencies have offices in the smaller towns, but it's best to deal with the Cape Town offices; you'll probably want to pick up a car at the airport anyway. ⇨ *For car-rental agencies, see the Cape Winelands.*

To get up the West Coast and to the Cederberg, take the N1 out of Cape Town. Just before Century City shopping center, take Exit 10, which is marked "Goodwood, Malmesbury, Century City Drive and Sable Road" and leads to the N7, the region's major access road. Though the highway is well marked, get yourself a good GPS or map from a bookstore or tourism office and explore some of the smaller roads, which offer surprising vistas or a glimpse into the rural heart of the Western Cape. The Versveld Pass, between Piketberg and the hamlet of Piket-Bo-Berg, at the top of the mountains, has views that stretch for miles.

Intercape Mainliner heads from Cape Town daily up the N7, which is the main route up to the Cederberg. The bus stops at Citrusdal and Clanwilliam, but not coastal towns such as Langebaan and Elands Bay. Expect to pay around R324 to Citrusdal and R333 to Clanwilliam. The journey to Clanwilliam from Cape Town takes about four hours. ⇨ *For detailed information about travel by bus, see Bus Travel in Travel Smart.*

Although there's public train service to major West Coast towns, it's not recommended, as there have been regular on-board muggings.

TOURS
To see the exceptional rock art in the Cederberg, it's recommended that you take a tour to fully appreciate and understand this ancient art form, about which experts still have questions.

Clanwilliam Living Landscape Project. The community-driven Clanwilliam Living Landscape Project has trained locals to act as guides. Expect to pay around R120 for a one-hour tour that includes a visit to two sites, and R220 for a full tour, which takes about three hours. If you don't have your own vehicle, the guide can pick you up, but you'll be charged a little extra for gas. To see some majestic scenery, take a three-day hike from the Living Landscape Project headquarters through the dramatic Cederberg mountain range. Donkey carts are used to transport your luggage from cottage to cottage in the Moravian Mission villages of Heuningvlei, Brugkraal, and Wupperthal. Expect to pay R2,175–R3,250 per person. ✉ *18 Park St., Clanwilliam* ☎ *027/482–1911* ⊕ *www.cllp.uct.ac.za.*

Donkey Cart Adventures. For something completely out of the ordinary, try a Donkey Cart Adventure, which starts at the top of the Pakhuis Pass and ends a couple of hours later in the tiny hamlet of Heuningvlei in the heart of the Cederberg Wilderness Area. The donkey-cart route is windy and takes you through some spectacular scenery and flora. It's best to plan this trip for spring, when the fynbos is at its best, or in autumn. In summer, temperatures soar in the Cederberg. ✉ *Pakhuis Pass, Clanwilliam* ✛ *20 km (12 miles) outside Clanwilliam* ☎ *027/492–3070 Heuningvlei Tourism* ⊕ *www.cedheroute.co.za.*

Elandsberg Eco Tourism. Rooibos tea is a big part of this region's economy, and a rooibos tour with Elandsberg Eco-Tourism should fill you in on all you need to know. The shorter tour, around 1½ hours, costs R100 for four or more people, and the 2½- to 3-hour tour costs around R175 for four or more people. They will still do a tour if there are fewer people, but they will charge a little extra to cover their costs. Because the tour is out on a farm, they will arrange to pick you up in town. Booking is essential. ✉ *Off R364, 22 km (14 miles) outside Clanwilliam, Graafwater* ☎ *027/482–2022* ⊕ *www.elandsberg.co.za.*

Goede Hoop Citrus. During the orange-harvest season (April–September), you can gain insight into the fruit industry with an hour-long tour through the packing sheds at Goede Hoop Citrus. These tours meet at the Citrusdal Tourism Bureau. ✉ *Voortrekker St., Citrusdal* ☎ *022/921–8100* ⊕ *www.ghcitrus.com.*

VISITOR INFORMATION

There are tourist offices in most small towns along the West Coast, but the West Coast Regional Tourism Organization has information on the entire area. Visit its website to get a good overview of the area.

The Flowerline is a central hotline that provides details about where the flowers are best seen each day. You can call 24 hours a day July–September.

Contacts Flowerline ☎ *072/938–8186.* **West Coast Regional Tourism Organization** ✉ *58 Long St., Moorreesburg* ☎ *022/433–8505* ⊕ *www.capewestcoast. org* ⊙ *Weekdays 7:45–4:30.*

DARLING

82 km (51 miles) north of Cape Town.

Darling is best known for three draws: its beautiful wildflowers; its sensational performer, Pieter-Dirk Uys, otherwise known as Evita Bezuidenhout; and the hugely popular rock music festival Rocking the Daisies, held each October on Cloof Wine Estate. Evita is at her best all year-round (⇨ *Nightlife and Performing Arts, below*). The wildflowers are usually at their best August–October, and an annual Wildflower and Orchid Show is held in September. Also in September, the whole town comes alive during the Voorkamerfest (directly translated as "Front

Room Festival"), when different homes host a variety of performers for the weekend and you can enjoy pop-up food stalls and wine tasting. When driving into Darling, ignore the rather unattractive new houses on the Cape Town side of the village and head straight through to the Victorian section of town, where pretty period houses line up amid lush gardens.

GETTING HERE AND AROUND
Darling is an easy hour's drive from Cape Town along the N7 north and then west on the R315. Alternately, you could go north on the R27 out of town, then east on the R315.

VISITOR INFORMATION
Contacts Darling Tourism Bureau ⊠ *Darling Museum, Pastorie and Hill Sts.* ☏ *022/492–3361* ⊕ *www.darlingtourism.co.za* ⊙ *Mon.–Thurs. 9–1 and 2–4, Fri. 9–1 and 2–3:30, weekends 10–3.*

EXPLORING
Darling Cellars. This large producer makes wines under a number of labels. In the Onyx range, look for the 2009 Sauvignon Blanc, with notes of peas, passion fruit, green figs, traces of guava on the nose, and a zingy aftertaste. Other suggestions include the 2008 Cabernet Sauvignon with aromas of wood, ripe blackberries, and cassis. Don't miss out on the Sweet Darling range, a selection of white, red, and rosé wines cultivated from local grapes. It's all good, drinkable stuff at very affordable prices. ⊠ *R315* ☏ *022/492–2276* ⊕ *www.darlingcellars.co.za* 🍷 *Tastings R20* ⊙ *Mon.–Thurs. 8–5, Fri. 8–4, Sat. 10–2; cellar tours by appointment.*

Groote Post Vineyard. Former dairy farmer Peter Pentz had enough of getting up at 4 am to milk his cows, so together with his son, Nick, he turned instead to wine farming at Groote Post Vineyard. Groote Post fans couldn't be happier. The large, environmentally sensitive winery got off to a fantastic start when its maiden 1999 Sauvignon Blanc was judged one of the best in the Cape, and Groote Post has been garnering awards ever since. Try the award-winning Groote Post Reserve Sauvignon Blanc 2012, packed with flavors of granadilla, green fig, and green pepper, or taste the Groote Post Reserve Pinot Noir 2009, with hints of plum, raspberry and dried beef(!). There are no cellar tours. The restaurant, Hilda's Kitchen, is a really excellent choice for lunch; regulars have been known to want to punch the chef if the Old Man's Steak Roll with its secret sauce isn't on the menu. A scrumptious picnic basket, teeming with local cheeses and cured meats, quiche, and chocolate brownies can be ordered in advance at around R350 per couple. A large portion of the farm has been left uncultivated and is covered with endangered *renosterveld* (literally, "rhino vegetation" in Afrikaans), which is found only in this area. These scrubby bushes might not look like much, but in the past they supported large herds of game. Because the vegetation grows in fertile soil, a lot of renosterveld has been lost to agriculture. Game drives (R130) through this unique vegetation for groups of 4 to 10 people are usually run by the charismatic owner, Peter; advanced bookings are essential. ⊠ *Off R307* ☏ *022/492–2825* ⊕ *www.grootepost.com* 🍷 *Tastings R25* ⊙ *Weekdays 8–5, weekends 10–4.*

3

Mamre Moravian Mission Station. As you head out of Cape Town on the
N1 or R27 on your way up the coast, it's easy to whiz past the tiny
whitewashed settlement of Mamre on the R304. But it's worth turning off here to check out the old thatch buildings that made up the
Moravian Mission Station, founded in 1808. The church here is almost
always open, but phone ahead to make sure. All the buildings dating
from this period have been restored and declared national monuments.
It is signposted in Afrikaans: Morawiese Kerk. Unfortunately, the rest
of the town is unlovely and crippled with the usual ills of unemployment and poverty. ⊠ *Main Rd., 650 feet from traffic circle, Mamre*
☎ *021/576–1134.*

OFF THE
BEATEN
PATH

Tienie Versfeld Wildflower Reserve. During the flower season, usually
August–October, the Tienie Versfeld Wildflower Reserve is just fantastic: a wonderful, unpretentious, uncommercialized little gem, boasting
a range of uniquely South African veld types, like renoster-, strand-,
riet-, and sandveld. This variation has produced some amazing flowers. Look out for the Geophytes (bulbous plants), which are striking
in their diverse sizes and colors. ⊠ *R315, 12 km (7½ miles) west of
Darling* ⊕ *www.sa-venues.com/game-reserves/wc_tienie-versveld.htm*
⊠ *Free* ☉ *Daily 24 hrs.*

WHERE TO STAY

$

B&B/INN

▥ **Darling Lodge.** You'll soon be made to feel at home at this pretty Victorian B&B set in a lovely garden in the heart of the village. **Pros:** centrally
located in Darling; perfect accommodation for families; only 15 minutes
from the coast. **Cons:** limited number of rooms; dinner and lunch only
on request. ⑤ *Rooms from: R960* ⊠ *22 Pastorie St.* ☎ *022/492–3062*
⊕ *www.darlinglodge.co.za* ⌁ *6 rooms* ◯ *Breakfast.*

$

B&B/INN

▥ **Trinity Guest Lodge and Restaurant.** This old Victorian house has been
elegantly transformed into a stylish and comfortable guest lodge; white
linen and subtle furnishings create a restful atmosphere. **Pros:** in-house
group cooking classes offered; fabulous on-site restaurant. **Cons:** close
quarters; prior arrangements need to be made if you're bringing the
kids. ⑤ *Rooms from: R800* ⊠ *19 Long St.* ☎ *022/492–3430, 083/325–
4148* ⊕ *www.trinitylodge.co.za* ⌁ *6 rooms* ◯ *Breakfast.*

NIGHTLIFE AND PERFORMING ARTS

Fodor'sChoice
★

Evita se Perron. One of Darling's main attractions is Evita se Perron, the
theater and restaurant started by satirist and drag-artist Pieter-Dirk
Uys. The theater is on the platform of the Darling station (*perron* is
the Afrikaans word for "railway platform"). Pieter-Dirk Uys has made
his alter ego, Evita Bezuidenhout, a household name in South Africa.
Performances cost R150 and take place Saturday afternoon and evening
and Sunday afternoon. Come early to enjoy a buffet meal in the restaurant (around R100 per person). In the same complex, **Evita's A en C** (get
the pun on the name of the ruling party, the ANC?) is the gallery of an
arts-and-crafts collective and skills-development center. Here you can
see and buy works from West Coast artists; it's open Tuesday–Sunday
10–4. ⊠ *Darling station, 8 Arcadia St.* ☎ *022/492–2851, 022/492–2831*
⊕ *www.evita.co.za.*

LANGEBAAN

50 km (31 miles) northwest of Darling.

Probably the most popular destination on the coast, Langebaan is a great base from which to explore the region, and the sheltered lagoon makes for fantastic water sports, especially windsurfing, kite surfing, and sea kayaking. The town has a truly laid-back, beachy feel. To quote a local: "There is nowhere in Langebaan you can't go barefoot." Lots of Capetonians have weekend houses and head here on Friday afternoon with boats, bikes, and boards in tow. If you're not into water sports and serious tanning, however, Langebaan doesn't have that much to offer. The town grew up around a slipway, yacht club, and cluster of brick-faced beach houses, and the main drag is unexciting. Though the town comes alive in summer as youngsters crowd the beach and flex their muscles, during the off-season Langebaan quickly reverts to a quiet settlement where people retire to fish and mess about on boats.

GETTING HERE AND AROUND

It's about 30 minutes by car from Darling to Langebaan.

VISITOR INFORMATION

Contacts **Langebaan Tourism Bureau** ✉ *Municipal Bldg., Bree St.* ☎ *022/772–1515* ⊕ *capewestcoastpeninsula.co.za/langebaan* ⊙ *Weekdays 9–5, Sat. 9–2.*

EXPLORING

FAMILY **West Coast Fossil Park.** About 20 minutes from Langebaan on the R45 on the way to Paternoster is the West Coast Fossil Park, one of the richest fossil sites in the world. It was discovered by chance while the area was being mined for phosphates in the 1950s. Since then, more than 200 kinds of fossilized animals have been collected, including the Africa bear, which used to roam this area. The park has been declared a national monument, and the curators have done much to make the park and information about the fossils as accessible as possible. There are interactive guided tours, cycling trails through the areas, and interesting archaeological workshops for all ages. There's also a children's play park and a simple coffee shop where you can have a toasted sandwich. ■TIP➜ **Kids will love the tour and the dinosaur digs they can take home.** ✉ *R27* ☎ *022/766–1606* ⊕ *www.fossilpark.org.za* 🖾 *R20, tours R55* ⊙ *Weekdays 8–4, weekends 10–1; tours on the hr.*

West Coast National Park. Even if you don't stop in West Coast National Park, consider driving the scenic road that runs through it rather than the R27 to Langebaan. The park is a fabulous mix of lagoon wetlands, pounding surf, and coastal fynbos. On a sunny day the lagoon assumes a magical color, made all the more impressive by blinding white beaches and the sheer emptiness of the place. Birders can have a field day identifying water birds, and the sandveld flowers are among the best along the West Coast. Postberg, the little mountain at the tip of the reserve where ships would drop off their mail on their trip around the Cape, is open only in flower season, which changes from year to year but usually falls between August and October. It's easy to run out of superlatives when describing West Coast flowers, but imagine acres of land carpeted in multicolored blooms—as far as the eye can see. If you're lucky, you may

Pieter-Dirk Uys: Everyone's Darling

It's fitting that Pieter-Dirk Uys (⊕ *www. pdu.co.za*) and his alter ego, Evita Bezuidenhout (⊕ *www.evita.co.za*), live in a village called Darling. He's the darling of South African satire, and his speech is peppered with dramatic and warmhearted "dahlings." *Tannie* (Auntie) Evita is as much a South African icon as braais and biltong.

Evita Bezuidenhout debuted in a newspaper column written by playwright Pieter-Dirk Uys in the 1970s. He dished the dirt as though he were an insider at the Nationalist Party. His mysterious source's voice grew so strong that she was soon nicknamed the "Evita of Pretoria." She hit the stage in the early 1980s, when apartheid was in full swing and the ruling Nationalist Party was short on humor.

Uys's first production, *Adapt or Dye*, was performed at a small venue in Johannesburg at 11 pm, a time when he hoped the censors would be in bed. The titles of his shows and some characters (all of which he plays himself) are intricately wound up with South African politics and life. *Adapt or Dye*, for instance, was based on a speech by former prime minister P. W. Botha, who said, "South Africans have to adapt to a changing world or die." Thirty-five years later his latest show is *Adapt or Fly*, a title out of the mouth of an ANC politician.

Every performance shows an intricate understanding of the country and her people. Over the years, Uys's richest material has come from the government. Most politicians were happy to be lampooned; in an inhumane society, laughing at themselves made them seem more human. If there's any criticism leveled at Uys, it's that for all his biting remarks, he played court jester to the apartheid government and held back too much. He would argue that too many punches don't put people in seats; too many tickles can be vacuous.

Uys is not just about comedy and satire, however. He's deeply committed to transforming society. Before the first democratic elections in 1994, he embarked on self-funded voter-education tours. He's now channeling his considerable energy into tackling HIV/AIDS. He speaks at schools, where he uses humor and intelligence and pulls no punches. During his presentation he demonstrates how to put a condom on a banana. This he swiftly replaces with a rubber phallus, "because," he explains with a twinkle, "men and boys don't have bananas between their legs. A condom on a banana on the bedside table is not going to protect you!" Of course, the kids shriek with laughter. As always, humor is his weapon of mass distraction.

In 2002, Uys was awarded the Truth and Reconciliation Award, as well as nominated a national living treasure by the South African Human Sciences Research Council. Tannie Evita also has more than a few fans. She received the Living Legacy 2000 Award in San Diego by the Women's International Center for "her contribution to the place of women in the last century." Pieter-Dirk Uys's autobiographies, *Between the Devil and the Deep—A Memoir of Acting and Reacting* and *Elections & Erections*, make for good reading. In 2015 Uys is 70 and Evita is 80. Here's to both of you, dahlings!

—Karena du Plessis

catch glimpses of zebra, wildebeest, or bat-eared fox. Accommodation in the park is rarer than hen's teeth, and families book cottages at the little village of Churchhaven here for years at a time. ⊠ *Off the R27, 11 km (7 miles) north of the R315* ☎ *022/772–2144* ⊕ *www.sanparks. org* ✉ *R120 in flower season, R60 out of season* ☉ *Park: daily 7–6:30. Postberg: flower season, daily 9–5*

WHERE TO EAT

$$$$
SEAFOOD

✕ **Die Strandloper Seafood Restaurant.** For a no-frills lunch on the beach, book a table at Die Strandloper. Bring your own drinks and games, and expect to linger for the afternoon. The focus is on the rustic outdoor *braai* (barbecue) area, where a 10-course feast is served over a couple of hours. If you're keen on seafood, this is the place to eat. Dishes include grilled snoek, smoked angelfish, *bokkoms* (dried, salted fish), crayfish, and mussels. For dessert there's *koeksisters* (braided pastries) and strong coffee. Adults eat for around R260, and children are charged according to height. ⑤ *Average main: R260* ☎ *022/772–2490* ⊕ *www.strandloper. com* ⌨ *Reservations essential* ▭ *No credit cards* ☉ *Closed Mon., Tues., and Thurs. No dinner.*

$$
SOUTH AFRICAN
FAMILY

✕ **Geelbek Restaurant.** Passionate about food and history, Elmarie Leonard created this restaurant to preserve the area's fast-disappearing old recipes. It's her way of paying homage to the different nationalities that helped shape the West Coast. The restaurant is in an old homestead dating to 1761, when it served as an outpost for people making the hard trip inland. Today the trip is a lot easier, but diners are still thrilled to tuck into Geelbek's fragrant Malay chicken curry and traditional bobotie. Every month the menu is planned around the ingredients, herbs, and fresh produce of the area. Geelbek is the only restaurant on the West Coast that serves *denningsvleis*, a Cape Malay lamb stew flavored with tamarind, which is a South African institution. The West Coast battered hake and calamari, golden french fries, and tartar sauce is a classic. This is also a great place for tea. The lemon-meringue pie stands a mile high, and the chocolate cake is delicious. You can sit in the garden or on the veranda and watch the weaver birds go crazy in the nearby trees. ⑤ *Average main: R120* ⊠ *West Coast National Park* ☎ *022/772–2134* ☉ *No dinner.*

WHERE TO STAY

$$
HOTEL

⚏ **The Farmhouse Hotel.** Centered on a restored farmstead built in the 1860s, this hotel has thick white walls, tile floors, and timber beams. **Pros:** great views over the lagoon; relaxed atmosphere. **Cons:** avoid rooms above the kitchen area, as they can be noisy; only two rooms have air-conditioning; area is very windy—expect a few bad hair days. ⑤ *Rooms from: R1900* ⊠ *5 Egret St.* ☎ *022/772–2062* ⊕ *www. thefarmhousehotel.com* ⇥ *18 rooms* ❍ *Breakfast.*

$
B&B/INN
FAMILY

⚏ **Friday Island.** If you like water sports or cycling or are generally active, then this guesthouse is a great choice: it's bright, airy, and right on the beach. **Pros:** perfect for family vacations; fall out of bed onto the beach. **Cons:** young, hip, and happening crowd might not suit those wanting a quiet escape; sports center next door can get noisy during the flower season in spring and the summer holidays over Christmas and New

Year. ⑤ *Rooms from: R720* ✉ *92 Main St.* ☎*022/772–2506* ⊕*www. fridayisland.co.za* ⇨*12 rooms* ⦿*Breakfast.*

SPORTS AND THE OUTDOORS

The sheltered Langebaan Lagoon is a haven for water-sports enthusiasts, but you don't have to be energetic all the time. There are expansive stretches of beach that are good for walking, sunbathing, and kite flying. Be warned, however: the water might look calm and idyllic, but it's still cold, and the wind can blow unmercifully for days at a stretch. It's fantastic for wind- or kite surfing, but not so great if you want to spend a peaceful day under your umbrella with a book.

Cape Sports Centre. You'll find everything you need here to kite surf, windsurf, kayak, or canoe or even learn how. You can rent gear or take lessons from qualified instructors, including packages consisting of a week of intensive lessons. Cape Sports Centre also rents mountain bikes. ✉ *98 Main St.* ☎*022/772–1114* ⊕ *www.capesport.co.za.*

PATERNOSTER

47 km (29 miles) northwest of Langebaan.

Paternoster is a mostly unspoiled village of whitewashed thatch cottages perched on a deserted stretch of coastline. The population here consists mainly of fisherfolk, who for generations have eked out a living harvesting crayfish and other seafood. Despite the overt poverty, the village has a character and sense of identity often lacking in larger towns. It helps if you turn a blind eye to the rather opulent houses on the northern side of the village.

GETTING HERE AND AROUND

Paternoster is about a half-hour drive from Langebaan. Take Langebaanweg out of town until you reach the junction with the R45. Turn left and head northwest toward Paternoster. At Vredenburg the road name changes to the R399.

EXPLORING

Columbine Nature Reserve. Along the coast just south of Paternoster, the Columbine Nature Reserve is a great spot for spring wildflowers, coastal fynbos, and succulents. Cormorants and sacred ibis are common here, and the population of the endangered African black oystercatcher is growing each year. You can walk anywhere you like in the 692-acre park (map provided); a round-trip through the reserve is 7 km (4 miles). It's very exposed, however, so don't plan to walk in the middle of the day, or you'll end up with some serious sunburn. Die-hard anglers and their families camp here during the Christmas holidays and revel in the abundant fish. The dusty road has no name, but head south out of town and ask directions of anybody along the way—it's impossible to get lost. There aren't that many roads to choose from. ✉ *8 km (5 miles) south of Paternoster* ☎*022/752–2718* ▨*R15.50* ☯ *Daily 7–7.*

WHERE TO EAT

$$ ✕**The Noisy Oyster.** The seaside shack ambience is a perfect foil for the
SEAFOOD   relaxed beach fare on offer here. A quirky and brightly decorated restaurant, this unpretentious gem is not to be missed. The menu changes

frequently as the freshest local ingredients are used. Not surprisingly, seafood is the main attraction—the oysters here are legendary—but meat-eaters will delight in a wide selection of pork, Chalmer steak, lamb, and quail. Enjoy your meal in front of a warm hearth when it's cold out, or dine under the canopy, dotted with fairy lights, on a clear night. $ *Average main: R120* ⊠ *St. Augustine Rd.* ☎ *022/752–2196* ⚠ *Reservations essential* ۞ *Closed Mon. and Tues. No dinner Sun.*

$$
SOUTH AFRICAN
✕ **Oep ve Koep.** Don't be fooled by the appearance of this tiny rustic bistro with a retro garden area. If you're looking for sensational cuisine, Oep ve Koep is the place to go. The chef-owner, Kobus van der Merwe, creates innovative, smart, and scrumptious dishes from traditional recipes. Local veldkos (foraged plants such as wild spinach and succulents) are incorporated into dishes. Oep ve Koep offers a limited menu, so fussy eaters beware. Those willing to take the plunge will not be disappointed, with dishes like pickled whitefish with grapefruit, and West Coast oysters with wild coastal herbs and seaweed flying out of the kitchen. Sunday lunch is a two- or three-course set menu of veldkos and seafood. Expect to pay around R250 per person. Bookings are essential, as Kobus opens the restaurant only on request. $ *Average main: R140* ⊠ *St. Augustine Rd.* ☎ *022/752–2105* ⚠ *Reservations essential* ۞ *On request* ۞ *No dinner.*

$$
SEAFOOD
✕ **Voorstrand.** A little West Coast gem, this old corrugated-iron shack on the beach stood empty for years, then suddenly metamorphosed into a truly innovative seafood restaurant. It's literally set on the sand, so you can almost hear the ones that got away; it's an ideal location to take in the sunset and watch the whales in the bay. Voorstrand serves all the expected seafood and fish, but the Malay-style fish curries and fresh local crayfish are favorites. You could also splash out and try the seafood platter, which includes prawns, oysters, hake, and calamari. Snoek samosas are a nice, local touch and so is the beef fillet served with a creamy mussel sauce. All dishes are freshly prepared while you wait. $ *Average main: R100* ⊠ *Strandloper St.* ☎ *022/752–2038* ⊕ *www.voorstrand.com* ⚠ *Reservations essential.*

WHERE TO STAY

$$$
HOTEL
🏨 **Abalone House and Spa.** This luxurious boutique hotel set in indigenous gardens has eclectic decor—a mix of restored antiques and modern furniture, with bold paintings adorning the walls. **Pros:** great restaurant with a vibey wine and cocktail bar; swimming pool; spa. **Cons:** no children under 12. $ *Rooms from: R3500* ⊠ *3 Kriedoring St.* ☎ *087/820–5974* ⊕ *www.southofafrica.co.za* ⤴ *10 suites* ⊙| *Breakfast.*

$
B&B/INN
🏨 **Paternoster Lodge & Restaurant.** This lodge makes the most of the sweeping views of the Atlantic Ocean; the rooms are simply decorated, but who needs artwork when at every turn you catch glimpses of the azure sea and pretty bay? **Pros:** easy stroll to the beach; kids under 6 stay free. **Cons:** hold your hat during summer as the wind can blow; rooms are close together. $ *Rooms from: R1200* ⊠ *64 St. Augustine Rd.* ☎ *022/752–2023* ⊕ *www.paternosterlodge.co.za* ⤴ *7 rooms* ⊙| *Breakfast.*

ELANDS BAY

75 km (46½ miles) north of Paternoster.

Mention eBay auctions here, and most people will stare at you blankly. But mention the E'bay left-hand break, and you'll get nods of approval and instant admission into the inner circle of experienced surfers, who make the pilgrimage to Elands Bay to experience some of the Western Cape's best surfing.

This lovely destination is at the mouth of the beautiful Verlorenvlei Lagoon. Verlorenvlei (Afrikaans for "lost wetland," a testimony to its remoteness) is a birder's delight; you're likely to see around 240 species, including white pelican, purple gallinule, African spoonbill, African fish eagle, and the goliath and purple herons. Nearby are some fantastic walks to interesting caves with well-preserved rock art that dates back to the Pleistocene era, 10,000 years ago.

GETTING HERE AND AROUND

Elands Bay is a two-hour drive from Paternoster. To get here, double back on the R399 to Vredenburg, then take the R399 north to Velddrif. You'll join the R27 at a junction just outside Velddrif. Follow the signs to Elands Bay through town and continue on to what looks like a secondary road. It may not seem to have a number, but it's still the R27.

WHERE TO EAT

$$$$
SOUTH AFRICAN

✕ **Muisbosskerm.** For the true flavor of West Coast life, come to the original open-air seafood restaurant, on the beach south of Lambert's Bay. It consists of nothing more than a circular *boma* (enclosure) of packed *muisbos* (a local shrub whose name means "mouse bush") and haphazardly arranged benches and tables. You'll watch food cook over blazing fires. Snoek is smoked in an old drum covered with burlap, bread bakes in a clay oven, and everywhere fish sizzles on grills and in giant pots. Prepare to eat as much as you can of the fixed-price meal (R210), using your hands or mussel shells as spoons. Be sure to try some of the local specialties like *bokkoms* (dried salty fish) and *waterblommetjiebredie* (water-flower stew). Crayfish costs extra, but don't order it unless you have an enormous appetite. The only drawback is high-season crowding: when the restaurant operates at full capacity, your 150 fellow diners can overwhelm the experience. Bookings are essential, as the restaurant operates only if there is a minimum of 15 diners. ■TIP➔ **Ask about the quaint Farm Cottage if you're looking for a place to stay.** ⑤ *Average main: R210* ✉ *Elands Bay Rd., 5 km (3 miles) south of Lambert's Bay* ☎ *027/432–1017* ⊕ *www.muisbosskerm.co.za* ⚓ *Reservations essential.*

CLANWILLIAM

46 km (28½ miles) northeast of Elands Bay.

Although the town itself is uninspiring, it's no surprise that half the streets are named after trees or plants. Clanwilliam is at the edge of one of the natural jewels of the Western Cape—the Cederberg Wilderness Area, which takes its name from the cedar trees that used to cover the mountains. In spring the town is inundated with flower-watchers. Clanwilliam is also the center of the rooibos-tea industry.

Clanwilliam was home to Dr. Christiaan Louis Leipoldt, poet and Renaissance man. He is buried in a lovely spot in the mountains a little way out of town; you can visit his grave, which is on the way to the Pakhuis Pass (R364; there's a small signpost). You could also pop into the Clanwilliam Museum, which houses a room devoted to Leipoldt.

GETTING HERE AND AROUND

Driving to Clanwilliam takes close to three hours from Cape Town without stopping, but half the fun is checking out what local farm stands have to offer and stopping to admire the scenery. In spring this trip will take much longer, as you'll likely want to stop to photograph the flowers that carpet the countryside.

VISITOR INFORMATION

Contacts Clanwilliam Tourism Bureau ⊠ *Main Rd.* ☏ *027/482–2024* ⊕ *www. clanwilliam.info* ⊗ *Weekdays 8:30–5, Sat. 8:30–12:30.*

EXPLORING

Cape Leopard Trust. Sheep farming in the Cederberg is a precarious business. Not only are the winters harsh, but valuable sheep may be killed by the leopards that live in the mountains. Farmers have resorted to using gin traps to keep their flocks safe, but with devastating consequences for any animals caught in them. Two researchers, Quinton and Nicole Martins, in conjunction with the farmers in the area, were keen to find a solution to this problem. They established the Cape Leopard Trust. The trust aims to track the movement of the predators to see exactly how many cats remain in the Cederberg and to pinpoint which farmers are most at risk. The trust is also working to introduce Anatolian shepherds—dogs that are bred to bond with sheep and act as their protectors against leopards. Several farmers have already had great success with these dogs. Their flocks are safe, and the leopards aren't at risk of dying an agonizing death in a trap. The Cape Leopard Trust does a lot of outreach and educational work with local schools and offers outdoor holiday programs for kids—and adults. ☏ *027/482–9923, 076/552–1201* ⊕ *www.capeleopard.org.za.*

Fodor's Choice ★ **Cederberg.** Clanwilliam is close to the northern edge of the Cederberg, a mountain range known for its San paintings, its bizarre rock formations, and, once upon a time, its cedars. Most of the ancient cedars have been cut down, but a few specimens still survive in the more remote regions. The Cederberg is a hiking paradise—a wild, largely unspoiled area where you can disappear from civilization for days at a time. About 172,900 acres of this mountain range constitute what has been declared the Cederberg Wilderness Area. Try to visit in spring when the flowers are out and the area is carpeted in orange, yellow, and white flowers. You can get hiking permits from Cape Nature or the local tourism offices in Clanwilliam or Citrusdal. Be sure to tell somebody if you are planning to hike in the area.

A scenic dirt road that heads south out of town, past the tourism bureau and museum, winds for about 30 km (18 miles) into the Cederberg to Algeria, a Cape Nature campsite with self-catering cottages and tent

San Rock Art

The Cederberg has astonishing examples of San rock art, and there is a concerted effort to find ways of managing these sites. On your explorations you'll come across paintings of elephants, eland, bees, people, and otherworldly beings that seem to be half human and half beast. Some examples are in pristine condition, whereas others are battered and scarred from a time when hikers saw nothing wrong with scribbling their names across the art, or lighting fires in the caves and overhangs where the paintings occurred. Luckily, this carelessness has waned. So, too, has our understanding of the art.

For centuries, people believed the rock art was simply a record of what happened during the daily lives of the San. But since about 1970, there has been a belief that the art is much richer and carries enormous spiritual meaning that tells us about the inner lives of the San. The art is riddled with metaphors, and it's unpacking the rich symbolism that poses a real challenge. Drawings of an eland, for instance, are not simply depictions of animals the San have seen or hope to hunt. Rather the eland serves as an intermediary between the physical and spiritual worlds.

sites set in an idyllic valley. Algeria is the starting point for several excellent hikes into the Cederberg. The short, one-hour hike to a waterfall is great, but it's worth going into the mountains for a day or two, for which you will need to book and obtain a permit through **Cape Nature** or from one of the local farms, many of which have simple, self-catering cottages on their land. ⊕ *www.capenature.co.za.*

Cederberg Private Cellar. The Cederberg might be the last place you'd expect to find a vineyard, but that's what makes Cederberg Private Cellar so unusual. It's been in the Nieuwoudt family for five generations. When old man Nieuwoudt, known to everyone as "Oom Pollie," planted the first vines in the 1970s, all his sheep-farming neighbors thought he had gone mad. Today, however, winemaker David Nieuwoudt and his viticulturist father, Ernst, are laughing all the way to the awards ceremonies. At an altitude of around 3,300 feet, this is the highest vineyard in the Western Cape, and consequently is almost completely disease-free. They don't have to spray for the mildew and mealybugs that are the bane of wine farmers in the Winelands and Constantia. All the wines are excellent; in fact you'll struggle to see the labels for all the wine accolades pasted on the bottles. Wine sales staff laugh when you ask them to identify their favorite wines and remark that it's like somebody asking you which child you like most. The farm has self-catering accommodation at Sanddrif, which is near the Wolfberg Cracks (cracks in the mountain that lure hikers), and Malgat (a huge rock pool), both well-known Cederberg attractions. The Cederberg Observatory also operates on this farm on Saturday. It's an open-air wonder run by passionate stargazers, who give a slide presentation when the weather permits and then help you spot faraway galaxies on their superpowerful telescopes. The little farm shop usually stocks delicious koeksisters served with strong coffee, which cuts through the sweetness. ⊠ *Dwarsrivier Farm, Algeria turnoff from the N7* ☎ *027/482–2827* ⊕ *www.cederbergwine.com* ☒ *Tastings R20* ☉ *Mon.–Sat. 9–noon and 2–4.*

Clanwilliam Museum (*Ou Tronk Museum*). The display is old-fashioned and not particularly well curated at the Clanwilliam Museum but still gives a sense of remarkable native son Dr. Christiaan Louis Leipoldt and early settler life in the mountains. The wagons, carts, and rudimentary household equipment speak of much harder times, when pioneers headed into the high country wanting to farm or escape colonial control in the cities. ⊠ *Main Rd.* ☎ *027/482–2024* ⊕ *clanwilliammuseum.webs. com* ☒ *R10* ☉ *Weekdays 8–1, Sat. 8–noon.*

Pakhuis Pass. East of Clanwilliam the R364 becomes a spectacularly scenic gravel road called Pakhuis Pass. Fantastic rock formations glow in the early morning or late afternoon. There's even a mountain range called the Tra-Tra Mountains, a completely fantastical name for a suitably fantastical landscape. A steep, narrow road to the right leads to the mission town of **Wuppertal,** with its characteristic white-thatch houses and sleepy air. This used to be a thriving Moravian mission station, and remnants of the old industries remain—a baker still turns out soft, yeasty loaves that are snapped up as fast as they come out of the oven, and you can see shoes being made in the local shoe factory. You can drive this road in an ordinary rental car, but be very careful in wet weather. Another way of seeing Pakhuis Pass is to take a Donkey Cart Adventures trip down to the tiny remote village of Heuningvlei, a former Moravian mission station. Currently only 20 families live here, making a modest living as subsistence farmers.

Ramskop Wildflower Garden. At its best in August—when the Clanwilliam Flower Show takes place at the old Dutch Reformed church, and almost every available space in town is filled with flowers—the Ramskop Wildflower Garden is a wonderful opportunity to see many of the region's flowers all growing in one place. The best time to go is between 11 am and 3 pm, when the sun is at its apex and the flowers are open. You pay to enter the flower garden at the entrance of the Clanwilliam Dam, on the road out of town past the garden. They won't charge you if the weather isn't great and the flowers aren't at their best—that's small-town hospitality for you. There is a simple coffee shop in the garden. Expect opening times to vary for no particular reason. ⊠ *Ou Kaapseweg* ☎ *027/482–8012* ☒ *R21.30* ☉ *Daily 8–5.*

WHERE TO STAY

$$$$
HOTEL
Fodor's Choice
★

🏨 **Bushmans Kloof Wilderness Reserve & Wellness Retreat.** It's no surprise that Bushmans Kloof garners awards each year—the lodge is in an area of rich cultural significance and a South African National Heritage site, and if you spend some time here, you're unlikely to want to leave. **Pros:** you can fly in to the reserve from Cape Town, which takes about an hour; many outdoor activities on offer; stunning rock art on the property; Western Cape is malaria-free, unlike other parts of the country with wildlife lodges. **Cons:** no small kids allowed at the lodge;

Rooibos Tea

Chances are you will either love or hate *rooibos* (red bush) tea, which South Africans drink in vast quantities. It has an unusual, earthy taste, and is naturally sweet. People drink it hot with lemon and honey or with milk or as a refreshing iced tea with slices of lemon and a sprig of mint. It's rich in minerals, such as copper, iron, potassium, calcium, fluoride, zinc, manganese, and magnesium; contains antioxidants; and is low in tannin. Best of all, it has no caffeine. Trendy chefs are incorporating it into their cooking, and you might see rooibos-infused sauces or marinades mentioned on menus. Good coffee shops also serve red cappuccinos and lattes—a delicious and healthful alternative to their coffee counterparts. Rooibos leaves are coarser than regular tea and look like finely chopped sticks. When they're harvested, they're green; then they're chopped, bruised, and left to ferment in mounds before being spread out to dry in the baking summer sun. The fermentation process turns the leaves red—hence the name.

very expensive. $ *Rooms from: R8000* ⊠ *Off Pakhuis Pass* ☎ *027/482–8200* ⊕ *www.bushmanskloof.co.za* ⇱ *16 rooms* ❢ *All meals.*

$
RESORT

⬚ **Traveller's Rest.** If you're on a tight budget, this farm is the place to stay; there are no frills at these basic but comfortable cottages, but the surrounding mountain scenery is spectacular. **Pros:** nearby rock-art route; cottages have self-catering facilities; very reasonable rates; the owner is a real character. **Cons:** amenities are basic; service at the restaurant can be annoyingly slow. $ *Rooms from: R400* ⊠ *Off Pakhuis Pass* ☎ *027/482–1824* ⊕ *www.travellersrest.co.za* ⇱ *25 cottages.*

SHOPPING

Strassberger Shoe Factory. *Veldskoen,* or *Vellies,* as they're fondly known, are something of a South African institution. All you have to do is think of the singer David Kramer and his signature red shoes to understand the place they hold in most South Africans' hearts. Vellies used to be the preserve of hardy farmers, who would wear these sturdy shoes with socks and shorts in winter, and without socks and shorts in summer. Thankfully, the styles have changed somewhat, and now you can get the softest shoes made to order from the Strassberger Shoe Factory. The shoemakers you see working here come from generations of craftspeople dating back to when the Moravian missionaries first started shoemaking in Wupperthal. ⊠ *12 Ou Kaapseweg* ☎ *027/482–1439* ⊕ *www.strassbergers.co.za.*

CITRUSDAL

53 km (33 miles) south of Clanwilliam.

As you might guess from the name, Citrusdal is a fruit-growing town. It sits by the Olifants River valley, surrounded by the peaks of the Cederberg, and is known as the gateway to the Cederberg. For the most part it's a sleepy farming town, but in spring the smell of fruit blossoms as you come over the Piekenaarskloof Pass (also known as the Piekenier-skloof Pass) is incredible.

GETTING HERE AND AROUND
It's usually 45 minutes on the N7 from Clanwilliam to Citrusdal, but factor in delays because of roadwork.

VISITOR INFORMATION
Contacts **Citrusdal Tourism Bureau** ✉ *Voortrekker St.* ☎ *022/921–3210* ⊕ *www.citrusdal.info* ⊗ *Weekdays 8–5, Sat. 8–noon.*

EXPLORING
Baths. After a grueling hike in the Cederberg, there's no better way to relax than at the Baths, where hot mineral water gushes from a natural spring. The waters' curative powers have been talked about for centuries, and although the formal baths were established in 1739, there's little doubt that indigenous San and Bushmen spent time here as well. In 1903 the hot springs were bought by James McGregor, and his great-grandchildren run them today. On-site are self-catering facilities and a restaurant. You can also go as a day visitor, but you must book at least a day in advance. ✉ *16 km (10 miles) outside Citrusdal; follow signs* ☎ *022/921–8026* ⊕ *www.thebaths.co.za* ✉ *Weekdays R40, weekends R80* ⊗ *Daily 8–5.*

RIEBEEK WEST AND RIEBEEK KASTEEL

104 km (65 miles) south of Citrusdal.

Drive through the small agricultural town of Malmesbury and over the Bothman's Kloof Pass to these twin towns named after Jan van Riebeeck, the 17th-century Dutch explorer of the Cape. The towns developed only a few miles apart because of a disagreement about where to build a church. In the end, two separate places of worship were built, and two distinct towns grew up around them.

Riebeek West is the birthplace of Jan Christiaan Smuts, one of the country's great politicians and leader of the United Party in the 1940s. D. F. Malan, prime minister of the Nationalist Party in 1948, was born on the farm Allesverloren, just outside Riebeek Kasteel. This wine estate produces some great red wines, an exceptional port, and world-class olives and olive oil. The *kasteel,* or castle, in question is the Kasteelberg (Castle Mountain), which stands sentinel behind the towns.

Disenchanted city dwellers have been buying up cottages here to use as weekend getaways, and others are moving out to the small towns and commuting into the city. It's not hard to understand why. Children play in the street and people keep sheep in their huge gardens—a far cry from Cape Town life. There are numerous restaurants, some galleries, and plenty of olive products to buy, including excellent olive oils and bottled olives. Huge groves in the area do well in the Mediterranean climate.

You'll hear the distinctive, rolling accent of the Swartland here. Known as the "Malmesbury *brei,*" it's characterized by long "ghrrrr" sounds that seem to run together at the back of the throat. In Afrikaans, *brei* means "to knit" or "temper," both of which make sense when listening to somebody from the Swartland.

GETTING HERE AND AROUND

The Riebeek Valley is an hour and a half from Citrusdal via the N7 and R311 without traffic. Roadwork will slow you down.

VISITOR INFORMATION

Contacts Riebeek Valley Information Centre ✉ *7 Plein St., Riebeek Kasteel* ☎ *022/448–1545* ⊕ *www.riebeekvalley.info* ⊘ *Weekdays 9–4, weekends 10–2.*

EXPLORING

Allesverloren. Translated from Afrikaans, Allesverloren means "all is lost." The bleak name derives from a story from the early 1700s, when the widow Cloete owned this farm. Legend has it that she left the farm for a few weeks to attend a church gathering in town, and in her absence the resentful indigenous tribespeople set her homestead alight. When she came back to a smoldering ruin, she declared, "Allesverloren," and the name stuck. Today the farm's prospects are a lot brighter. It has been in the Malan family for generations. The infamous D. F. Malan, regarded as one of the architects of apartheid, gave up the farm for politics. Happily, his descendants are doing a better job at wine making than he did at shaping a country's destiny, and their reds are big, bold, and delicious. Packed with black-currant and tobacco flavors, and with a lingering fruitcake finish, the port (called the Allesverloren Fine Old Vintage) is perfect for cool winter evenings. A family-friendly restaurant and pub on the premises means you can dine in a beautiful setting. ✉ *R311, between Riebeek Kasteel and Riebeek West* ☎ *022/461–2320* ⊕ *www.allesverloren.co.za* 🍷 *R20* ⊘ *Weekdays 9–5, Sat. 9–2.*

Kloovenburg Wine Estate. You have to move fast if you want to snap up any wines from the Kloovenburg Wine Estate. This family-run farm has many awards under its belt and is probably best known for its excellent Shiraz. Wines to take home are the Shiraz 2012, a ruby red wine with smoky flavors and a chocolaty aftertaste, and the Merlot 2012, with sweet berry and oak flavors and excellent aging potential. The 2010 Eight Feet is a fun but very drinkable testimony to the generations of du Toits who have worked the land: it alludes to the eight grape-stomping feet of the owners' four sons. Don't miss out on Annalene du Toit's olive products. Kloovenburg olives and olive oils are exceptional, and they manufacture olive oil beauty products too. A highlight is the annual market day in December, when everybody from the area displays their products and you can get a real taste of local produce and home-crafted goods. ✉ *R46, just outside Riebeek Kasteel as you come down pass into Riebeek Valley* ☎ *022/448–1635* ⊕ *www.kloovenburg.com* 🍷 *Wine tastings R20, olive tastings R10* ⊘ *Weekdays 9–4:30, Sat. 9–2.*

OFF THE BEATEN PATH

Swartland Winery. Because of its location in the less fashionable part of the Winelands, this large cellar a few miles outside Malmesbury has had to work hard for its place in the sun. Previously a well-kept secret among local cost- and quality-conscious wine experts, it's garnering an international reputation. In 2013 and 2014 alone, the winery won four bronze and two silver Decanter World Wine Awards. It is particularly proud of its Bushvine range, and the Bushvine Shiraz and Bushvine Pinotage were ranked among the top 100 SA wines in 2012. ✉ *R45,*

Dooringkuil, Malmesbury ☎ *022/482–1134* ⊕ *www.swwines.co.za*
✉ *Tastings free* ☉ *Weekdays 9–5, Sat. 9–2.*

WHERE TO EAT

$$ ✗ **Bar Bar Black Sheep.** This relaxed establishment offers rustic, slow-
ECLECTIC cooked country food with a twist; their dishes are hearty and big on
flavor. Fresh, seasonal ingredients are used to make up their menu, and
local boutique and garagiste wines are supplied by the Wine Kollektive
next door. The atmosphere is laid-back—enjoy alfresco dining in the
shaded courtyard or sit in the cozy dining room. The menu is not broad,
but there's likely something for everyone. For breakfast you might have
a duck egg frittata with chorizo, olives, capers, rosa tomatoes, and
Camembert, or soft-poached eggs with brown mushrooms and Greek
yogurt. Dinner gets off to an unusual start with a tapas platter with
stewed lamb hearts, panfried chorizo, marinated West Coast mussels,
and chili prawns. Service is friendly and efficient. ⑤ *Average main: R135*
✉ *Short St., Unit 7, Riebeek Kasteel* ☎ *022/448–1031* ⊕ *www.bbbs.*
co.za ☉ *Closed Mon. No dinner Sun.*

WHERE TO STAY

$$ ⊞ **Riebeek Valley Hotel.** At the top of town, with a great view over vine-
HOTEL   yards and mountains, this small luxury hotel in a converted farm-
house is an oasis from the sweltering Swartland summer heat as well
as a winter getaway. **Pros:** in-house spa treatments available; indoor
heated pool. **Cons:** avoid Room 8, as it's near the kitchen and can
get noisy. ⑤ *Rooms from: R1550* ✉ *4 Dennehof St., Riebeek West*
☎ *022/461–2672* ⊕ *www.riebeekvalleyhotel.co.za* ⇗ *23 rooms, 5 suites*
⑩ *Breakfast.*

THE NORTHERN CAPE

4

Visit Fodors.com for advice, updates, and bookings

Updated by
Angus Begg

South Africa's largest province, the Northern Cape, is also its least populated. Covering almost a third of the country, its deserts and semi-deserts—the Karoo, Kalahari, Namaqualand, and Richtersveld—stretch from the Orange River in the north to the Western Cape border in the south. From the small towns of Springbok and Port Nolloth in the west across 1,000 km (630 miles) to Pofadder and Hotazhel to the diamond capital, Kimberley, in the east, this is a place of large and rugged beauty—a far cry from the verdant greenness of Mpumalanga.

The Northern Cape's appeal is in its sense of loneliness, its sparse but remarkable vegetation, and its occasional lunar landscapes. All told, it covers an area of 363,389 square km (225,665 square miles), roughly a third bigger than the entire United Kingdom, but it has a population of less than a million people (only about two per square km), and most are concentrated in a handful of towns.

Many of the Northern Cape's attractions are linked to mining, which has been the province's economic backbone for more than a century. First there was the copper mania of the 1840s in Namaqualand, evidence of which is found in towns like Okiep and Nababeep. The deepest copper mines in the world are still operating here, although they are nearing the end of their productive lives. But the history of copper mining was eclipsed 30 years later by the frenzied scrabbling for diamonds on the other side of what is now the Northern Cape.

Kimberley, known as the City of Diamonds, is the provincial capital and in the 1870s was the site of one of the world's greatest diamond rushes. Thousands of hopeful diggers trekked to the hot, dusty diamond fields sitting in what is more or less the geographical center of South Africa. In Kimberley five diamond-bearing volcanic pipes were eventually discovered within a few miles of one another—a phenomenon unknown anywhere else in the world. But for real (and colorful) diamond tales, the far northern town of Port Nolloth is the real deal. In the Aukwatowa museum, veteran navy and diamond diver George Moyses is a colorful, unorthodox mine of information who can keep you engaged for hours. Apart from copper and diamonds, the province's mineral deposits range from manganese and zinc to lime, granite, gypsum, and other gemstones, and there are even oil and gas fields off the Namaqualand coast.

Although only a fraction of the province is regarded as arable because of low rainfall, the Orange River (known as the !ariep—the exclamation mark indicates a click of the tongue against the roof of the mouth—or "mighty river by the Nama") flows the breadth of the province, emptying into the Atlantic Ocean at Alexander Bay, on the Namibian border. South Africa's largest and longest river, the Orange supplies water to numerous irrigation schemes that sustain farming, most noticeably in the "Green Kalahari," which is a pleasant, roughly 70-km (43-mile) drive between Upington and Augrabies.

Agriculture employs the most people in the province, and you'll find varied agricultural production, from the second-largest date plantation in the world, at Klein Pella, near Pofadder (named after the highly poisonous puff adder snake), to thousands of acres of grapes under irrigation in the Orange River basin around Upington. The province boasts the country's second-largest national park, Kgalagadi Transfrontier Park, the first transfrontier (i.e., crossing a national border) park in Africa. Together with an adjoining national park in Botswana, this park forms one of the largest conservation areas in the world. Ecotourism also draws an annual pilgrimage of thousands, who come to see the spectacular Namaqualand flowers far southwest of the park.

The Northern Cape is a harsh province that begs to be driven—flying is an expensive luxury—but therein lies its beauty. There's plenty to see if you're the type who's not afraid to ask questions and to go where your nose leads you. You have to look hard if you're after luxurious accommodation and fine cuisine, but when you find it, it'll be worth it. Such is the joy of discovery in South Africa's less-traveled province. What you can expect, given a little time and patience, are sleepy villages and charming locals who appreciate visitors tremendously, albeit in very broken, accented English. This is a place of natural wonders—particularly the Khoi San first people—and unusual, unique crafts. It's an off-the-beaten-path getaway that could well turn out to be the highlight of your trip to South Africa.

ORIENTATION AND PLANNING

GETTING ORIENTED

The Northern Cape's vastness makes it a difficult place to travel, and on a first trip you'll probably see only a small part of it, such as Namaqualand in flower season, the Kalahari, or Kimberley. Namaqualand is most easily visited from Cape Town and the Western Cape, whereas Kimberley and the Kalahari are far more accessible from Johannesburg. If you are planning to drive from Johannesburg to Cape Town or vice versa, Kimberley makes an ideal stopover. The Kimberley route (along the N12) is less than 100 km (63 miles) longer than the sterile N1 route with its huge gas stations, toll plazas, and fast-food places. It's also more scenic and not as busy. Although Upington and the Kgalagadi Transfrontier Park are about the same distance from Cape Town as they are from Johannesburg, the roads from Johannesburg are far better.

North Cape and Namaqualand

Mata Mata

Kgalagadi Transfrontier Park

Koopan-Noord

Noenieput

NAMIBIA

10

Richtersveld National Park

Augrabies Falls National Park

Alexander Bay

Vioolsdrif

Orange R.

Onseepkans

7

Pella

Port Nolloth

382

Steinkopf

14

Pofadder

NAMAQUALAND

Kleinsee

◆ Goegap Nature Reserve

Springbok

358

K
A
M
I
E
S
B
E
R
G

355

Namegua National Park ◆

Kamieskroon

Koiingnaas

Leliefontein

Brandvlei

Hondeklip Bay

Garies

Loeriesfontein

357

H
A
N
T
A
M
B
E
R
G

ATLANTIC OCEAN

7

C
E
D
A
R
B
E
R
G

27

Calvinia

Vanrhynsdorp

Lambert's Bay

Clanwilliam

7

TOP REASONS TO GO

Getting Off the Beaten Path: This is South Africa's emerging, undiscovered province, where less is indisputably more.

Scenery: Mixed in with inevitable boring stuff, there is some awesome landscape with a rugged beauty.

Spring Flower Season: The magnificent wildflowers in Namaqualand must be seen to be believed, and

they are easily reachable from Cape Town.

Starry Skies: The Southern Hemisphere's largest telescope is in off-the-beaten-track Sutherland for good reason.

Desert Game: Excellent game reserves mean an experience very different from Kruger; you'll see more cheetahs and rhinos and fewer elephants.

PLANNING

WHEN TO GO

By South African standards the Northern Cape's climate is exceptionally hot in summer (late November–February), often rising to above 35°C (95°F). It's hottest in Kimberley and just about intolerable in Upington and the Kalahari. Conversely, the region can get seriously cold in winter (mid-May–early August), commonly dropping below 0°C (32°F) at night. In fact, the province has the dubious honor of being home to the hottest town in South Africa in summer (Upington) and the coldest in winter (Sutherland, in the Karoo), so come prepared to sweat or shiver (mostly by night). Any other time of year is fine, though. The best time to see the flowers in Namaqualand is usually between the middle of August and the end of September, depending on when and how much rain has fallen. The weather is generally milder in Namaqualand than in the rest of the province. Other dates to be aware of: the four-day Gariep Annual Festival (*Gariep* means "orange" in Tsetswana, the language of the Tswana people) in September. Sporting events also bring crowds to Kimberley, but dates change annually.

PLANNING YOUR TIME

To get the most out of this province, plan to visit between mid-August and late September, which would allow for a visit to Kgalagadi Transfrontier Park, a couple of days following the Orange River between Upington and Augrabies National Park, and taking in the culture and flowers of Namaqualand. Ten days would let you see the highlights. Most people have less time and choose to do one of these in two or three days.

3 Days: If you have three days, spend them soaking up the history and culture of Kimberley. On your first day, tour the town and its landmarks, perhaps starting your morning with one of the reasonably priced registered guides. Day 2 can be spent taking an underground tour of a working diamond mine, followed by an afternoon of diamond-rush history at a mine museum. To rest your weary feet, ride on a historic restored tram. On your third day take a side trip, either northwest of town toward Barkly West, where you can see alluvial diggings with a guide or view ancient rock engravings, or south of Kimberley to the evocative Anglo-Boer War battlefield Magersfontein. Take a picnic and have it under one of the ubiquitous thorn trees scattered across the battlefield.

5 Days: If it's spring (August–September), it's worth sharing five days between the florally quite phenomenal Nieuwoudtville, Springbok, and Port Nolloth to get the best of Namaqualand.

If you visit between mid-May and late July (winter in South Africa), head for the huge spaces of Kgalagadi, then spend a night along the Orange River between Upington and Augrabies Falls National Park. Some excellent accommodation and wining (this is serious grape country) and dining establishments have set up in the region in recent years, and these are viable alternatives to the better-known Cape Winelands. Take note that the Northern Cape is a renewable energy hub, and that Upington has a large solar energy project under way. Next try a few days of roughing it in the ruggedly beautiful Kgalagadi Transfrontier Park, cooking your own meals and driving your own vehicle in search of the black-maned Kalahari lions and the beautifully symmetrical gemsbok. Then head for the decadent luxury of two nights at Tswalu Kalahari Reserve, where you'll appreciate the game drives, bush walks, and attention to detail all the more for having roughed it for the past few days. A worthwhile, more affordable and geographically logical luxury option is Tutwa Desert Lodge, outside Augrabies Falls.

If you visit between October and mid-May, Port Nolloth makes an excellent entry point for the Richtersveld, South Africa's last true wilderness. The Port Nolloth region is undiscovered country of shipwrecks, diamonds, and crayfish, and is well worth at least two nights and a day in itself. Crayfish season begins in October, so during this time you may want to find a crayfish braai (barbecue) on the beach somewhere. This is off-the-beaten-track stuff. But note: there is no fresh fish in the winter months.

In summer Upington is a good base for day trips to Pella and Klein Pella (visually arresting date-palm plantations), Witsand (wildlife and white sand dunes), the occasional wine estate on the banks of the Orange River, and Augrabies Falls, but be sure to make your visits in early morning or late afternoon, leaving time for a rest or a swim in the midday heat.

7 or More Days: If you enjoy huge, empty spaces, take a week to drive from Kimberley to Springbok, taking in the Kalahari en route. There are some memorable places to stop and stay along the way, but beware: this is a long and lonely trip and really should be considered only if the flowers will be in bloom when you get to Namaqualand (July–mid-October). From Kimberley drive past Upington to the vast Kgalagadi Transfrontier Park some two hours north. Return just past Upington again and head for Kanon-Eiland in the middle of the Orange River, where your guesthouse experience can be as good as it gets Visit a local award-winning brandy and wine estate for lunch before or afterward. Then head north to visit Augrabies Falls National Park, where five-star accommodation has finally found its way. On Day 5 drive to Springbok, the heart of Namaqualand. Stay two nights here or in nearby Okiep, using this area as your base for exploring the picturesque towns of Leliefontein (and the nearby Namaqua National Park) to the south and Port Nolloth to the northwest. Head south down the N7 to Cape Town, where the madding crowds will catch you by surprise after the loneliness of the beautiful Northern Cape.

GETTING HERE AND AROUND
AIR TRAVEL

The small Kimberley Airport, 12 km (7½ miles) southwest of town, is served by South African Express, which connects to Johannesburg and Cape Town daily (except Saturday), and SA Airlink. Phakalane Airways is a relatively new entrant, flying exclusively in the Northern Cape between Kimberley, Upington, and Springbok. CEMAIR flies between Johannesburg and Sishen Kathu—an important mining hub, but these flights aren't really for tourists.

A five-minute drive from the city center, Upington International Airport has the longest runway in the Southern Hemisphere—5 km (3 miles)—and has been the scene of a few global land-speed records. Upington is the gateway to the Kalahari region of South Africa. SA Airlink operates daily service between Upington and both Johannesburg and Cape Town.

Airline Contacts Phakalane Airways. Phakalane Airways provides air connections between Kimberley, Upington, and Springbok in conjunction with the Northern Cape Provincial Department. ⊠ *Springbok* ☎ *053/492–0001* ⊕ *www. phakalaneairways.co.za.*

BUS TRAVEL

For those travelers with plenty of time, daily bus service between Kimberley and both Cape Town (about 11 hours, R389–R422) and Johannesburg (about 6 hours, R227) is offered by Greyhound and Translux. The local company Tickets for Africa provides schedules, prices, and other information and sells tickets for all buses in and out of Kimberley.

Intercape Mainliner runs daily service and night coach service three times a week between Upington and Johannesburg/Pretoria (approximately 10½ hours, R280) and Sunday–Friday service from Upington to Cape Town (about 12 hours, R250) and to Windhoek (approximately 12½ hours, R330).

Intercape Mainliner operates bus service up the West Coast from Cape Town to Springbok (nine hours) on Sunday, Tuesday, Thursday, and Friday evenings, stopping en route at Piketburg and Vanrhynsdorp in the Western Cape and Garies in the Northern Cape. Return service to Cape Town runs Sunday, Monday, Wednesday, and Friday late at night.

Contacts Tickets for Africa ⊠ *Kimberley Visitors' Centre, 121 Bultfontein Rd., Kimberley* ☎ *053/832–6040.*

CAR TRAVEL

From Johannesburg it is an easy 4½-hour drive (480 km/298 miles) to Kimberley on the N12 and N14; however, the trip from Cape Town is considerably longer, at 954 km (600 miles), and takes almost 13 hours. The trip from Kimberley to Upington can take another six hours. And it's another 2½ hours from Upington to Kgalagadi Transfrontier Park. The drive from Upington to Augrabies Falls is almost two hours, and this leg of the N14 is excellent.

Namaqualand, however, is considerably closer to Cape Town than it is to Johannesburg. The drive from Johannesburg to Springbok, the "capital" of Namaqualand, is 835 miles and takes a little over 12 hours driving straight through with refreshment stops; from Cape Town, it's only 7 hours driving (562 km/349 miles).

TRAIN TRAVEL

Trains between Kimberley and Johannesburg (eight hours) run daily, with extra trains on Wednesday, Friday, and Sunday. There are daily trains to Cape Town (seven hours), with an additional one on Thursday. Sleepers are available only in first and second classes, but you'll want to travel first or second class for safety reasons anyway, and preferably with a companion. Make sure you book tickets together so that they are issued for the same compartment. First- and second-class passengers must reserve in advance. The one-way fare between Kimberley and Johannesburg is R170, R340 between Kimberley and Cape Town, but prices increase for the December to January school vacation. Information on these routes can be obtained from Shosholoza Meyl, the long-distance passenger division of Spoornet. A private security company (Spoornet Security), train assistants, and a manager are on every train. ⇨ *See Train Travel in Travel Smart.*

HOTELS

The newest tourism kid on the South African provincial block, the Northern Cape is fast developing some outstanding product. Although homey cooking and accommodation remains the norm for this rural province, high-quality guesthouses and even luxury lodgings have emerged around the major business centers and tourist attractions. Guesthouses can be found in just about every little town; the bigger centers like Kimberley and Upington are brimming with them—from basic self-catering units with cooking facilities to luxurious bed-and-breakfasts. There are also comfortable farm accommodations, which offer overnight stays that can be a saving grace late at night on the province's long and lonely roads. In and near the parks and nature reserves, accommodations are in public rest camps, lodges, bungalows, and cottages, which often sleep up to six people, and the odd luxury lodge. Though the price categories given for all lodgings reflect the cost for two people, many places (especially chalets in the national parks) can hold more than two and are, therefore, often a better value if you're traveling as a family or larger party.

Remember that most safari lodges are all-inclusive experiences, with all meals, alcoholic beverages, and activities (like game-viewing) accounted for in the price, but that may not be the case in this region. *Hotel reviews have been shortened. For full information, visit Fodors.com.*

RESTAURANTS

The Northern Cape has never been gastronomically exciting, but some standout additions to the province's tourism map offer food as good as anything you'll find in Cape Town. In the larger towns of Kimberley, Upington, and Springbok—where local residents generally traditionally like their meat well done and regard chicken as salad—it may be hard to find what you're looking for. Your most memorable meal might be the legendary delicacy Karoo lamb—often roasted on a *braai*. It can be savored not only on the farms of the Karoo but also in restaurants in Kimberley, Upington, and the Kalahari. Vegetarians will find their needs very difficult to meet in large towns and almost unheard of in small villages. However, fresh fruits, especially grapes, are delicious and abundant in the summer months in the Orange River valley, from Upington to Kakamas. In winter look out for homemade preserves like peach chutney and apricot jam. Other than the more sophisticated hotels and such national steak-house chains as Spurs and Saddles, many restaurants are closed on Sunday evening. Unless you are a large group, reservations are not essential or even expected. Dining in the Northern Cape, even in Kimberley, is a casual affair in all but the few elegant and chic establishments. Wearing anything other than flip-flops is usually acceptable.

WHAT IT COSTS IN SOUTH AFRICAN RAND			
$	$$	$$$	$$$$
Restaurants	under R100	R100–R150	R151–R200	over R200
Hotels	under R1,500	R1,500–R2,500	R2,501–R3,500	over R3,500

Restaurant prices are the average cost of a main course at dinner or, if dinner is not served, at lunch. Hotel prices are the lowest cost of a standard double room in high season.

TOURS

The African Chapter Tours. This operator based near Johannesburg is forging a different path. Specializing in unusual experiences and vast landscapes—for those with both specific and general interests—owner Megan Alves impresses in that she's seen and tested everything she recommends. From the bed to the dinner to the itineraries, she never includes a feature without having had a firsthand look. She and her team will ensure that your tastes, styles, and wishes are satisfied. She offers a range of carefully crafted itineraries into the Northern Cape, and you can be assured that environmental, socioeconomic, and conservation ethics are carefully considered in every compelling journey. ✉ *Pretoria* ☎ *011/545–6100* ⊕ *www.africanchapter.co.za.*

VISITOR INFORMATION

Northern Cape Tourism Authority ✉ *15 Villiers St., Kimberley* ☎ *053/832–2657, 053/833–1434* ⊕ *www.experiencenortherncape.com.*

KIMBERLEY

480 km (298 miles) west of Johannesburg; 954 km (600 miles) north-west of Cape Town.

Kimberley was born in the dust, dreams, and disappointments of a rudimentary mining camp that grew into a city of grace and sophistication in some quarters, still evident in many of its early buildings. Today Kimberley is a city of about 200,000 people spread out around its diamond mines—giant holes in the earth, like inverted *koppies* (hills). Kimberley has a host of comfortable guesthouses, a few good restaurants, and many historical attractions, making it a wonderful place to spend a few days. It's an easy trip of about 4 to 4½ hours from Johannesburg on a good highway, but is almost 13 hours on much worse roads from Cape Town. (In South Africa the term *easy driving* means driving on good roads—no potholes, gravel, or single lanes—not distances, which are sometimes vast.)

Kimberley's colonial beginnings date to 1869, when diamonds were first discovered in the area. Through the late 1860s alluvial diamonds were mined on the banks of the Vaal River near Barkly West, about 30 km (19 miles) away. These were all but forgotten after the finds in Kimberley of five pipes bearing the diamondiferous Kimberlite, or "blue ground," so called because of its color. In 1871 the richest pipe of all, the Kimberley Mine (now known as the Big Hole), was discovered. Diggers from around the world flocked to stake claims in the mine, which produced more than 14.5 million carats before its closure in 1914, making it one of the richest diamond mines in history. At times there were as many as 30,000 people working in the hole, burrowing like a giant colony of termites. The history of the diamond fields is dominated by eccentric personalities, like Barney Barnato, who came to South Africa with so little, he had to walk to the diamond fields, yet died a magnificently wealthy man. Then there was Cecil John Rhodes, the diamond magnate and colonizer who aspired to paint the map of Africa red for Britain and to build a railroad from Cape Town to Cairo.

Both Rhodes and Barnato were shrewd businessmen. They watched diggers toiling at their individual claims in Kimberley's five holes. When the miners met what they perceived to be bedrock, they would often give up and stop digging, but what they were actually hitting was unweathered, hard blue ground that was fabulously rich in diamonds. The two men then snapped up claims at bargain prices, all the time increasing their shares in the mines. Eventually Barnato and Rhodes merged their companies into the De Beers Consolidated Mines Ltd. Today De Beers is the world's most powerful diamond-mining company. Its historic headquarters is still on Stockdale Street in Kimberley.

In addition to the allure of diamonds, another central part of Kimberley's history was its attack by the Boers during the Anglo-Boer War (1899–1902). Kimberley's proximity to the border of the then Boer Republic of the Orange Free State and its international fame as a diamond town occupied by prominent British citizens (including Rhodes) made it an ideal siege target. For four months in the summer of 1899 the town's citizens suffered dwindling rations, disease, Boer shell fire, and other hardships. British efforts to relieve the town were thwarted by the Boers at the famous Battle of Magersfontein, but eventually a sustained cavalry charge led by Major-General John French broke through to the beleaguered town. Kimberley's part in the Anglo-Boer War is brought to life everywhere through monuments, buildings, and statues.

GETTING HERE AND AROUND

If you arrive in Kimberley by air, you'll find only two local taxi companies. Although Rikkis Taxis try to meet most flights on arrival, their presence isn't guaranteed, so it's best to reserve a taxi in advance.

If you don't drive to Kimberley, renting a car there is a good idea (Avis, Budget, and Europcar can all be found at Kimberley Airport), as it gives you more freedom, but it's not mandatory if you're staying only a day or two and you hire a good tour guide. Strategically placed monuments and good signage make this an easy town to find your way around in. Just remember to drive within the speed limits, as there are plenty of hidden cameras. Parking is no problem, and gas stations are visible and plentiful. Roads out of town are very straight and generally do not have shoulders.

A restored 1914 tram travels through Kimberley between the other side of the Big Hole and City Hall. The cost is R10 round-trip. Trams leave from the Big Hole when at least four people are ready to go. (Kimberley was the first South African city to have tram service.)

Airport Contacts Kimberley Airport ✉ *N12* ☎ *053/851–1242.*

Airport Transfers Rikkis Taxis ☎ *053/842–1764, 083/342–2533* ⊕ *www. rikkistaxis.co.za.*

TOURS

Consider a tour by chartered township taxi (minibus), which will pick you up from wherever you wish. These tours focus on the history and culture of Galeshewe, Kimberley's largest township, named after an important Tswana chief. Places visited include the homes of legendary human-rights activists Sol Plaatje and Robert Sobukwe, as well as the Northern Cape legislature. The tours also take in a traditional *shebeen* (drinking place) and a restaurant serving traditional South African meals. Those wanting a longer township visit can stay at one of several guesthouses catering to tourists there. Galeshewe tours are offered by a variety of local operators; in most cases you'll need to take a taxi to Galeshewe to meet your tour operator, so ask hotel to make arrangements.

The Kimberley Ghost Route is another popular tour, starting at night with sherry inside the Honoured Dead Memorial and then proceeding to several of Kimberley's (purportedly) haunted places, such as the Kimberley Club and Rhodes's boardroom. The tour ends with a visit to the historic Gladstone Cemetery, where a certain Mr. Frankenstein and his wife are buried. Prices vary according to the size of the group. Book this one at least two days in advance, and make sure you specify that you want to go inside the haunted buildings, or the tour can be disappointing. The best guides for the ghost tour should be booked through Jaco (*Yako*) Powell or Steve Lunderstedt.

Guide fees are not regulated, and guides therefore charge different rates. A half-day tour should not cost more than R450 per person, a full day not more than R900. This excludes transportation, entrance fees, and refreshments.

Contacts Steve Lunderstedt. Steve is a reputable local tour operator, and will pick you up. He's an especially good guide for the Kimberley Ghost Route. ☎ 083/732–3189 ✉ From R450. **Jaco Powell.** Jaco will pick you up for a tour of the Kimberley Ghost Route. ☎ 082/572–0065. **Scotty Ross.** Military history of the Northern Cape is Scotty Ross's forte, and with his broad Scots lilt he conducts private tours of regional battlefields and diamond diggings—both old and new. Anything you want to see, he will show you and doubtless have a story to tell about it. ☎ 053/832–4083, 082/320–4380 ✉ murdochr10@gmail. com. **Taxi to Galeshewe.** Township tours in South Africa can be much more interesting when you visit a smaller place. If you've visited Soweto, a trip to Galeshewe offers an entirely different perspective. ☎ 083/763–5172.

VISITOR INFORMATION

The Northern Cape Tourism Authority, in Kimberley, has information on the entire province. The Kimberley Visitors' Centre has maps and brochures on the Northern Cape and the Kimberley region in particular, and can make referrals. Local guides can also provide good information (*see* ⇨ *Tours*).

Contacts Kimberley Visitors' Centre ✉ 121 Bultfontein Rd. ☎ 053/830–6779 ⊕ www.solplaatje.org.za.

EXPLORING

The hub of business activity, in the CBD (Central Business District), is defined by Jones Street, George Street, and Du Toitspan Road, with its small manufacturing concerns. Victorian-style architecture abounds in Belgravia, Kimberley's first residential suburb, which, beginning in the late 1880s, was associated with the town's mines. De Beers, another suburb that grew up around the De Beers mine, originally constituted part of Johannes Nicholas de Beer's farm. (Both the Kimberley and De Beers mines are now closed, leaving three remaining working mines.) Also on land originally owned by De Beers and of even greater historical interest, the residential area around the Civic Centre is similar to Cape Town's District Six in sociopolitical terms. Called Malay Camp, it was where freed Asian slaves (largely Muslim and erroneously lumped together under the name Cape Malays) settled. Given to the municipality as an open area in 1939, today it is a well-maintained, treed garden area stretching out from the base of the municipal building.

One of the two oldest townships in South Africa, Greenpoint, south of town, is populated by both coloured (a local term for people of mixed—white European, black African, or "Cape Malay"—heritage) and Africans (blacks). Despite its age, no standing buildings predate the 1930s. Galeshewe is the settlement to the west of town and is still where the majority of blacks in the area live.

Kimberley

TOP ATTRACTIONS

Africana Library. Housed in the old Kimberley Public Library, which was built in 1887, this is one of the country's premier reference libraries. Books are shelved from floor to ceiling, and an ornate wrought-iron staircase connects the floors. Included among the 20,000 books in the collection are such rarities as the Setswana Bible, the first-ever Bible in an African language, printed by Robert Moffat in the 1850s. The library also has four books dating from the 1400s and a good selection of locally published, limited-edition books for sale. If there's enough interest on tours or when requested by researchers, books are removed from the safe, and visitors can—under surveillance—have hands-on contact with some literary jewels. The library is said to be haunted by the ghost of Bertram Dyer, the first qualified librarian in the country. After he was caught defrauding the library of money, he committed suicide. He now purportedly stacks files on the floor and rattles teacups in the kitchen. ⊠ *63–65 Du Toitspan Rd.* ☎ *053/830–6247* ⊕ *www.africanalibrary. co.za* ✉ *Donations accepted* ☉ *Weekdays 8–12:45 and 1:30–4.*

FAMILY

Fodor'sChoice

★

Big Hole. If you do one thing in Kimberley, visit the Big Hole, at 2,690 feet deep, the largest hand-dug hole in the world. Although water now fill most of its depth, it's still an impressive sight, particularly from the observation post. On the lip is the extensive open-air Kimberley

Mine Museum, comprising a host of authentic 19th-century buildings, many of which were moved here from the city center instead of being torn down. They include the first house erected in Kimberley (1877), which was brought piece by piece from Britain to the diamond fields by ship and ox wagon; Barney Barnato's boxing academy; and a bar reminiscent of a Wild West saloon. Replicas of the world's most famous diamonds, including the Eureka, a 21-carat yellow diamond that was South Africa's first recorded diamond discovery in 1866, are also on view. Kids can dig through gravel for a real diamond, and learn about 19th-century attire at the museum. Allow a few hours here, and wear comfortable shoes. ⊠ *Tucker St.* ☎ *053/839–4600* ⊕ *www.thebighole. co.za* ✉ *R90* ☉ *Daily 8–5.*

OFF THE
BEATEN
PATH

Magersfontein Battlefield Museum. Where this evocative, barren national monument now stands, the Boers resoundingly defeated British forces marching to relieve besieged Kimberley in December 1899. An excellent museum screens an 11-minute multimedia display that does such a good job of recalling the battle in pictures and sound that it will give you goose bumps. You can also visit several monuments dotted around the battlefield. A pleasant tearoom and the on-site Bagpipe Lodge (bagpipes not included) offer a place to refuel and recline. This was the site of a major battle in the South African War, and is must for anyone with a sense of military, or South African history. ⊠ *Magersfontein Rd.* ✚ *31.5 km (20 miles) south of Kimberley off the N8* ☎ *053/833–7115* ⊕ *www. museumsnc.co.za* ✉ *R20* ☉ *Daily 8–4.*

McGregor Museum. This graceful Kimberley landmark, built at Rhodes's instigation, was first used as a sanatorium, then an upscale hotel, and later as a girls' convent school. Rhodes himself stayed here during the siege, and you can see rooms he once occupied. Today the building houses a museum that focuses on Northern Cape history (prehistoric to early 20th century) within a global context. It contains quite a good display on the Anglo-Boer War and the even more impressive Hall of Ancestors—an extensive exhibition on the history of humanity that includes prehistoric human skulls dating back some 3 million years. The natural history of the area can be seen in the EnviroZone, and a chapel once stood on what is today the Hall of Religion. ⊠ *Atlas St., Belgravia* ☎ *053/839–2700* ⊕ *www.museumsnc.co.za* ✉ *R25* ☉ *Week-days 8:30–5, Sat. 9–5, Sun. 2–5.*

William Humphreys Art Gallery. This renowned art museum in Kimberley's Civic Centre is at once sedate and lively. It's an air-conditioned haven of tranquillity on a hot summer day and an active site for community projects, such as the Whag Ubuntu Project, which teaches unemployed black women crafting skills. Come on a Monday, Wednesday, or Friday, and you'll see Tswana women embroidering and beading articles such as vests, pillowcases, and bags. The gallery's impressive collection features South African works as well as Dutch, Flemish, British, and French masters. One area is devoted to local work, and a very popular exhibit is a permanent display on rock art of the Northern Cape. Free guided tours (preferably booked two weeks in advance) cater to specific interests on request. Light meals are available in the gallery's downstairs tea-room, the Palette. ⊠ *Cullinan Cresent, Civic Centre* ☎ *053/831–1724,*

053/831–1725 ⊕ *www.whag.co.za* ⌨ *R5* ⊙ *Weekdays 8–4:45, Sat. 10–4:45, Sun.10–noon.*

WORTH NOTING

Duggan Cronin Gallery. This gallery houses early photographs of Africa and its inhabitants taken by A. M. Duggan Cronin, an Irishman who arrived in 1897 to work as a night watchman for De Beers. A keen photographer, he traveled widely through southern Africa, capturing his impressions—mostly of African peoples—on film. ⊠ *4 Edgerton, adjacent to McGregor Museum, Belgravia* ☎ *053/839–2743* ⊕ *www. museumsnc.co.za* ⌨ *Donations accepted* ⊙ *Weekdays 8–4:30.*

Dunluce. A well-known Kimberley landmark, the family home of merchant John Orr has a colonial wraparound veranda painted a distinctive green and white. To see the house you need to take a personalized tour (run by the McGregor Museum), on which you'll hear about such details as the swimming pool (the first in Kimberley) and the red dining room, which took a shell through its ceiling during the siege. *See* ⇨ *McGregor Museum.* ⊠ *Lodge Rd., Belgravia* ☎ *053/839–2700* ⊕ *www. museumsnc.co.za* ⌨ *R25* ⊙ *By appointment only.*

Rudd House. In the leafy suburb of Belgravia, Rudd House is the rambling home of Cecil John Rhodes's first business partner, the early diamond magnate Charles Dunnell Rudd. The house has been restored in the art deco style of the 1920s, when the Bungalow, as the house was then known, was in its heyday. Look for the croquet ground made out of kimberlite, and the massive snooker table surrounded by a multitude of animal heads from Rudd's trips north to Matabeleland. Like Dunluce, Rudd House can be seen only on a tour operated by the McGregor Museum (see ⇨ *McGregor Museum*). ⊠ *Loch Rd., Belgravia* ☎ *053/839–2700* ⊕ *www.museumsnc.co.za* ⌨ *R25* ⊙ *By appointment only.*

Sol Plaatje's House. Activist, author, and journalist Sol Plaatje (1876–1932) lived most of his multitalented life in this house. In addition to being the first general secretary of the African National Congress, he was the first black South African to publish a novel in English, an influential early black newspaper editor, and an energetic campaigner for human rights. His house is now a small reference library, publishing house, and museum with displays on his life and extracts from his diary. The reference library contains the works of previously exiled South Africans (in English) and a collection of Tsetswana literature; books are also for sale. ⊠ *32 Angel St., Albertynshof* ☎ *082/804–3266, 053/833–2526* ⊕ *www.museumsnc.co.za* ⌨ *R5 and donations* ⊙ *Weekdays 9–1 and 2–4.*

WHERE TO STAY

$

B&B/INN

Fodor's Choice

★

🛏 **Belgravia Bed and Breakfast.** In a 100-year-old house on leafy Elsemere Road, in the heart of historic Belgravia, this charming guesthouse is within easy walking distance of many of Kimberley's historic attractions, including the McGregor Museum, Dunluce, and the Rudd House. **Pros:** within easy walking distance of many historic attractions;

beautiful period-piece architecture; comfortable, small, and intimate. **Cons:** must be booked well in advance. $ *Rooms from: R600* ⊠ *10 Elsemere Rd., Belgravia* ☎ *053/832–8368, 082/224–3605* ⊕ *www. belgraviabb.co.za* ⇝ *2 rooms, 1 cottage* ⦿ *Breakfast.*

$$
B&B/INN
Estate Private Hotel. Built in 1907 as a wedding present to Lady Mary Oppenheimer, this exquisite guesthouse lets you see how the rich and famous lived it up at the turn of last century. **Pros:** good location; small, boutique feel; good value for money; excellent kitchen. **Cons:** limited room availability; bookings for restaurant essential. $ *Rooms from: R1050* ⊠ *7 Lodge Rd., Belgravia* ☎ *053/832–2668* ⊕ *www.theestate. co.za* ⇝ *5 rooms* ⦿ *Breakfast.*

$
B&B/INN
Langberg Guest Farm. On the west side of the Magersfontein Battle-field, Langberg is far removed from the buzz of city life. **Pros:** game-viewing (in game-farm context); relatively close to Kimberley; farm hospitality. **Cons:** not Big Five; still 21 km (13 miles) outside Kimberley. $ *Rooms from: R700* ⊠ *Beaconsfield* ✛ *21 km (13 miles) south of Kimberley on the N12 and another 2½ km (1½ miles) on farm road* ☎ *053/832–1001, 073/338–7314* ⊕ *www.langberg.co.za* ⇝ *10 rooms* ⦿ *No meals.*

$
B&B/INN
Milner House. In a tranquil part of the already sedate Belgravia, this big old, beautiful B&B offers all the comforts of home. **Pros:** refreshing swimming pool; the garden attracts 20 bird species; good breakfast. **Cons:** rooms don't maintain the Victorian period decor. $ *Rooms from: R650* ⊠ *31 Milner St., Belgravia* ☎ *053/831–6405* ⊕ *www.milnerhouse. co.za* ⇝ *10 rooms* ⦿ *Breakfast.*

NIGHTLIFE

Halfway House. Cecil John Rhodes used to stop for a drink at Halfway House, halfway between the Kimberley and Bultfontein mines. Because he was short and it was difficult for him to mount and dismount, he was served on his horse. Thanks to the building of a 6-foot wall to prevent people from drinking in public, this novel tradition still lives on. You can drive into the parking lot at "the Half," honk your horn, and a waiter will appear. Today, though, most of the action is inside, where the under-thirty crowd gets rowdy at night. If you go on a drinking spree, you can even spend the night at the attached hotel (locals describe the rooms as "shabby"), at which point no amount of noise will wake you. ⊠ *229 Du Toitspan Rd., Belgravia* ☎ *079/119–9266.*

SHOPPING

Africa Now. Africa Now, which is loaded with objects from just about every inch of Africa—in bone, bead, wood, and resin—has a big ware-house in town. The store closes for lunch daily from 1 to 2. ⊠ *37–39 Du Toitspan Rd., CBD* ☎ *053/832–5522, 082/413–6016.*

Annette's Gift Shop. The gift shop at Big Hole has Kimberley's best assortment of postcards, slides, books, videos, and knickknacks as well as a wide range of ethnic souvenirs such as T-shirts and pillow covers. (Postcards mailed in the pre-1902 Victorian mailbox outside the shop will receive a Kimberley Mine Museum postmark.) You can also buy diamonds and diamond jewelry here, but it may be useful to compare pieces and prices with the Jewel Box, down the road. ⊠ *Big Hole, W. Circular Rd.* ☎ *053/831–2681.*

Jewel Box & Big Hole Diamond Cutting Factory. The Jewel Box & Big Hole Diamond Cutting Factory specializes in diamond jewelry and can custom-make a piece if you will be in town for a day or two. Although the Jewel Box doesn't boast about its prices, they are among the country's most reasonable, and they draw customers from as far as Johannesburg. On weekdays you can watch goldsmiths at work in the on-premises factory. ⊠ *18 W. Circular Rd., Big Hole* ☎ *053/832–1731.*

Kimberley Jewellers. Kimberley Jewellers, around the corner from and a sister store of Africa Now, carries Euro-African jewelry, specializing in tanzanite and antique jewelry. It's open by appointment only. ⊠ *23 Jones St., CBD* ☎ *082/413–6016.*

SIDE TRIPS FROM KIMBERLEY

BARKLY WEST
32 km (20 miles) north of Kimberley on the R31.

The town of Barkly West, on the Vaal River, was the site of some of the earliest alluvial diamond diggings in South Africa.

EXPLORING
Canteen Kopje Archaeological Site. Today you can visit the open-air Canteen Kopje Archaeological Site to view both archaeological and geological treasures, ranging from Stone Age artifacts more than a million years old to rock axes, found in a recent excavation, that date from the late 1800s. Walk the 1-km (½-mile) trail to take in the exhibits. Students of history—and South Africa in particular—will really appreciate this off-the-beaten-path stuff. ⊠ *Barkly West* ✛ *10 km (6 miles) southeast of Barkly West, toward Kimberley* 🎫 *Free* ☯ *Weekdays 7:30–4:15, weekends 8:30–4.*

NEED A BREAK?

Pump House Bar. Finish off your tour of Barkly West with a drink or light snack at the Pump House Bar, on the important Vaal river and within a stone's throw of the museum. It's a great place to meet locals, enjoy a good steak or other pub fare, and contemplate the waters of the Vaal River. ⊠ *Barkly West* ☎ *053/531–0867.*

Fodor'sChoice
★
Wildebeest Kuil Rock Art Tourism Centre. At the Wildebeest Kuil Rock Art Tourism Centre, the half-mile-long San Rock Art Trail takes you on a short walk back through time. Billed as "helping to protect the future of the past," this memorable rock art experience includes engravings made by ancestors of the Khoisan, dating between 1,000 and 2,000 years ago. (Ancestors of the Khoisan are believed to be some of the earliest humans to walk the face of the earth.) Listening to an audio player, you take a boardwalk to the best of more than 400 images—eland, elephant, rhino, wildebeest, hartebeest, ostrich, and dancing human figures—on a low ridge of ancient andesite rock. The center also offers a 20-minute introductory film and display on the subject and a crafts shop run by the !Xun and Khwe San (refugees from the Angolan and

Namibian wars), whose land surrounds the site. ⊠ *Between Barkly West and Kimberly ✛ 15 km (9 miles) northwest of Kimberley on the R31, en route to Barkly West* ☎ *053/833–7069* ⊕ *www.museumsnc.co.za/ wildebeestkuil.htm* ⊒ *R30* ⊙ *Weekdays 9–4, weekends by appointment only.*

WHERE TO STAY

$$

RESORT

⛺ **Mattanu Private Game Reserve.** Accommodations at this small, family-operated game reserve are in luxury tents under the shade of the indigenous camel-thorn trees, with each intimate and secluded tent including a viewing deck overlooking a water hole. **Pros:** small and intimate atmosphere; eco-friendly environment; family-run by caring owners. **Cons:** popular local wedding venue, so it can be booked up. ⑤ *Rooms from: R1600* ⊠ *Barkly West ✛ 17 km (10½ miles) north of Barkly West* ☎ *083/235–1993* ⊕ *www.mattanu.com* ⮑ *5 luxury tents* ⦿| *Some meals.*

GRIQUATOWN

144 km (90 miles) west of Kimberley; 252 km (158 miles) east of Upington.

If you are driving from Kimberley to Upington, make a stop in Griquatown. The town, locally known as Griekwastad, was the center of a 19th-century state called Griqualand West, which had its own flag, coinage, and even language. The Griquas, a social group that came into being in the late 18th century, were at first a mixture of indigenous Khoisan and black peoples, runaway slaves, freebooters (pirates), adventurers, and criminals escaping the Cape Colony to the south. Some people still identify themselves as Griquas today.

Mary Moffat Museum. In 1803 the London Missionary Society established a mission here, and Mary Moffat, wife of explorer David Livingstone, was born here. The old mission house is now home to the Mary Moffat Museum, which has interesting displays and literature on the history of the Griquas, the missionaries, and the area. The phone number may not work, but it's definitely open. ⊠ *Main St., Griquatown* ☎ *053/343–0180* ⊒ *Donations accepted* ⊙ *Weekdays 8–1 and 2–5.*

THE KALAHARI

With Namibia to its west and Botswana to its north, the Kalahari is an area of arid dunelands that rightfully conjures up images of desolation. Much of the area is vast, semi-desert terrain with minimum rainfall, and it's largely uninhabited—by humans, that is. It is home to the oryx, springbok, and black-maned lion.

Paradoxically, the southern Kalahari—stretching west along the R64 from Upington to Kakamas and beyond—turns that stereotype on its head. This is the so-called Green Kalahari, the basin of the Orange River, South Africa's largest. It is where the hunter-gatherer San (Bushmen) marked the dry Kalahari as their home, and the fertile land around the Orange was originally occupied by the pastoral Khoi people. Here irrigation has created a literal oasis that today includes thousands of acres of vineyards and the largest date farm in the Southern Hemisphere.

4

Rock Art in the Northern Cape

An important key to understanding humankind's past, rock art is a fascinating aspect of South African and world heritage. In the Northern Cape, engravings (made by scratching into the rock surface), paintings, and finger paintings proliferate throughout the province and still carry an aura of mystique, since relatively little is known about them. Although some archaeologists have attributed the origins of rock art to ancient Egyptians, Phoenicians, and even extraterrestrial races, the rock art found here was created by ancestors of the San. Materials came from the immediate environment. Ocher (red iron-oxide clay) was used to obtain red, charcoal for black, and white clay for white. Blood, egg, and plant juices were used for binding, creating a paint with obvious staying power.

Most rock art illustrates the activities and experiences of the African medicine people, or shamans. Religious rituals, such as those for making rain and healing the sick, involved trances and inspired visions, from which rock-art images were created. The images included large animals, such as the highly regarded eland and rhino, which were believed to possess supernatural power. Half-animal, half-human representations and geometric patterns and grids are also featured. The shamans believed that when an image was drawn, power was transferred to the land.

Today some of the province's most significant examples of rock art are found at Wonderwerk Cave and Wildebeest Kuil. The former contains one of the country's oldest engravings—at some 10,200 years old—as well as finger paintings, a method used by older-era painters. The latter is well known because its animal engravings are easily accessible to visitors.

Along the roads, irrigation canals are punctuated with waterwheels, an old-fashioned irrigation technique that elevates water so it can be directed into the vineyards, particularly in Kakamas and Keimoes.

In winter the fields and vineyards are brown and bare, but in spring they turn from the neon green of new growth into a deep, lush summer green that makes the area look more like the Winelands of Paarl and Stellenbosch. Grapes are one of the province's major industries: 80% of South African sultanas are grown in the Northern Cape, and table grapes are a rapidly growing export.

Acting as a gateway to both these Kalaharis is the river town of Upington, known countrywide for its intense heat.

GETTING HERE AND AROUND

Because of its isolation, most people with limited time fly into the region via Upington, and many lodgings provide shuttle service from Upington Airport. You can also rent a car or 4x4 (Avis, Budget, and Europcar serve Upington Airport), but if you plan to do so, reserve it far in advance, because their numbers are limited.

If you are driving, Upington and the Kalahari are usually approached from Kimberley along the scenic and winding R64, a distance of 411

Sutherland, South Africa's Coldest Town

If you are looking for an interesting off-the-beaten-path destination between Cape Town and Upington, try this undiscovered gem. Home to beautiful spring flower displays, the only dormant volcano south of the equator—Salpeterkop—as well as the largest telescope in the Southern Hemisphere, Sutherland is home to bright, clear skies and genuine winters. You'll also find scatterings of Anglo-Boer (South African) War history, gorgeous solitude, period-piece accommodations, hiking and mountain-bike trails, and various other accoutrements of the road less traveled. Best of all, the town also boasts two remarkable characters, Rita and Jurg Wagener, who love to tell the story of the flowers and the stars at their establishment, which is about a 3½-hour drive from Cape Town. They can also give you the scoop on all the local happenings. Stop over at the delightful Matjiesfontein an hour before and make a trip of it. You could even fit in the flowers of Nieuwoudtville, just over two hours farther on down a drivable dirt road. There's plenty to do even when the wildflowers are not in bloom. The African Chapter (see ⇨ *Tours*) organizes trips to the region. The coldest town in the country (in winter, at least), it's quite fresh in the early mornings until November. Read more about the town at Discover Sutherland (⊕ *www.discoversutherland.co.za*).

km (257 miles). The N14, on the northern side of the Orange River, is a slightly longer alternative—450 km (313 miles)—but it's faster because it is straighter. Upington is 375 km (233 miles) from Springbok along an excellent paved road. There are several 4x4 trails within the Kgalagadi at Bitterpan and Gharagab, but it is not necessary to have one to get there or for getting around inside the park.

Most towns, game parks, and even remote areas have gas, but use common sense and anticipate long distances by refueling when passing a gas station. Roadside car wrecks bear testimony to what locals say is the biggest danger on these roads: falling asleep at the wheel.

Airport Contacts Upington International Airport ⊠ *Diedricks St., Upington* ☎ *054/337–7900.*

TOURS

Day trips from Upington to Augrabies Falls start at R630 per person. Kalahari Desert tours start at R2,500 per person for a few days. The latter are usually fully inclusive of entrance fees, food, and beverages.

Kalahari Safaris. Catering to all levels of the market, from budget to luxury, this popular company is widely praised and booked months in advance. The owner, Pieter Hanekom, was trained in bush lore by the San Bushmen and often says, "People say if the sand of the Kalahari gets in your shoes, you always come back." He calls the Kalahari one of the last true wilderness areas, and he brings his expertise to small groups of travelers. ⊠ *3 Orange St., Upington* ☎ *054/332–5653, 082/435–0007* ⊕ *www.kalaharisafaris.co.za.*

Kalahari Tours and Travel. Dantes Liebenberg of Kalahari Tours and Travel customizes trips to Kgalagadi Transfrontier Park from an afternoon to two weeks. Other specialties are the Witsand Nature Reserve, Augrabies Falls, the Kalahari, Namaqua flower tours (in season), and farther afield to Namibia and Botswana. The all-inclusive three-day desert experience, which includes interacting with the San community, is a must. Tours range from the four-star variety to backpacker style. Even better, the company is committed to responsible tourism and supports local communities and projects whenever possible. ⊠ *12 Mazurka Draai, Upington* ☎ *054/338–0375, 082/493–5041* ⊕ *www.kalaharitours.co.za.*

VISITOR INFORMATION

Local guides are often more reliable, knowledgeable, and helpful in disseminating information than the local government tourist office.

UPINGTON

411 km (257 miles) northwest of Kimberley.

Home to about 74,000 residents, Upington is a thriving agricultural center on the north bank of the Orange River. In the 1870s a Koranna (a group within the Na'ama culture) captain named Klaas Lucas invited missionary Christiaan Schroder to come to *Olyvenhoudtsdrift* (Ford at the Olive-wood Trees), as Upington was first known. Construction on the first mission buildings, now part of the Upington museum complex, was started in 1873. The town was renamed after Sir Thomas Upington, a Cape attorney general who was responsible for ridding the area of its notorious bandits in the 1880s. Although convention has it that the first person to irrigate crops from the Orange was Schroder himself, recent historical research has revealed that this honor should go to Abraham September, a freed coloured slave, who first led water from the Orange in about 1882.

EXPLORING

Bezalel Estate Cellars. If you are a fan of Cognac and liqueurs, then a stop here is a must. From his pot still, Tinus Bezuidenhout produces and sells really good brandies, and especially high-quality liqueurs. His (or his son Martiens's) generous hand with the tastings will be appreciated by all except the designated driver. It's a family-operated business, and Tinus also knows everyone in the area, so think of him as a tourism resource, too. ⊠ *N14, between Upington and Keimos* ☎ *2783/257–4736, 2754/491–1325* ⊡ *Free* ⊙ *Tastings weekdays 8:30–5, Sat. 8:30–1.*

Camel Statue. About 2 km (1 mile) from the Kalahari-Oranje Museum, in front of the Upington police station, the Camel Statue stands as a bronze monument to the police who used camels as mounts when they patrolled the Kalahari in frontier days. ⊠ *Schroder St.*

Kalahari-Oranje Museum. The Kalahari-Oranje Museum comprises simple whitewashed buildings that were erected by missionary Christiaan Schroder in the 1870s. It has displays on agriculture and local history and collections of minerals and artifacts used by area San. Just outside the complex is the Donkey Monument, a bronze sculpture by Hennie Potgieter that is a testimony to the role played by the animal in developing the Lower Orange River Valley. ⊠ *4 Schroder St.* ☏ *054/337–9300* ✉ *Donations accepted* ⊙ *Weekdays 8–4.*

Orange River Wine Cellars. In Upington's industrial area is Orange River Wine Cellars, the second-largest wine cooperative in the world (the largest is also in South Africa). Tastings of a variety of white wines— from the sweet and rich dessert wine Hanepoort to the lighter steens and chenin blancs—as well as grape juice are offered. Between January and March you can also take a tour of the cellars. ⊠ *32 Industrial Rd.* ☏ *054/337–8800* ⊕ *orangeriverwines.com* ✉ *Tastings R10 for 5 wines, R20 for 10 wines* ⊙ *Weekdays 9–4:30, Sat. 9–11:30.*

Sakkie se Aartjie (*Sakkie's Ark*). If you're missing the sea, a sedate sunset cruise on the Orange River may be just the thing. Sakkie se Aartjie offers a 90-minute trip on a double-decker raft complete with cash bar. After dark you may see monkeys, fish, eagles, and other birds, as well as catfish. ⊠ *Park St., below O Hagans Restaurant* ☏ *082/564–5447* ⊕ *www.arkie.co.za* ✉ *R80* ⊙ *Weekends and public holidays.*

OFF THE BEATEN PATH

Spitskop Nature Reserve. This 12,000-plus-acre private reserve is about 14 km (9 miles) from Upington, and it's a good fallback if you don't have time to make it all the way to Kgalagadi Transfrontier Park. You'll get to see some wildlife, especially the iconic oryx (or gemsbok, as it is called in South Africa), eland, mountain zebra, and decent herds of springbok. Apart from such typical Kalahari game species, other predators to be seen are the jackal and caracal; resident bird species include the kori bustard, ostrich, and Namaqua sandgrouse. Whether you are a day visitor or staying over in one of the chalets (or in an RV), you should make a point of climbing to the top of the Spitskop at dawn or dusk, where you're likely to see a beautiful Kahalari sunrise or sunset. The cooler hours are also advised because day temperatures in summer in this desert reserve can hit 40°C–45°C (104°F–113°F). ⊠ *15 km (8 miles) north of Upington on the R360* ☏ *061/457–8262* ✉ *R50* ⊙ *Daily sunrise–sunset.*

WHERE TO EAT

$
ITALIAN

✗ **Die Dros.** You can drop in for a meal or just a drink at the bar in this large and rowdy franchise steak house which its owner has dubbed a "grill and wine cellar." Bottles are packed into the walls from floor to ceiling, and numerous archways give the place a Mediterranean feel. In addition to steak, specialties include hamburgers and pizza. Overlooking a car park, there is seating outside and inside, and it's open daily from 9 am until late. ⑤ *Average main: R44* ⊠ *Pick 'n Pay Centre, Le Roux St.* ☏ *054/331–3331* ⊕ *www.dros.co.za.*

WHERE TO STAY

$
B&B/INN

⊡ **African Vineyard Guesthouse.** Just outside Upington on Kanon-Eiland, an island in the Orange River (South Africa's largest), this luxurious and peaceful guesthouse sits among expansive vineyards, perhaps as many rows of grapes as you've ever seen. **Pros:** brilliant mix of accommodation styles (warehouse-loft look to cottage-y); superb cuisine; convivial hosts. **Cons:** if you walk too far down the road outside, you'll come across laborers in awful conditions on the farm next door. ⑤ *Rooms from: R800* ⊠ *Kanon-Eiland, Plot 79, Upington* ☎ *083/461–1724, 071/607–4582* ⊕ *www.africanvineyard.co.za* ⤴ *7 rooms* ⦿ *Breakfast.*

$　⬚ **Kalahari Guest House.** A perfect overnight stop on the way to or from
B&B/INN　the Kgalagadi National Park, this typical South African homestead, 50 km (31 miles) north of Upington, caters to all budgets. **Pros:** countryside atmosphere with a lot of local flavor; proximity to Kgalagadi Transfrontier Park. **Cons:** basic accommodations. ⑤ *Rooms from: R300* ⊠ *R360* ☎ *054/902 and ask for 918704, 073/194–2864* ⊕ *www.upington.co.za/ kalahariguesthouse* ⤴ *1 room, 1 guesthouse, 1 bush camp* ▭ *No credit cards* ⦿ *No meals.*

$　⬚ **A Riviera Garden B&B.** In the middle of a row of guesthouses, the
B&B/INN　Riviera is an oasis of personal attention, charm, and tasteful interiors. **Pros:** beautiful garden on the river; very good breakfast; secure parking. **Cons:** you have to prepay to confirm booking; only two units. ⑤ *Rooms from: R920* ⊠ *16 Budler St.* ☎ *054/332–6554* ⊕ *upington.co.za/ariviera* ⤴ *2 rooms* ▭ *No credit cards* ⦿ *Breakfast.*

$　⬚ **Witsand Kalahari Nature Reserve Lodge.** It's worth staying a few nights
RESORT　in one of the chalets or bungalows at this beautiful site in the southern Kalahari, especially if you can't get all the way to Kgalagadi. **Pros:** roaring sand dunes; good game; desert bush sounds at their best. **Cons:** off the well-worn track, unless you're moving between Upington and Kimberly; self-catering. ⑤ *Rooms from: R480* ⊠ *Postmasburg* ✛ *220 km (137 miles) east of Upington on road to Griquatown and then another 45 km (28 miles) down sometimes rocky road to Witsand* ☎ *053/313–1061* ⊕ *www.witsandkalahari.co.za* ⤴ *10 3-bedroom chalets, 7 bungalows* ⦿ *No meals.*

AUGRABIES FALLS NATIONAL PARK

120 km (75 miles) west of Upington; 40 km (25 miles) northwest of Kakamas.

The Khoi, early pastoralists who lived in this area for thousands of years before the arrival of Europeans, called these falls Aukoerabis (Place of Great Noise), and though Augrabies is a relatively small national park (696,850 acres), its falls are truly impressive. Reports of sightings of a river monster in the gorge have been made frequently but are probably fanciful accounts of shoals of giant barbels, which reach about 7 feet in length. A half-day tour should not cost more than R350 per person, a full day not more than R640. This excludes transportation from Upington, entrance fees, and refreshments.

Augrabies Falls National Park. South Africa's largest falls in volume of water, Augrabies plunges 653 feet over terraces and into a gorge 18 km (11 miles) long, which was carved into smooth granite over millions of years. It is strangely otherworldly. Legend has it that an unplumbed hole beneath the main falls is filled with diamonds washed downriver over millennia and trapped there.

Depending on what you're looking for, you can hike in the park for an hour or several days. You don't need a guide. You can also drive around the park to its beautiful and well-appointed lookout points, which offer spectacular views of the gorge below the falls. Unfenced Ararat provides the best views. Oranjekom, which is fenced with a shaded hut, is particularly welcome in the blistering summer heat, and the Swartrante lookout offers a view over the rugged, barren areas of the park. All are easily accessible and well-marked. For the energetic, the Gariep 3-in-1 Adventure is a day trip that consists of canoeing down the Orange for 4 km (2½ miles), hiking another 4 km (2½ miles), and taking a 12-km (7½-mile) mountain-bike ride. During peak times, the park also offers worthwhile night drives (around R60 per person). Recently renovated, reception is at the main gate, and the visitor center, with an information office, shop, and restaurant, is a few miles down the road. All accommodations here were renovated in mid-2014. ⊠ *Augrabies* ☎ *054/452–9200* ⊕ *www.sanparks.org/parks/augrabies* ⬥ *R60 per person per day.*

WHERE TO EAT

$$$$ ✕ **Kalahari Sushi & Cocktail Bar.** The current owner of this restaurant was
JAPANESE so impressed by a sushi-cum-cocktail bar in Cape Town that he bought it and moved it—plus the barman—to the table-grape farming town of Kakamas. Rave reviews (even in the *New York Times* of all places) are probably due more to its novelty value. But it's a fun place, and although local menu additions like springbok won't appeal to everyone, real sushi is served here, and there's a good cocktail bar. It's definitely worth a visit. There are also rooms for rent in the hotel. ⑤ *Average main: R690* ⊠ *Kalahari Gateway Hotel, 19 Voortrekker Way, Kakamas* ☎ *2754/431–0838* ⊕ *www.kalaharigateway.co.za* ⬥ *Reservations essential.*

WHERE TO STAY

$ ⊡ **Augrabies Rest Camp.** South African National Parks (SANParks) offers
RESORT a variety of modern, clean units near both the main visitor center and the falls that were renovated in mid-2014. **Pros:** beautiful, peaceful environment; great hikes and walks; chalets recently renovated (some with better views). **Cons:** satellite TV in the chalets; SANParks food is not the best (better to bring your own). ⑤ *Rooms from: R880* ⊠ *Augrabies* ☎ *012/428–9111 parks board, 054/452–9200 park* ⊕ *www.SANParks. org* ⬥ *50 chalets, 9 cottages* ⦿ *No meals.*

$ ⊡ **Damas Guesthouse.** In a real story of community uplift, a Nama
B&B/INN teacher (originally from Namibia) and her family in the Augrabies Falls village have uniquely decorated rooms in their old house near the hot springs on the Riemvasmaak community trust land. **Pros:** a real community project, given an extra boost by a white Afrikaner helping a local Nama woman; beautiful environment; solitude and peace. **Cons:** the owner is new to the business, so not all the boxes will always be checked off. ⑤ *Rooms from: R350* ⊠ *Riemvasmaak Community, Augrabies* ☎ *078/215–1634* ✍ *damasguesthouse@gmail.com* ⬥ *3 rooms* ⊟ *No credit cards* ⦿ *No meals.*

$ ⊡ **Dundi Lodge.** Situated just 3 km (2 miles) from the falls, this stylish
HOTEL luxury lodge, which oozes hospitality, is a recent addition to this desert oasis. **Pros:** phenomenal cuisine; beautiful rooms; dirt runway outside for that 4-km (2.5-mile) morning run. **Cons:** unfortunately, you can't see Augrabies Falls from here. ⑤ *Rooms from: R1350* ⊠ *4 Airport Blvd.,*

Rooipad, Augrabies ☎ *054/451 9201* ⊕ *www.dundilodge.co.za* ⊅ *11 rooms* ⦿| *Breakfast.*

$$$ 🔲 **Tutwa Desert Lodge.** Only a few lodges in South Africa are blessed
ALL-INCLUSIVE   with phenomenal locations, and Tutwa is one of them, but it's not for
Fodor's Choice   the seekers of the Big Five. **Pros:** a standout South African location;
★   acceptable isolation and solitude; attention to details. **Cons:** few major animals; fairly isolated. ⑤ *Rooms from: R3500* ⊠ *Southern Cross Game Reserve, Schuitdrift, Augrabies* ☎ *2754/453–0001* ⊕ *www.tutwalodge. co.za* ⊅ *9 rooms, 3 self-catering houses* ⦿| *All-inclusive.*

$$ 🔲 **Vergelegen Guesthouse.** This well-placed guesthouse for travelers on
HOTEL   the road from Upington to Riemvasmaak Hot Springs also has a good restaurant, curio shop, and cocktail lounge (and even swings for kids in the garden). **Pros:** nice, modern rooms; good restaurant; accepts pets. **Cons:** isolated, so you aren't likely to stay here unless you are on the way somewhere in the vicinity. ⑤ *Rooms from: R920* ⊠ *Kakamas* ☎ *054/431–0976* ⊕ *www.augrabiesfalls.co.za* ⊅ *18 rooms* ⦿| *Breakfast.*

SPORTS AND THE OUTDOORS

Khamkirri Private Game Reserve. Located 25 km (15 miles) from Kakamas, the Khamkirri Private Game Reserve offers white-water rafting, horseback riding, and game drives. It's also inexpensive to stay overnight in one of their chalets or in the campground. ⊠ *Riemvasmaak Rd., Kakamas* ☎ *082/790–1309* ⊕ *www.khamkirri.co.za.*

KGALAGADI TRANSFRONTIER PARK

260 km (162 miles) north of Upington on the R360.

If you're looking for true wilderness, remoteness, and stark, almost surreal landscapes and you're not averse to forgoing luxury and getting sand in your hair, then this uniquely beautiful park within the Kalahari Desert is for you.

In an odd little finger of the country jutting north between Botswana in the east and Namibia in the west lies South Africa's second-largest park after Kruger. The "reborn" Kgalagadi was officially launched in 2000 as the first transfrontier, or "peace park," in southern Africa by merging South Africa's vast Kalahari Gemsbok National Park with the even larger Gemsbok National Park in Botswana. The name Kgalagadi (pronounced kala-*hardy*) is derived from the San language and means "place of thirst." It's now one of the largest protected wilderness areas in the world—an area of more than 38,000 square km (14,670 square miles). Of this awesome area, 9,600 square km (3,700 square miles) fall in South Africa, and the rest fall in Botswana.

Passing through the Twee Rivieren Gate, you'll encounter a vast desert under enormous, usually cloudless skies and a sense of space and openness that few other places can offer. With the rest camp to the left, just a little farther down the dirt road to the right is the dry Nossob River, lined by camel-thorn trees, which winds its way to Botswana, into which the park continues.

The Kgalagadi Transfrontier is less commercialized and developed than Kruger. The roads aren't paved, and you'll come across far fewer people and cars. There's less game on the whole than in Kruger, but because there's also less vegetation, the animals are much more visible. Also, because the game and large carnivores are concentrated in two river-beds (the route that two roads follow), the park offers unsurpassed game-viewing and photographic opportunities. Perhaps the key to really appreciating this barren place is in understanding how its creatures have adapted to their harsh surroundings to survive—like the gems-bok, which has a sophisticated cooling system allowing it to tolerate extreme changes in body temperature. There are also insects in the park that inhale only every half hour or so to preserve the moisture that breathing expends.

The landscape—endless dunes punctuated with blond grass and the odd thorn tree—is dominated by two *wadis* (dry riverbeds): the Nos-sob (which forms the border between South Africa and Botswana) and its tributary, the Auob. The Nossob flows only a few times a century, and the Auob flows only once every couple of decades or so. A single road runs beside each riverbed, along which windmills pump water into man-made water holes, which help the animals to survive and provide good viewing stations for visitors. There are 82 water holes, 49 of which are along tourist roads. Park management struggles to keep up their maintenance; it's a constant battle against the elements, with the elements often winning. Similarly, the park constantly maintains and improves tourist roads, but again it's a never-ending struggle. A third road traverses the park's interior to join the other two. The scenery and vegetation on this road change dramatically from two river val-leys dominated by sandy banks to a grassy escarpment. Two more dune roads have been added, and several 4x4 routes have been developed. From Nossob camp a road leads to Union's End, the country's north-ernmost tip, where South Africa, Namibia, and Botswana meet. Allow a full day for the long and dusty drive, which is 124 km (77 miles) one way. It's possible to enter Botswana from the South African side, but you'll need a 4x4. The park infrastructure in Botswana is very basic, with just three campsites and mostly 4x4 terrain.

The park is famous for its gemsbok, the desert-adapted springbok, and its legendary, huge, black-maned Kalahari lions. It also has leopard, cheetah, eland, blue wildebeest, jackal, and giraffe, as well as meerkat and mongoose. Rarer desert species such as the elusive aardvark, and the pretty Cape fox, also make their home here. Among birders, the park is known as one of Africa's raptor meccas; it's filled with bateleurs, lappet-faced vultures, pygmy falcons, and the cooperatively hunting red-necked falcons and gabar goshawks.

The park's legendary night drives (approximately R200 per person) depart most evenings around 5:30 in summer, earlier in winter (check when you get to your camp), from Twee Rivieren Camp and Nossob. The drives set out just as the park gate closes to everyone else. You'll have a chance to see rare nocturnal animals like the brown hyena and the bat-eared fox by spotlight. The guided morning walks—during which you see the sun rise over the Kalahari and could bump into a lion—are also a must. Reservations are essential and can be made when you book your accommodations.

WHEN TO GO

The park can be superhot in summer and freezing at night in winter (literally below zero, with frost on the ground). Autumn—from late February to mid-April—is perhaps the best time to visit. It's cool after the rains, and many of the migratory birds are still around. The winter months of June and July are also a good time. It's best to make reservations as far in advance as possible, even up to 11 months if you want to visit at Easter or in June or July, when there are school vacations.

GETTING HERE AND AROUND

Upington International Airport is 260 km (162 miles) south of Kgalagadi Transfrontier Park; many lodgings provide shuttle service, or you can rent a car at the airport. If you reserve a car through an agency in Upington, you can pick it up from the Twee Rivieren Camp. If you drive from Johannesburg, you have a choice of two routes: either via Upington (with the last stretch a 60-km [37-mile] gravel road) or via Kuruman, Hotazel, and Vanzylrus (with about 340 km [211 miles] of gravel road). The gravel sections on both routes are badly corrugated, so don't speed.

VISITOR INFORMATION

There's a daily conservation fee, but Wild Cards, available at the gates or online, are more economical for stays of more than a few days. Reservations for all accommodations, bush drives, wilderness trails, and other park activities must be made through South African National Parks.

EXPLORING

Kgalagadi Transfrontier Park. Originally called Kalahari Gemsbok National Park when it was first incorporated in 1931, Kgalagadi was combined with Botswana's Gemsbok National Park to create this internationally protected area of nearly 9 million acres. Unlike Kruger, South Africa's other mammoth national park, this is a desert park, with sparse vegetation and even sand dunes. The game seen here is mostly concentrated around two roads, which follow the park's two (mostly) dry riverbeds. Black-maned Kalahari lions, springbok, oryx, pygmy falcons, and martial eagles are among the star animal attractions. You will not find the broad range of animals that you see in Kruger, but because of the sparse vegetation and limited grazing areas, they are more visible here. Among the noteworthy plant species are plenty of beautiful camel-thorn acacia trees. The park has several lodges and more rustic rest camps for accommodations, but its isolation means that it's never as crowded as Kruger. ✉ *Twee Rivieren Rest Camp* ☎ *054/561–2000* ⊕ *www.sanparks.co.za* ✉ *R248 per person per day.*

WHERE TO STAY

Accommodations within the park are in three traditional rest camps and several highly sought-after wilderness camps (try to reserve these if possible) that are spread around the park. All of the traditional rest camps have shops selling food, curios, and some basic equipment, but Twee Rivieren has the best variety of fresh fruit, vegetables, milk, and meat, and is the only camp with a restaurant. Twee Rivieren is also the only camp with telephone and cell-phone reception (although cell-phone reception quickly disappears as you head into the dunes) and 24-hour electricity; the other camps have gas and electricity, but the electricity runs only part of the day, at different times in each camp.

For all national park accommodations, contact South African National Parks (✐ *reservation@sanparks.org*), or you can reserve directly through the park if you happen to be there and would like to stay a night or add another night onto your stay.

For a private luxury lodge, !Xaus, owned by the Khomani San community, is deep in the west of the park. Because it's roughly 50 km (32 miles) in from the gate, guests are met by a vehicle at the Kumqwa rest area, where they park their car. From there it is exactly 91 dunes to the lodge in a 4x4—and well worth it.

BOOKING

South African National Parks. Usually safest to book through this central booking office in Pretoria, although often-times when that office says "full," the camp itself has vacancies. ☎ *012/428–9111 Pretoria, 021/552–0008 Cape Town* ⊕ *www.sanparks.org.*

A limited number of campsites (R195) are available at Nossob (20) and Twee Rivieren (24). All campsites have a *braai* and access to electricity and water, and there are communal bathroom facilities and a basic communal kitchen. Before you arrive, be sure to arm yourself with the "blue camping plug"—available from any camping–RV shop—to plug into the electrical system and a long extension cord. Try to find a shady spot.

LODGES

$ ⊡ **!Xaus Lodge.** If you want to experience one of South Africa's most
ALL-INCLUSIVE   beautiful and isolated parks without hassle, then this luxury lodge
Fodor'sChoice   owned by the Khomani San and Mier communities and jointly man-
★   aged with SANParks is the place for you. **Pros:** unique wilderness setting; only private lodge in area; opportunities to interact with the local people. **Cons:** It doesn't get much more remote than this; not a Big Five destination. ⑤ *Rooms from: R3670* ⊠ *Dune 92 Kgalagadi, Kgalagadi Transfrontier Park* ☎ *021/701–7860* ⊕ *www.xauslodge.co.za* ⇆ *12 chalets* ⦿ *All-inclusive.*

REST CAMPS

$ ⊡ **Kalahari Trails.** Offering clean, comfortable self-catering accommoda-
B&B/INN   tions a few miles from the Twee Rivieren gate to the Kgalagadi Transfrontier Park, this is the kind of unique place that's worth seeking out. **Pros:** individual and unique; Anna is engaging and a font of information; Anna's relationship with the meerkats is good. **Cons:** the accommodation is a bit basic. ⑤ *Rooms from: R400* ⊠ *Andriesvale, Kgalagadi Transfrontier Park* ☎ *072/277–2377* ⊕ *www.kalaharitrails.co.za* ⇆ *5 rooms, 1 2-bedroom chalet* ⦿ *No meals.*

$ ⊡ **Nossob Rest Camp.** In the central section of the park, this camp is on
RESORT   the Botswana border, 166 km (103 miles) from Twee Rivieren. **Pros:** riverbed location in a desert landscape makes it a great place place to see predators, particularly lions; predator information center. **Cons:** barren, unattractive camp; no phone reception. ⑤ *Rooms from: R750*

San Culture and Language

The Northern Cape has a long and rich human history. Also called the !Xam, the hunter-gatherer San (most of whom prefer to be called Bushmen, as it describes their skill) have a culture that dates back more than 20,000 years, and their genetic origins are more than 1 million years old, contemporary humans' oldest. Fast-forward a few years—about 2,000 years ago, to be inexact—when Korana or Khoi (Khoe) herders migrated south, bringing their livestock and settling along the Orange (Gariep/Garieb), Vaal, and Riet rivers. During the 18th and 19th centuries the Griquas—thought to be part Khoi and part African and Malay slaves—moved into the Northern Cape with their cattle and sheep.

At one time 20–30 languages pertaining to various San/Bushmen clans flourished, but colonialism brought with it devastating results for most of these languages, which lost out to Tswana and Afrikaans. In the nick of time in the 1870s, British doctor Wilhelm Bleek (who spoke !Xam) and Lucy Lloyd recorded the last activities of !Xam culture and tradition. (Some of these records can be found at the McGregor Museum in Kimberley.)

Still thousands of Northern Cape residents today acknowledge an ancestral connection to the largest San or !Xam group of the 18th and 19th centuries. The two biggest remaining groups are the !Xu and the Khwe, who live at Schmidtsdrift, 80 km (50 miles) from Kimberley. Among the best-known groups in South Africa today is the Khomani San, some of whom still speak the ancient Nu. For a good overview on the languages, culture, and peoples who migrated to the Northern Cape, check out the McGregor Museum.

⊠ *Kgalagadi Transfrontier Park* ☎ *012/428–9111 reservations* ⊕ *www.sanparks.org* ⊅ *15 chalets, 1 cottage, 2 guesthouses, 21 campsites* ⎟◎⎟ *No meals.*

$

RESORT

FAMILY

⛺ **Twee Rivieren Rest Camp.** On the Kgalagadi's southern boundary, this camp is home to the park's headquarters. **Pros:** modern, well-equipped chalets; on-site grocery store selling basics; not-to-be-missed guided morning and night drives; 24-hour electricity. **Cons:** the biggest and noisiest camp in the park; not particularly attractive ⑤ *Rooms from: R1110* ⊠ *Kgalagadi Transfrontier Park* ☎ *012/428–9111 reservations* ⊕ *www.sanparks.org* ⊅ *1 cottage, 30 bungalows* ⎟◎⎟ *No meals.*

WILDERNESS CAMPS

Kgalagadi is the first national park to provide accommodation deep in the wilderness, where several unfenced wilderness camps with their own water holes for game-viewing put you deep in the heart of the Kalahari. These enchanting camps are very popular, so make your reservations well in advance—11 months ahead, if possible. Each camp is slightly different, but all have the same facilities and are similarly priced. All have an equipped kitchen with a gas-powered refrigerator, solar-powered lights, gas for hot water, and a deck with braai facilities. You do need to supply your own water and firewood.

Because all of these camps are unfenced (which is part of their desirability and charm), it's probably best not to walk outside your accommodation at night. There's a very real chance of face-to-face encounters with nocturnal hunters like lions, leopards, and hyenas.

$
RENTAL

Bitterpan. This camp overlooks an enormous expanse of sand and a water hole, where you can watch game come and go from your deck or from the communal areas. **Pros:** spectacular game-viewing from your accommodation; beautiful desert scenery; only four cabins. **Cons:** 4x4s only; no children under 12; communal kitchen and eating area (cross fingers you share the camp with amenable visitors); it's a long drive to get here from any starting point; guests have to bring their own drinking water and firewood. $ *Rooms from: R1165* ⊠ *Kgalagadi Transfrontier Park* ☎ *012/428–9111 reservations* ⊕ *www.sanparks.org* 🛏 *4 cabins* ⏺ *No meals.*

$
RENTAL

Gharagab. Although you'll need a 4x4 to negotiate the two-track road to Gharagab, it's worth every dusty mile for the chance to feel like you're the only person on earth. **Pros:** you've probably never experienced solitary wilderness such as this. **Cons:** 4x4s only; no children under 12; not much in the way of big game; guests must bring their own drinking water and firewood. $ *Rooms from: R1300* ⊠ *Kgalagadi Transfrontier Park* ☎ *012/428–9111 reservations* ⊕ *www.sanparks. co.za* 🛏 *4 cabins* ⏺ *No meals.*

$
RENTAL

Grootkolk. Surrounded by camelthorn trees and close to the Nossob River bed, this lovely camp has good game-viewing, with lions, cheetahs, hyenas, and lots of antelope, including oryx and springbok, and it can book up months in advance. **Pros:** spotlighted water hole; sublime wilderness; ceiling fans in the cabins. **Cons:** 4x4s or 2x4s only; no children under 12; chalets are made from canvas and sandbags, so if you prefer something more substantial, stay away. $ *Rooms from: R1350* ⊠ *Kgalagadi Transfrontier Park* ☎ *012/428–9111 reservations* ⊕ *www.sanparks.org* 🛏 *4 cabins* ⏺ *No meals.*

$
RENTAL
FAMILY

Kalahari Tent Camp. Many visitors say that this good game-viewing camp overlooking the Auob River bed and water hole is one of the most beautiful places in the park, so try to stay for more than one night. **Pros:** near Mata Mata, which has a shop and gas; excellent game; family-friendly; lovely honeymoon tent; ceiling fans in the tents, pool. **Cons:** guests must bring their own drinking water and firewood. $ *Rooms from: R1355* ⊠ *Kgalagadi Transfrontier Park* ☎ *012/428–9111 reservations* ⊕ *www.sanparks.org* 🛏 *10 tents, 4 family tents, 1 honeymoon tent* ⏺ *No meals.*

$
RENTAL

Kieliekrankie. Perched high on a big sand dune only 8 km (5 miles) from the game-rich Auob River road, this small camp overlooks seemingly infinite red Kalahari sands, creating an amazing sense of space and isolation. **Pros:** easily accessible with a sedan; you can start your game drives before residents of the other camps reach the area so you have the game to yourself for a while; the red Kalahari sands are unforgettable. **Cons:** no children under 12; guests must bring their own drinking water and firewood, although it is a happily interactive. $ *Rooms from: R1350* ⊠ *Kgalagadi Transfrontier Park* ☎ *012/428–9111 reservations* ⊕ *www.sanparks.org* 🛏 *4 cabins* ⏺ *No meals.*

$ **Urikaruus.** Four cabins with kitchens, bedrooms, and bathrooms are
RENTAL   built on stilts among camelthorn trees overlooking the Auob River.
Pros: accessible with a sedan; stunning location; game to yourself on
early-morning and late-afternoon drives; cabins have their own kitchen.
Cons: no children under 12; guests must bring their own drinking water
and firewood. **$** *Rooms from: R1350* ✉ *Kgalagadi Transfrontier Park*
☎ *012/428–9111 reservations* ⊕ *www.sanparks.org* ⟿ *4 cabins* ⦿ *No
meals.*

TSWALU KALAHARI RESERVE

*250 km (155 miles) southeast of Kgalagadi Transfrontier Park; 262
km (163 miles) northeast of Upington; 145 km (90 miles) northwest
of Kuruman.*

Near the Kgalagadi Transfrontier Park is the malaria-free Tswalu Kalahari Reserve, at 1,000 square km (386 square miles) the largest privately
owned game reserve in Africa; it's the perfect place to photograph a
gemsbok against a red dune and big blue sky. Initially founded as a
conservation project by the late millionaire Stephen Boler (how he made
his money is a story in itself), primarily to protect and breed the endangered desert rhino, he left it to the Oppenheimer (of De Beers diamonds
fame) family in his will. Today it spreads over endless Kalahari dunes
covered with tufts of golden veld and over much of the Northern Cape's
Korannaberg mountain range. Its initial population of 7,000 animals
has grown, and it's now home to lions, cheetahs, buffalos, giraffes,
and a range of antelope species—including rare species such as roan
and sable antelope, black wildebeest, and mountain zebra. For (sadly)
financial reasons a fence keeps the lion and the sable antelope separate
in this massive reserve. There's not as much game as in some of Mpumalanga's private reserves because the land has a lower carrying capacity
(the annual rainfall is only about 9¾ inches). But when you do see the
animals, the lack of vegetation makes sightings spectacular.

GETTING HERE AND AROUND
The lodge operates a direct flight between its Johannesburg airport han-
gar and Tswalu (this has to be booked directly through the reserve). It's
also easy (and cheaper) to fly to Kimberley or Upington and be picked
up from there by the lodge. Daily charter flights are available from
Johannesburg, Durban, and Cape Town with Airlink and Federal Air.
Road transfers from Kimberley or Upington can be arranged, or you
can book a charter flight from Johannesburg.

EXPLORING
FAMILY   **Tswalu Kalahari Reserve.** This reserve northeast of Upington is one of
the most child-friendly game reserves in southern Africa. Children are
welcomed and well catered to, with lots of freedom and special activities. No other game reserve offers such flexibility, and the dedication
of the field guides and butlers here allows you to plan your days as
you please: you might prefer a Champagne breakfast in your stunning
accommodation to going out on a game drive, or you may want to
sleep under the stars on the "Malori" open deck. The reserve plays a
particularly important conservation role: backed by funds from the De

Beers family, its desert black rhino population represents one-third of South Africa's entire remaining animals. In addition to rhino sightings, the interactive experience with the meerkats is a highlight when staying at Tswalu, as are visits to 380,000-year-old rock engravings from the earliest residents of these phenomenal landscapes.

A stop on your game drive from one of the many spacious hills affords a peace and serenity not often experienced in Africa, as you sip sundowners on red dunes while the typically sensational sunsets are the cherry on top. The reserve is a must-visit if you're in the area, and there are easy connections via Johannesburg by charter flight. Kuruman is the nearest town. ⊠ *Kuruman* ☎ *053/781–9331* ⊕ *www.tswalu.com.*

WHERE TO STAY

$$$$
RESORT
FAMILY

🛏 **The Motse.** Tswalu's main lodge is made up of freestanding thatch-and-stone suites clustered around a large main building with a heated natural-color pool and a floodlighted water hole. **Pros:** special children's room and babysitting services and nannies available; unique desert landscape; same great wildlife as Tarkuni; wonderful library with rare books. **Cons:** no elephants; sable antelopes kept separate from the lions, making the experience feel a little manufactured. $ *Rooms from: R10600* ⊠ *Tswalu Kalahari Reserve* ⊕ *www.tswalu.com* 🛏 *8 suites* ⦿ *All meals.*

$$$$
RENTAL
FAMILY

🛏 **Tswalu Tarkuni Lodge.** In a private section of Tswalu, Tarkuni is an exclusive, self-contained house decorated similarly to the Motswe and offering a comparable level of luxury. **Pros:** this is excellent value for money, and if there are 10 of you, it works out to be far more affordable than most other luxury lodges; a children's paradise; black-maned Kalahari lions, occasional wild dogs, cheetah, and one-third of South Africa's endangered desert black rhino population; if you're a fan of TV's *Meerkat Manor,* you'll be in a seventh heaven. **Cons:** no elephants. $ *Rooms from: US$5711* ⊠ *Tswalu Kalahari Reserve* ⊕ *www.tswalu.com* 🛏 *1 house* ⦿ *All meals.*

KURUMAN

250 km (156 miles) northeast of Upington.

If you have a car while in the Kalahari region, it's worth stopping in Kuruman, the hub of a dairy, cattle, and game-farming area. With flat, wide streets, the town is a rush of green in the middle of the Kalahari. Camel-thorn and stinkwood trees are everywhere, but cleanliness is not high on this municipality's priority list, so arrive without expectations. Follow signs to "The Eye" or "Die Oog," an amazing natural spring that bubbles out 5 million gallons of water daily. This is the source of the Kuruman River and of massive significance to the arid Northern Cape, though the river's polluted appearance can be a bit disappointing.

EXPLORING

Kuruman Moffat Mission. Established in 1816, the Kuruman Moffat Mission is the most famous mission station in Africa. It was headed by Robert Moffat from 1820 until his retirement in 1870. The site, with stone-and-thatch buildings dating from the 1820s and 1830s and surrounded by huge trees, represents an interface between precolonial history and the present. A complete Setswana Bible was printed here in 1857—the first time the Bible was printed in its entirety in a previously unwritten African language. The mission served as a springboard for many early adventures into the interior, including David Livingstone's expeditions. It's a lovely and gentle place full of memories. It still functions as a mission and community center, and has an excellent curio shop. ⊠ *Moffat La., Kuruman* ✛ *5 km (3 miles) north of Kuruman on Hotazel Rd.* ☎ *078/589–0644* ✍ *R10* ⊘ *Daily 8–5.*

OFF THE BEATEN PATH

Wonderwerk Cave. This fascinating heritage site contains a spectacular 460-foot-long cave that shows evidence of 800,000 years of Stone Age occupation and early fire use. Some 10,000-year-old engravings were found in the deposit, and the cave has unusual rock paintings on its walls. A good museum adjacent to the cave provides detailed interpretation, and a resident guide will show you around. The cave is administered by Kimberley's McGregor Museum, which can provide additional information, and advance reservations are advised. ⊠ *Off the R31, 50 km (31 miles) south of Kuruman* ☎ *053/839–2700, 053/839–2707 ask for Archaeology Department* ⊕ *www.museumsnc. co.za* ✍ *R25* ⊘ *Daily 9–5.*

NAMAQUALAND

This huge, semi-desert region extending north from the West Coast to Namibia, hundreds of miles north of Cape Town and west of Kimberley, is a highlight of South Africa. It's a remote, unpopulated area, with few facilities and comforts. In spring, however, it puts on a spectacle that must be the greatest flower show on earth. Vast fields that seemed barren only a month before blush with blossoms—and in two months they're gone again. *Vygies* (a type of succulent fynbos) and Namaqualand daisies brightly splash the hillsides and valleys with color. Known as the Succulent Karoo, the area is dependent on the right weather conditions—staggered and regular rainfall and particular temperature and light—to show off its full beauty. As with many South African village businesses, the flowers tend to open at 10 and close at 4. Unless it's flower season, think twice about trekking to Namaqualand. As in parts of the American West, distances are vast, and the landscape looks harsh, mostly hills dotted with giant boulders and swollen-trunked *kokerbooms* (quiver trees, so named because Bushmen cut arrow quivers from them).

Khoisan people have lived in Namaqualand for thousands of years. The first Europeans to venture into the area were Dutch settlers from the Cape, who came in search of the copper they knew existed here because the Khoi had used it in trade. Though Simon van der Stel, a governor of the Cape Colony, sank test shafts in 1685 and realized there were rich quantities of copper in the hills around Okiep and Carolusberg, it wasn't until the 1840s, when the Okiep Copper Mining Company came to Namaqualand, that copper was mined on a large scale. Today the region's commercial activity is clustered in the *dorps* (villages) of Okiep, Concordia, and Nababeep, and in the region's most prominent town,

Springbok—all of whose roots lie in copper. The area is littered with heritage sites harking back to the early copper days, from the smoke-stack in Okiep to the Messelpad Pass, south of Springbok.

The life of the mines is now almost at an end, and most of Namaqualand is poverty-stricken but still intriguing. As the copper mines reach the end of their lives, tourism is becoming the region's great hope, and a tourism infrastructure has been put into place to serve the significant number of locals and foreigners who visit for the flowers (all high-quality establishments are booked up—and there aren't too many of them, at least not yet). Hotels and restaurants are largely still basic, and Namaqualand isn't the easiest place to get to. It's 909 km (568 miles) from Kimberley and 375 km (233 miles) from Upington. But as this is one of the most memorable experiences of a visit to South Africa, it's worth the effort if you're here during the right time of the year.

Although Namaqualand is part of the Northern Cape Province, it's actually more accessible from Cape Town, and many travelers choose this approach. It's 544 km (340 miles) from Cape Town to Springbok, and a four- to five-hour drive from Cape Town just to reach Kamieskroon, the closest Namaqualand hamlet with a decent hotel. The N7, the main road linking Cape Town to Namibia, is being widened (finally, to locals' relief) between Citrusdal and Vanrhynsdorp, so the stop-and-go road-work does slow the journey somewhat. A recommended stop on the way up would be the coffee shop and information center at Bitterfontein for yummy homemade burgers, about three hours from Cape Town. To do the area justice, you need to budget four days or more. The order of towns assumes you are driving up from Cape Town. If you are driving to Springbok from Upington, read the towns in reverse.

GETTING HERE AND AROUND

Phakalane Airways connects Springbok with Kimberley and Upington. Heading out of town on the R355 toward the Goegap Nature Reserve, the airport is a roughly 8-km (5-mile) journey. ⇨ *For more information, see Air Travel in Travel Smart.*

Intercape Mainliner provides bus transportation to Springbok from both Cape Town and Johannesburg. ⇨ *For more information, see Bus Travel in Travel Smart.*

Namaqualand is more than 320 km (200 miles) north of Cape Town and 900 km (563 miles) west of Kimberley. With the great distances involved and the absence of any real public transportation, the only way to get around is by car. Roads are generally well paved, but signage to tourist attractions is not always good. From Springbok to Hondeklip-baai there is an 80-km (50-mile) stretch of sandy gravel road. Traffic to Springbok picks up on Friday and Saturday, when people from neigh-boring communities converge on the town.

If you arrive by bus or air, you can rent from Titis or Namaqualand 4x4 Hire, which also rents camping equipment. Make your reservations early. If you're going to the Richtersveld, rent a bakkie (pickup truck) or 4x4, as sedans are not permitted.

Car-Rental Contacts **Namaqualand 4x4 Hire** ✉ *Voortrekker Rd., opposite information center, Springbok* ☎ *027/718–1905.* **Titis Car Rental** ✉ *7 van den Heever, Springbok* ☎ *027/718–2544.*

TOURS

Local trips around Springbok lasting several hours start from R200 per person. Three-day Richtersveld trips cost around R4,850 per person, all-inclusive, with a minimum of two people.

Photographer and tour and river guide Rey van Rensburg caters to adventure tourists on 4x4 trails to the mountainous desert of the Richtersveld, Namibia, Namaqualand, and Kaokoland (home of the Himba), in northern Namibia, one of the most remote and unspoiled areas left on the continent. He has a good eye for spotting the unusual. He also does botanical tours.

Contacts **Aukwatowa Tours.** The complexity of this area and its history is exactly why a good guide is imperative here. When there is so much that is beyond our daily lives to interpret, you need the right person, with the right people skills, to do it. Conrad Mouton is an ex-soldier–turned–tour guide who communicates his passion for the environment and the inhabitants of the far reaches of the Northern Cape, where he takes tours to South Africa's last wilderness, the Richtersveld, and within Port Nolloth. His shipwreck and crayfish (in season) tours—crayfish braais and excellent sunsets "guaranteed"—plus his vast knowledge of the flora in the area afford visitors a local introduction to this remarkable province. His tours are simply brilliant. ⊕ *www.aukwatowatours.co.za.*

VISITOR INFORMATION

The Namakwa tourism office is across from the Agenbag gas station in Springbok. Springbok Lodge's tourist-friendly, welcoming approach often makes it the first place visitors stop for information and free maps.

TOURIST OFFICES

Namakwa Tourism. Ask for Pearl; she's very helpful. ✉ *Voortrekker Rd., Springbok* ☎ *027/712–8034 or 8035 or 8036, 027/718–2985* ⊕ *www. namakwa-dm.gov.za.*

Springbok Lodge/Tourist Information. Unparalleled local knowledge of the area resides in owner Jopie's head. He's a sort of "Mr. Springbok" who knows everyone, both in business and in leisure. There's likely not much he does not know about the region, and he also tends the Jewish graves (the early Jewish merchants in this area were known in Afrikaans as *smouse)* in the Okiep cemetery, for which he's been thanked by an international Zionist organization. ✉ *37 Voortrekker St., Springbok* ☎ *027/712–1321* ⊕ *www.springboklodge.com.*

GARIES

58 km (36 miles) northeast of Vanrhynsdorp.

Garies is a one-horse town cradled amid sunbaked, granite-dominated hills, and one of the best flower routes runs just north of it for 100 km (60 miles) to Hondeklipbaai, on the coast. The road winds through rocky hills before descending onto the flat coastal sandveld. Flowers in this region usually bloom at the end of July and early August. If you're lucky, fields along this route will be carpeted with purple vygies, but also look for Namaqualand daisies, aloes, and orchids. Quiver trees are common along this route, too.

WHERE TO STAY

$

RESORT

🏕 **Agama Tented Camp.** This camp is open in and out of Namaqualand's world-renowned wildflower season. **Pros:** phenomenal scenery, especially in the (spring) flower season; beautiful atmosphere; good meals. **Cons:** isolation could be an issue out of flower season. ⑤ *Rooms from: R800* ⊠ *20 km (12 miles) past Garies, Klipfontein* ✛ *20 km (12.5 miles) north of Garies* ☎ *2772/0400–614* ⊕ *www.agamacamp.co.za* ⬚ *5 tents* �託 *Some meals.*

KAMIESKROON

49 km (30 miles) north of Garies; 72 km (45 miles) south of Springbok on the N7.

Another base for exploring Namaqualand in spring, Kamieskroon is the only place to stay close to Namaqua National Park—unless you're in the park itself. The Kamieskroon Hotel, although no great shakes for accommodations, is a good source of information on wildflowers in Namaqualand. The SANParks information center at the gate to the park should also help.

EXPLORING

NEED A
BREAK?

Kamieskroon Padstal. Some nibbles may be required on your journey, and this would be the ideal place for a snack, particularly because stops in this area are few and far between. ⊠ *Kamieskroon.*

Namaqua National Park. During its flower season (August through early October), Namaqua National Park can usually be counted on for superb wildflower displays, even when there are no flowers anywhere else. Covering an area of almost 200,000 acres, 21 km (11 miles) west of Kamieskroon, the park is the world's only arid biodiversity hot spot. Recent and planned upgrades include more routes and new rest camps; game (tsetsebe, oryx, springbok, and eland) has been reintroduced. Visitors look for Namaqua daisies in oranges and yellows as well as succulents, such as the many-color vygies in hues of purple, magenta, and orange. Roads are good throughout the park. Driving from Soebatsfontein toward Springbok yields spectacular views over the coast from the top of the Wildeperdehoek Pass. Two short hiking trails take a few hours each. A visitor center is at the Skilpad entrance, and an on-site restaurant across the road caters for those in need. ⊠ *Skilpad Rd., Kamieskroon* ☎ *027/672–1948* ⊕ *www.sanparks.co.za* ⬚ *R60* ⊙ *Daily 8–5.*

OFF THE
BEATEN
PATH

Leliefontein. A 29-km (18-mile) detour from Kamieskroon brings you to this old Methodist mission station at the top of the Kamiesberg, which has spectacular views across the desert to the sea. The church, a national monument, was finished in 1855, but the adjacent parsonage is much older. The wildflowers in Leliefontein bloom much later than those on the coast, often lasting as late as the end of October. Even if there are no flowers, it's a beautiful drive back down the Kamiesberg to Garies, 72 km (45 miles) away. ⊠ *Liliefontein.*

WHERE TO STAY

$
RESORT

🏨 **Namaqua Flower Skilpad Camp.** During flower season, this rustic camp operated by An African Anthology puts you in the middle of things, as you are surrounded by low-lying mountains and, of course, fields of orange, yellow, and white flowers with superb views all around. **Pros:** gorgeous setting, with low-lying mountains on the surrounding horizon; the Namaqua National Park never fails to deliver a natural flower spectacular. **Cons:** pricey for what you get; unsatisfactory meals for the price; food is served in indoor dining room rather than the hopitality tent, which is on the hill already offering great views ⑤ *Rooms from: R1500* ⊠ *Skilpad Nature Reserve, Kamieskroon* ☎ *071/688–8201* ⊕ *www.africananthology.co.za* ➴ *20 tents* ⊙ *Closed Sept. 16–July* ⑪ *All meals.*

SPRINGBOK

117 km (73 miles) north of Kamieskroon; 375 km (233 miles) southwest of Upington.

The capital of Namaqualand is set in a bowl of rocky hills that form part of the Klipkoppe, a rocky escarpment that stretches from Steinkopf, in the north, to Bitterfontein, in the south. Quiver trees proliferate in the area, and flower season brings the town alive with multicolored carpets. Though the town owes its existence to the discovery of copper, its architecture is mostly modern, with very few buildings dating from the 1800s. Compared with most of the dorps in the Northern Cape, Springbok is a buzzing little town, with a fair number of things to see in the area if you need to take a break from flower gazing.

EXPLORING

Namaqualand Museum. Displays at the Namaqualand Museum tell the history of Namaqualand, the town of Springbok, and the people who lived here. Articles range from some 17th-century pieces to an old fridge and washing machine made from *kokerboom* wood (from the distinctive "half-man" tree). The museum is housed in an old synagogue, and pays tribute to the era when Jews lived in Springbok (180 Jews lived here until 1972, but there are none left today). The earliest Jewish traders had a significant impact on the the growth of business not only in the area, but in the country as a whole. The massive and nationwide Lewis chain of stores had its origins here in the little town of Springbok. ⊠ *Monument St.* ☎ *027/718–8100* ✉ *Donations accepted* ⊙ *July–mid-Oct., weekdays 8–5, Sat. 9–2, Sun. 10–1; mid-Oct.–June, weekdays 8–5.*

George Swanson Enterprises. This is odd and quite unexpected establishment is an interesting find. If you've grown frustrated driving past land you know contains quartz crystals quietly whiling away eternity, stop at George Swanson Enterprises to dig up some treasures without a permit. Swanson's yard is full of raw rock crystals, water sapphires, turquoise, and blue lace agate along with the entire gamut of semiprecious minerals found in Namaqualand (and Namibia, where Swanson apparently found his first "treasures"). Even if you don't find a piece of rock that speaks to you, Swanson, who "turns rock into bread," will regale you with anecdotes from his "famous past with American presidents' wives," including his ecology award for the discovery of blue lace agate, which had remained hidden for more than 50 million years until he found it in the 1960s. Swanson's is primarily a working yard, and watching the splitting of the rock is fascinating. Having the option to buy something is a bonus. ⊠ *28 van Riebeeck St.* ☎ *027/712–2058* ⊗ *Daily 8–5.*

Goegap Nature Reserve. Each spring this reserve transforms into a wildflower mosaic, which you can discover on either of two short—4- and 6-km (2½- and 4-mile)—walking trails. Goegap is also home to the Hester Malan Wildflower Garden, which displays an interesting collection of succulents, including the bizarre *halfmens,* or "half person" (*Pachypodium namaquanum*), consisting of a long, slender trunk topped by a passel of leaves that makes it resemble an armless person—hence the name. ⊠ *R355, 16 km (10 miles) southeast of town via airport road* ☎ *2727/718–9906* 🖅 *R30* ⊗ *Oct.–July, daily 7:30–4; Aug. and Sept., daily 7:30–6.*

WHERE TO EAT

$ ╳ **Caffe Bella.** What a nice and welcome surprise! Good coffee is gener-
ECLECTIC ally hard to find in such remote parts, but the owners here have got this right. Though they are not quite baristas, their "flat whites" nevertheless taste like real coffee. The café is also a deli, stocking yummy chutneys (try the peach), relishes, and more. It's got a nice atmosphere and serves good, hearty lunches (it closes at 5). One interesting fact to know is that the owners' husbands work for opposing engineering firms, but that hasn't hindered their cooperation. If you're headed toward Springbok, it's worth calling ahead for a table; there are not many good places to eat here. ⑤ *Average main: R30* ⊠ *50 Voortrekker St.* ☎ *027/712–3588* 🖘 *Reservations essential* ⊗ *No dinner.*

WHERE TO STAY

$ 🛏 **Apollis Cottage.** Remote in location 30 minutes from Springbok, this is
B&B/INN the real deal if you want comfort and solitude with big skies in a desert-like location. **Pros:** remote location provides solitude; modern accommodations. **Cons:** bedroom color combinations (green and red) are not attractive; parts of the road are rough when it rains; credit cards not accepted. ⑤ *Rooms from: R800* ⊠ *Homeb 6, 20 km (12 miles) off the N2* ☎ *087/233–9194* ⊕ *www.theapolliscottage.com* 🖘 *3 rooms* ⊟ *No credit cards* ⦿❘ *Breakfast.*

$ 🛏 **Naries Namakwa Retreat.** This upscale Cape Dutch–style guesthouse
HOTEL west of Springbok looks out over the mountains of the Spektakelberg. **Pros:** beautiful location in the mountains; excellent cuisine, beautiful bedrooms. **Cons:** location is isolated; if the guesthouse is not full, then the dining room can feel a bit large and empty. ⑤ *Rooms from: R995* ⊠ *Kleinzee Rd.* ⊹ *27 km (17 miles) west of Springbok on the R355*

☎ *021/872–0398, 027/712–4262* ⊕ *www.naries.co.za* ⇆ *5 rooms, 2 suites, 2 cottages* ⎢◯⎢ *Some meals.*

$ ⊡ **Okiep Country Hotel.** About 8 km (5 miles) from Springbok, this hotel
HOTEL is one of the nicest places to stay in Namaqualand, not only for the above-average accommodations and dining ($–$$), but also because owner Malcolm Mostert has created a homey atmosphere and goes out of his way to be helpful and friendly. **Pros:** hands-on, longtime owner/manager; good food; great value. **Cons:** style is a subjective matter. ⑤ *Rooms from: R910* ⊠ *Main St., Okiep* ☎ *082/569–7158, 082/744–1000* ⊕ *www.okiep.co.za* ⇆ *34 rooms, 1 self-catering unit* ⎢◯⎢ *No meals.*

$ ⊡ **Springbok Lodge and Restaurant.** People come here as much for the
B&B/INN living museum that owner extraordinaire Jopie Kotze has created as for the rest of the establishment, which originated as private homes, but it's a serviceable place to stay if you need to sleep over in Springbok. **Pros:** interesting owner; laundry service available; reasonable rates. **Cons:** spread out over quite a large area; some accommodations very basic. ⑤ *Rooms from: R240* ⊠ *37 Voortrekker St.* ☎ *027/712–1321* ⎙ *027/712–2718* ⊕ *www.springboklodge.com* ⇆ *51 rooms, 19 suites, 2 houses* ⎢◯⎢ *No meals.*

EN
ROUTE For an excellent **flower drive,** take a 320-km (200-mile) rectangular route that heads north on the N7 from Springbok to Steinkopf and then west on the paved R382 to Port Nolloth. From there a dirt road leads south through the Sandveld to Grootmis, then east along the Buffels River before climbing the Spektakel Pass back to Springbok. If the rains have been good, the route offers some of the best flower viewing in the region. Note that this depends entirely on the time of the season and the rains—there might be little in obvious evidence. Try to time your return to Springbok to coincide with the sunset, when the entire Spektakel Mountain glows a deep orange red.

PORT NOLLOTH

110 km (69 miles) northwest of Springbok.

Port Nolloth—a lovely drive from Springbok, particularly during flower time—started life as a copper port, but it's better known today as a fishing and diamond center. With only one (decent) road leading into it, the flat, desertlike coastal dorp is a ghost town at night, as the little life that exists by day dies completely after dark. If the few establishments in town are full, MacDougall Bay a mile down the coast has accommodation.

Port Nolloth is also the springboard to the Richtersveld, the vast region of mountains and desert to the north, which is well known for its exquisite succulents and other flora but should be visited only on an organized tour or once you have armed yourself with a considerable amount of information. It's extremely remote, and you'll definitely need a 4x4 or *bakkie* to avoid breakdowns. If you're a newbie to deserts, a guide will help you get the most out of your visit to the Richtersveld. In fact this arid country comes alive when interpreted, whether that means learning about its flowers or the Richtersveld mountains (look out for Conrad Mouton of Aukwatoa Tours).

Port Nolloth's bay is safe for swimming, although the water is freezing cold almost any time of the year. Head over to the harbor to check out the diamond-vacuuming boats, with their distinctive hoses trailing astern. Divers use the hoses to vacuum under boulders on the seabed in search of any diamonds that have washed into the sea from the Orange River over many millennia. It's a highly lucrative endeavor but not without its dangers; at least one diver has been sucked up the vacuum hose to his death.

George Mouyses, at the local museum, has done it all (except for the diamond-vacuum). He can keep you enthralled for hours and asks only for a small donation for his time, which may feel invaluable as you depart.

WHERE TO STAY

$ ⚑ **Bed Rock Accommodation.** The interiors of this guesthouse (made up
RENTAL   of some of the very first houses in town) is delightful, decorated with an eclectic collection of Africana and antiques; each room has its own bathroom, although not always in the room. **Pros:** beautiful period-piece accommodations; convenient location. **Cons:** management can have an attitude. ⓢ *Rooms from: R325* ✉ *Beach Rd., Port Nolloth* ☎ *027/851–8865* ⊕ *www.bedrocklodge.co.za* ☞ *9 units* ⦿ *No meals.*

$ ⚑ **Indigo Bay Guesthouse.** A range of spotless, fully equipped, self-catering
RENTAL   units across the road from the beach can accommodate individuals and groups. **Pros:** friendly hosts; the rooms have everything a traveler needs; across the road from the beach. **Cons:** ugly facade; no soul. ⓢ *Rooms from: R1450* ✉ *1245 Kamp St., McDougalls Bay, Port Nolloth* ☎ *027/851–8012, 2782/892–6344* ⊕ *www.portindigo.co.za* ☞ *6 units with various configurations, each accommodating 2–8 people.*

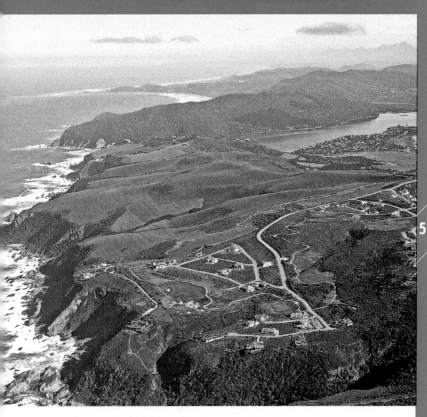

5

THE GARDEN
ROUTE AND THE
LITTLE KAROO

Updated by
Andrea Weiss

This region is a study in contrasts. The forested mountain ranges of the Outeniqua and Tsitsikamma that shadow the coastline trap moist ocean breezes that then fall as rain on the verdant area known as the Garden Route. Meanwhile, these same mountains rob the interior of water, creating the arid semi-deserts of the Little and Great Karoo. Even within these areas, however, there is significant variety.

The Garden Route, which generally refers to the 208-km (130-mile) stretch of coastline from Mossel Bay to Storms River, encompasses some of South Africa's most spectacular and diverse scenery, with long beaches, gentle lakes and rivers, tangled forests, impressive mountains, and steep, rugged cliffs that plunge into a wild and stormy sea. It's this mix that has earned the Garden Route its reputation for being one of the most scenic routes in South Africa. Though the ocean may not be as warm as it is in KwaZulu-Natal, the quality of accommodations tends to be far superior and the atmosphere more tranquil.

The Garden Route also offers great variety for all ages. The backpacking crowd loves it for its great beaches, adventure activities, and accessibility, whereas more sophisticated visitors revel in the excellent seafood, scenery, golf courses, and superior guesthouses and hotels—many with attached spas—where pampering is the name of the game. A Garden Route trip also makes a fabulous family vacation destination, where little ones can frolic on a beach, visit an animal sanctuary like Monkeyland or Birds of Eden, or go for a magical forest walk. Few would wish to pass up the opportunity to see whales and dolphins. With numerous guided, catered, and portered multiday hikes and loads of pretty day walks, the Garden Route is ideal for avid ramblers.

A trip into the Little Karoo in the interior, on the other hand, offers a glimpse of what much of South Africa's vast hinterland looks like. This narrow strip of land, wedged between the Swartberg and Outeniqua ranges, stretches from Barrydale in the west to Willowmore in the east. It's a sere world of rock and scrub, famous for its ostrich farms and the subterranean splendors of the Cango Caves. Unlike more classic safari destinations, the Little Karoo's treasures are not handed to you on a plate. Scour the apparently dry ground to spot tiny and beautiful plants. Hike into the hills to admire the fascinating geological formations of the Cape Fold Mountains and to look for rock art. Or simply pause and drink in the space and the silence. Also special to the Little Karoo are the many dramatic mountain passes that traverse the mountains to the coast or even deeper into the interior, the most famous and precipitous of these being the Swartberg Pass between Oudtshoorn and Prince Albert.

■**TIP➜** The national parks of Wilderness, Knysna, and Tsitsikamma, once separate entities, are now part of the Garden Route National Park. Each area offers a distinct experience from lakeside to forest to dramatic shoreline.

ORIENTATION AND PLANNING

GETTING ORIENTED

Although it *is* possible to get from place to place by bus, the best way to explore this region is by car. There are two practical routes from Cape Town to Port Elizabeth. You can follow the N2 along the Garden Route, or you can take Route 62, which goes through the Little Karoo. These two roads are separated by the Outeniqua Mountains, which are traversed by a number of scenic passes. So it is possible—even desirable, if you have the time—to hop back and forth over the mountains, alternating between the lush Garden Route and the harsher Little Karoo. The inland border of the Little Karoo is formed by the Swartberg Mountains; the Great Karoo is on the other side, beyond the mountains.

Garden Route. This beautiful 208-km (130-mile) stretch of coast takes its name from a year-round riot of vegetation. Here you'll find some of the country's most inspiring scenery: forest-cloaked mountains, rivers and streams, and golden beaches. The area draws a diverse crowd, from backpackers and adventure travelers to family vacationers and golfers. The main towns along the route are (from west to east) Mossel Bay, George, Wilderness, Knysna, Plettenberg Bay, the Crags, Tsitsikamma, and Storms River.

Little Karoo. Presenting a striking contrast to the Garden Route is the semiarid region known as the Little Karoo (also known as the Klein Karoo). In addition to a stark beauty that comes with its deep gorges and rugged plains, the Little Karoo offers the chance to visit ostrich farms, to stay at the Sanbona Wildlife Reserve, to explore the impressive Cango Caves, and to relax at vineyards.

PLANNING

WHEN TO GO

There's no best time to visit the Garden Route, although the water and weather are warmest November through March. The high season is from mid-December to mid-January, when South African schools break for the summer holidays and families flock to the coast. Between May and September the weather cools down with some rain (though there is no single rainy season here). The winter months are the low season, and some establishments choose this time of year to take a break. Yet, even in these colder months it's rarely cold for more than two or three days at a stretch, after which you'll get a few days of glorious sunshine. Wildflowers bloom along the Garden Route from July to October, the same time as the annual Southern Right whale migration along the coast.

The Little Karoo can be scorchingly hot in summer. In winter, days are generally warm and sunny, though it does get cold at night.

Garden Route
and Little Karoo

TOP REASONS TO GO

Whale-Watching. Some of the best boat-based whale- and dolphin-watching in the world can be found at Plettenberg Bay on the Garden Route. And although Plett is the best, there are also good trips to be had at Mossel Bay and Knysna. You can often watch these friendly cetaceans frolicking from the shore, as well. If you really want to feel part of the ocean, your best bet is a kayaking trip in Plett.

Animal Encounters. The Crags area, just outside Plettenberg Bay, is the place to go if you want to spend a day with the animals. Visit with rescued primates at Monkeyland Primate Sanctuary or amble through the world's largest free-flight aviary next door at Birds of Eden. Other spots for animal-watching include the ostrich farms and Cango Wildlife Ranch at Oudtshoorn and—for free-roaming big game like elephants and lions—the Sanbona Wildlife Reserve close to Barrydale.

Adventure Sports. If you're itching for a taste of freefall, you've come to the right place. The highest commercial bungee jump in the world (at 700 feet) can be found at Bloukrans Bridge. If you really have an appetite for heights, you can leap out of a plane with Skydive Plett. For something a little bit closer to the ground, nothing beats the canopy tour at Tsitsikamma, where you fly through the trees (via cables and a harness) with the greatest of ease.

Scenic Hiking. Enjoy the best of nature in comfort on an escorted, guided, portered, and catered hike, locally called "slackpacking." The Dolphin Trail, in the Tsitsikamma section of the Garden Route National Park, offers the chance to walk along remote and rugged coastal terrain but with indulgent accommodation. The Oystercatcher Trail in Mossel Bay lets you explore a wide range of coastal scenery, from cliff-top paths to long beaches, and the food emphasizes traditionally cooked local seafood. The Garden Route Trail combines long and short day hikes with some paddling through the wonderful wetlands of the Wilderness section of the Garden Route National Park.

GETTING HERE AND AROUND
AIR TRAVEL

The only major airport serving the Garden Route and the Little Karoo is George Airport, 10 km (6 miles) southwest of town. George is well served by Airlink, SA Express, Mango, and Kulula airlines with daily flights from South Africa's three major cities (Cape Town, Durban, and Johannesburg). Flying times are two hours from Johannesburg, 1½ hours from Durban, and one hour from Cape Town. There are only a handful of flights from Johannesburg or Cape Town to the little airfield in Plett, 6 km (4 miles) west of town, but from here African Ramble runs charters to anywhere you may wish to go that has a landing strip (most commonly to the Eastern Cape game reserves). These scenic trips fly over the Robberg Peninsula and out over the bay (where you may see whales or dolphins) and then hug the coast up to Nature's Valley before heading inland. ⇨ *For additional airline contact information, see Air Travel in the Travel Smart South Africa chapter.*

Airlines African Ramble Air Charter ✉ *Plettenberg Bay Airport* ☎ *083/375–6514* ⊕ *www.africanramble.co.za.*

Airport George Airport (*GRJ*). ✉ *George Airport, George* ☎ *044/876–9310* ⊕ *www.airports.co.za.*

BUS TRAVEL

Intercape Mainliner and Greyhound offer regular service between Cape Town and Port Elizabeth, stopping at all major Garden Route destinations on the N2, although they often don't go into town but drop passengers off at gas stations along the highway. Another excellent service is the Baz Bus, which offers a handy door-to-door, hop-on, hop-off service to backpacking hostels along the Garden Route and beyond (all the way up to the Wild Coast in the Eastern Cape).

CAR TRAVEL

Most of the towns in this chapter can be found along the N2 highway. The road is in good condition and well signposted. A cautionary note, however: there is a wide shoulder along most of the route, but pull onto it to let faster cars overtake you *only* when you can see a good few hundred yards ahead. Also, stick to the speed limit, as speed traps are common.

■TIP→ An alternative to the N2 is the less traveled—some say more interesting—inland route, dubbed Route 62, even though some of it is on the R60. From Worcester, in the Breede River valley *(⇨ Chapter 3)*, you can travel the R60 and R62 to Oudtshoorn.

PLANNING YOUR TIME

3 Days: Choose a home base in the Garden Route: Wilderness, Knysna, and Plettenberg Bay (Plett) are all excellent options. You'll encounter wonderful crafts shops and studios in all these towns, so keep your credit card handy. On your first day, take a half-day walk through Plett's Robberg Nature Reserve, visit the Woodville Big Tree in Wilderness, or explore Knysna's Garden of Eden. Devote the afternoon to a boat or kayak trip; you may see dolphins, seals, and/or whales, particularly around Plett. Dedicate the second day to whatever activity suits your fancy—lounging on the beach, paddling, horseback riding, or abseiling (rappelling). If you're staying in Plett, you could drive out to Storms River on the third day to do the treetop canopy tour. If you're staying farther west, head over one of the scenic passes to Oudtshoorn, visit the Cango Caves, and take a different scenic drive back.

5 Days: Start with the three-day itinerary *above*. Then spend the next two days at the Little Karoo's Sanbona Wildlife Reserve, where you can see the Big Five and take in lovely flora. Alternatively, you could spend some extra time at any of the Garden Route destinations from the first itinerary; you may want to linger, for example, in Storms River, which will put you right near the spectacular Tsitsikamma section of the Garden Route National Park.

8 Days: Spend the first day or two at Sanbona Wildlife Reserve. Then head east along the R62 to Oudtshoorn, stopping for lunch at the Joubert-Tradauw winery near Barrydale. The next day, visit the Cango Caves before heading over the Robertson, Montagu, or Outeniqua pass to Mossel Bay, Plettenberg Bay, Knysna, or Wilderness, where you'll have no trouble filling the rest of your time with shopping, beach lounging, kayaking, whale-watching, or any combination thereof. If you have an adventurous bent, spend the last two or three days at Storms River Village, where you can take the treetop canopy tour, hit a mountain-bike trail, or go for a long walk in the Tsitsikamma section of the Garden Route National Park. Want still more adventure? En route to Storms River, make the world's highest bungee jump at the Bloukrans River Bridge.

HEALTH AND SAFETY

The whole area is malaria-free, the climate is mild, and the water is safe to drink. Avoid sunburn by wearing a hat and slathering on sunscreen, and take care when swimming, as some beaches have dangerous currents. Never feed wild animals, especially vervet monkeys, who can become a nuisance.

Most towns have late-night pharmacies, and if they don't, pharmacies usually have an emergency number on the door. Call the general-emergencies number (10111 from landline; 112 from mobile phone) for all emergencies. If you break down while driving, call your car-rental company or the company's designee. If you are a member, you can also call the Automobile Association (AA) for assistance.

HOTELS

The region would not have such allure if it weren't for its exclusive seaside getaways and colonial manor houses, as well as its more rustic inland farms and national-park log cabins. Many of the better establishments are set on little islands of well-tended gardens within wild forests. Breakfast is included in most lodgings' rates, and if your guest-house serves dinner, eating the evening meal in situ often has a welcome intimacy after a day of exploring. On the flip side, some cottages are self-catering (with cooking facilities), giving you the chance to pick up some local delicacies and make yourself a feast.

Note that the prices listed are for high season, generally October–April. In some cases these prices are significantly higher than during low season, and they may go up higher still for the busiest period—mid-December to mid-January. (If you're traveling during South Africa's winter, be sure to inquire about seasonal specials.) *Hotel reviews have been shortened. For full information, visit Fodors.com.*

RESTAURANTS

Most medium-size towns along the Garden Route offer a decent selection of restaurants, and the smaller towns of the Little Karoo usually have one or two good restaurants and a handful of lesser eateries. On the Garden Route the emphasis is often on seafood in general and oysters in particular. (Knysna has an oyster festival in July.) Restaurants in the Little Karoo feature fresh ostrich meat and organic mutton or lamb, which is delicious accompanied by a good South African red wine. Look out for farm shops between towns. These make excellent comfort stops where you can buy traditional home-baked fare, dried fruit, and other snacks for the road.

WHAT IT COSTS IN SOUTH AFRICAN RAND			
	$	$$	$$$	$$$$
Restaurants	under R100	R100–R150	R151–R200	over R200
Hotels	under R1,500	R1,500–R2,500	R2,501–R3,500	over R3,500

Restaurant prices are the average cost of a main course at dinner or, if dinner is not served, at lunch. Prices are the lowest price for a standard double room in high season.

VISITOR INFORMATION

Most local tourism bureaus are very helpful. Typical hours are weekdays 8:30 to 5, Saturday 8 to 1. In peak season (generally October to April), you may find them open longer; in very quiet periods the staff may close up shop early.

MOSSEL BAY

384 km (238 miles) east of Cape Town.

Mossel Bay's main attractions are an excellent museum complex; several beautiful historic stone buildings (some of which are exceptionally well preserved); some of the best oysters along the coast; excellent golf; and good beaches with safe, secluded swimming. The area has some of the only north-facing (read: sunniest) beaches in South Africa, which means it's very popular with local families and is always packed in December. Dolphins—sometimes hundreds at a time—frequently move through the bay in search of food, and whales swim past during their annual migration (July–October). You could take a cruise out to Seal Island, home to a breeding colony of more than 2,000 Cape fur seals or, if you're feeling brave, a cage dive to view the numerous white sharks (blue pointers) that hang around the seal colony.

GETTING HERE AND AROUND

Mossel Bay, at the western end of the Garden Route, lies 384 km (238 miles) east of Cape Town along the N2 highway. It usually takes about four hours to drive from Cape Town to Mossel Bay—unless you stop to take in a view, have lunch, or browse in a roadside produce or crafts store.

VISITOR INFORMATION

Contacts Mossel Bay Tourism ✉ *Mossel Bay Tourism Office, Church and Market Sts.* ☎ *044/691–2202* ⊕ *www.visitmosselbay.co.za.*

EXPLORING

Bartolomeu Dias Museum Complex. Named for the 15th-century Portuguese navigator, the Bartolomeu Dias Museum Complex concentrates on the early history of Mossel Bay, when it was a regular stopover for Portuguese mariners en route to India from Europe. The most popular exhibit is the full-size (340-foot-long) replica of Dias's ship (a caravel), which was sailed to Mossel Bay from Lisbon as part of the quincentenary celebrations in 1988. If you pay the extra fee to board it, you'll find it all pretty authentic, except for the modern galley and heads. Also here is the Post Office Tree. In the 15th century a few sailors decided that the tree—then a lone tree on a deserted beach on an unexplored coast—stood out sufficiently and left some letters here in an old boot, under a stone, in the hope they would be found and delivered. They were. Pop a postcard into the shoe-shape mailbox and see if the service is still as good. Your mail will arrive with a special postmark. ⊠ *Church and Market Sts.* ☎ *044/691–1067* ⊕ *www.diasmuseum.co.za* ✉ *Free Mon.–Thurs., otherwise R20; caravel additional R40* ☾ *Weekdays 9–4:45, weekends 9–3:45.*

WHERE TO EAT

$$ ✕ **Café Gannet.** Tour-bus crowds occasionally descend on this popular
SEAFOOD spot, located right next to the Dias Museum and Old Post Office Tree but don't let that put you off. This is Mossel Bay's premium seafood house. The oysters, both wild and cultivated, are extremely fresh and served three ways. Try them with the mango, sweet bell pepper, and coriander salsa for a bit of zing. For something besides fish, try the ostrich fillet with caramelized onions and port-soaked apricots. In summer, it's virtually mandatory to sip a cocktail on the deck of the Blue Oyster bar with its great sea view. The restaurant has been incorporated into the Protea Hotel Mossel Bay and also has a private dining room. ⑤ *Average main: R150* ⊠ *Church and Market Sts.* ☎ *044/691–1885* ⊕ *www.cafegannet.co.za.*

$ ✕ **Delfino's Espresso Bar and Pizzeria.** Good coffee, yummy pizzas and
ITALIAN pastas, tables on the lawn right next to the beach, and a fantastic view of the bay and the Cape St. Blaize lighthouse make this a great place to spend a sunny afternoon. ⑤ *Average main: R60* ⊠ *2 Point Village* ☎ *044/690–5247* ⊕ *www.delfinos.co.za.*

WHERE TO STAY

$$ ⊡ **Protea Hotel Mossel Bay.** Just yards away from the museum complex,
HOTEL this stylish hotel is close to most of what's happening in Mossel Bay. **Pros:** location very central for museum, restaurants, and the beach; stylish and modern rooms. **Cons:** swimming pool is small and overlooked by the terrace; street-facing rooms can be noisy, view is slightly obstructed by building below. ⑤ *Rooms from: R2055* ⊠ *Church and Market Sts* ☎ *044/691–3738* ⊕ *www.proteahotels.com* ⇱ *22 rooms, 7 suites.*

$ ⊡ **Santos Express Train Lodge.** And now for something completely dif-
B&B/INN ferent: In an old train parked on the beach, this lodging uses real train compartments for accommodations. **Pros:** all the cabins face the sea; town center is a 10-minute walk away. **Cons:** compartments are a bit cramped; you need to supply your own towel and soap; no a/c. ⑤ *Rooms from: R500* ⊠ *Munro Rd., Santos Beach* ☎ *083/900–7797* ⊕ *www.santosexpress.co.za* ⇱ *27 compartments, 16-bed dormitory, 1 Caboose, 4 Royal Suites* ⑩ *Breakfast.*

SPORTS AND THE OUTDOORS

BOATING

Romonza Boat Trips. For a closer look at the Cape fur seals lounging around on Seal Island or to check out whales and dolphins, take a trip with Romonza Boat Trips on a 54-foot sailing yacht. One-hour Seal Island trips (all year) cost R140 and whale-watching trips cost R640 (from June to October). ⊠ *Church St.* ☎ *044/690–3101, 082/701–9031* ⊕ *www.mosselbay.co.za/romonza.*

HIKING

Fodor'sChoice ★ **Oystercatcher Trail.** The guided, catered Oystercatcher Trail offers the best of both worlds, providing a multiday hiking experience along the beach and over rocky shorelines while you carry only a day pack. The trail starts in Mossel Bay, with the first day spent on the lovely cliff-top Cape St. Blaize Trail, and continues to the mouth of the Gouritz River. Nights are spent in a guest house or a thatched cottage, where delicious traditional food is prepared for you on open fires. Knowledgeable guides point out birds and plants and discuss local history and customs along the way. Walking on the beach can be hard if the tide is in, but most people of average fitness should manage. A typical trip is four days and five nights but shorter hikes of one or two days can be arranged. ⊠ *Sandpiper Safaris, Boggoms Bay* ☎ *044/699–1204* ⊕ *www.oystercatchertrail.co.za.*

EN ROUTE The small town of Albertinia, about 40 km (25 miles) west of Mossel Bay, is an interesting place to break your journey into the Garden Route from Cape Town or the Winelands. It's the center of the aloe ferox industry. The gel of this indigenous aloe has even greater therapeutic benefits than the better-known aloe vera. Two factories in Albertinia make cosmetics and health-care products from this interesting plant and sell them on-site.

Alcare House of Aloes. Situated next to the N2 highway on the outskirts of the town of Albertinia, the House of Aloes is a good place for a pit stop. There's a garden, play area, coffee shop, and restroom—in addition to the shop which sells aloe-based cosmetic and health products. ⊠ *39 Industrial Rd.* ☎ *028/735–1454* ⊕ *www.aloe.co.za* ☾ *Weekdays 8–5, weekends 8–4.*

GEORGE

45 km (28 miles) northeast of Mossel Bay; 50 km (31 miles) southeast of Oudtshoorn.

About 11 km (7 miles) from the sea, George is the largest town and the de facto capital of the Garden Route. Although the surrounding countryside is attractive and there is a thriving farming and crafts community on its outskirts, George itself is not particularly appealing unless you are a golfer or a steam train enthusiast eager to visit its excellent transportation museum.

GETTING HERE AND AROUND

The only true airport serving the Garden Route and the Little Karoo is George Airport, 10 km (6 miles) southwest of town. Most people who arrive by plane rent a car to continue their journey on the Garden Route. Avis, Budget, Europcar, and Hertz all have car-rental offices at George Airport.

It takes about half an hour to get to Mossel Bay and Oudtshoorn from George, and the roads are good. ⚠ **The area between George and Wilderness is notorious for speed traps, especially in the Kaaimans River Pass, just west of Wilderness.**

VISITOR INFORMATION

Contacts George Tourism Information ✉ *124 York St.* ☎ *044/801–9295* ⊕ *www.georgetourism.co.za.*

EXPLORING

Outeniqua Transport Museum. This museum in a huge hangarlike building is a steam train enthusiast's delight, with 13 beautifully kept steam locomotives and other examples of vintage vehicles. One of the museum's highlights is the original "White Coach" in which Queen Elizabeth and her sister Margaret slept during their 1947 visit to South Africa. ✉ *2 Mission Rd.* ☎ *044/801–8289* ⊕ *www.outeniquachootjoe.co.za* 🎫 *R20* ⊙ *Weekdays 8–4:30, Sat. 8–2.*

WHERE TO EAT

$ ✕ **Meade Café.** This light and airy bistro-style restaurant, with a lovely
CONTEMPORARY outdoor seating area, is in an 18th-century town house in George's shopping district. For breakfast you can indulge in eggs Benedict or French toast, among other things, and lunch features homemade fish cakes and burgers, traditional beer-battered hake, and chicken curry. They also have an excellent selection of salads and sandwiches with interesting ingredients such as hickory-smoked pork loin, roasted vegetables, or marinated chickpeas and apricots. $ *Average main: R65* ✉ *91 Meade St.* ☎ *044/873–6755* ⊕ *meadecafe.co.za* ⊙ *Closed Sun. No dinner.*

WHERE TO STAY

$$$$ 🏨 **Fancourt Hotel and Country Club Estate.** If you're one of those peo-
RESORT ple who believe we were created with opposable thumbs for the sole purpose of gripping a golf club, you'll *love* Fancourt, a luxury resort in the shadow of the Outeniqua Mountains that resembles a country club with numerous leisure and business facilities. **Pros:** on-site spa; kids' program; spectacular golf. **Cons:** nongolfers might feel out of place; little nightlife in George. $ *Rooms from: R3455* ✉ *Montagu St., Blanco* ☎ *044/804–0000* ⊕ *www.fancourt.com* 🛏 *125 rooms, 18 suites in Manor House* ⦿ *Breakfast.*

SPORTS AND THE OUTDOORS

GOLF

The Links, Outeniqua, and Montagu golf courses (all at Fancourt near George) regularly make the list of South Africa's top 20 courses. There are some other notable courses in the area, including the public George Golf Club.

Fancourt Hotel and Country Club Estate. Fancourt's three golf courses are all regularly featured among South Africa's top 20 golf courses. To play at the Gary Player–designed championship courses, Montagu and Outeniqua, you have to stay at the Fancourt Hotel and Country Club Estate. The Links, a private club exclusively for members and Fancourt hotel guests, is particularly challenging and was the venue of the 2003 Presidents Cup. It is currently ranked number 1 in South Africa and 34th in the world by *Golf Digest USA*. There is a golf academy on-site. ⊠ *Montagu St.* ☎ *044/804–0000* ⊕ *www.fancourt.com* ☞ *R795 for Outeniqua and Montagu; R1,500 for the Links* ⅃. *Outeniqua Course: 18 holes, 6902 yards, par 72. Montagu Course: 18 holes, 7342 yards, par 72. The Links: 18 holes, 7578 yards, par 72.*

George Golf Club. This 108-year-old, picturesque public course is a long-time favorite. It kicks off with a tricky first hole, with water to the left and trees to the right and a well-placed bunker that makes the approach to the green difficult. The course highlight is the 17th hole, which has been described as one of the best par-3s in the world (and certainly the best in South Africa), leaving no room for error. Golf-cart rental is R220, and caddies are R145. You can rent clubs (R150–R300 for 18 holes) and pull carts (R30) from the George Golf Shop at the course. ⊠ *George Golf Club, Langehoven Rd.* ☎ *044/873–6116 club, 044/874–7597 shop* ⊕ *www.georgegolfclub.co.za* ☞ *R380* ⅃. *18 holes, 6738 yards, par 72.*

EN ROUTE From George the N2 descends steeply to the sea through a heavily forested gorge formed by the Kaaimans River. Look to your right to see a curved railway bridge spanning the river mouth. This is one of the most photographed scenes on the Garden Route. As you round the point, a breathtaking view of mile upon mile of pounding surf and white beach unfolds before you. There is an overlook from which you can often see dolphins and whales in the surf, and if you look up, you may see a colorful paraglider floating overhead.

WILDERNESS

12 km (7 miles) southeast of George.

Wilderness is a popular vacation resort for good reason. Backed by thickly forested hills and cliffs, the tiny town presides over a magical stretch of beach between the Kaaimans and Touw rivers, as well as a spectacular system of waterways, lakes, and lagoons strung out along the coast, separated from the sea by towering vegetated dunes. Many of the Garden Route's other attractions are within an hour or two's drive, making Wilderness a good base for exploring.

GETTING HERE AND AROUND

Many hotels offer a transfer from George airport, but your best bet is to rent a car there and drive yourself, as the roads are good and you'll be able to see a lot more of the country.

EXPLORING

Wilderness Section of the Garden Route National Park. This 299,000-acre reserve stretches east along the coast for 31 km (19 miles). A wetlands paradise, the park draws birders from all over the country to its two blinds. Several walking trails wind through the park alongside lakes, rivers, and the sea. A relatively gentle option is the 45-minute Woodville Big Tree Walk, which takes you past an 800-year-old yellowwood tree and into the indigenous forest. ☎ 044/877–0046 ⊕ www.sanparks.org ✉ R100 ۞ Daily 7–6.

WHERE TO EAT

$$$$

SOUTH AFRICAN

Fodor's Choice

★

✕**Serendipity.** Start your evening at this award-winning restaurant with predinner drinks on the patio overlooking the river, then move inside to a candlelit table for a fabulous five-course menu. The menu, which changes daily, is imaginative, taking classic South African ingredients and giving them an original, modern twist; chef Lizelle Stolze's passion is evident in the creative combination of flavors and attention to detail in presentation. Dishes could include perfectly cooked venison medallions served with a wild mushroom "lasagna" made of thin slices of *mieliepap* (a kind of polenta) or Cape salmon served with sautéed niçoise vegetables and hollandaise sauce. Desserts also have a South African touch, such as Amarula crème brûlée or saffron-infused milk tart. There are also four luxurious guest rooms upstairs ($$), all with river views and a large communal balcony. ⑤ *Average main: R380* ✉ *Freesia Ave.* ☎ *044/877–0433* ⌚ *Reservations essential* ۞ *No lunch. Closed Sun.*

$$

SOUTH AFRICAN

FAMILY

Fodor's Choice

★

✕**Zucchini.** Since 2007, owner Stephen Henning has been producing food that is free-range, organic, locally sourced, and seasonal, and chances are the garnishes on your plate will have been freshly picked from the organic herb garden outside. The result is tasty, imaginative, healthful fare that's served in generous portions, with vegetarians well catered for. The menu changes regularly and features homemade pastas, soups, sandwiches, and a range of salads served either roasted or raw. Meat eaters take heart: you have not been neglected. Venison *frikkadells* (meatballs) are served with a buttery potato mash and beetroot chutney, hearty steaks come with potato wedges, and slow-cooked lamb shanks are dished up with potato mash and roasted vegetables. You can also sample more than 10 craft beers, including two on tap. The setting is a charming, rustic wooden cottage where guests are encouraged to linger over their meal. Zucchini's is part of Timberlake Farm Stall, which has a number of artisan and organic shops, and a children's adventure playground. ⑤ *Average main: R134* ✉ *Timberlake Farm Stall, off the N2* ☎ *044/882–1240* ⊕ *www.zucchini.co.za.*

5

WHERE TO STAY

$
RESORT
Ebb and Flow Restcamp, Wilderness Section of the Garden Route National Park. This rest camp, along a lovely, meandering stretch of river, is divided into two sections (north and south) and includes a variety of accommodation, ranging from cottages and cabins to huts and campsites. **Pros:** activities like hiking and canoeing available; tranquil; good base. **Cons:** accommodation fairly utilitarian, in style of national parks; rondavels a bit worn; river is prone to flooding. ⑤ *Rooms from: R760* ⊠ *Wilderness section of Garden Route National Park* ☎ *044/877–1197* ⊕ *www.sanparks.org* ⤴ *5 family cottages, 9 log cabins, 20 forest cabins, 12 rondavels, 10 with bath.*

$$$
HOTEL
Fodor's Choice
★
Views Boutique Hotel & Spa. This boutique hotel offers stupendous views of the seemingly endless Wilderness beach from rooms that have floor-to-ceiling windows and private verandas looking straight onto the ocean. **Pros:** superb ocean views; a pillow menu for picky guests; service is attentive and friendly. **Cons:** about 3 km (2 miles) from village center and safe swimming area; limited dining options on-site. ⑤ *Rooms from: R3150* ⊠ *South St.* ☎ *044/877–8001* ⊕ *www.viewshotel.co.za* ⤴ *20 suites, 1 penthouse.*

$
B&B/INN
Fodor's Choice
★
Xanadu. Deep-pile carpets, double-volume spaces, spectacular floral arrangements, and voluminous drapes framing the sea-view windows add to the sense of opulence at this beachfront establishment. **Pros:** just a short walk to the beach; bathrooms are modern and large; free Wi-Fi. **Cons:** too far to walk into town; breakfast is eaten communally; only one restaurant in immediate vicinity. ⑤ *Rooms from: R1200* ⊠ *Xanadu, 43 Die Duin* ☎ *044/877–0022* ✎ *stay@xanaduvilla.co.za* ⊕ *www.xanadu-wilderness.co.za* ⤴ *6 suites* ❢❢ *Breakfast.*

SPORTS AND THE OUTDOORS

The Wilderness section of the Garden Route National Park and its environs provide opportunities for lovely walks, paddling, and birding.

ADVENTURE TOURS

Eden Adventures. Based close to the Wilderness section of the Garden Route National Park, Eden Adventures offers canyoneering in Kaaimans Gorge (R500), which includes a leisurely walk through indigenous forest to the confluence of the Kaaiman and Silver rivers. You then have to jump into deep pools and swim through canyons on your way back. Wet suits are provided. Other adventures in their bag of tricks include abseiling (rappelling) and canoeing. Custom tours can also be arranged. ⊠ *Fairy Knowe Hotel* ☎ *044/877–0179* ⊕ *www.eden.co.za.*

HIKING

Fodor's Choice
★
Garden Route Trail. Mark Dixon is the highly qualified nature guide behind this operation. Excursions include guided day walks and multiday hikes in the forest and around the lakes and beaches of this beautiful part of the world. His signature offering is the five-day guided Garden Route Trail, starting at the Ebb and Flow Restcamp at Wilderness. The trip takes you east along the coast, with long beach walks and coastal forest included, before ending at Brenton on Sea near Knysna.

The emphasis is on the natural environment rather than covering great distances, with Mark's expert guiding along the way. The trip is catered and portered, and you do some canoeing in addition to hiking. Another popular offering is the Moonlight Meander on the beach at full moon. ☎ *044/883–1015, 082/213–5931* ⊕ *www.gardenroutetrail.co.za.*

PARAGLIDING

Cloudbase Paragliding. Wilderness is one of the best paragliding spots in the country. You can ridge-soar for miles along the dune front, watching whales and dolphins in the sea. If you've never done it before, don't worry: you can go tandem (R550) with an experienced instructor from Cloudbase Paragliding. Their season is from mid-September to mid-April as weather conditions in winter are not suitable for paragliding. They also use launch sites at Sedgefield and Brenton-on-Sea depending on weather conditions. ☎ *082/777–8474* ⊕ *www.cloudbase.co.za.*

KNYSNA

5

40 km (25 miles) east of Wilderness.

Knysna (pronounced *nize*-nuh) is one of the most popular destinations on the Garden Route. The focus of the town is the beautiful Knysna Lagoon, ringed by forested hills dotted with vacation homes. Several walking and mountain-bike trails wind through Knysna's forests, many offering tremendous views back over the ocean. With luck you may spot the Knysna turaco, a brilliantly plumed forest bird also known as the Knysna loerie, or the brightly colored but even more elusive Narina trogon.

Towering buttresses of rock, known as the Heads, guard the entrance to the lagoon, funneling the ocean through a narrow channel. The sea approach is often hazardous, which is why Knysna never became a major port, and may explain why it developed instead into the modern resort town it is today, with the attendant hype, commercialism, and crowds, especially in summer. About the only aspect of the town that hasn't been modernized is the single-lane main road (the N2 goes straight through the middle of town), so traffic can be a nightmare. Walking is the best way to get around the town center, which is filled with shops, galleries, restaurants, and coffeehouses. Knysna's main claims to fame are edible and drinkable. The former are cultivated oysters, and the latter is locally brewed Mitchell's beer, on tap at most bars and pubs.

GETTING HERE AND AROUND

The main N2 highway travels straight through the center of Knysna, so the road can get rather busy (and noisy) in the high season.

VISITOR INFORMATION

Contacts Knysna Tourism ✉ *40 Main St., Knysna* ☎ *044/382–5510* ⊕ *www. visitknysna.com.*

EXPLORING

Featherbed Nature Reserve. Unlike its eastern counterpart, the western side of the Heads (part of the Featherbed Nature Reserve) is relatively unspoiled. In addition to a bizarre rock arch and great scenery, the reserve is home to various small mammals, more than 100 species of birds, and 1,000 plant species. There are two standard trips here, plus more in high season (generally October–April). The morning trip costs R490, leaves at 10, and lasts four hours. It consists of a ferry ride across the Lagoon to the Western Head, a 4x4 tractor ride onto the reserve, and a guided 2.2-km (1.3-mile) downhill walk through the Reserve and along the coastline. After this there's a buffet lunch under the trees. The afternoon trip leaves at 2:30, costs R345, takes three hours, and is identical except that it does not include lunch. ⊠ *Cruise Cafe Bldg., Waterfront Dr., Knysna* ☎ *044/382–1693* ⊕ *www.knysnafeatherbed.com.*

Heads. You can't come to Knysna without making a trip out to the Heads, at the mouth of the lagoon. The rock sentinels provide great views of both the sea and the lagoon. Only the developed, eastern side is accessible by car, via George Rex Drive off the N2. You have two options: to park at the base of the Head and follow the walking trails that snake around the rocky cliffs, just feet above the crashing surf, or drive to the summit, with its panoramic views and easy parking. ⊠ *Knysna.*

Holy Trinity Church, Belvidere. One of the most interesting buildings in the area stands across the lagoon from Knysna, in the exclusive community of Belvidere. The Anglican Holy Trinity Church, built in 1855 of local stone, is a lovely replica of a Norman church of the 11th century. The interior is notable for its beautiful stinkwood and yellowwood timber and stained-glass windows. ⊠ *Belvidere, Knysna* 🖭 *Free.*

BEACHES

Although Knysna is very much a seaside destination, there are no beaches actually in the town—unlike in Plett or Mossel Bay—but there are some fabulous ones nearby.

Brenton on Sea. The beach at Brenton on Sea, past Belvidere, is a beautiful, long, white-sand beach popular for its 6-km (4-mile) walk to neighboring Buffalo Bay. It's about a 10-minute drive from the exit off the N2 highway, about 12 km (7½ miles) west of Knysna. Although spectacular, this beach is not particularly good for swimming because of a strong undertow (hence the warning signs in German!). Lifeguards are present in season, but swimmers are cautioned to swim only between the flags where indicated. **Amenities:** food and drink; lifeguards; parking; toilets. **Best for:** sunrise; sunset; walking. ⊠ *Brenton-on-Sea.*

Buffalo Bay Beach. About 20 km (12 miles) from Knysna, Buffalo Bay Beach offers safe swimming and excellent surfing and body-boarding conditions. It's around a half-moon bay with a sandy beach next to a grassy peninsula. The little village has been spared overdevelopment because of its proximity to the nearby Goukamma Nature Reserve. There is a popular beach walk in the direction of Brenton-on-Sea, and there are accommodations in the nature reserve (booked through Cape Nature). **Amenities:** food and drink; lifeguards; parking; showers; toilets; water sports. **Best for:** surfing; swimming; walking. ⊠ *Buffalo Bay.*

Leisure Isle. In the middle of the Knysna lagoon, Leisure Isle has a few tiny strands of beach but is essentially a low-lying island populated with vacation and residential homes. The surrounding mudflats of the lagoon provide bait for the local fisherfolk. For those lucky enough to stay here, the best views are out toward The Heads of Knysna, but the only swimming to be had is knee-height paddling. **Amenities:** parking. **Best for:** solitude; swimming; windsurfing. ⊠ *Knysna.*

WHERE TO EAT

Of course there are restaurants that don't serve seafood, but very few of them are in Knysna. It's what the town's all about.

$ ╳ **Ile de Pain.** Almost every South African you meet on the Garden Route will tell you to visit Ile de Pain. Its stellar reputation is well deserved; owners Liezie Mulder and Markus Farbinger have an uncompromising attitude toward quality that shows in their wonderful bread and pastries, as well as on the short, perfectly executed menu. Local and organic suppliers are used wherever possible, the menu changes seasonally, and everything is made on the premises. For breakfast you could opt for a croissant with scrambled egg, salmon, capers, and horseradish cream or brioche French toast with berry fruit compote and marscapone cream. Lunch favorites include a slice of ciabatta bread with sirloin steak, balsamic caramelized onions, rocket (similar to arugula), and tomato. Not all the menu items are bread-based; the duck confit with accompanying mash and honey quince compote is outstanding. They also supply baked goods to an outlet on Hedge and Gordon streets called Mon Petit Pain, which focuses on handheld pocket breads with fillings such as scrambled eggs and salmon. $ *Average main: R80* ⊠ *The Boatshed, Thesen Island, Knysna* ☎ *044/302–5707* ⊕ *www.iledepain. co.za* ☉ *Closed Mon. No dinner.*

ECLECTIC
Fodor'sChoice
★

$$ ╳ **34° South.** Right on the water's edge in what appears to be a dolled-up warehouse, this place gives off a sense of abundance, with shelves, baskets, and display stands overflowing with all kinds of delicious goodies. Defying convention, 34° South manages to combine elements of a fishmonger, a bar, a bistro, a deli, a coffee shop, and a seafood restaurant. Choose from the huge array of fresh fish, including sushi; opt for a rustic pizza; or just fill a basket with tasty breads, pickles, cheeses, meats, and other delights. Whatever your choice, enjoy your feast while sitting on the jetty looking out at the boats. There's also a good selection of wines and a gift-shop section. $ *Average main: R100* ⊠ *Knysna Quays* ☎ *044/382–7331.*

SEAFOOD

$$$$ ╳ **Zachary's.** Knysna is a bit of a gourmet destination, and Zachary's, at the Pezula Resort Hotel and Spa, about a 10- to 15-minute drive from Knysna, has helped to cement that reputation. The restaurant specializes in high-quality organic and seasonal produce served in a stylish dining room with decor featuring splashes of orange, amber, bronze, and copper. The menu changes seasonally. First-course options might

MODERN
EUROPEAN

5

include dishes like shiitake mushroom broth or butter-poached crayfish, and main dishes run to venison (eland, anyone?), line fish, scallops, and Karoo lamb. The Gourmand set menu is a six-course feast offered with wine pairings. As expected, there's an excellent wine list and a sommelier on hand to make recommendations. $ *Average main: R250* ✉ *Pezula Resort Hotel and Spa, Lagoon View Dr., Knysna* ☎ *044/302–3364* ⊕ *www.zacharys.co.za* ⌁ *Reservations essential.*

WHERE TO STAY

There are more bed-and-breakfasts than you can possibly imagine, as well as some fantastic guesthouses, self-catering resorts, and hotels, so you will not be short of choices.

$$
B&B/INN
Belvidere Manor. There are lovely views across the lagoon to Knysna, some 6½ km (4 miles) away, at this attractive establishment where accommodation is offered in airy cottages that face each other across a lawn sloping down to a jetty. **Pros:** British-style pub on-site; great views; well-equipped cottage accommodations. **Cons:** out of town, so dining options are limited; no a/c; in the center of a retirement village. $ *Rooms from: R2100* ✉ *169 Duthie Dr.* ☎ *044/387–1055* ⊕ *www.belvidere.co.za* ⇲ *34 cottages* ⚭ *Breakfast.*

$
B&B/INN
Brenton on the Rocks. This understated bed-and-breakfast is on a cliff top in the quiet coastal hamlet of Brenton-on-Sea, with breathtaking ocean views from the suites and spacious public rooms. **Pros:** great views; self-catering facilities; restaurant nearby for convenience. **Cons:** standard double rooms have limited views and no bathtubs; Wi-Fi only in reception area; not the safest swimming beach in the area. $ *Rooms from: R1050* ✉ *276 Steenbras St., Brenton-on-Sea* ☎ *044/381–0489, 083/249–3644* ⊕ *www.brentononrocks.co.za* ⇲ *2 rooms, 5 suites, 1 3-bed house, 1 4-bed house.*

$$$$
HOTEL
Fodor's Choice
★
Phantom Forest Eco Reserve. On a private 450-acre nature reserve, this stunning lodge, set in the tree canopy of the indigenous Knysna forest, offers guests the opportunity to sleep in luxury tree houses built from sustainable woods. **Pros:** spacious and luxurious bathrooms, with under-floor heating; lodge has a secluded feel although it's in the center of Knysna; food and service are excellent. **Cons:** lodge is up a steep hill so you need to be ferried up the hill by a lodge vehicle; the N2 highway is some distance away, but the road noise does filter through; views of the Knysna lagoon only from the Eyrie lounge area. $ *Rooms from: R4274* ✉ *Phantom Pass* ☎ *044/386–0046* ⊕ *www.phantomforest.com* ⇲ *14 suites* ⚭ *Some meals.*

$$
B&B/INN
St. James of Knysna. This elegant lodging right on the edge of Knysna Lagoon offers individually decorated rooms with uninterrupted views of the water, a landscaped formal garden with tranquil koi ponds, and a private pier with free use of canoes or fishing equipment. **Pros:** some rooms are enormous, and all are decorated individually; views of the lagoon are stunning; rooms have a/c. **Cons:** old-fashioned decor; swimming pool is on the small side; a bit out of town. $ *Rooms from: R1770* ✉ *Eastford, The Point, Knysna* ☎ *044/382–6750* ⊕ *www.stjames.co.za* ⇲ *2 rooms, 13 suites* ⚭ *Breakfast.*

SPORTS AND THE OUTDOORS

BOATING

Featherbed Company. In addition to running the ferry to the nature reserve, the Featherbed Company operates sightseeing boats on the lagoon (trips start at R100 per person), as well as a Mississippi-style paddle steamer that does lunch and dinner cruises. ☒ *Off Waterfront Dr., Knysna* ☎ *044/382–1693* ⊕ *www.knysnafeatherbed.com.*

Springtide Charters. This charter company operates a luxury 50-foot mono-hull yacht, Outeniqua, that takes visitors out on scenic cruises on the lagoon and through the Heads (weather permitting). The boat takes a maximum of 12 passengers, and can also be rented out for private parties. Their most popular outing is the sunset cruise (R750 per person) which includes Mediterranean-style snacks and a couple of glasses of bubbly. Springtide Charters also operates the Ocean Odyssey, Knysna's only accredited close-encounter whale watching vessel, which takes visitors through the Heads to the open ocean (R700 per person). ☒ *Knysna Quays, Knysna* ☎ *082/470–6022* ⊕ *www.springtide.co.za.*

GOLF

Pezula Championship Golf Course. Perched on the cliff top of the Eastern Head, the challenging 18-hole Pezula Championship Golf Course is one of South Africa's most scenic courses. Designed by Ronald Fream and David Dale, it features among the top 20 in the country and is also one of the most popular courses on the Garden Route. Also on-site is a comfortable clubhouse, and lessons from resident pros are available. ☒ *Lagoonview Dr., Knysna* ☎ *044/302–5300* ⊕ *www.pezula.com* ☒ *R705* ⚑ *18 holes, 6521 yards, par 72.*

HIKING

Diepwalle Elephant Walk. This lovely trail takes you deep into the indigenous forest. The full trail is about 20 km (12 miles) long and should take around six to seven hours. For those who don't have a whole day to spare, there are three color-coded shorter routes of 9 km (5½ miles), 7 km (4½ miles), and 6½ km (4 miles). These should take between two and four hours. Day hikes cost R20. ☒ *Off N2, Uniondale Rd., Diepwalle Forest Estate, 24 km (15 miles) east of Knysna, Knysna* ☎ *044/382–9762/3.*

Garden of Eden. If you'd like to sample the Harkerville Forest but don't want to commit to a strenuous, two-day hike, try the easy stroll in the Garden of Eden. The short trail goes into the forest on a wheelchair-friendly wooden boardwalk. You'll see some big old trees, plus tables where you can picnic. The kiosk at the Garden of Eden is open daily 8–5 and on weekends 8–6, and entry is R12 per person. ☒ *Off N2 between Plett and Knysna, Knysna* ☎ *044/532–7770* ⊕ *www.sanparks.org.*

Harkerville Trail. The two-day, 26-km (16-mile) Harkerville Trail passes through the indigenous forests, pine plantations, and "islands" of fynbos, as well as fairly taxing sections on the coast. (This is not a beginner's trail.) Homesick Californians can hug a familiar tree in a small stand of huge redwoods (*Sequoia sempervirens*), planted as part of a forestry experiment years ago. Overnight accommodation is in a hut with beds and mattresses, water, and firewood, but you'll need to bring your own bedding and food provisions. There's also no electricity. The trail costs R195 per person. ⊠ *Off N2, 15 km (9 miles) east of Knysna, Knysna* ☎ *044/532–5606* ⊕ *www.sanparks.org.*

Knysna Forest Tours. If you don't fancy heading off into the forest on your own, take a guided walk or even a trail run through the area with Knysna Forest Tours. Prices start at R350 for a trail run while a full day outing, including lunch, will cost R950. The parent company, Tony Cook Adventures, also offers surfing, kiteboarding, standup paddle boarding, and sea and river kayaking trips. ⊠ *Thesen Island, Knysna* ☎ *082/783–8392* ⊕ *www.knysnaforesttours.co.za.*

MOUNTAIN BIKING

The Garden Route is ideal for mountain biking, and Harkerville, 20 km (12 miles) east of Knysna, is where mountain bikers usually head first. Here you'll find four color-coded circular trails of varying length and difficulty, starting and ending at the Garden of Eden. The most challenging of these is the Red route, which is a 22-km (13½-mile) ride through forest with some coastal scenery along the way. The others are Blue (11 km/7 miles), Yellow (13 km/8 miles), and Green (14 km/9 miles). There's a fifth 22-km (13½-mile) trail, Petrus se Brand, that is not circular but can be ridden in either direction between Diepwalle and Garden of Eden. It's tight and twisty, and you'll zip downhill (if you start at Diepwalle) over the springy forest floor, dodging enormous trees. It costs R35 to cycle any of these trails.

Outeniqua Biking Hire. You can rent mountain bikes (R150) from Outeniqua Bike Hire, which is conveniently located right on the forest edge and close to the trails. Only adult bikes are available and booking is essential. The SANParks entrance fee is R35. ⊠ *Off N2, 20 km (12.4 miles) east of Knysna, Harkerville* ☎ *044/532–7644, 083/252–7997.*

PLETTENBERG BAY

32 km (20 miles) east of Knysna.

Plettenberg Bay is South Africa's premier beach resort, as the empty houses on Beachy Head Road (known as Millionaires' Mile) during the 11 months when it's not high season will attest. But in December inland visitors with all their teenage offspring arrive en masse. Even then you can find yourself a stretch of lonely beach if you're prepared to walk to the end of Keurboomstrand or drive to Nature's Valley. Plett, as it is commonly known, is one of the best places in the world to watch whales and dolphins. Boat-based trips are run from Central Beach, as are sea-kayaking trips.

GETTING HERE AND AROUND

There is an airport in Plett, but it's not currently in operation. There's no public transportation to and around Plett, so your best bet is renting a car and driving yourself.

Contacts Plettenberg Bay Tourism Association ⊠ *Shop 35, Melville's Corner, Marine Dr. and Main Rd.* ☎ *044/533–4065* ⊕ *www.pletttourism.co.za.*

BEACHES

Plett presides over a stretch of coastline that has inspired rave reviews since the Portuguese first set eyes on it in 1497 and dubbed it *bahia formosa* (the beautiful bay). Three rivers flow into the sea here, the most spectacular of which—the Keurbooms—backs up to form a large lagoon. For swimming, surfing, sailing, hiking, and fishing you can't do much better than Plett, although the water is still colder than it is around Durban and in northern KwaZulu-Natal.

⚠ **Keep in mind that the beach facilities (i.e., lifeguards, food concession, and so on) are available only during the summer months (November–April).**

Central Beach. All the dolphin-watching boats and kayak trips leave from Central Beach. A constant stream of tenders going out to the fishing boats moored in the bay makes this area quite busy, but it's still a great spot. Just keep away from the boat-launching area and swim in the southern section. **Amenities:** food and drink; lifeguards; parking; toilets. **Best for:** surfing; swimming; walking.

Keurboomstrand. This beach is about 10 km (6 miles) from Plett—right on the eastern edge of the bay. If you're fit, you can walk all the way from here to Nature's Valley, but you need to watch both the tides and the steep, rocky sections. It's best to ask locals before tackling this. Even if you're not fit, you can walk about a mile down the beach, relax for a while, and then walk back. **Amenities:** food and drink; lifeguards; parking; showers; toilets. **Best for:** walking.

Lookout Beach. Traditionally one of Plettenberg Bay's most popular beaches, Lookout Beach underwent radical change in recent years after the beach was washed away when the Keurbooms River flooded. Since then, a large swath of sand has been restored through natural tidal action, although the vegetation that separated it from the lagoon is gone. However, it is once again a popular spot with swimmers and surfers, and families and toddlers enjoy paddling on the lagoon side of what is essentially a large sandy spit. Happily, its Blue Flag status has also been restored. **Amenities:** food and drink; lifeguards in season; parking; toilets; water sports. **Best for:** surfing; swimming; walking.

Robberg Beach. Just on the other side of the Beacon Isle hotel, the unmissable building at the end of the tombolo (a sand spit linking the island to the mainland), is Robberg Beach, a great swimming beach that continues in a graceful curve all the way to Robberg Peninsula. You can get pretty good sightings of dolphins and whales just behind the back break. **Amenities:** food and drink; lifeguards; parking; showers; toilets. **Best for:** swimming; sunbathing. ⊠ *Beachy Head Dr.*

WHERE TO STAY

Plett has plenty of fabulous places to eat and overnight, although dining options are generally better in Knysna, so guests in Plettenberg Bay usually eat in their hotel.

$$ 🏠 **Bitou River Lodge.** About 3 km (2 miles) upstream from the Keurboom
B&B/INN Lagoon, this lovely, quiet, restful B&B has a wonderful location on the
Fodor's Choice bank of the Bitou River, with rooms overlooking a pretty garden and a
★ quiet bird-rich and lily-filled pond. **Pros:** beautiful river running past the
property; owner Sue Scheepers is friendly and helpful; private verandas.
Cons: no a/c in the rooms; 10-minute drive to restaurants; self-catering
facilities limited. ⑤ *Rooms from: R1500* ⊠ *About 3 km (2 miles) on
the R340 to Wittedrif (off the N2)* ☎ *044/535–9577, 082/978–6164*
⊕ *www.bitou.co.za* 🛏 *5 rooms* ⦿❘ *Breakfast.*

$$ 🏠 **The Grand Café and Rooms.** Although the entrance is on the town's
B&B/INN main street, walking into the Grand is like walking into a different
world. **Pros:** central location; unique, quirky decor. **Cons:** rooms can
be a bit dark; on main road ⑤ *Rooms from: R1500* ⊠ *27 Main Rd.*
☎ *044/533–3301* ⊕ *www.grandafrica.com* 🛏 *7 rooms* ⦿❘ *Breakfast.*

$$$$ 🏠 **The Plettenberg.** High on a rocky point in Plettenberg Bay, this luxury
HOTEL hotel has unbelievable views of the bay, the Tsitsikamma Mountains,
Fodor's Choice and Keurbooms Lagoon; miles of magnificent beach; and, in season,
★ whales frolicking just beyond the waves. **Pros:** watch dolphins frolicking
from your room; walk down to the beach in minutes; the view from the
breakfast terrace is incredible. **Cons:** standard rooms are small; some
rooms look out onto the car park. ⑤ *Rooms from: R5000* ⊠ *Lookout
Rocks* ☎ *044/533–2030* ⊕ *www.collectionmcgrath.com* 🛏 *25 rooms,
12 suites, 2 villas* ⦿❘ *Breakfast.*

$$$$ 🏠 **Plettenberg Park.** The setting of this stylish, minimalist lodge—in
HOTEL splendid isolation on a cliff top in a private nature reserve on the western (wild) side of Robberg Peninsula—is one of the best anywhere,
and the view of the open ocean across fynbos-clad hills is spectacular.
Pros: spacious rooms; on-site spa; private beach. **Cons:** no cell phone
reception; no a/c; out of town. ⑤ *Rooms from: R5400* ⊠ *Off Robberg Rd.* ☎ *044/533–9067* ⊕ *www.plettenbergpark.co.za* 🛏 *10 rooms*
⦿❘ *Some meals.*

$$$$ 🏠 **Tsala Treetop Lodge.** Built on the same property as Hunter's, and also
HOTEL run by the Hunter family, this lodge combines the best of sleek design
Fodor's Choice with spectacular natural surroundings. **Pros:** beautiful infinity plunge
★ pools; vegetarians are well looked after; Wi-Fi throughout. **Cons:**
suites don't have valley views as trees are in the way; pools not heated.
⑤ *Rooms from: R8080* ⊠ *Hunter's Estate, off N2, 10 km (6.2 miles)
west of Plettenberg Bay* ☎ *044/501–1111* ⊕ *www.hunterhotels.com*
🛏 *10 suites, 6 villas* ⦿❘ *Breakfast.*

SPORTS AND THE OUTDOORS

KAYAKING

Dolphin Adventures. This company offers regular trips in sleek but stable
tandem kayaks (all gear provided). From May to the end of August their
trips depart at 10 and 2; the rest of the year the times are 6, 9, noon,
and 3. They also offer surf rentals. ⊠ *Central Beach* ☎ *083/590–3405*
⊕ *www.dolphinadventures.co.za.*

Ocean Blue Adventures. Ocean Blue runs regular paddling trips on which
you may see whales and dolphins. They go out at 9, noon, and 3; fees

are R250 per person. ✉ *Hopwood St., Central Beach* ☎ *044/533–5083* ⊕ *www.oceanadventures.co.za.*

Plettenberg Bay. Kayaking on Plettenberg Bay is a great way to see the sights and possibly enjoy a visit from a whale or dolphin. Though you aren't likely to see as many animals as the people on the big boats will, it's a far more intimate and exciting experience if you do. You also get to paddle past the Cape fur seal colony on Robberg.

SKYDIVING

Skydive Plett. If you want your views with a bit of adrenaline thrown in, consider a tandem skydive with Skydive Plett. Tandem jumps cost about R1,850, and it's worth the extra R400 to get the DVD so you can show your friends back home. You get nearly half a minute of free fall, during which you get to see Robberg and the whole of the Tsitsikamma coast. ✉ *Plettenberg Bay Airport* ☎ *082/905–7440* ⊕ *www.skydiveplett.com.*

WHALE-WATCHING

FAMILY

Fodor'sChoice

★

Plettenberg Bay is one of the very best locations worldwide for boat-based whale- and dolphin-watching. Most days, visitors see at least two cetacean species and Cape fur seals, as well as a variety of seabirds, including Cape gannets and African penguins. On some days people have seen up to six cetacean species in the course of a few hours.

Two similar operators, Ocean Blue Adventures and Ocean Safaris, have you step directly onto a boat at the beach. Boats are fast, safe, and dry, even though the beaching after a trip can be a bit adventurous, as it's a bumpy ride. Both operators offer similar trips, and boats are licensed to come as close as 164 feet to the whales.

Ocean Blue Adventures. Ocean Blue has a 1½–2-hour whale-watching trip that costs R700 and a dolphin-watching trip that costs R440. Sightings are not guaranteed, but the adventure of going out to sea in a launch and beaching again is worth the trip alone. En route, they take you past Robberg, which is home to a colony of Cape fur seals. ✉ *Hopwood St., Central Beach* ☎ *044/533–5083* ⊕ *www.oceanadventures.co.za.*

Ocean Safaris. This group runs regular whale-watching trips from the beach area. These last 1½ to 2 hours and cost R700. Trips to see dolphins cost R450. ✉ *Hopwood St., Central Beach* ☎ *082/784–5729* ⊕ *www.oceansafaris.co.za.*

SHOPPING

Old Nick Village. Plenty of shops in and around town sell crafts, but for a good concentration of crafts and designer items in one place, you can't beat Old Nick. Originally just a pottery and weaving studio, it has grown to include a host of other shops and galleries selling items such as outdoor ceramics, woven homeware, designer clothing, and more—there's enough that you could spend a whole day here. There are several workshops on-site as well as a licensed restaurant (i.e., one that serves alcohol). ✉ *N2, east of town* ☎ *044/533–1395* ⊕ *www.oldnickvillage.co.za.*

THE CRAGS

16 km (10 miles) northeast of Plettenberg Bay.

Although technically part of Plett, the Crags is very different. It's rural and forested and is home to a primate refuge as well as a free-flight aviary. Although there's no beach, the Crags region is close to the lagoon and beautiful beach at Nature's Valley—although swimming here can be dangerous because of the currents. There are loads of accommodation options and exciting activities, most of which are part of a great little marketing initiative called Cruise the Crags.

GETTING HERE AND AROUND

The Crags falls within the greater Plett area, so the same travel information applies. There's no public transportation to and around Plett, so renting a car and driving yourself is your best option.

VISITOR INFORMATION

Contacts Cruise the Crags ☎ 082/261–0542 ⊕ www.cruisethecrags.co.za.

EXPLORING

FAMILY **Birds of Eden.** Built over a natural valley in the indigenous forest, Birds of Eden is a giant free-flight aviary spanning five dome-enclosed acres. A stream, waterfalls, ponds, paths, benches, and rest areas make it a great place to spend the day. About 200 species of birds, some of which are quite tame, stay here, among them many African species. ⊠ *16 km (10 miles) east of Plettenberg Bay along the N2, just before Nature's Valley turnoff* ☎ *044/534–8906* ⊕ *www.birdsofeden.co.za* ⊠ *R160; combined ticket with visit to Monkeyland R260; plus Jukani cat sanctuary R335* ⊗ *Daily 8–5.*

FAMILY **Monkeyland.** This refuge is houses abused and abandoned primates, most of which were once pets or laboratory animals. They now roam in a huge enclosed area of natural forest and are free to play, socialize, and do whatever it is that keeps primates happy. There are lemurs, gibbons, spider monkeys, indigenous vervet monkeys, howler monkeys, and many more. Guided walks are offered throughout the day, and the tamer "inmates" often play with guests. You can also just visit the coffee shop without paying an entrance fee. ⊠ *16 km (10 miles) east of Plettenberg Bay along the N2, The Crags* ☎ *044/534–8906* ⊕ *www. monkeyland.co.za* ⊠ *R160, combined ticket with Birds of Eden R260 and R335 including Jukani (big cat sanctuary)* ⊗ *Daily 8–5.*

WHERE TO STAY

$$$

B&B/INN

Fodor's Choice

★

▥ **Hog Hollow Country Lodge.** This lovely lodge, set on the edge of a forested gorge with the Tsitsikamma mountains beyond, is well-located for many of the Garden Route's most popular attractions, although you will be hard-pressed to find a reason to leave your room with its private veranda, sumptuous views, and cozy in-room fire place. **Pros:** excellent service; lavish breakfasts; privacy and space. **Cons:** dining is communal (although you can opt to have a separate table); Wi-Fi only available in the main lounge area; vervet monkeys (while cute) might pester you while you're sitting out on your veranda. $ *Rooms from: R2830* ✉ *Askop Rd., The Crags* ☎ *044/534–8879* ⊕ *www.hog-hollow. com* ➪ *16 suites, 3 are family suites* ⦿ *Breakfast.*

$$$$ ⊡ **Kurland.** On the road to Tsitsikamma, this magnificent 1,500-acre
HOTEL estate offers spacious guest suites that make you feel like you're staying
Fodor's Choice in your own country home. **Pros:** excellent Wi-Fi; rooms are individu-
★ ally decorated and supremely comfortable; suites have loft rooms for
children. **Cons:** about a 15-minute drive out of Plettenberg Bay; no
other dining options nearby; far from beach. $ *Rooms from: R5800*
✉ *The Crags* ☎ *044/534–8082* ⊕ *www.kurland.co.za* ➪ *2 rooms, 6
luxury suites, 4 superior suites* ⦿ *Multiple meal plans.*

EN
ROUTE

As you travel on the N2 east from Plett, you cross a flat coastal plain of
fynbos, with the forested Tsitsikamma Mountains to your left. Just after
The Crags, turn off onto the R102, an alternative to the toll road and a
far more interesting and scenic route. The road passes through farmland
before dropping suddenly to sea level via the Groot River Pass. It's a
great descent, with the road worming back and forth through a tunnel
of greenery, impenetrable bush pressing in on either side. At the bottom
of the pass, turn right into **Nature's Valley,** where the Groot River forms
a magnificent lagoon hemmed in by bush-cloaked hills before crossing
a long, beautiful beach to enter the sea. An almost fairy-tale settlement
can be found here beneath a canopy of indigenous trees. This is the end
point of the Otter Trail. At a small restaurant-cum-shop near the beach,
weary hikers give their boots a solemn resting place if they're not fit for
another hike. A walk to Salt River is another great way to spend the
day, and there is a reasonable chance of spotting an otter.

From Nature's Valley the R102 climbs out of the Groot River valley and
meets up with the N2. Here you must turn back onto the N2, because
sadly, the incredibly scenic Bloukrans Pass road has been closed to
through traffic. Look out for the turnoff to the Tsitsikamma section
of the Garden Route National Park and the wild and beautiful Storms
River Mouth. The pretty and rather remote Storms River village is
another 4 km (2½ miles) farther east on the N2 and is where adven-
ture lovers congregate for its treetop canopy tours, mountain biking,
and hiking trails.

TSITSIKAMMA

*31 km (19 miles) east of Nature's Valley; 42 km (26 miles) east of
Plettenberg Bay.*

Administered as its own park, the Tsitsikamma section of the Garden
Route National Park is a narrow belt of coastline extending for 80 km
(50 miles) from Oubosstrand to Nature's Valley, encompassing some
of the most spectacular coastal scenery in the country, including deep
gorges, evergreen forests, tidal pools, and beautiful empty beaches.

GETTING HERE AND AROUND
Pickup can be arranged with most lodges. There's no public transporta-
tion in this area, so your best bet is renting a car and driving yourself.
The roads are in good condition.

EXPLORING

Tsitsikamma Section of the Garden Route National Park. If you want to see some of the most fantastic scenery along the Garden Route by foot, then this area that hugs the coast between Nature's Valley and Plettenberg Bay, should be your top choice. One of the best ways to see this section of the park is on the five-day Otter Trail, one of South Africa's most popular hikes—but this is usually booked out a year ahead. The somewhat easier and more comfortable portered Dolphin Trail is another option. A less strenuous highlight is to visit the suspension bridge at Storms River Mouth, where the river enters the sea through a narrow channel carved between sheer cliffs. Storms River was aptly named: when gale winds blow, as they often do, the sea flies into a pounding fury, hurling spray onto the rocks and whipping spume high up the cliffs. From the Tsitsikamma section's visitor center, a trail descends through the forest (different tree species are all labeled) and over a narrow suspension bridge strung across the river mouth. It's a spectacular walk, a highlight of any trip to the Garden Route. On the other side of the bridge a steep trail climbs to the top of a bluff overlooking the river and the sea—the turning point of the Storms River MTB (mountain bike) Trail, which starts and finishes in Storms River village. Other trails, ranging from 1 to 3 km (½ to 2 miles), lead either to a cave once inhabited by hunter-gatherers or through the coastal forest. The Cattle Baron restaurant (part of a steak-house chain) has great views of the river and ocean. It serves breakfast, lunch, and dinner to park visitors. ✉ *Storms River* ☎ *042/281–1607* ⊕ *www.sanparks.org* 🎫 *R80.*

WHERE TO STAY

$
HOTEL
🏨 **Storms River Mouth Rest Camp.** The lodgings here are clean and comfortable (as are most lodgings in South Africa's national parks), and the setting, almost within soaking distance of the pounding surf, is spectacular, making this spot a must-visit for international visitors. **Pros:** you couldn't get closer to the sea; restaurant and shop on-site; everything is well cared for and clean. **Cons:** there's a daily conservation fee on top of accommodation rates; the Otter Trail is generally booked out a year ahead; inclement weather means activities like kayaking and snorkeling are not always available. ⑨ *Rooms from: R500* ✉ *Storms River Mouth, Storms River* ☎ *012/428–9111* ⊕ *www.sanparks.org* 🛏 *21 cottages, 20 huts, 17 oceanettes, 16 chalets, 6 cabins.*

SPORTS AND THE OUTDOORS

BOATING

Spirit of Tsitsikamma. For a really good look at the gorge, take a boat trip (R80) on the Spirit of Tsitsikamma. The boat departs every 45 minutes between 9:30 and 2:45 from the jetty below the suspension bridge. ☎ *042/281–1607* ⊕ *www.sanparks.org.*

HIKING

Fodor's Choice **Dolphin Trail.** This trail is the perfect marriage of exercise and relaxation,
★ rugged scenery and comfort. Starting at Storms River Mouth, the trail
continues east along the coast, with scenery similar to the Otter Trail
but with infinitely more comfortable lodging. The trail covers 17 km
(10½ miles) over two days, and the best part is that you carry only
a day pack (your luggage is transported by vehicle to the next spot).
Accommodations on the first night are in very comfortable cabins with
private baths at Storms River Mouth. The next two nights are spent
in lovely guesthouses with awesome views and great food. The price
includes a guide, all meals from dinner on arrival to breakfast on the last
day, transportation, and three nights' accommodation. ⊠ *Tsitsikamma*
☎ *042/280–3588* ⊕ *www.dolphintrail.co.za.*

STORMS RIVER

5

*4 km (2½ miles) east of Tsitsikamma section of the Garden Route
National Park.*

Although it's a small, isolated village, Storms River absolutely buzzes
with activity. A hotel, a couple of guesthouses, and a few backpackers'
lodges all cater to the numerous adrenaline junkies and nature lovers
who frequent this hot spot for adventure and ecotourism activities. Bear
in mind that Storms River Mouth, the SANParks camp in the Tsitsikamma section of the Garden Route National Park, and Storms River
village are not the same place.

GETTING HERE AND AROUND

Storms River Mouth is 18 km (11 miles) south of the Storms River
Bridge. There's no public transportation around the area, so you will
need your own transport, though the Baz Bus will drop you off at various hostels around town.

WHERE TO STAY

$ 🏨 **At the Woods Guest House.** Built with care and attention to detail, this
B&B/INN lovely owner-managed guesthouse is a winner. **Pros:** rooms are spacious; there's a comfortable guest lounge; knowledgeable hosts. **Cons:**
swimming pool is small; dining options in the area are limited; no a/c
(ceiling fans only); some rooms don't have mountain views. ⑤ *Rooms
from: R1100* ⊠ *Formosa St., Storms River Village* ☎ *042/281–1446*
⊕ *www.atthewoods.co.za* ⇨ *8 rooms* ⦿| *Breakfast.*

$ 🏨 **Tsitsikamma Backpackers.** This small, tidy hostel is quieter than most,
B&B/INN so it's a good place to stay if you're on a budget and the lovely garden
has great mountain views where you can even sleep in a safari tent.
Pros: huge garden; it's as environmentally friendly as possible; they
offer Segway tours of the village and into the forest. **Cons:** shuttle to
take you to nearby activities is not free; tented accommodation can get
hot in summer; Wi-Fi doesn't reach all the tents. ⑤ *Rooms from: R400*
⊠ *54 Formosa St.* ☎ *042/281–1868* ⊕ *www.tsitsikammabackpackers.
co.za* ⇨ *5 rooms, 2 dormitories, 6 tents.*

$ ▦ **Tsitsikamma Village Inn.** The guest rooms here are in pretty, colorful
HOTEL   buildings that are neatly arranged around a village green, and the public
rooms are in an old hunting lodge built in 1888. **Pros:** good restaurant
on-site; pretty, spacious gardens; adventure center close by. **Cons:** it's
also a conferencing center so can get busy; on the main road (although
it is a very quiet, little town). ⑤ *Rooms from: R1400* ⊠ *Darnell St.,*
Storms River Village ☎ *042/281–1711* ⊕ *www.tsitsikammahotel.co.za*
↪ *49 rooms,* ⦿ *Breakfast.*

SPORTS AND THE OUTDOORS

BUNGEE JUMPING

Fodor's Choice   **Face Adrenalin.** If you do only one bungee jump in your life, do it from
★   the Bloukrans River bridge with Face Adrenalin. At 700 feet, it's the
highest commercial bungee jump in the world. The span is the third-
highest bridge in the world and the highest in the Southern Hemisphere.
The jump costs R850, and a USB loaded with pictures and video to
show your friends back home is an extra R400. If you want to see what
it's all about but have no intention of flinging yourself off the bridge,
you can do a walking tour for R100, but even that's not for the faint of
heart, as it is pretty high, exposed, and scary. ⊠ *Off the N2, Bloukrans*
☎ *042/281–1255* ⊕ *www.faceadrenalin.com.*

CANOPY AND FOREST TOUR

Fodor's Choice   **Storms River Adventures.** Want a turaco's-eye view of the treetops? Storms
★   River Adventures will take you deep into the forest, where you don
a harness, climb up to a platform, clip in, and "fly" on long cables
from platform to platform. You can even control your speed. The cost
is R495 (including a light lunch), and a double DVD with video and
downloadable photos costs an extra R160. Storms River Adventures
also offers the Woodcutter's Journey, a gentle, open-vehicle tour of the
forest and the old Storms River Pass. Knowledgeable guides expound on
the flora and fauna, as well as the interesting history of the region. You
end it all with lunch or tea at a beautiful picnic site next to the Storms
River, where wagons would stop more than a century ago. The tea trip
costs R200, and the lunch trip R250. ⊠ *Main Rd.* ☎ *042/281–1836*
⊕ *www.stormsriver.com.*

MOUNTAIN BIKING

Storms River Mountain Bike Trail. This trail, in the Plaatbos area of the
Garden Route National Park, is a scenic, circular 22-km (14-mile) trail
that navigates the old Storms River Pass (fitness is a prerequisite here).
The 5-km (3-mile) descent through the forest to the bottom of the pass
offers beautiful gorge views and a refreshing dip in the river. The starting point is near the police station at Storms River; be sure to pick up a
self-issue permit at the start of the trail. ⊠ *Main Rd.* ☎ *042/281–1557*
⊕ *www.sanparks.org.*

Tsitsikamma Segway Tours. Part of the Tsitsikamma Backpackers hostel, Tsitsikamma Segway Tours rents mountain bikes and offers Segway tours. A two-hour Segway tour into the forest costs R400 per
person (including a short safety lesson in advance). ⊠ *54 Formosa St.*
☎ *042/281–1868* ⊕ *www.tsitsikammasegwaytours.com.*

LITTLE KAROO

The landscape of the Little Karoo—austere, minimal, and dry—stands in stark contrast to the Garden Route. In summer it resembles a blast furnace, and winter nights are bitterly cold. In its own way, however, it is absolutely beautiful. The Little Karoo, also called the Klein Karoo (*klein* is Afrikaans for "small"; *karoo* derives from the San [Bushman] word for "thirst"), should not be confused with the Great Karoo, a vast semi-desert scrubland on the interior side of the Swartberg Mountains. Everything here is a little surreal—giant birds of prey soar overhead, huge caves stretch for miles underground, and bright-green vineyards contrast with intricately eroded, deep-red hills.

Ronnie's Sex Shop. No, your eyes are not playing tricks on you. That sign definitely says Ronnie's Sex Shop. And no, it's not a country brothel or a sex shop. It's actually a Route 62 icon that started out as a joke. Ronnie Price (a real person) planned to open a shop here near the road, but his friends painted the word "sex" in big red letters next to the sign to read "Ronnie's Sex Shop." It stayed like that for years—a local landmark—until Ronnie thought he would cash in on the unintentional marketing, and opened a pub instead. It's a far cry from a sophisticated venue, but it's a great place to meet the locals, some of whom spend a large proportion of the day here. It's also a mandatory stop on most motorcycle rallies. It's open from 10 in the morning until the last person leaves at night, which is usually pretty late. You can't miss it—it's right on Route 62, just on the Ladysmith side of Barrydale. You may not want to go in, but you'll probably want to photograph it. ⊠ *Off R62, Barrydale* ☏ *028/572–1153* ⊕ *www.ronniessexshop.co.za.*

EN
ROUTE **Joubert-Tradauw.** Set between Montagu and Barrydale on the R62, the Op-de-Tradouw region, named after a pass through the mountains, is best known for its excellent wines. Joubert-Tradauw is a great place to stop for a wine tasting or for lunch or tea. Owner Meyer Joubert makes wine in the age-old French tradition—unfiltered and unrefined. His chardonnay is sublime, and he has publicly stated that it is his ambition to make the best Syrah in the world. (Try it; he's definitely on the right track.) While he works his magic in the winery, his wife Beate waves her star-spangled wand over the small deli–coffee shop, where you can sit under the pergola and spend ages over a superb cheese plat-ter or Gruyère salad, or just have a quick coffee and cheesecake. It's tapas alfresco with a traditional Afrikaner touch. ⊠ *R62, 12 km (7½) miles west of Barrydale, Barrydale* ☏ *028/572–1619* ⊕ *www.joubert-tradauw.co.za* ⊠ *Free* ☉ *Weekdays 9–5, Sat. 9–2*

SANBONA WILDLIFE RESERVE

27 km (17 miles) west of Barrydale.

Roughly the size of Singapore, this enormous private wildlife reserve supports a free-roaming population of wild animals that were indig-enous to the Western Cape before European settlers arrived. Here you'll find the Big Five (lion, rhino, elephant, buffalo, and leopard) and many smaller desert creatures. One of the more unique experiences is to spend time on foot with the wild cheetahs that have grown accustomed to being approached by the rangers. But don't expect to be able to touch them. Remote, tranquil, and beautiful, Sanbona has the added benefits of offering luxurious accommodation options and being malaria-free.

GETTING HERE AND AROUND

There's no public transportation in the area, so you will need a car to get around. The drive from Cape Town is about three hours along the N1, R60, and then R62.

EXPLORING

Fodor'sChoice ★ **Sanbona Wildlife Reserve.** Arguably the Western Cape's most authentic Big Five reserve, Sanbona Wildlife Reserve is within relatively easy reach of Cape Town (270 km/168 miles). Animals like elephants, lions, and cheetahs roam free in the reserve's some 135,000 acres, and guides make use of tracking devices to locate them. The scenery is spectacular, too. Rugged gorges alternate with gently rolling plains featuring unique plant life that comes into its own in spring. Crystal-clear night skies promise exceptional stargazing. Three luxury lodges cater to a variety of tastes and life stages: historic Tilney Manor has an old-world farmhouse feel, Gondwana Lodge is geared toward families, and Dwyka Tented Camp, magnificently situated beneath soaring cliffs, is styled as a honeymoon camp. ✉ *Montagu* ✛ *Off the R62 about 43 km (27 miles) from Montagu, en route to Oudtshoorn* ⊕ *www.sanbona.com.*

WHERE TO STAY

$$$$ HOTEL **Dwyka Tented Camp.** This luxury tented camp, on a horseshoe bend of a dry riverbed at the foot of soaring cliffs, is a great place to reconnect with yourself, your partner, and nature. **Pros:** luxuriously appointed tents; spa treatments available; no kids under 16. **Cons:** paths to tents are unpaved and a bit rough; wilderness environment might not be to everyone's taste. $ *Rooms from: R10260* ✉ *Sanbona Wildlife Reserve, Montagu* ☎ *028/572–1365* ⊕ *www.sanbona.com* ⤴ *9 luxury tents* ⦿| *All meals.*

$$$$ HOTEL FAMILY **Gondwana Lodge.** Within easy striking distance of the best game-viewing areas and overlooking the Bellair Dam, Gondwana Lodge marries contemporary design with traditional thatched, Karoo-style architecture and is unashamedly family-friendly. **Pros:** staff are attentive and accommodating; lots of options for kids; on-site spa. **Cons:** stairs to the upper level are steep; not ideal for couples looking for a secluded stay. $ *Rooms from: R9720* ✉ *Sanbona Wildlife Reserve, Montagu* ☎ *028/572–9914* ⊕ *www.sanbona.com* ⤴ *12 rooms* ⦿| *All meals.*

$$$$ HOTEL Fodor'sChoice ★ **Tilney Manor.** A warm welcome awaits when you arrive at the historic manor house at Tilney Lodge, where staff wait outside to greet new arrivals with hot face towels to freshen up after the hour-long drive from the reserve entrance. **Pros:** hands-on staff will attend to every need; indoor and outdoor dining; on-site spa. **Cons:** Wi-Fi connectivity does not reach all rooms; communal dinner tables may not suit everyone's tastes. $ *Rooms from: R9720* ✉ *Sanbona Wildlife Reserve, Montagu* ☎ *028/572–1365* ⊕ *www.sanbona.com* ⤴ *6 rooms* ⦿| *All meals.*

OUDTSHOORN

85 km (53 miles) north of Mossel Bay.

Oudtshoorn has been famous for its ostriches since around 1870, when farmers began raising them to satisfy the European demand for feathers to adorn women's hats and dresses. In the years leading up to World War I, ostrich feathers were almost worth their weight in gold thanks to the continuing demands of fashion, and Oudtshoorn experienced an incredible boom. Many of the beautiful sandstone buildings in town date from that period, as do the "feather palaces," huge homes built by prosperous feather merchants and buyers. Although feathers are no longer a major fashion item, these huge birds are now bred for their tough and distinctive leather and almost completely fat- and cholesterol-free red meat. Almost as much of a moneymaker, though, is the tourist potential of these weird and wonderful birds. In addition to visiting an ostrich farm, you can buy ostrich products ranging from the sublime— feather boas—to the ridiculous—taxidermic baby ostriches emerging from cracked eggs. Several farms compete for the tourist buck, offering almost identical tours and a chance to eat an ostrich-based meal. Be warned—these can be real tourist traps: glitzy, superficial, and crowded.

Note that most of the restaurants, guesthouses, and attractions listed here are on Baron van Reede Street. This street becomes the R328, which heads north from Oudtshoorn to the Cango Caves, the Swartberg Pass, and Prince Albert.

GETTING HERE AND AROUND

As there's no public transportation in this area, the most convenient and efficient way of getting around is driving yourself. The roads are good, and parts are very scenic. Intercape buses now travel to Oudtshoorn.

VISITOR INFORMATION

Contacts Oudtshoorn Tourism Bureau ⊠ *12 Baron van Reede St.* ☎ *044/279–2532* ⊕ *www.oudtshoorn.com.*

EXPLORING

Cango Caves. Between Oudtshoorn and Prince Albert, the huge and stunningly beautiful Cango Caves, filled with weird and wonderful stalactite and stalagmite formations, are deservedly one of the most popular attractions in the area. Only a small fraction of the caves, which extend for several miles through the mountains, is open. Unfortunately, due to shortsighted tourism schemes in the 1960s and vandalism, there's some damage, especially to the first chamber, but they are still very impressive and get more magnificent the more the tour progresses. One of the highlights is "Cleopatra's Needle," which is 29 feet high and at least 150,000 years old. You can choose between two tours: the hour-long standard tour and the aptly named adventure tour, which lasts 1½ hours. Think long and hard before opting for the latter if you're overweight, very tall, claustrophobic, or have knee or heart problems. It's exhilarating, but the temperature and humidity are high, there's not much oxygen, and you'll be shimmying up narrow chimneys on your belly, wriggling your way through tiny tunnels, and sliding on your bottom. Wear old clothes and shoes with a good tread. Standard tours leave on the hour, adventure tours on the half hour. ☒ *Off R328, 29 km (18 miles) north of Oudtshoorn* ☏ *044/272–7410* ⊕ *www.cango-caves.co.za* ✉ *Standard tour R80, adventure tour R100* ☾ *Daily 9–4.*

FAMILY **Cango Ostrich Farm.** Cango Ostrich Farm is probably the least commercialized of the ostrich show farms. Guides explain the bird's extraordinary social and physical characteristics, and there are lots of interactive opportunities, including feeding and petting the ostriches and posing on one for a photograph. People who weigh less than 75 kilograms (165 pounds) are permitted to ride the ostriches. Some people don't like this practice, but the farm complies with strict regulations, meaning that you can ride for no longer than 30 seconds, although generally it's hard to stay on for longer than that in any event. The farm is conveniently located en route to the Cango Caves from town. From September to February, you may see babies hatching. ☒ *R328, 14 km (9 miles) north of Oudtshoorn* ☏ *044/272–4623* ⊕ *www.cangoostrich.co.za* ✉ *R80* ☾ *Daily 8:30–4:30.*

FAMILY **Cango Wildlife Ranch.** The name Cango Wildlife Ranch is a bit misleading, as this is really just a glorified zoo, crocodile farm, and cheetah-breeding center, but it is great fun—especially for children. In addition to the crocodiles and cheetahs, you may see white Bengal tigers and lions in large pens. Other attractions include a snake park, pygmy hippos, a tropical house with birds and giant fruit bats: in short, loads of different animals that will keep the little ones amused for ages. You can even do a croc cage dive (R340), which isn't as bizarre as it sounds: it's not really diving as you can stand up for a breath of air whenever you feel the need. ☒ *Caves Rd.* ☏ *044/272–5593* ⊕ *www.cango.co.za* ✉ *R145* ☾ *Daily 8:30–4:30.*

C. P. Nel Museum. This museum focuses on the ostrich and Oudtshoorn's boom period at the beginning of the 20th century. The section on fashions of the feather-boom period are by far the most picturesque. The display that depicts the contribution of Lithuanian Jews to the economic development of Oudtshoorn and the feather industry contains a reconstruction of the town's first synagogue. The most interesting remnants of the glory of the boom period in Oudtshoorn are the magnificent palaces built by successful farmers. Most are private homes, but you can visit the sandstone Le Roux's Town House (now the Town House Museum), built in 1909 and furnished in period style, to see just how good they had it in those heady days. It forms part of the C. P. Nel Museum. ☒ *Baron van Reede St.* ☏ *044/272–7306* ⊕ *www.cpnelmuseum.co.za* ✉ *R20 (includes admission to Town House Museum)* ☾ *Weekdays 8–5, Sat. 9–1.*

NEED A BREAK?

Wilgewandel. At the turnoff to the Cango Caves, Wilgewandel serves well-cooked simple food such as hamburgers, toasted sandwiches, ostrich steaks, and sweet treats. Shady outdoor tables overlook a big lawn and duck-filled pond. Trampolines are offered for children, as well as camel, pony, and boat rides. ☒ *R328, 2 km (1 mile) from caves* ☏ 044/272-0878 ⊕ *www.wilgewandel.co.za.*

Back and Forth

Part of the beauty of the Garden Route and Little Karoo is found in the spectacular passes that connect the two and in those between the Little and Great Karoo. Be sure to drive at least one.

Between Oudtshoorn and George, you'll encounter the Outeniqua Pass (via the paved N12) or the more historic Montagu Pass (off the N9, after it diverges from the N12, on a narrow gravel road built in 1843 by Henry Fancourt White). The latter offers excellent views, picnic sites, and examples of Victorian road building, including a five-span arch bridge, railway viaduct, and expertly laid dry-stone embankments. An old tollhouse still sits at the bottom of the pass.

The Robertson Pass, between Oudtshoorn and Mossel Bay, is an easy, paved road with some fabulous views. One of the most interesting things about this route (especially if you're traveling from Mossel Bay) is that you can see the abrupt change of vegetation as you crest the ridge and drive over into the rain shadow.

For a great loop between the Great and Little Karoo, drive counterclockwise from Oudtshoorn through De Rust and the spectacularly scenic Meiringspoort. This road runs along the bottom of a deep gorge, crossing the pretty Meirings River 25 times as it cuts through red cliffs. Halfway through the pass is a rest area, where a path leads to a 200-foot waterfall. Local legend is that a mermaid lives in the pool at the base of this waterfall. Head west on the R407 to the pretty Karoo town of Prince Albert; then head south over the Swartberg Pass on the R328 back to Oudtshoorn. (The views are more dramatic from this direction.) This pass, built between 1881 and 1886, is regarded as the legendary road engineer Sir Thomas Bain's masterpiece. At times the road barely clings to the mountainside, held only by Bain's stone retaining walls. From the top, at 5,230 feet, you can look out toward the hot plains of the Great Karoo and the distant mountains of the Nuweveldberg or down at the huge gorge and sheer walls of deep-red rock.

WHERE TO EAT

$$

ECLECTIC

✕ **Jemima's Restaurant.** Named after the mythical guardian angel of love, good taste, and good cooking, this restaurant would not disappoint its muse. All the ingredients are sourced locally from farmers in the district, and the menu focuses on such local delicacies as olives, Karoo mutton, and, of course, ostrich. Meat lovers often opt for the Trilogy—medallions of beef, ostrich, and venison fillet. Herbivores love the butternut cheesecake. There's an extensive list of local wines. $ *Average main: R140 ⊠ 94 Baron van Reede St.* ☎ *044/272–0808* ⊕ *www.jemimas.com* ⚘ *Reservations essential.*

WHERE TO STAY

$

B&B/INN

⛺ **Backpackers Paradise.** A communal kitchen, pool table, swimming pool, bar, and TV lounge combine to create that vibe where everyone becomes friends in half an hour in this hostel that specializes in daily cycling trips down the Swartberg Pass, with stops at the Cango Caves and an ostrich farm. **Pros:** good value; bar away from the hostel sleeping area; centrally located. **Cons:** small pool; Wi-Fi free but not available throughout premises; some dorms a bit of a squeeze because of double bunks. $ *Rooms from: R450* ✉ *148 Baron van Reede St.* ☎ *044/272-3436* ⊕ *www.backpackersparadise.net* ⤴ *11 rooms, 5 with bath* ⫰◉⫰ *Some meals.*

$
B&B/INN
⊞ **Hlangana Lodge.** Conveniently situated on the edge of town on the road out to the caves, this great option is warm and friendly and has a lovely garden surrounding a swimming pool. **Pros:** Superior rooms have huge bathrooms; staff is friendly and helpful. **Cons:** rooms not very private; lodge is on the main road; they don't serve dinner. $ *Rooms from: R1240* ✉ *Baron van Reede and North Sts.* ☎ *044/272-2299* ⊕ *www. hlangana.co.za* ⤴ *18 rooms, 1 suite* ⫰◉⫰ *Breakfast.*

$
B&B/INN
⊞ **Kleinplaas.** Comfortable, well-appointed chalets with fully equipped cooking facilities are neatly arranged in a huge, shady lawn area at Kleinplaas, which means "small farm"—although it isn't really a farm despite the ostriches and ducks on the premises. **Pros:** chalets serviced daily; a private patio area for each chalet; conveniently located at edge of town. **Cons:** only the open-plan chalets have a/c; Wi-Fi available only in the office; not particularly scenic. $ *Rooms from: R897* ✉ *171 Baron van Reede St.* ☎ *044/272-5811* ⊕ *www.kleinplaas.co.za* ⤴ *54 chalets* ⫰◉⫰ *No meals.*

$
B&B/INN
⊞ **La Plume Guest House.** This stylish guesthouse is set on a working ostrich farm on the Calitzdorp side of Oudtshoorn. **Pros:** beautiful views of the valley from the patio; spacious bedrooms and en suite bathrooms; terrific attention to detail (candles in bathrooms, sprigs of lavender on the pillow, etc.). **Cons:** a 10-minute drive out of town; no room phones. $ *Rooms from: R1280* ✉ *Volmoed, 14 km (9 miles) west of Oudtshoorn* ☎ *044/272-7516, 082/820-4373* ⊕ *www.laplume.co.za* ⤴ *6 rooms, 4 suites, 2 2-bedroom cottages* ⫰◉⫰ *Some meals.*

$
B&B/INN
⊞ **Le Petit Karoo.** Perched high on a hill just off the R328, three en-suite bush tents, with spa-baths on the veranda, have fabulous mountain views where you can feel like you're in your own little private paradise. **Pros:** breakfasts (not included) are great; the Jacuzzis in the tents are wonderful; the French owner/hosts are charming. **Cons:** it's rustic; tents can get hot in summer; dinners only by arrangement. $ *Rooms from: R800* ✉ *Off the R328, about 14 km (9 miles) north of Oudtshoorn* ☎ *044/272-7428* ⊕ *www.lepetitkaroo.za.net* ⤴ *4 tents, 4 rooms* ▭ *No credit cards.*

$$$
B&B/INN
⊞ **Rosenhof.** For luxury and indulgence in the heart of Oudtshoorn, look no further than Rosenhof, where you'll be greeted with fresh cut flowers in garden cottages boasting underfloor heating, baths and showers, and patios facing a pretty stone fountain. **Pros:** excellent restaurant; attentive staff; lovely gardens, with many places to sit and relax; on-site art gallery. **Cons:** outside areas of rooms are not private; small pool area; close to main road. $ *Rooms from: R3300* ✉ *264 Baron van Reede St.* ☎ *044/272-2232* ⊕ *www.rosenhof.co.za* ⤴ *12 rooms, 2 suites* ⫰◉⫰ *Some meals.*

SPORTS AND THE OUTDOORS

BALLOONING

Oudtshoorn Ballooning. Oudtshoorn Ballooning offers a scenic balloon flight over the town and neighboring farms at dawn. Flights are R2,500 per person and include tea and coffee on arrival and sparkling wine on landing. In the high season, book well in advance. ☎ 082/784–8539 ⊕ *www.oudtshoornballooning.co.za.*

MOUNTAIN BIKING

Joyrides. Joyrides, based at Backpackers Paradise, runs a fabulous mountain-biking trip. You get transported to the top of the Swartberg Pass, where you (and your fellow cyclists) are left with a mountain bike, helmet, and water. It's pretty much downhill all the way back to town, and the route passes Cango Caves (it's a bit of a steep uphill detour to get there), Wilgewandel coffee shop, Cango Ostrich Farm, Cango Wildlife Ranch, and Le Petit Karoo and then back to Backpackers Paradise. So you've got all day to visit the main tourist attractions. The tour costs R390 and an extra R100 if you want to be picked up somewhere on route. ✉ *148 Baron Van Reede St.* ☎ 044/272–3436 ⊕ *www.backpackersparadise.net.*

SHOPPING

Oudtshoorn has loads of stores selling ostrich products, but it pays to shop around, as prices vary significantly. The smartest shops strung out along Baron van Reede Street have a great variety but are a tad pricey.

Klein Karoo Boutique. The Klein Karoo Co-op, that coordinates the marketing of ostrich products, has a boutique on its premises near the airport, on the western side of town. (This is really just an airfield, but it's called the airport.) Here you can purchase bags, feather boas, shoes, and other smaller items. It can be a little tricky to find, so it's best to phone for directions or ask for help at your hotel. ✉ *Kooperasie St.* ☎ *044/203–5270* ⊕ *www.kleinkaroo.com/showroom.*

Lugro Ostrich. This small factory in town manufactures ostrich handbags and wallets, as well as belts and smaller items such as key rings. These can be bought in the shop on the premises. ✉ *133 Langenhoven Rd.* ☎ *044/272–7012, 082/788–7916* ⊕ *www.lugro-ostrich.co.za.*

DE RUST

40 km (25 miles) northeast of Oudtshoorn.

De Rust is a sleepy Little Karoo village. The main road is lined with crafts stores, coffee shops, restaurants, and wineshops.

GETTING HERE AND AROUND

There's no public transportation here. You will need your own vehicle to travel around, but the roads are good, and the scenery is very beautiful.

VISITOR INFORMATION

Contacts De Rust Tourism Bureau ✉ *29 Schoeman St.* ☎ *044/241-2109* ⊕ *www.derust.org.za.*

EXPLORING

Domein Doornkraal. This one-stop farm shop features wines from 25 cellars and has an excellent selection of pot-still brandies, dessert wines, dry wines, and blends. They also make their own superb range of fortified wines and an inexpensive white blend (Chenin Blanc, Sauvignon Blanc, and Colombard). The shop also stocks local olive oil products from 10 local suppliers, preserves, honey, sweets, and cookies, all sourced from local farms and bakers. In season, they operate a small outdoor restaurant focusing on old-fashioned home cooking. ⊠ *R62, about 10 km (6 miles) southwest of De Rust* ☎ *044/251–6715* 🖙 *Free* ☉ *Weekdays 8–5, Sat. 8–1.*

Mons Ruber Estate. This estate is named after the Red Hills that dominate the landscape and whose soil creates the perfect environment for growing grapes with a high sugar content. So it's not surprising that this winery specializes in dessert wines as well as a fine brandy. There is a lovely restored 19th-century kitchen, and an easy hiking trail stretches 1½ hours into the fascinating Red Hills. ⊠ *N12, about 15 km (9 miles) southwest of De Rust* ☎ *044/251–6550* 🖙 *Free* ☉ *Weekdays 9–5, Sat. 9–1.*

THE EASTERN CAPE

Updated by
Christopher
Clark

The Eastern Cape is South Africa's most diverse province and has some of its best vacation destinations, yet it is perhaps the most glossed over by overseas visitors. Starting where the Garden Route stops, it includes much of the Great Karoo—a large, semidesert region of ocher plains, purple mountains, dramatic skies, and unusual, hardy vegetation—and abuts KwaZulu-Natal in the northeast and Lesotho's mountain lands in the north. But a glance at a map will reveal the region's main attraction: its coastline, still largely undeveloped and running for some 640 km (400 miles) from temperate to subtropical waters.

The climate is mild across the region and throughout the year, with temperatures at the coast ranging between winter lows of 5°C (41°F) and summer highs of 32°C (90°F). It has many of the country's finest and least crowded beaches, Afro-montane forests (one of South Africa's eco-regions) and heathlands, an ever-increasing number of fantastic malaria-free game reserves, and some of the most interesting cultural attractions in South Africa.

There are a few areas of note. Frontier Country, formerly known as Settler Country, stretches from the outskirts of Port Elizabeth to Port Alfred in the east, Grahamstown in the northeast, and the Zuurberg Mountains in the north. It was here that the early-19th-century immigrants (colloquially called the 1820 Settlers) tried to set up farms, some successfully, some not. Toward the end of the 20th century, many of the unprofitable farms were bought up and redeveloped as game reserves, thus adding superb game-viewing to the already existing cultural attractions.

Frontier Country also overlaps with the Sunshine Coast, an almost invariably sunny 500 km (310 miles) stretch of coastline (hence the name) running from the pretty and pristine coastal towns and villages around Cape St Francis and St Francis Bay all the way to the city of East London, taking in a range of great family-friendly beaches, eco-trails, lagoons, and forests, and the surfing mecca of Jeffreys Bay along the way.

Another noteworthy region on the Eastern Cape is the Wild Coast. Unfortunately, the Wild Coast lost a lot of its allure during the political uncertainty of the 1980s—more because of the perceived threat of violence than anything else. Hotels went out of business, the overnight huts on the fantastic Wild Coast Hiking Trail fell into disrepair, and the Transkei—the name given to this previously designated Xhosa "homeland" by the former apartheid government—sank further into economic depression. For many years it was only die-hard locals with strong emotional ties and small groups of backpackers who frequented these still-lovely and little-known places. Happily, the area has gone through a significant revival in recent years. Coastal hotels have been renovated one by one, and community projects are continually being put in place to ensure that the tourist dollar goes where it should. In addition to long, lovely beaches, the Wild Coast has crystal-clear turquoise lagoons, some of which can be paddled for miles. The area's still largely unspoiled, and the people who live here are mostly subsistence farmers and fisherfolk. It's not uncommon for a family who can't afford a loaf of bread to dine (reluctantly) on oysters and lobster.

Then there's the Amatole region that comprises the casual coastal hub of East London as well as the idyllic, secluded bay at Cintsa just a little farther along the coast. Head inland for an hour or so and you'll find yourself in the foothills of the dramatic mountain range that gives this area its name. The forests, waterfalls, peaks, and rock formations of Amatole are an outdoor enthusiast's dream, and some of the picturesque towns and villages in the valleys below are strangely reminiscent of rural England; this area was said to be the inspiration behind J.R.R. Tolkien's Middle Earth and the living trees in The Lord of the Rings. It's also an important region in South Africa's history of struggle—Nelson Mandela, among others, attended university here, and black consciousness leader Steve Biko was born here. Though a popular region with a handful of South Africans in the know, Amatole isn't on many international tourists' maps yet. That's slowly beginning to change, but for now it's another large part of Amatole's appeal.

ORIENTATION AND PLANNING

GETTING ORIENTED

The Eastern Cape is a big space with many tiny gems. The towns, and even the cities, of the province are relatively small and often quaint, and the distances between them are often fairly large. Since the only airports are in Port Elizabeth, East London, and Mthatha (previously Umtata), the best way to experience the region is on a self-driving tour, leaving yourself plenty of time to explore (but be prepared for some poorly maintained roads in some regions of the Transkei).

Frontier Country and the Sunshine Coast. Formerly known as Settler Country, the Frontier Country stretches from the outskirts of Port Elizabeth to Port Alfred in the east, Grahamstown in the northeast, and the Zuurberg Mountains in the north. The area also encompasses Addo Elephant National Park and the game reserves at Shamwari, Kwandwe, and Grahamstown itself. The Sunshine Coast overlaps part of this area, running roughly from Cape St Francis for 500 km (310 miles) as far as East London via Port Elizabeth.

Amatole. This undulating region stretches along the coast from just beyond Port Alfred almost up to Port St Johns, overlapping with the Wild Coast from East London onward. But the larger part of this region stretches far into the hinterland, almost to Queenstown, with

TOP REASONS TO GO

Take a Walk on the Wild Side The Wild Coast is a fabulous "slackpacking" destination. You can walk all day on long, lovely beaches, past turquoise lagoons and through unspoiled villages. Wonderful day-hiking opportunities include the 37-km (23-mile) walk between Bulungula and Coffee Bay—which takes you along beaches, cliff tops, and rolling hills—plus guided hikes run by many of the lodges.

Take a Look at the Wildlife With its rich and varied topography and flora, the Eastern Cape supports a wide range of game, much of which was once hunted to near extinction by farmers and settlers. Initiatives to reclaim this area for its original inhabitants include Addo Elephant National Park, Shamwari Game Reserve, and Kwandwe Private Game Reserve. Most of the terrain here is hilly with thick bush, so you won't see vast herds of animals wandering across open plains, and some areas bear visible scars from farming. But the game is here: elephants, antelope, rhinos, buffalo, and much more. And best of all—it's malaria-free.

Take a Dive on the Wild Side If you've cage-dived with great whites, plumbed the depths of dark and narrow caves, and dived under ice, you probably think you've done it all. Wrong. Diving with a "baitball"—fish herded together by dolphins

for dining purposes—in the sardine run off the Wild Coast is the ultimate adrenaline dive. Sharks, Cape gannets, Bryde's whales, and even humpbacks have all been known to join in the feast.

Take in the Culture and History From unsullied Xhosa villages—where women paint their faces with ocher clay and boys undergo circumcision rites of passage—to colonial mansions, the range and depth of the Eastern Cape's cultural heritage is amazing. Since the early 19th century, the Eastern Cape has been a frontier and a focus of black resistance. In almost every town you'll find fascinating museums and art galleries and a good tour operator who can expose you to the history and culture of this heterogeneous society. The cultural highlight of South Africa is the annual National Arts Festival, which runs for 10 action-packed days every late June and/or July in Grahamstown.

See the Other Side The Transkei is a truly unadulterated vision of rural South Africa. Taking a tour will allow you to interact with locals while traversing the spectacular Wild Coast on foot, horse, bicycle, or ATV. If you're more interested in culture than adventure, a visit to Bulungula will let you meet locals and generally interact on a far more personal level.

the picturesque mountain village of Hogsback found more or less at its heart.

Wild Coast. Lovely, long beaches stretch as far as the eye can see, with only a few cows and a small herder to break the isolation. Strictly speaking, the Wild Coast originally stretched from the Kei River mouth to Port Edward (which were the borders of the then nominally independent Transkei), but today it has spread almost to the outskirts of East London.

PLANNING

WHEN TO GO

Although winters are pretty mild, especially farther north along the Wild Coast, summer—from September to April—is the most popular time to visit, especially for sun worshippers. (The beaches are best avoided at Christmas and New Year's, as they become severely overcrowded with hordes of reveling locals.) But even winter has its attractions. The sardine run, usually in June or early July (⇨ *"The Food Chain Up Close" box, in Wild Coast*), is becoming a major draw, and July's (sometimes late June's) National Arts Festival draws thousands of cultural pilgrims to the delightful university town of Grahamstown.

PLANNING YOUR TIME

3 Days: Fly in to Port Elizabeth in the morning and head straight out to Grahamstown. Do a historical tour in the afternoon followed by dinner at your guesthouse or one of the restaurants in town. The next morning, drive out to Shamwari, Kwandwe, or Addo; plan to spend two days in one of these reserves (staying at one of the private luxury lodges or, at Addo, at an inexpensive SANParks camp) and then drive back to Port Elizabeth to fly out. Or if you choose to visit Kwandwe, you can cut the game-viewing down to one day, keep heading north of Grahamstown, and spend the third day exploring the pretty village of Hogsback and taking a brisk hike into the Amatola Mountains. Alternatively, you could spend two days in Port Elizabeth or its beautiful coastal environs—soaking up the sun, playing a round of golf, taking a cultural tour, and just relaxing—and a third day on a day trip to Addo for an animal fix.

5 Days: With five days you could fly in and out of East London to join the Wild Coast Meander tour with Wild Coast Holiday Reservations (⇨ *East London*)—your days filled with walking this wonderful coastline, and each night spent at a different beach hotel. For a glimpse of South Africa not on the usual tourist route, fly to Mthatha from Johannesburg; spend two days and three nights at Bulungula, immersing yourself in the local culture, and then drive from Mthatha to Addo, Shamwari, or Kwandwe for a good game fix. If you spend these last couple of nights at one of the private lodges, you can revel in the indulgence of absolute luxury after a few days of roughing it. Or if game parks aren't your thing, head to Hogsback and hike through the mountains and forests for a day or two before returning to Port Elizabeth to fly out. A third option is to start in Grahamstown, as for the three-day itinerary; two days in Grahamstown will give you the opportunity to appreciate the history and culture of this lovely city. Then spend two days at the game destination of your choice—Addo, Shamwari, or Kwandwe—and one more day on the Sunshine Coast soaking up some culture, lounging on the beach, or playing golf.

7 Days: Start off as you would for the three-day itinerary but spend two days in Grahamstown and three days at your game destination. Then opt for some beach time on the Sunshine Coast, at Coffee Bay, or Cintsa. Alternatively, fly into East London to join the Wild Coast Meander or head inland toward the Amatola mountain range, with a few cultural

6

stop-offs along the way; then spend two days at Addo, Shamwari, or Kwandwe. Head to Port Elizabeth or its environs and try to work in time to relax on the beach, play golf, or join a tour before flying out.

GETTING HERE AND AROUND

AIR TRAVEL

Port Elizabeth (PLZ) airport, small and easy to navigate, is the primary air entry point for the Eastern Cape and has a number of daily services with South African Airways, and the affiliated SA Airlink and SA Express, as well as British Airways (operated by Comair). Mango and Kulula, two local no-frills budget airlines, also offer good service but usually have only one or two flights a day. You can fly here from Cape Town (1 hour), Johannesburg (1½ hours), and most other major cities; there are no direct international flights.

The small and easy-to-navigate East London (ELS) airport is the best entry for the Amatole region and is served daily by South African Airways, SA Express, SA Airlink, and British Airways.

SA Airlink also flies between the tiny airport at Mthatha (UTT)—for travel to the Wild Coast—and Johannesburg. There are three flights a day, which take about an hour and 40 minutes. ⇨ *For information on airlines, see Air Travel in Travel Smart.*

Contacts East London Airport (*ELS*). ☎ *043/706–0306* ⊕ *www.acsa.co.za.* **Mthatha Airport** (*UTT*). ☎ *047/536–0023.* **Port Elizabeth Airport** (*PLZ*). ☎ *041/507–7319* ⊕ *www.acsa.co.za.*

BUS TRAVEL

Greyhound and Intercape Mainliner have pretty reliable and reasonably priced bus services, but the distances are long. Both services depart and arrive at Greenacres shopping complex, in the Newton Park suburb 3 km (2 miles) from the city center. This area is perfectly safe during the day, but you do need to arrange to be picked up in advance. If you are concerned about your budget, consider saving money by staying at a backpackers' lodge and spending a bit more on the Baz Bus (which travels door-to-door); an added benefit is that you won't have to wander around town with your luggage. ⇨ *For information on buses, see Bus Travel in Travel Smart.*

CAR TRAVEL

Traveling by car is the easiest and best way to tour this area. The major rental agencies have offices at the airport and in downtown PE. One-way rentals are available. Roads are generally in fairly good shape. ⇨ *For information on car-rental agencies, see Car Travel in Travel Smart.*

SAFETY AND PRECAUTIONS

One thing to keep in mind is that although most of the Central area of PE is safe, a few parts of it can be dicey. The lower section along Govan Mbeki is lively and vibrant, and the upper section is quiet and peaceful, but the parts in between have seen some crime. The area is slowly improving, but it's still best to get advice from your hotel or the tourism office before wandering around.

The Eastern Cape is malaria-free, and the climate is generally healthy. The tap water in the deep rural areas may be a bit unpredictable, but it's fine in the cities and towns. Avoid driving east of Grahamstown at night: the roads are unfenced and animals wander onto—or even sleep on—the warm tarmac, which is a serious hazard. Be sure to bring protection against sunburn, and be careful swimming in the sea. The Wild Coast beaches don't have lifeguards.

In case of an emergency, call the general emergencies number. For vehicle breakdown, call your car-rental company.

HOTELS

Most hotels along the coast get booked up over summer vacation (December to January), and the Wild Coast hotels are even busy over the winter school vacation, usually around June. Most establishments run winter specials, but there are exceptions. Grahamstown is packed in late June and/or early July for the National Arts Festival; every guesthouse is full, the campsite bulges, and even school and university dorms rent out rooms. Hotels on the Wild Coast often offer packages for the sardine run, usually in June or early July, but it's always a bit of a gamble, as the sardines are just not as reliable as the artists of the Grahamstown festival.

The best way to secure a reservation is by phone or via the lodging's website, if they have one. Another thing to keep in mind is that some of the more remote or rural lodgings on the Eastern Cape (particularly on the Wild Coast) still have limited Internet services provided for guest use, though almost all lodgings in the urban areas have good, fast Wi-Fi service these days. ■TIP➔ If the ability to connect to the Web is important to you, it's always worth clarifying the type of service available when you make your reservation.

Hotel reviews have been shortened. For full information, visit Fodors. com.

RESTAURANTS

Generally speaking, the restaurants of the Eastern Cape are good but not great. Of course there are always a few exceptions to every rule, and in the Eastern Cape the number of these exceptions is always increasing. But for really good food, choose a great hotel or guesthouse, some of which are noted for their cuisine. Not surprisingly, most restaurants are reasonably casual, and there are none where men would be expected to wear a tie.

WHAT IT COSTS IN SOUTH AFRICAN RAND			
$	**$$**	**$$$**	**$$$$**
Restaurants	under R100	R100–R150	R151–R200	over R200
Hotels	under R1,500	R1,500–R2,500	R2,501–R3,500	over R3,500

Restaurant prices are the average cost of a main course at dinner or, if dinner is not served, at lunch. Hotel prices are the lowest cost of a standard double room in high season.

TOURS

African Dive Adventures. This tour company offers Sardine Run Packages along the Wild Coast from a base at Coffee Bay. The best time to see the run is usually between late June and late July. ☎ *039/317–1483, 082/456–7885 mobile* ⊕ *www.afridive.com* ✉ *Five nights and four days diving and food costs R25,500.*

Calabash Tours. The tour company offers some of the best cultural, township, and shebeen tours in Port Elizabeth. In recognition of its commitment to community development, this operator is the only one of its kind that has been accredited by Fair Trade Tourism in South Africa. A tour of the local townships costs R450. An evening shebeen tour (R550) includes visits to a couple of township taverns, dinner, and, almost certainly, some good music. For a more intimate and personal experience, a new storytelling route has recently been added to the list, incorporating a traditional lunch with one of the local storytellers (R695). Calabash also has multiday tours to Addo Elephant National Park, as well as three- to five-day African heritage tours. ✉ *31 Cuyler St., Central, Port Elizabeth* ☎ *041/585–6162* ⊕ *www.calabashtours.co.za.*

Mosaic Tourism. From a short and informative city or township tour to an all-day game-viewing excursion or an elephant ride, Mosaic Travel offers a variety of tours in and around Port Elizabeth and across the Eastern Cape. Almost all of the tours are conducted by the irreverent and unbelievably knowledgeable company founder, Craig Duffield, who is also a certified game ranger and has free Wi-Fi services in all his vehicles. ☎ *083/656–8329 mobile* ⊕ *www.mosaictourism.co.za.*

VISITOR INFORMATION

Contacts **Nelson Mandela Bay Tourism** ✉ *Donkin Reserve, Belmont Terr., Central, Port Elizabeth* ☎ *041/585–8884* ⊕ *www.nmbt.co.za.*

FRONTIER COUNTRY AND THE SUNSHINE COAST

Frontier Country and the Sunshine Coast offer the perfect mix of well-maintained sunny coastal towns, beaches and resorts, historic and cultural sites, and a plethora of great game reserves all within a relatively concentrated (and malaria-free) area. Combined with good roads and infrastructure and a fine climate almost throughout, it's not hard to see why this part of the Eastern Cape is a particularly popular playground for South African tourists. It's richer and more developed here than in many other parts of the Eastern Cape, and although towns like Jeffreys Bay can become a little overrun during the holidays, there's a lot to see and do here, with most of the highlights within very short and easy driving distances of each other. Sometimes unkindly referred to as the Detroit of South Africa, Port Elizabeth is the Sunshine Coast's (as well as the whole of the Eastern Cape's) main urban hub and has great transport links to and from the rest of the region and beyond. Both the city and the surrounding region also boast many of the province's best accommodation options and restaurants.

PORT ELIZABETH

770 km (477 miles) east of Cape Town.

Port Elizabeth, or PE, may not have the range of attractions found in Cape Town or on the Garden Route, but it's a pleasant town that's worthy of a couple of days' exploration. There are some beautiful beaches (although you'll need to visit them early in the day in summer, as the wind tends to pick up by midday) and some wonderfully preserved historic buildings in the older part of the city, called Central. A large part of the town's charm lies in its small size and quiet environment, but PE is not a total sleepy hollow. If you feel the need for a bit of nightlife, head to the Boardwalk complex near the beach, for its restaurants, cafés, theater, and casino, or to the pedestrianized Parliament Street in Central, which has a vibrant restaurant and nightlife scene.

GETTING HERE AND AROUND

PE is a good base for exploring some other fantastic destinations, both wild and cultural, including Addo Elephant National Park. If you are traveling to any of the luxury game reserves east of Port Elizabeth (such as those in Addo, Shamwari, or Kwandwe), it may be a good idea to spend the night before in PE, as many places advise you to check in before lunch and it could be a scramble to get there if you're driving or flying in that morning.

Port Elizabeth's suburbs can be a little confusing. Humewood and Summerstrand are PE's two main coastal suburbs, with Humewood closer to the city center. The Humewood Golf Course, one of South Africa's best, is in Summerstrand, not Humewood, however (just to keep you on your toes).

There's a minibus shuttle at the Port Elizabeth airport that will drop you off at your hotel (about R90 one way, much less than a metered taxi), but you'll need to book in advance.

Contacts Blunden Minibus Shuttle ☏ *041/581–0411* ⊕ *www.blunden.co.za.*

VISITOR INFORMATION

Port Elizabeth's Nelson Mandela Bay Tourism is open weekdays 8–4:30 and Saturday 9:30–3:30.

EXPLORING

Art Route 67. Consisting of 67 public artworks by the Eastern Cape's local artists, the route symbolizes the 67 years that the late Nelson Mandela dedicated to the South African fight for freedom. The route runs from the city center to Donkin Reserve and the old lighthouse above that overlook the harbor and the ocean beyond. Here there's a large pyramid built by the city's former governor Rufane Shaw Donkin in honor of his deceased wife, Elizabeth, from whom Port Elizabeth gets its name. Stretching from the pyramid toward a towering South African flag is a long and colorful mosaic that references various important parts of Port Elizabeth's and the Eastern Cape's history and cultural heritage. Beneath the huge flag is a life-size metal cutout of Mandela (he was taller than you might think) with his fist raised in triumph, and snaking down the steps behind him is a line of South Africans (also life-size) of all ages, colors, and creeds lining up to vote in the 1994 elections. Sixty-seven colored steps lead from this point back to the city below, and along the way you'll find a number of inspiring quotes from Mandela on sheets of metal made to look like pages ripped from a book. Combined with all the other colorful wall paintings, sculptures, and texts, the route has both revitalized and contextualized some of the previously more run-down areas of central Port Elizabeth, and tells important stories about where South Africa came from and where it is headed. ⊠ *Donkin Reserve.*

South End Museum. South End was once the most vibrant part of Port Elizabeth, until it was flattened by the apartheid-era government to "tidy up" the city and put everything and everyone in their places. At the South End Museum a map, photographs, and paintings give you an idea of what the old South End was like in its heyday. ⊠ *Humewood Rd. and Walmer Blvd., Summerstrand* ☎ *041/582–3325* ⊕ *www. southendmuseum.co.za* ✉ *Donations welcome* ⊗ *Weekdays 9–4.*

BEACHES

The beaches listed here are lined with restaurants, shops, and coffee bars, and there are flea markets on weekends. Beyond Hobie Beach the seafront is still built up with houses and apartments, but the frenetic commercialism is missing.

Hobie Beach. The pier marks the beginning of Hobie Beach, where sailing catamarans and Jet Skis launch, and where a number of annual events and festivals are held. There are a number of restaurants along the other side of the promenade, including Ginger at the Beach Hotel. The Hobie Beach Guesthouse is also close by. The section of beach closest to the pier is great for swimming and sunbathing, and there are also a number of rock pools to explore. Hobie Beach can get very busy on a hot summer's day. **Amenities:** lifeguards; toilets; showers; food and drink; parking. **Best for:** swimming; snorkeling. ⊠ *Marine Dr.*

FAMILY **Humewood Beach.** Humewood Beach runs from King's Beach to Shark Rock Pier. This beach has fine white sand and is a great place for families, with shaded areas supplied by an overhead promenade. A convenient parking lot is behind the beach (behind John Dory's restaurant), and there are excellent facilities, including picnic tables, plus lifeguards on duty during peak times. Some grassy areas lead into Happy Valley, but it's not recommended that you walk into the valley, as it's often completely deserted and you may be in danger of being mugged. The beach slipway has a little reef, and the water beside it is great for snorkeling. Humewood Beach is close to the bustling Boardwalk Hotel and all its facilities (including a casino and mall) and the Beach Hotel. **Amenities:** lifeguards; toilets; showers; parking. **Best for:** swimming; snorkeling. ⊠ *Marine Dr.*

King's Beach. Within the bay and starting closest to the city center and harbor (which is best avoided), the first beach you come to is King's Beach, so named because King George VI slept in the Royal Train here during a visit to the city before World War II. You may want to avoid the far end of King's Beach, as it can get pretty crowded. The beach is one of three Blue Flag beaches in PE (along with Hobie Beach and Humewood Beach), meaning that it has met international standards of cleanliness, safety, and facilities. It's another very family-friendly beach, too. The McArthur Baths pool complex is along the promenade. The Garden Court King's Beach Hotel offers rooms with views across King's Beach. **Amenities:** lifeguard; toilets; showers; parking lot. **Best for:** swimming; walking. ⊠ *Kings Rd.*

FAMILY **McArthur Baths.** The section of beach near McArthur Baths is great for swimming and very popular. If you'd rather swim in flat water, head for the bath complex (R50, open September–April), which has a range of pools, two of which are heated to a few degrees above sea temperature. There's no natural grass here, however, so you will need to rent a lounge chair (R10) to be comfortable. **Amenities:** lifeguard; toilets; showers. **Best for:** swimming. ⊠ *McArthur Baths, Beach Rd., Humewood* ☎ *041/582–2282*

Pollock Beach. Adjacent to the suburb of Summerstrand, Pollock Beach is one of the better swimming beaches, with a lovely small natural tidal pool. It also offers great surfing. (Generally the surfing in PE is not too challenging, unlike at Jeffreys Bay, just over an hour's drive to the west, which has some pretty exciting waves.) The far end of Pollock Beach is best avoided, as it can get crowded with somewhat boisterous, picnicking, partying crowds. **Amenities:** lifeguard; toilets; food and drink; parking lot. **Best for:** surfing; partiers. ⊠ *10th Ave., off Marine Dr.*

Sardinia Bay. For a truly fantastic Port Elizabeth beach experience, very little can beat Sardinia Bay Beach, outside the bay and about a 20-minute drive from the main beaches. Here, miles and miles of deserted, snow-white sand are great for long walks. It's best to come on weekends, however, as during the week it can be isolated and there have been a few incidents of muggings. On weekends there are plenty of people, and you will be perfectly safe. It's also a popular beach for scuba-diving and this part of the coast has been declared a marine reserve, so no fishing is allowed. There are also fire pits so come prepared for a braai. **Amenities:** lifeguard; toilets; food and drink; parking lot. **Best for:** swimming; walking; snorkeling. ⊠ *Sardinia Bay Dr.*

WHERE TO EAT

The beachfront is lined with reasonably priced hotels and restaurants, as well as a few higher-quality ones.

$$$

SOUTH AFRICAN

Fodor's Choice

★

✕ **Ginger.** This is Port Elizabeth's most well-established fine-dining option, a stalwart in the expanding beachfront dining scene. It's located in the Beach Hotel opposite the pier. Glass doors open onto a terrace, with sea views, or you can sit inside at tables placed around the bar, which is located in the center of the restaurant. Cuisine is contemporary with local flavors and the menu is expansive; the seafood options are hard to beat, but there's also a large selection of steaks and game meats. For dessert try a Spice Route ice-cream plate, with four different flavors of homemade ice cream: ginger, cinnamon, fennel, and honey. The wine list is excellent, and the service is crisp and efficient. Prices are reasonable, especially considering the size of the portions. A lighter lunch menu features warm salads, sandwiches, burgers, and pastas, as well as some seafood and steak dishes. ⓢ *Average main: R160* ⊠ *The*

Beach Hotel, Marine Dr., Summerstrand ☎ *041/583–1229* ⊕ *www. ginger-restaurant.co.za.*

$ ✕ **The Stage Door.** Accessed by the back entrance of Port Elizabeth's
SOUTH AFRICAN oldest hotel, the Phoenix Hotel, the Stage Door is one of the city's best-kept secrets and has long been a favorite with locals in the know for its cheap and cheerful menu, good range of beers, and that old-fashioned pub feel with a healthy measure of quirkiness thrown in. The floor of the restaurant section is covered in sawdust, and the walls glare with an array of retro signs, slogans, number plates from vehicles, posters, and advertisements that recall America in the 1950s. The menu offers advice such as "Want great service—we suggest you try somewhere else." Although a sense of humor is a must here and it can get very busy, the service remains excellent, as do the steaks. The bar area is less colorful than the restaurant but equally interesting, as much for the characters it attracts as for the original, dark-wood furnishings. ■ **TIP→ This is definitely worth a visit even just to have a quick drink and soak up the rich atmosphere and history of the place.** ⑤ *Average main: R75* ⊠ *5 Chapel St.* ☎ *041/586–3553* ⊕ *www.phoenixhotel.co.za.*

WHERE TO STAY

$ ⊞ **Forest Hall Guesthouse.** Located in the leafy and affluent suburb of
B&B/INN Walmer, just a 5- to 10-minute drive from the airport, the friendly and family-run guesthouse is a great place to stop and recuperate for a night or two before traveling on from PE. **Pros:** owners are approachable and helpful; prices are very reasonable; private airport shuttle service; a number of tours can also be organized. **Cons:** it's popular with business and conference groups so can get noisy at night; it's a bit of a trek to any of PE's best restaurants or attractions; no meals aside from breakfast except on special request. ⑤ *Rooms from: R675* ⊠ *84 River Rd., Walmer* ☎ *041/581–3356* ⊕ *www.foresthall.co.za* ⌇ *10 rooms* ⦿ *Breakfast.*

$$ ⊞ **Hacklewood Hill Country House.** For superbly comfortable and gracious
B&B/INN lodgings, try this inn set in English-style gardens in the leafy suburb of
Fodor's Choice Walmer. **Pros:** it has a great air of tranquillity; service and food are both
★ excellent and prices are reasonable. **Cons:** decor is a bit old-fashioned; it's not in walking distance of the beachfront; not particularly well-suited to the business traveler. ⑤ *Rooms from: R2360* ⊠ *152 Prospect Rd., Walmer* ☎ *041/581–1300* ⊕ *www.hacklewood.co.za* ⌇ *8 rooms* ⦿ *Breakfast.*

$ ⊞ **Jikeleza Lodge.** In a quiet part of the Central neighborhood, this hostel
B&B/INN tends to attract mature backpackers who are more interested in culture and adventure activities than partying. **Pros:** within walking distance of restaurants and bars in less touristy area than the beachfront; tables in the garden make dining (either brought in or cooked in the communal kitchen) a pleasure; free Wi-Fi. **Cons:** you will need to take a taxi to the beachfront; service is a little sloppy; bookings and deposits have been known to go awry on occasion. ⑤ *Rooms from: R300* ⊠ *44 Cuyler St., Central* ☎ *041/586–3721* ⊕ *www.jikelezalodge.co.za* ⌇ *6 rooms* ⦿ *No meals.*

$ ⊞ **Summerstrand Hotel.** Two major attractions of this hotel are its good
HOTEL prices and its location—close to the beach on the quieter side of the

6

bay and virtually on top of the excellent Humewood Golf Course. **Pros:** excellent on-site help with arranging tours and onward travel; friendly staff; good restaurant. **Cons:** exterior and bathrooms could use an update; it's a popular conference venue so can get a bit noisy. ⑤ *Rooms from: R880* ✉ *Marine Dr., Summerstrand* ☎ *041/583–3131* ⊕ *www.summerstrandhotel.co.za* ➥ *127 rooms* ⦿ *Breakfast.*

SPORTS AND THE OUTDOORS

GOLF

Humewood Golf Course. Consistently listed as one of the country's top courses, the challenging championship Humewood Golf Course is set in undulating dunes on the edge of Algoa Bay, making it one of South Africa's few natural links courses. The late South African golfer Bobby Locke considered it the finest course in the country and compared it favorably to the best of British links courses. At 7,030 yards and exposed to stiff sea breezes, it's not for the fainthearted. ✉ *Marine Dr., Summerstrand* ☎ *041/583–2137* ⊕ *www.humewoodgolf.co.za* ➥ *R375 for 18 holes; R250 for 9 holes* ⛳ *18 holes, 7030 yards, par 72.*

CAPE ST FRANCIS

111 km (69 miles) west of Port Elizabeth; 693 km (430 miles) east of Cape Town.

Weaving its way between beautiful nature reserves, indigenous fynbos, wetlands, plush marinas, and rolling sand dunes, Cape St Francis is a pretty beachfront eco-village at the heart of the St Francis peninsula, which also includes the equally pristine St Francis Bay and Oyster Bay. Though it's increasingly popular with South African tourists during the summer holiday season, it retains an air of calm and tranquility throughout the year, and there's plenty of sunshine even in the depths of winter, when the area's mostly empty. There's a historic lighthouse (the highest masonry building in Southern Africa), a challenging links golf course, a handful of good restaurants and watering holes, and any number of fine accommodation options among the pretty whitewashed, thatch-roofed Cape Dutch–style beach cottages and villas that dominate the area's architecture. It's also a great destination for surfers and water-sports enthusiasts.

GETTING HERE AND AROUND

The best way to get here is to rent a car from Port Elizabeth and drive yourself; it's an easy and pleasant 1½-hour drive on the N2 and then the R330, and the roads are pretty good. There's no direct public transport between Cape St Francis and Port Elizabeth. There are local minibus taxis around, but they run fairly infrequently, as evinced by the many hitchhikers you'll see on the side of the road. If you're riding the Baz Bus from Cape Town, Cape St Francis is your first stop within the Eastern Cape. You can also book a private shuttle from Port Elizabeth's airport with J-Bay Cabs (R750 one-way for one person, or R375 per person for more than one passenger). St Francis Bay is roughly 10 km (6 miles) north of Cape St Francis, and Oyster Bay is 14 km (9 miles) west of St Francis Bay on a dirt road. ⇨ *For information on car rentals, see Car Travel in Travel Smart.*

WHERE TO STAY

$$$
RESORT
FAMILY
Cape St Francis Resort. This big, bright beachfront resort offers a wide range of different accommodations, from luxury self-catering villas with direct beach access over the dunes to simple backpacker rooms with shared bathrooms. **Pros:** great location; a wide range of activities can be organized at reception; very family-friendly. **Cons:** it can get overcrowded during holidays; because of the size, it can feel a little impersonal; it's not the quietest place with so many children about. $ *Rooms from: R3500* ⊠ *Da Gama Way, Cape St. Frances* ☎ *042/298–0054* ⊕ *www.capestfrancis.co.za* ↝ *10 rooms, 11 suites, 71 apartments* ¶◯¶ *Some meals.*

$$
B&B/INN
Fodor'sChoice
★
Oyster Bay Lodge. Set on a secluded coastal reserve that incorporates magnificent dunes, woods, river deltas, lagoons, a 3½-km (2-mile) expanse of beach, free-roaming horses, and a plethora of birdlife, Oyster Bay Lodge truly is a hidden gem. **Pros:** location and activities are superb; service is smooth; room rates are very reasonable. **Cons:** set dinner menu is a little overpriced and doesn't include drinks; Wi-Fi can be temperamental; some of the standard rooms don't get a lot of daylight. $ *Rooms from: R1600* ⊠ *Humansdorp, Cape St. Frances* ⨯ *Take the 632 Palmietvlei exit off the N2 highway and follow signs to Oyster Bay Lodge for 24 km (15 miles)* ☎ *042/297–0150* ⊕ *www.oysterbaylodge. com* ↝ *10 rooms, 4 suites* ¶◯¶ *Breakfast.*

SPORTS AND THE OUTDOORS

GOLF

St Francis Links Golf Course. This beautiful and unique links course was designed by the famous American golfer Jack Nicklaus, and appears regularly on many of South Africa's top 10 golf course lists. It's a varied, undulating, and very challenging course that has been designed to mirror the terrain on which it was built; the shape of the greens comes from the natural contours of the sand beneath, and the course incorporates various wetlands areas and weaves its way between dense outcrops of indigenous fynbos as well as along parts of the rugged coastline of St Francis Bay. There's also a decent family-friendly clubhouse restaurant and bar. ⊠ *Lyme Rd., St Francis Bay* ☎ *042/200–4500* ⊕ *www. stfrancislinks.co.za* ⊡ *R350 for 9 holes, R550 for 18 holes; club rentals R290* ⚑ *18 holes, 7874 yards, par 72.*

ADDO ELEPHANT NATIONAL PARK

72 km (45 miles) north of Port Elizabeth.

GETTING HERE AND AROUND

The closest airport to Addo Elephant Park is Port Elizabeth (PLZ) airport. Flights arrive daily from all of South Africa's main cities via South African Airways, SA Express, SA Airlink, British Airways, and the budget airlines Mango and Kulula. Flights from Cape Town take roughly 1 hour and from Johannesburg 1½ hours.

Traveling by car is the easiest and best way to tour this area, as public transport is limited. Some roads are unpaved but in decent condition. Most lodges will organize airport transfers for their guests. ⇨ *For information on airlines, see Air Travel in Travel Smart.*

EXPLORING

Addo Elephant National Park. Smack in the middle of a citrus-growing and horse-breeding area, Addo Elephant National Park is home to a staggering 700 elephants not to mention plenty of buffalo, black rhino, leopards, spotted hyena, hundreds of kudu and other antelopes, and lions. At present the park has about 400,000 acres, but it's expanding all the time and is intended to reach a total of about 600,000 acres, including a fully incorporated marine section. The most accessible parts of the park are the original, main section and the Colchester, Kabouga, Woody Cape, and Zuurberg sections. The original section of Addo still holds most of the game and is served by Addo Main Camp. The Colchester section, in the south, which has one SANParks camp, is contiguous with the main area. The scenic Nyati section is separated from the main section by a road and railway line. Just north of Nyati is the mountainous Zuurberg section, which doesn't have a large variety of game but is particularly scenic, with fabulous hiking trails and horse trails. It is also the closest section of the park to Addo Elephant Back Safaris. You can explore the park in your own vehicle, in which case you need to heed the road signs that claim "dung beetles have right of way." Addo is home to the almost-endemic and extremely rare flightless dung beetle, which can often be seen rolling its unusual incubator across the roads. Watch out for them (they're only about 2 inches long, but have sharp spines that can puncture tires), and watch them: they're fascinating. Instead of driving you could take a night or day game drive with a park ranger in an open vehicle from the main camp. A more adventurous option is to ride a horse among the elephants. Warning: no citrus fruit may be brought into the park, as elephants find it irresistible and can smell it for miles. ⊠ *Addo Elephant National Park* ☎ *042/233–8600* ⊕ *www. addoelephantpark.com* ✉ *R50* ⊗ *Daily 7–7 (may vary with seasons).*

FAMILY **Addo Elephant Back Safaris.** This company lets you get up close and personal with a small group of trained African elephants. You get to do a short elephant ride and then go for a scenic walk through the bush with them. You can touch them, feed them, and watch them as they bathe themselves with sand, water, or both (i.e., mud). The whole experience lasts about two to three hours and includes a meal either before or after the safari. You can also arrange for a fly-in day trip from Port Elizabeth. ⊠ *Addo Elephant National Park* ☎ *086/123–3672, 042/235–1400* ⊕ *www.addoelephantbacksafaris.co.za* ✉ *R975* ⊗ *Visits by appointment only.*

Schotia Safaris. If you're short on time or budget, Schotia offers a good value, family-run, no-frills safari experience taking place in a privately owned wildlife reserve bordering the eastern side of Addo. Due to its small size (4,200 acres) and the fact that it's very densely stocked (more than 2,000 animals and 40 species) you're almost guaranteed to see a wide variety of wildlife—lion, giraffes, hippos, white rhinos, crocodiles, zebras, and all kinds of buck. The popular Tooth and Claw safari starts at 2:30 pm and includes a game drive and a tasty, generous buffet dinner served in an attractive open-air area with roaring fires. After dinner you're taken on a short night drive back to the reception area—keep your eyes peeled for some unusual nocturnal animals. There's also the option of going on a morning game drive into Addo, with lunch, and then the Tooth and Claw safari. Other packages include one or two nights' accommodation on the reserve. Although you may see other vehicles during your drive, tours are very good value and well run, and the guides are excellent. The Tooth and Claw half-day safari can be done easily as a day trip from Port Elizabeth, as it's only a 45-minute drive away. ⊠ *Orlando Farm, Paterson, Addo Elephant National Park* ☎ *042/235–1436* ⊕ *www.schotia.com.*

WHERE TO STAY

$
RESORT

Addo Elephant National Park Main Camp. One of the best SANParks rest camps, this location has a range of self-catering accommodations, such as safari tents, forest cabins, rondavels, cottages, and chalets, and a shop that sells basic supplies as well as souvenirs. **Pros:** great value; you get to enter the game area before the game gates open and go on night drives. **Cons:** the shop has only basic supplies; the rondavels have shared cooking facilities. ⑤ *Rooms from: R1300* ⊠ *Addo Elephant National Park* ☎ *012/428–9111* ⊕ *www.addoelephant.com* ⮌ *65 suites* ⦿ *No meals.*

$$$$
ALL-INCLUSIVE

Gorah Elephant Camp. A private concession within the main section of Addo, this picturesque colonial-themed camp has accommodations in spacious, luxurious safari tents with thick thatch canopies and furnished in antiques from the colonial era. **Pros:** the food and service are top-notch; guests are not required to sit together at meals; the location and colonial style are special. **Cons:** rooms don't have bathtubs; rooms can get cold at night in winter; you often have to leave the private concession area to find the best game. ⑤ *Rooms from: R10000* ⊠ *Addo Elephant National Park* ☎ *044/501–1111* ⊕ *www.hunterhotels.com* ⮌ *11 tents* ⦿ *All-inclusive.*

$$
B&B/INN
Fodor's Choice
★

Hitgeheim Country Lodge. This lovely lodge is set on a steep cliff overlooking the Sundays River and the town of Addo. **Pros:** personal touches, such as a turndown service and luxury bath products by the South African company Charlotte Rhys; very friendly and helpful owners; very reasonable prices. **Cons:** not for independent travelers, as the owners like to arrange your activities for you; the restaurant is not open to nonguests. ⑤ *Rooms from: R2500* ⊠ *Addo Elephant National Park* ✛ *18 km (11 miles) from Addo Main Gate on R335, then follow R336 to Kirkwood* ☎ *042/234–0778* ⊕ *www.hitgeheim-addo.co.za* ⮌ *8 suites* ⦿ *Breakfast.*

$$$$
B&B/INN
FAMILY

River Bend Lodge. Situated on a 34,594-acre private concession within the Nyati section of Addo, River Bend perfectly balances the feel of a sophisticated, comfortable country house with all the facilities of a game lodge. **Pros:** kids are welcome, and there's an enclosed playground; the food is excellent, especially the seven-course dinner menu; all food and drinks are included in the rack rates. **Cons:** decor is more English colonial than African; only the honeymoon suite has a plunge pool; it's not the most exciting section of the park in terms of game. ⑤ *Rooms from: R11000* ⊠ *Zuurberg, Addo Elephant National Park* ☎ *042/233–8000* ⊕ *www.riverbendlodge.co.za* ⮌ *8 suites* ⦿ *All meals.*

6

SHAMWARI GAME RESERVE

72 km (45 miles) from Port Elizabeth.

GETTING HERE AND AROUND

The closest airport to Shamwari Game Reserve is the one in Port Elizabeth (PLZ), about 72 km (45 miles) away. Small and easy to navigate, the airport is served daily by South African Airways, SA Airlink, SA Express, British Airways, and Mango. Flights arrive from Cape Town (1 hour) and Johannesburg (1½ hours). From here it's best to rent your own car, as there isn't any reliable public transport. If you are flying into Port Elizabeth and visiting only Shamwari, it may be easier to arrange an airport transfer with the reserve. As with all of the luxury game reserves, it's advised that you arrive by midday so you can check in and have lunch before the afternoon game drive. ⇨ *For information on airlines, see Air Travel in Travel Smart. For information on car rentals, see Car Travel in Travel Smart.*

EXPLORING

Shamwari Game Reserve. In the Eastern Cape, an easy hour and a half's drive from Port Elizabeth, Shamwari Game Reserve is, in every sense of the word, a conservation triumph. Unprofitable farmland has been turned into a successful tourist attraction, wild animals have been reintroduced, and alien vegetation has been, and is still being, eradicated. The reserve, which officially opened in 1992, is constantly being expanded and now stands at about 62,000 acres. Its mandate is to conserve not only the big impressive animals (which are abundant), but everything else: indiginous plants, buildings, history, and culture of the area. The reserve's six lodges are all top notch and each offers its own unique flavor, from the romantic colonial decadence of Long Lee Manor to the contemporary cool of Eagle's Crag. ⊠ *Shamwari Game Reserve* ☎ *041/509–3000* ⊕ *www.shamwari.com.*

Born Free Centres. Part of the reserve has been set aside as the Born Free Centres (there's one in the northern part and one in the southern part of the reserve). Here African leopards and lions rescued from zoos, circuses, and even nightclubs around the world are allowed to roam in large enclosures for the rest of their lives, as they cannot safely be returned to the wild. Although these are interesting tourist attractions, the main purpose is educational, and about 500 local schoolchildren tour the centers every month. ⊠ *Shamwari Game Reserve* ⊕ *www.bornfree.org.uk.*

WHERE TO STAY

$$$$
ALL-INCLUSIVE

🛏 **Bayethe Tented Lodge.** Huge air-conditioned safari tents under thatch roofs create comfortable accommodations, and private decks with plunge pools overlook the Buffalo River. **Pros:** each tent has an amazing outside shower and deck; tents have fabulous bathrooms; the king-size beds have comfortable 400-thread-count sheets. **Cons:** for those seeking privacy, the communal meals might be a nuisance; Wi-Fi is not available in the suites. ⑤ *Rooms from: R8700* ⊠ *Shamwari Game Reserve* ☎ *041/509–3000* ⊕ *www.shamwari.com* ☜ *12 suites* ◎ *All-inclusive.*

$$$$
ALL-INCLUSIVE
Fodor's Choice
★

☐ **Eagles Crag.** Very different from the other Shamwari options, this sleek, modern lodge makes use of light wood, pale sandstone, and stainless-steel finishes. **Pros:** a carefully selected choice of top local wines and spirits is included; the rooms are enormous; the food and service are excellent. **Cons:** the reception areas are very large and can feel impersonal; drinks are not included in the rates; the decor in the dining area doesn't live up to the rest of the lodge ⑤ *Rooms from: R8310* ✉ *Shamwari Game Reserve* ☎ *041/509–3000* ⊕ *www.shamwari.com* ↩ *9 suites* ⍒ *All-inclusive.*

$$$$
ALL-INCLUSIVE

☐ **Long Lee Manor.** Originally built in 1910 as the manor house of one of the private farms that would later be incorporated into Shamwari, this colorful and richly furnished Edwardian property continues to evoke the colonial era and all the romanticism and opulence that went with it. **Pros:** the food and service are spectacular; the dining area is the best of any of Shamwari's lodges; there are spa facilities and a gym with great views. **Cons:** it's one of the bigger lodges at Shamwari, so not the most intimate; it's not as deep into the heart of the reserve as other lodges; it's certainly not for those looking for something more "African." ⑤ *Rooms from: R8310* ✉ *Shamwari Game Reserve* ☎ *041/509–3000* ⊕ *www. shamwari.com* ↩ *10 suites, 5 rooms* ⍒ *All-inclusive.*

$$$$
ALL-INCLUSIVE
FAMILY

☐ **Riverdene Lodge.** Riverdene combines the great food and service of Shamwari's other lodges with a much more child-friendly atmosphere and facilities. **Pros:** there are are special "Kids on Safari" programs for kids of all ages; seven of the nine suites are connectable; it's probably Shamwari's friendliest lodge. **Cons:** all those children means it can get noisy; not the place for privacy; has less character than the likes of Long Lee or Bayethe. ⑤ *Rooms from: R8310* ✉ *Shamwari Game Reserve* ☎ *041/509–3000* ⊕ *www.shamwari.com* ↩ *9 suites* ⍒ *All-inclusive.*

GRAHAMSTOWN

134 km (83 miles) northeast of Port Elizabeth.

Although billed as a city, Grahamstown looks more like an English village than anything else—if you discount that alter ego of most South African towns, the contiguous shanty townships. These are a big part of Grahamstown, and they contribute to the city's wealth of cultural history. Established as a garrison town to enforce the arbitrarily assigned border of the British Cape Colony, Grahamstown was the center of several battles during the last couple of centuries.

It's worth spending a day or two to explore the sights and to perhaps take a tour—just to reinforce the fact that history, no matter how accurately portrayed, is always subjective.

GETTING HERE AND AROUND

It's easiest and best to tour this area by car. Roads are generally in good shape, though there is a slight difference in road conditions east and west of Grahamstown. To the west (that is, on the PE side) roads are wide, often dual lane, and well maintained. East of Grahamstown the N2 is a single-lane road and there are some sections with no shoulders, but for the most part it's good.

From PE, the drive is approximately 1½ hours. Bus services (Greyhound, Intercape) stop in the center of town. There's also Mini-Lux, a minibus shuttle that runs from PE Airport to Grahamstown on Tuesday, Thursday, and Friday and then on to East London.

Grahamstown is small enough that you can easily walk around on foot, although you should take a taxi late at night. ⇨ *For information on car rentals, see Car Travel in Travel Smart. For information on buses, see Bus Travel in Travel Smart.*

TOURS

Ottours "Spirit of Life." One of South Africa's most seminal historical incidents was the 1819 Battle of Grahamstown, when the Xhosa prophet Makana tried to rid his area of British colonizers. Makana was arrested and sent to Robben Island, where he died trying to escape. You can relive this battle and other interesting parts of Grahamstown's history with Ottours "Spirit of Life" tours. Your guide, Otto Nteshebe, will inform you about the traditional way of life of the Xhosa people, and can also organize local township and shebeen tours, as well as give you a greater insight into the beautiful historic architecture of Grahamstown. ✉ *63 High St.* ☎ *046/637–1025.*

VISITOR INFORMATION

In Grahamstown, Makana Tourism is open weekdays 8:30–5 and Saturday 9–noon.

Contacts Makana Tourism ✉ *63 High St.* ☎ *046/622-3241* ⊕ *www.grahamstown.co.za.*

EXPLORING

Home to Rhodes University and some of the country's top schools, Grahamstown is considered by many to be the seat of culture and learning in South Africa.

National Arts Festival. The 10-day National Arts Festival, which takes place in late June and/or early July and is purported to be second in size only to the Edinburgh Festival in Scotland, is the country's premier cultural event. ☎ *046/603–1103* ⊕ *www.nationalartsfestival.co.za.*

TOP ATTRACTIONS

Cathedral of St. Michael and St. George. This is Grahamstown's most prominent landmark, as much by virtue of its steeple—the highest in South Africa at 176 feet—as the strict geometry of the town. High Street runs in a straight line from the cathedral doors through the Drostdy Arch to the doors of the administration buildings of Rhodes University. The cathedral's eight bells, which you can hear ringing out on Sundays, were the first and still are the heaviest in Africa. Though construction on the cathedral started in 1824, it wasn't completed until 1952. ✉ *108 High St.* ☎ *046/622–2445* 🎟 *Free* ⊙ *Weekdays 8–1.*

FAMILY **Observatory Museum.** An intriguing study of Victorian-era cutting-edge science, the building was constructed by a watchmaker and amateur astronomer, H. C. Gulpin, who built a cupola above his shop to house his instruments. The museum contains a two-story pendulum and the only genuine Victorian camera obscura in the Southern Hemisphere. You can stand in the tower and watch what's happening in the town

CLOSE UP

Grahamstown's Arts Festival

The National Arts Festival (⊕ *www. nationalartsfestival.co.za*) began in 1974 with some 60-odd performances, and now offers a staggering variety of entertainment. Besides theaters, every conceivable kind of venue is used, including churches, school halls, museums, and pubs. There is a formal program, an official fringe festival, and even a fringe of the fringe that gets seriously alternative. Some offbeat productions have included families of giant puppets and stilt workers roaming the streets and a theater ensemble who create hair installations on its audience. You can also see local and international music, theater, ballet, and modern dance performances. There's a Children's Festival and a large outdoor market with vendors selling everything from hand-painted T-shirts to local crafts.

The large festival events and the film festival are staged at the **1820 Settlers National Monument,** a concrete edifice on Gunfire Hill, next to the old garrison, Fort Selwyn. Sundowner concerts at 5 pm in the monument's foyer give previews of the various shows.

TICKETS
Tickets are available via the official festival website (⊕ *www. nationalartsfestival.co.za*) up to two months before the festival.

GETTING TO AND AROUND THE FESTIVAL
If you are flying into Port Elizabeth, you can rent a car to make the 1½-hour-long journey to Grahamstown, or you can take the festival minibus that meets passengers at the airport (until 8 pm, R250 per person). Check out the festival website for booking information.

In Grahamstown, the Festival Hopper Bus travels between the monument and various venues throughout the day. Timetables and booking information for all festival-related events are on the comprehensive website.

WHERE TO STAY
A wide variety of accommodation is available, ranging from rooms in university halls to private-home stays. It's advisable to plan your trip three months in advance or more, but it's still possible to find something at the last minute. Many overseas visitors stay in surrounding towns or on game farms in the area (which often have special packages) and make day trips into the town.

BE PREPARED
The festival takes place in midwinter, and it's always very cold at night. Days can be hot and sunny, so it's advisable to wear layers, and to bring a coat and scarf.

6

below—pretty useful if you've lost your companions. ⊠ *10 Bathurst St.* ☎ *046/622–2312* ⊠ *R10* ☉ *Weekdays 9–4:30.*

WORTH NOTING
Drostdy Arch. When Grahamstown was a garrison town, the Drostdy Arch, erected in 1841, was the original entrance to the military parade ground. Now it is the gateway through which thousands of Rhodes students pass when leaving campus for town. There is a small crafts market "under the Arch" on weekdays 9–5 and Saturday 9–1. ⊠ *High St.*

International Library of African Music. A teaching and research center for indigenous music, the library has a collection of more than 200 traditional African musical instruments, including *djembes* (drums), *mbiras* (thumb pianos), and marimbas (xylophones). ⊠ *Rhodes University, Prince Alfred St.* ☎ *046/603–8557* 🖭 *Free* ☉ *Weekdays 8–1 and 2–4.*

> ## THE ELASTIC CITY
>
> Most of the year Grahamstown is pretty small, but around festival time (late June/early July) this elastic city expands to accommodate the tens of thousands of festivalgoers. Come December, it shrinks to a mere ghost of itself as the students and scholars go home.

National English Literary Museum. The National English Literary Museum houses a comprehensive collection of books, articles, and press clippings on South African writers in the English language, including some unpublished works. There is also a bookshop. ⊠ *87 Beaufort St.* ☎ *046/622–7042* ⊕ *www.ru.ac.za/static/institutes/nelm/* 🖭 *Free* ☉ *Weekdays 8:30–4:30.*

Winged Angel of Peace. The statue of the Winged Angel of Peace commemorates the dead of the Second South African War (1899–1902), also called the Boer War. The site was chosen as one that was "in the midst of our daily work," so it would be seen often and would serve as an inspiration for peace. ⊠ *Bathurst St.*

WHERE TO EAT

You won't find the greatest choice of dining establishments here, particularly when it comes to fine dining, as Grahamstown is largely a student town. However, there are a number of cafés on High Street that are adequate.

$$
SOUTH AFRICAN

✕ **Haricot's.** Centrally located with a pretty outside courtyard area, Haricot's simple, bright, and clean decor and its good array of reasonably priced and very fresh fare has helped it become a local stalwart since it opened a few years ago. More café and deli by day, it's popular with Rhodes University students and professors thanks to its great coffee, homemade cakes and baked goods, and good lunch menu. By night it's a little more sophisticated and has a decent local wine list to accompany the à la carte dinner menu, which changes weekly. There's a traditional French or Italian twist to many of the dinner offerings, and to the feel of the place, but portion sizes remain distinctly South African and student-friendly, and so do the prices. Order three courses at your peril! $ *Average main: R100* ⊠ *32 New St.* ☎ *046/622–2150* ⊕ *www.haricots.co.za.*

$
CAFÉ

✕ **137 High St.** Conveniently located right on High Street, this warm, friendly coffee shop is popular with students, and there's outside seating in a pretty, sunny courtyard. It serves the usual pastas, sandwiches, and salads—and arguably the best coffee in town. The seven-room bed-and-breakfast ($) upstairs has fabulous yellowwood floors in the residents' lounge. One room has a tub; the others have showers only. There's a self-catering one-bedroom flat, too. Accommodation is a little on the basic side, but the place has plenty of charm. $ *Average main: R80* ⊠ *137 High St.* ☎ *046/622–3242* ⊕ *www.137highstreet.co.za* ☉ *No dinner Sun.*

WHERE TO STAY

If you need help finding accommodations, the Grahamstown Accommodations Bureau should be able to give you a hand.

Grahamstown Accommodation Central Booking Office. Your best bet for help with lodging, especially at festival time, is the Grahamstown Accommodation Central Booking Office. ☎ *046/622–5777, 071/316–574* ⊕ *www.grahamstownaccom.co.za.*

$
B&B/INN
🖼 **The Cock House.** Over the years, this charming building, a National Monument built in 1826, has been the home of distinguished citizens, most notably academic and novelist André Brink, so it's fitting that the individually decorated rooms are named after previous owners. **Pros:** a small, lovely garden in the back; good restaurant; plenty of character. **Cons:** rooms are on the small side; no air-conditioning in the hotel. ⑤ *Rooms from: R980* ✉ *10 Market St., at George St.* ☎ *046/636–1295* ⊕ *www.thecockhouse.co.za* ⤵ *9 rooms, 4 apartments* ⍟ *Breakfast.*

$
B&B/INN
🖼 **High Corner Guesthouse.** This popular, quaint, and centrally located guesthouse is in the oldest cottage in Grahamstown (built in 1814) and is just a few paces from the main entrance to Rhodes University and most of Grahamstown's shops, cafés, restaurants, and bars. **Pros:** free Wi-Fi throughout the property; prices are reasonable; great breakfast. **Cons:** it's popular with visiting professors and businessmen, so it can be hard to get a room; the rooms are not the biggest around; no meals apart from breakfast available. ⑤ *Rooms from: R680* ✉ *122 High St.* ☎ *046/622–8284* ⊕ *www.highcorner.co.za* ⤵ *5 suites, 2 apartments* ⍟ *Breakfast.*

KWANDWE PRIVATE GAME RESERVE

38 km (24 miles) northeast of Grahamstown.

GETTING HERE AND AROUND

Kwandwe is a 30-minute drive from Grahamstown, and air and road shuttles are available from Port Elizabeth, which is a 1½-hour drive.

EXPLORING

Kwandwe Private Game Reserve. Kwandwe Private Game Reserve is tucked away in the Eastern Cape, near the quaint, historic cathedral city of Grahamstown. Little more than a decade ago, the area was ravaged farmland and goat-ridden semidesert. Today it is a conservation triumph—more than 55,000 acres of various vegetation types and scenic diversity, including rocky outcrops, great plains, thorn thickets, forests, desert scrub, and the Great Fish River—that's home to more than 7,000 mammals, including the Big Five. Your chances of seeing the elusive black rhino are very good, and it's likely you'll see fauna you don't always see elsewhere, such as black wildebeest and the endangered blue crane (*Kwandwe* means "place of the blue crane" in Xhosa). If you come in winter, you'll see one of nature's finest floral displays, when thousands of scarlet, orange, and fiery-red aloes are in bloom, attended by colorful sunbirds. The reserve also has a strong focus on community development, as evinced by the Community Centre and village within the reserve, both of which are worth a visit. ☎ *046/603-3400* ⊕ *www. kwandwe.com.*

WHERE TO STAY

There are four great places to stay within the reserve; guests can choose between classic colonial or modern chic. You'll be cosseted, pampered, well fed, and taken on some memorable wildlife adventures. Kwandwe is a member of the prestigious Relais & Châteaux group. All the lodges listed here have cable TV in a communal area as well as a safari shop, and massages are available upon request. The child-friendly lodges have movies and games. In the single-use lodges, these are hidden away in a cupboard, so you can keep their existence a secret from your brood unless a rainy day makes them essential.

$$$$
RESORT

☷ **Ecca Lodge.** This classy lodge combines understated modern elegance with vibrant African colors. **Pros:** superb food; an extensive self-service bar; magnificent open outdoor and indoor showers. **Cons:** some guides are young and slightly inexperienced; service can be a little disorganised; the lounge can feel big and impersonal. ⑤ *Rooms from: R9875 ⊠ Kwandwe Private Game Reserve ☎ 046/603–3400 ⊕ www. kwandwe.com ⇩ 6 rooms* ⦿ *All meals.*

$$$$
RESORT
Fodor's Choice
★

☷ **Great Fish River Lodge.** If you have an artistic eye, you'll immediately notice how the curving thatch roof of the main buildings echoes the mountain skyline opposite. **Pros:** spectacular river views; unusual habitats (it's not often you find lions clambering up and down rocky outcrops); ultrafriendly staff. **Cons:** avoid if you're a bit unsteady as there are lots of tricky steps; also avoid if you don't like open camps and predators potentially wandering around the lodge at night. ⑤ *Rooms from: R9875 ⊠ Kwandwe Private Game Reserve ☎ 046/603–3400 ⊕ www.kwandwereserve.co.za ⇩ 9 suites* ⦿ *All meals.*

$$$$
RESORT

☷ **Melton Manor.** Slightly bigger than Uplands, the Manor accommodates up to eight guests and offers the same superb service and exclusivity. **Pros:** exclusivity deluxe; great food; great service. **Cons:** as you're in your own group you miss out on the opportunity to meet other lodge guests; unlike other Kwandwe lodges, there are no private plunge pools and decks; you can only book for a minimum of four people. ⑤ *Rooms from: R7900 ⊠ Kwandwe Private Game Reserve ☎ 046/603–3400 ⊕ www.kwandwereserve.co.za ⇩ 4 rooms* ⦿ *All meals.*

$$$$
RESORT

☷ **Uplands Homestead.** If you're a small family or a bunch of friends and want to have a genuine, very exclusive, out-of-Africa experience, then stay at this restored 1905 colonial farmhouse. **Pros:** perfect for that special family occasion or friends' reunion; great food and service. **Cons:** can only be booked for families or parties of up to six; the colonial nostalgia might be a little overwhelming for some. ⑤ *Rooms from: R7900 ⊠ Kwandwe Private Game Reserve ⊕ www.kwandwereserve. co.za ⇩ 3 rooms* ⦿ *All meals.*

SAMARA PRIVATE GAME RESERVE

55 km (34 miles) southeast of Graaff-Reinet; 258 km (160 miles) north of Port Elizabeth.

GETTING HERE AND AROUND

There are daily flights from Johannesburg, Durban, and Cape Town to Port Elizabeth. Air charters from Port Elizabeth to Samara (gravel airstrip) can be arranged on request; it's a 45-minute drive from the airstrip to the reserve. Transfers to and from the airport or airstrip can be arranged through the reserve.

The drive from Port Elizabeth should take about three hours. Take the R75 toward Graaff-Reinet for 258 km (160 miles). Turn right onto the R63 toward Pearston/Somerset East for 7 km (4 miles). Turn left onto the Petersburg gravel road and drive 23 km (14 miles) to reach Karoo Lodge.

EXPLORING

Samara Private Game Reserve. Nestled among 70,000 acres of achingly beautiful wilderness, Samara Private Game Reserve is located in a hidden valley deep in the Karoo Mountains of South Africa's Eastern Cape. Owners Sarah and Mark Tompkins opened the reserve in 2005 with a promise to return former farmland to its natural state. The malaria-free reserve now encompasses 11 former farms and is home to a variety of protected species that have been reintroduced, including cheetah, Cape mountain zebra, white rhino, giraffe, black wildebeest, and a variety of antelope; there are even meerkats and aardvarks. Because there aren't any big predators to pose a threat, rangers stop the trucks often and guests get a completely different safari experience on foot. The lack of predators also makes this a great place for families with children. ⊠ *Samara Private Game Reserve* ☎ *023/626–6113* ⊕ *www.samara.co.za.*

WHERE TO STAY

$$$$
ALL-INCLUSIVE
▦ **Karoo Lodge.** From the moment you reach this lovingly restored, 19th-century, green-roofed farmhouse set among purple mountains, 800-year-old trees, and rolling plains where cheetahs, rhinos, and giraffes roam, you'll forget another more stressful world even existed. **Pros:** unique beauty; exclusivity; great for families. **Cons:** lack of accessibility; Samara is not Big Five country, so some might find the game drives lacking. ⑤ *Rooms from: R5000* ⊠ *Samara Private Game Reserve* ☎ *023/626–6113* ⊕ *www.samara.co.za* ➳ *3 rooms, 3 suites* ⫿◎⫿ *All-inclusive.*

$$$$
ALL-INCLUSIVE
▦ **The Manor House.** If you're looking for the perfect place to share a safari with a group of people, then look no further. **Pros:** complete run of the house for your group; attentive personal staff; lunch in the bush is an experience you'll not soon forget. **Cons:** not close to major airports; climate can get very hot and dry; if you're after the Big Five, this is not for you. ⑤ *Rooms from: R9900* ⊠ *Samara Private Game Reserve* ☎ *023/626–6113* ⊕ *www.samara.co.za* ➳ *4 suites* ⫿◎⫿ *All-inclusive* ⟳ *4 guest minimum.*

AMATOLE

The Amatole region takes its name from the spectacular Amatola mountain range, which is home to a number of ancient indigenous forests, waterfalls, and rare flora and fauna, all presided over by impressive peaks that reach up to 5,905 feet above sea level. All of this sets the backdrop for the six-day Amatola hiking trail, one of the coun-

> **DID YOU KNOW?**
>
> East London is part of Buffalo City, the name given to the towns clustered in this area: East London, King William's Town, and Bhisho, the administrative center of the province.

try's best trails. There are also game parks, beautiful beaches, and a number of cultural pursuits to discover in Amatole, in addition to plenty of history. Aside from the region's important role in South Africa's anti-apartheid struggle, towns like Cathcart and Adelaide began their life as 19th-century British military outposts intended to defend the border of the Cape Colony and the white farmers in the area from the Xhosa nation to the east. One of the frequent border wars between these two sides was dubbed the Amatola War. There's still something distinctly reminiscent of rural England about parts of the region, and farming remains a central facet of life. As with the Wild Coast, there's certainly little risk of overdevelopment here.

East London, the largest city in the region, has excellent transport links with the rest of the country and is a good starting point for heading into the hinterland as well as joining the Wild Coast.

EAST LONDON

150 km (93 miles) east of Grahamstown.

The gateway to both the Wild Coast and Amatole, East London was built around the mouth of the Buffalo River, which forms South Africa's only river port. Although fairly urban, East London is still close to the rural heartland, so it retains a pleasantly small-town air. There's a great museum here, and you can take a half-day city tour, an escorted visit to a local township, or a full-day tour of a rural village (⇨ *Tours, below*). Although the beaches on the outskirts of the city are wonderful, those within the central business district are crowded and not very pleasant.

GETTING HERE AND AROUND

The East London airport has all the expected facilities. There's also an airport shuttle service called the Little Red Bus, which will drop you off at your hotel, but you'll need to book it in advance.

Greyhound and Intercape Mainliner have pretty reliable and reasonably priced bus services from the country's major cities, including Johannesburg and Cape Town, but the distances are long. The Mini-Lux minibus service also travels from Port Elizabeth to East London via Grahamstown. All the buses stop and depart from the coach terminal in town. A more convenient option is the Baz Bus, which travels to East London, Cintsa, and Coffee Bay and will drop you off at your lodgings. ⇨ *For information on buses, see Bus Travel in Travel Smart.*

It's easiest and best to tour this region by car. The major rental agencies have offices at East London's airport and in the city's downtown. One-way rentals are available. Roads are wide, often dual lane, and well maintained. Northeast of East London there are long sections of road that are relatively broad and well maintained, but they are all unfenced—meaning livestock can wander onto the road—and some stretches have potholes. ⇨ *For information on car rentals, see Car Travel in Travel Smart.*

TOURS

Imonti Tours. Based in East London, Imonti Tours runs a three- to four-hour tour through the local township, including a visit to a sangoma (traditional healer) and a local shebeen where you can enjoy a braai (barbecue) lunch and drinks with the locals, and listen to some awesome jazz (R320). On Sunday, the tour includes a church visit. A tour of a rural Xhosa village takes the whole day and costs R420. Imonti's full-day Nelson Mandela Freedom Trail takes in Mandela's childhood home in Qunu and the Nelson Mandela Museum in Mthatha, as well as some beautiful Transkei scenery. The price is R750 per person for groups of four (two people minimum) and includes lunch. The Pride of Amatole Heritage Tour (R480) is another full-day tour that takes you to a number of sites related to the iconic Steve Biko, as well as to the historical town of Alice, where most of South Africa's greatest black political figures received their education. ☎ *083/487–8975* ⊕ *www.imontitours.co.za.*

Fodor's Choice **Wild Coast Holiday Reservations.** The Wild Coast has been a favorite
★ hiking destination for years, but the overnight huts have practically disintegrated. Perhaps they will be repaired, but until then you can take advantage of some good options—perhaps better than the original—offered by the East London–based Wild Coast Holiday Reservations. The Wild Coast Meander and the Wild Coast Amble are five- or six-day guided hikes during which you walk between hotels and/or resorts on the southern section of the coast. Farther north, the Hole-in-the-Wall and Wild Coast Pondo walks traverse more remote and less densely populated terrain. The Pondo Walk is a series of treks to and from a comfortable base camp over far more spectacular, but also much steeper, terrain than what you'll find on the other hikes. The trips are all catered, and you can arrange to have your luggage driven or portered. Costs start at R3,900 per person. Shorter walks can be organized by request. This really is the best of both worlds. You walk on deserted beaches during the day and stay in comfy hotels with all the modern conveniences at night. ☎ *043/743–6181* ⊕ *www.wildcoastholidays.co.za.*

VISITOR INFORMATION

Tourism Buffalo City, in East London, is open weekdays 8–4:30.

Contacts Tourism Buffalo City ⊠ *Fire Station, Fleet St., 2nd fl.* ☎ *043/736–3019* ⊕ *www.bctourism.co.za.*

EXPLORING

East London Museum. There's definitely something fishy going on at the East London Museum. In addition to a whole section on the discovery of the coelacanth, the museum has a large display of preserved fish, including an enormous manta ray. For a different kind of fishy, check out what is claimed to be the world's only surviving dodo egg. *Jurassic Park,* here we come! Probably the most worthwhile exhibit, though, is the extensive beadwork collection; it's culturally interesting and just plain beautiful. ✉ *319 Oxford St.* ☎ *043/743–0686* ⊕ *www.elmuseum. za.org* 🎫 *R15* ⊙ *Weekdays 9–4.*

Steve Biko Heritage Centre. The state-of-the-art heritage center, which opened in 2012, is in King William's Town's Ginsberg township, where Steve Biko grew up. It's actually about a 40-minute drive out of East London, but it's well worth a visit for anyone interested in South Africa's "struggle" history, as well as the development of its young democracy. There's a museum, an archive, a library resource center, a commemorative garden honoring human rights activists, performance and production spaces, training rooms, and a community media center. The center is also the focal point for a new heritage trail that consists of various sites that pay tribute to Steve Biko, the South African activist and leading Black Consciousness Movement proponent, who died in police custody in 1977 at the age of 31. Biko has often been held up as one of the greatest martyrs of the anti-apartheid movement. You can organize a tour from East London with Imonti Tours that will also incorporate lunch in the township. ✉ *1 Zotshie St., Ginsberg, King William's Town* ☎ *043/605–6700* ⊕ *www.sbf.org.za* 🎫 *Free* ⊙ *Weekdays 9–5, Sat. 9–1.*

BEACHES

East London is just far enough north of PE that the water and the weather are a bit warmer, but the inner-city beaches are not that great and would appeal more to surfers than to general loungers.

FAMILY **Gonubie Beach.** Gonubie Beach is at the mouth of the Gonubie River, about half an hour north east of the city. The riverbank is covered in dense forest, with giant *strelitzias* (wild banana trees) growing right to the water's edge. A lovely white sandy beach, tidal pools, and a 500-yard-long wooden walkway make this a fantastically user-friendly beach. It's also a good place to watch whales and dolphins, and compared to some of the more central beaches it's pretty quiet. There are picnic tables, fire pits, and a playground. **Amenities:** lifeguard; toilets; showers; food and drink; parking lot. **Best for:** swimming; walking. ✉ *Riverside Rd., Gonubie.*

Nahoon Beach. Nahoon Beach, at the mouth of the Nahoon River, is about a 10-minute drive from the city. There's some fantastic surf—but only for people who know what they're doing. It's also just a beautiful beach for sunbathing, watching surfers, and evening walks, and the lagoon is good for swimming and snorkeling. From the end of the beach nearest the lagoon you can look straight across to the Blue Lagoon Hotel on the other side of the water. The walk from the parking lot to the beach takes you through a beautiful forest, which helps make the beach feel secluded despite its proximity to the city. There are picnic tables, fire pits, and a playground, making a perfect spot for a braai. **Amenities:** lifeguards; toilets; food and drink; parking. **Best for:** walking; sunsets. ✉ *Beach Rd., Nahoon.*

WHERE TO EAT

$ ✕ **Buccaneers.** An East London institution, Buccaneers has been open
SOUTH AFRICAN   and under its current ownership since 1992, and not a lot has changed
FAMILY   here in the last twenty years or so: hearty and unpretentious pub fare
and atmosphere, lots of seafood, sports, draft beer a plenty, live music,
raucous student nights, and spectacular sea views from the big sun-
soaked wooden deck all remain the order of the day. The food and
service aren't great, and neither is the decor inside, but there's usually
plenty of atmosphere and on a hot, sunny Sunday afternoon it's an
absolute must, at least for a drink or two, especially if you're staying at
Sugarshack Backpackers next door. It's also a favorite with families and
it has kids' menu. $ *Average main: R85* ⊠ *Marina Glen, Beachfront*
☎ *043/743–5171* ⊕ *www.buccaneers.co.za.*

$ ✕ **Sanook.** This youthful, trendy, and very welcome newcomer to the
BURGER   East London dining scene is constantly busy and bustling thanks to its
Fodor's Choice   simple formula of good, well-presented gourmet burgers and great thin-
★   crust pizzas topped with only the freshest ingredients, combined with
sharp but always friendly service. The decor and layout of the place are
equally simple and effective, with heavy wooden tables and exposed
brick walls and pillars, and lots of air and light. There's also a bar area
with comfy couches and cushions. If the weather suits (which it generally does in these parts), you can eat outside in the courtyard. It can be
hard to get a table unless you book ahead, and the menu isn't the most
extensive, but the atmosphere is great, helped by the good selection of
South African craft beers as well as a decent wine list. $ *Average main:*
R95 ⊠ *11 Chamberlain Rd.* ☎ *043/721–3215* ⚓ *Reservations essential.*

WHERE TO STAY

$$ ⛱ **Blue Lagoon Hotel.** Overlooking the mouth of the beautiful Nahoon
HOTEL   River and within easy reach of Nahoon Beach, this is a great place for
FAMILY   a low-key family beach break. **Pros:** staff are friendly and warm; there's
an airport shuttle; location is hard to beat. **Cons:** it's a conference venue
so can get noisy; only the suites have river or sea views; service can
be a little disorganized. $ *Rooms from: R1600* ⊠ *17–19 Blue Bend*
Pl. ☎ *043/748–4821* ⊕ *www.bluelagoonhotel.co.za* ⇥ *67 rooms, 36*
suites ❙◎❙ *Breakfast.*

$ ⛱ **Meander Inn.** In the leafy suburb of Selborne, Meander Inn is close
B&B/INN   to the East London Museum, restaurants, and shops. **Pros:** pool and
gardens are lovely; good business facilities are available; there's an air-
port shuttle. **Cons:** groups about to embark on the Wild Coast Mean-
der stay here the night before, so it could get noisy; rooms don't have
air-conditioning or telephones. $ *Rooms from: R990* ⊠ *8 Clarendon*
Rd., Selborne ☎ *043/726–2310* ⊕ *www.meanderinn.co.za* ⇥ *10 rooms*
❙◎❙ *Breakfast.*

$ ⛱ **Stratfords Guest House.** It's worth staying at this friendly, stylish guest-
B&B/INN   house just to see the building, a masterpiece of design that makes excel-
lent use of space and utilizes unusual materials like corrugated iron,
bare concrete, wood, and glass in incredibly innovative ways to create a
comfortable, stimulating environment. **Pros:** the building is unusual and
was designed by the owner; the garden is sheltered from the elements;
the business facilities are superb. **Cons:** as it's a conferencing venue it

6

can get noisy; there are no meals available apart from breakfast; bathrooms are a little basic. $ Rooms from: R990 ✉ 31 Frere Rd., Vincent ☎ 043/726–9765 ⊕ www.stratfordsguesthouse.co.za ⤴ 11 rooms, 3 suites ⧖ Breakfast.

$ ⛱ **Sugarshack Backpackers.** The numerous wet suits and surfboards lying
B&B/INN   around make it clear that this fun, casual hostel is the place to go if you're after some waves. **Pros:** in easy walking distance of the bus station, or the Baz Bus will drop you off here; prices are very reasonable; views are great. **Cons:** no on-site restaurant; no meals included; kitchen/lounge area needs some serious TLC. $ Rooms from: R290 ✉ Eastern Beach, 50 Esplanade St. ☎ 043/722–8240 ⊕ www.sugarshack.co.za ⤴ 5 rooms without baths, 4 dormitories ⧖ No meals.

CINTSA

40 km (25 miles) northeast of East London.

This lovely, quiet little seaside town a half-hour drive from East London is a winner. A nice long beach, pretty rock pools, and a beautiful lagoon on which to paddle make this a coastal paradise. Not much happens here, which is its main attraction. The town—if it can be called a town—is divided by the river mouth into an eastern and a western side. It's a drive of about 10 km (6 miles) between them, although you can walk across the river at low tide (most of the time). The town has a couple of restaurants and small shops, plus a good choice of accommodations.

GETTING HERE AND AROUND

It's best to tour this area by car, and the road from East London to Cintsa is paved and in good condition. The Baz Bus drops passengers off in Cintsa. Intercape and Greyhound buses go as far as East London on the coast and then carry on slightly inland to Mthatha before rejoining the coast at Durban. Neither go via Cintsa.

TOURS

African Heartland Journeys. African Heartland Journeys arranges excellent tours into the Transkei and Wild Coast. They cost anywhere from R700 to R2,000 daily, depending on the nature of the trip and the number of guests. Tours generally focus on the people and culture but all include an element of adventure and are tailor-made to suit the needs, interests, and fitness levels of participants. You can choose to travel by vehicle, ATV, horse, canoe, mountain bike, on foot, or a combination thereof. Overnight accommodation may be in a village or at hotels—again, usually a combination of the two. The company also offers working holidays and volunteering programs focusing on education, conservation, and social betterment. ☎ 043/738–5523, 082/269–6421 ⊕ www.ahj.co.za.

WHERE TO STAY

$ ⛱ **Buccaneers Lodge and Backpackers.** Half hostel, half B&B, this very
RESORT   casual establishment is a shirts-and-shoes-optional sort of place, and it does get quite lively. **Pros:** has an airport shuttle; sociable environment; restaurant can cater for dietary restrictions. **Cons:** most activities are not run from the lodge itself; some accommodations can be a little

basic. $ *Rooms from: R310* ✉ *Vincent* ✛ *From the N2 toward Durban, follow signs for Wild Coast and Jikileza, take Cintsa West turnoff and follow signs for lodge on left* ☎ *043/734–3012* ⊕ *www.cintsa.com* ➡ *5 cottages, 8 suites* ⦿ *No meals.*

$$$$
RESORT
Fodor's Choice
★

▦ **Prana Lodge.** With seven luxury suites tucked away inside a thick, lush indigenous dune forest, the exclusive Prana Lodge is Cintsa's first and best luxury offering, and you won't find a much better spot in which to unwind anywhere in the Eastern Cape. **Pros:** fantastic relaxation and wellness location; you can organize a combined luxury "Bush Beach" experience in conjunction with Kwandwe Private Game Reserve; great for romantic getaways. **Cons:** service can be a little overzealous at times; it's a bit of a walk from the main reception area to some of the suites; vervet monkeys can be a nuisance. $ *Rooms from: R4200* ✉ *Chintsa Dr., Chintsa East* ☎ *043/704–5100* ⊕ *www.pranalodge.co.za* ➡ *7 suites* ⦿ *Breakfast.*

HOGSBACK

139 km (87 miles) northwest of East London; 170 km (105 miles) northwest of Cintsa.

This peaceful and picturesque village is the perfect place from which to embark on some of South Africa's best hiking trails and experience a number of its finest waterfalls and oldest Afro-montane forests. Hogsback allegedly takes its name from the shape of the three striking peaks that overlook the village, referred to as the Three Hogs. One of the village's earliest inhabitants was a gardener from Oxford by the name of Thomas Summerton, who set about trying to re-create the English countryside in his new homeland; he's responsible for many of the pretty gardens, apple orchards, and tree-lined avenues that give the village its distinctly rural English feel. Today, Hogsback has become a mecca for artists and artisans, as well as a few other endangered species. The village has long been associated with J. R. R. Tolkien's *Lord of the Rings*, though there is nothing to actually prove this connection. But spend some time in this magical place and it's not hard to see why the rumors might have gained so much credence.

GETTING HERE AND AROUND

As is the case throughout most of Amatole, it's best to tour this area by car, and the roads to and from East London (2 hours) and Cintsa (2½ hours) are pretty good for the most part, aside from the occasional pothole. The Baz Bus also runs services to Hogsback from East London. Once you're in the village itself, most of the points of interest are within walking distance of the accommodations.

WHERE TO STAY

$
B&B/INN

▦ **The Edge Mountain Retreat.** This property boasts some of the best views in Hogsback, as well as 15 acres of gardens, a range of self-catering cottages that are perfect for families or groups—some are perched right on the cliff's edge—and 10 simple but comfortable en suite rooms with rustic whitewashed walls. **Pros:** breathtaking views; there's a lot of space; great for families. **Cons:** food can be a little disappointing; it's not the easiest place to get to; service is a bit disorganized. $ *Rooms from:*

6

CLOSE UP

The Food Chain Up Close

Hailed by locals as "the greatest shoal on earth," the sardine run is, in terms of biomass, the world's largest animal migration. Cold water traveling up the coast moves closer to shore and brings with it untold millions of sardines (actually pilchards). These tiny fish are, of course, highly edible, so they have quite a following. Cape gannets, Cape fur seals, common and bottlenose dolphins, sharks, and Bryde's whales all follow this movable feast. The run coincides with the northern migration of the humpback whales, so the sea is teeming with life. Local fishing folk revel in the huge catches to be had simply by wading into the shallows with make-shift nets, and sightseers can watch for the bubbling water and attendant cloud of seabirds that signal shoals moving past.

There are boat trips aplenty to take you out for a closer look, but the real thrill is in diving the run. It's awesome just being amid all those fish, but you often are also among a thousand common dolphins. What everyone is really hoping for is a "baitball"— when dolphins herd a big school of sardines into a circle, keep them there by swimming around them, and pick them off at will. Sharks almost always join in, and an acrobatic seal or two might take advantage of the free lunch. Bryde's and even humpback whales have been known to take a (rather large) passing bite out of the ball, and the sight of Cape gannets from underwater as they dive-bomb the fish is memorable. African Dive Adventures (⊕ www.afridive.com) offers Sardine Run Packages along the Wild Coast from a base at Coffee Bay. Five nights and four days diving and food costs R25,500. The best time to see the run is usually between late June and late July.

R450 ⊠ Redcoat La., Hogsback ☎ 045/962–1159 ⊕ www.theedge-hogsback.co.za ⇆ 10 rooms, 12 cottages ⍩ Breakfast.

$ ⊞ **Nutwoods Park.** Nowhere better encapsulates the general feel of Hogs-
B&B/INN   back than this lovely old guesthouse, nestled amid 7 acres of beauti-
Fodor'sChoice   fully well-kept gardens with expansive views across the treetops to the
★   dramatic mountain peaks, and with easy access to all of Hogsback's outdoor pursuits. **Pros:** great location with lots of space and privacy; family-friendly options; prices are very reasonable. **Cons:** all meals must be arranged at least a day in advance; some of the room furnishings are a little gaudy. ⑤ Rooms from: R730 ⊠ Nutwoods Dr. and Orchard La., Hogsback ☎ 045/962–1043 ⊕ www.nutwoodspark.co.za ⇆ 2 suites, 2 cottages ⍩ Breakfast.

WILD COAST

As the name suggests, the Wild Coast is a haven of unspoiled wilderness. Whereas other areas of the country have become tourist playgrounds, the coast's lack of infrastructure has resulted in the large and mostly undeveloped swath of country east of Cintsa. The coastline consists of more than 280 km (174 miles) of desolate white-sand beaches, ragged cliffs, and secluded bays. Inland it's green and forested, with abundant birdlife. With mild year-round weather, this is a great destination for the adventure traveler.

To many, though, this part of the Eastern Cape is a glimpse of a very different South Africa. The mostly Xhosa population farm the land communally, domestic animals roam free, and traditional thatched *rondavel* huts dot the landscape. This is also one of South Africa's poorest regions, but the introduction of responsible tourism is helping to raise employment levels while simultaneously giving visitors unique insights into the traditional Xhosa culture.

BULUNGULA

295 km (183 miles) northeast of East London.

Bulungula is a tiny community near the mouth of the Bulungula River, about a 25-km (16-mile) walk from Coffee Bay's Hole-in-the-Wall. There are no shops, no banks, and no post office. There isn't even a decent road. The one lodge is run in partnership with the local community, making it a completely different destination for adventure travelers. Bulungula is a great place to just chill out on the beach, but there are also loads of great activities—all owned and run by members of the community in conjunction with the lodge. You can choose from a horseback ride, a canoe or fishing trip, an educational walk through the bush with an herbalist, a visit to a local restaurant, or a day spent with the women of the village, learning how they live. You might learn to carry water and firewood on your head, harvest wild foods and cook them for your lunch, make mud bricks, work in the fields, or weave baskets.

This is a really worthwhile destination, although it's not for everyone. But because Bulungula is such a small, isolated community, crime is practically nonexistent and it is very safe.

GETTING HERE AND AROUND

You'll need to travel on unpaved roads to get to Bulungula. The driving time from East London is 4½ hours. The lodge will provide you with a detailed map if you're driving yourself. Your best bet is to leave your car in the secure parking provided by the lodge at a small grocery store about 1½ km (1 mile) away, from which you can walk to the lodge (downhill for 45 minutes) or be picked up. If you arrive after 5 pm, leave your vehicle at the larger grocery store 15 km (9 miles) away and arrange for a pickup, as it's not advisable to drive the dirt road in the dark. In both instances, the owners of the stores will look after your vehicles for R15 per night. The lodge also runs a shuttle service to and from the bus stop at Mthatha.

WHERE TO STAY

$ **Bulungula Lodge.** Even though it is relatively isolated, Bulungula's one lodge is, in spirit, just an extension of the village. **Pros:** interaction with local Xhosa people means you learn a lot about their culture; eco-friendly credentials; warm and friendly staff. **Cons:** accommodation is simple and low on creature comforts; not much privacy or solitude. ⑤ *Rooms from: R370* ⊠ *Bulungula River Mouth, Nqileni Village,*

HOTEL
Fodor's Choice
★

6

Mthatha ☎ *047/577–8900, 083/391–5525* ⊕ *www.bulungula.com* ⤶ *10 rooms* ⊘| *No meals.*

COFFEE BAY

295 km (183 miles) northeast of East London.

The village of Coffee Bay is a bit run-down, but the beaches and the scenery are great. (The surf is fantastic, but don't head out alone if you don't know what you're doing.)

You can do a fabulous 37-km (23-mile) hike from Coffee Bay to Bulungula (or vice versa) via Hole-in-the-Wall, across the cliff tops, and along the beach. It's best to take a guide, who can cut about two or three hours from the journey by taking a shortcut through rolling hills dotted with thatched huts. Arrange for a guide through Bulungula Lodge *(⇨ above)*, where you should plan to overnight at the end of your hike; the lodge can transport your luggage while you walk. The cost for the guide and luggage transfer is R70 (R50 going from Bulungula to Coffee Bay).

GETTING HERE AND AROUND
Coffee Bay is about 1½ hours from Mthatha. Greyhound buses and the Baz Bus stop at the Shell Ultra City just outside the town. The Coffee Shack *(⇨ below)* will also pick guests up from here (R70 each way). Otherwise, local minibus taxis run from Mthatha to Coffee Bay for about R50 one way. They leave from the taxi stand in the center of town and change at Mqanduli, a small town on the way. They are a cheap and convenient way of getting around but are not always the safest option.

If you are driving, take the N2 to Viedgesville (about 20 km [12 miles] south of Mthatha) and then follow signs for Coffee Bay road. The coastal road is paved, but there are lots of potholes, and you're advised to travel only during daylight. The drive takes about 3½ hours from East London.

Coffee Bay itself is small, so you can walk to most places or take local minibus taxis to get around.

EXPLORING
Hole-in-the-Wall. What makes Coffee Bay stand out from all the other lovely destinations, though, is its proximity—only 9 km (5½ miles)—to the spectacular Hole-in-the-Wall, a natural sea arch through a solid rock island. You can go here on a rather adventurous road from Coffee Bay, and it's included on almost any tour of the Wild Coast. The Xhosa name, Esikaleni, means "place of the water people," and it is believed to be a gateway to the world of our ancestors. If you try swimming through it in rough seas, it certainly will be, but some intrepid souls have made it on calm (very calm) days. ⊠ *African Dive Adventures* ⊹ *9 km (5.6 miles) south of Coffee Bay, along coastal path.*

WHERE TO STAY
$ ⊞ **Coffee Shack on the Beach.** The main (but certainly not the only) attrac-
B&B/INN   tion of this vibey backpackers' lodge are the surfing lessons (R50 for two hours, including surfboard and wet suit)—possibly from former world pro-am surfing champion Dave Malherbe, who moved here so he could surf the perfect wave whenever he wanted. **Pros:** surf lessons

are great value; stay for four nights and get the fifth free throughout the year; dinner is free on a Sunday night. **Cons:** can have a noisy, party atmosphere; although quieter accommodation is located across the river; you need to book ahead; no meals are included in your room rates. $ *Rooms from: R350* ⊠ *Bomvu Beach, Mqanduli* ☎ *047/575–2048, 083/656–4350 mobile* ⊕ *www.coffeeshack.co.za* ⇨ *9 rooms* ⦿ *No meals.*

$$ ⛱ **Ocean View Hotel.** This old Wild Coast hotel is light and bright, with

HOTEL white walls and blue fabrics with marine motifs. **Pros:** child-friendly;

FAMILY there are tons of adventure activities to participate in; the hotel is close to the beach. **Cons:** rooms are basic but comfortable; it's a family resort, so there may be children around; service is not always the friendliest. $ *Rooms from: R2500* ⊠ *Main Beach* ☎ *047/575–2005, 047/575–2006* ⊕ *www.oceanview.co.za* ⇨ *30 rooms* ⦿ *Some meals.*

MTHATHA

295 km (183 miles) northeast of East London; 100 km (62 miles) northwest of Coffee Bay.

Mthatha is largely poor and overcrowded, and a little dilapidated, though it's certainly not boring. Most people don't stay here beyond making a travel connection elsewhere; strangely, accommodation here is generally very expensive too. However, if you're traveling on your own and have some free time, be sure to see the Nelson Mandela Museum in town, as well as the center at Qunu about 19 km (12 miles) outside the city. The museum can arrange a tour for you, which is advised. And if you want some good, cheap local food, try one of the numerous large storage containers around the center of Mthatha that serve as makeshift (and very popular) restaurants.

GETTING HERE AND AROUND

Because Mthatha is a really small airport, it doesn't have all the expected facilities. Greyhound and Baz Bus drop passengers off at the Shell Ultra City just outside Mthatha. You can rent a car from either Avis or Budget. ⇨ *For information on buses, see Bus Travel in Travel Smart. For information on car-rental agencies, see Car Travel in Travel Smart."*

EXPLORING

Nelson Mandela Museum. The Nelson Mandela Museum stands as evidence of the love and respect that this awesome statesman inspired in people all over the world, from rural schoolchildren to royalty. The many gifts Mandela received through his life say more about the givers than the receiver, and the exhibitions display the political and personal journey of this beloved politician. In addition to the building in Mthatha, there are three other sites. **Qunu,** the area where Mandela spent part of his childhood, was also the site of his family residence in the years prior to his death; the house can be seen from the N2, 32 km (20 miles) south of Mthatha, as can his grave on the hill inside the property behind the house. On another hill on the opposite side of the road is the Nelson Mandela Youth and Heritage centre, a beautifully designed building that combines natural stone and unfinished wattle branches to create an interesting pattern of light and shade that complements the black-and-white photographs documenting Mandela's early life and his period of activism and incarceration. There's also a reconstruction of his prison cell on Robben Island. Huge glass windows overlook the fields where Madiba (an affectionate sobriquet for Mandela) herded cattle as a boy, and you can also take a short walk to a smooth rock face that he and his young friends used to use as a slide, and maybe even have a go at it yourself. **Mvezo** was the birthplace of Mandela. Although the foundations of the house in which Mandela was born are visible and there is a small open-air museum, Mvezo is more a place of pilgrimage than a museum (since there isn't very much to see here). It's best to visit Mvezo as part of a tour—both because it's hard to find and because you'll get much more out of it with a knowledgeable guide—which you can arrange through the museum, or with Imonti Tours. But you can get directions from the museum in Mthatha if you want to go on your own. You'll need to travel down a 19 km (12 miles) gravel road, but a 4x4 is not required. You can take a similar gravel road north of the N2 to **Mqhekezweni**, which is where Mandela went to live with his cousin under the guardianship of Jongintaba Dalindyebo, regent of the Tembu people, and where he began his education. The rondavel he and his cousin shared remains exactly as it would have been then, as does the great tree where Mandela used to sneak up and secretly listen to the elders during their meetings. ■ TIP→ **It's possible to visit the Nelson Mandela Museum on Saturday afternoon and Sunday if you make an arrangement in advance.** ✉ *Bhunga Bldg., Owen St. and Nelson Mandela Dr. (N2)* ☎ *047/532–5110* ⊕ *www.mandelamuseum.org.za* ✑ *Free* ⊙ *Weekdays 9–4, Sat. 9–noon.*

7

DURBAN AND
KWAZULU-NATAL

Updated
by Christine
Marot and
Kate Turkington

Durban isn't slick or sophisticated, but 320 days of sunshine a year entices visitors and locals alike to the vast stretches of beautiful beach that hug the coastline. The proximity to the beach has given the province's largest city a laid-back vibe that makes it a perfect vacation destination and the ideal springboard from which to visit the diverse beauty of the rest of the province of KwaZulu-Natal.

As one of the few natural harbors on Africa's east coast, Durban developed as a port city after the first European settlers landed in 1824 with the intention of establishing a trading post. It's the busiest port in South Africa, as it exports large volumes of sugar and is home to the country's largest import/export facility for the motor industry. The port also has a passenger terminal for cruise liners that operate mostly between November and May.

The city's Golden Mile (an area much larger than the name implies) consists of high-rise hotels flanked by a popular promenade and beaches, with the Moses Mabhida Stadium in the background. The colonial-inspired suburbs of Berea and Morningside overlook the city and offer boutique hotels and packed restaurants.

Residential and upscale commercial development has seen coastal spots like Umhlanga to the north earn cult status with tourists, and collections of small villages along both the north and south coasts have access to pristine beaches. Add to the mix two World Heritage Sites (uKhahlamba-Drakensberg Park and iSimangaliso Wetland Park), and KwaZulu-Natal itself embodies South Africa's mantra: the world in one country. More important, it's truly representative of South Africa's rainbow nation.

KwaZulu-Natal—commonly referred to as KZN—is a premier vacation area for South Africans, and, despite being a comparatively small province, has the country's second-largest province population, at more than 10 million people. It's all but impossible to resist the subtropical climate and the warm waters of the Indian Ocean. In fact, the entire 480-km (300-mile) coastline, from the Wild Coast in the south to the Mozambique border in the north, is essentially one long beach, attracting hordes of swimmers, surfers, and anglers.

KwaZulu-Natal's two-part moniker is just one of the many changes introduced since the 1994 democratic elections. Previously the province was known simply as Natal (Portuguese for "Christmas"), a name bestowed by explorer Vasco da Gama, who sighted the coastline on Christmas Day in 1497. KwaZulu, "the place of the Zulu," was one of the nominally independent homelands created by the Nationalist government (1948–94), but with the arrival of democratic South Africa the two were merged to form KwaZulu-Natal. The province is now defined as the Kingdom of the Zulu, and the local Zulu population (about 2.2 million) is characterized by warm hospitality and friendly smiles. The Indian population—originally brought here by the British in the late 1860s as indentured laborers to cut sugarcane—has also made an indelible mark and now represents about 1 million of Durban's total population of 3.5 million.

ORIENTATION AND PLANNING

GETTING ORIENTED

Hugging the country's east coast, Durban's requisite amount of sunshine has earned the city the nickname "South Africa's playground." Here you'll find the colonial-inspired suburbs of Berea and Morningside, the coastal village of Umhlanga, and the warm waters and vacation towns that populate the areas known as the Dolphin Coast and South Coast. Head inland to the KwaZulu-Natal Midlands and the dramatic Drakensberg Mountains for the antithesis of coastal beauty. Farther north you'll find the Battlefields and Zululand that portray the province's bloody history, as well as the Big Five (lion, elephant, Cape buffalo, leopard, rhinoceros) roaming in various game reserves.

Durban. South Africa's third-largest city, Durban is southern Africa's busiest port (chiefly cargo). The city's chief appeal to tourists is its long strip of high-rise hotels and its popular promenade—known as the Golden Mile (though it's actually several miles long)—fronting its beaches.

Side Trips from Durban. To find beaches unmarred by commercial development, you need to travel north to the Dolphin Coast or south to the aptly named South Coast. Moving inland takes you to the KwaZulu-Natal Midlands, just off the N3 between Durban and Johannesburg. Here racehorse and dairy farms stud rolling green hills and lush pastures that are reminiscent of England. The Midlands Meander (a series of routes set up by the local tourism board) is a great way to experience the area's farms and crafts shops.

Zululand and the Battlefields. Zululand, the region north of the Tugela River and south of Swaziland and Mozambique, is the traditional home of the Zulu people. Prominent towns (though these are all relatively small) in this region are the industrial towns of Empangeni and Richards Bay, Eshowe, Pongola, and Ulundi. The farther north you go, the less populated and more rural the area becomes, with traditional Zulu huts and herds of long-horn brown-and-white and black-and-white Nguni cattle, tended by boys or young men, scattered over the hills.

The Battlefields (Anglo-Zulu and Anglo-Boer) are inland, to the north of the Midlands and northeast of the Drakensberg. The towns dotted among the Zululand battlefields tend to be a little ugly and dusty during the dry winter months, but this is an area to visit more for its historic than its scenic value.

SWAZILAND

MOZAMBIQUE

KwaZulu–
Natal

N2

Ithala
Game
Reserve

Phongola

Jozini

Phongola

Maputaland
Coastal Forest
Reserve

Louwsburg

Mkuze

Amazulu Private
Game Reserve

uMkhuze
KZN
Park

Phinda
Private
Game
Reserve

ELEPHANT COAST

Nongoma

Msunduze

Black Umfolozi

R66

Thanda Private
Game Reserve

Hluhluwe

ZULULAND

N2

Simangaliso
Wetland Park

Hluhluwe-iMfolozi
Game Reserve

Cape Vidal

White Umfolozi

St. Lucia

2

Mtubatuba

R34

Ngwelezana

Empangeni

Shakaland

Richards Bay

Ezikhawini

Gingindlovu

N2

Dolphin Coast

Dukuza

INDIAN OCEAN

Umhlanga
see detail
map

0   30 miles

0   30 kilometers

TOP REASONS TO GO

Beautiful Beaches: Durban's beaches are some of the world's safest and most beautiful. The long, sandy beaches and inviting water temperatures extend all the way up the Dolphin (north) Coast and beyond, as well as south from Durban, down the Sapphire Coast, the Hibiscus Coast, and into the Eastern Cape.

Reliving History: Explore the battlefields of the Anglo-Zulu and Anglo-Boer wars, making sure you visit the legendary sites of Isandlwana, Rorke's Drift, and Blood River.

Game-Viewing: Although smaller than Kruger, the easily accessible Hluhluwe-iMfolozi Park, Mkuze,

Ithala (aka Itala), and Pongola game reserves are all teeming with game, including the Big Five.

Amazing Natural Wonders: KZN has two World Heritage Sites—the uKhahlamba-Drakensberg and iSimangaliso Wetland Park—as well as numerous game reserves.

A Vibrant City: Durban, Africa's busiest port, has a distinct feel, flavored by its diverse populations. In the city center, you'll find mosques, temples, and churches. Take a rickshaw ride along the beachfront after browsing for Zulu beadwork, or try a local "bunny chow" (curry inside a hollowed-out loaf of bread).

PLANNING

WHEN TO GO

The height of summer (December and January) brings heat, humidity, higher prices, and crowds, who pour into "Durbs," as it's fondly known, by the millions. Locals know never to brave the beach on holidays or over the Christmas season except for an hour or two from 6 AM—one of the nicest times there. June and July are Durban's driest months, and although you can never predict the weather, expect warm, dry days and cool nights.

The best time to tour KwaZulu-Natal is early autumn through winter and into spring (April to October), with the coast particularly pleasant in winter—you'll see people swimming. April is a lovely time to visit the city (avoid Easter weekend if you can), with warm air and sea temperatures.

Some facilities in the Zululand game reserves close in summer because of the extreme and unpleasantly high temperatures.

FESTIVALS

In addition to choosing the right season, it's worth considering timing your visit to coincide with one or more of the exciting events hosted within this region.

Comrades Marathon. This is the world's oldest and largest ultramarathon—approximately 90 km (56 miles) between Pietermaritzburg and Durban, the race route changes annually. It's a South African institution, creating an unparalleled camaraderie between runners. Many runners have earned their 'life' permanent race number, after competing in the grueling marathon 10 times. ✉ *Durban* ☎ *033/897–8650* ⊕ *www.comrades.com.*

Durban July. South Africa's most prestigious horse race sees tens of thousands of spectators descend on Greyville Racecourse to partake in one of the year's biggest social events and to watch the ponies run.

Fashionistas have a day in the sun as they compete for "best-dressed" prizes. ✉ *Greyville Racecourse, 150 Avondale Rd., Durban* ☎ *031/314–1651* ⊕ *www.vodacomdurbanjuly.co.za.*

Dusi Canoe Marathon. Paddlers compete in this 120-km (76-mile) kayak race between Pietermaritzburg and Durban along the Msindusi (Dusi) River. It's regarded as one of the toughest canoe events in the world and takes place over three days. The race is run by Natal Canoe Club. ☎ *033/394–9994, 033/342–1528* ⊕ *www.dusi.co.za.*

Mr Price PRO. Around the end of June and the beginning of July, top surfers and surfing fans head to Ballito for one of the longest-running professional surfing events in the world, established in 1969. ✉ *Ballito* ☎ *031/310–8000* ⊕ *www.mrpricepro.com.*

Sardine Run. Dubbed "The Greatest Shoal on Earth," the Sardine Run is regarded as one of nature's most amazing migrations. Starting along the South Coast and moving up to Durban, sardine shoals of 20–30 km (12–18 miles) are followed by some 23,000 dolphins, 500 whales, 1,000 sharks and countless birds. The spectacle can be viewed from the beach or at various dive spots. You can even grab a bucket and catch your own dinner. Ancillary events take place on land. ✉ *Durban* ☎ *039/682–7944 South Coast Tourism Information* ⊕ *www.sardinerun.co.za.*

Splashy Fen. South Africa's longest-running and most renowned annual music festival showcases the country's top bands, famous performers, and up-and-coming musicians. The outdoor event takes place every Easter long weekend on a Midlands farm. It's great fun, has great music and a great vibe—think a bonsai Woodstock. ✉ *Bushmansnek Rd., Underberg* ☎ *031/563–0824, 078/065–9389 24-hr line* ⊕ *www. splashyfen.co.za.*

PLANNING YOUR TIME

2 Days: If you have just two days, spend it in Durban. Start with an early morning walk along the Golden Mile to watch the surfers. ⚠ **Always leave jewelry and valuables in your hotel safe.** Spend three or four hours on a guided walking tour of the Indian District or downtown Durban. Tours (reservations are a must) leave from the Tourist Junction (Old Station Building). Wilson's Wharf, which overlooks the Durban harbor, and Morningside's trendy Florida Road offer great options for lunch or dinner. If you dine on Florida Road, make sure you stop by the African Arts Market for beautiful Zulu beadwork, baskets, prints, and other crafts and curios. You can also spend the afternoon strolling around Mitchell Park, which is known for its colorful flower beds at the top of Florida Road (also be sure to visit the small zoo here). On your second day, visit the aquarium at uShaka Marine World, one of the largest and best in the world, perhaps lunching on seafood at Cargo Hold, adjacent to the shark tank. In the afternoon, visit the Natal Sharks Board for a show and fascinating shark dissection—yes, they actually do a dissection (Tuesday–Thursday only). You could also visit the Umgeni River Bird Park, whose live bird shows are a must-see (11 and 2 daily, except Monday).

5 Days: Spend at least one day in Durban *(see above)* before or after you explore KwaZulu-Natal following the Zululand and the more northern section option, which takes in the coastal strip and some of the northern game parks and private lodges. Start out with a tour of the battlefield sites of Isandlwana, Rorke's Drift, and the Talana Museum at Dundee. Afterward, travel north and take the R103 to pick up the Midlands Meander, which stretches north all the way to Mooi River, through the tranquil KZN Midlands.

If you decide to head up the north coast, spend a night at Shakaland or Simunye Zulu Lodge to get the total Zulu cultural experience. Then schedule at least two days in Hluhluwe-iMfolozi Park or Phinda Private Game Reserve to see the wildlife for which these reserves are known. A trip to iSimangaliso Wetland Park to see hippos and crocodiles in the wild is another great experience.

7–10 Days: Spend a day or two exploring Durban and Umhlanga and then head up to Zululand to start your grand loop. Visit iSimangaliso Wetland Park on your way to the incredible wildlife of Hluhluwe-iMfolozi Park or Phinda Private Game Reserve. A three-day trek in the wilderness of iMfolozi could be the high point of your trip. For something more sedate, spend three days at Rocktail Beach Camp in the Maputaland Coastal Reserve, close to the Mozambique border; it's especially interesting during turtle-breeding season, November through early March. Another distant park near the edge of the province is the delightful, less-visited Ithala Game Reserve. On the way back to Durban, drive through the battlefields.

GETTING HERE AND AROUND
AIR TRAVEL
Durban's King Shaka International Airport, at La Mercy, on the north coast, became operational in 2010 and is three times the size of the old airport. About 17 km (11 miles) from Umhlanga and about 32 km (20 miles) north of Durban, it operates under the management of the Airports Company South Africa.

South African Airways (SAA) flies to Durban via Johannesburg. Domestic airlines serving Durban are SAA, BA/Comair, Kulula, SA Express, SA Airlink, and Mango. Perhaps the easiest way to book a ticket to or from Durban is online. Kulula and Mango are the budget-priced airlines, so expect to buy your own snacks and drinks on board. SAA is usually the more expensive option, unless you're looking for a ticket at short notice (next day or two), when it may turn out to offer the lowest price.

The most inexpensive ground transfer into Durban and back is the Airport Shuttle Service, which costs R70 and departs every 30 to 45 minutes after incoming flights arrive and leaves the city center every hour. Its drop-off points are flexible within the city and include all hotels on the North Beach and South Beach, the Central Business District, the International Convention Centre, and the Moses Mabhida Stadium. On request, the driver is likely to drop you anywhere en route. Call ahead and the bus will pick you up at any hotel in the city; there's no need to reserve for the trip into Durban. A taxi ride into Durban will cost around R4450. If you plan to go farther afield, call Magic Transfers or catch a cab from outside the terminal building. ⇨ *For airline contact information see Air Travel in Travel Smart South Africa.*

Airports Airports Company South Africa ☏ *011/921–6262* ⊕ *www.acsa. co.za.* **King Shaka International Airport** ☏ *011/921–6262* ⊕ *kingshakainternational.co.za.*

Airport Transfers Airport Shuttle Service ☏ *031/465–5573.* **Aqua Tours** ☏ *082/410–7116* ⊕ *www.aquatours.co.za.* **Magic Transfers** ☏ *031/263–2647.*

BUS TRAVEL

Greyhound and Translux Transfers offer long-distance bus service to cities all over South Africa from Durban. All intercity buses leave from the Durban Station on Masabalala Yengwa Avenue (N.M.R. Avenue), between Archie Gumede Road (Old Fort Road) and Sandile Thusi Road (Argyle Road). Bear in mind that you can often fly for much the same prices as traveling by bus, especially if you book well in advance or find a discount.

Three primary bus services are available in and around the city: Durban Transport, Mynah, and People Mover buses, operated by eThekwini Transport Authority. All of the fleet's buses are air-conditioned and equipped with electronic ramps for wheelchair access and strollers. All bus stops are staffed by security people. Small Mynah buses are ideal for short trips within the inner city, costing a couple of rand per ride; you pay as you board and exact change isn't required. Larger, more comfortable People Mover buses make longer city trips, including to the Golden Mile, the Central Business District (aka CBD), and out to the beachfront and back; fares are R5.50 per ride or R16 for a day pass, and buses arrive every 15 minutes between 6:30 am and 10 pm. Durban Transport services city-to-suburb routes. If you plan to make frequent use of public transportation, it would be worth investing in a Muvo Card. This is a single secure smartcard that can be used interchangeably across the three bus lines. Call Muvo at ☏ *080/000–6886.*

The main bus depot is on Monty Naicker Road (Pine Street) between Samora Machel (Aliwal) and Dorothy Nyembe (Gardiner) streets. Route information is also available at an information office at the corner of Samora Machel Street and Monty Naicker Road.

Contacts eThekwini Transport Authority (*Durban City Transport*). ☏ *031/309–3250* ⊕ *www.durban.gov.za.*

CAR TRAVEL

Durban is relatively easy to navigate because the sea is a constant reference point. Downtown Durban is dominated by two parallel one-way streets, Dr. Pixley kaSeme Street (West Street) going toward the sea and Anton Lembede Street (Smith Street) going away from the sea, toward Berea and Pietermaritzburg; together they get you in and out of the city center easily. Parking downtown is a nightmare; head for an underground garage whenever you can. As with the rest of South Africa, wherever you go, self-appointed car guards will ask if they can watch your car. The going rate for a tip—if you want to give one—is R5, depending on how long you're away. The guards directly outside Joe Kool's, between North and South beaches, are said to be very trustworthy. ⚠ **Don't leave your keys with anyone.**

The M4 (Ruth First Highway), which stretches north up to the Dolphin Coast—from Umhlanga to Ballito, about 40 km (25 miles) and beyond—is a particularly pretty coastal road, offering many views of the sea through lush natural vegetation and sugarcane fields. It's much nicer than the sterile N2 highway, which takes a parallel path slightly inland and offers no views.

Avis, Budget, Europcar, and Tempest have rental offices at the airport. Rates start at around R400 per day, including insurance and 200 km (125 miles), plus R2.10 per additional kilometer (half mile), or about R500 for the weekend. Avis offers unlimited mileage to international visitors, as long as you can produce your return ticket, international driver's license, and passport as proof.

RICKSHAW TRAVEL

Colorfully decorated rickshaws are unique to Durban—you won't find them in any other South African city. Though their origins lie in India, these two-seat carriages with large wheels are pulled exclusively by Zulu men dressed in feathered headgear and traditional garb. Limited to the beachfront, the rickshaw runners ply their trade all day, every day, mostly along the Golden Mile section. The going rate is R40 per person for about 15 minutes, and R15 for a photo (don't assume you can take a picture without paying for the privilege). Although it's worth doing because it will be memorable and you won't have the opportunity anywhere else, negotiate the rate before climbing on.

TAXI TRAVEL

Taxis are metered and start at R5, with an additional R12 per kilometer (half mile); after-hours and time-based charges apply. Fares are calculated per vehicle for up to four passengers. Expect to pay about R50 from City Hall to North Beach and R400 to Durban International Airport. The most convenient taxi stands are around City Hall, in front of the beach hotels, and outside Spiga d'Oro on Florida Road in Morningside. Some taxis display a "for-hire" light, whereas others you simply hail when you can see they're empty. Major taxi companies include Eagle Taxi, Mozzies, Umhlanga Cabs, and Zippy Cabs. If you're headed to the Indian Market on a weekend, consider having your taxi wait for you, as it can be difficult to flag a taxi in this neighborhood.

There's no need to contact a taxi yourself. They will either be easy to find or your hotel or restaurant can call one for you. Once a driver has dropped you off, he or she will usually give you a card so you have contact details for the return trip.

Contacts Umhlanga Cabs ☎ *031/561–1846.*

HOTEL AND RESTAURANT PRICES

WHAT IT COSTS IN SOUTH AFRICAN RAND			
	$	$$	$$$	$$$$
Restaurants	under R100	R100–R150	R151–R200	over R200
Hotels	under R1,500	R1,500–R2,500	R2,501–R3,500	over R3,500

Restaurant prices are the average cost of a main course at dinner or, if dinner is not served, at lunch. Hotel prices are the lowest cost of a standard double room in high season.

VISITOR INFORMATION

The Tourist Junction, in the restored Old Station Building, houses the Tourism KwaZulu-Natal offices, where you can find information about almost everything that's happening in the province of KwaZulu-Natal. It's open weekdays 8–4:30 and weekends 9–2. There's also a satellite office, conveniently located along the Golden Mile, one of the city's premier destinations. Sugar Coast Tourism (covering the Umhlanga and nearby Umdloti areas), is open weekdays 8:30–4:45 and Saturday 9–1, and Sapphire Coast Tourism (covering Amanzimtoti to Umkomaas) is open weekdays 8–4 and Saturday 9–2.

Contacts Durban Tourism Office ✉ *90 Florida Rd.* ☎ *031/322–4164* ⊕ *www. durbanexperience.co.za* ⊗ *Weekdays 8:30–5.* **Durban Tourism Beach Office** ✉ *1 K.E. Masinga Rd., Beachfront* ☎ *031/322–4173* ⊕ *www.durbanexperience. co.za.* **Sapphire Coast Tourism** ✉ *95 Beach Rd., Amanzimtoti* ☎ *031/903– 7498* ⊕ *www.sapphirecoasttourism.co.za.* **Sugar Coast Tourism** ✉ *Shop 1A, Chartwell Centre, 15 Chartwell Dr., Umhlanga* ☎ *031/561–4257* ⊕ *www. zulu.org.za.* **Tourism KwaZulu-Natal** ☎ *031/366–7500* ⊕ *www.zulu.org.za.* **Tourist Junction** ✉ *160 Monty Naicker Rd. (Pine St.), at Soldiers Way, City Centre* ☎ *031/366–7500* ⊕ *www.zulu.org.za.* **Umhlanga Tourism** ✉ *Chartwell Centre, 15 Chartwell Dr., shop 1A, Umhlanga* ☎ *031/561–4257* ⊕ *www. umhlangatourism.co.za.*

DURBAN

Updated by Christine Marot

Durban has the pulse, the look, and the complex face of Africa. It may have something to do with the summer heat, a clinging sauna that soaks you with sweat in minutes. If you wander into the Indian District or drive through the Warwick Triangle—an area away from the sea around Julius Nyerere (Warwick) Avenue—the pulsating city rises up to meet you. Traditional healers tout animal organs, vegetable and spice vendors crowd the sidewalks, and minibus taxis hoot incessantly as they trawl for business. It is by turns colorful, stimulating, and hypnotic.

It's also a place steeped in history and culture. Gandhi lived and practiced law here, and Winston Churchill visited as a young man. It's home to the largest number of Indians outside India; the massive Indian townships of Phoenix and Chatsworth stand as testimony to the harsh treatment Indians received during apartheid, though now thousands of Indians are professionals and businesspeople in Durban.

⚠ Street names have all been updated, but the old ones remain in brackets, as some maps and locals still refer to streets by the old names.

SAFETY AND PRECAUTIONS

Durban has not escaped the crime evident in every South African city. Particularly in the city center but also elsewhere, smash-and-grab thieves roam the streets, looking for bags or valuables in your car, even while you're driving, so lock any valuables in the trunk and keep your car doors locked and windows up at all times. Although there's no need to be fearful, be observant wherever you go. Hire a guide to take you around Durban, don't wander around the city center or outside your hotel alone at night, and keep expensive cameras and other possessions concealed. The Durban Beachfront (with recently upgraded security features), Umhlanga, and the outlying areas are safe to explore on your own, though you'll need a taxi or car to get between them. If you plan to take a dip while you're at the beach, ask a neighboring beachgoer or lifeguard to keep an eye on your belongings, or put them in a locker—available in the vicinity of North and South beaches and on Umhlanga Main Beach.

TOURS

Durban Tourism. Three-hour walking tours depart from the Tourist Junction on weekdays at 9:30 and 1:30: the Oriental Walkabout explores the Indian District, including Victoria Market and several mosques, and the Historical Walkabout covers major monuments and museums. Reservations are essential; a two person minimum applies. Durban Tourism can also provide details of various guided township tours by local tour operators, which offer an insight into the social history and modern-day challenges of the townships. ☎ *031/322–4164* ⊕ *www. durbanexperience.co.za* ✉ *R100.*

Isle of Capri. This company offers sightseeing cruises around Durban Bay or out to sea, plus whale- and dolphin-watching tours. Boats depart from Wilson's Wharf on Margaret Mncadi Avenue. ⊠ *14–18 Boatman's Rd., Canal Rd., Victoria Embankment* ☎ *031/305–3099* ⊕ *www. isleofcapri.co.za.*

Ricksha Bus Tours. An inexpensive way to see the main attractions Durban has to offer is to join one of the bus tours, operated by Durban Tourism. They depart daily at 9 am and 1 pm from the North Beach Tourism Office and take 2½–3 hours to complete the circuit. The route includes the Beachfront, uShaka Marine World, Emmanuel Cathedral, Victoria Market, Florida Road, City Hall, KwaMuhle Museum, Mitchell Park, Moses Mabhida Stadium, Suncoast Casino, and more, and a tour guide provides commentary en route. ☎ *031/322–4209* ✉ *R100.*

Sarie Marais Pleasure Cruises. Trips around the bay or out to sea are offered by this company. Half-hour harbour cruises run on the hour from 9–4 and hour-long sea cruises run noon–3 daily. Charters for up to 57 people are also available. ⊠ *Wilson's Wharf, 14–18 Boatman's Rd., Victoria Embankment* ☎ *031/305–4022* ⊕ *www.sariemaraiscruises. co.za* ✉ *Harbor cruise R80; sea cruise R120; private charter R2,500.*

EXPLORING

By no means should you plan an entire vacation around Durban, because there is so much more to see beyond the city. Nevertheless, it's definitely worth a stopover. To get the most from your visit, get ready to explore the Central Business District (CBD), which includes the Indian District; the Beachfront; and Berea and Morningside. If you're concerned about safety within the CBD, book tours through Tourist Junction.

CITY CENTER

The center of the city is indicative of South Africa's third-world status and first-world leanings. Large office buildings dominate streets filled with African taxis and buses, but every so often you'll stumble across a building that speaks of an imperial past. It can get horribly humid from December through February, so if you visit then, avoid walking too much during the midday heat. Browse the air-conditioned museums when it's hot, and save walking outside for later in the afternoon, making sure you get to the museums and galleries before they close, around 4:30.

TOP ATTRACTIONS

Durban Art Gallery. A vibrant, contemporary mix of local, southern African, and international work is presented here, though the main focus is on work from KwaZulu-Natal. Exhibits have included the cultural diversity of art and craft from KwaZulu-Natal and the rest of South Africa. Look out, too, for the traditional, patterned *hlabisa* baskets, regularly displayed at the gallery. Exhibits change every few months. ⊠ *City Hall, Anton Lembede (Smith) St. entrance, 2nd fl.* ☎ *031/311–2264* ⊕ *www.durban.gov.za/city_services/parksrecreation/durban_art_gallery/Pages/default.aspx* ⊠ *Free* ⊗ *Mon.–Sat. 8:30–4, Sun. 11–4.*

KwaMuhle Museum. Pronounced kwa-*moosh*-le (with a light *e*, as in *hen*), this small museum, housed in what used to be the notorious Department of Native Affairs, tells of Durban's apartheid history. During apartheid the department was responsible for administering the movement of black people in and out of the city, dealing with the dreaded passes that blacks had to carry at all times, and generally overseeing the oppressive laws that plagued the black population. Ironically, the name means "place of the good one," Kwa meaning "place of" and "Muhle" meaning "good one" (after J. S. Marwick, the benevolent manager of the municipal native affairs department from 1916 to 1920). Exhibits provide the often heartbreaking background on this period through old photographs and documents, replicas of passbooks, and lifelike models of people involved in the pass system, including *shebeen* (informal bar) queens, who had to apply for permits to sell alcohol at a time of prohibition. ⊠ *130 Bram Fischer (Ordnance) Rd.* ☎ *031/311–2223* ⊠ *Free* ⊗ *Mon.–Sat. 8:30–noon.*

WORTH NOTING

City Hall. Built in 1910 in Edwardian neo-baroque style, the hall looks as if it has been shipped straight from the United Kingdom column by column—hardly surprising, since it's an exact copy of Belfast City Hall. The main pediment carries sculptures representing Britannia, Unity, and

Durban

Patriotism, and allegorical sculptures of the arts, music, and literature adorn the exterior. City Hall houses not only the mayor's parlor and other government offices, but also the Durban Art Gallery, the Natural Science Museum, and the City Library. Ask the guard to let you in to see the huge theater's ornate molding and grand parterre boxes, or join an official tour run by City of Durban. ⊠ *Dr. Pixley kaSeme (West) and Church Sts.* ☎ *031/304–4934* ⊕ *www.durban.gov.za* ✉ *Free* ☉ *Daily 10–2.*

NEED A BREAK?

Royal Coffee Shoppe. This is a popular meeting place for daytime breaks and for pre- and posttheater crowds. Crystal chandeliers, etched glass, formally dressed staff, and live piano music in the nearby lounge at lunchtime create a rich atmosphere of old-time colonial Durban. The café serves light breakfasts and lunch as well as coffees, teas, cakes, quiches, salads, and sandwiches. ⊠ *Royal Hotel, 267 Anton Lembede (Smith) St.* ☎ *031/333–6000* ⊕ *www.theroyal.co.za.*

FAMILY **Durban Natural Science Museum.** Despite its small size, this museum provides an excellent introduction to Africa's numerous wild mammals (the displays include a stuffed elephant and leopard, as well as smaller mammals like wild dogs and vervet monkeys), plants, birds, reptiles, and insects. It's a great place to bring the kids or to familiarize yourself with the local wildlife before heading up to the game parks in northern KwaZulu-Natal. At one popular gallery, the KwaNunu Insect Arcade, giant insect replicas adorn the wall; another, the bird gallery, showcases a variety of stuffed birds, including flamingos, ostriches, eagles, and penguins. ⊠ *City Hall, Anton Lembede (Smith) and Church Sts., 1st fl.* ☎ *031/311–2256* ✉ *Free* ☉ *Mon.–Sat. 8:30–4, Sun. 11–4.*

Francis Farewell Square. In the heart of Durban, the square is a lovely shady plaza bordered by some of the city's most historic buildings, including City Hall, the Central Post Office, and the Royal Hotel. Walkways lined with stately palms and flower beds crisscross the square and lead to monuments honoring some of Natal's important historic figures. The square stands on the site of the first European encampment in Natal, established by Francis Farewell and Henry Fynn in 1824 as a trading station to purchase ivory from the Zulus. A statue representing Peace honors the Durban volunteers who died during the Second South African War (1899–1902), also known as the Boer War or Anglo-Boer War. The Cenotaph, a large stone obelisk, commemorates the South African dead from the two world wars. In the same block is the Old Court House Museum, one of the city's oldest buildings. Apart from the historic attractions, it's an energetic, bustling part of the city center, with inexpensive street stands selling flowers, clothes, and food for the locals. You'll really feel the vibe of the city here. ⚠ **Pay attention to your valuables while walking in the square.** ⊠ *Bounded by Anton Lembede (Smith), Dr. Pixley Kaseme (West), and Dorothy Nyembe (Gardiner) Sts. and the Church St. pedestrian mall* ⊕ *www.heritagekzn.co.za.*

Tourist Junction. The city's principal tourist information outlet occupies Durban's old train station, an attractive brick building constructed in 1894 in Flemish Revival style. The "NGR" above the main entrance

7

stands for Natal Government Railways. KwaZulu-Natal tourism authority also has a large office here, so it's a good place to pick up pamphlets and information about the city and province. ⌧ *160 Monty Naicker Rd. (Pine St.), at Soldier's Way* ☏ *031/366–7500* ⊕ *www.zulu. org.za* ⊙ *Weekdays 8–4:30.*

MORNINGSIDE

Dating back to Durban's colonial past, Morningside is an upscale suburb featuring prestigious residential properties such as the Dr John L Dube House, where the state president resides when in Durban. Below Jameson Park and Mitchell Park a slew of fashionable restaurants, boutique hotels, pubs, and clubs welcome patrons to trendy Florida Road.

WORTH NOTING

FAMILY   **Mitchell Park.** The magnificent rose garden, colorful floral displays, and leafy lawns here are a real treat on a hot summer day. Attached to the park is a small zoo, named after Sir Charles Mitchell, an early governor of Natal. It was opened at the turn of the 19th century, and the Aldabra tortoises that were donated to the park in the early 1900s—now massive—are still in residence. There are also small mammals, reptiles, tropical fish, and birds in large aviaries. The park has a popular playground, and the leafy terrace of the park's Blue Zoo Restaurant is a great place for breakfast or a light lunch. ⌧ *Bordered by Innes, Nimmo, and Ferndale Rds., and Havelock Crescent* ☏ *031/303–2275* ⌦ *Gardens free, zoo R10* ⊙ *Daily 8–4.*

NEED A
BREAK?

Vida e Caffè. Right across the street from Mitchell Park you'll find perfect coffees in various forms (accompanied by a piece of Lindt chocolate), and freshly squeezed orange juice, muffins, rolls, and a few pastries. ⌧ *Oakwood Centre, 465–471 Innes Rd., Shop 2* ☏ *031/312–4606* ⊕ *www. vidacaffe.co.za.*

BEACHFRONT

Of any place in Durban, the Beachfront most defines the city. Either you'll hate it for its commercial glitz, or love it for its endless activity. It extends for about 7 km (4½ miles) from uShaka Marine World, at the base of Durban Point, all the way past North Beach and the Suncoast Casino to Blue Lagoon, on the southern bank of the Umgeni River. The area received a R500 million upgrade that included creating a 65-foot-wide uninterrupted promenade and an additional pedestrian walkway linking the Beachfront to the Kings Park Sports Precinct and the Moses Mabhida Stadium. There are refreshment stands and places to relax every 980 feet. The section of Beachfront between South Beach and the Suncoast Casino is particularly safe, as police patrol often, though don't walk there late at night. It's lovely to take a stroll along here early or late in the day when it's less busy. Walk out onto one of the many piers and watch surfers tackling Durban's famous waves.

Depending on the weather, parts of the Beachfront can be quite busy, especially on weekends. There's always something to see, even in the early mornings, when people come to surf or jog before going to work.

The Florida Road Strip

Florida Road leads a double life. By day, shoppers and tourists stroll up and down the tree-lined avenue, browsing art galleries and boutiques; by night it transforms into a neon-lighted nightclub, where hordes of young and not-so-young revelers overflow from restaurants, lounges, and bars.

The thing that sets Florida Road apart is its historic character, with fine Edwardian architecture, well-preserved historic buildings, and half a dozen churches creating a timeless atmosphere that attracts the city's trendy set to meet and eat.

Since the strip is only about 0.8 km (less than ½ mile) long, you can enjoy it on foot in fine weather, but Mynah buses pass regularly, so there's transportation if you need it, and taxis are another option.

For a daytime visit, start in the morning at the top of the road where it meets Innes, opposite Mitchell Park, and work your way downhill, rather than battling an incline from the other end, where it intersects with Sandile Thusi (Argyle) Road.

Along the way, a trio of coffee shops beckon for a light bite and good coffee, with designer jeweler Mark Gold's breakfasts edging out Vida e Caffe. Clothing boutique Gorgeous and designer outlet Colleen Eitzen flank the eateries.

Chic home design outlet Ceclie & Boyd's showcases opulent style in a repurposed original home. After stopping there, head across the road to see the hundreds of locks that adorn the fence at Mandela Legacy Park.

Smokers will want to seek out the road's high-quality tobacconists selling imported cigars and cigarettes, of which the Cairo Smokeshop, Coffee and Cigar Lounge is the best.

There's an Apple Store, looking a little incongruous among the restaurants, and Botica's leather bags and shoes woo passersby, but it's worth pressing on to the African Art Centre, which supports local artists and artisans and offers a good choice of unique and high-quality gifts and mementos. For more art, the Elizabeth Gordon Gallery showcases established South African artists in mixed media, and a small display of African artwork and wooden masks makes a stop at Art on Florida worthwhile.

Most of the numerous restaurants remain open all day, so there's no shortage of lunch venues. Spiga d'Oro, Cappello, or Butcher Boys are good choices.

As the sun goes down and Florida Road puts on its party face, restaurants begin filling up, and pubs and lounges—Absolut, Velvet Lounge, Uber Zulu, Keys on Florida, Boulevard, and Ice Bar—do a brisk trade. Find Italian fare at Mama's, Spiga d'Oro, Piatto, and Cappello; Spanish tapas at Vicky-Cristina's; hot and spicy food at House of Curries; Mexican-inspired cuisine at Taco Zulu; and steaks at Butcher Boys.

Should you choose to stay overnight on Florida Road, Quarters on Florida or the Benjamin are two classy boutique hotels at the lower end of the road, offering some respite from the hustle and bustle.

7

TOP ATTRACTIONS

FAMILY **uShaka Marine World.** This aquatic complex combines the uShaka Sea World aquarium and the uShaka Wet 'n Wild water park. The largest aquarium in the Southern Hemisphere, it has a capacity of nearly 6 million gallons of water, more than four times the size of Cape Town's aquarium. Enter through the side of a giant ship and walk down several stories to enter a "labyrinth of shipwrecks"—a jumble of five different fake but highly realistic wrecks, from an early-20th-century passenger cruiser to a steamship. Within this labyrinth are massive tanks, housing more than 350 species of fish and other sea life and the biggest variety of sharks in the world, including ragged-tooth and Zambezi (bull sharks). Try to catch the divers hand-feeding fish and rays in the morning. The complex includes dolphin, penguin, and seal shows, and a variety of reptiles and amphibians populate the Dangerous Creatures exhibit.

The extensive water park comprises slides, pools, and about 10 different water rides. The intensity ranges from toddler-friendly to adrenaline junkie. Durban's moderate winter temperatures make it an attraction pretty much year round, though it's especially popular in summer. ■TIP→ Avoid on public holidays, and call ahead during winter when hours may change. ⊠ *1 King Shaka Ave.* ☎ *031/328–8000* ⊕ *www. ushakamarineworld.co.za* ⊠ *Sea World R149; Wet 'n Wild R149; combo ticket R199. Dangerous Creatures Exhibit R40* ☉ *Daily 10–5.*

WORTH NOTING

Suncoast Casino & Entertainment World. Part of the rejuvenation of Durban's Golden Mile, this casino is done in the art deco style for which Durban is famous. Colorful lights make it a nighttime landmark, but it's established itself as a daytime hot spot as well. There are deck chairs beneath umbrellas on a grassy sundeck and a pretty beach. A paved walkway dotted with benches is a pleasant place to sit and watch cyclists, inline skaters, and joggers. Fairly regularly there's a band playing directly in front of the complex on weekends, with amphitheater-like stairs where you can sit and enjoy the show. ⊠ *20 Suncoast Blvd.* ☎ *031/328–3000* ⊕ *www.suncoastcasino.co.za* ⊠ *Free* ☉ *24 hrs.*

NEED A BREAK? **Milky Lane.** Take respite from the summer sun and enjoy a cool treat at this ice-cream parlor, one of 20 or so restaurants, fast-food outlets, and coffee shops in the Suncoast Casino complex. Even in winter, the creamy ice-cream waffles and creative shakes are a welcome indulgence. ⑤ *Average main: R30* ⊠ *Sun Coast Mall, Marine Parade, shop L11* ☎ *031/332–1849* ⊕ *www.milkylane.co.za.*

BEREA

Durban's colonial past is very much evident in this suburb overlooking the city. Built on a ridge above the sea, it's characterized by old homes with wraparound balconies, boutique hotels, and strips of fashionable restaurants. Durban formed the coastal hub of the British Colony of Natal, declared in 1843 after the annexation of the former Boer Republic of Natalia. In 1910 Natal combined with three other colonies to form the Union of South Africa. One of the most sought-after addresses in the upscale Berea suburb is Musgrave Road. Tree-lined avenues feature luxury homes and apartment blocks interspersed with parks, schools and sports clubs. The Musgrave Centre shopping hub is a major drawing card.

TOP ATTRACTIONS

Campbell Collections. Amid bustling, suburban Berea, Muckleneuk is a tranquil Cape Dutch home in a leafy garden. It was built in 1914 upon the retirement of Sir Marshall Campbell, a wealthy sugar baron and philanthropist who lived here with his wife, Ellen, and daughter, Killie. Today it is administered as a museum by the University of KwaZulu-Natal, and is furnished in similar style to when the Campbells lived here, with some excellent pieces of the family's Cape Dutch furniture. In addition to the **William Campbell Furniture Museum** (William was the son of Sir Marshall) there is an extensive collection of works by early European traveler artists, such as Angas, and paintings by prominent 20th-century black South African artists, including Gerard Bhengu, Daniel Rakgoathe, and Trevor Makhoba. The **Mashu Museum of Ethnology** displays the best collection of traditional Zulu glass beadwork in the country, plus African utensils, like tightly woven wicker beer pots, carvings, masks, pottery, and musical instruments. There are also weapons dating from the Bambatha Uprising of 1906, during which blacks in Natal rebelled against a poll tax and were brutally put down. Paintings of African tribespeople in traditional dress by artist Barbara Tyrrell, who traveled around South Africa from the 1940s to 1960s gathering valuable anthropological data, add vitality to the collection. The **Killie Campbell Africana Library,** open to the public, is a treasure trove of historical information on KwaZulu-Natal. It includes the papers of James Stuart, a magistrate and explorer during the early 20th century; the recorded oral tradition of hundreds of Zulus; a collection of pamphlets produced by the Colenso family in their struggle for the recognition of the rights of the Zulu people; and a good collection of 19th-century works relating to game hunting. ✉ *220 Gladys Mazibuko (Marriott) Rd., at Stephen Dlamini (Essenwood) Rd.* ☎ *031/207–3432, 031/260–1722* ⊕ *campbell.ukzn.ac.za* ✍ *Muckleneuk tours R20; library free* ☉ *Muckleneuk tours daily 8:30–4 (reservations essential); library weekdays 9–noon and 2–4:30, Sat. 9–noon.*

WORTH NOTING

FAMILY **Durban Botanic Gardens.** Opposite the Greyville Racecourse, Africa's oldest surviving botanical garden is a delightful 150-year-old oasis of greenery interlaced with walking paths, fountains, and ponds. The gardens' orchid house and collection of rare cycads are renowned. The Garden of the Senses caters to the blind, and there's a lovely tea garden where you can take a load off your feet and settle back with a cup of hot tea and cakes—crumpets with "the works" are the best in town. On weekends it's a popular place for wedding photographs. During the Music at the Lake events, which happen on some Sundays, various musical acts perform in the gardens (additional fee) and people take along picnics. ✉ *70 St. Thomas Rd.* ☎ *031/322–4021* ⊕ *www.durbanbotgardens.org.za* ✍ *Free* ☉ *Daily 7–5.*

INDIAN DISTRICT

The biggest Indian population outside of India resides in Durban, and the influence on the city is much in evidence, from the architecture to the cuisine. Under apartheid's Group Areas Act that designated where various race groups could live and own businesses, Indian traders set up shop on Dr Yusuf Dadoo Street (Grey Street). Here you can eat vegetarian curry, bargain for goods, buy fabrics, or just browse shops whose ownership spans generations, and soak up the Eastern vibe. ⚠ **Watch your belongings closely.** In addition, this part of town can be quite grubby, and in the midday summer heat it can get unpleasantly humid.

TOP ATTRACTIONS

Jumah Mosque. Built in 1927 in a style that combines Islamic and colonial features, this is the largest mosque in the Southern Hemisphere. Its colonnaded verandas, gold-domed minaret, and turrets give the surrounding streets much of their character. Tours (the only way to visit) are free and can be arranged through the Islamic Propagation Center, in a room at the entrance of the mosque, or through the Durban Tourism offices at Tourist Junction. ■ **TIP→ If you plan to go inside, dress modestly: women should bring scarves to cover their heads and shoulders and skirts should extend below the knees; men should not wear shorts.** It's a good idea to keep a *kikoi* (a lightweight African sarong readily available in local markets) in your bag to use as a skirt or scarf. Men can use them, too, to cover bare legs. You'll have to take off your shoes as you enter, so wear socks if you don't want to go barefoot. No tours are offered during Islamic holidays, including Ramadan, which varies but lasts a whole month in the latter part of the year. ⊠ *Dr Yusaf Dadoo (Grey) and Denis Hurley (Queen) Sts.* ☎ *031/306–0026* ⊡ *Free* ⏰ *Weekdays 8–12:30 and 2–3:45.*

Madressa Arcade. There's a Kiplingesque quality to this thoroughfare, recalling the bazaars of the East. Built in 1927, it's little more than a narrow, winding alley perfumed by spices and thronged with traders. You can buy everything from plastic trinkets to household utensils and recordings of Indian music. Bursts of color—from bright yellow fabric to dark red spices—create a refreshing and photogenic sight. You can buy striking costume jewelry that would cost three times as much at major shopping centers, but be wary of pickpockets while browsing through the stores. ⊠ *Entrances on Denis Hurley (Queen) and Cathedral Sts.* ⏰ *Daily 9–5.*

Muti Market. For a uniquely African experience, hire a guide through Durban Tourism at Tourist Junction to take you to southern Africa's largest and most extensive *muti* (traditional medicine, pronounced moo-tee) market. The market also serves as a distinctive traditional-medicine facility, where *sangomas* (traditional healers) offer consultations to locals in a bustling, urban atmosphere. If you're feeling bold, you might wish to consult a sangoma on matters of health, wealth, or personal problems. ⚠ **Don't go without a guide.** ⊠ *Warwick Junction, Julius Nyerere Ave.* ⏰ *Weekdays 8–6, Sat. 8–1.*

Victoria Street Market. Masses of enormous fish and prawns lie tightly packed on beds of ice while vendors competing for your attention shout

Bunny Chow

Contrary to what you might think, bunny chow is not about lettuce and carrots. This Durban specialty, prevalent in the Indian District, is a hollowed-out loaf of bread traditionally filled with bean curry, although mutton and sometimes beef and chicken are also used. The dish was popularized in the 1940s, during apartheid, when blacks were prohibited from entering Kapitan's Restaurant, in the city center, where traditional Indian beans in roti (pancakelike bread) were sold. The manager, known fondly as Bhanya, started offering takeout on the pavement, but the rotis often fell apart.

So he started using a hollowed-out quarter loaf of bread as a small pot for the beans, and the soft bread was used to soak up the gravy. "Bhanya's chow" became bunny chow, and meat was soon added as filling.

Good bunnies can be found at several Indian District eateries. Try **Little Gujarat** for great vegetarian bunnies in simple surroundings; family-run **Patel Vegetarian Refreshment House**, which has been satisfying customers since 1912; and **Victory Lounge**, which is usually very busy, and for good reason.

---

their respective prices. In the meat section, goat and sheep heads are stacked into neat piles (a spectacle for those with iron stomachs), and butchers slice and dice every cut of meat imaginable. The noise is deafening. In an adjacent building—where all the tour buses pull up—you'll discover a number of curio shops whose proprietors are willing to bargain over wood and stone carvings, beadwork, and basketry. You'll also find shops selling spices, recordings of African music, and Indian fabrics. The current structures stand on the site of an original, much-loved market, a ramshackle collection of wooden shacks that burned down during the years of Nationalist rule. ⚠ **Watch your belongings closely. Ask your taxi to wait for you, or visit as part of a guided tour.** ✉ *Denis Hurley (Queen) and Jospeh Nduli (Russell) Sts.* ☎ *031/306–4021* ⊙ *Weekdays 8–5, weekends 9–2.*

VICTORIA EMBANKMENT

Margaret Mncadi Avenue (formerly Victoria Embankment or the Esplanade) skirts Durban harbor from Maydon Wharf with its sugar terminal in the west, past Wilson's Wharf and the yacht mall to the docksides in the east.

TOP ATTRACTIONS

BAT Centre. This vibrant center (though perhaps a little on the seedy side these days) is abuzz with artists and musicians. Most days—and some nights—you can watch sculptors and painters at work, hear poetry readings, and see Africology (African teachings and traditions) dancers and musicians. The center is home to several small galleries that showcase the work of local artists. The center contains a coffee bar overlooking the bay and shops that sell an excellent selection of high-quality African crafts, including fabrics and ceramics. ✉ *Small Craft*

Harbour, 45 Maritime Pl. ☎ *031/332–0451* ⊕ *www.batcentre.co.za* 🖅 *Free* ⊙ *Daily 8:30–4:30.*

Walk over to Wilson's Wharf (⊕ www.wilsonswharf.co.za) in the nearby Maydon Wharf neighborhood, where you can have a cool cocktail or a meal on a deck overlooking the harbor at one of several restaurants ranging from an oyster bar to fast-food outlets.

GREYVILLE

Between the foot of the Berea ridge and the beachfront, this suburb of older homes and apartment blocks is dominated by the legendary Greyville Racecourse, where Durban's social highlight, the Durban July horse race, takes place. Greyville is bounded in the south by the Botanical Gardens and in the north by Morningside.

WORTH NOTING

Kendra Hall and Ekta Mandir. One of the most easily accessible and opulent temples in the city, the Kendra, next to the Durban Botanic Gardens, opened in 2001 after two years of intricate work by sculptors in India. The structure is unmistakably Eastern, with golden domes that tower above a palm tree supported by ornately decorated columns and arches that give the temple an East-meets-West look. Inside are two halls: a small one on the ground level and a larger one upstairs, which is a popular venue for weddings and leads to the temple. Huge statues of Hindu gods, notably Ganesha, Krishna, and Ram, are garlanded and clothed in exquisite Indian fabric. You can join an early morning or evening prayer daily at 6:30 am and 6:30 pm. ⊠ *5 John Zikhali (Sydenham) Rd.* ☎ *031/309–1824* 🖅 *Free* ⊙ *Daily 8:30–4.*

MAYDON WHARF

Maydon Wharf is an extensive cargo handling section of Durban's harbor, sandwiched between the suburb of Congella and the ocean. Its northern section features the Wilson's Wharf entertainment node, with a number of restaurants and the Catalina Theatre.

WORTH NOTING

S. A. Sugar Terminal. Much of Durban's early economy was built on the sugar industry, and even today the hills and fields around the city and along the north and south coasts are covered with sugarcane. It's not surprising then that Durban's Sugar Terminal is the largest in southern Africa and one of the most advanced in the world. A short video presentation provides background to the sugar industry, and then you'll be taken on an educational tour of the terminal. Together, the tour and video presentation take 45 minutes. It's extraordinary to see the terminal's three enormous silos piled high to the domed ceiling with tons of raw sugar. The architectural design of the silos has been patented and used in other parts of the world. ⊠ *25 Leuchars Rd.* ☎ *031/365–8100, 031/365–8153* 🖅 *R16* ⌔ *Reservations essential* ⊙ *Tours Mon.–Thurs. at 8:30, 10, 11:30, and 2, Fri. at 8:30, 10, and 11:30.*

Zack's. This popular spot overlooks the Durban harbor and often hosts live music. It serves breakfast until late, as well as lunch and dinner. ⊠ *Wilson's Wharf, 14 Boatman's Rd., Shop 23* ☎ *031/305–1677.*

Wilson's Wharf. On the edge of the harbor, this pleasant, privately developed section of waterfront is a lovely place to while away a few hours, soaking up the atmosphere, admiring the harbor view, and maybe having a meal or drink at one of the open-air restaurants on the expansive wooden deck. In addition to restaurants and fast-food outlets, there are boat rentals, sightseeing cruises, and a market with stands selling local crafts or cheaper trinkets from India and China. ⊠ *Boatman's Rd.* ☎ *031/305–3099* ⊕ *www.wilsonswharf.co.za* ☯ *Market Mon.–Sat. 10–5, some restaurants daily 9 am–11 pm.*

CHATSWORTH

The predominantly Indian inner-city suburb of Chatsworth is a vibrant, cosmopolitan mix of old and new architecture complemented by myriad home-based businesses and a couple of large shopping malls. It comprises seven residential wards along the Higginson Highway, bounded to the north by the Umhlatuzana River and to the south by the Umlaas River. It's home to one of South Africa's most spectacular Hare Krishna temples.

WORTH NOTING

Hare Krishna Temple of Understanding. This magnificent lotus-shape temple, opened in 1985, is at the heart of activities run by the city's International Society for Krishna Consciousness. Gold-tinted windows add a glow to the interior, floored with imported Italian marble. Colorful laser drawings depicting the life of the Hindu god Krishna cover the ceiling, and statues of Krishna and his consort Radha are elaborately dressed in traditional Indian attire. Love fests and traditional singing and dancing take place on Sunday (1:30–5) and all are welcome. You need to remove your shoes when entering the temple. ⊠ *50 Bhaktivedanta Swami Circle, Unit 5* ☎ *031/403–3328* ⊠ *Free* ☯ *Mon.–Sat. 10–1 and 4:15–6:30, Sun. 10–9.*

NEED A
BREAK?

Govinda's. This is an inexpensive yet excellent vegetarian restaurant catering to Hare Krishna devotees, who do not use onions, garlic, or mushrooms in their food. The traditional Indian *biryani*, a rice dish, is a favorite. ⊠ *Hare Krishna Temple of Understanding, 50 Bhaktivedanta Swami Circle, Unit 5* ☎ *031/403–4600.*

DURBAN NORTH AND GLENASHLEY

Along the eastern coastline north of the Umgeni River, you'll find the well-established middle- to upper-income suburb of Durban North, the highlight of which is the superb Umgeni River Bird Park. One of the city's older suburbs, Glenashley sits between Durban North and La Lucia. Palatial properties line its beachfront, whereas more modest yet upscale homes fill the inland area. The Ruth First Highway (M4) connects these suburbs southward to the city and northward to the more upscale Umhlanga Rocks region.

TOP ATTRACTIONS

FAMILY **Umgeni River Bird Park.** Ranked among the world's best, this bird park shelters beneath high cliffs next to the Umgeni River and has various walk-through aviaries containing more than 800 birds. The variety of birds, both exotic and indigenous, is astonishing. You'll be able to take close-up photographs of macaws, giant Asian hornbills, toucans, pheasants, flamingos, and three crane species, including the blue crane, South Africa's national bird. Try to time your visit to take in the free-flight bird show, which is a delight for both children and adults. Drinks and light lunches are available at the park's kiosk. ✉ *490 Riverside Rd., off the M4, Durban North* ☎ *031/579–4600* ⊕ *www.umgeniriverbirdpark. co.za* ✉ *R50* ☼ *Daily 9–5; bird shows Tues.–Sun. at 11 and 2.*

GLENWOOD

Dotted with parks, schools, churches and sports clubs, Glenwood is a quiet family suburb. Helen Joseph Road is the social hub, where restaurants, bistros, pubs, and clubs attract hordes of partygoers on weekends.

WORTH NOTING

KwaZulu-Natal Society of Arts Gallery. This arts complex houses four exhibition areas, in addition to a crafts shop, the Durban Center for Photography, and a classy open-air restaurant. The center does not have a particular focus but is committed to promoting emerging talent in the province. Exhibition media ranges from photos and paintings to video installations. The center's clean architectural lines and leafy setting make this a popular venue with Durban's trendy set, and it's a lovely place to cool off after a hot morning touring the town. The gallery and crafts shop support and promote local art, so it's worth seeking out for tasteful souvenirs. Local musicians are given a platform fairly regularly on Friday nights. The daytime-only restaurant is a wonderful child-friendly pit stop. ✉ *166 Bulwer Rd.* ☎ *031/277–1700* ⊕ *www. kznsagallery.co.za* ✉ *Free* ☼ *Tues.–Fri. 9–5, Sat. 9–4, Sun. 10–3.*

CATO MANOR

This neighborhood came about when black South Africans settled in the area during the 1920s, renting land from Indian landlords. The area saw race riots in the 1950s and 1960s when squatters and police clashed, but since the 1980s new infrastructure and urban development has created a more formal, working-class suburb with schools, a market, and a community center.

WORTH NOTING

Shree Ambalavaanar Alayam Temple. One of Durban's most spectacular Hindu shrines is in Cato Manor. The temple's facade is adorned with brightly painted representations of the Hindu gods, notably Ganesha, Shiva, and Vishnu. The magnificent doors leading to the cellar were salvaged from a temple built in 1875 on the banks of the Umbilo River and subsequently destroyed by floods. During an important Hindu festival held annually in March, unshod fire walkers cross beds of burning, glowing coals. There are no set visiting hours. If the temple is open you'll be welcome to go inside; if not, the exterior of the building is still worth seeing. ✉ *890 Bellair Rd.* ⟴ *Take the M13 (from Leopold St.) out of city; at major fork in road after Westridge Park and high school, veer left onto Bellair Rd.* ☎ *031/304–1518* ✉ *Free* ☼ *Hrs vary.*

UMHLANGA

Umhlanga's village charm and lovely beaches have entrenched it as one of the most sought-after vacation destinations for locals and foreigners, and it has many of Durban's top hotels. Also known as Umhlanga

Rocks (meaning "Place of the Reeds"), this area used to be a small vacation village, but Durban's northward sprawl has incorporated it into a popular and upscale residential and business suburb, much like Sandton is to downtown Johannesburg. To the north are the nicest sea views; to the south is Umhlanga's lighthouse.

TOP ATTRACTIONS

FAMILY

Fodor's Choice

★

Gateway Theatre of Shopping. The largest mall in the Southern Hemisphere, Gateway has been designed to let in natural light and is surprisingly easy to navigate. Shopping ranges from surfing paraphernalia and imported and local fashions to electronics and art and crafts. Gateway also has a large variety of entertainment options including an IMAX theater and the art nouveau Barnyard Theatre, which hosts live music compilation shows in an informal "barn" environment. The Wave House, has various levels of artificially generated waves for surfing and waterslides, and there's a funfair, karting track, and sports arena. ⊠ *New Town Centre, 1 Palm Blvd.* ☎ *031/514–0500* ⊕ *www. gatewayworld.co.za* ⊗ *Mon.–Thurs. 9–7, Fri. and Sat., 9–9, Sun. 9–6 (longer hrs for entertainments and activities).*

FAMILY

KwaZulu-Natal Sharks Board. Most of the popular bathing beaches in KwaZulu-Natal are protected by shark nets maintained by this shark-research institute, the world's foremost. Each day, weather permitting, crews in ski boats check the nets, releasing healthy sharks back into the ocean and bringing dead ones back to the institute, where they are dissected and studied. One-hour tours are offered, including a shark dissection (sharks' stomachs have included such surprising objects as a boot, a tin can, and a car license plate!) and an enjoyable and fascinating audiovisual presentation on sharks and shark nets. An exhibit area and good curio shop are also here. You can join the early morning trip from Durban harbor to watch the staff service the shark nets off Durban's Golden Mile. Depending on the season, you will more than likely see dolphins and whales close at hand. Booking is essential for trips to the shark nets, and a minimum of six people is required; no one under age six is allowed. ■TIP→ **Book well in advance for this—it may turn out to be a highlight of your trip.** ⊠ *1a Herrwood Dr.* ☎ *031/566–0400* ⊕ *www. shark.co.za* ☜ *Presentation R45, boat trips R300* ⊗ *Presentation Tues., Wed., and Thurs. at 9 and 2, Sun. at 2. Boat trips to shark nets, daily (weather dependent) 6:30–8:30 am.*

WORTH NOTING

Hawaan Forest. This 114-acre coastal forest grows on a dune that dates back 18,000 years and has 175 species of indigenous trees, fungi (during wet months), and various species of birds. Guided walks take two to three hours and are conducted on the first Saturday of every month (except in January or February), but if you call ahead you may be accommodated at another time. ■TIP→ **Be sure to wear closed-toe shoes.** ⊠ *Portland and Herald Drs.* ☎ *031/566–4018, 083/275–2216* ☜ *R30* ⊗ *First Sat. of every month; reservations essential.*

O'Connor Promenade. Join tourists and locals for a gentle stroll or vigorous run along the 3 km (1.8 mile) paved stretch that reaches from Durban View Park in the south to Umhlanga Lagoon Nature Reserve in the

7

Umhlanga

KWAZULU-NATAL

Theatre of Shopping Gateway 25
KwaZulu Natal Sharks Board 24
Hawaan Forest 26
Souvenirs 23
Sibaya Casino & Entertainment Kingdon ..28
Swallow View Site 27

north. This is a great way to check out the local coastline and bathing areas, and you'll pass Umhlanga's landmark lighthouse (closed to the public) and the pier, with steel arches designed to look like a whale's skeleton. ⊠ *Umhlanga Beach.*

NEED A BREAK?

La Spiaggia. As close to the Indian Ocean as you can get, this restaurant overlooking the main bathing beach has outside tables that are always packed with families sipping milk shakes or friends sharing a bottle of wine and having a bite to eat off a menu with broad appeal. ⊠ *O'Connor Promenade* ☎ *031/561–4388.*

Sibaya Casino & Entertainment Kingdom. Sibaya is expansive—in size, appearance, and number of activities—but is worth seeing for its grandiose, Zulu-themed design. The buildings themselves, for example, echo a giant and opulent Zulu *kraal* (compound/dwelling). Huge bronze statues of Zulu warriors and buffalos at the entrance provide a truly African welcome. Wherever you are at Sibaya—all 48 hectares (119 acres) of it—a breathtaking view of the ocean is only a window or a balcony away. As you might expect, there are plenty of dining options, and there's a 36-room, five-star hotel. It's quite a way out of town, north of Umhlanga and about halfway between the city center and Ballito. ⊠ *1 Sibaya Dr.* ☎ *031/580–5000, 0860/742–292* ⊕ *www.sibaya.co.za* ⊠ *Free* ⊙ *24 hrs.*

Souvenirs. For years a group of informal traders has sold its wares, ranging from woven baskets to straw hats, carvings, and various traditional beadworks, on the roadside opposite the Cabana Beach Hotel. There are about eight stalls, open daily, and the vendors rarely change. Bring cash and a penchant for bargaining. ⊠ *Lagoon Dr.*

Swallow View Site. If you're in the area between November and February, be sure to take in this amazing natural phenomenon that sees 3 million barn swallows returning to their nests at sunset. Arrive 45 minutes before sunset armed with something to sit on, binoculars, camera, sundowners, and some mosquito repellent. ⊠ *Mount Moreland* ✛ *From N2 take Umdloti/Verulam off-ramp and follow signs to Verulam Dr. for less than 1 km (600 yards), turn at Umdloti Estate and follow signs* ☎ *031/568–1557* ⊕ *www.barnswallow.co.za* ⊠ *R10.*

BEACHES

The sea near Durban, unlike that around the Cape, is comfortably warm year-round: in summer the water temperature can top 27°C (80°F), whereas in winter 19°C (65°F) it's considered cold. The beaches are safe, the sand is a beautiful golden color, and you'll see people swimming year-round. KwaZulu-Natal's main beaches are protected by shark nets and staffed by lifeguards, and there are usually signs giving the wind direction, water temperature, and warnings about any dangerous swimming conditions. Directly in front of uShaka Marine World, **uShaka Beach** is an attractive public beach. The **Golden Mile,** stretching from South Beach all the way to Snake Park Beach, is packed with people who enjoy the waterslides, singles' bars, and fast-food joints. A little farther north are the **Umhlanga beaches,** and on the opposite side of the bay are the less commercialized but also less accessible and safe beaches on **Durban's Bluff.** Another pretty beach and coastal walk, just north of the **Umhlanga Lagoon,** leads to miles of near-empty beaches backed by virgin bush. You should not walk alone on deserted beaches or carry jewelry, phones, or cameras, and never walk the beaches at night.

BEREA

Bluff Beaches. South of Durban's harbor, these beaches offer a less crowded alternative to the more central city beaches, although it can get rough at times, with big waves. Brighton Beach and Anstey's Beach are popular surf spots, with southerly surf swells breaking on the rocky reef below. Cave Rock at low tide is a paradise for anyone who enjoys exploring rock pools; at high tide it's a wave ride for the fearless. **Amenities:** lifeguards. **Best for:** surfing; swimming. ⊠ *Marine Dr.*

UMHALANGA

Umhlanga Beaches. Some of the country's finest beaches are on this stretch of the coast, and they can be less crowded than those in central Durban. Safe and clean—Umhlanga Rocks beach has a Blue Flag award—the beaches are easily accessed via pathways from parking lots down to a promenade skirting the busy beachfront. Vacation apartments and premier hotels like the Oyster Box, Cabanas, and Beverly Hills line this paved walkway southward to Umhlanga's famous lighthouse. If you're driving here, arrive early at peak times so you'll have a better chance of finding a parking spot. **Amenities:** food and drink; parking. **Best for:** sunrise; surfing; swimming; walking. ⊠ *Lighthouse Rd. or Marine Dr.*

BEACHFRONT

Golden Mile. From Vetch's Pier in the south to Suncoast in the north, the Golden Mile is a series of golden, sandy beaches divided by piers. Beaches are cleaned regularly, and each has a beach report board warning of bluebottles, jellyfish, strong currents, or dangerous conditions. Bodyboarders favor North Beach, and New Pier and Bay are preferred surfing spots. Swimmers should remain between the flags or beacons and away from the sides of piers, where strong currents wash straight out to sea. Chairs and umbrellas can be rented. Just off the sand, popular beachfront hotels like the Edward, Blue Waters, Elangeni, Belaire, Tropicana, and Garden Court jostle for visitors' favor. **Amenities:** food and drink; lifeguards; parking; showers; toilets. **Best for:** surfing; swimming. ⊠ *O. R. Tambo Parade.*

uShaka Beach. In front of uShaka Marine World aquarium and water theme park this beach has small waves and calm conditions, making it great for families. Sand sculptors are often here, too, creating intricate artwork. Grassy banks offer an alternative to the sand (which isn't always as clean as the more central beaches), and the local surf school is busy all year round. A block inland, in the rejuvenated Point area, is the trendy Docklands hotel. **Amenities:** parking. **Best for:** swimming; walking. ⊠ *Escombe Terr.*

WHERE TO EAT

Durban's dining public is fickle by nature, and restaurants tend to change hands fairly often. But don't be discouraged—Durban offers some superb dining options, provided you eat to its strengths. Thanks to a huge Indian population, it has some of the best curry restaurants in the country.

Durbanites eat lunch and dinner relatively early because they're early risers, particularly in summer, when it's light soon after 4. They're also generally casual dressers—you'll rarely need a jacket and tie, and jeans are rarely frowned upon.

⇨ *For more information on South Africa food, see Flavors of South Africa, in Chapter 1.*

CITY CENTER

$$$ ╳**Roma Revolving.** In business since 1973, this slowly revolving restaurant, which takes about an hour to do one full rotation, offers what has to be the most spectacular views of the city, especially the harbor. It's run by the original Italian owners, and the extensive menu runs the gamut from pasta to seafood. From old-school waiters to the hard-to-resist dessert trolley, there's something pleasingly old-fashioned about the place. While the restaurant is perched atop a high-rise building, its entrance is in an area that has become rather run-down over the years; the parking lot is fenced in. $ *Average main: R160* ⊠ *John Ross House, Margaret Mncadi Ave., 32nd fl.* ☏ *031/368–2275* ⊕ *www.roma.co.za* ⚐ *Reservations essential* ⊙ *Closed Sun. No lunch Mon.–Thurs.*

ITALIAN

MORNINGSIDE

$$ ╳**Joop's Place.** No trip to South Africa would be complete without a good traditional steak, and without a doubt, Joop's (pronounced *yopes*) is the best and most popular steak house in Durban. It goes without saying that most customers are regulars. It has an intimate, homey atmosphere, though the interior design is certainly nothing special. The food is the true focus, with Joop—a butcher by trade—himself selecting and preparing the steaks in an open kitchen. The specialty here is panfried steak; the pepper steak and Hollandse (Dutch-style) *biefstuk* (a center-cut fillet panfried in black butter and flambéed in brandy) are tasty favorites. The exceptionally hungry should try the 800-gram (about 21-ounce) T-bone. $ *Average main: R100* ⊠ *Avonmore Centre, shop 14, 9th Ave.* ☏ *031/312–9135* ⚐ *Reservations essential* ⊙ *Closed Sun. No lunch Sat.–Thurs. Jan.–Nov.*

STEAKHOUSE

$$$ ╳**9th Avenue Bistro.** Chef-patron Graham Neilson has a dedicated following, and deservedly so. While his dishes are based on classic principles, he continues to interpret them with a modern twist. Think pepper-seared tuna sashimi on Japanese radish and cucumber salad with wasabi, soy, and pickled ginger, or crispy roasted free-range duck served on potato rosti with butternut puree and lentil ragout with grilled zucchini and honey and cumin jus. The food is decadent but the setting is less so, with friendly waiters who work happily to indulge diners. The wine list contains a good choice of South African and international wines, and your waiter will be able to advise on any unfamiliar

ECLECTIC

7

Restaurants ▼
Café 1999 .... **4**
Cargo Hold **9**
Havana Grill **7**
Jack Salmon
Fish House **1**
Joop's Place **6**
9th Avenue
Bistro **5**
Roma Revolving ..**8**
Spiga d'Oro **2**
VickyCristina's **3**

Hotels .... ▼
The Benjamin **1**
Durban Hotel **6**
Garden Court
Marine Parade ...**7**
Protea Hotel
Edward Durban ..**8**
Quarters on
Avondale **2**
Quarters on
Florida **3**
Suncoast Hotel
and Towers **4**
Tsogo Sun Elangeni
& Maharani **5**

Where to Eat and Stay in Durban

local labels. $ *Average main: R150* ✉ *Avonmore Centre, shop 2, 9th Ave.* ☎ *031/312–9134* ⊕ *www.9thavenuebistro.co.za* ⊘ *Closed Sun. No lunch Mon. and Sat.*

$ ✕ **Spiga d'Oro.** On the fashionable Florida Road, Spiga is something of
ITALIAN a Durban institution, and it certainly represents the attitude and overall feeling of Durban—unpretentious with an animated atmosphere that makes diners feel part of the crowd. The Italian menu is not always classical in its interpretation, but you can count on it being delicious and a good value (pasta dishes come in medium or large portions). The Linguine à la Shaik, done with a tomato and basil sauce with a touch of chili, is perennially popular. And, if you enjoy taking your time over a meal, there are no over-zealous staff trying to turn your table. Open from breakfast, the kitchen doesn't close until the early hours of the next morning, and it's constantly abuzz with a steady stream of hungry patrons. Be prepared for a wait. $ *Average main: R80* ✉ *200 Florida Rd.* ☎ *031/303–9511* ⊕ *www.spiga.co.za* ⩑ *Reservations essential.*

$ ✕ **VickyCristina's.** This L-shape restaurant opens onto a veranda over-
CATALAN looking the buzz of Florida Road. A red-and-black interior with ornamental silver mirrors and loads of celebrity photographs creates a vibe in keeping with tasty Spanish cuisine. A spicy, hot tapas selection—think grilled crispy baby calamari, panfried sardines, grilled artichoke hearts—with Catalonian flatbread makes for a light meal, and you can add more if you're hungry. House-made sangria is a good accompaniment. $ *Average main: R85* ✉ *275 Florida Rd.* ☎ *031/561–1000* ⊕ *www.vickycristinas.com* ⊘ *Closed Mon.*

BEREA

$$ ✕ **Café 1999.** Trendy this restaurant may be, but the food is infinitely
MEDITERRANEAN more memorable than the shopping center setting. The husband-and-wife owners encourage you to celebrate taste with a menu of dishes that are meant for sharing, from the "titbits" (small servings) to the "bigbits." Let your fork and fingers wander between dishes like breaded olives stuffed with ricotta cheese and beef skewers with peanut satay and crisp sheets of pancetta. The triple-chocolate brownies with white chocolate and poppy seed ice cream makes for a sweet finish. $ *Average main: R120* ✉ *Silvervause Centre, shop 2, 117 Vause Rd., Musgrave* ☎ *031/202–3406* ⊕ *www.cafe1999.co.za* ⩑ *Reservations essential* ⊘ *Closed Sun. No lunch Sat.*

DURBAN NORTH AND GLENASHLEY

$$ ✕ **Jack Salmon Fish House.** A short drive north of the city, the small sub-
SOUTH AFRICAN urb of Glenashley has an elevated position that offers diners a pleasant sea view, but this restaurant's fresh seafood, prepared in unique and traditional ways, is the drawing card, with excellent service keeping the place busy during lunch and dinner. For starters go for the Falkland Island calamari tubes stuffed with prawns and peri-peri dressing and then chargrilled, or the black mussels. The catch of the day—dorado, swordfish, or Cape salmon—or Thai-inspired seared tuna are recommended mains. If you have room, round out the meal with deep-fried brownies with ice cream and chili. $ *Average main: R110* ✉ *Glenore*

7

Centre, shop 15, 1 Aubrey Dr., Glenashley ☎ *031/572–3664* ⊕ *www. jacksalmon.co.za* ⚲ *Reservations essential.*

UMHLANGA

$$ ✕ **Barbacoa.** This is an Argentinean-styled mecca for red-meat lovers
SOUTH where steaks are cooked on an open charcoal fire and South American
AMERICAN music dictates the atmosphere. There's also an on-site butchery where
local grain-fed beef is aged and cut to size to suit all appetites. Cuts
are served with a choice of sauces (mushroom and red wine, cheese, or
garlic to name a few) and vegetable sides. Alternates include deboned
chicken and freshly seared tuna. Their exclusive Malbec is an obvious
wine choice, with a range of other high and low vintage reds and whites
to choose from. Ⓢ *Average main: R130* ✉ *Lighthouse Mall, Chartwell
Dr.* ☎ *031/561–4106* ⊕ *www.barbacoa.co.za* ⚲ *Reservations essential.*

$$$ ✕ **Bel Punto.** Follow your stomach 15 minutes north of Umhlanga to
ITALIAN Umdloti where you'll dine on Italian fare with a contemporary twist.
The seafood is outstanding—think line fish baked in the wood-fired
pizza oven and perfectly cooked calamari or prawns done in a garlic,
white wine, tomato, cream, and chili sauce. Italian staples like pastas,
pizzas, and risotto also hit the spot. The wine list is noteworthy and
waiters are knowledgeable, although there are sometimes delays with
food when the restaurant is busy. To make the most of the gorgeous
sea views, book for lunch or an early dinner. Ⓢ *Average main: R150*
✉ *Umdloti Centre, 1 South Beach Rd.* ☎ *031/568–2407* ⚲ *Reservations
essential* ☾ *Closed Mon. No lunch Tues.*

$$$ ✕ **Ile Maurice.** One of Umhlanga's culinary gems, this restaurant was
FRENCH built up over many years by the charming Mauvis family. Today own-
Fodor's Choice ership is shared by Jean Mauvis and Christian Lenferna de la Motte.
★ The soft-hue interior and pretty veranda that overlooks the Umhlanga
beach hark back to the area's colonial roots. On the menu you'll find
classic French Mauritian fare such as soupe de poisson à la mauricienne
and octopus curry. Although seafood is a specialty, meat-lovers have
plenty to choose from, with fillet de chateau a popular option. A well-
considered wine list complements the menu. Ⓢ *Average main: R150* ✉ *9
McCausland Crescent* ☎ *031/561–7609* ⊕ *www.ilemauricerestaurant.
co.za* ⚲ *Reservations essential* ⚱ *Jacket required* ☾ *Closed Mon.*

$$ ✕ **Kashmir.** The menu features mainly North Indian dishes that are so
INDIAN large and filling that—take our word for it—appetizers are not needed.
Standout curries include butter chicken, lamb *gosht pasanda* (done in an
almond-and-cream sauce with saffron), and the *navratan korma* (mixed
vegetables cooked in cashew gravy with fruit). The interior provides a
sophisticated dining experience, which continues onto an enclosed terrace. There's a good, reasonably priced buffet on Friday and Saturday
nights and a carvery for Sunday lunch. Ⓢ *Average main: R130* ✉ *11
McCausland Crescent* ☎ *031/561–7486.*

$$ ✕ **Olive & Oil.** You can't go wrong here. Fantastic Mediterranean-
MEDITERRANEAN inspired fare is good value for the money. The best way to start your
meal is with a mezze platter to share among two or three people. Main
courses range from melt-in-your-mouth calamari to steaks, pastas, and
pizzas. The large restaurant is not suitable for a romantic night out,
but it's great for families and offers consistently good food and service.

Where to Eat and Stay in Umhlanga

KEY
① Hotels
● Restaurants

KWAZULU-NATAL

Restaurants ▸

Barbacoa	2
Bel Punta	3
lie Maurice	4
Kashmir	5
Olive & Oil	1

Hotels ▸

Beverly Hills Hotel	2
Breakers	4
Cabana Beach	3
Oyster Box	1
Teremok Marine	5

INDIAN OCEAN

If the weather's warm, try for a table on the veranda. $\boxed{S}$ *Average main: R120* ⌨ *Chartwell Centre, 15 Chartwell Dr., shop 19* ☎ *031/561–2618* ⊕ *oliveandoil.co.za/branches/umhlanga/* ⌂ *Reservations essential.*

BEACHFRONT

$$　✕ **Cargo Hold.** You might need to book several weeks in advance to
SEAFOOD　secure a table next to the shark tank at here, but if you do it'll be one of your most memorable dining experiences. Enjoy a duo of carpaccios—smoked ostrich or peppered beef—while massive ragged-tooth sharks drift right by your table and sandsharks stir up the sandy bottom. Aside from the array of fish dishes like salmon trout in a phyllo pastry wrap or *peri-peri* (spicy chili pepper sauce) calamari with basmati rice, Cargo Hold also serves meat dishes like slow-braised lamb shank in tomato, honey, lemon, and Dijon mustard. The restaurant is done up like a shipwreck; both floors have tank frontage. ■ **TIP→ The view of the shark tank is best from the bottom floor, so ask for this when booking.** The restaurant is part of the building known as the Phantom Ship, accessed from the promenade next to the ship's giant propeller; you don't need to pay admission to uShaka Marine World to eat here. $\boxed{S}$ *Average main: R130* ⌨ *uShaka Marine World, 1 King Shaka Ave.* ☎ *031/328–8037* ⊕ *www.ushakamarineworld.co.za/restaurants/cargohold* ⌂ *Reservations essential.*

$$$　✕ **Havana Grill.** Attention to detail and freshly prepared, quality food
SOUTH AFRICAN　combine to make this one of Durban's finest restaurants. It offers spec-
Fodor's Choice　tacular sea vistas (ask for a table with a view when making your reserva-
★　tion) and a contemporary interior, with white leather-upholstered chairs, wall-length couches, and antelope horns on the walls. Steak—prepared and aged in the in-house butchery—and seafood are specialties. Try the tasting platter for starters (minimum of two people sharing): a mix of nachos; jalapeños stuffed with cheese; grilled calamari; bruschetta; lamb and spring rolls. For mains, consider the grain-fed rib-eye steak with a duo of peppercorn and red wine sauce; seasonal varieties of venison; or line fish (likely swordfish, dorado, or Cape salmon). There's a good basic domestic wine list, but take the opportunity to make a selection from a walk-in cellar lined with lesser-known wines. $\boxed{S}$ *Average main: R150* ⌨ *Suncoast Casino & Entertainment World, shop U2, 20 Suncoast Blvd.* ☎ *031/337–1305* ⊕ *www.havanagrill.co.za* ⌂ *Reservations essential* ☞ *No children after 6 pm.*

WHERE TO STAY

Many of Durban's main hotels lie along the Golden Mile, but there are some wonderful boutique hotels and bed-and-breakfasts (especially in Berea, Morningside, and Umhlanga) that offer a more personalized experience.

In northern Zululand and Maputaland, game reserves and lodges—both publicly and privately owned and managed—are smaller than what you'd find in Mpumalanga, but offer delightful game-viewing experiences. Many are all-inclusive (or nearly so), though some have self-catering options. *Hotel reviews have been shortened. For full information, visit Fodors.com.*

■TIP→ Prices, especially along the coast, tend to rise with the summer heat.

CITY CENTER

$$
HOTEL
🏨 **Durban Hilton.** This massive luxury hotel adjacent to the International Convention Centre is a short taxi ride from the city center and beachfront and is favored by business people and conference-goers. **Pros:** close to convention center; good gym; beauty salon offers unusual treatments such as the bamboo massage. **Cons:** not within walking distance of restaurants; unsafe to walk outside hotel after dark. ⑤ *Rooms from: R2590* ✉ *12–14 Walnut Rd.* ☎ *031/336–8100* ⊕ *www.hilton. com* ⇲ *327 rooms, 16 suites* ❑ *No meals.*

MORNINGSIDE

$
HOTEL
🏨 **The Benjamin.** In one of Durban's transformed historic buildings, this small hotel offers excellent value and its location on trendy Florida Road is ideal for excellent restaurants and nightlife, and only a short distance from the city center and beaches. **Pros:** within walking distance to restaurants; covered swimming pool; historic building's charm has been retained; approximately five minutes from beaches and city center. **Cons:** limited secure parking; no on-site restaurant; no elevator. ⑤ *Rooms from: R1255* ✉ *141 Florida Rd.* ☎ *031/303–4233* ⊕ *www. benjamin.co.za* ⇲ *43 rooms* ❑ *Breakfast.*

$$
HOTEL
🏨 **Quarters on Florida.** Four converted Victorian homes comprise the city's most intimate boutique hotel, a contemporary European-style property that's been reinvented with a colonial African makeover. **Pros:** tasteful rooms; on-site restaurants; close to restaurants and nightlife of Florida Road. **Cons:** despite efforts, street-facing rooms are noisy; no pool; limited off-street parking. ⑤ *Rooms from: R1620* ✉ *101 Florida Rd.* ☎ *031/303–5246* ⊕ *www.quarters.co.za* ⇲ *24 rooms* ❑ *Breakfast.*

UMHLANGA

$$$$
HOTEL
Fodor's Choice
★
🏨 **Beverly Hills Hotel.** In a high-rise building right on the beach, this upscale hotel is popular with both vacationers and businesspeople and has a longstanding reputation for gracious hospitality. **Pros:** unbeatable sea views; hotel has its own demarcated piece of beach with lounge chairs; great cocktail bar. **Cons:** some rooms are smaller than you might expect; prices increase in-season. ⑤ *Rooms from: R6018* ✉ *54 Lighthouse Rd.* ☎ *031/561–2211* ⊕ *www.tsogosunhotels.com/deluxe/ beverly-hills-hotel/* ⇲ *88 rooms, 7 suites, 8 garden villas* ❑ *Breakfast.*

$$
RESORT
FAMILY
🏨 **Breakers Resort.** This property enjoys an enviable position at the northern tip of Umhlanga, surrounded by the wilds of the Hawaan Forest (⇨ *See Exploring*) and overlooking the unspoiled wetlands of Umhlanga Lagoon. **Pros:** babysitting services; sprawling gardens; great pool; family-friendly. **Cons:** taxi is required to get to local restaurants, especially at night; overrun with families in-season. ⑤ *Rooms from: R2380* ✉ *88 Lagoon Dr.* ☎ *031/561–2271* ⊕ *www.breakersresort.co.za* ⇲ *80 rooms* ❑ *No meals.*

$$
RESORT
FAMILY
🏨 **Cabana Beach.** Families who want a traditional beach vacation can't do better than this large resort, where children under 18 stay free, the bathing beach is directly in front of the hotel, and there are tons of activities to keep kids happy. **Pros:** at main swimming beach;

7

adults-only pool; within walking distance to village. **Cons:** basic, no-frills, no-fuss interiors; teeming with children in-season. $⑤ Rooms from: R1800 ⌧ 10 Lagoon Dr. ☏ 031/561–2371 ⊕ www.tsogosunhotels.com/resorts/cabana-beach/ ↝ 217 apartments ⑩ No meals.$

$$$$ ⬚ **Oyster Box.** The iconic multiaward-winning Oyster Box hotel has
HOTEL   achieved a perfect marriage between old colonial and African contem-
FAMILY   porary style in its luxurious accommodations and offers an eye-popping
Fodor'sChoice   range of services and complimentary extras. **Pros:** fabulous food and
★   service; spa includes complimentary healthful buffet; free shuttle to
Gateway Shopping Centre; free snacks and treats all over the place;
kids' vacation club. **Cons:** lots of steps and only one elevator; insuf-
ficient signage to rooms and public areas. $⑤ Rooms from: R5875 ⌧ 2 Lighthouse Rd. ☏ 031/514–5000 ⊕ www.oysterboxhotel.com ↝ 69 rooms, 17 suites ⑩ Breakfast.$

$$$ ⬚ **Teremok Marine.** Translated from Russian as "little hideaway," this
HOTEL   delightful boutique lodge has individually styled rooms, each offering a
Fodor'sChoice   different sensory experience—its own specific body-product fragrance,
★   mood CD, candy—and the three rooms at the top have beautiful ocean
views. **Pros:** close to Umhlanga village and one block from the sea;
personalized service; free Internet; free transfers to village; complimen-
tary laundry service. **Cons:** 1 km (½ mile) from nearest restaurants;
open-plan bathrooms in all but one room. $⑤ Rooms from: R3250 ⌧ 49 Marine Dr. ☏ 031/561–5848 ⊕ www.teremok.co.za ↝ 8 rooms ⑩ Breakfast.$

BEACHFRONT

$$ ⬚ **Garden Court Marine Parade.** You can't beat the location of this pleas-
HOTEL   ant hotel midway between South and North beaches and only a five-
minute drive from the city center. **Pros:** central location on Golden
Mile; sea views; friendly staff. **Cons:** hotel lobby and bar area lack
atmosphere; recommended restaurants a taxi ride away; inadvisable to
walk in area after dark. $⑤ Rooms from: R1799 ⌧ 167 Tambo (Marine) Parade ☏ 031/337–3341 ⊕ www.tsogosun.com ↝ 346 rooms, 6 suites ⑩ Breakfast.$

$$ ⬚ **Protea Hotel Edward Durban.** Built in 1939 in classic colonial style,
HOTEL   the Edward is one of Durban's oldest hotels. **Pros:** don't be put off by
the facade, the interior is old-world elegance; on Golden Mile; you can
catch a rickshaw right outside hotel; 24-hour business center. **Cons:**
recommended restaurants are a taxi trip away; inadvisable to walk
in the area after dark. $⑤ Rooms from: R2397 ⌧ 149 Marine Parade ☏ 031/337–3681 ⊕ www.proteahotels.com ↝ 101 rooms, 10 suites ⑩ No meals.$

$$ ⬚ **Suncoast Hotel and Towers.** This hotel mostly attracts businesspeople
HOTEL   and gamblers, but it's a stone's throw from the beach and has some
great sea views. **Pros:** closest hotel to Moses Mabhida Stadium; spa;
access to beach. **Cons:** smallish rooms. $⑤ Rooms from: R2220 ⌧ 20 Battery Beach Rd. ☏ 031/314–7878 ⊕ www.tsogosunhotels.com/deluxe/suncoast-towers/pages/overview.aspx ↝ 165 rooms, 36 suites ⑩ Breakfast.$

$$ ⬚ **Tsogo Sun Elangeni & Maharani.** Overlooking North Beach along the
HOTEL   Golden Mile, this combination of two adjacent high-rise hotels is a

two-minute drive from the city center and attracts a mix of business, conference, and leisure travelers. **Pros:** tour and travel desk; business center; sea views; discounted rates on weekends. **Cons:** not for those who prefer an intimate hotel experience; breakfast not included in price during peak times; minimum stay requirements in peak season. ⑤ *Rooms from: R2600* ✉ *63 Tambo (Snell) Parade* ☎ *031/362–1300* ⊕ *www.tsogosunhotels.com* ⟿ *734 rooms, 19 suites* ⎪⊚⎪ *Multiple meal plans.*

BEREA

$$$
HOTEL
⚏ **Quarters on Avondale.** The superior, and quieter, of the two Quarters boutique hotels (⇨ *see also Quarters on Florida*), Quarters on Avondale offers rooms in Edwardian style with a modern twist. **Pros:** quiet; close to restaurants and nightlife on Florida Road. **Cons:** breakfast is the only meal served; no pool. ⑤ *Rooms from: R2900* ✉ *335 Avondale Rd.* ☎ *031/303–5246* ⊕ *www.quarters.co.za* ⟿ *17 rooms* ⎪⊚⎪ *Breakfast.*

NIGHTLIFE

What's On in Durban, a free bimonthly publication put out by the tourism office and distributed at popular sites, lists upcoming events.

Billy the BUMS. This place hums from the early evening until late. It also serves tasty small meals, like jalapeño poppers. ✉ *504 Lilian Ngoyi (Windermere) Rd.* ☎ *031/303–1988.*

Velvet Lounge. African-Indian cuisine teamed with white-and-gold interior design sets the style in this bar/lounge, a see-and-be-seen place for local movers and shakers. ✉ *178 Florida Rd.* ☎ *031/312–0864.*

SPORTS AND THE OUTDOORS

BOATING

It's easy to charter all manner of boats, from a paddleski (a flat fiberglass board that you paddle) for a few rand to a deep-sea fishing vessel for a few thousand. Inexpensive harbor tours lasting a half hour, booze cruises, and dinner cruises can all be booked from the quayside at Wilson's Wharf. Shop around to find something that suits your budget, taste, and time frame.

DOLPHIN-WATCHING AND DIVING

Calypso Dive and Adventure Centre. This PADI five-star Instructor Development Center organizes dives, rents equipment and conducts dolphin viewing tours. ☎ *031/332–0905, 082/976–6018* ⊕ *www.calypsoushaka. co.za.*

FISHING

Deep-sea fishing is a popular activity, as there's almost always something biting. Summer (November–May) brings game fish like barracuda, marlin, sailfish, and dorado, whereas winter is better for the bottom fishes, like mussel crackers, salmon, and rock cod.

Casea Charters. Trips on a ski boat depart from Granny's Pool, in front of Umhlanga's Cabana Beach. Various trips are available, ranging from one to six hours. The popular three- and four-hour trips are priced per person at R500 and R600 respectively; otherwise you need to get a group together and hire the whole boat (R1,250–R4,500 depending on the length of time you want). Fish for dorado, yellowfin tuna, king and queen mackerel, garrick, rock cod, salmon, and other species. Bait and equipment are supplied, but bring your own food and drinks. You can keep the fish you catch. Booking is essential, and you need to obtain a fishing license (from any post office) in advance of the trip. ☎ *031/561–7381, 083/690–2511 ⊕ www.caseacharters.co.za.*

Lynski Charters. Deep-sea fishing trips for barracuda, sailfish, marlin, shark, and reef fish head out from Durban's harbor at 5 am in a 30-foot game-fish boat, returning at 2 pm. The cost is R5,500 for up to six people fishing for a day trip, although the boat can take 12 people. The price includes equipment, tackle and bait. Bring your own refreshments. ☎ *031/539–3338, 082/445–6600 ⊕ www.lynski.com.*

Swissroll Charters. Deep-sea fishing trips depart from the harbor. For R6500, skipper-owner Ralph Nussbaumer takes a maximum of six people for a day on his 30-foot boat with a cabin. Sometimes he sets up a gas cooker and fries some fresh fish. ☎ *031/467–2185, 082/451–6567 ⊕ www.swissroll.co.za.*

GOLF

Durban is a great destination for golfers, with a number of internationally acclaimed courses in subtropical settings. Lush, forest-fringed fairways make for a scenic and challenging golfing experience, and thanks to Durban's sunshine and perennially warm climate, golf can be enjoyed throughout the year.

Beachwood Country Club. This course is currently rated 29 in the *Golf Digest* Top 100 Courses in South Africa. The layout is challenging to the links-course golfer, with most fairways running parallel in a N-NE/S-SW direction. The sixth and ninth fairways feature doglegs, and 74 bunkers lure wayward shots. Four holes have water features and tree-lined fairways. Set high in the dunes, the par-4 sixth is a hugely demanding hole at 448 yards from the back tee. The hole doglegs left, with a stream, bush, and water hazard to be negotiated before reaching the green. ⊠ *Beachwood Pl., off Fairway ⊕ www.dcclub.co.za/index.php/golf/golf_beachwood/ ☜ R240 for 18 holes in the morning, R320 for 18 holes in the afternoon and on Sat.* ⚐ *18 holes, 6016 yards, par 71.*

Fodor's Choice ★   **Durban Country Club.** Durban Country Club is the only public course on the African continent to be rated in the Top 100 Golf Courses of the World by *Golf Magazine USA.* Lush subtropical vegetation, sand dunes and elevated views of the Indian Ocean lend this course its unique and challenging appeal. Classic features include large undulating fairways on the 5th, 8th, and 17th and massive sand dunes that form part of the design. The 1535-foot par 5 third hole—high tee-off to a narrow fairway with dense vegetation and a left-hand fairway bunker—is rated among the world's best. ⊠ *Walter Gilbert Rd.* ☎ *031/313–1777 ⊕ www.dcclub.co.za ☜ Weekdays R475, Sat. R525* ⚐ *18 holes, 6683 yards, par 72.*

Mount Edgecombe Country Club. This two-course championship estate—Mount Edgecombe One and Mount Edgecombe Two—is set in rolling hills inland from Umhlanga. Designed by Sid Brews in 1936, Course One was upgraded in 1992 and modernized by Hugh Baiocchi to meet USGA specifications. Both feature indigenous vegetation that attracts a variety of birdlife. Course One's water features and multitiered greens demand accurate play, whereas Course Two has more undulating terrain that tests the serious golfer and hones the amateur's skill. Signature holes are the 13th to 16th, referred to by locals as "Amen corner." ⊠ *Golf Course Dr., Gate 2, Mount Edgecombe ⊕ www.mountedgecombe.com/ golf ✉ R295 for tee-off before 8:30 am weekdays; R345 Sat. and after 8:30 am weekdays. Prices are the same for both courses, and include golf cart rental. ⅃ 18 holes, 6302 yards, par 71.*

Royal Durban Golf Club. Tucked in the centre of the Greyville Racecourse, the Royal Durban Golf Club course, built in 1898, appears deceptively easy. However there's no wind protection, so hitting narrow fairways is difficult, and subtle green breaks are challenging. On the plus side, its centrally located, surroundings are attractive, the course flat and trees are minimal. The par four 7th is the most difficult with palm trees punishing a sliced or blocked tee shot. First tee-off is at 6.30 am. ⊠ *16 Mitchell Cres., Gate 15, Greyville ☎ 031/309–1373 ⊕ www. royaldurban.co.za ✉ R260 ⅃ 18 holes, 6444 yards, par 73.*

Umhlali Country Club. This Peter Matkovich–designed golf course is a premier golf destination on the North Coast. It features sweeping greens, exotic palms, and manicured fairways that offer an easy walk for golfers of all abilities. Strategically positioned tee boxes and seven water holes test the mettle of competitive golfers, and longer handicappers can take advantage of front markers. The fourth and eighth present more of a challenge, with greens surrounded by water. ⊠ *Compensation Rd., Ballito, Umhlali ☎ 032/947–1181 ⊕ www.umhlaliclub.co.za/sports/golf ✉ R360 for 18 holes on weekdays; R515 for 18 holes on weekends ⅃ 18 holes, 6,228 yards, par 72 ⊙ Mon.–Thurs. and Sun. 6 am–5 pm, Fri. and Sat. 6 am–6:30 pm.*

Zimbali Country Club. This prestigious eco-friendly course, 1.2 km (¾ mile) from Ballito, embraces one of the region's few remaining natural forests. It holds a Five-star Golf Experience Award from Complete Golfer, reflecting its standards of service, the quality of its clubhouse facilities, and the condition of the course. Designed by Tom Weiskopf, the course lies amid sand dunes above a secluded beach, natural springs, and a lake. Weiskopf's philosophy of "presenting a fair challenge to any level of play" is seen at Zimbali. The club's Crowned Eagle Restaurant serves breakfasts and lunches. ⊠ *Zimbali Estate, M4, Ballito ☎ 032/538–1041 ⊕ www.zimbali.co.za/GolfCourse.aspx ✉ R495 weekdays, R525 weekends (includes compulsory golf cart rental) ⅃ 18 holes, 6618 yards, par 72.*

HELICOPTER TOURS

JNC Helicopters. Flips (a short flight on a helicopter) are undertaken with up to three people leaving from Virgina Airport. Take a scenic trip to Umhlanga (10 minutes), Umdloti (14 minutes), Durban harbor (14 minutes), or to Ballito (25 minutes). Seeing the coast from the air is quite breathtaking. ✉ *Virgina Airport, Hangar 1, 220 Fairway, Umhlanga* ☎ *031/563–9513* ⊕ *www.jncheli.co.za* 🖅 *R500–R820.*

SURFING

Surfing has a fanatical following in Durban, and several local and international tournaments are staged on the city's beaches, at nearby Umhlanga, Ballito, or on the Bluff. Crowds of more than 10,000 are not unusual for night surfing competitions or the annual Mr. Price Pro championship (formerly the Gunston 500) held in Ballito, a top World Qualifying Series event on the world surfing circuit. When the conditions are right, New Pier is one of the best beach breaks in the world.

Just on the other side of Durban's protected bay, Cave Rock, on the Bluff, offers a seething right-hander that can handle big swell. It can be a tough paddle and is not for amateurs. Farther down the South Coast, surfers head for Scottburgh, Green Point, Park Rynie, or Southbroom. North of Durban, popular spots include Umhlanga, Ballito, Richard's Bay, and Sodwana Bay.

The more popular spots can get crowded, and locals are known to be territorial about certain sections. Be sure to obey the laws of surfing etiquette. Usually the best waves are found at dawn and dusk. If the southwester blows, the Durban beaches are your best bet. In the winter months look out for an early-morning land breeze to set up good waves along the whole coastline.

Surfing lessons are offered at uShaka Beach, where experienced coaches supply boards and advice. Surf shops along the beachfront will put you in touch with surf coaches, including professional surfers and bodyboarders who offer one-on-one coaching and group lessons. You can also rent surfing equipment from the surf shops, by the hour or by the day, at nominal rates during peak vacation season.

Learn2Surf. Run by a surfer-lifeguard, this surf school just north of uShaka Beach at Addington Beach caters to beginners and improvers for individuals or groups—and can even organize surf parties. Equipment is supplied. Prices depend on your individual requirements. ✉ *Erskine Terr., Beachfront* ☎ *083/414–0567 SMS hotline* ⊕ *www.learn2surf. co.za.*

Ocean Ventures. Based on the beachfront at uShaka Marine World, this company offers surf instruction suitable for beginners for $100 per hour. You can rent surfboards and bodyboards here, too. ✉ *Escombe Terr., Beachfront* ☎ *086/100–1138, 31/332–9949 from outside South Africa* ⊕ *www.oceanventures.co.za.*

SHOPPING

Durban offers a great array of shopping experiences, from the Beachfront, where you can buy cheap beadwork and baskets, to enormous Western-style malls such as Gateway in Umhlanga. In general, bargaining is not expected, though you might try it at the Beachfront or with hawkers anywhere. Look out for goods indigenous to the province: colorful Zulu beadwork and tightly handwoven baskets.

MORNINGSIDE

African Art Centre. An outstanding collection of art and crafts from local artisans is on offer at this nonprofit center dedicated to promoting their work. Purchases can be shipped overseas. ⊠ *94 Florida Rd.* ☎ *031/312–3804* ⊕ *www.afriart.org.za.*

Cécile & Boyd's. Super-stylish interiors here cleverly combine the best of African and colonial design in a contemporary space. ⊠ *253 Florida Rd.* ☎ *031/303–1005* ⊕ *www.cecileandboyds.com.*

Elizabeth Gordon Gallery. This small gallery carries a wide selection of work—including prints—by local and international artists and photographers. ⊠ *120 Florida Rd.* ☎ *031/303–8133.*

Mark Gold Jewels. Contemporary handcrafted jewelry, many pieces featuring diamonds, is sold here. ⊠ *Oakwood Centre, 469 Innes Rd.* ☎ *031/303–4177* ⊕ *www.markgold.net.*

SIDE TRIPS FROM DURBAN

VALLEY OF A THOUSAND HILLS

Updated by
Kate Turkington

45 km (27 miles) northwest of Durban.

In the early part of the 19th century, before cars were introduced, wagons traveled from the port of Durban up along the ridge of this region of plunging gorges, hills, and valleys into the hinterland, where the mining industry was burgeoning. Today the Old Main Road (M103) still runs between Durban and Pietermaritzburg, winding through a number of villages and offering stunning views of hills and valleys dotted with traditional Zulu homesteads. It is along this route that the Comrades Marathon—South Africa's most famous road race—is run.

For purposes of exploring, the area has been organized into routes by the local tourism office. A favorite with Durbanites, the routes wind through villages and past coffee shops, art galleries, restaurants, quaint pubs, small inns, farms, and nature reserves. There are a number of excellent B&Bs, small inns, and lodges in the area, often with fantastic views of the gorges.

GETTING HERE AND AROUND

The main route—the T1, or Comrades Route—follows the M13 out of Durban, up Field's Hill, through the village of Kloof, and past Everton, Gillits, and Winston Park; it then joins the Old Main Road (M103) at Hillcrest. A number of small shopping centers along the M103 sell a variety of goods, from crafts to old furniture, and there are some excellent coffee shops, restaurants, and small hotels as well as cultural attractions. At the end of the M103 is the small town of Monteseel. Drive along the dirt roads to the signposted overlook for one of the best uninterrupted views of the Thousand Hills. Other well-marked routes in the area are the T2 Kranzkloof Route, T3 Assagay Alverstone Route, T4 Isithumba Route, and T5 and T6 Shongweni Shuffle, all of which make for scenic drives.

VISITOR INFORMATION

Contacts **Thousand Hills Tourism Association** ⊠ *47 Old Main Rd., Botha's Hill* ☎ *031/777–1874* ⊕ *www.1000hillstourism.co.za.*

EXPLORING

Assagay Coffee. Take a tour to see how this 100% homegrown coffee, very popular with locals, is grown, roasted, and packaged. You may also find this distinctive, delicious coffee—from dark roast through to espresso—in your local specialty coffee store. Look for the distinctive calico bag packaging. ⊠ *D157, No. 21, Harrison, Cato Ridge* ☎ *031/782–1268* ⊕ *www.assagaycoffee.co.za* ⊠ *Tours R50* ⊙ *By appointment only.*

FAMILY **PheZulu Safari Park.** Popular with big tour buses, PheZulu is the equivalent of fast-food tourism, good for people who want a quick-fix African experience. A tour of the cultural village with its traditional beehive huts gives some insight into African traditions, and there are performances of traditional Zulu dancing, but the operation is not as vibrant or professional as the cultural villages up north in Zululand. An old-fashioned crocodile farm and snake park is fairly interesting, if a little tacky. The curio shop is enormous; you can probably get just about any type of African memento or booklet imaginable. Impala and zebra are frequently spotted on the hour-long game drive (additional fee). ⊠ *Old Main Rd., Drummond* ☎ *031/777–1000* ⊕ *www.phezulusafaripark. co.za* ⊠ *Park R140, game drive R220* ⊙ *Daily 9–3; shows daily at 10, 11:30, and 2.*

DOLPHIN COAST

48 km (30 miles) northwest of Durban.

About an hour north of Durban, the Dolphin Coast (North Coast) lies along the warm waters of the Indian Ocean, with lifeguards and shark-netted beaches making it a popular vacation choice. Bordered by the Tugela River in the north and Zimbali in the south, it includes Ballito, Chaka's Rock, Salt Rock, Sheffield Beach, Blythedale, and Zinkwazi. Four excellent golf courses, a crocodile farm, cultural villages, and historical Indian, British, and Zulu sites are easily accessible at KwaDukuza, Shakaskraal, and Sheffield.

Large shopping malls straddle the entry into Ballito, and the Gateway Theatre of Shopping and La Lucia malls are just 15 minutes' drive away. All types of accommodations are covered, from hotels to camping, and a host of restaurants are available.

Culture and history form an integral part of life on the Dolphin Coast. Indian, Zulu, and colonial cultures can all be explored on one estate at The Kingdom in Sheffield. You can visit the King Shaka Memorial in KwaDukuza/Stanger, the Dukuza Museum, or the grave and home of Nobel Peace Prize winner Chief Albert Luthuli in Groutville. There are also many temples and mosques in the Shakaskraal and KwaDukuza/Stanger area.

GETTING HERE AND AROUND

A rental vehicle will afford you the flexibility needed to visit select destinations. You can take the N2, but the M4 north is a more scenic option. King Shaka International Airport lies 22 km (14 miles) north.

VISITOR INFORMATION

Contacts **North Coast Tourism** ☎ *031/366–7500* ⊕ *www.zulu.org.za/discover/ destinations/northcoast.*

WHERE TO EAT

$$$$　✕ **Gigi's.** Although it's on the Hotel iZulu property, you don't have to
ECLECTIC　be a guest to eat at this excellent restaurant. Only the finest ingredients are used, and they are locally sourced whenever possible, like South African cheeses, lamb from the KZN Midlands, venison, and fresh seafood. Try the Hotel Izulu curry of the day—always delicious. Dining is fairly formal but lunch is best enjoyed poolside. There's an excellent wine cellar, so take the opportunity to sample some of the best South African wines. ⑤ *Average main: R200* ⊠ *Hotel iZulu, 3 Rey's Pl., Ballito* ☎ *032/946–3444* ⊕ *www.hotelizulu.com.*

$$$　✕ **Mo-zam-bik.** Sample the authentic tastes of Mozambique without ever
AFRICAN　crossing the border at this funky, vibrant restaurant. The eatery's rus-
FAMILY　tic charm extends from the interior design to the service to the food. Mozambiquan food is often, mistakenly, equated with Portuguese cuisine, but it also has Arab, Indian, and Goan influences. Seafood and chicken are specialties and appear in some irresistible combinations—try the specialty seafood platter—and you can enjoy a cocktail while the kids are entertained in their own section. Dining here is definitely a case of eat, mess, and be merry. Be sure to check out the historic Arab dhow on-site. It's usually busy, so not ideal for a quiet rendezvous. ⑤ *Average main: R165* ⊠ *Boulevard Centre, shops 4 and 5, Jack Powell Rd., Ballito* ☎ *032/946–0979* ⊕ *www.mozambik.co.za.*

WHERE TO STAY

$$$$　🏨 **Fairmont Zimbali Resort.** Zimbali's tranquil 700 hectare (1,730-acre)
HOTEL　setting is in one of the few remaining coastal forests in the province with direct access to the beach, and the award-winning resort is a stylish mix of African and Balinese, with lots of glass, dark wood, and rough woven fabrics. **Pros:** access to unspoiled beach; professional service; good golf course. **Cons:** overly formal for some. ⑤ *Rooms from: R5000* ⊠ *M4, Ballito* ✚ *20 km (12 miles) north of Umhlanga* ☎ *032/538–5000* ⊕ *www.fairmont.com* ⇱ *133 rooms, 21 suites* �◉| *Breakfast.*

$$$　🏨 **Hotel iZulu.** The buildings of this five-star hotel—a disparate but har-
HOTEL　monious mix of Tuscan and Balinese architecture—are the centerpiece of an intimate estate ensconced in lush, tropical gardens. **Pros:** excellent on-site restaurant; one private Jacuzzi per two suites; **Cons:** not close to beach. ⑤ *Rooms from: R3390* ⊠ *3 Rey's Pl., Ballito* ☎ *032/946–3444* ⊕ *www.hotelizulu.com* ⇱ *19 suites* �◉| *Breakfast.*

7

SOUTH COAST

60 km (37 miles) southwest of Durban.

Vacation towns like Scottburgh, Margate, Ramsgate, Trafalgar, and Palm Beach dot KwaZulu-Natal's southern coast, which stretches for more than 200 km (125 miles) from Durban in the north to Port Edward in the south. The area has some of the country's best beaches, set against a tropical background of natural coastal jungle and palm trees. In fact, Blue Flag status has been conferred on Alkantstrand, Lucien, Marina (San Lameer), Ramsgate, Southport, Trafalgar, and Umzumbe beaches.

The South Coast is also famous for the annual sardine run, dubbed the Greatest Shoal on Earth, which usually occurs in June or July. Colder currents in Antarctica at this time bring millions of sardines to local waters, and they often wash right up on the beach. Dolphins, seabirds, sharks, and whales follow in a feeding frenzy. Paddle into the sea and collect your own lunch in a bucket.

GETTING HERE AND AROUND

The best and really only way to explore this area is with your own transportation. Main roads (the N2 and R61) are easy to navigate, and following the coastal road (turn off the R61 toward the coast) is picturesque.

If you're looking to explore the South Coast, Sapphire Coast Tourism can provide relevant information. It's also worth checking out the *Southern Explorer* magazine (⊕ *www.southern explorer.co.za*) and its website, which includes maps of the various tourist routes, along with details of restaurants, sights, and accommodations.

VISITOR INFORMATION

Contacts Tourism South Coast ✉ *16 Bisset St., Port Shepstone* ☏ *039/682–7944* ⊕ *www.tourismsouthcoast.co.za.*

WHERE TO STAY

$$$

RENTAL

FAMILY

🏠 **San Lameer Villas.** The vacation rental properties in this exclusive resort between Ramsgate and Palm Beach offer a great getaway for a group of friends or a family, and golfers are drawn by the on-site championship course. **Pros:** on a Blue Flag beach; championship golf course on-site. **Cons:** estate is very large; it's a car ride away from off-site restaurants; busy in-season. $ *Rooms from: R3600* ✉ *Lower South Coast Main Rd., San Lameer* ☏ *039/313–0450* ⊕ *www.sanlameer.com* 🛏 *40 rooms, 22 villas* ❌ *No meals*

THE KWAZULU-NATAL MIDLANDS

104 km (65 miles) northwest of Durban.

Set amid the rolling green foothills of the Drakensberg, the Midlands encompass waterfalls, lakes, reservoirs, forests, fields, Zulu villages, game reserves, and battle sites. The climate is pleasant most of the year, though summers tend to be hot. The area has long been an enclave for craftspeople—weavers, potters, woodcrafters, metalworkers, cheese makers, and beer brewers—who escaped the cities.

As a way to draw customers to the area, the crafters created four routes, called the Midlands Meander, in 1983, which include more than 160 shops, galleries, cultural activities, restaurants, and accommodations. Running through the towns of Curry's Post and Howick in the northeast and the little village of Nottingham Road, Mooi River, Balgowan, the Dargyle District, Lion's River, and Midmar in the southwest, the routes provide a great opportunity to shop for authentic, high-quality South African arts and crafts while enjoying the tranquility and beauty of the countryside. The area is filled with top accommodations and dining options.

The most popular time to do the Meander is in the autumn (March to May), when it's not too hot or too cold. Many South Africans love the winters here; it often snows, particularly on the higher ground, and many establishments burn fires. Don't be surprised to experience four seasons in one day! No matter what time of year you visit, though, there's always something to see and do, most of which involves shopping.

GETTING HERE AND AROUND
The only way to explore this area is in your own transportation. Roads are easy to navigate, and all establishments are well marked. The N3 is the quickest route between places, but the R103 is a scenic route that passes through all areas.

VISITOR INFORMATION
If you plan to explore the area, contact the Midlands Meander Association for its magazine that includes maps of the routes and details of the various establishments. Members of the association also stock the magazine.

Contact Howick Tourism Office ✉ *Lawton Rd., Howick* ☎ *033/330–7959* ⊕ *www.howicktourism.co.za.* **Midlands Meander Association** ☎ *033/330–8195* ⊕ *www.midlandsmeander.co.za.*

EXPLORING

Howick Falls. Although this area in the heart of the KwaZulu Natal Midlands is mainly about dining, shopping, and the arts, this lovely waterfall is definitely worth a stop. In the town of Howick, the Umgeni River plunges an impressive 300 feet into a deep pool in the gorge. Local people and sangomas (traditional Zulu healers) believe the waterfall is inhabited by ancestral spirits and has mystical powers. Take photographs from the viewing platform, or if you have more time, there are numerous hikes of varying difficulty that provide different vantages of the falls. Contact or visit the Howick Tourism Office, which is just a few hundred yards from the falls, for information. ✉ *Falls Dr., Howick.*

Fodor's Choice ★ **Nelson Mandela Capture Site.** In 2012, on the 50th anniversary of Nelson's Mandela's capture, this breathtakingly dramatic steel sculpture was unveiled and the visitor center opened. You will never have seen anything quite like this—don't miss it. The magnitude of what happened here is remarkable: on August 5, 1962, after 17 months on the run, Nelson Mandela, disguised as a chauffeur, was arrested at this very spot on his way from Durban to Johannesburg. He was convicted of incitement and illegally leaving the country and was sentenced to five years in jail before being prosecuted in the Rivonia Trials that led to his 27-year incarceration, most of it served on Robben Island. The tiny on-site gift shop is open daily 8–5; the Truth Café, also on-site, is open Friday and Saturday 8–4. ✉ *R103, Howick* ✛ *From the N3 take Tweedie Interchange and get onto the R103; the monument is just outside Howick.*

Nottingham Road Brewery. On the same premises as Rawdon's Hotel, this rustic microbrewery has developed a cult following. With names like Pickled Pig Porter, Whistling Weasel Pale Ale, Pye-Eyed Possum Pilsner, and Tiddly Toad Lager, you may have a tough time choosing which brew to taste first, so order a tasting paddle in the hotel's pub to sample them all. Call ahead if you would like to do a tour of the small brewery; otherwise just pop into the shop to stock up on beer, accessories, and clever merchandising. Guaranteed you'll head home with a "pickled as a pig" or "I'm as possed as a pye-eyed pissum" T-shirt. ✉ *R103, Nottingham Rd.* ☎ *033/266–6044* ⊕ *www.rawdons. co.za* ⊗ *By appointment.*

FAMILY　**Swissland Cheese.** Expect to be greeted by white free-roaming Saanen goats grazing happily in luscious green pastures when you visit this family owned-and-run cheesery. In the Swiss-chalet-style tasting room, you can sample a range of goat cheeses including *chevin*—similar to a cream cheese but a little crumblier—and a mild blue cheese, and learn about the cheese-making practices that Fran Isaac and her family have been following here for more than two decades. Kids love the *insinyani* cheese, which is also great as pizza topping. If you're here between August and May, you can watch the daily goat milking between 3 and 4:30 pm. ✉ *R103 Old Main Rd., Balgowan* ☎ *078/239–3975* ⊕ *www. swisslandcheese.net* ⊗ *Thurs.–Tues. 9:30–4:30.*

WHERE TO STAY

$$$$　☒ **Brookdale Health Hydro.** This is an exclusive yet unpretentious genu-
RESORT　ine health hydro, set in one of the province's prettiest locations, only
Fodor's Choice　an hour's drive from Durban, and five hours from Johannesburg. **Pros:**
★　authentic health hydro; rates include meals and certain treatments; day spa. **Cons:** no one-night stays; you won't want to leave. ⓈRooms from: R3850 ✉ *R103, Nottingham Rd., Howick* ☎ *033/266–6208, 033/266–6507* ⊕ *www.brookdale.co.za* ⇱ *17 rooms, 5 suites* ⏐◯⏐ *All meals.*

$$$$　☒ **Fordoun Hotel and Spa.** In the heart of a lush dairy farm that dates
HOTEL　back to the 1800s, original stone buildings have been converted into a five-star luxury hotel and spa. **Pros:** complimentary sauna, steam room, and gym; tranquil country setting. **Cons:** not all suites face mountains or dam. ⓈRooms from: R4800 ✉ *R103, Nottingham Rd., Howick* ✛ *3 km (2 miles) off the N3* ☎ *033/266–6217* ⊕ *www.fordoun.com* ⇱ *22 suites* ⏐◯⏐ *Breakfast.*

$$$$　☒ **Granny Mouse Country House.** One of the best-loved and oldest hotels
B&B/INN　on the Meander, Granny Mouse has cozy thatch rooms, all slightly different, with a bush view, fireplace, and homey, though upmarket, atmosphere. **Pros:** lovely setting in rolling green countryside; highly

regarded restaurant; on-site spa. **Cons:** popular wedding venue so can be noisy. ⑤ *Rooms from: R3840* ⊠ *R103, Balgowan* ✛ *25 km (15½ miles) south of Nottingham Road exit off the N3* ☎ *033/234–4071* ⊕ *www.grannymouse.co.za* ↩ *32 rooms* |○| *Breakfast.*

$$$
B&B/INN
Fodor's Choice
★

🏠 **Hartford House.** Deliciously luxurious, if rather formal, this 1875 inn, high up on the Meander in the foothills of the Drakensberg, is steeped in history and misty beauty. **Pros:** gourmet getaway; beautiful English-styled garden. **Cons:** dinner is served at 7:30 on the dot for all guests. ⑤ *Rooms from: R3020* ⊠ *Hlatikulu Rd., off road to Giant's Castle, Mooi River* ☎ *033/263–2713* ⊕ *www.hartford.co.za* ↩ *15 suites* |○| *Breakfast.*

SPORTS AND THE OUTDOORS

ZIPLINES

Karkloof Canopy Tours. Zip along steel cables through the treetops of the Karkloof Forest, the second-largest indigenous forest in South Africa. The 1,800-foot-long *foefie* (zip) course is divided into eight slides—the longest an exhilarating 574 feet long—that are interspersed with wooden platforms. Designed by a civil engineer, safety is paramount, and two trained guides (well versed in the forest and ecology) accompany each group; group size ranges from one to eight people. Tours (R495) take 2 hours and leave every hour in most weather conditions; call ahead to reserve your spot. Anyone from the ages of 7 to 70 can participate, but there's a weight limit of 130kg (286 pounds). Light refreshments, lunch, and a 4x4 trip up the mountain are included. ⊠ *Karkloof Rd., Howick* ✛ *From Howick, take Karkloof Rd. for 19 km (12 miles) and follow signs to Canopy Tours for another 2 km (1¼ miles)* ☎ *033/330–3415, 076/241–2888* ⊕ *www.karkloofcanopytour. co.za* ▱ *R495.*

SHOPPING

Though on the whole the route is known for its quality, you can also find some establishments that are not quite up to standards of others. If you've only a limited time, head for the concentration of crafts shops on the R103 between Nottingham Road and Lion's River. Or visit the one-stop Piggly Wiggly Country Village, which showcases the work of many of the Meander members. If you have a couple of days, base yourself at one of the hotels and explore the Meander using the large-format, free guide available at most Meander stops. Many of the better establishments offer shipping services for those unusual items large and small.

ART AND CRAFTS

Culamoya Chimes. As you enter the gardens of Culamoya Chimes, in the Dargyle District, your ears will be gently assailed with harmonious chimes of every description. There's a 13-foot chime in the garden as well as other chimes inside the shop that mimic the sounds of Big Ben and St. Paul's Cathedral down to gentle tinkles of fairy magic. The chimes are handmade and can be shipped to your home. ⊠ *3 km*

(2 miles) off the R103, Lidgetton, Howick ☎ *083/627–6195* ⊕ *www. facebook.com/culamoyachimes.*

Dargyle Valley Pottery. Established over three decades ago, this pottery is where renowned potter Ian Glenny, whose work is in private collections and galleries worldwide, founded the Midlands Meander in 1983. The pottery has an earthy, rugged appeal and you can choose from porcelain, stoneware, or terra-cotta pots, bowls, and vases—or even invest in a fireplace. ⊠ *D666, off Dargle Rd. and R103, Howick* ☎ *082/420–7729, 074/102–0189.*

Piggly Wiggly Country Village. If you're short of time, but still want to experience some of the best of the Midland Meander's arts and crafts, drop in at the one-stop Piggly Wiggly, where more than 20 shops—all representing Meander destinations and selling their products—are clustered round a central green with a Piggly putt putt course. There are fast-food outlets serving pizza and hamburgers, but be sure to sample the award-winning cappuccino and a slice of freshly baked cheesecake at Piggly Wiggly's famous coffee shop. ⊠ *1 Dargle Rd., Lions River* ☎ *033/234–2911, 076/803–1110* ⊕ *www.pigglywiggly.co.za.*

Weaver's Hut. The beautiful 100% handmade rugs sold here are produced in Donnybrook village. The company provides employment and skills to the local rural community. ⊠ *2 Morling St., Howick* ☎ *033/330–4026* ⊕ *www.weavershut.com.*

Woodturner. Andrew Early specializes in making elegant wooden bowls, modern wood sculptures, and one-of-a-kind furniture pieces using salvaged, exotic woods like jacaranda and local varieties like African mahogany and stinkwood. The pieces are often snapped up by studios in New York and elsewhere. Ask if you can visit the delightful studio behind the sprawling farmhouse, which you'll find 6 km (4 miles) from Rosewood, down the Dargyle road. ⊠ *Dargyle Rd., Lions River* ☎ *072/365–6270* ⊕ *www.andrew-early.com.*

CLOTHING

Mole Hill. Near Culamoya and Granny Mouse, 8 km (5 miles) south of Nottingham Road, Mole Hill, established in 1997, has a good reputation for high-quality, hard-wearing men's and women's shirts with an African twist. If you've always fancied a colorful Mandela-type, mandarin-collared shirt, you may well find one here, and both ladies' and men's shirts come in a wide range of sizes. Custom shirts can also be made to order. ⊠ *Millgate Cottage, R103, Nottingham Rd.* ☎ *083/289–7696* ⊕ *www.millgatecottage.com.*

FOOD AND CANDY

Peel's Honey. Established in 1924, Peel's Honey is the oldest honey label in the country. Snack on peanut honey brittle, or other tasty treats, or take a jar of creamed honey with you for *padkos* (the popular South African word for "road food," to munch as you drive). It's on the N3 below the Midmar Dam ⊠ *1 Boston Rd., Merrivale* ☎ *033/330–3762* ⊕ *www.peelshoney.co.za* ⊗ *Daily 8–5.*

SHOES, LUGGAGE, AND LEATHER GOODS

Groundcover. This is a great place to buy handmade leather goods, especially shoes, beautiful bags, and briefcases. ⌧ *Curry's Post Rd., Howick* ☎ *033/330–6092* ⊕ *www.groundcover.co.za.*

THE DRAKENSBERG

240 km (150 miles) west of Durban.

Afrikaners call them the Drakensberg: the Dragon Mountains. To Zulus they are uKhahlamba (pronounced Ooka-hlamba)—"Barrier of Spears." Both are apt descriptions for this wall of rock that rises from the Natal grasslands, forming a natural fortress protecting the mountain kingdom of Lesotho. Although you don't come here for big game, or much game at all, it's well worth visiting this World Heritage Site, the first in South Africa to be recognized for both its natural and cultural attractions, with some of the finest rock art in the world.

If possible plan your visit to the Berg during the spring (September and October) or late autumn (late April–June), because although summer sees the Berg at its greenest, it's also the hottest and wettest time of the year. Vicious afternoon thunderstorms and hailstorms are an almost-daily occurrence. In winter the mountains lose their lush overcoat and turn brown and sere. Winter days in the valleys, sites of most resorts, are usually sunny and pleasant, although there can be cold snaps, sometimes accompanied by overcast, windy conditions. Nights are chilly, however, and you should pack plenty of warm clothing if you plan to hike high up into the mountains or camp overnight. Snow is common at higher elevations.

GETTING HERE AND AROUND

The main resort area of the Drakensberg is almost a direct shot along the N3 from Durban. A car is not strictly necessary for a trip to the Berg, although it is certainly a convenience, and though a 4x4 would be an advantage, it, too, is not a necessity. Gas stations can be found in Bergville, Winterton, and at the foot of Champagne Castle. Driving in this area is time consuming. Trucks often slow up traffic, and you should watch for animals on and attempting to cross the road.

VISITOR INFORMATION

Ezemvelo KZN Wildlife. For more information on viewing rock-art sites, contact Ezemvelo KZN Wildlife, the province's official conservation organization. ☎ *033/845–1999* ⊕ *www.kznwildlife.com.*

EXPLORING

The Natal Drakensberg is not conducive to traditional touring because of the nature of the attractions and the limited road system. It's best to check into a hotel or resort for two or three days and use it as a base for hiking and exploring the immediate area. If you decide to stay at one of the self-catering camps, do your shopping in one of the bigger towns, such as Winterton or Harrismith for Tendele, and Bergville or Estcourt for Giant's Castle, Kamberg, and Injasuti. For more information on touring the area, visit the Drakensberg Tourism Association website (⊕ *www.drakensberg.org.za*).

The Drakensberg. The Drakensberg is the highest range in southern Africa and has some of the most spectacular scenery in the country. The blue-tinted mountains seem to infuse the landscape, cooling the "champagne air," as the locals refer to the heady, sparkling breezes that blow around the precipices and pinnacles. It's a hiker's dream, and you could easily spend several days here just soaking up the awesome views.

The Drakensberg is not a typical mountain range—it's actually an escarpment separating a high interior plateau from the coastal lowlands of Natal. It's a continuation of the same escarpment that divides the Transvaal Highveld from the hot malarial zones of the lowveld in Mpumalanga. However, the Natal Drakensberg, or Berg, as it is commonly known, is far wilder and more spectacular than its Transvaal counterpart. Many of the peaks—some of which top 10,000 feet—are the source of crystalline streams and mighty rivers that have carved out myriad valleys and dramatic gorges. The Berg is a natural watershed, with two of South Africa's major rivers, the Tugela and the Orange, rising from these mountains. In this untamed wilderness you can hike for days and not meet a soul, and the mountains retain a wild majesty missing in the commercially forested peaks of Mpumalanga. ☎ *036/448–1557 Drakensberg Tourism Association* ⊕ *www.drakensberg.org.za.*

WHERE TO STAY

$$$
HOTEL
FAMILY

☷ **Cathedral Peak Hotel.** You'll get breathtaking views from almost every spot in this friendly, delightful hotel nestled among the mountains, 43 km (18 miles) from Winterton. **Pros:** well-organized activities make it ideal for families. **Cons:** crowded in season. ⑤ *Rooms from: R3130* ⊠ *Cathedral Peak Rd., Winterton* ☎ *036/488–1888* ⊕ *www. cathedralpeak.co.za* ⇨ *104 rooms, 1 suite* |○| *Some meals.*

$$$$
B&B/INN
Fodor'sChoice
★

☷ **Cleopatra Mountain Farmhouse.** This truly enchanting hideaway tucked away at the foot of the Drakensberg Range near Rosetta overlooks a trout-filled lake encircled by mountains and old trees. **Pros:** exclusive yet modish accommodations. **Cons:** stay away if you're on a diet. ⑤ *Rooms from: R4190* ⊠ *Highmoor Rd., off Kamberg Rd., Kamberg* ☎ *033/267–7013* ⊕ *www.cleomountain.com* ⇨ *5 rooms, 4 suites, 2 cottages* |○| *Some meals.*

$$
RESORT

☷ **Tendele Hutted Camp.** Smack in the middle of Royal Natal National Park west of Bergville, amid some of the most spectacular mountain scenery in the Drakensberg, this very affordable popular camp makes a great base for hikes into the mountains. **Pros:** great views from every room. **Cons:** not for urban party animals. ⑤ *Rooms from: R2100* ⊠ *Royal Natal National Park* ☎ *033/845–1000* ⊕ *www.royalnatal. info* ⇨ *26 chalets, 2 cottages* |○| *No meals.*

San Paintings

Besides the hiking opportunities and the sheer beauty of the mountains, the other great attraction of the Berg is the San (Bushman) paintings. The San are a hunter-gatherer people who once roamed the entire country from 8,000 years ago to the 1800s. With the arrival of the Nguni peoples from the north and white settlers from the southwest in the 18th century, the San were driven out of their traditional hunting lands and retreated into the remote fastnesses of the Drakensberg and the Kalahari Desert. San cattle raiding in Natal in the late 19th century occasioned harsh punitive expeditions by white settlers and local Bantu tribes, and by 1880 the last San had disappeared from the Berg. Today only a few clans remain in the very heart of the Kalahari Desert. More than 40,000 of their paintings enliven scores of caves and rock overhangs throughout the Berg in more than 550 known San rock-art sites—one of the finest collection of rock paintings not only in the country, but also in the world. They tell the stories of bygone hunts, dances, and ceremonies as well as relating and representing spiritual beliefs and practices. Images of spiritual leaders in a trance state, their visions, and their transformation of themselves into animals have now been studied and written about, although some of the meanings are still not fully understood. ■TIP➔ **Be sure to bring binoculars with you.**

ZULULAND AND THE BATTLEFIELDS

Zululand stretches north from the Tugela River all the way to the border of Mozambique. It's a region of rolling grasslands, gorgeous beaches, and classic African bush. It has also seen more than its share of bloodshed and death. Modern South Africa was forged in the fiery crucible of Zululand and northern Natal. Here Boers battled Zulus, Zulus battled Britons, and Britons battled Boers. Some of the most interesting historic sites, however, involve the battles against the Zulus. Names like Isandlwana, Rorke's Drift, and Blood River have taken their place in the roll of legendary military encounters.

No African tribe has captured the Western imagination quite like the Zulus. A host of books and movies have explored their warrior culture and extolled their martial valor. Until the early 19th century the Zulus were a small, unheralded group, part of the Nguni peoples who migrated to southern Africa from the north. King Shaka (1787–1828) changed all that. In less than a decade Shaka created a military machine unrivaled in black Africa. By the time of his assassination in 1828, Shaka had destroyed 300 tribes and extended Zulu power for 800 km (500 miles) through the north, south, and west.

Fifty years after Shaka's death, the British still considered the Zulus a major threat to their planned federation of white states in South Africa. The British solution, in 1879, was to instigate a war to destroy the Zulu kingdom. They employed a similar tactic 20 years later to bring the Boer republics to heel and the rich goldfields of the Witwatersrand into their own hands.

Interest in the battlefields continues to grow, particularly since the Boer and Zulu War centenary celebrations in 2000. If you're not a history buff, the best way to tour the battlefields is with an expert guide, who can bring the history to life, because many of the battle sites are little more than open grassland graced with the occasional memorial stone.

GETTING HERE AND AROUND

Unless you're on a tour, it's almost impossible to see this part of the country without your own car. Your best bet is to rent a car in Durban and perhaps combine a trip to the battlefields with a self-driving tour of KwaZulu-Natal's game reserves. Roads are in good condition, although some of the access roads to the battlefields require more careful and slower driving, as dirt roads can be bumpy and muddy when wet.

TOURS

The visitor information offices at Dundee's Talana Museum and in Ladysmith have lists of registered battlefield guides. Information about battlefield guides and guides specializing in authentic Zulu culture can be obtained at any information center or tourism office.

Ken Gillings. A Registered National Tourist Guide, Ken Gillings specializes inAnglo-Zulu War and Anglo-Boer War sites. The length of a tour depends on the client's requirement, but Ken suggests ideally one night away—preferably two, Longer tours are available if, for example, iSimangaliso Wetland Park and the Drakensberg are included. Tours are available year round. Ken also offers personalized copies of his books relating to the wars. ☎ *031/702–4828, 083/654–5880* ✉ *R1,950 per day (accommodations, meals, transport, toll fees and admission fees are extra).*

Pat Rundgren. An official registered guide, Pat Rundgren offers 68 battlefield tours dealing with the Anglo-Zulu and Anglo-Boer wars. He will tailor tours to your requirements, but his most popular day tour is Isandlwana and Rorke's Drift for the Zulu War, or Spioenkop/Ladysmith for the Boer War. He has also introduced a 3-day tour which includes a visit to Nambiti, a Big Five game reserve. Prices range according to length of trip and type of accommodation. Pat also offers 'novelty' tours to coincide with annual reenactments of battles at Isandlwana in January and Talana in October. ☎ *034/212–4560, 082/690–7812* ✉ *From R1,500 for day trip (not including site entrance fee and lunch).*

Rob Gerrard. The resident historian at Isandlwana Lodge leads the lodge's flagship daily tours to Isandlwana and Rorke's Drift. Rob, author and Fellow of the Royal Geographical Society, or one of his associates, dramatically plays out the history of the Anglo-Zulu War on the actual battlefields of Isandlwana and Rorke's Drift. Reservations for tours can be booked through your travel operator or direct with the Lodge. ✉ *Off R68, Isandlwana* ☎ *034/271–8301* ⊕ *www.isandlwana.co.za* ✉ *R500.*

VISITOR INFORMATION

Battlefields Route is a good source for information on the battlefields. For a good overview covering this area, go to Tourism KwaZulu-Natal's website.

CLOSE UP

Boers, Brits, and Battlefields

The Second Anglo-Boer War (1899–1902), now referred to as the South African War, was the longest, bloodiest, and costliest war fought by Britain for nearly 100 years. The Brits and the Boers, Afrikaner descendants of 17th-century Dutch settlers fighting for independence from Britain, engaged in numerous battles in which the little guys (the Boers) often made mincemeat of the great British colonial army sent out to defeat them. Britain marched into South Africa in the spring of 1899, confident that it would all be over by Christmas. However, the comparatively small bands of volunteers from the republics of the Transvaal and the Orange Free State were to give Queen Victoria's proud British army, as Kipling wrote, "no end of a lesson." Today history has also revealed the part played by hundreds of thousands of black South Africans in the war as messengers, scouts, interpreters, and laborers— hence the renaming of the war.

The most famous—or infamous—battle was fought on top of Spioenkop, in KwaZulu-Natal, where the mass grave of hundreds of British soldiers stretches from one side of the hill to the other. Of interest is that three men who were to change the course of world history were there on that fateful day: war correspondent Winston Churchill (who wrote "The shallow trenches were choked with dead and wounded"), Mahatma Gandhi (who was a stretcher bearer), and Louis Botha, the first prime minister of the Union of South Africa.

—Kate Turkington

Contacts Battlefields Route. ☎ 082/802–1643 ⊕ www.battlefieldsroute.co.za. **Tourism KwaZulu Natal** ✉ 160 Monty Naicker Rd., Durban ☎ 031/366–7500 ⊕ www.zulu.org.za.

LADYSMITH

160 km (99 miles) northwest of Pietermaritzburg.

Ladysmith, dating back to the middle of the 19th century, became famous around the world during the South African War, when it outlasted a Boer siege for 118 days. Nearly 20,000 people were caught in the town when the Boers attacked on November 2, 1899. Much of the early part of the war revolved around British attempts to end the siege. The incompetence of British general Sir Redvers Buller became apparent during repeated attempts to smash the Boer lines, resulting in heavy British losses at Spioenkop, Vaalkrans, and Colenso. Finally, the sheer weight of numbers made possible the British defeat of the Boers in the epic 10-day Battle of Tugela Heights and ended the siege of Ladysmith on February 28, 1900.

Today Ladysmith is a small provincial town with a haphazard mix of old colonial and newer buildings and the same inhospitable climate (scorchingly hot in summer, freezing in winter). Seek out the elegant, historic Town Hall built in 1893 and visit the gleaming white Soofie Mosque on the banks of the Klip River—this national monument is regarded as one of the most beautiful mosques in the Southern Hemisphere. On Murchison Street (the main street) is Surat House, a shop built in the 1890s, where Gandhi used to shop on his way through Ladysmith. On the same street is the Siege Museum, and in its courtyard stands a replica of a Long Tom, the 6-inch Creusot gun used by the Boers during the siege to terrify the inhabitants of Ladysmith. In front of the town hall are two howitzers used by the British and christened Castor and Pollux.

GETTING HERE AND AROUND

There are only two ways to get around the battlefields: with your own rental car or with an organized tour.

VISITOR INFORMATION

Contacts Ladysmith Information Bureau ⊠ *Siege Museum, Town Hall, 151 Murchison St.* ☎ *036/637–2992* ⊕ *www.ladysmith.co.za* ⊙ *Weekdays 7:30–4.*

EXPLORING

Ladysmith Siege Museum. Formerly an 1884 market house, this is regarded as the best South African (Anglo-Boer) War Museum in South Africa. Step back into history and into the siege itself with electronic mapping, old uniforms, memorabilia, artifacts from the period, and black-and-white photos. The museum can arrange guided tours, but it also sells two pamphlets that outline self-guided tours: the Siege Town Walkabout and the Siege Town Drive-About. ⊠ *151 Murchison St.* ☎ *036/637–2992* ⊕ *www.ladysmith.co.za* ⊠ *R11* ⊙ *Weekdays 8–4, Sat. 9–noon.*

WHERE TO STAY

$$$
HOTEL
🖼 **Royal Hotel.** This historic South African country hotel shares much of Ladysmith's tumultuous past—it was built in 1880, just 19 years before the town was attacked by the Boers during the South Africa (Anglo-Boer) War. **Pros:** convenient, central location; great 1800s facade and front door; steeped in South African (Anglo-Boer) War history. **Cons:** undistinguished, bland rooms; roadside rooms are noisy. ⓢ *Rooms from: R2700* ⊠ *140 Murchison St.* ☎ *036/637–2176* ⊕ *www.royalhotel. co.za* 🛏 *71 rooms* ⍾⊙⍾ *Breakfast.*

SPIOENKOP

38 km (24 miles) southwest of Ladysmith.

The Second Anglo-Boer War (1899–1902) (now called South African War) was the biggest, the longest, the costliest, the bloodiest, and the most humiliating war that Great Britain had ever fought. The **Battle of Spioenkop** near Ladysmith was a focal point, where the Boers trounced the British, who suffered 243 fatalities during the battle; many were buried in the trenches where they fell.

WHERE TO STAY

$$$
RESORT
🖼 **Spionkop Lodge.** This lovely secluded lodge, with the spectacular Drakensberg mountains as a backdrop, lies in a 700 hectare (1,730 acre) nature reserve and is a perfect base for touring the battlefields, discovering the mountains and rock art, birding, or looking for big game. **Pros:** superb location and hospitality; knowledgeable and friendly hosts. **Cons:** cold winters. ⓢ *Rooms from: R3400* ⊠ *Off the*

R600 ☎ *036/488–1404* ⊕ *www.spionkop.co.za* ⇱ *8 rooms, 2 cottages* ⎮○⎮ *All meals.*

$$$$
RESORT
FAMILY
Fodor's Choice
★

🔲 **Three Trees Lodge.** This quaint little Victorian lodge is run by a safari- and mountain-guide couple who follow Fair Trade, sustainability, and social ethics, and also offer guided walks and activities. **Pros:** Superb hosts and food; fabulous tours, including game walks and rhino track- ing. **Cons:** bleak in winter. ⑤ *Rooms from: R4600* ⊠ *D564, about 25 km (16 miles) northeast of Bergville* ☎ *036/448–1171* ⊕ *www. threetreehill.co.za* ⇱ *7 suites, 1 cottage* ⎮○⎮ *All meals.*

DUNDEE

74 km (46 miles) northeast of Ladysmith.

Once a busy coal-mining town, Dundee still has straight roads wide enough for the ox wagons of pioneer days to turn in, but today it's just a small commercial center in an area of subdued farming activity.

GETTING HERE AND AROUND
To get to Dundee from Ladysmith, take the N11 north and then the R68 east. For a more scenic route, take the R602 toward Elandslaagte from the N11 and then go east on the R68.

VISITOR INFORMATION
Tourist Offices Dundee Tourism ⊠ *Civic Gardens, Victoria St.* ☎ *034/212– 2121* ⊕ *www.tourdundee.co.za.*

EXPLORING
Battle of Blood River Site. One of the most important events in the history of South Africa, this battle, fought between the Boers and the Zulus in 1838, predates the Anglo-Zulu War by more than 40 years. After the murder of Piet Retief and his men at Mgungundlovu in February 1838, Dingane dispatched Zulu impis to kill all the white settlers in Natal. But by November Andries Pretorius' new Boer commando of 464 men and 64 wagons moved to challenge the Zulus and took a vow that should God grant them victory, they would forever remember that day as a holy day. On December 16 an enormous Zulu force armed only with spears attacked the armed Boers. At the end of the battle 3,000 Zulus lay dead, but not a single Boer had fallen. The long-term effects of the battle were dramatic. The intensely religious Voortrekkers saw their great victory as a confirmation of their role as God's chosen people which led to the apartheid system that surfaced more than a century later. Two powerful monuments—one to the Boers, the other to the Zulus—today commemorate the battle. ⊠ *Off R33, between Dundee and Vryheid* ☎ *034/632–1695, 087/808–2964* ⊕ *www.bloedrivier.org. za* 🖃 *R30* ⊗ *Daily 8–4.30.*

FAMILY

Talana Museum. The first-rate Talana Museum, set in an 8-hectare (20- acre) heritage park, on the outskirts of Dundee, is well worth a visit. Fascinating exhibits, spread over 17 buildings, trace the history of the area, from the early San hunter-gatherers to the rise of the Zulu nation, the extermination of the cannibal tribes of the Biggarsberg, and, finally, the vicious battles of the South African (Anglo-Boer) War. The museum stands on the site of the Battle of Talana (October 20,

1899), the opening skirmish in the war, and two of the museum buildings were used by the British as medical stations during the battle. The military museum here is an excellent starting point for the Battlefields Route, where Zulus, Brits, and Boers battled it out for territory and glory. Reenactments, living history, and special events are regular features. ⊠ *R33, 2 km (1 mile) east of Dundee* ☎ *034/212–2654* ⊕ *www. talana.co.za* 🖃 *R25 (cash only)* ⊙ *Weekdays 8–4:30, weekends and holidays 9–4:30.*

NEED A BREAK?

Miners' Rest Tea Shop. In a delightfully restored pre-1913 miner's cottage at the Talana Museum, the tea shop serves light refreshments as well as more substantial home-cooked meals. The food is excellent and the atmosphere most welcoming. You can also take advantage of the braai and picnic sites on the museum grounds. ⊠ *Talana Museum.*

RORKE'S DRIFT

35 km (22 miles) southwest of Dundee.

From the British perspective the Battle of Rorke's Drift was the most glorious battle of the Anglo-Zulu War, all the more so because it took place just hours after the British humiliation at Isandlwana on January 22, 1879. For 12 hours, a British force numbering just 140 men, many of them wounded in the previous battle, fought off and ultimately repelled more than 3,000 Zulu warriors. The 1964 movie *Zulu* brought the story to the masses.

GETTING HERE AND AROUND
Rorke's Drift is southwest of Dundee on the R68.

EXPLORING
Fugitives' Drift. This drift (ford) was where, on 22 January 1879, the British survivors of the Battle of Isandlwana crossed the Buffalo River, and it was here that Lieutenants Melvill and Coghill were killed as they tried to save the Queen's Colour. They are buried on the hillside above drift, which is now on the grounds of what is now the Figutives' Drift Lodge. The Queen's Colour was later recovered and now restored, hangs in Brecon Cathedral in Wales. ■TIP→ There's no information on site, so read up about it before your visit, or hire an accredited battlefields guide. ⊠ *Rorke's Drift Rd., Rorke's Drift* ☎ *034/271–8051* ⊕ *www. fugitivesdrift.com.*

Rorke's Drift. This is by far the best of the Zulu War battlefields to see without a guide. An excellent small museum and orientation center retells the story of the battle, with electronic diagrams, battle sounds, and dioramas. The British force at Rorke's Drift consisted of just 140 men, of whom 35 were ailing or wounded. They occupied a Swedish mission church and house, which had been converted into a storehouse and hospital. The Zulu forces numbered some 3,000–4,000 men, composed of the reserve regiments from the earlier battle of Isandlwana. When a survivor from Isandlwana sounded the warning at 3:15 pm, the tiny British force hastily erected a stockade of flour bags and biscuit boxes around the mission. The Zulus attacked 75 minutes later, and the fighting raged for 12 hours before the Zulus faltered and retreated. A record number of 11 Victoria Crosses (Britain's highest military honor) were awarded at Rorke's Drift. ⊠ *Rorke's Drift Rd., off the R68, Rorke's Drift* ☎ *034/642–1687* 🎫 *R15* 🕙 *Weekdays 8–4, weekends 9–4.*

WHERE TO STAY

$$$$ 🏨 **Fugitives' Drift Lodge.** Set in a 5,000-acre natural heritage site, this
RESORT attractive lodge lies just a couple of miles from the famous battle site of Rorke's Drift and overlooks the drift where survivors of the British defeat at Isandlwana fled across the Buffalo River. **Pros:** lovely garden settings; you'll be contributing to the local communities through the David Rattray Foundation. **Cons:** pricey; can be full of groups of old military gentlemen. Ⓢ *Rooms from: R7650* ⊠ *Rorke's Drift Rd., Dundee* ☎ *034/642–1843* ⊕ *www.fugitives-drift-lodge.com* 🛏 *8 chalets, 1 cottage* 🍽 *All meals.*

$$$$ 🏨 **iSibindi Lodge.** This lodge within the iSibindi Eco Reserve, 9 km (4
HOTEL miles) from Rorke's Drift, combines game-viewing and Zulu cultural experiences with battlefield tours led by excellent local guides and historians. **Pros:** lovely eco-reserve with game (not predators). **Cons:** very hot in summer; no a/c. Ⓢ *Rooms from: R4320* ⊠ *Dundee* ☎ *035/474–1473* ⊕ *www.isibindiafrica.co.za* 🛏 *6 huts* 🍽 *Some meals.*

SHOPPING

Rorke's Drift ELC Art and Craft Centre. Rorke's Drift is still a mission station, run by the Evangelical Lutheran Church, and this center at the mission sells handmade bags, handwoven rugs, curios and beadwork, all created by local artists. ⊠ *Rorke's Drift Rd., off R68, Dundee* ☎ *034/642–1627* ⊕ *www.centre-rorkesdrift.com* 🎫 *Weekdays 8–4,weekends 9–4.*

ISANDLWANA

35 km (22 miles) southeast of Rorke's Drift on R68.

The name of Isandlwana went down in British military history on January 22, 1879, when the then mighty British Empire suffered a resounding defeat at the hands of the 20,000-strong Zulu army. Today, the site remains a poignant reminder, dotted with memorials to the fallen—about 1,000 Zulus and 1,329 British soldiers.

EXPLORING

Isandlwana. The Battle of Isandlwana, on January 22, 1879, was a major defeat for the British army. Coming as it did at the very beginning of the Zulu War, the humiliating defeat shocked Imperial Britain. Lt., Gen. Lord Chelmsford was in charge of one of three invasion columns that were supposed to sweep into Zululand and converge on Cetshwayo's capital at Ulundi. On January 20 Chelmsford crossed the Buffalo River into Zululand, leaving behind a small force at Rorke's Drift to guard the column's supplies.

Unknown to Chelmsford, the heart of the Zulu army—20,000 men—had taken up a position just 5 km (3 miles) away. Using Shaka's classic chest-and-horns formation, the Zulus swept toward the British positions. The battle hung in the balance until the Zulus' left horn outflanked the British. The fighting continued for two hours before the British fled the field, with the Zulus in triumphant pursuit. About 1,000 Zulus perished in the attack, as did 1,329 British troops. Today the battlefield is scattered with whitewashed stone cairns and memorials marking the resting places of fallen soldiers. ■ TIP→ The visitor center houses a small but excellent museum of mementos and artifacts, following the course of the battle in marvelous detail—a good place to start if you're here without a guide. Allow at least two or three hours for a visit. ⊠ Off R68, Dundee ☎ 034/271–8165 ☒ R30 ⊙ Weekdays 8–4, weekends 9–4.

GETTING HERE AND AROUND

The site of the Battle of Isandlwana is halfway between Dundee and Babanango, just off the R68.

WHERE TO STAY

$$$$ 🏨 **Isandlwana Lodge.** It's said that on January 22, 1879, during the Battle
HOTEL of Isandlwana, which was a major defeat for the British army, the chief of the Zulu army stood on Nyoni Rock where this lodge is now built. **Pros:** amazing views; battle tours on-site. **Cons:** area a bit bleak if the weather's bad. ⑤ Rooms from: R4190 ⊠ Off R68 ☎ 034/271–8301 ⊕ www.isandlwana.co.za ⮡ 12 rooms, 1 guesthouse ⦿ All meals.

BABANANGO

33 km (20 miles) east of Isandlwana on R69.

The tiny hamlet of Babanango is a major agricultural center.

GETTING HERE AND AROUND

A dirt road connecting the R34 to Babanango passes through some of the most beautiful countryside in Zululand, with seemingly endless views over rolling grasslands. The road ends at the tarred R68. Turn right and drive less than 2 km (1 mile) into the pleasant hamlet of Babanango.

WHERE TO STAY

$ 🏨 **Babanango Valley Lodge.** This tiny guest lodge sits at the head of a
B&B/INN steep valley, in a 2,000-acre nature reserve that's far from any other buildings, and has tremendous views of acacia-studded grasslands and hills. **Pros:** ultrafriendly, knowledgeable hosts; great personal service. **Cons:** quite remote but worth the drive. ⑤ Rooms from: R1430 ⊠ Off R68 ☎ 082/709–7951 ⊕ www.babanangovalley.co.za ⮡ 9 rooms, 1 cottage ⦿ Some meals.

$$ 🏨 **Protea Simunye Zulu Lodge.** If you find Shakaland too commercial, then
RESORT consider delving into Zulu culture at this small settlement in a remote valley of Zululand, 60 km (37 miles) from Babanango. **Pros:** smaller and more intimate than Shakaland. **Cons:** food not great. ⑤ Rooms from: R2040 ⊠ R68, Melmoth ☎ 035/450–0101, 079/786–3784 reservations ⊕ www.simunyelodge.co.za ⮡ 24 rooms ⦿ Some meals.

SHAKALAND

13 km (8 miles) north of Eshowe; 96 km (59 miles) southeast of Babanango.

If you're interested in learning more about the fierce warrior Shaka Zulu or the Zulu people, this living history museum will give you a glimpse into this amazing culture, its social structure, ceremonies, and crafts.

EXPLORING

Shakaland. A living museum of Zulu culture, Shakaland is one of the most popular tourist stops in the region. Originally the movie set for *Shaka Zulu* (1987), it consists of a traditional 19th-century Zulu kraal, with thatch beehive huts arranged in a circle around a central cattle enclosure. Watch traditionally dressed Zulus making beer, forging spears, and crafting beadwork. Opt for a three-hour day tour with lunch or spend the night. A Zulu cultural adviser leads you through the kraal, explaining the significance of the layout and the roles played by men and women in traditional Zulu society. A highlight is a performance of traditional Zulu dances. This is undoubtedly an excellent introduction to Zulu culture, but some critics have labeled it Zulu Disneyland. ⊠ *Normanhurst Farm, off R66, Nkwalini, KwaZulu-Natal* ✛ *13 km (8 miles) north of Eshowe* ☎ *035/460–0912, 087/740–9292 central reservations* ⊕ *www.shakaland.com* ☒ *R460* ☉ *Tours daily at 11 and noon.*

WHERE TO STAY

$$ ⊡ **Shakaland.** For a more in-depth exploration of Shakaland, stay the
HOTEL night at the 55-room Shakaland. **Pros:** warm, friendly staff; one-off
FAMILY experience. **Cons:** fake but fun. ⑤ *Rooms from: R2250* ⊠ *Normanhurst Farm, off R66, KwaZulu-Natal* ✛ *13 km (8 miles) north of Eshowe* ☎ *035/460–0912, 087/740–9292 central reservations* ⊕ *www.shakaland.com* ⇖ *55 rooms* ⍟ *Some meals.*

THE ELEPHANT COAST

The Elephant Coast is bordered in the northwest by the Ubombo Mountains, in the east by the Indian Ocean, and in the south by the Umfolozi River, which is just below the St. Lucia Estuary. The estuary is part of the iSimangaliso Wetland Park (Greater St. Lucia Wetland Park), South Africa's very first World Heritage Site. Although the area is only 200 km (124 miles) long and 70 km (43 miles) wide, its eco-diversity offers some of South Africa's most varied and gorgeous scenery: pristine coastal bird-rich forests, floodplains and inland lakes, unspoiled miles-long beaches, deep rivers, and unique sand forests. It's an outdoor lover's paradise, where you can swim (with sharks!), snorkel, surf, watch turtles, go hiking, mountain biking, deep-sea fishing or diving, check out the Big Five, or see dolphins and whales.

KwaZulu-Natal's best private lodges lie in northern Zululand and Maputaland, a remote region close to Mozambique. With one exception, the lodges reviewed here do not offer the Big Five. However, they are sufficiently close to one another and to the Hluhluwe-iMfolozi Game Reserve to allow you to put together a bush experience that delivers the Big Five and a great deal more, including superb bird-watching opportunities and an unrivaled beach paradise. Malaria does pose a problem, however, and antimalarial drugs are essential. Summers are hot, hot, hot. If you can't take heat and humidity, then autumn, winter, and early summer are probably the best time to visit.

WHEN TO GO

This area is hot and humid in summer, but if you can stand the heat, it's a great time to visit, because the scenery is at its greenest and most spectacular. Want to see turtles or whales? November through March is turtle-tracking time, and July through December is whale-watching time. Witnessing these magnificent creatures leaping or breaching above the waves is an unforgettable sight. From July to September you can spot humpback whales, and occasionally see Southern Right whales moving north to their breeding grounds off Mozambique; in September and November you can spot them on their way back to their Antarctic feeding grounds.

GETTING HERE AND AROUND

The Richards Bay airport is the closest to the Hluhluwe-iMfolozi area—about 100 km (60 miles) south of Hluhluwe-iMfolozi and about 224 km (140 miles) south of Ithala.

There are daily flights from Johannesburg to Richards Bay; flight time is about an hour. Private lodges will arrange your transfers for you.

If you're traveling to Hluhluwe-iMfolozi from Durban, drive north on the N2 to Mtubatuba, then cut west on the R618 to Mambeni Gate. Otherwise, continue up the N2 to the Hluhluwe exit and follow the signs to the park and Memorial Gate. The whole trip takes about three hours, but watch out for potholes.

If you're headed to Ithala from Durban, drive north on the N2 to Empangeni, and then head west on the R34 to Vryheid. From here cut east on the R69 to Louwsburg. The reserve is immediately northwest of the village, from which there are clear signs. The journey from Durban takes around 5 hours and from Hluhluwe-iMfolozi about 2½ hours. Roads are good, and there are plenty of gas stations along the way.

Contacts Richards Bay Airport ✉ *Fish Eagle Rd., Richards Bay* ☎ *035/786–0986.* **Upington International Airport** ☎ *054/337–7900* ⊕ *www.upingtonairport.com.*

TOURS

umHluhluwe Safaris. By far the largest tour operator in Zululand, this company offers a full range of three- and six-hour game drives in Hluhluwe-iMfolozi, as well as night drives and bush walks. The company also leads game drives into the Mkuze Game Reserve and guided tours to the bird-rich wetlands and beaches of St. Lucia. ☎ *035/562–0519, 082/964–2547. cell* ⊕ *www.hluhluwesafaris.co.za* ✍ *3-hr game drive R533, 6-hr game drive R715 (minimum of 4 people).*

VISITOR INFORMATION

Ezemvelo KZN Wildlife can provide information about the Hluhluwe-iMfolozi and Ithala game reserves and can help you book hikes on wilderness trails.

The Elephant Coast's website has information about dining and lodging, as well as attractions, towns you'll pass through, sports facilities, and much more. If you're visiting the Hluhluwe-iMfolozi Park, all activities can be booked through the website of the province's official conservation organization, Ezemvelo KZN Wildlife.

Contacts Elephant Coast ☎ *035/562–0966* ⊕ *www.elephantcoast.kzn.org.za.* **Ezemvelo KZN Wildlife** ☎ *033/845–1000* ⊕ *www.kznwildlife.com.*

RICHARDS BAY

177 km (110 miles) northeast of Durban.

Founded in the 1880s during the Anglo-Zulu colonial wars, Richards Bay was named after British Rear Admiral Sir Frederick William Richards, who landed a naval force here. An early claim to fame came in 1891, when colonial adventurer John Dunn killed a 22-foot crocodile in the estuary—still one of the largest ever documented—but the town remained a backwater with a population of less than 200 people until as recently as 1968. Today, Richards Bay is the major port in the region and is adjacent to significant mineral deposits, which have contributed to the town's massive growth. Visitors may be more interested in what awaits beyond in the hinterland. Richards Bay is the gateway to the land of the Zulu, one of Africa's most fascinating tribal peoples, and from here you have easy access to some of the world's finest wildlife game parks, including the Hluhluwe-Umfolozi Game Reserve, which protects the highest concentration of white rhino left in Africa.

EXPLORING

Richards Bay Game Reserve. Just south of town, the lagoon formed by the confluence of the Mzingazi and Mhlatuzi rivers has populations of hippos, crocodiles, monkeys, fish, and eagles. In 1935, 1,198 hectares (2,961 acres) of the lagoon was saved from development and named the Richards Bay Game Reserve. It is particularly important as a bird habitat, with more than 300 documented species, and offers permanent hides from which you can watch wading birds on the tidal flats and swamp wetlands. ⊕ *www.sa-venues.com/game-reserves/kzn_richardsbay.htm* 🖼 *Small entrance fee* ☉ *Daily 7–5.*

WHERE TO EAT

$ ✕**Dockside Shack.** You'll dine on wooden picnic tables at this rustic no-frills seafood shack near (but not on) the bay, where the food is fresh, plentiful, and unfussy—fresh lobster, prawns, whole grilled fish, and a range of salads. Cocktails are taken seriously, and you'll find a surfeit of colorful frozen drinks plus wine and beer. There's entertainment on weekends. ⑤ *Average main: R90* ⊠ *Pioneer Rd.* ☎ *35/788–0320.*

SEAFOOD

$ ✕**Elephant & I.** The question is what *won't* you find to eat at this popular restaurant in the Boardwalk Inkwazi shopping center. You name it, they've got it: from burgers, wraps, salads, bagel sandwiches, and paninis, to a jumble of international dinner dishes, like moussaka, lasagna, quiche, shepherd's pie, or stir fry, topped off with dessert. Early opening hours are a big bonus, all the better to enjoy an extensive menu of breakfast classics or a muffin and a great selection of coffee drinks.

FAST FOOD

If you want to come for dinner, be aware that they close early evening (3 pm on Sunday), so call to check. [$] *Average main: R80* ⊠ *Shop L26, Boardwalk Centre* ☎ *35/789–7269* ⊕ *www.elephant-and-i.co.za* ⚮ *Reservations not accepted.*

$ ✕ **The Hot Spot Food Fusion.** A welcome change from the soulless chain
MODERN INDIAN   restaurants that dominate the wharf, this humble mom-and-pop restaurant (opposite the parking area, not the waterfront) serves up its own delightful mix of Italian-Indian cuisine. Portions are large and you can choose from a variety of Indian dishes, like spicy lamb curry, butter chicken, and traditional garlic naan, along with burgers and fish and chips. Everything is served fresh and with a friendly smile. [$] *Average main: R80* ⊠ *6 Newark Rd.* ☎ *35/788–0563* ⚮ *Reservations not accepted* ☉ *Closed Mon.*

WHERE TO STAY

$ 🏠 **Aristo Manor Guesthouse.** Minutes from the airport and close to Rich-
B&B/INN   ard's Bay and Lake Mzingazi, this elegant seven-room guesthouse combines all the personalized service of a bed-and-breakfast with the amenities of an inn or small hotel. **Pros:** owners go out of their way to be accommodating; plenty of privacy; parking. **Cons:** not in the city center. [$] *Rooms from: R1000* ⊠ *16 Whydah Wing* ☎ *35/786–1212* ⊕ *www.aristomanor.com* ↪ *7 rooms* ◉ *No meals.*

$ 🏠 **Duck Inn.** You'll benefit from abundant peace and quiet at these six
B&B/INN   appealing guest rooms and three independent self-catering cottages—a pleasant, good-value alternative to the local hotels. **Pros:** only 2 km (1 mile) from Richard's Bay dining, shopping, and beach; wonderful service; very private. **Cons:** payment in advance required; suburban location, away from the center. [$] *Rooms from: R1000* ⊠ *3 Dageraad Meerensee* ☎ *35/753–4147* ⊕ *www.duckinn.co.za* ↪ *6 rooms, 3 cottages* ◉ *Breakfast.*

$$ 🏠 **Protea Hotel Waterfront Richards Bay.** Views are not an issue at this
HOTEL   modern hotel right on the bay, as all of the rooms face the water (some on the second and third floors also have balconies). **Pros:** close to the beach. **Cons:** service spotty; breakfast buffet scanty; Internet access only via phone lines. [$] *Rooms from: R1615* ⊠ *Corner of Pioneer and Bridgetown Rds., TuziGazi Waterfront* ☎ *35/788–0448* ⊕ *www.proteahotels.com/hotels/Pages/protea-hotel-waterfront-richards-bay.aspx* ↪ *75 rooms* ◉ *No meals.*

SHOPPING

Zulu art and handicrafts are the must-have souvenirs from a visit to Richards Bay. The beadwork objects are of particular interest because the traditional colors and patterns on the belts and bands were developed as secret coded messages from the Zulu women who made them, telling of love, jealousy, and loneliness. Needless to say, these days most pieces produced for the tourist market are simply pleasing to the eye rather than having any symbolic significance. Other handcrafted objects include pottery, used as everyday utensils, and carved wooden spears and shields once carried into battle by the Zulu warriors. The skill of carving is also put to good, and less bloody, use to produce statues of warriors and African animals (make sure that any wooden artifacts you buy have been treated against termites). Zulu handicrafts are best bought directly from the artisans at tribal villages, but they can also be found in craft markets and street stalls throughout the region. In Richards Bay, the Tuzi Gazi Waterfront shopping mall has a range of shops and, with its restaurants, boardwalk, and leisure marina, is a great place for strolling and browsing.

Boardwalk Inkwazi Shopping Centre. Richards Bay's most popular shopping mall has the kinds of chain stores you'd expect, plus some surprises. There's also a large selection of fast food and a movie theater. ⊠ *Krugerrand Grove* ☎ *35/789–7251* ⊙ *Mon.–Thurs. 9–6 , Fri. and Sat. 9–7, Sun. 10–8.*

HLUHLUWE-IMFOLOZI PARK

264 km (165 miles) northeast of Durban.

Renowned for its conservation successes—most notably with white rhinos—this reserve is a wonderful place to view the Big Five and many other species. Until 1989 it consisted of two separate parks, Hluhluwe in the north and iMfolozi in the south, separated by a fenced corridor. Although a road (R618) still runs through this corridor, the fences have been removed, and the parks now operate as a single entity. Hluhluwe and the corridor are the most scenic areas of the park, notable for their bush-covered hills and knockout views, whereas iMfolozi is better known for its broad plains.

EXPLORING

Dumazulu Cultural Village. This village has a royal connection, having been opened by the current King of the Zulu, Goodwill Zwelithini. It's the largest traditional cultural settlement in KwaZulu-Natal and home to 50 permanent residents. Visitors can experience Zulu culture, including traditional crafts, music, and cuisine. Artisans also sell their craftwork. ⊠ *Lot H29, Bushlands Rd., Hluhluwe* ☎ *35/562–2260.*

Hluhluwe-iMfolozi Park. Reputedly King Shaka's favorite hunting ground, Zululand's Hluhluwe-iMfolozi (pronounced shloo-*shloo*-ee im-fuh-*low*-zee) incorporates two of Africa's oldest reserves: Hluhluwe and iMfolozi, both founded in 1895. In an area of just 906 square km (350 square miles), Hluhluwe-iMfolozi delivers the Big Five plus all the plains game and species like nyala and red duiker that are rare in other parts of the country. Equally important, it encompasses one of the most biologically diverse habitats on the planet, with a unique mix of forest, woodland, savanna, and grassland. You'll find about 1,250 species of plants and trees here—more than in some entire countries.

The park is administered by Ezemvelo KZN Wildlife, the province's official conservation organization, which looks after all the large game reserves and parks as well as many nature reserves. Thanks to its conservation efforts and those of its predecessor, the highly regarded Natal Parks Board, the park can take credit for saving the white rhino from extinction. So successful was the park at increasing white rhino numbers that in 1960 it established its now famous Rhino Capture Unit to relocate rhinos to other reserves in Africa. The park is currently trying to do for the black rhino what it did for its white cousins. Poaching in the past nearly decimated Africa's black rhino population, but as a result of the park's remarkable conservation program, 20% of Africa's remaining black rhinos now live in this reserve—and you won't get a better chance of seeing them in the wild than here. ⊠ *Hluhluwe iMfolozi* ☎ *033/845–1002* ⊕ *www.kznwildlife.com* 🖃 *R130.*

ACTIVITIES

BUSH WALKS

Armed rangers lead groups of eight on two- to three-hour bush walks departing from Hilltop or Mpila Camp. You may not spot much game on these walks, but you do see plenty of birds, and you learn a great deal about the area's ecology and tips on how to recognize the signs of the bush, including animal spoor. Walks depart daily at 5:30 am and 3:30 pm (6 and 3 in winter) and cost R250. Reserve a few days in advance at **Hilltop Camp** reception (☎ *035/562–0848*).

GAME DRIVES

A great way to see the park is on game drives led by rangers. These drives (R300 per person) hold several advantages over driving through the park yourself: you sit high up in an open-air vehicle with a good view and the wind in your face, a ranger explains the finer points of animal behavior and ecology, and your guide has a good idea where to find animals like leopards, cheetahs, and lions. Game drives leave daily at 5:30 am in summer, 6:30 am in winter. The park also offers three-hour night drives, during which you search with powerful spotlights for nocturnal animals. These three-hour drives depart at 7, and you should make advance reservations at **Hilltop Camp reception** (☎ *035/562–0848*).

WILDERNESS TRAILS

The park's **Wilderness Trails** are every bit as popular as Kruger's, but they tend to be tougher and more rustic. You should be fit enough to walk up to 16 km (10 miles) a day for a period of three days and four nights. An armed ranger leads the hikes, and all equipment, food, and baggage are carried by donkeys. The first and last nights are spent at Mndindini, a permanent tented camp. The other two are spent under canvas in the bush. While in the bush, hikers bathe in the iMfolozi River or have a hot bucket shower; toilet facilities consist of a spade and toilet-paper roll. Trails, open March–October, are limited to eight people and should be reserved a year in advance (R3,450 per person per trail).

Fully catered two- or three-night **Short Wilderness Trails** (R2,250 per person) involve stays at a satellite camp in the wilderness area. You'll sleep in a dome tent, and although there's hot water from a bucket shower, your toilet is a spade.

If that sounds too easy, you can always opt for the four-night **Primitive Trail**. On this trek hikers carry their own packs and sleep out under the stars, although there are lightweight tents for inclement weather. A campfire burns all night to scare off animals, and each participant is expected to sit a 90-minute watch. A ranger acts as guide. The cost is R2,400 per person.

A less rugged wilderness experience can be had on the **Base Camp Trail**, based out of the tented Mndindini camp, where you're guaranteed a bed and some creature comforts. The idea behind these trails is to instill in the participants an appreciation for the beauty of the untamed bush. You can also join the Mpila night drive if you wish. Participation is limited to eight people and costs about R3,900 per person.

The Explorer Trail, two nights and three days, combines the most comfortable Base Camp trail with the Primitive Trail. On this trail you sleep out under the stars at a different spot each night. The cost is R2,350 per person.

WHERE TO STAY

Hluhluwe-iMfolozi offers a range of accommodations in government-run rest camps, with an emphasis on self-catering (only Hilltop has a restaurant). The park also has secluded bush lodges and camps, but most foreign visitors can't avail themselves of these lodgings, as each must be reserved in a block, and the smallest accommodates at least eight people. Conservation levies are R80 per person.

$$ **Hilltop Camp.** This delightful lodge in the Hluhluwe half of the park
RESORT matches some of South Africa's best private lodges. **Pros:** floodlit water
FAMILY hole. **Cons:** watch out for marauding monkeys. $ *Rooms from: R2188*
⊠ *Hluhluwe* ☎ *033/845–1000/1 central reservations, 035/562–0848*
⊕ *www.kznwildlife.com* ⮌ *20 rondavels, 49 chalets, 2 lodges* ⦶*No meals.*

$$ **Hluhluwe River Lodge.** Overlooking False Bay Lake and the Hluhluwe
ALL-INCLUSIVE River flood plain—follow signs from Hluhluwe village—this fantastic-
FAMILY value, family-owned lodge is the ideal base for visiting the game reserves and the iSimangaliso Wetland Park. **Pros:** only 25 minutes from Hluhluwe-iMfolozi; great for families. **Cons:** lots of kids in holiday times; activities cost extra. $ *Rooms from: R2390* ⊠ *Hluhluwe* ☎ *035/562–0246* ⊕ *www.hluhluwe.co.za* ⮌ *12 chalets* ⦶ *All-inclusive.*

$$ **Mpila Camp.** In the central iMfolozi section of the park, Mpila is
RENTAL reminiscent of some of Kruger's older camps. **Pros:** free-roaming game; lovely location. **Cons:** electricity only 7 am–10 pm; watch out for hyenas stealing your braai meat. $ *Rooms from: R1640* ⊠ *Hluhluwe iMfolozi* ☎ *033/845–1000/1 central reservations, 035/550–8476/7 reception* ⊕ *www.kznwildlife.com* ⮌ *2 cottages, 18 chalets, 13 safari tents, 2 lodges* ⦶ *No meals.*

$$$$ **Zululand Tree Lodge.** About 16 km (10 miles) from Hluhluwe-iMfolozi
HOTEL Park, this lodge lies in a forest of fever trees on the 3,700-acre Ubizane
FAMILY Game Reserve and makes a great base from which to explore Hluhluwe, Mkuze, and St. Lucia. **Pros:** bird's-eye views over lovely surroundings; friendly staff. **Cons:** smelly crocodile pool in front of dining deck. $ *Rooms from: R4560* ⊠ *1020 Main Rd., Hluhluwe* ☎ *035/562–1020* ⊕ *www.ubizane.co.za* ⮌ *24 rooms* ⦶ *All meals.*

UMKHUZE KZN PARK

48 km (30 miles) north of Hluhluwe-iMfolozi.

Wildlife—and amazing birdlife—abounds in this 400-square-km (154-square-mile) reserve in the shadow of the Ubombo Mountains. Lying between the uMkhuze and Msunduzi rivers, it makes up the northwestern spur of the iSimangaliso Wetland Park, a World Heritage Site. It has been a protected area since 1912.

EXPLORING

OFF THE BEATEN PATH

Jozini Dam. It may be off the main tourist routes, but if you've time head for the huge, beautiful 160-square-km (62-square-mile) Jozini Dam (or Lake Jozini), that lies in northern KwaZulu Natal and borders Swaziland. Easily accessible from Gauteng, it's approximately five hours southeast by road from Johannesburg, via Pongola, and approximately three hours northeast from Durban. The dam is lined by the Pongola Game Reserve—one of South Africa's oldest reserves (proclaimed in 1894)—so all sorts of game meanders along the banks, from black and white rhinos to elephants and hippos. If you're a birder you'll be in avian heaven, as the dam is a magnet for waterbirds of every description. ■ TIP→ **The dam has the best tiger fishing in South Africa (in season), but if you don't catch and release a tiger, maybe you'll hook a yellowfish, carp, or tilapia.** ⊠ *Mkuze* ⊕ *www.kznwildlife.co.za.*

uMkhuze KZN Park. If you're a birder, then you'll find yourself in seventh heaven in this reserve, 48 km (30 miles) north of Hluhluwe-iMfolozi, which is famous for its birds: more than 420 bird species have been spotted here, including myriad waterfowl drawn to the park's shallow pans in summer. Several blinds, particularly those overlooking Nsumo Pan, offer superb views. Don't miss out on the amazing 3-km (2-mile) walk through a spectacular rare forest of towering, ancient fig trees. This is a good place to spot rhinos and elephants although lions, cheetah and leopard, are much harder to find. However, there's is plenty of other game, including hippos, zebras, giraffes, kudus, and nyalas. ■ TIP→ **There are variant spellings of Mkuze in the area; you may also see Mkuzi or Mkhuzi.** ⊠ *Off N2, Mkuze* ☎ *035/573–9004* ⊕ *www. kznwildlife.com* ☝ *R40 per vehicle plus R40 per person* ☉ *Daily 6–6.*

WHERE TO STAY

$$
B&B/INN

Ghost Mountain Inn. Swaths of scarlet bougainvillea run riot in the lush gardens of this family-owned country inn with tastefully furnished rooms that each have a small veranda. **Pros:** good value for money; generous buffet; good curio shop. **Cons:** hotel-like atmosphere; tour buses overnight here. ⑤ *Rooms from: R2020* ⊠ *Fish Eagle Rd., uMkhuze* ☎ *035/573–1025* ⊕ *www.ghostmountaininn.co.za* ☝ *50 rooms* ⑩ *Breakfast.*

$$$
ALL-INCLUSIVE

Shayamanzi Houseboats. Cabins with floor-to-ceiling windows allow you to lie on your king-size bed and view hippos, water birds, elephants, giraffe, zebra, crocodiles, and even an occasional rhino without even getting up. **Pros:** friendly staff; tasty food; tiger fishing in season. **Cons:** off the beaten track; very hot and humid in summer. ⑤ *Rooms from: R2950* ⊠ *Jozini Tiger Lodge, 1 Main Rd., Jozini* ☎ *034/413–2299* ⊕ *www.shayamanzi.co.za* ☝ *16 cabins* ⑩ *All-inclusive.*

ITHALA GAME RESERVE

221 km (138 miles) northwest of Hluhluwe-iMfolozi.

The topography of this reserve, from mountaintop to deep river valleys, incorporates varied terrain and plantlife, and makes for superior game-viewing in relation to its relatively small size. Thousands of years of human habitation have also provided archaeological and historical interest.

EXPLORING

Ithala Game Reserve. Close to the Swaziland border, Ithala (sometimes spelled "Itala"), founded in 1972 and run by KZN Wildlife, is a rugged region that drops 3,290 feet in just 15 km (9 miles) through sandstone cliffs, multicolor rocks, granite hills, ironstone outcrops, and quartz formations. Because it's a small reserve (296 square km [114 square miles]), and has no lions, it's often bypassed, even by South Africans. The other four of the Big Five are here—it's excellent for black and white rhinos—and you could spot cheetahs, hyenas, giraffes, and an array of antelopes among its 80 mammal species. It's also an excellent spot for birders. The stunning landscapes and the relaxed game-viewing make this area a breath of fresh air after the Big Five melee of Kruger. ⌧ *Pongola* ☏ *033/845–1002* ⊕ *www.kznwildlife.com* ⌦ *R40 per person and R40 per vehicle.*

WHERE TO STAY

Although Ithala has several exclusive bush camps, these are booked up months in advance by South Africans, making the chalets at its main camp the only practical accommodations for foreign visitors.

$$
RENTAL
Fodor's Choice
★

Ntshondwe Camp. Arriving at the award-winning Ntshondwe Camp is nothing short of dramatic. **Pros:** tarred road access; game drives; self-guided walks. **Cons:** busy conference and wedding venue. ⑤ *Rooms from: R1680* ⌧ *Ithala Game Reserve* ☏ *033/845–1000/1* ⊕ *www. kznwildlife.com* ⌦ *67 chalets, 1 lodge* ⑩ *No meals.*

> ### SELF-GUIDED TRAILS
>
> An unusual feature of Ithala is its self-guided walking trails, in the mountainside above Ntshondwe Camp. The trails give you a chance to stretch your limbs if you've just spent hours cooped up in a car. They also let you get really close to the euphorbias, acacias, and other fascinating indigenous vegetation that festoon the hills. Ask at the camp reception for further information.

PHINDA PRIVATE GAME RESERVE

134 km (83 miles) from Richards Bay; 300 km (186 miles) from Durban.

Where Phinda excels is in the superb quality of its rangers, who can provide fascinating commentary on everything from local birds to frogs. It's amazing just how enthralling the love life of a dung beetle can be! There are also Phinda adventures (optional extras) down the Mzinene River for a close-up look at crocodiles, hippos, and birds; big-game fishing or scuba diving off the deserted, wildly beautiful Maputaland coast; and sightseeing flights over Phinda and the highest vegetated dunes in the world.

GETTING HERE AND AROUND

Phinda is 300 km (186 miles) from Durban by road, with a journey time of just over four hours. Before you decide to drive, bear in mind that you won't use your vehicle after you arrive at Phinda—all transportation is provided by open game-viewing vehicles. There are scheduled flights daily from Johannesburg to King Shaka International Airport and to Richards Bay Airport (check with the lodge for latest schedules). Phinda will also arrange road transfers from the airports.

EXPLORING

FAMILY **Phinda Private Game Reserve.** This eco-award-winning flagship &Beyond reserve, established in 1991, is a heartening example of tourism serving the environment with panache. *Phinda* (*pin*-duh) is Zulu for "return," referring to the restoration of 220 square km (85 square miles) of overgrazed ranchland in northern Zululand to bushveld. It's a triumph. Today Phinda has a stunning variety of five healthy ecosystems: sand forest (which grows on the fossil dunes of an earlier coastline), savanna, bushveld, open woodland, and verdant wetlands. The Big Five are all here, plus leopards, cheetahs, spotted hyenas, hippos, giraffes, impalas, and the rare, elusive, tiny Suni antelope. Birdlife is prolific and extraordinary, with some special Zululand finds: the pink-throated twin spot, the crested guinea fowl, the African broadbill, and the crowned eagle. The reserve is a little more than a two-hour drive from Richards Bay or four hours by road from Durban. ⊠ *Phinda Game Reserve* ☎ *011/809–4300* ⊕ *www.andbeyond.com.*

WHERE TO STAY

$$$$ 🏨 **Forest Lodge.** Hidden in a rare sand forest, this fabulous lodge
ALL-INCLUSIVE overlooks a small water hole where nyalas, warthogs, and baboons
Fodor's Choice frequently come to drink. **Pros:** magical feeling of oneness with the
★ surrounding bush. **Cons:** being in a glass box could make some visitors nervous; not for traditional tastes. ⑤ *Rooms from: R12000* ⊠ *Phinda Game Reserve* ☎ *011/809–4300 reservations* ⊕ *www.andbeyond.com* ⌁ *16 suites* ⦿*| All-inclusive.*

$$$$ 🏨 **Mountain Lodge.** This attractive thatch lodge sits on a rocky hill over-
ALL-INCLUSIVE looking miles of bushveld plains and the Ubombo Mountains. **Pros:**
FAMILY great mountain views; very family-friendly. **Cons:** rather bland interiors; pricey if you take the kids (pricey even if you don't take the kids). ⑤ *Rooms from: R12000* ⊠ *Phinda Game Reserve, off R22, Hluhluwe* ☎ *011/809–4300 reservations* ⊕ *www.andbeyond.com* ⌁ *25 suites* ⦿*| All-inclusive.*

$$$$ 🏨 **Rock Lodge.** If you get tired of the eagle's-eye view of the deep val-
ALL-INCLUSIVE ley below from your private veranda, you can write in your journal in your luxurious sitting room or take a late-night dip in your own plunge pool. **Pros:** personal plunge pools; amazing views. **Cons:** stay away if you suffer from vertigo. ⑤ *Rooms from: R14340* ⊠ *Phinda Game Reserve* ☎ *011/809–4300 reservations* ⊕ *www.andbeyond.com* ⌁ *6 suites* ⦿*| All-inclusive.*

$$$$
ALL-INCLUSIVE
Fodor's Choice
★
⬛ **Vlei Lodge.** Your suite at this comfortable lodge, tucked into the shade of a sand forest, is so private it's hard to believe there are other guests. **Pros:** superb views over the floodplains. **Cons:** lots of mosquitoes and other flying insects. $ *Rooms from: R14340* ✉ *Phinda Game Reserve* ☎ *011/809–4300* ⊕ *www.andbeyond.com* ↪ *6 suites* ⦿ *All-inclusive.*

$$$$
ALL-INCLUSIVE
FAMILY
⬛ **Zuka Lodge.** An exclusive, single-use lodge for a family or small group of friends, Zuka (*zuka* means "sixpence" in Zulu) is a couple of miles from the bigger lodges. **Pros:** exclusivity; it's like having your own private holiday retreat; gives you the feeling of immediate celebrity status. **Cons:** this exclusivity comes at a high price; entire property must be rented as a whole; choose your fellow guests carefully—you're on your own here. $ *Rooms from: R13650* ✉ *Phinda Game Reserve* ☎ *011/809–4300 reservations* ⊕ *www.andbeyond.com* ↪ *4 cottages* ⦿ *All-inclusive.*

THANDA PRIVATE GAME RESERVE

23 km (14 miles) north of Hluhluwe; 400 km (248 miles) north of Durban.

One of KwaZulu-Natal's newer game reserves, Thanda offers a more intimate nature experience than some. Game may sometimes be elusive, but the highly experienced and enthusiastic rangers work hard to find the Big Five and other wildlife. Enjoyable cultural interactions with local people are a highlight of any visit.

GETTING HERE AND AROUND
Road transfers from Richards Bay and Durban airports can be arranged with the reserve.

EXPLORING
Thanda Private Game Reserve. In wild, beautiful northern Zululand, the multi-award-winning 150-square-km (60-square-mile) Thanda reserve, which turned 10 in 2014, continues to restore former farmlands and hunting grounds to their previous pristine state, thanks to a joint venture with local communities and the king of the Zulus, Goodwill Zwelitini, who donated some of his royal hunting grounds to the project. Game that used to roam this wilderness centuries ago has been reestablished, including the Big Five. *Thanda* (*tan*-duh) is Zulu for "love," and its philosophy echoes just that: "for the love of nature, wildlife, and dear ones." There's a main lodge, a private villa, and a small tented camp and opportunities to interact with the local people. ✉ *D242, off N2, Hluhluwe* ⊕ *www.thanda.com.*

WHERE TO STAY
$$$$
ALL-INCLUSIVE
FAMILY
⬛ **Thanda Main Lodge.** This exquisite lodge blends elements of royal Zulu with an eclectic pan-African feel. **Pros:** luxury unlimited. **Cons:** some might say it's Hollywood in the bush. $ *Rooms from: R12500* ✉ *Off N2 and D242, Hluhluwe* ☎ *035/573–1899* ⊕ *www.thanda.com* ↪ *9 chalets* ⦿ *All-inclusive.*

$$$$
ALL-INCLUSIVE
FAMILY
⬛ **Thanda Tented Camp.** Perfect for a family or friends' reunion (although it's great for individual travelers too), this intimate, luxurious camp deep in the bush brings you into close contact with your surroundings.

7

Pros: five-star luxury on a bonsai scale; solar power. Cons: not for the nervous type; no a/c; no children. ⑤ *Rooms from: R7100* ⊠ *Off N2, D242, Hluhluwe* ☎ *035/573–1899* ⊕ *www.thanda.co.za* ⇨ *15 tents* ⑩ *All-inclusive.*

AMAZULU PRIVATE GAME RESERVE AND AMAKHOSI LODGE

155 km (14 miles) southeast of Hluhluwe; 400 km (248 miles) north of Durban.

Amazulu Private Game Reserve incorporates mountains, wetlands, and savanna and in addition to the Big Five, many other mammals and hundreds of bird species make their home here. Zululand has more frog species than the whole of Europe, and to go on a frogging safari at Amakhosi is a unique and unforgettable experience.

GETTING HERE AND AROUND

Roads are good here, so you can drive yourself. The nearest airport is Richards Bay, which has scheduled flights from all major cities. If necessary, AmaKhosi Lodge does road transfers from Richards Bay.

EXPLORING

Amazulu Private Game Reserve and AmaKhosi Lodge. More than 100 square km (39 square miles) of pristine wilderness on the perennial Mkhuze River are the attraction at this private reserve, where habitats range from rocky hillsides to thick bushveld, tamboti forests to broad wetlands. AmaKhosi has all of the Big Five, in addition to wildebeests, zebras, giraffes, and a variety of antelopes, including the shy nyala. Most animals have been reintroduced, with the exception of leopards, which remain secretive and very difficult to spot. Hundreds of birds, however, are much easier to see. ■TIP➜ Try something really special— after a day spotting big game, join a guided frogging safari at night. Armed with a lighted miner's helmet, you'll discover a whole new exciting amphibian world. The reserve is 40 km (21 miles) south of Pongola. ⊠ *Pongola* ☎ *034/414–1157* 🖷 *034/414–1172* ⊕ *www.amakhosi.com.*

WHERE TO STAY

$$$$
RESORT
🖫 **AmaKhosi Lodge.** This spectacular lodge overlooks the Mkhuze River in the heart of northern KwaZulu Natal, where birdlife is abundant and the Big Five are all present. **Pros:** exciting night time frogging expeditions. **Cons:** off the beaten track. ⑤ *Rooms from: R7800* ⊠ *Off the N2, Pongola* ☎ *034/414–1157* 🖷 *034/414–1172* ⊕ *www.amakhosi.com* ⇨ *9 suites* ⑩ *All meals.*

MAPUTALAND COASTAL FOREST RESERVE

300 km (186 miles) from Richards Bay.

Expect great swaths of pale, creamy sand stretching to far-off rocky headlands, a shimmering, undulating horizon where whales blow. Watch out for pods of dolphins leaping and dancing in the morning sun. If you're here in season (November to early March), one of nature's greatest and most spiritually uplifting experiences is waiting for you— turtle tracking.

GETTING HERE AND AROUND

Visitors fly into Richards Bay from Johannesburg and are picked up by the lodge's transportation—they will make all the flight and pickup arrangements, and if you'd like to travel by road instead of air, they can arrange a car service to get you to and from Johannesburg. You could drive yourself, but it's really an unnecessary waste of time and car-rental fees, as you won't be able to use the vehicle once you're on the property. Plus, you'd need to rent a 4x4, because the last part of the road is very bumpy and muddy.

WHEN TO GO

The loggerhead and leatherback turtle egg-laying season goes from November through early March. During these months rangers lead after-dinner drives and walks down the beach to look for turtles, and you can expect to cover as much as 16 km (10 miles) in a night. From a weather standpoint, the best times to visit the lodge are probably spring (September–October) and autumn (March–May). In summer the temperature regularly soars past 38°C (100°F), but this is when the turtles come ashore to dig their nests and lay their eggs—an awesome spectacle. Swimming during winter is a brisk proposition, and August is the windiest month.

EXPLORING

iSimangaliso Wetland Park. Declared a UNESCO World Heritage Site (South Africa's first) in 1999, the iSimangaliso Wetland encompasses a number of disparate natural African environments including the Umfolozi Swamp Forest and the Maputaland Marine Reserve, an important nesting site for endangered loggerhead and leatherback turtles. The most carefree way to enjoy the reserve is on a boat trip, where you'll be able to get close to hippos and immense Nile crocodiles and try to spot some of the more than 500 species of birds that call the park home. Two-hour trips run by the park (R140/person) leave daily at 10, noon, and 3, and require a minimum of 6 people. The park protects myriad river and coastal environments, including the estuary of the St. Lucia River, coral reefs, sandy beaches, coastal dunes, inland and tidal lakes, swamps, mangrove forests, and papyrus wetlands. ⊠ *KwaZulu-Natal* ☎ *35/590–1633* ⊕ *isimangaliso.com.*

Maputaland Coastal Forest Reserve. The highlight of a visit here, if it's timed right, is to view the loggerhead and leatherback turtles. Nothing—not photographs, not wildlife documentaries—prepares you for the size of these creatures. On any given night, you might see a huge, humbling leatherback, 6 feet long and weighing up to 500 kg (1,100 pounds), drag her great body up through the surf to the high-water mark at the back of the beach. There she will dig a deep hole and lay up to a 120 gleaming white eggs, bigger than a golf ball but smaller than a tennis ball. It will have taken her many, many years to achieve this moment of fruition, a voyage through time and across the great oceans of the world—a long, solitary journey in the cold black depths of the sea, meeting and mating only once every seven years, and always coming back to within about 300 feet of the spot on the beach where she herself had been born. And if your luck holds, you might even observe the miracle of the hatchlings, when perfect bonsai leatherback turtles

7

dig themselves out of their deep, sandy nest and rush pell-mell toward the sea under a star-studded sky. ⊠ *Off Hwy. 2, south of Mtunzini.*

WHERE TO STAY

$$$$
RESORT
FAMILY

⛺ Rocktail Beach Camp. Tucked away in the Maputaland Coastal Forest, with glorious unspoiled beaches, this lovely lodge is perfect for families, though it's great for individual travelers and honeymooners, too. **Pros:** pristine reefs; loggerhead and leatherback turtle nesting sites. **Cons:** 20-minute walk to beach; difficult to access. ⑤ *Rooms from: R5738 ⊠ D1850, Maputaland Coastal Forest Reserve ☎ 011/807–1800 reservations ⊕ www.wilderness-safaris.com ⇗ 17 rooms* ⦿| *All meals.*

$$$$
RESORT
Fodor's Choice
★

⛺ Thonga Beach Lodge. Dramatically sited, this lovely beach lodge a stone's throw from the sea has air-conditioned, thatch suites decorated in chic Robinson Crusoe style with wooden floors, reed interior walls, cane and wooden furniture, gorgeous bathrooms with sea views, and personal decks looking out over rolling coastal dunes and the blue Indian Ocean. **Pros:** Robinson Crusoe deluxe; turtle tracking; spa treatments. **Cons:** difficult to get to, so pricey. ⑤ *Rooms from: R8280 ⊠ Maputaland Coastal Forest Reserve ☎ 035/474–1490, 035/474–1473 reservations ⊕ www.isibindi.co.za ⇗ 12 chalets* ⦿| *All meals.*

8

JOHANNESBURG

Updated by
Tara Turkington

Johannesburg, or Jo'burg, Egoli ("City of Gold"), or Jozi, as it is affectionately known by locals, is the commercial heart of South Africa and the primary gateway for international visitors. Historically it is where money is made and fortunes are found. The city has a (perhaps rather unfair) reputation for being an ugly, dangerous place you ought to avoid on any trip to South Africa. On the contrary, much of Johannesburg is quite pretty, largely because of the millions of trees that cover it (it has, purportedly, the largest human-planted forest in the world), and statistically speaking it is less dangerous than Cape Town.

But like all big cities in the world, there are some areas that are safer than others; you should keep your wits about you in Jo'burg and not flaunt expensive equipment or jewelry in public places. Johannesburg is South Africa's most-visited city by far, and it's well worth a stopover of at least two or three days. There's plenty to see here, including the Apartheid Museum and Constitution Hill in the city, not to mention the nearby city of Soweto, and the Cradle of Humankind World Heritage Site about 90 minutes away. All the attractions listed in this chapter, including areas like Sandton, Rosebank, Greenside, and Parkhurst, are perfectly safe to visit on your own.

Ask a *jol* (lively party) of Jo'burgers what they love about their hometown, and they may point to its high-paced energy; its opportunity; afternoon thunderstorms in the summer; the Pirates versus Chiefs derby (the Orlando Pirates and Kaizer Chiefs are South Africa's most loved—and hated—soccer teams); spectacular sunsets; jacaranda blooms carpeting the city in purple in October and November; a great climate; the dog walks around Emmarentia Dam; the fast-paced lifestyle; the can-do attitude; the down-to-earth nature of its people; and the city's rich history. For many, Johannesburg is the gateway to the rest of Africa, and it may very well be the continent's most cosmopolitan city.

Johannesburg's origins lie in the discovery of gold. The city sits at the center of a vast urban industrial complex that covers most of the province of Gauteng (the *g* is pronounced like the *ch* in Chanukah), which means "Place Where the Gold Is" in the Sotho language and is home to the world's deepest gold mines (more than 3.9 km [2.4 miles] deep). More than 100 years ago it was just a rocky piece of unwanted Highveld land. But in 1886 an Australian, George Harrison, officially discovered gold, catapulting Johannesburg into a modern metropolis that still helps to power the country's economy (though gold mining has been winding down in recent years).

TOP REASONS TO GO

History in Your Lifetime. Do a self-guided tour of the Constitutional Court, built on the site of a prison whose inmates included Mahatma Gandhi and Nelson Mandela. The Apartheid Museum takes a holistic look at South Africa's road to democracy.

Iconic Soweto. Visit the site of some dramatic anti-apartheid struggles, including the Hector Pieterson Museum, as well as former homes of Nobel Peace Prize laureates Nelson Mandela and Archbishop Desmond Tutu.

African Arts and Crafts. The African Craft Market in Rosebank showcases ornaments, masks, and fabrics from across Africa, ranging from the cheap and cheerful to one-off collector's items.

Cradle of Humankind. Visit the Sterkfontein Caves and Maropeng Visitor Centre at this World Heritage Site, about 90 minutes from Johannesburg, to view humankind's evolutionary pathway, fossils, and paleontology, presented in a fun, kid-friendly manner.

With a population between 8 and 10 million—if you include the surrounding cities like Soweto, the East Rand, and the West Rand—greater Jo'burg is a fairly populous city by world standards (bigger than New York but smaller than Tokyo) and is by far the country's largest city. Despite its industrial past, Jozi remains a green city, with more than 10 million trees and many beautiful parks and nature reserves, which is all the more exceptional considering it is the largest city in the world not built on a river or near a significant water source.

In addition, local government has invested in an extensive new public transportation system that serves the local working population and tourists alike. This includes the Gautrain rapid rail system that connects Johannesburg with Pretoria and the O. R. Tambo International Airport, moving Jo'burg steadily toward its goal of being—as the city's government is eager to brand it—"a world-class African city."

ORIENTATION AND PLANNING

GETTING ORIENTED

South Africa's biggest city is in the middle of Gauteng, South Africa's smallest but wealthiest province. The greater metropolitan area is a massive 1,645 square km (635 square miles), most of which is made up of suburban sprawl. The M1, a major highway, runs centrally through the city and its suburbs. Two adjoining highways circle the city: the N3 to the east and the N1 to the west; the M1 bisects this circle.

Johannesburg City Center. Jo'burg was born as a mining camp, and its downtown area—the oldest part—is a jumbled grid of one-way streets heading in opposite directions, reflecting its hasty start to life. A number of important attractions, such as Constitution Hill, are found here.

Soweto and the South. About 20 km (12 miles) south of downtown Johannesburg, the vast township of Soweto is where the 1976 anti-apartheid student uprisings began; Soweto is now officially part of greater Johannesburg, though during apartheid, they were regarded as poles apart. Take a full- or half-day township tour and visit the Hector Pieterson Memorial and Museum and former homes of Nelson Mandela and Desmond Tutu. City Sightseeing also offers a Soweto add-on.

Northern Suburbs. Most of the city's good hotels and major malls are in the northern suburbs: notably Sandton, the new financial center of South Africa, and Rosebank, a chic commercial center. Greenside and Parkhurst, close to Rosebank, are popular for eating out.

PLANNING

WHEN TO GO
Jo'burgers boast that they enjoy the best climate in the world: not too hot in summer (mid-September–mid-April), not too cold in winter (mid-April–mid-September), and not prone to sudden temperature changes. Summer (especially during December and January) may have the edge, though: it's when the gardens and open spaces are at their most beautiful.

GETTING HERE AND AROUND
It's difficult but not impossible to see the Johannesburg area without a car. A good bet is to rent one, decide what you want to see, and get a good road map or rent a GPS navigator. If you're reluctant to drive yourself, book a couple of full-day or half-day tours that will pick you up from your hotel or a central landmark. The City Sightseeing bus can give you an excellent overview of the city and enable you to hop on and off at most of Johannesburg's attractions. Spend a half day or a full day doing this.

AIR TRAVEL
O. R. Tambo International Airport is about 19 km (12 miles) from the Johannesburg city center and is linked to the city by a fast highway, which is always busy but especially before 9 am and between 4 and 7 pm. The best way to travel to and from it is via the Gautrain, a high-speed train that connects Sandton, Johannesburg, and Pretoria directly with O. R. Tambo. It takes about 30 minutes to travel from the airport to Sandton. The train runs from between 5 or 5:30 am and 9 or 9:30 pm every day, depending on the station.

Alternatively, Magic Bus offers private transfers to all major Sandton hotels (R575 per vehicle for one or two people, R630 for three people, R670 for four to seven people). The journey takes 30 minutes to an hour. Getthere Transfers and Tours charges R450 from the airport to anywhere in Johannesburg for the first rider and R30 for each additional person (R500 to Pretoria and R50 for each additional person). Airport Link will ferry you anywhere in the central Johannesburg area for R490 per person.

Wilro Tours runs from the airport to Sandton (R835 for one to three people, R1,230 for four to seven).

In addition, scores of licensed taxis line up outside the airport terminal. By law they must have a working meter. Expect to pay about R500 for a trip to Sandton. Negotiate a price before you get into a taxi.

Lines at the airport can be long: plan to arrive two to three hours before an international departure and at least an hour before domestic departures. The airport has its own police station, but luggage theft has been a problem in recent years. Keep your belongings close to you at all times.

If your hotel or guesthouse does not have a shuttle, ask a staff member to arrange for your transportation with a reliable company. Most lodgings have a regular service they use, so you should have no problem arranging this in advance.

Prices vary, depending on where you are staying, but plan on R400–R500 for a ride from your hotel or guesthouse in Sandton, Rosebank, or the city center to the airport. Some companies charge per head, whereas others charge per trip, so be sure to check that in advance. The Gautrain is less expensive, quick, and safe, but you'll have to handle your own luggage. Most guesthouses or hotels will be able to drop you at the closest Gautrain station.

⇨ *For airline contact information, see Air Travel, in the Travel Smart South Africa chapter.*

Airport Contacts O. R. Tambo International Airport ☏ *086/727–7888* ⊕ *www.acsa.co.za.*

Airport Transfers Airport Link ☏ *011/794–8300, 083/625–5090* ⊕ *www.airportlink.co.za.* **Gautrain** ☏ *0800/428–87246* ⊕ *www.gautrain.co.za.* **Getthere Transfers and Tours** ✉ *Johannesburg* ☏ *076/6324235.* **Legend Tours and Transfers** ☏ *021/704–9140* ⊕ *www.legendtours.co.za.* **Magic Bus** ☏ *011/548–0822* ⊕ *www.megabus.co.za.*

BUS TRAVEL

Intercity buses depart from Park Station in Braamfontein in the Johannesburg city center. Greyhound, Translux, and Intercape Mainliner operate extensive routes around the country. The Baz Bus operates a hop-on, hop-off door-to-door service, stopping at backpackers' hostels between Johannesburg and Durban or Jo'burg and Cape Town via the Drakensberg. You can buy Greyhound, Intercape Mainliner, and Translux bus tickets through Computicket. Airfares with budget airlines in South Africa, such as Mango, or Kulula (⇨ *Air Travel in Travel Smart)* are more expensive than bus fares, but traveling by plane is much more efficient and comfortable, because the distances in South Africa can be vast. Be sure to book as far in advance as you can if you are going to fly or go by bus, as tickets can get more expensive as you approach the date of travel, and during peak holiday times (especially over Easter in April and December/January) tickets can sell out.

CAR TRAVEL

Traveling by car is the easiest way to get around Johannesburg, as the city's public transportation is not that reliable or extensive, though this is changing (the Gautrain, for example, is incredibly reliable). The general speed limit for city streets is 60 kph (37 mph); for main streets it's often 80 kph (50 mph), and for highways it's 100 kph or 120 kph (62 mph or 75 mph). But be warned that Johannesburg drivers are known as the most aggressive in the country, and minibus taxis are famous for ignoring the rules of the road, often stopping for passengers with little or no warning. Most city roads and main countryside roads are in good condition, with plenty of signage. City street names are sometimes visible only on the curb, however. Avoid driving in rush hours, 7 to 8:30 am and 4 to 6:30 pm, as the main roads become terribly congested. Gas stations are plentiful in most areas. (Don't pump your own gas, though; stations employ operators to do that for you.)

Almost everywhere there are security guards who look after parked cars. It's customary to give these guards a small tip (R2 or R5) when you return to your car. Most big shopping centers have parking garages (about R8 per hour).

If you plan to drive yourself around, get a *good* map of the city center and northern suburbs or buy or rent a GPS (available at the airport and most car-rental agencies). MapStudio prints excellent complete street guides, available at bookstores and many gas stations and convenience stores.

Major rental agencies have offices in the northern suburbs and at the airport. (⇨ *For information on roadside assistance or national car-rental companies, see Car Travel, in the Travel Smart South Africa chapter.*)

TAXI TRAVEL

Minibus taxis form the backbone of Jo'burg's transportation for ordinary commuters, but you should avoid using them since they're often not roadworthy, drivers can be irresponsible, and it's difficult to know where they're going without consulting a local. Car taxis, though more expensive, are easier to use. They have stands at the airport and the train stations, but otherwise you must phone for one (be sure to ask how long it will take the taxi to get to you). Taxis should be licensed and have a working meter. Meters usually start at R50 (includes first 3 km [2 miles]) and are about R13 per kilometer (½ mile) thereafter. Expect to pay about R500 to the airport from town or Sandton and about R300 to the city center from Sandton. Uber is a popular, safe, and inexpensive taxi service, but it can be accessed only from an app.

Contacts Maxi Taxi ☎ *011/648–1212, 011/648–1200.* **Quick Cab** ☎ *086/166–5566.* **Rose Taxis** ☎ *011/403–9625, 011/403–0000* ⊕ *www.rosetaxis.com.* **Uber** ⊕ *www.uber.com/cities/johannesburg.*

TRAIN TRAVEL

Johannesburg's train station, Park Station, is in Braamfontein, at Leyds and Loveday streets. The famous, luxurious Blue Train, which makes regular runs to Cape Town, departs from here, as do Shosholoza Meyl trains to cities around the country, including the Trans-Karoo to Cape Town, the Komati to Nelspruit in Mpumalanga, and the Trans-Natal to Durban. Many of these trains have overnight service. They vary a lot in terms of comfort levels and price, and the more expensive ones such as the Blue Train are often booked up far in advance (though it's always worth a try if you want to make a reservation on short notice).

Locally, you can catch the Gautrain from O. R. Tambo, Pretoria, Sandton, or Rosebank to Park Station (see ⇨ *Airport Transfers in Air Travel*).

TOURS

Township tours (to Soweto in particular) are offered by a number of local operators. One of the best options is to do a Soweto tour with the City Sightseeing bus, which partners with local operators for tours of Soweto. Wilro Tours and JMT Tours and Safaris offer half-day and full-day tours of Johannesburg and Soweto. For more recommendations of reputable tour operators, inquire at Johannesburg Tourism.

Africa Explore. Africa Explore offers full-day and half-day tours of the Cradle of Humankind area; the full package includes the Kromdraai Gold Mine, Sterkfontein Caves, and the Rhino and Lion Park. ☎ *011/917–1999, 072/242–2281* ⊕ *www.africa-explore.co.za* ✉ *From R925.*

Fodor's Choice **City Sightseeing Bus.** The City Sightseeing bus is a great and very safe ★ way to see the Johannesburg city center and all its main attractions. The bus departs from 12 locations every 30 minutes from 9 to 5 every day, but the best places to catch it are either at Gold Reef City or Park Station (accessible via the Gautrain). Adults and kids alike will love the experience; there's a special children's soundtrack, and the adult commentary is available in 16 languages. The total trip takes about two hours if you don't get off (though you should consider at least getting off at the Apartheid Museum and Constitution Hill); you can get a one- or two-day pass. There is also an option to pair it with a Soweto tour, also highly recommended. You can buy your tickets at O. R. Tambo, at Gold Reef City, or Park Station (or you can wait and buy tickets on any City Sightseeing bus), but there's a discount for purchasing them online. ☎ *0861/733–287* ⊕ *www.citysightseeing.co.za* ✉ *From R150.*

JMT Tours and Safaris. JMT Tours and Safaris can arrange tailor-made trips for small groups to a number of destinations. Prices will vary according to where you want to go and how many people are in your group. JMT Tours and Safaris specializes in tours of Soweto but also does the Cradle of Humankind and can take you farther afield. ☎ *010/233–0073, 083/307–4390* ⊕ *www.jmttours.com* ✉ *From R690.*

Johannesburg Heritage Foundation. Interested in checking out hundreds of heritage buildings? Most are closed to the public, but the Johannesburg Heritage Foundation organizes tours of the houses and gardens, which will give you a glimpse of turn-of-the-20th-century grandeur. Prearranged tours looking at different aspects of Johannesburg's history are arranged for most Saturday mornings and many Wednesday mornings and take about 2½ hours. It's also possible to arrange a private tour if you can do it far enough in advance. ■ TIP→ **Departure points vary by the tour.** ☎ *011/482–3349* ⊕ *www.joburgheritage.co.za* ✉ *From R100.*

Mynhardts Diamonds. Mynhardts Diamonds sells diamonds and jewelry, and specializes in women's and men's rings, especially engagement and wedding rings. The company makes up the rings from loose stones on demand and even offers a 3-D rendering so you can see how your ring will look. It's best to make an appointment. ☎ *011/484–1719* ⊕ *www. mynhardts.com.*

8

Palaeo-Tours. Palaeo-Tours specializes in half-day tours to the Cradle of Humankind World Heritage Site. Participants are given the opportunity to observe a working dig at Drimolen, where more than 100 early hominid fossils have been found, among many other paleontological discoveries. The experience, guided by a scientist, will be extra-special because so few people have access to this site. It's certainly not a cheap tour, though the per-person price drops if you have more than two in your group. Transportation from Pretoria is R1,600 from Johannesburg or Pretoria (above and beyond the cost of the tour). Palaeo-Tours will also do a full-day tour on request. ☎ *011/023–4234* ⊕ *www.palaeotours.com* ✉ *From R3700.*

Springbok Atlas. Springbok Atlas offers two- to three-hour tours (including self-drive tours) of Johannesburg to the city center, Soweto, the Apartheid Museum, Gold Reef City, and other points of interest. Other tours explore Tshwane, the diamond-mining town of Cullinan, Sun City, and the Pilanesberg Game Reserve. ☎ *011/396–1053* ⊕ *www.springbokatlas.com* ✉ *From R450.*

Wilro Tours. Wilro Tours is one of the best-known operators in Johannesburg and offers tours of Soweto, Johannesburg, and farther afield, such as the Pilanesberg Game Reserve. With Wilro, you hire the car and guide for a number of hours, and can mix and match attractions and activities such as shopping as you wish. Tours have a base price, so per-person rates drop dramatically the more people you have on the tour. ☎ *011/789–9688* ⊕ *www.wilrotours.co.za* ✉ *From R2340.*

PLANNING YOUR TIME

1 or 2 Days: If you have only one day in Jo'burg, take a tour of Soweto and visit the Apartheid Museum, then stop by Constitution Hill if you have a chance. Spend the evening having dinner at an African-style restaurant, such as Moyo. If you have a second day, focus on what interests you most: perhaps a trip to the Cradle of Humankind, where you can explore the sites of some of the world's most significant paleontological discoveries; a trip to Cullinan, where you can visit a working diamond mine; or a fun day or two at Sun City and/or the Pilanesberg Game Reserve, a 2½-hour drive west of Johannesburg.

3 to 5 Days: Spend your first day touring Soweto and visiting the Apartheid Museum and Constitution Hill, followed by an African-style dinner. The next day, leave early and do Sterkfontein Caves and Maropeng in the Cradle of Humankind, then overnight at one of the establishments in the Magaliesberg, perhaps at the luxurious Maropeng Hotel, which offers beautiful views of the Magaliesberg; the De Hoek Country House; or Mount Grace Country House Hotel. Then head out early to the Pilanesberg Game Reserve, a lovely reserve in the hills of an ancient volcano, where you're likely to see rhinos and elephants. Stay a night or two in one of the reserve's lodges, and treat yourself to an early-morning balloon ride over the reserve.

SAFETY

Johannesburg is notorious for being a dangerous city—it's quite common to hear about serious crimes such as armed robbery and murder. That said, it's safe for visitors who avoid dangerous areas and take reasonable precautions. Do not leave bags or valuables visible in a car, and keep the doors locked, even while driving (to minimize the risk of smash-and-grab robberies or carjackings); don't wear flashy jewelry or carry large wads of cash or expensive equipment. ⚠ **Don't visit a township or squatter camp on your own.** Unemployment is rife, and foreigners are easy pickings. If you wish to see a township, check with reputable companies, which run excellent tours and know which areas to avoid. The Apartheid Museum and Constitution Hill within the city and the Cradle of Humankind just outside are perfectly safe to visit on your own.

⚠ **If you drive yourself around the city, it's safest to keep your doors locked and windows up, and to not leave valuables such as bags, cameras, or phones on the seat or visible.** That said, it is safe to drive yourself around Johannesburg. If you prefer, though, you could order a car service or transportation from your hotel for trips in and around the city.

VISITOR INFORMATION

The helpful Gauteng Tourism Authority has information on the whole province, but more detailed information is often available from local tourism associations—for example, the Soweto Accommodation Association lists more than 20 lodgings. Joburg Tourism has a good website, with information about Johannesburg and up-to-date listings of events happening around the city.

Contacts City of Johannesburg ⊕ *www.joburg.org.za.* **Gauteng Tourism Authority** ☎ *011/085–2500* ⊕ *www.gauteng.net.* **Joburg Tourism** ☎ *011/214–0700* ⊕ *www.joburgtourism.com.* **Soweto.co.za** ☎ *011/312–9228* ⊕ *www.soweto.co.za.*

EXPLORING

Johannesburg epitomizes South Africa's paradoxical makeup—it's rich, poor, innovative, and historic all rolled into one. And it seems at times as though no one actually comes *from* Johannesburg. The city is full of immigrants: Italians, Portuguese, Chinese, Hindus, Swazis, English, Zimbabweans, Nigerians, Zulus, Xhosas. The streets are full of merchants. Traders hawk *skop* (boiled sheep's head, split open and eaten off newspaper) in front of polished glass buildings as taxis jockey for position in rush hour. *Sangomas* (traditional healers) lay out herbs and roots next to roadside barbers' tents, and you never seem to be far from women selling *vetkoek* (dollops of deep-fried dough) beneath billboards advertising investment banks or cell phones.

The Greater Johannesburg metropolitan area is massive—more than 1,600 square km (618 square miles)—incorporating the large municipalities of Randburg and Sandton to the north. Most of the sights are just north of the city center, which degenerated badly in the 1990s but is now being revamped.

To the south, in Ormonde, are the Apartheid Museum and Gold Reef City; the sprawling township of Soweto is just a little farther to the southwest. Johannesburg's northern suburbs are its most affluent. On the way to the shopping meccas of Rosebank and Sandton, you can

Posing on a Gold Mine

In 1952, Dolly Rathebe, a young black woman who was to become a jazz-singing legend, and a white German photographer, Jürgen Schadeberg, scrambled to the top of a gold-mine dump for a *Drum* magazine photo shoot. The photograph looks like it was taken on some strange beach: Rathebe smiles, posing in a bikini. They were spotted by the police and arrested under the Immorality Act, which forbade intercourse between blacks and whites. This dump was at Crown Mines, and is now the site of the Crown Mines Golf Course. Today there's a street in Newtown named

after Rathebe, who died in 2004 at the age of 76. Schadeberg is still alive and lives in South Africa.

Today you can see gold-mine dumps along the edge of town marching east and west along the seam of gold. Some are close to 300 feet high. Many people are fond of them—they are one of the city's defining characteristics—but those who live nearby are blinded by the dust, and little vegetation grows on the dumps. Because they're also rich in minerals, they're slowly being chipped away and remined, and in years to come, they will probably be completely gone.

find the superb Johannesburg Zoo and the South African Museum of Military History, in the leafy suburb of Saxonwold.

CITY CENTER

Although the city center is experiencing a revival, it's not a place everyone will choose to visit. You'll find plenty to do downtown, including a visit to the Maboneng precinct, an up-and-coming area in the inner city. Diagonal Street runs—you guessed it—diagonally through the city center. The Hillbrow Tower is 883 feet, the tallest structure in Jo'burg, and is used for telecommunications, as is the 768-foot Brixton Tower in Auckland Park. The tall, round Ponte City apartment block near Hillbrow is another focal point that can be seen from almost all parts of the city.

Located in the western section of the city, Newtown, which is connected to Braamfontein via the Nelson Mandela Bridge, was once one of the city's most run-down neighborhoods. Today it is one of the city's cultural precincts, as it's the home of MuseuMAfricA, the SAB World of Beer, and the Market Theatre, among other attractions.

Braamfontein is home to Constitution Hill and the University of the Witwatersrand, one of South Africa's oldest and most respected universities.

TOP ATTRACTIONS

Fodor'sChoice   **Constitution Hill.** Overlooking Jo'burg's inner city and suburbs, Constitu-
★   tion Hill houses the **Constitutional Court,** set up in 1994 with the birth of democracy, as well as the austere **Old Fort Prison Complex** (also called Number Four), where thousands of political prisoners were incarcerated, including South African Nobel Peace laureates Albert Luthuli

Johannesburg City Center

PARKTOWN

Wits Education Campus

Peter Roos Park

HILLBROW

BEREA

BRAAMPARK

Johannesburg Theatre Complex

University of the Witwatersrand

DOORNFONTEIN

Braamfontein Cemetery

Joubert Park

BRAAMFONTEIN

NEWTOWN

Sophiatown Bar and Lounge

FORDSBURG

MARSHALLTOWN

TO O.R. TAMBO AIRPORT →

0   1/2 mile
0   1/2 kilometer

and Nelson Mandela, and iconic Indian leader Mahatma Gandhi. The court decides on the most important cases relating to human rights, much like the Supreme Court in the United States. Exhibits in the visitor center portray the country's journey to democracy. You can walk along the prison ramparts (built in the 1890s), read messages on the We the People Wall (and add your own), or view the court itself, in which large, slanting columns represent the trees under which African villagers traditionally met to discuss matters of importance. If the court isn't in session, you can walk right into the courtroom, where many of the country's landmark legal decisions have been made in recent years and where the 11 chairs of the justices are each covered in a different cowhide, representing their individuality. A small but good shop carries interesting titles about South African history. Group tours of the Old Fort Prison Complex are given every hour on the hour from 9 to 4 and include a visit to the Women's Jail, where there are photographs and exhibits of how women were treated in the prison system and how they contributed to the struggle against apartheid. You can also take a private tour, which departs at any time. ⊠ *Joubert and Kotze Sts., entrance on Joubert St., Braamfontein* ☎ *011/381–3100* ⊕ *www. constitutionhill.org.za* ⊠ *Court free; Old Fort group tour R50, private tour R70* ☉ *Court daily 9–5 (Wed. 9–1), last entry at 4. Old Fort group tours daily on the hr, 9–4; private tours by appointment.*

MuseuMAfricA. Founded in 1935, this was the first major museum to acknowledge black contributions to the city's development. The museum, which is in the city's block-long former fruit and vegetable market, houses geological specimens, paintings, African artifacts, costumes, and photographs relating to South Africa's complex history. Another display illustrates the life of Mahatma Gandhi, who once lived in Jo'burg. ⊠ *121 Bree St., Newtown* ☎ *011/833–5624* ⊠ *Free* ☉ *Tues.–Sun. 9–5.*

FAMILY
Fodor's Choice
★

Origins Centre. This modern museum is dedicated to exploring human development over the past 100,000 years, and in particular the tradition of rock art—of which southern Africa has the oldest and some of the richest in the world. The center is complementary to Maropeng (⇨ *Cradle of Humankind, in Side Trips from Johannesburg*), which details the past 5 million years or so of human evolution and the history of Earth since its formation. The two experiences enhance each other rather than compete. Origins is spacious and elegantly designed, with multimedia displays and photographs catering to a range of tastes, from kids to visiting professors. The shop sells high-quality crafts and hard-to-source books on rock art in southern Africa, and the center's coffee shop, Café Fino, serves good, light meals. ⊠ *University of the Witwatersrand, Yale Rd., Braamfontein* ☎ *011/717–4700* ⊕ *www.origins.org. za* ⊠ *R75, including audio guide* ☉ *Daily 10–5.*

WORTH NOTING

Diagonal Street. This street in the city center is lined with African herbalists' shops, where you can acquire a mind-boggling array of homeopathic and traditional cures for whatever ails you. If you're lucky, a *sangoma* (traditional healer) might throw the bones and tell you what the future holds. This is also the site of the old Johannesburg Stock Exchange building (the modern version is in Sandton). ⊠ *Diagonal St.*

Nelson Mandela Bridge. A symbol of the renewal process going on in the city, this modern, 931-foot-long bridge with sprawling cables spans the bleak Braamfontein railway yard, connecting Constitution Hill and Braamfontein to the revamped Newtown Cultural Precinct. The bridge is especially beautiful at night. Do not walk over the bridge, however, as it is a known spot for muggings. ⊠ *Bertha St., Braamfontein* ✛ *Take Queen Elizabeth St. from Braamfontein, or follow signs from central Newtown or from M1 South.*

Ponte City. If there's a symbol of Johannesburg, it's Ponte City, a massive, hollow 54-story cylinder of apartments perched on the edge of the central business district. Built in 1975, and standing at a height of 568 feet with a flashing cell-phone advertisement at the top, it's the tallest residential building in the Southern Hemisphere. ⊠ *1 Lily Ave., Hillbrow.*

SAB World of Beer. SABMiller is Africa's largest brewing company, and its unusual museum is dedicated to that great South African favorite—beer. You can find out all about the history of beer brewing in South Africa and the process of beer-making, including African brewing traditions. After a 75-minute tour you can enjoy two complimentary beers in the taproom. ⊠ *15 President St., Newtown* ☎ *011/836–4900* ⊕ *www.worldofbeer.co.za* ⊠ *R75* ☉ *Tues.–Sat. 10–6.*

Standard Bank Gallery. At the home of the Standard Bank African art collection you can admire contemporary South African artwork. The gallery hosts high-quality, ever-changing local and international exhibitions, including the annual traveling World Press Photo show. ⊠ *Frederick and Simmonds Sts., Marshalltown* ☎ *011/631–4467* ⊕ *www.standardbankarts.com* ⊠ *Free* ☉ *Weekdays 8–4:30, Sat. 9–1.*

SOWETO AND THE SOUTH

An acronym for *South Western Townships*, Soweto was founded in 1904, when city councilors used an outbreak of bubonic plague as an excuse to move black people outside the town. Today the suburb, which is 20 km (12 miles) south of the city, is home to about a million residents. What it lacks in infrastructure (though it's been vastly upgraded since the first democratic elections in 1994) it more than makes up for in soul, energy, and history. The largely working-class population knows how to live for today, and Soweto pulsates with people, music, and humor.

Some areas of Soweto that are worth touring include old-town neighborhood Diepkloof, just beyond Orlando West, and its neighbor, the new Diepkloof Extension, which dates from the mid-1970s, when bank loans first became available to black property owners. The difference between the two is startling: the dreary, prefabricated matchbox houses of Diepkloof next to what looks like a middle-class suburb anywhere. In nearby Dube, many of the evicted residents of Sophiatown—a freehold township (where blacks were allowed to own property) west of the city and a melting pot of music, bohemianism, crime, and multiracialism

Soweto

that insulted Afrikaner nationalism—were resettled in 1959, bringing an exciting vibe to the dreary, homogenous dormitory town. The area remains a vibrant suburb, with an exciting mix of people and a festive atmosphere.

Between downtown Johannesburg and Soweto lie several suburbs less affluent than their northern counterparts, including Ormonde, where Gold Reef City and the Apartheid Museum are. Both attractions are well signposted from the N1 highway going both south and north and are easy to find if you have hired a car, but many tour operators do include a stop at the Apartheid Museum in their Soweto tours.

GETTING HERE AND AROUND

Various companies offer bus tours, but we suggest hiring a private guide or joining a smaller group tour, because you'll get one-on-one attention and be able to ask any and all questions. You can also ask for a special-interest tour, such as one centered on art, traditional medicine, restaurants, nightlife, or memorials. Most tours start in Jo'burg, and you can arrange to be collected from your hotel. ■TIP→ **We strongly suggest that you take a guided tour if you decide to visit Soweto** (⇨ *Tours, in Planning*). **It is a chaotic, virtually indistinguishable sprawl. Even if you found your way in, you'd struggle to find your way out—let alone around.**

TOP ATTRACTIONS

Fodor's Choice ★ **Apartheid Museum.** The Apartheid Museum takes you on a journey through South African apartheid history—from the entrance, where you pass through a turnstile according to your assigned skin color (black or white), to the myriad historical, brutally honest, and sometimes shocking photographs, video displays, films, documents, and other exhibits. It's an emotional, multilayered journey. As you walk chronologically through the apartheid years and eventually reach the country's first steps to freedom, with democratic elections in 1994, you experience a taste of the pain and suffering with which so many South Africans had to live. A room with 121 ropes with hangman's knots hanging from the ceiling—one rope for each political prisoner executed in the apartheid era—is especially chilling. ⊠ *Northern Pkwy. and Gold Reef Rd., Ormonde* ☎ *011/309–4700* ⊕ *www.apartheidmuseum.org* ☞ *R70* ☼ *Daily 9–5.*

> ### FAMOUS RESIDENTS
>
> What other place on earth can boast of having had two Nobel Peace Prize laureates living within a block of each other? For most of his adult life Anglican Archbishop Desmond Tutu lived on Vilakazi Street, in Soweto's Orlando West neighborhood. His neighbor would have been an attorney named Nelson Mandela, had Mandela not spent most of *his* adult life incarcerated on Robben Island (⇨ *Chapter 2, Cape Town*). The archbishop's home is a gray, two-story building that is not open to the public, but you can visit the nearby Mandela house. It became a museum in 1997 and was revamped in 2009.

Fodor's Choice ★ **Hector Pieterson Memorial and Museum.** Opposite Holy Cross Church, a stone's throw from the former homes of Nelson Mandela and Archbishop Desmond Tutu on Vilakazi Street, the Hector Pieterson Memorial and Museum is a crucial landmark. Pieterson, a 13-year-old scholar, was the first victim of police fire on June 16, 1976, when schoolchildren rose up to protest their second-rate Bantu (black) education system. The memorial is a paved area with benches for reflection, an inscribed stone and simple water feature; inside the museum are grainy photographs and films that bring that fateful day to life. A total of 562 small granite blocks in the museum courtyard are a tribute to the children who died in the Soweto uprisings. ⊠ *Khumalo and Phela Sts., Orlando West* ☎ *011/536–2253* ⊕ *www.joburg.org.za* ☞ *R30* ☼ *Mon.–Sat. 10–5, Sun. 10–4:30.*

WORTH NOTING

FAMILY **Gold Reef City.** This theme park lets you step back in time to 1880s Johannesburg and see why it became known as the City of Gold. One of the city's most popular attractions, it has good rides that kids will enjoy and is based on the history of Jo'burg. In addition to riding the Anaconda, a scary roller coaster on which you hang under the track, feet in the air, and you can (for an additional fee) descend into an old gold mine and see molten gold being poured. The reconstructed streets are lined with operating Victorian-style shops and restaurants. And for those with money to burn, the large, glitzy Gold Reef Village Casino beckons across the road. ⊠ *Northern Park Way, Shaft 14, Ormonde* ✛ *6 km*

8

Hector Pieterson and the Soweto Uprising

On June 16, 1976, hundreds of schoolchildren in Soweto marched to protest the use of Afrikaans as the primary language of education in the overcrowded, much neglected Bantu schools in the townships. This was a highly charged political issue. Not only was Dutch-based Afrikaans considered the language of the oppressor by blacks, but it also made it more difficult for students to learn, as most spoke an African language and, as a second language, English.

The march quickly turned nasty. The police started firing into the youthful crowd. One of the first people of 200 to 500 to die in what was the beginning of a long and protracted struggle was 13-year-old Hector Pieterson. A

picture taken by photographer Sam Nzima of the dying Pieterson in the arms of a crying friend, with Pieterson's sister running alongside them, put a face on apartheid that went around the globe.

Pieterson was just a schoolboy trying to ensure a better life for himself and his friends, family, and community. He and the many students who joined the liberation movement strengthened the fight against apartheid. Eventually Afrikaans was dropped as a language of instruction, and more schools and a teaching college were built in Soweto. Today, Hector Pieterson's name graces a simple memorial and museum about the conflict, and June 16 is Youth Day, a public holiday.

(4 miles) south of city center ☎ *011/248–6800* ⊕ *www.goldreefcity. co.za* ✉ *R165; R90 for mine tour* ⊙ *Wed.–Sun. (except for school holidays, when it's open daily) 9:30–5; mine tours hourly 10–4.*

Mandela House. The former president lived in this small house until his arrest in 1961, with his ex-wife Winnie Madikizela-Mandela, who owns a high-security mansion in Orlando West. The house is now a museum containing Mandela memorabilia from the 1960s. ✉ *Vilakazi St., Orlando West* ☎ *011/936–7754* ⊕ *www.mandelahouse.org* ✉ *R60 (South African citizens R40)* ⊙ *Daily 9–4:45.*

Orlando Towers. The brightly painted Orlando Towers complex in Soweto is a well-known landmark in Johannesburg. Originally a coal-fired power station, the site has been transformed into an adrenalin junkie's paradise, where you can do base and bungee jumping from the top of the 33-story structure. Afterwards, go on a unique and highly memorable quad bike tour of Soweto, or relax at the popular restaurant, Chaf Pozi, located on the premises. The Orlando Towers complex and all activities on-site are administered by Soweto Outdoor Adventures. ✉ *Sheffield Rd., just off Chris Hani Rd., Orlando* ☎ *072/692–8159* ⊕ *www.sowetooutdooradventures.co.za.*

Oppenheimer Park. Named after mining magnate Ernest Oppenheimer, who established the De Beers diamond mining company as a powerful global brand, this park is one of the few green spaces in Soweto and is rich in flora and birdlife. The park is dominated by a large tower built as a tribute to Oppenheimer, who helped resettle people displaced by the apartheid government in the 1950s. Here you can also see **Khayalendaba,** a cultural village built in the 1970s by South Africa's best-known traditional healer, artist, and oral historian, Credo Mutwa. Some of his statues here portray African gods, warriors, and mythical figures, even sculptures of prehistoric African animals. ■ **TIP→ It's best to visit the park with a guide in the daytime for safety reasons.** ⊠ *991 Majoeng St., Central Western Jabavu* ◨ *Free* ☉ *Daily 24 hrs.*

Regina Mundi Church. Central to the liberation struggle, this Catholic church was a refuge of peace, sanity, and steadfast moral focus for the people of Soweto through the harshest years of repression. Archbishop Desmond Tutu often delivered sermons in this massive church during the apartheid years. It has a black Madonna and Child painting inside and a photographic exhibition showcasing the history of Soweto and its transformation over the past 40 years upstairs. A few years ago, former U.S. President Bill Clinton and Hillary Clinton caused a stir here by accepting communion at a service, even though they are not Catholic. ⊠ *1149 Khumalo St., Rockville* ☏ *011/986–2546* ⊕ *reginamundichurch.co.za* ◨ *Donations requested* ☉ *Weekdays 9–4.*

Walter Sisulu Square *(Formerly Freedom Square).* In 1955 the Freedom Charter was adopted here by the Congress Alliance, a gathering of political and cultural groups trying to map a way forward in the repressive 1950s. The charter, the guiding document of the African National Congress, envisaged an alternative nonracial dispensation in which "all shall be equal before the law." Its significance in South Africa is similar to that of the Declaration of Independence in the United States, and it influenced South Africa's new constitution, adopted in 1995 and widely considered one of the best and most progressive in the world. ⊠ *Close to Union Ave. and Boundary Rd., Kliptown.*

NORTHERN SUBURBS

Johannesburg has dozens of northern suburbs, ranging in size from the huge and diverse Sandton, which includes the entire township of Alexandra, among other suburbs, to the smaller, leafy Saxonwold near the zoo. The northern suburbs highlighted here, in order from southernmost to northernmost, are by no means the only ones—they simply have the most attractions and are where most tourists stay.

ROSEBANK

Originally a farm known as Rosemill Orchards, today **Rosebank** is home to upmarket shopping malls, restaurants, hotels, and art galleries. It's frequented by well-to-do locals and tourists. At the Rosebank Mall you'll find all the international brands, along with the best in uniquely South African boutiques and outlets like Exclusive Books, which has an excellent range, including reference and coffee-table books on Africa. The Rosebank Mall is smaller than its larger and even swankier mall, the nearby Sandton City. The **African Craft Market,** open daily, is adjacent to the Rosebank Mall and is open every day. It is popular for its curios and African art. Clubs, bars, galleries, and an art-house cinema add flavor to this trendy area.

O.R. TAMBO AIRPORT TO ↑

Rosettenville Rd.

Turf Rd.

Turffontein Rd.

ROSETTENVILLE

Geranium St.

Main St.

Prairie St.

Verona Rd.

Rifle Range Rd.

Booysens Rd.

Heronmere Rd.

Bellavista Rd

Klip Rivier Dr.

Ophir Booysens Rd.

Booysens Rd.

Alamein Rd.

Northern Parkway Rd.

De Villiers Graaff Motorway

Xavier St.

Rifle Range Rd.

Southern Bypass

Soweto Hwy

Nasrec Rd.

Rand Show Rd.

Western Bypass

Ben Naude Dr.

Immink Dr.

Potchefstroom Rd.

Soweto
see detail
map

← TO NAMBITHA AND
WANDIE'S PLACE

1 mile

1 kilometer

0

0

Apartheid Museum **5**
Gold Reef City **6**
Johannesburg
Botanical Gardens and
Emmarentia Dam **1**
Johannesburg Zoo **3**
Melville Koppies
Nature Reserve **2**
South African
National Museum of
Military History **4**

GREENSIDE AND EMMARENTIA

Close to Rosebank, the suburb of **Greenside** is filled with popular restaurants. **Gleneagles Road** is lined with small eateries, including Italian,
Indian, Portuguese, and Japanese restaurants, along with those offering
a more conventional range of meats, fish, and pasta. Over the weekend,
cars fill the streets and people pack the sidewalks. The adjacent suburb
of **Emmarentia** is also benefiting from Greenside's popularity, with small
restaurants popping up. The **Emmarentia Dam** and gardens, a popular
dog-walking and picnic spot, is also a draw.

FAMILY **Johannesburg Botanical Gardens and Emmarentia Dam.** The large and
beautiful botanical gardens here are five minutes from Greenside. This
gigantic parkland, dotted with trees, statues, fountains, and ponds, is a
wonderful haven. You can relax on benches beneath weeping willows
surrounding the dam and lake, where canoeists and windsurfers brave
the water, or wander across to the 24-acre rose and herb gardens. The
gardens' flowers include an alpine collection and a cycad collection.
On weekends bridal parties use the gardens as a backdrop for photographs. ⊠ *Thomas Bowler Rd., at Beyers Naude, Roosevelt Park*
☎ *011/782–0517* ⊠ *Free* ☉ *Daily sunrise–sunset.*

FAMILY **Melville Koppies Nature Reserve.** A small nature reserve and heritage site
on the southern side of the Johannesburg Botanical Gardens, Melville
Koppies has guided ecology walks, and many of the guides are members
of the local botanical society and can introduce you to the rich diversity of Highveld flora found here. Bird-watching is also excellent: more
than 200 varieties of grassland and Highveld birds recorded, as well as
suburban garden species and small mammals. An archaeological site
contains a 500-year-old furnace dating from the Iron Age. The reserve
is managed by volunteers, and you can take a three-hour tour with
them. ⚠ **Don't go alone, as it isn't safe to do so.** ⊠ *Judith Rd., Emmarentia* ☎ *011/482–4797* ⊕ *www.mk.org.za* ⊠ *R50 for guided tour; special
group tours by prior arrangement* ☉ *Sun.; times vary, check website.*

PARKTOWN, PARKVIEW, SAXONWOLD,
AND WESTCLIFF

Perched on the Braamfontein Ridge, Parktown was once the address
du jour for the city's early mining magnates. Most of the magnificent
houses have since met their demise, but those that are left are worth a
look, and they are all lovely areas in which to stay or to take a walk.
The small but picturesque suburbs of Westcliff, Parkview, and Saxonwold are nearby.

FAMILY **Johannesburg Zoo.** Smaller than its Pretoria counterpart but no less
impressive, the city's zoo makes for a pleasant day-trip, and with plenty
of lawns and shade, it's a good place to picnic. The large variety of species (more than 250) includes rare white lion and highly endangered
red panda. The Temple of the Ancients is a relatively new attraction
that houses freshwater fish, snakes, as well as other reptiles, amphibians, spiders, and fruit bats. Perhaps the best way to see the zoo is to
take the ferry to various parts for R5 per person. Afterward, stroll past
Zoo Lake in the large, peaceful park across the road. ⊠ *Jan Smuts Ave.,*

opposite Zoo Lake, Parkview ☎ *011/646–2000* ⊕ *www.jhbzoo.org.za* ✆ *R65* ⊙ *Daily 8:30–5:30.*

South African National Museum of Military History. In a park adjacent to the Johannesburg Zoo, this museum has two exhibition halls and a rambling outdoor display focusing on South Africa's role in the major wars of the 20th century, with an emphasis on World War II. On display are original Spitfire and Messerschmidt fighters (including what is claimed to be the only remaining ME110 jet night fighter), various tanks of English and American manufacture, and a wide array of artillery. Among the most interesting objects are the modern armaments South Africa used in its war against the Cuban-backed Angolan army during the 1980s, including French-built Mirage fighters and Russian tanks stolen by the South Africans from a ship en route to Angola. More recent exhibits include the national military art collection, memorabilia from the Anti-Conscription Campaign of apartheid days, and an exhibit on the history of Umkhonto we Sizwe (Spear of the Nation, or MK, the African National Congress's military arm). The tall, freestanding South African (Anglo-Boer) War Memorial, which looks like a statue-adorned mini Arc de Triomphe, is the most striking landmark of the northern suburbs. ✉ *22 Erlswold Way, Saxonwold* ☎ *011/646–5513* ⊕ *www. militarymuseum.co.za* ✆ *R30* ⊙ *Daily 9–4:30.*

MELROSE ARCH

Close to both Rosebank and Sandton, **Melrose Arch** is an upscale shopping, dining, and business district that features good restaurants and boutiques. This European-style lifestyle center offers pleasant accommodations, shopping, and dining in a relaxed and safe setting.

ROODEPOORT

Roodepoort is a residential suburb to the west of Johannesburg in what is known as the West Rand, a drive of about 45 minutes to an hour from the city center. Its top attraction is the Walter Sisulu National Botanical Garden, and it's also relatively close to the Cradle of Humankind World Heritage Site.

OFF THE BEATEN PATH

Cullinan Diamond Mine. Anyone can go to a jewelry store and bring home South African diamonds, but how many people can say they got their sparkler from an actual mine? At Cullinan Diamond Mine, you can not only buy diamonds, but get custom-made pieces from the resident jeweler, though don't expect your piece to include the world's largest diamond—the 3,106-carat Cullinan Diamond unearthed here in 1905 is now in the crown jewels in London. Ninety-minute surface tours of the mine are every day, and four-hour underground tours are offered every day but Sunday. You must reserve all tours in advance; children under 16 are not permitted underground, and children younger than 10 are not permitted on the surface tour. Cullinan has a series of delightful tea gardens to choose from. For pleasant outdoor dining, the Whispering Oaks Garden Café (closed Tuesday) serves breakfast, lunches, and homemade sweets. ✉ *99 Oak Ave., Cullinan* ☎ *012/734–0081* ⊕ *www. diamondtourscullinan.co.za* ✆ *Surface tours R110, underground tours R500* ⊙ *Surface tours daily at 10, noon, and 2; underground tours Mon. and Fri. at 10:30, Tues.–Thurs. at 9:30, Sat. at 8*

8

Walter Sisulu National Botanical Garden. More than 220 birds species and a variety of small mammals add to a biodiverse garden named in honor of late ANC stalwart Walter Sisulu. The Witpoortjie Falls dominate the garden, providing a backdrop to a succulent rockery, cycads, an arboretum, birds and butterfly garden, wild flowers, a children's section, and more. Most of the garden is accessible by wheelchair, and there are refreshment facilities. The garden is famous for a pair of Verreaux eagles that breed in early spring (August/September). ⊠ *End of Malcolm Rd., Poortview, Roodepoort* ☎ *086/100–1278* ⊕ *www.sanbi.org/gardens/walter-sisulu* ⊠ *R35* ⊙ *Daily 8–5.*

SANDTON

Originally a residential area, **Sandton** is now home to the Johannesburg Stock Exchange and the enormous Sandton Convention Centre, which hosts large conferences and concerts. In the large and expensive **Sandton City Shopping Centre** and adjacent open-air **Nelson Mandela Square** (also known as Sandton Square), you'll find trendy restaurants selling good but pricey food. There's also a small theater, Theater on the Square, which favors short, lightweight productions such as stand-up comedy. The convention center is next to the square.

But Sandton is not all glitz and glamour—a few miles from the Sandton City Shopping Centre and part of the large suburb is the township of **Alexandra,** home to an estimated 500,000 people, mostly living in overcrowded, squalid conditions in shacks and rented run-down houses.

FOURWAYS

Fourways is one of Johannesburg's newer suburbs, in the far north of the city. It's home to many upscale housing estates, as well as good shopping centers, and places to stay. It's a journey of at least 30 minutes to an hour into Sandton or Johannesburg from Fourways.

BRYANSTON

Bryanston is an old, treed residential suburb that is farther north (toward Fourways) of the city center than suburbs like Rosebank and Sandton. It's one of Johannesburg's wealthier suburbs, and is characterized by tree-lined streets and homes with large gardens.

WHERE TO EAT

Jo'burgers love eating out, and there are hundreds of restaurants throughout the city to satisfy them. Some notable destinations for food include Melrose Arch, Parkhurst, Sandton, and Greenside. Smart-casual dress is a good bet. Many establishments are closed on Sunday night and Monday.

There's no way to do justice to the sheer scope and variety of Johannesburg's restaurants in a few examples. What follows is a (necessarily subjective) list of some of the best. Try asking locals what they recommend; eating out is the most popular form of entertainment in Johannesburg, and everyone has a list of favorite spots, which changes often.

⇨ *For more information on South Africa food, see Flavors of South Africa, in Chapter 1.*

WHAT IT COSTS IN SOUTH AFRICAN RAND			
$	**$$**	**$$$**	**$$$$**
Restaurants	under R100	R100–R150	R151–R200	over R200

Restaurant prices are the average cost of a main course at dinner or, if dinner is not served, at lunch.

OAKLANDS

Oaklands is an old residential suburb not far from Rosebank and Melrose. It's known for its wide streets, large homes (most often behind high walls), and trees. The whole area seems to turn purple when the jacarandas bloom in October and November.

$ ✕ **Sophiatown Bar and Lounge.** Although not in the same league as the
SOUTH AFRICAN more famous Nambitha and Wandie's traditional township restaurants in Soweto, the Sophiatown Bar and Lounge in Newtown is popular and much easier to get to. The restaurant is decorated with photos and murals of 1950s musicians like Miriam Makeba, and patrons gather around braziers on chilly winter nights. Jazz music vies for attention with the rather boisterous crowd, and the place has the feel of a shebeen (township bar). The food is a good example of black South African cuisine. A specialty is pap-and-wors—a traditional South African maize-meal porridge (*pap*) that is white and stiff with *boerewors* (a South African sausage). The restaurant serves other dishes popular in the townships such as *mogodu* (tripe) with *samp* (stewed corn kernels) and beans, as well as ostrich steaks or burgers. Simpler meals like steak and fresh salads are also served. ⑤ *Average main: R80* ⊠ *Jeppe and Henry Nxumalo Sts., Newtown* ☎ 011/836–5999, 073/598–8581 ⊕ *www.sophiatownbarlounge.co.za.*

$$ ✕ **Tortellino d'Oro.** This small and unpretentious restaurant and deli has
ITALIAN legendary food, especially the pasta. Run by an Italian family, Tortel-
Fodor'sChoice lino's is popular for both lunch and dinner. Try the Parma ham and
★ melon as an antipasto, and then get a pasta for your main course, such as the tortellini, which is filled with a mixture of ham, mortadella sausage, chicken, and Parmesan cheese then served with mushroom cream, Napoletana, or butter and sage sauce. The service is as outstanding, as is the food, and there's an excellent wine list. Be sure to book ahead. ⑤ *Average main: R120* ⊠ *Oaklands Shopping Center, Pretoria St. at Victoria St.* ☎ 011/483–1249 ⊕ *www.tortellino.co.za* ⊲ *Reservations essential* ⊙ *Closed Sun. dinner.*

SOWETO AND THE SOUTH

$ ✕ **Nambitha.** You can't actually see Nelson Mandela's old house from
AFRICAN this popular restaurant, which means that you're less likely to run into a tour bus. Nambitha has evolved from a township restaurant catering only to African tastes into a more versatile establishment. It plays an eclectic selection of music—soul, jazz, R&B, and more traditional African—and is constantly buzzing with people. Meals include mutton

BEST BETS FOR JOHANNESBURG DINING

With hundreds of restaurants to choose from, how will you decide where to eat? Fodor's writers and editors have selected their favorite restaurants by price, cuisine, and experience. In the first column, Fodor's Choice properties represent the "best of the best" in every price category. You can also search by neighborhood for excellent eats—just peruse our reviews on the following pages.

Fodor's Choice

Moyo, $$$, p. 436, 438
Tortellino d'Oro, $$, p. 433
Wombles, $$$$, p. 438

Best by Price

$

Mike's Kitchen, Parktown, p. 437
Nambitha, p. 433
Nice, p. 438
Trabella Pizzeria, p. 437

$$

Bellinis, p. 436
Doppio Zero, p. 438
Parea, p. 437
Tortellino d'Oro, p. 433
Turn 'n Tender, p. 437
Wandie's Place, p. 436

$$$$

Wombles, p. 438

Best by Cuisine

ITALIAN

Bellinis, p. 436
Tortellino d'Oro, p. 433

MEDITERRANEAN

Parea, p. 437

PIZZA

Trabella Pizzeria, p. 437

SOUTH AFRICAN

Nambitha, p. 433
Turn 'n Tender, p. 437
Wandie's Place, p. 436
Wombles, p. 438

Best by Experience

CHILD-FRIENDLY

Doppio Zero, p. 438
Moyo (Parkview/Zoo Lake), p. 438
Turn 'n Tender, p. 437

GOOD FOR GROUPS

Doppio Zero, p. 438
Mike's Kitchen, Parktown, p. 437
Moyo, p. 436
Turn 'n Tender, p. 437
Wombles, p. 438

GREAT VIEW

Moyo (Parkview/Zoo Lake), p. 438

MOST ROMANTIC

Bistro Vine, p. 437
Wombles, p. 438

Where to Eat and Stay in the Northern Suburbs

KEY

1 Restaurants
1 Hotels

curry served with pap, dumplings, rice, or samp, spinach and pumpkin; *mogodu* (tripe); marinated traditional chicken, lamb shank, and oxtail. Meals are relatively inexpensive, but food is less Nambitha's strength than its busy vibe. Many locals pop in just to chat and mingle. $\boxed{S}$ *Average main: R75* ⊠ *6877 Vilakazi St., Orlando West* ☎ *011/936–9128* ⊕ *www.nambitharestaurant.co.za.*

$$ ✕ **Wandie's Place.** Wandie's Place isn't the only good township restau-
AFRICAN rant, but it's the best known and one of the most popular spots in Jo'burg. The decor is eclectic township (a bit makeshift), and the walls are adorned with signatures and business cards of tourists who have crossed its path. The waiters are smartly dressed in bow ties, and the food is truly African. Meat stews, *imifino* (a leafy African dish), sweet potatoes, beans, corn porridge, traditionally cooked pumpkin, chicken, and tripe are laid out in a buffet in a motley selection of pots and containers. The food is hot, the drinks are cold, and the conversation flows. You may end up here with a tour bus, but it's big enough to cope. It's not that difficult to find, and parking is safe, but it's probably better to organize a visit on a guided trip. $\boxed{S}$ *Average main: R120* ⊠ *618 Makhalamele St., Dube* ☎ *011/982–2796* ⊕ *www.wandiesplace.co.za.*

NORTHERN SUBURBS

ILLOVO AND MELROSE ARCH

Illovo and Melrose Arch are two small suburbs between the trendy suburbs of Rosebank and Sandton. Illovo is home to several shopping centers, office parks, and small restaurants; Melrose Arch is a smaller development with shops, offices, and restaurants. Both are popular with locals and very safe to visit.

$$ ✕ **Bellinis.** This small, friendly restaurant offers both memorable food
ITALIAN and quick and professional service. Many people return again and again to this local favorite. Although mostly relaxed, the atmosphere can also be quite noisy and energy-packed, as friends catch up over lunch and business people chat animatedly about work. The potato rostis are almost legendary: try one with smoked salmon or a pepper fillet. There's also a good wine list. $\boxed{S}$ *Average main: R129* ⊠ *18 Chaplin Rd., Illovo* ☎ *011/880–9168/9* ⊕ *www.bellinis.co.za* ⚏ *Reservations essential* ☉ *Closed Sun.*

$$$ ✕ **Moyo.** From the food and decor to the music and live entertainment,
AFRICAN Moyo is strongly African in theme. The focus of the rich and varied
Fodor's Choice menu is pan-African, incorporating tandoori cookery from northern
★ Africa, Cape Malay influences such as lentil bobotie, Moroccan-influenced tasty *tagines* (stews with lamb, chicken, fish, or seven vegetables), and ostrich burgers and other dishes representing South Africa. Diners are often entertained by storytellers, face painters, and musicians. The restaurant has six locations in South Africa. At night or in winter, the branch at Melrose Arch is the best bet of the two Jo'burg outposts. In summer and during the day, the Zoo Lake branch (*1 Prince of Wales Dr., Parkview, 011/646–0058*) is the nicest. $\boxed{S}$ *Average main: R180* ⊠ *Melrose Arch, High St., shop 5, Melrose North* ☎ *011/684– 1477* ⊕ *www.moyo.co.za* ⚏ *Reservations essential.*

$$ ✕ **Parea.** This Greek taverna, grill, and meze café is the best of its kind
GREEK   in the city. Greek music floats above the buzz of conversation, a souv-
laki spit turns slowly near the door, and a refrigerated case displays an
array of *meze* (small appetizers). Most people sit on the roofed terrace
or at the few street-side tables (in summer). Start with a meze platter of
souvlaki, feta, olives, cucumber, and tomato, followed by the line fish,
grilled on an open flame with olive oil and lemon, or *kleftiko* (lamb
slow-cooked in a clay oven) and a carafe of wine. On weekend evenings,
belly dancers perform between the tables, and Greek dancers do the
Zorba to a backdrop of "controlled" plate breaking—all while patrons
find it hard to resist a glass of ouzo. Even the manager is known to let
his hair down and perform for the patrons once in a while. The dress is
casual and the atmosphere very relaxed. Choose the set menus or the à
la carte menu. ⑤ *Average main: R105* ⊠ *3 Corlett Dr., at Oxford Rd.,
Illovo* ☎ *011/788–8777* ⊕ *www.parea.co.za.*

$ ✕ **Trabella Pizzeria.** This restaurant is on a busy street corner around the
ITALIAN   corner from Parea—an accessible but not attractive position. Trabella's
strength is its designer pizza, some of the best you'll ever taste, whether
it's with the Brie and cranberry topping; Parma ham, rocket (arugula),
and Parmesan; or smoked salmon, sour cream, and caviar, sprinkled
with spring onion. The pasta and gnocchi are good options as well.
⑤ *Average main: R80* ⊠ *Illovo Junction, Oxford Rd. 3, at Corlett Dr.,
Illovo* ☎ *011/442–0413, 011/442–0414* ⊗ *Closed Mon. No lunch Sun.*

$$ ✕ **Turn 'n Tender.** This upmarket steak house chain was founded by four
AFRICAN   brothers in the 1970s, and the restaurants are still among Jo'burg's
FAMILY   most popular for easy dining. Meat is the specialty, with a wide range
of steaks, ribs, and burgers to choose from. For something very South
African—and yet a little different from the popular oxtail dish—try the
Karoo lambtail braised in thick tomato sauce. Aside from the Illovo
branch, there are other Turn 'n' Tender outlets in Bryanston, Park-
town North, Bedfordview, and Boksburg. Details for each can be found
on the chain's website. ⑤ *Average main: R130* ⊠ *Thrupps Center, 204
Oxford Rd., Illovo* ☎ *011/268–2107* ⊕ *www.turnntender.co.za.*

PARKHURST AND PARKTOWN NORTH

$$ ✕ **Bistro Vine.** This is a small and intimate restaurant is Parkhurst's
FRENCH   famous 4th Avenue, one of the best-known streets for restaurants in
the country. With only a dozen or so tables the place can be crowded
when full, but the food is good and the service excellent. Try the *moules
frites,* fresh Saldhana bay mussels simmered in their own stock, dry
white wine, lemon, cream, leeks, celery, herbs, and served with deli-
ciously crunchy fries and homemade mayonnaise. Order one of many
excellent South African white wines on the menu. ⑤ *Average main:
R129* ⊠ *24 4th Ave., Parkhurst* ☎ *011/327–4558* ⊕ *www.bistrovine.
co.za* ⌕ *Reservations essential* ⊗ *Closed Mon.*

$ ✕ **Mike's Kitchen, Parktown.** A good choice for a meal near Wits Univer-
STEAKHOUSE sity and the city center is the Mike's Kitchen in Parktown, where you'll
FAMILY   find hearty fare (the steaks are excellent) and a convivial atmosphere.
The restaurant is housed in an old restaurant called Eikenlaan, which
was built in 1903 for James Goch, a professional photographer and the
first to use flash photography in South Africa. In 1985 the home was

8

turned into a franchise of the Mike's Kitchen steak-house chain. There's a garden for kids to play in. $ *Average main: R89* ⊠ *15 St. Andrew's Rd., Parktown North* ⊕ *www.mikeskitchen.co.za.*

$
CAFÉ
✗ **Nice.** This easygoing, unpretentious café serves only breakfast and lunch but is always busy, mostly because the food is so fresh and good. Breakfast is a specialty, with wholesome breakfast baskets made from toast and piled with succulent tomatoes, bacon, and a poached egg. Fresh open sandwiches are also good, with a wide range of options on the frequently changing menu. It's open from 7:45 am until 3 pm. $ *Average main: R80* ⊠ *4th Ave. and 14th St., Parkhurst* ☎ *011/788–6286* ⊙ *Closed Mon. No dinner.*

$$$$
STEAKHOUSE
Fodor's Choice
★
✗ **Wombles.** Wombles is an upmarket steak house with a warm, yet rather formal atmosphere. Steaks are their specialty, and portions are generous. If you want to try something very South African, go for the springbok shank with savory green peppercorn sauce and stewed fruit on the side. If you still have space, try the rosewater ice cream with chocolate rose petals, made from an old family recipe. As good as the food is, Wombles is also an experience, with rich decorations and impeccable service. $ *Average main: R200* ⊠ *17 3rd Ave., Parktown North* ☎ *011/880–2470* ⊕ *www.wombles.co.za* ⌕ *Reservations essential* ⋒ *Jacket required.*

PARKTOWN, PARKVIEW, SAXONWOLD, AND WESTCLIFF

$$$
AFRICAN
Fodor's Choice
★
✗ **Moyo.** Of the two Moyo locations in Johannesburg, this Parkview branch, at Zoo Lake, is the nicest during the day, as you can dine with a view of the lake and take a stroll or a ride in a rowboat afterward. The branch retains the quintessential Moyo vibe, with the option to dine outside in the lush gardens or to enjoy the African decor indoors. The deck is a wonderful spot to enjoy a relaxing lunch or a late-afternoon drink. $ *Average main: R150* ⊠ *Zoo Lake Park, 1 Prince of Wales Dr., Parkview* ☎ *011/646–0058* ⊕ *www.moyo.co.za* ⌕ *Reservations essential.*

SANDTON

$$$
STEAKHOUSE
✗ **The Butcher Shop and Grill.** This is a good place for hungry meat lovers. It specializes in prime South African meat aged to perfection by Alan Pick, the butcher-owner. An operating butcher shop features prominently in the restaurant, and special cuts can be ordered for the meal or to take home. Kudu, springbok, ostrich, and other game are often on the specials list, and only the most tender cuts are served. For lighter choices, try the chicken or linefish. Jelly and custard pudding is a favorite with regulars. There's an excellent wine cellar. $ *Average main: R167* ⊠ *Nelson Mandela Sq., shop 30, Sandton* ☎ *011/784–8676* ⊕ *www.thebutchershop.co.za.*

ROSEBANK

$$
MEDITERRANEAN
✗ **Doppio Zero.** This chain of restaurants is found across Johannesburg, but the Rosebank branch is well-located if you are peckish after a morning shopping at the nearby African Craft Market or Rosebank shopping centers. Doppio Zero serves wholesome, tasty Mediterranean-inspired meals. The sandwiches are excellent and contain ingredients like grilled

holoumi (a salty mozzarella-texture Greek cheese), fresh tomato, arugula, avocado, and salmon. More substantial meals such as pastas and pizzas are also on the menu. ⑤ *Average main: R110* ✉ *The Firs Shopping Centre, Cradock and Bierman Sts.* ☎ *011/447–9538* ⊕ *www.doppio.co.za.*

WHERE TO STAY

You can find just about every type of lodging in Johannesburg, from the stately and classic Saxon to the fun and funky Ten Bompas or the Peech. Although these varied options are all worthy places to lay your head, the truth is that most travelers stop here only for an overnight or two before they head out to their safari destination. With that in mind, we have compiled a list of places that are easy to get to from the airport and are in well-secured areas so that you will feel safe and comfortable.

Most, if not all, of the good hotels are in the northern suburbs. Many of them are linked to nearby malls and are well policed. Boutique hotels have sprung up everywhere, as have bed-and-breakfasts from Melville to Soweto. Hotels are quieter in December and January, when many locals take their annual vacations and rates are often cheaper. But beware: if there's a major conference, some of the smaller hotels can be booked months in advance.

All the hotels we list offer no-smoking rooms, and many have no-smoking floors.

Hotel reviews have been shortened. For full information, visit Fodors.com.

8

WHAT IT COSTS IN SOUTH AFRICAN RAND			
$	$$	$$$	$$$$
Hotels	under R1,500	R1,500–R2,500	R2,501–R3,500	over R3,500

Prices are the lowest price for a standard double room in high season.

NORTHERN SUBURBS

KEMPTON PARK

$$$$
HOTEL
🏨 **InterContinental Johannesburg O.R. Tambo Airport.** A few paces from international arrivals and adjacent to the car-rental companies, this is a good choice for those who have a one-night layover. **Pros:** ideal for those who don't need to go into Johannesburg or who have a layover before a connecting flight; free Wi-Fi; free meet-and-greet service with escort to the hotel. **Cons:** large and impersonal; you won't see much of Johannesburg without leaving the hotel. ⑤ *Rooms from: R3850* ✉ *O.R. Tambo Airport, Kempton Park* ☎ *011/961–5400* ⊕ *www.ihg.com* ⤳ *138 rooms, 2 suites* ⑩ *Breakfast.*

BEST BETS FOR JOHANNESBURG LODGING

Fodor's offers a selective listing of high-quality lodging experiences in every price range, from the city's best budget beds to its most sophisticated luxury hotels. Here, we've compiled our top recommendations by price and experience. The very best properties—in other words, those that provide a particularly remarkable experience in their price range—are designated in the listings with the Fodor's Choice logo.

Fodor's Choice

Four Seasons The Westcliff, $$$$, p. 443

The Orient Hotel, $$, p. 453

The Saxon Hotel, Village & Spa, $$$$, p. 443

By Price

$$

Clico Boutique Hotel, p. 441

Crowne Plaza Johannesburg–The Rosebank, p. 441

InterContinental Johannesburg Sandton Towers, p. 442

Maropeng Hotel, p. 457

Mount Grace Country House & Spa, p. 460

The Orient Hotel, p. 453

Palazzo at Montecasino, p. 443

The Peech, p. 441

Sandton Sun, p. 442

$$$

Hyatt Regency Johannesburg, p. 441

InterContinental Johannesburg O.R. Tambo Airport, p. 439

The Michelangelo, p. 442

$$$$

Fairlawns Boutique Hotel & Spa, p. 442

Four Seasons The Westcliff, p. 443

The Saxon Hotel, Village & Spa, p. 443

By Experience

BEST FOR ROMANCE

Fairlawns Boutique Hotel & Spa, p. 442

Palazzo at Montecasino, p. 443

BEST GYM

Fairlawns Boutique Hotel & Spa, p. 442

Hyatt Regency Johannesburg, p. 441

InterContinental Johannesburg O.R. Tambo Airport, p. 439

BEST HOTEL BARS

Hyatt Regency Johannesburg, p. 441

BEST INTERIOR DESIGN

Crowne Plaza Johannesburg–The Rosebank, p. 441

Sandton Sun, p. 442

The Saxon Hotel, Village & Spa, p. 443

BEST-KEPT SECRET

Fairlawns Boutique Hotel & Spa, p. 442

The Peech, p. 441

BUSINESS TRAVEL

Hyatt Regency Johannesburg, p. 441

InterContinental Johannesburg Sandton Towers, p. 442

The Michelangelo, $$$, p. 442

Sandton Sun, p. 442

HIPSTER HOTELS

Crowne Plaza Johannesburg–The Rosebank, p. 441

ROSEBANK

$$ 🏨 **Clico Boutique Hotel.** This small, upmarket guesthouse in central Rose-
HOTEL bank is an old Cape Dutch house with a gracious garden that offers good
value in an area known for expensive accommodation. **Pros:** 24-hour
manned security and CCTV cameras; free Wi-Fi throughout the hotel;
restaurant serves breakfast daily, and lunch and dinner are available
upon request. **Cons:** Some of the on-site parking spaces are difficult to
negotiate; noise from the pool activity can travel to the suites; dining at
lunch and dinner times needs to be booked in advance. $ *Rooms from:
R1936* ✉ *27 Sturdee Ave., at Jellicoe Ave.* ☎ *011/252–3300* ⊕ *www.
clicohotel.com* ➳ *9 suites, including 1 room with kitchen* ⦿ *Breakfast.*

$$ 🏨 **Crowne Plaza Johannesburg–The Rosebank.** Notable for its quirky public
HOTEL spaces—Louis XVI reproduction armchairs, white shaggy rugs, and the
very popular Circle Bar with its beaded booths—The Rosebank Crowne
Plaza is an "it" spot for late-night revelry. **Pros:** hip nightspot; great
spa and gym. **Cons:** popular with partying locals; bathrooms in deluxe
suites lack privacy. $ *Rooms from: R1700* ✉ *Tyrwhitt and Sturdee
Aves.* ☎ *011/448–3600* ⊕ *www.therosebank.co.za* ➳ *294 rooms, 24
suites* ⦿ *Breakfast.*

$$$ 🏨 **54 on Bath.** Most of the visitors to 54 on Bath are international busi-
HOTEL ness travelers and foreign tourists drawn to the modern yet intimate
elegance behind the towering brick facade and Doric columns, though
the popular champagne bar does draw locals. **Pros:** free Wi-Fi for guests
throughout the hotel; direct access to malls via sky bridge; free trans-
portation to the Gautrain station. **Cons:** construction in the area can
be noisy; not on airport shuttle route, although the hotel will arrange
transport from the airport for a fee. $ *Rooms from: R3200* ✉ *54 Bath
Ave.* ☎ *011/344–8500* ⊕ *www.54onbath.com* ➳ *56 rooms, 19 suites*
⦿ *Breakfast.*

$$$ 🏨 **Hyatt Regency Johannesburg.** This Hyatt Regency hotel is trendy and
HOTEL opulent, with lots of black, gold, and glass and enormous picture win-
dows revealing stunning views of the northern suburbs. **Pros:** direct
basement access to the adjoining malls; very cosmopolitan atmosphere;
bustling lobby area is frequently used for meetings. **Cons:** busy area
with lots of traffic; an expensive option for the area. $ *Rooms from:
R3300* ✉ *191 Oxford Rd.* ☎ *011/280–1234* ⊕ *johannesburg.regency.
hyatt.com* ➳ *244 rooms, 15 suites* ⦿ *Breakfast.*

$$ 🏨 **The Peech.** The smart traveler stays at this upscale boutique hotel
HOTEL for uncluttered, but comfortable interiors and quality restaurant. **Pros:**
fabulous rain showerheads and Molton Brown toiletries in every bath-
room; free Wi-Fi throughout the hotel and iPod docking stations in
every room; every room has a private outdoor space. **Cons:** rooms and
the neighboring gym overlook the pool; fee to use the gym. $ *Rooms
from: R2400* ✉ *61 North St.* ☎ *011/537–9797* ⊕ *www.thepeech.co.za*
➳ *16 rooms* ⦿ *Breakfast.*

MELROSE ARCH

$$$ 🏨 **African Pride Melrose Arch Hotel.** Primarily catering to business travel-
HOTEL ers, this ultramodern hotel is within the Melrose Arch shopping, din-
ing, and residential enclave. **Pros:** Melrose Arch is a high-security gated
community with good dining and shopping options within safe walking

8

distance; the Library bar is a favorite with well-heeled executives. **Cons:** hipster decor might not appeal to everyone; some might find it hard to relax in a high-energy environment; no on-site gym, but a Virgin Active Gym, one of the country's best, is available at R200 per visit within easy walking distance. $ *Rooms from: R3500* ✉ *1 Melrose Sq.* ☎ *011/214–6666* ⊕ *www.africanpridehotels.com* ⤳ *117 rooms, 1 suite* |O| *Breakfast.*

SANDTON

$$$$ 🕮 **Fairlawns Boutique Hotel & Spa.** In a residential area, this gracious bou-
HOTEL   tique hotel was once a private home owned by the Oppenheimer family. **Pros:** well-stocked library; complimentary shuttle service to Sandton City mall. **Cons:** service can be slow. $ *Rooms from: R4870* ✉ *Morningside Manor, 1 Alma Rd.* ☎ *011/804–2540* ⊕ *www.fairlawns.co.za* ⤳ *40 suites* |O| *Breakfast.*

$$ 🕮 **InterContinental Johannesburg Sandton Towers.** Directly connected to
HOTEL   Sandton City via a sky bridge, this hotel is particularly attractive to keen shoppers and businesspeople who value proximity and easy access to Johannesburg's premier mall and meeting venues. **Pros:** free Wi-Fi throughout the hotel; free morning newspaper; international adapters provided in the rooms; room windows open; great location. **Cons:** large and not as personal as a smaller hotel; public areas used extensively by locals for meetings. $ *Rooms from: R2300* ✉ *Maude and 5th Sts.* ☎ *011/780–5555* ⊕ *www.ihg.com* ⤳ *231 rooms, 17 suites* |O| *Breakfast.*

$$ 🕮 **The Maslow.** Conveniently situated in the heart of bustling Sandton,
HOTEL   the Maslow is a case study in modern, seamless sophistication. **Pros:** one of the best business-orientated hotels in the province; stellar attention to detail; great location. **Cons:** people have complained that the breakfast buffet does not reflect the high standard of the hotel. $ *Rooms from: R2300* ✉ *146 Rivonia Rd.* ☎ *010/226–4600, 011/780–7810* ⊕ *www. suninternational.com/maslow/* ⤳ *281 rooms* |O| *Breakfast.*

$$$$ 🕮 **The Michelangelo.** As though taken from a street in Florence, this
HOTEL   hotel forms the northern facade of much-touted piazza-inspired Nelson Mandela Square, also called Sandton Square. **Pros:** great shopping (especially for designer labels and high-fashion items from Gucci and Louis Vuitton) in the Square and adjoining Sandton Sun Mall; high security is omnipresent. **Cons:** Nelson Mandela Square is very popular and never quiet; service can be inattentive at times. $ *Rooms from: R3510* ✉ *135 West St., Nelson Mandela Sq.* ☎ *011/282–7000* ⊕ *www. legacyhotels.co.za* ⤳ *242 rooms* |O| *Breakfast.*

$$ 🕮 **Radisson Blu Gautrain.** Located just across the road from the Sandton
HOTEL   Gautrain station (55 steps, to be exact), the Radisson Blu Gautrain hotel is a popular destination for both international travelers and city locals. **Pros:** Great value for money; 24-hour gym; beautiful views of surrounding Sandton. **Cons:** no free parking; not child friendly. $ *Rooms from: R1850* ✉ *Cnr Rivonia Rd. and West St.* ☎ *011/286–1000* ⊕ *www. radissonblu.com/hotelsandton-johannesburg* ⤳ *216 rooms, 2 suites* |O| *Breakfast.*

$$$$ 🕮 **Sandton Sun.** One of the first luxury hotels to open in Sandton, the Sun
HOTEL   has a very upmarket designer African feel. **Pros:** linked to Sandton City,

Johannesburg's premier mall, by a first-floor sky bridge; business suites have home-automation technology and video conferencing; excellent restaurants are within easy walking distance. **Cons:** shopping's the name of the game here; if conspicuous consumption bothers you, stay elsewhere; pricey. $ *Rooms from: R3850* ⊠ *Sandton City, 5th St. and Alice La.* ☎ *011/780–5000* ⊕ *www.tsogosunhotels.com/deluxe/sandton-sun/* ⬦ *334 rooms* ❑ *Breakfast.*

SANDHURST

$$$$
HOTEL
Fodor'sChoice
★

The Saxon Hotel, Village & Spa. In the exclusive suburb of Sandhurst, adjacent to the commercial and shopping center of Sandton, the Saxon Hotel has repeatedly received awards for its excellence. **Pros:** possibly the most exclusive address in Gauteng; exceptional spa on-site; good for business travelers or high-profile folk who'd rather not see anyone else in the corridors. **Cons:** some might find the atmosphere a bit snooty; children under 14 not welcome in restaurant; pricey. $ *Rooms from: R5210* ⊠ *36 Saxon Rd.* ☎ *011/292–6000* ⊕ *www.saxon.co.za* ⬦ *53 suites* ❑ *Breakfast.*

WESTCLIFF

$$$$
HOTEL
Fodor'sChoice
★

Four Seasons The Westcliff. The iconic Westcliff, now under the Four Seasons banner and with a $56-million revamp has been transformed into the paragon of a luxurious urban resort, while renowned chef Dirk Gieselmann has been whisked from France to oversee both the new View and Flame restaurants. The restaurants are perched at the top of Westcliff hill and accessible via panoramic glass elevators. Exquisite dining aside, the view of Johannesburg's urban forest below makes the trip up worthwhile. All 117 rooms have been overhauled, each offering immaculate accommodation and all the refinements you'd expect from a five-star establishment. The resort's business facilities are equally impressive. Staff exude a love for Johannesburg and are quick to recommend places of interest to international visitors. Guests are also offered escorted tours of inner-city cultural hubs like Maboneng and Braamfontein. **Pros:** great location; spectacular views over Johannesburg; impeccable service. **Cons:** all this luxury and service comes at a high cost; rather formal atmosphere, which may not be to everyone's liking; rooms spread out along a steep hill, sometimes requiring a shuttle. $ *Rooms from: R3795* ⊠ *67 Jan Smuts Ave.* ☎ *011/481–6000* ⊕ *www. fourseasons.com/johannesburg/* ⬦ *81 rooms, 36 suites* ❑ *Breakfast.*

FOURWAYS

$$
HOTEL

Palazzo at Montecasino. Built in the style of a Tuscan villa, the hotel is set among formal herb gardens in a location far north of Johannesburg that's good for shopping but somewhat distant from most of the city's sights and the business center of Sandton and the city center itself. **Pros:** neighboring casino complex has malls, cinemas, and major theater; the hotel's grounds contain great gardens and a pool; service is impeccable. **Cons:** gridlocked traffic in the area means longer than usual traffic jams; as in the casino, the decor is faux-Tuscan. $ *Rooms from: R2500* ⊠ *Montecasino Blvd.* ☎ *011/510–3000* ⊕ *www.tsogosunhotels.com/ deluxe/the-palazzo-montecasino/* ⬦ *246 rooms, 12 suites* ❑ *Breakfast.*

8

NIGHTLIFE AND PERFORMING ARTS

NIGHTLIFE

Johannesburg comes alive after dark, and whether you're a rebellious punk rocker or a suave executive, there's always something to do. Rivonia and the business district of Sandton have become trendy spots for young, hip professionals and their style-conscious friends, and the old neighborhood of Greenside still has streets filled with lively little bars and restaurants and a sprinkling of clubs. The suburb of Norwood also has a central street with a good selection of small restaurants and bars. To dine and dance in one go, you should venture to one of these suburbs or visit one of the casino complexes, such as the popular Montecasino in Fourways or Emperor's Palace next to the O. R. Tambo Airport.

JHBLive. A useful website for event details is JHBLive. ⊕ *www.jhblive. com.*

The Star. A good place to find out what's going on is in the "Tonight" section of *The Star*, Johannesburg's major daily. ⊕ *www.tonight.co.za.*

BARS AND PUBS

Café Vacca Matta. Dress stylishly for Café Vacca Matta, a trendy bar and restaurant where a sometimes-snobbish crowd dances to Top 40 hits. ⊠ *Montecasino, William Nicol Dr., Fourways* ☎ *011/511–0511.*

Capitol Music Café. Capitol Music Café is a happening vinyl shop and bar, where DJs play what they have just bought and an eclectic crowd gathers. ⊠ *Tyrwhitt and Keyes Aves., Rosebank* ☎ *011/880–0033.*

CLUBS

Jo'burg's clubs are usually not too expensive. On a normal club night, you'll pay between R100 and R250 to get in, though you won't always have to pay for entrance. When dance parties or bigger events take place (or big-name DJs and musicians appear), expect to pay upward of R200. Here are just some of the city's established clubs.

PERFORMING ARTS

For a comprehensive guide to events, read the "Friday" section of the weekly *Mail & Guardian,* which is also available online.

TICKETS

Computicket. Almost all major performances and many smaller ones can be booked through Computicket. ☎ *0861/915–8000, 011/340–8000* ⊕ *www.computicket.com.*

THEATER

Joburg Theatre. Joburg Theatre is Jo'burg's main cultural venue and the home of the Joburg Ballet Theatre. It contains the enormous Nelson Mandela Theatre and the smaller People's and Fringe theaters. Many international productions are staged here, but there's also a good balance of local material, such as the annual pantomime by Janice Honeyman, which satirizes South Africans uproariously. ⊠ *163 Civic Blvd., Braamfontein* ☎ *011/877–6800* ⊕ *www.joburgtheatre.com.*

Kwaito

Kwaito is a uniquely South African music genre, rooted in house, raga (a subgenre of reggae), hip-hop, and local rhythms. It emerged from the country's townships after apartheid and gets its name, some say, from township slang for "cool talk." Its hard-pumping bass beats, lightly slowed down from a house rhythm, are topped with rambled-off lyrics in a style reminiscent of American rap. It's as much a lifestyle as it is a music genre, with its own ways of dancing and dressing.

The best-selling kwaito musicians (and kwaito DJs) have superstar status in South Africa, but they have a less unsavory reputation than their American hip-hop equivalents. Though some kwaito acts stand accused of sexism and vulgar lyrics, the kwaito attitude is generally quite respectable. Lyrics are often about banning guns or respecting women, or they comment on murder, rape, AIDS, and unemployment. One kwaito star, Zola—named after an impoverished Soweto community—enjoyed a long-running TV series, in which he worked to improve people's lives. His music is featured in the 2006 Academy Award–winning movie *Tsotsi*. Other chart-topping kwaito stars include Mandoza, whose catchy, powerful songs have earned him several awards and cross-over appeal; Arthur Mafikizolo; Mdu; the Brothers of Peace; and Mzekezeke, an enigmatic masked singer.

—Riaan Wolmarans

Teatro at Montecasino. The Teatro opened at the Montecasino leisure and casino complex in 2007, introducing patrons to a world-class theater facility with its debut production, *The Lion King*. Since then, it's staged dozens of world-class productions, including shows as diverse as *Phantom of the Opera*, *War Horse*, and *Swan Lake*. like the Although it seats more than 1,800, no seat is more than 33 metres (100 feet) from the action—and there's plenty of that. Expect large-scale music productions, cirque arts, drama performances, stand-up comedy, and National Theatre productions. Teatro is one of the world's 10 largest lyric theaters. ⊠ *Montecasino, Nelson Mandela Sq., Sandton* ☎ *011/510–7472* ⊕ *www.montecasino.co.za.*

Theatre on the Square. Located on Nelson Mandela Square in Sandton, this intimate, 200-seater theater has hosted hundreds of shows since it opened in 1996. An extensive repertoire includes comedy shows, cultural celebrations, author interviews, jazz concerts, plays, and music recitals. Friday lunchtime performances are a boon to Sandton-based workers. ⊠ *Nelson Mandela Sq., Sandton* ☎ *011/883–8606* ⊕ *www.theatreonthesquare.co.za.*

SHOPPING

Whether you're after designer clothes, the latest books or DVDs, high-quality African art, or glamorous gifts, Johannesburg offers outstanding shopping opportunities. In fact, many people, particularly from other African countries, come here with the express aim of shopping.

Dozens of malls, galleries, and curio shops are scattered throughout the city, often selling the same goods at widely different prices. It's best to shop around.

NORTHERN SUBURBS

ROSEBANK
AFRICAN ARTS AND CRAFTS
Everard Read Gallery. The Everard Read Gallery, established in 1912, is one of the largest privately owned galleries in the world. It acts as an agent for several important South African artists. The gallery specializes in wildlife paintings and sculpture. ⊠ *6 Jellicoe Ave.* ☎ *011/788–4805* ⊕ *www.everard-read.co.za.*

MARKETS
At the city's several markets, bargaining can get you a great price. At the African Craft Market in particular, bargain hard by offering half the asking price, and then work your way up to about two-thirds of the price if you're interested in the item. Take your time before you buy anything, as you will see similar crafts at different stalls, and the prices may vary considerably.

Fodor's Choice **African Craft Market.** The African Craft Market, between the Rosebank ★ Mall and the Zone, has a huge variety of African crafts from Cape to Cairo, all displayed to the background beat of traditional African music. Drive a hard bargain here—the vendors expect you to! If you want to save your shopping until the end of your trip, then this should be your destination. It's the best place in Jo'burg to buy African crafts, and it's an entertaining place to visit as well. ⊠ *Mall of Rosebank, Cradock Ave. and Baker St.* ☎ *072/614–5506* ⊕ *www.rosebankmall.co.za/art-crafts-rosebank-mall* ۞ *Daily 9–6.*

Rooftop Market. Rosebank's Rooftop Market has become a Sunday tradition in the city. More than 600 stalls sell African and Western crafts, antiques, books, food, art, trinkets, CDs, jewelry, and clothes. Frequently, African musicians, dancers, and other entertainers delight the crowds. ⊠ *The Mall of Rosebank, 50 Bath Ave.* ☎ *011/442–4488* ⊕ *www.craft.co.za* ۞ *Sun. 9–5.*

BRYANSTON
MARKETS
Bryanston Organic and Natural Market. If you're into healthful living, visit the Bryanston Organic and Natural Market. More than 140 stalls feature artisanal, organic, and naturally sourced fresh produce. There's a dairy section, delicatessen and bakery, choice of five coffee shops, flowers, crafts in wood, leather, glass and metal, handmade clothes and shoes, and many other products clamoring for your clean-living attention. ⊠ *Michael Mount Waldorf School, Culross Rd., off Main Rd.* ☎ *011/706–3671* ⊕ *www.bryanstonorganicmarket.co.za* ۞ *Thurs., Sat., and public holidays 9–3.*

PARKTOWN, PARKVIEW, SAXONWOLD, AND WESTCLIFF

AFRICAN ARTS AND CRAFTS

Art Africa. Art Africa brings together a dazzling selection of ethnic arts, crafts, and artifacts from across the continent and also sells funky items, such as tin lizards and wooden animals, that are produced in community empowerment projects that uplift and benefit the craftsmen and their communities. ⊠ *62 Tyrone Ave., Parkview* ☎ *011/486–2052.*

Goodman Gallery. The highly successful, five-decade-old Goodman Gallery presents exciting monthly exhibitions by the stars of contemporary African and African diaspora art, including William Kentridge, David Goldblatt, and Kudzanai Chiurai. ⊠ *163 Jan Smuts Ave., Parkwood* ☎ *011/788–1113* ⊕ *www.goodman-gallery.com.*

SANDTON

GOLD AND DIAMONDS

Krugerrands, which carry images of President Paul Kruger and a springbok on either side, are among the most famous gold coins minted today. They lost some of their luster during the apartheid years, when they were banned internationally. Krugerrands are sold individually or in sets containing coins of 1 ounce, ½ ounce, ¼ ounce, and 1/10 ounce of pure gold. You can buy Krugerrands through most city banks, and at reputable coin shops such as the Scoin chain of shops, which you'll find in upmarket malls. The most convenient branches are in the Sandton City Shopping Centre and in Rosebank.

Charles Greig. Charles Greig is a reputable jeweler with a long-standing record, and a reputation for excellence, making this shop a good choice if you wish to buy a special South African piece, such as a ring or necklace containing diamonds. ⊠ *Hyde Park Corner, Jan Smuts Ave., Hyde Park* ☎ *011/325–4477* ⊕ *www.charlesgreig.co.za.*

Schwartz Jewellers. Schwartz Jewellers is a diamond wholesaler and manufacturing jeweler. It offers a large range of classical and ethnic African pieces and a custom-design service. You can also take a one-hour tour of its workshops in Sandton by appointment. You can see stone grading, diamond setting, and gold pouring, plus get tips on what to look for when buying diamonds, as well as a brief history of South Africa's diamond industry. And, of course, you can buy the finished product. Tours are free and include refreshments; you need your passport for security reasons. ⊠ *Nelson Mandela Sq., shop L3, on bridge* ☎ *011/783–1717.*

8

SIDE TRIPS FROM JOHANNESBURG

About an hour north of Johannesburg (depending on the traffic—on a bad day it can take more than two hours), Pretoria, the country's capital, is within the larger metropolitan area of Tshwane (pronounced *chwa*-ah-neh). About an hour and a half from Johannesburg is the Cradle of Humankind, declared a World Heritage Site for its rich fossil record reflecting the history of humanity over the past 3 million years or so. To the north of Johannesburg, not far from the Cradle of Humankind, lies the Magaliesberg (pronounced muh-*xuh*-lees-berg, where the first *g* is pronounced like the *ch* in *Chanukah*), a gentle, ancient mountain range and leisure area, where you can get a restful break amid lovely mountain scenery, farmlands, and quiet country roads. Sun City, a multifaceted entertainment and casino complex comprising hotels, championship golf courses, and a water park, and the adjacent Pilanesberg Game Reserve are about a three-hour drive from Johannesburg—well worth a visit if you have the time.

PRETORIA

48 km (30 miles) north of Johannesburg.

The city of Pretoria lies within the greater Tshwane metropolitan area, which was formed in 2000 when Pretoria and its surrounding areas—Centurion, the townships of Atteridgeville, Mamelodi, and Shoshanguve, and neighboring areas—merged under a single municipal authority. The country's administrative capital and home to many senior politicians and diplomats, Pretoria is a pleasant city, with historic buildings and a city center that is easily explored on foot.

Founded in 1855, the city was named after Afrikaner leader Andries Pretorius, one of the Voortrekkers (pronounced *fooer*-trekka) who moved from the Cape to escape British rule. In 1860 it became the capital of the independent Transvaal Voortrekker Republic. After the South African War of 1899–1902 (the Second Anglo-Boer War), the city became the capital of the then British colony, and in 1910 it was named the administrative capital of the Union of South Africa. In 1948, when the National Party came to power, Pretoria became the seat of the apartheid government. In 1964 the Rivonia Treason Trial (named for the Johannesburg suburb where 19 ANC leaders were arrested in 1963) was held here, and Nelson Mandela and seven of his colleagues were sentenced to life in prison.

GETTING HERE AND AROUND

There are a few options for getting to Pretoria. The Gautrain offers a safe, convenient, and high-speed connection between O.R. Tambo International Airport, Johannesburg, and Pretoria. Alternatively, a rental car gives you the flexibility to explore the city at your leisure, and private transfers are offered by all of O.R. Tambo's airport transfer companies (⇨ *Air Travel, in Planning, at the beginning of the chapter*). It takes at least an hour to travel from Johannesburg to Pretoria in the Tshwane metropolitan area on the N1 (two hours if the traffic is bad, which happens quite regularly, especially between about 7 and 9 am and 4 and 7 pm).

TIMING AND PRECAUTIONS

If you want to see everything, schedule an entire day or even couple of days here. A side trip to the Cullinan Diamond Mine will take at least half a day. Pretoria is not as notorious as Johannesburg for crime, but drive with your car doors locked, and don't have bags or valuables visible or you could become a target of a "hit-and-grab."

Pretoria

↑ TO
TSWAING CRATER
MUSEUM

R101

M5 RIVIERA

M22

PRINSHOF

Apies

Boom

Dr. Savage

ASIATIC
BAZAAR

N4

← TO
SUN CITY

Heroes
Acre

WF Nkomo

M1

PRETORIA
CENTRAL

R101   R101

Nana Sita

PRETORIA
WEST

Soutter

Visagie

Jeff Masemola St.

Kgosi Mampuru

Bosman

Sophie de Bruyn

Paul Kruger

M22

M22

Boom

Bloed

Struben

Thabo Sehume St.

Vermeulen

Helen Joseph St.

Pretorius St.

Francis Baard St.

Lilian Ngoyi St.

Burgers
Park

Scheiding

Rhodes
Berea
Park

M18

J. Ramohoase

J. Ramohoase St.

Madiba

M5

M5

ARCADIA

Stanza Bopape St.

East

N4

Park St.

Pretorius St.

M2

TREVENNA

R. Sobukwe St.

Korze

Rissik

Steve Biko Rd.

M6

M11

M11 Justice Mahomed St.

Nelson Mandela Dr.

TO →
NATIONAL BOTANICAL
GARDENS AND
SAMMY MARKS MUSEUM

N4

N4

M5

Troye

Walkerspruit

M6

SUNNYSIDE

Jorissen

MUCKLENEUK

LUKASRAND

SALVOKOP

Groenkloof
Nature
Reserve

M1

R101

Jan Smuts

Ben-Schoeman

Vortrekker
Monument
Nature Reserve

TO
JOHANNESBURG
AND CRADLE OF
HUMANKIND

George Storrar

M7

0   1/2 mile

0   1/2 kilometer

Locations:
1
2
3
4
5
6
7
8
9
10
11
12

VISITOR INFORMATION

Covering Pretoria, Centurion, Atteridgeville, Mamelodi, and the surrounding area, the Tshwane Tourism Information Centre has friendly staff, plenty of pamphlets and printed guides, and a 24-hour info line.

Visitor Information **Tshwane Tourism Information Centre** ⊠ *Bitss Centre, Church Sq., Paul Kruger St. and Parliament St., Pretoria* ☎ *012/358–1430* ⊕ *www.tshwane.gov.za* ⊙ *Open weekdays 7:30 am–4 pm; closed weekends.*

EXPLORING

TOP ATTRACTIONS

Ditsong National Museum of Cultural History. This museum offers an insightful look at the country's indigenous cultures. You can marvel at San rock art, African headdresses, clay sculptures, and several permanent collections of archaeological material dealing with Pretoria, South Africa, and the many people who call this country home. The museum also has a restaurant. ⊠ *149 Visagie St., between Bosman and Schubart Sts., Pretoria* ☎ *012/324–6082* ⊕ *www.ditsong.org.za* ☞ *R25* ⊙ *Daily 8–4.*

Freedom Park. Opened in 2013, the 129-acre Freedom Park is dedicated to the struggle for freedom and humanity, as well as other aspects of South African heritage, including human evolution. At Salvokop, a prominent hill at the entrance to Pretoria on the highway from Johannesburg, and within view of the Voortrekker Monument, the site comprises a memorial, interactive museum, archives, and a garden of remembrance. The park was launched in 2002 by President Thabo Mbeki, who said, "We dedicate this day to all the heroes and heroines in this country and the rest of the world who sacrificed in many ways and surrendered their lives so that we could be free." Individual South African, African, and global leaders who made significant contributions to the struggle against oppression, exploitation, racism, and other forms of discrimination are honored here. ⊠ *Koch and 7th Ave., Salvokop, Pretoria* ☎ *012/336–4000* ⊕ *www.freedompark.co.za* ☞ *R90* ⊙ *Daily 8–2:30.*

FAMILY
Fodor's Choice
★

National Zoological Gardens. The city's zoo, covering nearly 200 acres, is considered one of the world's best, with about 9,000 animals from almost every continent (including rare Komodo dragons, the world's largest lizards). The animal enclosures here are much larger than those of most zoos. Like any modern zoo worth its name, this is just the public facade for a much larger organization that specializes in the research and breeding of endangered species. It includes an aquarium (with Africa's largest collection of freshwater fish) and reptile park, where the king crocodiles and the impressive collection of snakes don't fail to intimidate. A cable car transports you high above the zoo to a hilltop lookout, and it's a fun, worthwhile ride. It's also a good idea to rent a golf cart, so you can move more quickly between enclosures for the staggered feeding times each morning and afternoon. ⊠ *Boom St., Pretoria* ☎ *012/328–3265* ⊕ *www.nzg.ac.za* ☞ *R75* ⊙ *Daily 8:30–5:30.*

WORTH NOTING

Church Square. Anton van Wouw's statue of President Paul Kruger, surrounded by sentries, dominates this pleasant square, which is flanked by some of the city's most historic buildings: the Old Raadsaal (Council

Chamber), designed by Dutch architect Sytze Wierda; the Palace of Justice (used as a military hospital during the South African War), built in early Italian Renaissance style; and the modern Provincial Administration Building. On Wednesday mornings you can watch a military parade and flag-raising. ⊠ *Bordered by Paul Kruger and Church Sts., Pretoria.*

NEED A BREAK?

Café Riche. In a building dating from 1904, Café Riche is one of the better coffee shops in the center of town. It also serves *tramezzini* (toasted sandwiches) and salads. ⊠ *Church Sq., Pretoria* ☎ *012/328–3173.*

City Hall. This imposing structure has an Italianate style that borrows freely from classical architecture. A tympanum on the front, by Coert Steynberg, one of South Africa's most famous sculptors, symbolizes the growth and development of the city. Statues of Andries Pretorius, the city's founder, and his son Marthinus, stand in the square fronting the building, and relief panels depict the founding in 1855. ⊠ *Visagie and Paul Kruger Sts., Pretoria* ☎ *012/358–1088* ⬚ *Free* ☉ *Weekdays 7:45–4.*

Ditsong National Museum of Natural History. This massive natural-history museum has an extensive collection of land and marine animals from around the world, with an emphasis on African wildlife. The beautiful building also contains the Austin Roberts Bird Collection, the most comprehensive display of taxidermied African birds in southern Africa. Of particular interest are the Genesis exhibits, tracing the evolution of life on Earth, and the geology section, with displays of weird and wonderful rocks and minerals. Mrs. Ples, the famous Australopithecus skull found at the Sterkfontein Caves in the Cradle of Humankind, resides here. ⊠ *Paul Kruger St., across from City Hall, Pretoria* ☎ *012/000– 0040* ⊕ *www.ditsong.org.za* ⬚ *R30, tours R35* ☉ *Daily 8–4.*

Kruger Museum. This was once the residence of Paul Kruger, president of the South African republic between 1883 and 1902 and one of the most revered figures in South African history. The home, still fully furnished, is humble and somber, befitting this deeply religious leader who loved to sit on the front *stoep* (veranda) and watch the world go by. Exhibits in the adjoining museum trace Kruger's career, culminating in his exile by the British and eventual death in Switzerland in 1904. Of particular interest are the letters of support that Kruger received from all over the world, including the United States, when Britain instigated the South African War (1899–1902), also known as the Anglo-Boer War. Across the road is the Dutch Reformed Church, where Kruger's wife is buried. ⊠ *70 Church St. W, at Potgieter St., Pretoria* ☎ *012/000–0010* ⊕ *www. ditsong.org.za* ⬚ *R35* ☉ *Weekdays 8:30–4:30, weekends 9–4:30.*

Lillian Ngoyi Square. This square, once called the J. G. Strijdom Square, was in apartheid times dominated by a huge bust of former pro-apartheid prime minister J. G. Strijdom. However, on May 31, 2001— exactly 40 years to the day after the government declared South Africa a republic—the supporting structure of the whole edifice crumbled, and Strijdom fell unceremoniously into the parking garage under the square. The public square has since been renamed the Lillian Ngoyi

Square. Ngoyi was a prominent anti-apartheid activist. ⊠ *Church and van der Walt Sts., Pretoria.*

Melrose House. Built in 1886, this opulent structure is one of South Africa's most beautiful and best-preserved Victorian homes, furnished in period style. It has marble columns, mosaic floors, lovely stained-glass windows, ornate ceilings, porcelain ornaments, and richly colored carpets. On May 31, 1902, the Treaty of Vereeniging was signed in the dining room, ending the South African War. You can view a permanent exhibit on the war or arrange for a guided tour. ⊠ *275 Jeff Masemola St., Pretoria* ☎ *012/322–2805* ⊕ *www.tshwane.gov.za* ⊠ *R22, guided tour R170 per hr* ☾ *Tues.–Sun. 10–5. Closed Mon. and public holidays.*

FAMILY   **Pretoria National Botanical Garden.** Natural grassland and lawns fringed by indigenous flowers provide a welcome contrast to city life in Pretoria. Within the main garden a succulent garden, cycad garden, and dassie trail provide added interest, and more than 220 bird species have been recorded. Look out for hawks, falcons, kestrels, and Verreaux's eagle. An Enabling Garden near the entrance is dedicated to the physically challenged. ⊠ *2 Cussonia Ave., off Church St., Pretoria* ☎ *012/843–5000* ⊕ *www.sanbi.org/gardens/pretoria* ⊠ *R26* ☾ *Daily 8–6 (last entry at 5).*

OFF THE BEATEN PATH

Sammy Marks Museum. About 23 km (14 miles) east of Pretoria's city center, this furnished, 48-room Victorian mansion, in a mixture of grand styles, and its outbuildings, surrounded by gardens, were built in 1884 for mining and industrial magnate Sammy Marks. Guided tours take place every hour on weekends; every 90 minutes on weekdays; and there are ghost tours at night by appointment. A restaurant is on-site, and you can picnic on the grounds. ⊠ *Off N4, Riamarpark* ✛ *Exit at Hans Strijdom and follow signs* ☎ *012/755–9541* ⊠ *R45* ☾ *Tues.–Sun. 10–4.*

Smuts House. This small wood-and-iron country house in Irene, an outlying suburb of Pretoria, was the residence of three-time South African prime minister Jan Christian Smuts, who played active roles in the South African War and World Wars I and II and was instrumental in setting up the League of Nations (forerunner of the United Nations). Despite his military background, he was committed to working for peace and remains one of South Africa's most interesting historical characters. His home illustrates the simple manner in which he lived until his death in 1950. There's a tea garden on the large grounds, an adjacent campsite, and easy trails up a nearby hill. On the second and last Saturday of each month, a crafts market takes to the grounds. ⊠ *Off Nelmapius Rd., Irene, Pretoria* ☎ *012/667–1176* ⊠ *R20* ☾ *Daily 9:30–4.*

OFF THE BEATEN PATH

Tswaing Crater Museum. The huge Tswaing meteorite crater was formed about 220,000 years ago. Today the area is a nature reserve home to 240 bird species, zebra, impala, kudu, steenbok, reptiles, and even more trees and plant species. Browse through the crater's eco-museum to learn more. A three-hour guided tour includes a walk to the crater and an informative talk. Self-guided tour options are also available. The site is of great significance to traditional healers because of the mythical snake believed to live in the salty crater lake. Picnic tables and rustic accommodation are also available. ⊠ *Old Soutpan Rd. (M35),*

Soshanguve ⚜ About 40 km (25 miles) north of Tshwane ☎ 079/829–5464 ⌨ R20, tours R200 ⊗ Daily 7:30–4.

Union Buildings. Built in 1901, this impressive cream-sandstone complex—home to the administrative branch of government—was designed by Sir Herbert Baker, one of South Africa's most revered architects. It is his masterpiece and closely resembles the Parliament Buildings in New Delhi, where he went on to work. The complex incorporates a hodgepodge of styles—an Italian tile roof, wooden shutters inspired by Cape Dutch architecture, and Renaissance columns—that somehow works beautifully. Expansive formal gardens step down the hillside in terraces, which are dotted with war memorials and statues of former prime ministers. There's no public access to the building, but the gardens are perfect for a picnic lunch. ⌂ *Off Church St., Pretoria* ⊗ *Gardens open 24 hrs.*

Voortrekker Monument and Museum. This famous landmark is regarded as a symbol of Afrikaner nationalism and independence. Completed in 1949, the monument honors the Voortrekkers, who rejected British rule and trekked into the hinterland to found their own nation. The Hall of Heroes traces in its marble frieze their momentous Great Trek, culminating in the Battle of Blood River (December 16, 1838), when a small force of Boers defeated a large Zulu army without losing a single life. The Voortrekkers considered this victory a special gift from God. An adjoining museum displays scenes and artifacts of daily Voortrekker life, as well as the Voortrekker Tapestries, 15 pictorial weavings that trace the historical high points of the Great Trek. The monument is in a nature reserve, which has a picnic area and hiking and biking trails. You can dine in the restaurant and tea garden if you don't like to rough it. Also on-site is **Fort Schanskop**, the best preserved of four area forts commissioned by President Paul Kruger in about 1897. The fort houses a South African (Anglo-Boer) War museum and gift shop. ⌂ *Eeufees Rd., Pretoria* ☎ *012/326–6770, 012/325–7885* ⊕ *www.vtm. org.za* ⌨ *R55* ⊗ *May–Aug., daily 8–5; Sept.–Apr., daily 8–6.*

WHERE TO STAY

$$
HOTEL
Fodor's Choice
★

The Orient Hotel. This exquisite, Asian-themed boutique hotel is aimed at the discerning traveler who is looking for an unusual and memorable experience and wants to be out of the center of the Johannesburg business district. **Pros:** superb cuisine; majestic surroundings; extraordinary service. **Cons:** no Wi-Fi; poor mobile phone reception; need a car to get around. ⑤ *Rooms from: R3000* ⌂ *Francolin Conservancy, Crocodile Valley Rd., Pretoria* ☎ *012/371–2902* ⊕ *www.the-orient.net* ⟳ *10 suites* ❘⊗❘ *Breakfast.*

CRADLE OF HUMANKIND

72 km (45 miles) northwest of Johannesburg.

This World Heritage Site stretches over an area of about 470 square km (181 square miles), with about 300 caves. Inside these caves, paleo-anthropologists have discovered thousands of fossils of hominids and other animals, dating back some 4 million years. The most famous

8

of these fossils are Mrs. Ples, a skull more than 2 million years old, and Little Foot, a skeleton more than 3 million years old. Although the Cradle does not have the world's oldest hominid fossils, it has the most complete fossil record of human evolution of anywhere on earth, has produced more hominid fossils than anywhere else, and has been designated a UNESCO World Heritage Site.

Archaeological finds at the Cradle of Humankind include 1.7-million-year-old stone tools, the oldest recorded in southern Africa. At Swartkrans, near Sterkfontein, a collection of burned bones tells us that our ancestors could manage fire more than a million years ago.

Not all the fossil sites in the Cradle are open to the public, but a tour of the Sterkfontein Caves and the visitor center provides an excellent overview of the paleontological work in progress, and a trip to Maropeng, a much larger visitor center 10 km (6 miles) from the Sterkfontein Caves, provides even more background. Special tours to fossil sites with expert guides can be booked via tour operator Palaeo-Tours.

GETTING HERE AND AROUND
Public transportation to the Cradle of Humankind area is limited, so using a rental car or taking an organized tour is best. Some hotels in the area will arrange transportation on request. The Cradle of Humankind is about a 90-minute drive from Johannesburg or Pretoria, but isn't well signposted, so use a GPS or download instructions on how to get there from the Maropeng website if you don't visit on a guided tour.

VISITOR INFORMATION
The Maropeng Visitor Centre provides information about the various sites in the Cradle of Humankind, and you can pick up many different promotional pamphlets here about things to do and see in the area. (*See* ⇨ *Exploring.*)

Maropeng Visitor Centre ☎ 014/577–9000 ⊕ www.maropeng.co.za.

EXPLORING
Lion Park. This highly rated drive-through safari park offers a rare chance to get up close with Africa's iconic predator. And while the experience might be trumped by seeing lion in more natural, expansive settings like the Kruger National Park, the opportunity to interact with a lion cub, take a guided walk with a cheetah, or feed a giraffe is not to be passed up. A leisurely drive around the small park will also guarantee sights of lion and other carnivores roaming through grassland, but try visit when it's a little cooler (early evening is a good time), as they tend to seek shady refuge during hot days. The lunch menu is reasonably priced. ⊠ *Lion Park, R114, just off Malibongwe Dr., Nietgedacht, Muldersdrift* ☎ *087/150–0100, 011/691–9905* ⊕ *www.lion-park.com* 🖃 *R200* ⊙ *Daily 8:30 am–9 pm.*

FAMILY
Fodor's Choice
★

Maropeng Visitor Centre. Maropeng is the official visitor center of the Cradle of Humankind World Heritage Site and offers much more than information about the region: it's a modern, interactive museum dedicated to the history of humanity. It provides information about the various fossil sites in the area. About a 90-minute drive from either Johannesburg or Pretoria, it's one of the area's top attractions. It's best

8

visited in parallel with the nearby fossil site of Sterkfontein Caves (about 5 km/3 miles away), but to visit both you'll need to set aside at least half a day. ⌧ *Off R563 Hekpoort Rd., Sterkfontein, Johannesburg* ☎ *014/577–9000* ⊕ *www.maropeng.co.za.*

Old Kromdraai Gold Mine. For more recent history of South Africa's Gold Rush era (as opposed to the ancient history of humanity you'll find in the Cradle of Humankind like Maropeng and the Sterkfontein Caves), tour the small but fascinating Old Kromdraai Gold Mine, one of the country's oldest mines begun in 1881. Frankly, it's a little spooky. You don a miner's helmet and wander into the mine's murky depths on one-hour guided tours. It's not a difficult walk, and if you're lucky, you'll see bats roosting. ⌧ *Ibis Ridge Farm, Kromdraai Rd., Kromdraai* ☎ *082/259–2162, 073/147–8417* ⊕ *www.gauteng.net* ⌧ *R100* ⊗ *Tours weekends 9–5, on the hr, last tour at 3; weekdays by appointment.*

FAMILY **Rhino and Lion Nature Reserve.** Rhinos, lions, wild dogs, cheetahs, hippos, and crocodiles are among the animals you can see at the Rhino and Lion Nature Reserve. You can spot about 600 head of game; visit the lion, wild dog, and cheetah enclosures (be careful of lions approaching vehicles) or vulture blind, or be thrilled by live snake shows on weekends and holidays. You can also visit the endangered-species breeding center and the magnificent white lions or cuddle a baby animal at the nursery for young orphaned animals. In addition to the self-driving tour, you can book an escorted game drive or horseback ride. The visitors' area has a pool, the Croc Pub and Diner, and a curio shop, as well as three basic chalets (no electricity) for overnights. ⌧ *Kromdraai Rd., Kromdraai* ☎ *011/957–0109* ⊕ *www.rhinolion.co.za* ⌧ *R140* ⊗ *Weekdays 8–5, weekends 8–6.*

FAMILY **Sterkfontein Caves.** It was in the Sterkfontein Caves, in 1936, that Dr. Robert Broom discovered the now famous Mrs. Ples, as she is popularly known—a skull of an adult *Australopithecus africanus* that is more than 2 million years old. The find reinforced the discovery of a skull of an *Australopithecus* child, the Taung Skull, by Professor Raymond Dart in 1924, which was the first hominid ever found. At the time, Dart was ostracized for claiming the skull belonged to an early human ancestor. Scientists in Europe and the United States simply didn't believe that humanity could have originated in Africa. Today, few disagree with this theory. Another important find was the discovery in the 1990s of Little Foot, a near-complete skeleton of an *Australopithecus*, embedded in rock deep inside the caves. Guided tours of the excavations and caves, which are spacious and not claustrophobic, last an hour. Wear comfortable shoes. Spend some time in the small but excellent **Sterkfontein Visitor Centre**, which has exhibits depicting the origins of the earth, life, and humanity. A small on-site restaurant is open daily. ⌧ *Sterkfontein Caves Rd., off R563, Maropeng* ☎ *014/577–9000* ⊕ *www.maropeng. co.za* ⌧ *R150* ⊗ *Tours daily 9–4 on the ½ hr; last tour departs at 4.*

Fodor'sChoice
★

FAMILY **Wonder Cave.** Wonder Cave is a huge single-chamber cave with a number of intact stalagmites and stalactites and formations up to 50 feet high. An elevator takes regular guided tours all the way down, but if you're feeling adventurous you can rappel down (by prior arrangement only). Groups of 20 or more may book evening tours. ⊠ *Kromdraai Rd., Kromdraai* ☎ *011/957–0106, 011/957–0109* 🖅 *R90* ⊙ *Weekdays 8–5, weekends 8–6.*

WHERE TO EAT

$ ✕ **The Carnivore.** Don't come expecting a quiet romantic dinner, as the
AFRICAN huge space lends itself to a loud and sometimes frenetic scene. Game meat such as warthog, impala, and crocodile vies with tamer fare such as pork and mutton for space around an enormous open fire in the center of the restaurant. Great hunks of meat are brought around to your table on Masai spears and carved directly onto your plate until you surrender by lowering the flag on your table. It's an African twist on the traditional Argentinian *churrascaria*. An excellent vegetarian à la carte menu features uniquely African dishes such as *aviyal* (a spicy mixed vegetable dish cooked in coconut milk). $ *Average main: R100* ⊠ *Misty Hills Country Hotel, 69 Drift Blvd., Muldersdrift* ☎ *011/950–6000* ⊕ *www.carnivore.co.za.*

$$ ✕ **The Cradle.** The Cradle is a great choice for a lunch or dinner if you're
SOUTH AFRICAN spending the day or more in the Cradle of Humankind area, which is about a 90-minute drive from Johannesburg or Pretoria, but it's only open on weekends. Tables here overlook a 7,413-acre game reserve. The overall impression is one of space and silence. The frequently changing menu is impressive, including among other dishes sage pork chops, springbok shank, veal saltimbocca, and venison-and-pancetta stew. The extensive wine list has many local specialties. $ *Average main: R125* ⊠ *Kromdraai Rd., Mogale City* ☎ *011/659–1622* ⊕ *www.thecradle. co.za* ⌕ *Reservations essential* ⊙ *Closed Mon.–Thurs.*

WHERE TO STAY

$$$ 🏨 **Forum Homini.** This boutique hotel in a game estate within the Cradle
HOTEL of Humankind aptly alludes to the mysterious and fascinating story of the development of humanity in every bit of its decor and can be a good option if you want to spend some time outside but near Johannesburg. **Pros:** luxury accommodation; daily changing menu. **Cons:** hotel can be overwhelmed with wedding parties on weekends; not suitable for children. $ *Rooms from: R3500* ⊠ *Letamo Game Estate, Bartlet Rd., Kromdraii, Mogale City* ☎ *011/668–7000* ⊕ *www.forumhomini.com* 🛏 *14 suites* ⦿ *Breakfast.*

$$ 🏨 **Maropeng Hotel.** The Maropeng Hotel offers peace and tranquillity
HOTEL with magnificent views of the Magaliesberg and Witwatersberg mountain ranges just 90 minutes from Johannesburg. **Pros:** attentive service; easy access to the Maropeng Visitor Centre and Cradle of Humankind; delicious, fresh food. **Cons:** rooms on the small side; difficult to access without a car. $ *Rooms from: R1640* ⊠ *R400, off the R563 Hekpoort Rd., Kromdraai* ☎ *014/577–9100* ⊕ *www.maropeng.co.za* 🛏 *24 rooms* ⦿ *Some meals.*

$$ 🏨 **Toadbury Hall.** This small, upscale country hotel is well-located for
HOTEL trips into the Cradle of Humankind World Heritage Site, though less so if the focus of your trip is Johannesburg. **Pros:** luxurious spa facilities; fresh, tasty cuisine at the in-house restaurant; romantic setting. **Cons:** difficult to reach without a car; not a family destination. $ *Rooms from:*

8

R2100 ⊠ *Beyers Naude Dr. Extension, Plot 64, Elandsdrift* ☎ *010/593–7523* ⊕ *www.toadburyhall.co.za* ↩ *5 rooms, 5 suites* ℍ *Breakfast.*

THE MAGALIESBERG

The Magaliesberg are about 100 km (62 miles) northwest of Johannesburg.

The Magaliesberg Mountains (actually rolling hills) stretch 120 km (74 miles) between Pretoria and the town of Rustenburg. The South African War once raged here, and the remains of British blockhouses can still be seen. The region is most remarkable, however, for its natural beauty—grassy slopes, streams running through the ferns, waterfalls plunging into pools, and dramatic rock formations. It's an outdoor lover's paradise: go hiking, mountain biking, zip lining, or horseback riding; swim in crystal streams; picnic in one of the natural hideaways; or take a balloon flight at dawn followed by a Champagne breakfast. It's also home to the large Hartbeespoort Dam, a water-sports hot spot. You can get a great view of the Magaliesberg from atop them by riding up in the Hartbeespoort Aerial Cableway, a highly recommended attraction.

GETTING HERE AND AROUND

About a 90-minute drive northwest of Johannesburg, the region is fairly isolated, requiring a rental car or private transfer. Some of the hotels and lodges in the area can arrange transfers on request.

TIMING AND PRECAUTIONS

The main areas and attractions become crowded on weekends. On Friday evenings and Sunday afternoons there's always a wait—sometimes half an hour or more—to cross the one-way bridge over the Hartbeespoort Dam. The area is relatively small, and two to three days is more than enough time to spend exploring.

VISITOR INFORMATION

Magalies Reservations covers accommodations and attractions in the Magaliesberg area.

EXPLORING

Fodor's Choice ★ **Ann van Dyk Cheetah Centre.** The Ann van Dyk Cheetah Centre (formerly the De Wildt Cheetah Centre, it has been renamed after its founder) is respected for its conservation and breeding programs. It offers three-hour guided tours in vehicles (included in the price of admission); at an additional cost you can witness a cheetah run. A beautiful stone lodge has nine guest rooms if you would like to spend the night in the area. No children under six are permitted. Visits to the center must be booked in advance. The center is in an area of the Magaliesberg called De Wildt, near Harbeespoort, about a 90-minute drive from Johannesburg. ⊠ *Pretoria North Rd., entrance to farm at No. 22* ✚ *Take R513; center is near Hartbeespoort Dam* ☎ *012/504–9908* ⊕ *www.dewildt.co.za* 🖂 *R300, R400 with cheetah run* ☺ *Tours Mon., Wed., Fri. 8:30–4:30, Tues., Thurs., Sat., Sun. 8–11:30 and 1:30–4:30.*

Elephant Sanctuary. The Elephant Sanctuary is home to five of the big mammals and has elephant rides. Visits must be prearranged and include interactive educational sessions. As part of the session, you can groom and feed the elephants; learn about their habits, personalities, and anatomy; and ride one of Africa's largest mammals. A small on-site lodge sleeps up to 12. This is a good option if you're spending a day in the Hartbeespoort area (do the Ann van Dyk Cheetah Centre and the Hartbeespoort Aerial Cableway on the same day), or visit it on the way to Pilanesberg or Madikwe if you're headed there. ✛ *Rustenburg Rd. (R512), about 2 km (1 mile) from Hartbeespoort Dam* ☎ *012/253–9920* ⊕ *www.elephantsanctuary.co.za* ✉ *R650; elephant rides are an extra R465* ⊗ *Sessions daily at 8, 10, and 2.*

Harties Cableway. Take the longest mono-cableway in Africa to savor panoramic views of the Magaliesberg mountains and Hartbeespoort Dam. A circular pathway at the top takes in indigenous flora and signposts points of interest. Look for mementoes and branded items at the curio shop or top shop. A restaurant at the base and self-service at the top sell pizzas, pastas, sandwiches and burgers. Treat yourself to a late afternoon cocktail at the mountaintop bar. ✉ *Melodie Agricultural Holdings, Plot 3, Hartbeespoort* ☎ *072/241–2654* ⊕ *www. hartiescableway.co.za* ✉ *R160* ⊗ *Daily 8:30–5 (last car down at 4:45).*

Lesedi Cultural Village. This is not just a place to stay and eat (although you can stay here in a very comfortable hut); it's a place to learn about the cultures and history of South Africa's Basotho, Ndebele, Pedi, Xhosa, and Zulu nations. Daily shows of dancing and singing, tours of traditional homesteads, and a crafts market complement the dining, lodging, and conference facilities. The large Nyama Choma restaurant serves food from all over the continent so you can taste North African fare, East African cuisine, or opt for a South African barbecue. Dishes include roast meats, porridge and vegetables, often cooked in traditional African three-legged iron pots. Most of the Africa-theme guest rooms have two beds. Packages can include breakfast, dinner, and the tours, but most people just come for a day visit and a meal. ✉ *R512 (Lanseria Rd.), Pelindaba Rd., Broederstroom* ☎ *087/940–9933, 087/740–9292 central reservations* ⊕ *www.lesedi.com* 🛏 *38 rooms* ❙⊚❙ *Some meals.*

Snake and Animal Park. The Snake and Animal Park is not big (you can walk through in less than two hours) but it has lions, tigers, pumas, jaguars, hyenas, many primate species, and birds of prey. Its selection of reptiles is overwhelming. Snake cages line the walkways, containing anything from harmless little garden snakes to poisonous cobras and giant pythons. Keep an eye out for snake shows, especially on weekends. The park offers a ferry boat cruise and a tea garden. ✉ *1 Scott St., Hartbeespoort* ☎ *012/253–1162* ⊕ *www.hartbeespoortsnakeandanimalpark. co.za* ✉ *R100* ⊗ *Daily 8–5.*

WHERE TO STAY

Although it's an hour drive from the city center, Hartbeespoort is these days almost a suburb of Johannesburg. You might choose to stay here for the night if you're en route from O. R. Tambo International (or the even-closer domestic airport of Lanseria) to a game reserve like the Pilanesberg or Madikwe, rather than staying in Johannesburg itself. It's on the way, after all, and has a pleasant, relaxed atmosphere, and you could more easily squeeze in a trip up the cableway, which is well worth doing. There are loads of bed-and-breakfasts and guesthouses to choose from.

$ ⚏ **Budmarsh Private Lodge.** Surrounded by a lush garden in the heart of
HOTEL   the Magaliesberg, this lodge has rooms with beautiful antique furniture and is a good place to base yourself if you just want to get into the country for a river ramble or a mountain hike. **Pros:** relaxing setting; peaceful library; rooms have Jacuzzis and outdoor showers. **Cons:** can be busy on weekends; inaccessible without a car. $ *Rooms from: R1385* ✉ *T1, Magalies Meander Rd., R96* ☎ *011/728–1800* ⊕ *www.budmarsh. co.za* ↝ *18 rooms* ⦿ *Some meals.*

$$ ⚏ **De Hoek Country House.** In France this exclusive establishment would
ALL-INCLUSIVE   be called an *auberge*—a small destination hotel with a great restaurant suitable for an overnight or weekend jaunt—and the two-story stone-and-heavy-timber building along the river would not be out of place in Provence. **Pros:** plenty of activities; attentive service; lovely setting; fabulous food. **Cons:** difficult to access with public transport; pricey. $ *Rooms from: R2270* ✉ *Off R24, north of Magaliesberg, adjacent to Bekker School* ☎ *014/577–9600* ⊕ *www.dehoek.com* ↝ *28 rooms, 2 suites* ⦿ *All-inclusive.*

$ ⚏ **Goblin's Cove.** You can find this delightful little restaurant and hotel,
B&B/INN   the creation of sculptor Charles Gotthard, amid trees next to a river. **Pros:** an unusual and memorable getaway; beautiful location; easy access from Johannesburg. **Cons:** visitors might find it a bit twee; the hotel is at least an hour drive from Johannesburg. $ *Rooms from: R890* ✉ *Off R96, Bekker School Rd.* ☎ *014/576–2143 landline, 081/043– 1155 cell phone* ⊕ *www.thegoblinscove.co.za* ↝ *3 rooms* ⊙ *No overnights Sun.–Thurs.* ⦿ *Breakfast.*

$ ⚏ **Jameson Country Cottages.** These pretty, well-appointed, self-catering
B&B/INN   cottages can sleep four or six people and have stoves, refrigerators, TVs, and a good selection of culinary appliances. **Pros:** fully equipped with modern amenities; facilities to keep the kids entertained. **Cons:** additional cost for folding beds; difficult to reach without a car. $ *Rooms from: R750* ✉ *R509, Koster Rd.* ✛ *10 km (6 miles) from Magaliesberg* ☎ *014/577–4619, 083/301–5791* ⊕ *www.westcane.co.za* ↝ *6 cottages* ⦿ *No meals.*

$$$ ⚏ **Mount Grace Country House & Spa.** This village-style bed-and-breakfast
HOTEL   near Magaliesberg offers accommodations in a variety of delightful, scattered country-style buildings in a wide variety of accommodations categories. **Pros:** luxury accommodation; top-rated spa facilities; complimentary Wi-Fi. **Cons:** no children under 12; expensive. $ *Rooms from: R2900* ✉ *Hekpoort* ✛ *Take the R24 to Hekpoort, near Magaliesberg* ☎ *014/577–5600* ⊕ *www.mountgracecountryhouseandspa. com* ↝ *121 rooms* ⦿ *Breakfast.*

$ ⚏ **Mountain Sanctuary Park.** This wilderness retreat offers both campsites
RESORT   and comfortable self-catering cottages with electricity, hot water, and cooking facilities. **Pros:** inexpensive; peaceful, rural setting; unspoiled nature reserve. **Cons:** rustic accommodation; it's just a self-catering experience, so not good if you don't like to do it yourself. $ *Rooms from: R400* ✛ *40 km (25 miles) from Magaliesberg on dirt road, 15 km (9 miles) from N4* ☎ *014/534–0114, 082/707–5538 Stacy* ⊕ *www.*

mountain-sanctuary.co.za ➳ 7 cosy huts, 4 chalets, 8 log cabins ❤ No meals.

$$$ ⌂ **Valley Lodge & Spa.** Although it's too big to be called a hideaway, this
HOTEL beautiful lodge on a 250-acre nature reserve with a stream running
through it also has a bird sanctuary. **Pros:** excellent food and good
wine list; peaceful surroundings; spacious accommodation. **Cons:** can
get busy with conference groups; pricey. ⑤ *Rooms from: R2650 ⊠ 13
Jennings St. ☎ 014/577–1301, 014/577–1305 ⊕ www.valleylodge.co.za
➳ 76 rooms ❤ Breakfast.*

SPORTS AND THE OUTDOORS

BALLOONING

Bill Harrop's "Original" Balloon Safaris. A fun and fascinating way to start
the day is with an early-morning balloon ride. Bill Harrop's "Origi-
nal" Balloon Safaris flies daily at sunrise from a site close to the Hart-
beespoort Dam for about an hour, weather permitting. A flight costs
R2,575, including breakfast and sparkling wine. Bill Harrop's will pick
you up from Johannesburg at an additional price, if necessary. ⊠ *R560,
near Skeerpoort Rd.* ☎ *011/705–3201 ⊕ www.balloon.co.za.*

Flying Pictures. Flying Pictures offers daily (though dependent on good
conditions) hot-air balloon trips at sunrise over the Magaliesberg and
Cradle of Humankind, and are a reputable operator, having been in
business for many years. The flight costs approximately R1,900, lasts
about an hour, and includes sparkling wine and a full English break-
fast on landing. You can be picked up from any hotel in the Magalies-
berg. The company also partners with Airtrackers, which operate daily
flights over the Pilanesberg Game Reserve. ☎ *082/990–6924 ⊕ www.
flyingpictures.co.za; www.airtrackers.co.za.*

SHOPPING

Chameleon Village Lifestyle Junxion. The Chameleon Village Lifestyle
Junxion has shops, fast-food outlets, a Sunday food market, and
restaurants lined up alongside art studios. You can visit the nearby
lion park, browse through the Crafters Junxion market, or enjoy live
music on weekends. ⊠ *Hartbeespoort Dam* ☎ *012/253–1451 ⊕ www.
chameleonvillage.co.za.*

Welwitschia Country Market. The Welwitschia Country Market sells arts
and crafts among other goodies at dozens of shops and stalls. There's
live weekend entertainment, and it's especially busy on weekends.
⊠ *Rustenburg Rd.* ✛ *R104, 2 km (1 mile) from Hartbeespoort Dam, at
Damdoryn 4-way stop* ☎ *083/302–8085 ⊕ www.countrymarket.co.za.*

SUN CITY

177 km (110 miles) northwest of Johannesburg.

A huge entertainment and resort complex in the middle of dry bush-
veld in the North West Province, Sun City is popular with golfers and
families—and with South Africans and foreign tourists alike. Sun City's
appeal is vastly enhanced by the Pilanesberg Game Reserve, which is
only a few miles from the resort, and by a full round of outdoor sports
and activities, including two Gary Player–designed world-class golf

8

courses. Developed by the same company that built the elaborate Atlantis resorts in the Bahamas and Dubai, this is a real destination resort.

Sun City was built in 1979, in the rocky wilds of the Pilanesberg Mountains, themselves the remains of an ancient volcano. The area was in the then Bantustan of Bophuthatswana—one of several semi–self-governed areas during apartheid set aside for black ethnic groups. As such, it was exempt from South Africa's then strict anti-gambling laws. Today Sun City comprises four luxurious hotels; one casino with slot machines, card tables, and roulette wheels; major amphitheaters that host international stars; and an array of outdoor attractions. The complex is split into two parts: the original Sun City, where the focus is on entertainment and gambling, and the Lost City, anchored by the magnificent Palace Hotel, which offers guests an opportunity to enjoy outdoor adventure at the Valley of the Waves.

In addition to its casinos, the original Sun City also stages rock concerts, major boxing bouts, the annual Nedbank Golf Challenge, and many major conferences. At the Lost City, painted wild animals march across the ceilings, imitation star-spangled skies glitter even by day, lush jungles decorate the halls, and stone lions and elephants keep watch over it all. The Lost City has hosted a long list of celebrities, including Michael Jackson, Frank Sinatra, and Oprah.

GETTING HERE AND AROUND
Ingelosi, the official Sun City shuttle, travels between Johannesburg (pickups are in various locations, including O. R. Tambo) and Sun City twice daily, and once a day from Pretoria. The tickets cost R1,000 one-way for one or two people, though the per-person price drops quickly with a larger group. Otherwise, to get to the area you'll need to arrange a private transfer or a rental car.

Within the Sun City complex are shuttle buses that ferry visitors between the entertainment complex and the various hotels, and the Sky Train monorail transports day visitors from the parking lot to the resort's entertainment complex.

TIMING AND PRECAUTIONS
There is plenty to keep you entertained in the area, so a few days are needed to do justice to the entertainment complex and adjacent Pilanesberg Game Reserve.

VISITOR INFORMATION
Covering the entire North West Province (including Magaliesberg, Sun City, and the Pilanesberg Game Reserve), the North West Tourism Information website offers plenty of useful information on what to do and where to stay in the province. The Sun International website also offers useful information on Sun City.

Visitor Information **North West Province Tourism Information**
☎ *0861/111–866* ⊕ *www.tourismnorthwest.co.za.* **Sun International** ⊕ *www. suninternational.com.*

WHERE TO STAY

There's a wide variety of dining options in and near Sun City (mostly pricey), from upmarket and glitzy to poolside cafés selling light meals like toasted sandwiches.

$$ ▣ **The Cabanas.** Paths thread through pleasant gardens to rooms in these
RESORT small apartment blocks overlooking a man-made lake. **Pros:** great for
FAMILY kids; more affordable than other Sun City accommodation; access to activities. **Cons:** not a particularly tranquil setting; smallish rooms. ⑤ *Rooms from: R2500* ✉ *Sun City complex, Sun City* ☎ *014/557–1580, 011/780–7800 reservations* ⊕ *www.suninternational.com/suncity/cabanas* ➷ *380 rooms* ⦿ *Breakfast.*

$$$$ ▣ **Palace of the Lost City.** You might think a hotel based on the concept of
HOTEL a lost African palace would suffer from theme-park syndrome, but happily that's not the case here. **Pros:** luxury accommodation; impeccable service. **Cons:** pricey; some would think find it unbearably ostentatious. ⑤ *Rooms from: R5930* ✉ *Lost City Complex, Sun City* ☎ *014/557–3131, 011/780–7800 reservations* ⊕ *www.sun-city-south-africa.com/palace.asp* ➷ *338 rooms* ⦿ *Breakfast.*

$$$$ ▣ **Sun City Hotel and Casino.** This is the original Sun City hotel, housing
HOTEL spacious and comfortable rooms in the complex that houses the resort's gaming casino, banks of slot machines, and other gaming activities. **Pros:** classic turn-down and chocolate-on-the-pillow service; easy access to all the entertainment facilities. **Cons:** casino can be noisy; crowded during high season; expensive food and drink. ⑤ *Rooms from: R3600* ✉ *Sun City Complex, Sun City* ☎ *014/557–5370, 011/780–7800 reservations* ⊕ *www.sun-city-south-africa.com/suncity.asp* ➷ *340 rooms* ⦿ *Breakfast.*

8

PILANESBERG GAME RESERVE

200 km (124 miles) northwest of Johannesburg.

The 150,000-acre Pilanesberg Game Reserve is often called the Pilanesberg National Park. It isn't actually a South African national park these days, though it was one in the days when Bophutatswana was independent Bantustan. The game reserve is centered on the caldera of an extinct volcano dating back 1.3 billion years that may well have once been Africa's highest peak. Concentric rings of mountains surround a lake filled with crocodiles and hippos. Open grassland, rocky crags, and densely forested gorges provide ideal habitats for a wide range of plains and woodland game, including rare brown hyenas and cheetahs, and wildebeests and zebras, which are abundant in this reserve. Since the introduction of lions in 1993, Pilanesberg (pronounced pee-*luns*-berg) can boast the Big Five. One of the best places in the country to see rhinos, it's also a bird-watcher's paradise, with a vast range of grassland species, waterbirds, and birds of prey. It's also malaria-free and an excellent choice for game-viewing if you're short on time and can't make it all the way to Kruger National Park, for instance. You can drive around the park in your own vehicle or join guided safaris with Pilanesberg Mankwe Safaris. The entertainment and resort complex of Sun City is nearby.

GETTING HERE AND AROUND

To get to the Pilanesberg from Johannesburg, get on the N4 highway to Krugersdorp and take the R556 off-ramp and follow the signs. The drive is about 2½ to 3 hours. There is a shuttle from Johannesburg to Sun City, just outside the park, but public transportation in and around the park is limited, so you'll need to rent a car or hire a transfer company.

TOURS

Several major tour operators in Johannesburg offer trips to Pilanesberg, including Springbok Atlas and Wilro Tours (*see Tours in Planning*).

Booking these tours ahead of time is essential.

EXPLORING

Pilanesberg Game Reserve. The 150,000-acre Pilanesberg Game Reserve is centered on the caldera of an extinct volcano. Concentric rings of mountains surround a lake filled with crocodiles and hippos. Open grassland, rocky crags, and forested gorges provide ideal habitats for a wide range of plains and woodland game, especially wildebeests and zebras, which are plentiful here. The Pilanesberg (pronounced pee-*luns*-berg) can boast the Big Five (you have a great chance of seeing elephants and rhinos here on almost any single drive) and is malaria-free. It's a bird-watcher's paradise, with a vast range of grassland species, waterbirds, and birds of prey. The entertainment and resort complex of Sun City is nearby. ⊠ *Pilanesberg Game Reserve, Sun City* ☎ *014/555–1600* ⊕ *www.pilanesbergnationalpark.org* ✉ *R20 per vehicle, R65 per person* ☉ *Mar., Apr., Sept., and Oct., daily 6 am–6:30 pm; May–Aug., daily 6:30–6; Nov.–Feb., daily 5:30 am–7 pm.*

WHERE TO STAY

$$$$ 🏨 **Bakubung Bush Lodge.** Abutting Pilanesberg, this lodge sits at the head
HOTEL of a long valley with terrific views of a hippo pool that forms the lodge's central attraction—it's not unusual to have hippos grazing 100 feet from the terrace restaurant. **Pros:** malaria-free; resident hippos; cheerful atmosphere. **Cons:** close to a main gate; always crowded. ⑤ *Rooms from: R4430* ⊠ *Bakubung, Pilanesberg Game Reserve* ☎ *014/552–6000 lodge, 014/552–4006 reservations* ⊕ *www.legacyhotels.co.za* ⤶ *76 rooms, 66 chalets* ⑩ *Some meals.*

$$$$ 🏨 **Kwa Maritane Bush Lodge.** The greatest asset of this hotel, primarily
HOTEL a time-share resort, is its location: in a bowl of rocky hills on the edge
FAMILY of the national park. **Pros:** malaria-free; you've got the best of both worlds: bushveld on your doorstep and Sun City only 20 minutes away by free shuttle bus; lovely swimming pools. **Cons:** you can't get away from the hotel feel; busy during school holidays; it gets noisy around reception, pool, and dining areas. ⑤ *Rooms from: R5316* ⊠ *Kwa Maritane, Pilanesberg Game Reserve* ☎ *014/552–5100 hotel, 014/552–5161 reservations* ⊕ *www.legacyhotels.co.za* ⤶ *90 rooms* ⑩ *Some meals.*

$$ 🏨 **Manyane.** In a thinly wooded savanna east of Pilanesberg's volcanic
RESORT ridges, this resort offers affordable accommodations in the Sun City area for those travelers who want to experience the region but can't pay five-star prices. **Pros:** accommodations are very basic but a good value; there is a good restaurant if you want a break from self-catering; lovely

pool, which is a delight on a hot day. **Cons:** more downmarket than other options in the area; can be full of noisy campers and late-night revelers. ⑤ *Rooms from: R1760 ⊠ Manyane, Pilanesberg National Park* ☎ *014/555–1000* ⊕ *www.manyaneresort-pilanesberg.com* ⇨ *14 4-bed chalets, 10 2-bed chalets* ⑩*No meals.*

$$$$
ALL-INCLUSIVE
🏠 **Tshukudu Bush Lodge.** Tshukudu Bush Lodge is built into the side of a steep, rocky hill and overlooks open grassland and a large water hole where elephants bathe. **Pros:** malaria-free; luxurious and secluded accommodation; high on a hill with great views. **Cons:** it's a 132-step climb to the main lodge from the parking area so avoid it if you're not sound of wind and limb; game good, but not as abundant as Kruger. ⑤ *Rooms from: R8630 ⊠ Tshukudu, Pilanesberg Game Reserve* ☎ *014/552–6255* ⊕ *www.legacyhotels.co.za* ⇨ *6 cottages* ⑩*All-inclusive.*

MADIKWE GAME RESERVE

300 km (186 miles) northwest of Johannesburg (or farther, depending on which gate you enter).

Just as leopards and Sabi Sand Game Reserve are synonymous, think of Madikwe Game Reserve and wild dogs in the same way. This is probably your best chance in South Africa to have an almost guaranteed sighting of the "painted wolves."

More than two decades ago the 765-square-km (475-square-mile) area bordering Botswana was a wasteland of abandoned cattle farms, overgrown bush, and rusting fences. A brilliant and unique collaboration between the North West Parks Board, private enterprise, and local communities changed all that when Operation Phoenix—one of the most ambitious game relocation programs in the world—relocated more than 8,000 animals of 27 different species to Madikwe. Soon after, it became one of the fastest-growing safari destinations in South Africa.

Madikwe today is teeming with game. Spot the Big Five, plus resident breeding packs of the endangered painted wolves—the wild dogs of Africa. On your morning, evening, or night game drive, you also might spot cheetahs, hippos, lions, elephants, and buffalos, but you'll certainly see zebras, wildebeests, and several kinds of antelope (South Africans refer to all antelope generically as buck, whether they're male or female). Birders can spot more than 350 birds. Be dazzled by the crimson-breasted shrike, the lilac-breasted roller, yellow-billed and red-billed hornbills, blue waxbills, and many more.

GETTING HERE AND AROUND
Madikwe is an easy drive on good roads from Johannesburg. Go to Sun City via Hartbeespoort Dam and follow the signs to Madikwe, which is about an hour's drive from Sun City (though your trip could be an hour longer if your lodge is in the north of the park). Ask at your lodge for detailed instructions. You'll be driven around in an open game vehicle by a staff member of your lodge; guided bush walks are also available. No day visitors are allowed.

EXPLORING

Madikwe Game Reserve. This 187,500-acre game reserve in the North-West Province (about four hours from Johannesburg) close to the Botswana border is open only to overnight visitors, who can choose from more than 20 lodges to stay at, most of them five-star. The reserve is famous for its wild dog population, but is also known for cheetah, the Big Five, and its general game, such as zebra, wildebeest, giraffe, and impala. It was established in 1991 and is fast becoming one of the most popular private reserves in the country, because of its abundance of game, proximity to Johannesburg, and the fact that it is malaria-free (so is very safe for children). ⊠ *Madikwe Game Reserve* ⊕ *www. parksnorthwest.co.za/madikwe/.*

WHERE TO STAY

In the south, choose between the ultraluxurious Tuningi Lodge, where a 300-year-old fig tree stands sentinel over a busy water hole, or either of Jaci's delightful lodges. Madikwe Safari Lodge, managed by the More family of Mpumalanga's Lion Sands, is another example of this company's high standards of luxury, service, and game-viewing.

Tau Lodge in the north of the reserve is more like a small resort than a private safari lodge, but the accommodations are excellent, the food is good, and the game drives are well done. Always check for special offers at any of the Madikwe lodges. You can often get very affordable rates, especially off-season.

$$$$
HOTEL
FAMILY
⊡ **Jaci's Lodges.** The two lodges that make up Jaci's Lodges are family owned and have a longstanding reputation for friendliness, superb game drives, and comfortable accommodations that has made them synonymous with the name Madikwe Game Reserve. **Pros:** friendly, welcoming atmosphere, great children's activities and facilities, great game. **Cons:** if children aren't your thing, stay away from Jaci's Safari Lodge; pricey. ⑤ *Rooms from: R9590* ⊠ *Madikwe Game Reserve* ☎ *083/700–2071* ⊕ *www.madikwe.com* ⇥ *8 tented suites per camp, 2 family suites at Safari Lodge* ⦿ *All meals.*

$$$$
RESORT
FAMILY
⊡ **Madikwe Safari Lodge.** This stunning five-star lodge in the central eastern region of the park is managed by the More family of Lion Sands, and their attention to detail, reputation for fine food and excellent service, and thrilling game drives are readily apparent. **Pros:** malaria-free; superb accommodation; great food; excellent game viewing. **Cons:** not as scenically beautiful as the Mpumalanga and KwaZulu-Natal reserves; long walks between suites. ⑤ *Rooms from: R13960* ⊠ *Madikwe Game Reserve* ☎ *018/350–9902* ⊕ *www.madikwesafarilodge. co.za* ⇥ *20 suites* ⦿ *All meals.*

$$$$
RESORT
⊡ **Tuningi Safari Lodge.** A 300 year-old fig tree dominates the the ultra-luxurious Tuningi Lodge overlooking a busy water hole that will keep you entranced all day. **Pros:** superb accommodation, service, and food. **Cons:** pricey but look out for special offers particularly in the off-season. ⑤ *Rooms from: R9000* ⊠ *Madikwe Game Reserve* ☎ *011/781–5384* ⊕ *www.seasonsinafrica.com* ⇥ *2 family units, 4 double suites* ⦿ *All meals.*

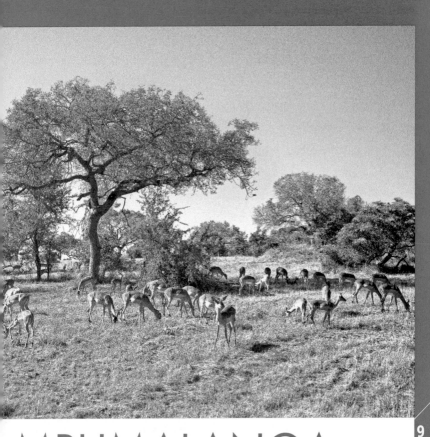

MPUMALANGA & KRUGER NATIONAL PARK

Updated by
Kate Turkington

In many ways Mpumalanga ("where the sun rises") is South Africa's wildest and most exciting province. Its local history is action packed: local wars, international battles, and a gold rush every bit as raucous and wild as those in California and the Klondike. Kruger National Park and the private game reserves abutting its western borders provide the country's best and most fulfilling game experience; in fact, it's highly probable that you will see all of the Big Five (lion, elephant, Cape buffalo, leopard, rhinoceros) during an average two- to three-night stay at one of the private reserves.

If you look at a map of South Africa, Mpumalanga is in the top right just below Limpopo. It spreads east from Gauteng to the border of Mozambique. The 1,120-km (700-mile) Drakensberg Range, which originates in KwaZulu-Natal, divides the high, interior plateau from a low-lying subtropical belt that stretches to Mozambique and the Indian Ocean. The lowveld (the subtropical region of northeastern South Africa), where Kruger National Park alone covers a 320-km (200-mile) swath of wilderness, is classic Africa, with as much heat, dust, untamed bush, and big game as you can take in.

The Drakensberg Escarpment rises to the west of Kruger and provides a marked contrast to the lowveld; it's a mountainous area of trout streams and waterfalls, endless views, and giant plantations of pine and eucalyptus. The escarpment has some of South Africa's most spectacular scenery, including the Blyde River (Motlatse) Canyon—one of the world's largest canyons and one of its greenest because of its luxuriant subtropical foliage—waterfalls, amazing vistas, great hiking, and river rafting. People come to the escarpment to unwind, soak up its beauty, and get away from the summer heat of the lowveld. Touring the area by car is easy and rewarding—the 156-km (97-mile) Panorama Route winds along the lip of the escarpment—and you can reach many of the best lookouts without stepping far from your car. You'd miss fabulous sightseeing opportunities if you failed to stop on the way to or from Kruger to take in some of Mpumalanga's fantastic sightseeing opportunities.

From the escarpment, the landscape plunges down to banana, mango, and papaya groves and the lowveld. It's here you'll find Kruger National Park, undoubtedly one of the world's finest game parks. Apart from its ease of access (there are nine entry gates along its western border), there is plenty of excellent accommodation ranging from bushveld and tented camps to luxury lodges. Mbombela (Nelspruit), south of Kruger, is the nearest big town.

ORIENTATION AND PLANNING

ORIENTATION

In a nutshell: imagine Mpumalanga as a large horizontally squashed ball in the northeast of South Africa with Limpopo to the north, Gauteng to the west, and Swaziland and KwaZulu-Natal to the south. The Drakensberg mountain range divides the high escarpment (where you'll find the Blyde River [Motlatse] Canyon and more stunning scenery) from the low, lush, subtropical lowveld, home of Kruger National Park and other smaller game reserves, all teeming with game.

Mpumalanga. Mpumalanga (Mm-puma-langa) has activities galore, from poking around cultural villages and hiking on mountain trails to driving through game reserves. The best way to get around Mpumalanga is by car, either from Johannesburg or from the airports at Mbombela (Nelspruit), Hoedspruit, Skukuza, or Phalaborwa (if you're going into the central section of Kruger). Plan your road trip with booked-in-advance accommodations (there are superb options all over the province), and visit at least one of the farm stalls that dot country roads for fresh fruit and veggies (in season), nuts, and creamy farm milk.

Kruger National Park. Larger than Israel and approximately the same size as Wales, Kruger National Park encompasses diverse terrain ranging from rivers filled with crocodiles and hippos to rocky outcrops where leopards lurk and thick thorn scrub shelters lions and buffalo. Roaming this slice of quintessential Africa are animals in numbers large enough to make a conservationist squeal with delight: in all, there are nearly 150 mammal species and more than 500 species of birds.

Sabi Sand Game Reserve. Named after the Sabie and Sand rivers that flow through it, and situated adjacent to Kruger's western boundary at its southern end (no fences separate the two), South Africa's oldest private reserve is famous for its abundant game and world-famous luxury lodges. You'll find the Big Five here, including the best opportunities in South Africa of spotting leopards, plus hundreds of birds. It's easily accessible by road and air.

West of Kruger. Manyeleti, Timbavati, Thornybush, and Kapama game reserves all lie north of Sabi Sand Game Reserve, but also border Kruger's western boundary. Although the reserves are less well known than Sabi Sand, they offer much the same game experiences, often at more affordable prices.

PLANNING

Where you stay on the escarpment may well dictate the kind of weather you get. High up, around Pilgrim's Rest and Sabie, the weather can be chilly, even in summer. Pack a sweater whatever the season. At these elevations fog and mist can be a hazard, especially while driving. On the other hand, the lowveld, especially in summer, is downright sultry.

TOP REASONS TO GO

Classic Africa Apart from the tarred roads and rest camps, Kruger Park is the legendary Africa of Dr. Livingstone, the Rain Queen, and Karen Blixen, where countless animals, birds, insects, and reptiles freely roam the plains, rivers, and forests.

Discovery Channel Comes Alive From grasses and flowers to trees and shrubs, from comical dung beetles to gaudy butterflies, from tiny colorful lizards to huge dozing crocodiles, from dainty bushbuck to giant giraffes, from leaping bush babies to languorous lions, you'll marvel at them all.

A Total Escape When you're steeped in the bush, watching that approaching elephant or a pod of harrumphing hippos, you'll forget all the pressures of today's living.

Safari Opulence Stay for a couple of nights at one of Sabi Sand's private game reserves. You're guaranteed luxury accommodation, impeccable service, and probably Big Five sightings. Kids are usually welcome, but check before you book.

Blyde River Canyon The gigantic rocks, deep gorges, and high mountains of the Three Rondawels create one of South Africa's great scenic highlights.

WHEN TO GO

Kruger National Park is hellishly hot in midsummer (November–March), with afternoon rain a good possibility, though mostly in the form of heavy short showers that don't interfere with game-viewing for long. If you plan your drives in the early morning (when the gates first open) or in the late afternoon, you will manage even if you are extremely heat sensitive. ■**TIP→ Don't drive with the windows up and the air conditioner on—you'll cocoon yourself from the reason you're there.** In summer the bush is green, the animals are sleek and glossy, and the birdlife is prolific, but high grasses and dense foliage make spotting animals more difficult. Also, because there's plenty of surface water about, animals don't need to drink at water holes and rivers, where it's easy to see them. There are also more mosquitoes around then, but you'll need to take malaria prophylactics whatever time of year you visit.

In winter (May through September), the bush is at its dullest, driest, and most colorless, but the game is much easier to spot, as many trees are bare, grasses are low, and animals congregate around the few available permanent water sources. Besides, watching a lion or leopard pad across an arid but starkly beautiful landscape could be the highlight of your trip. It gets very cold in winter (temperatures can drop to almost freezing at night and in the very early morning), so wear layers of warm clothes you can shed as the day gets hotter. Lodges sometimes drop their rates during winter (except July), because many foreign tourists prefer to visit in the South African summer months, which coincide with the Northern Hemisphere winter.

Spring (September and October) and autumn (March to early May) are a happy compromise. The weather is very pleasant—warm and sunny but not too hot—and there are fewer people around. In October migratory birds will have arrived, and in November many animals give birth. In April some migrating birds are still around, and the annual rutting season will have begun, when males compete for females and are often more visible and active.

PLANNING YOUR TIME

If you have more than a handful of days in the area, split them between the mountain scenery of the escarpment and wildlife-viewing in the lowveld. You could complete a tour of the Drakensberg Escarpment area in two days, but you're better off budgeting three or more if you plan to linger anywhere. To take in parts of Kruger National Park or one of the private game lodges, which are simply a must, add another three days or more.

3 Days: One of the prime reasons for visiting Mpumalanga is for big game, so fly into the airport nearest your destination and either rent a vehicle and take off into Kruger or get picked up by the private game lodge of your choice. Driving anywhere else in such a short time is not really an option.

5 Days: Your biggest decision will be how much time to spend wildlife-watching and how much to spend exploring the escarpment and its historic towns. A good suggestion is two days for the mountains and three in Kruger. Driving from Johannesburg, plan an overnight in Sabie after driving the awesome Long Tom Pass. The next day, head to the former mining town of Pilgrim's Rest and soak up some of the colorful local history. Spend the night there or at one of the friendly and superb value-for-the-money bed-and-breakfasts in the area, and start out early the next morning for Blyde River (Motlatse) Canyon, with its hiking trails and magnificent escarpment scenery. Then it's off to Kruger, Sabi Sand, Manyeleti, Timbavati, Thornybush, or any of the other game reserves adjacent to Kruger, but make sure you get to Kruger or your private lodge in time for the afternoon game drive.

7 to 10 Days: Spend four or more days in the bush—half at Kruger and half at a private lodge, perhaps. A minimum of two nights at either one is nonnegotiable. Then split the rest of your time between the escarpment and the lowveld outside Kruger, as in the previous itinerary.

GETTING HERE AND AROUND

AIR TRAVEL

Two airlines—SA Airlink, SA Express—link Johannesburg to KMIA (Kruger Mpumalanga International Airport), at Mbombela (Nelspruit), which is equipped to handle the largest and most modern aircraft. KMIA has a restaurant, curio shops, banking facilities, car-rental agencies, VIP lounges, information desks, and shaded parking. SA Airlink has daily flights; SA Express also flies daily. SA Airlink also flies directly to MalaMala airstrip, which serves the Sabi Sand lodges and has daily flights to Skukuza Airport, in the middle of Kruger. ⇨ *For information on airlines, see Air Travel in Travel Smart.*

Hoedspruit Airport is an attractive little Africa-themed airport with a restaurant and curio shop. Connected to Johannesburg by SA Express daily, it's close to Kruger's Orpen Gate and serves the Timbavati Game

Reserve. SA Airlink has daily flights between Johannesburg and Phalaborwa Airport, which is near Kruger's Phalaborwa Gate.

Contacts Hoedspruit Airport (*HDS*). ⊠ *Eastgate Airport, Hoedspruit* ☎ *015/793–3681* ⊕ *www.eastgateairport.co.za.* **Kruger Mpumalanga International Airport (KMIA)** ☎ *013/753–7500* ⊕ *www.kmiairport.co.za.* **Phalaborwa Airport** (*PHW*). ⊠ *Access Rd., near Phalaborwa Gate, Phalaborwa.* **Skukuza Airport** (*SZK*). ⊠ *Skukuza* ⊕ *www.skukuzaairport.com.*

BUS TRAVEL

Greyhound runs daily between Johannesburg and Mbombela (Nelspruit), stopping in the city of Louis Trichardt opposite the Promenade Hotel.The direct trip takes five to six hours, but there are also buses that stop along the way. A round-trip ticket is R570, one way R285. Mbombela (Nelspruit) is 50 km (31 miles) from Kruger's Numbi Gate and 64 km (40 miles) from Kruger's Malelane Gate.

Public bus service is limited or nonexistent in Mpumalanga. If you don't have your own car, you're dependent on one of the tour companies to get around the escarpment and into the game reserves. Many of these companies also operate shuttle services that transfer guests between the various lodges and to the airport. It's usually possible to hire these chauffeured minibuses at an hourly or daily rate.

Only tour-company buses actually go through Kruger, but they're not recommended. Being in a big tour bus in the park is like being in an air-conditioned bubble, totally divorced from the bush. Also, the big tour buses aren't allowed on many of Kruger's dirt roads and have to stick to the main paved roads. ⇨ *For information on buses, see Bus Travel in Travel Smart.*

CAR TRAVEL

The road system in Mpumalanga is excellent, making it a great place to travel by car. Three principal routes—the N4, N11, and R40—link every destination in the province. From Johannesburg drive north on the N1, and then head east on the N4 to Mbombela (Nelspruit), which is close to many of Kruger's well-marked gates. It's best to arm yourself in advance with up-to-date maps, available at most large gas stations or bookstores, and plan your route accordingly.

The N4 is an expensive toll road (approx R250–R300 for the one-way trip between Johannesburg and Kruger). You can *only* use cash at the toll booths; foreign credit cards are not accepted. Though it's a very good, well-maintained road, always look out for the ubiquitous, often reckless taxi drivers in their overcrowded *combis* (vans). Traffic jams are common on weekends and at the beginning and end of school vacations. Secondary roads are also well maintained, but watch out for goats and donkeys that stray from the villages.

The best places to pick up rental cars are at the KMIA, Hoedspruit, and Phalaborwa airports. Avis, Budget, and Europcar all have desks at KMIA and Phalaborwa, whereas Hoedspruit offers Avis and Budget. Rental cars also available at Skukuza. ⇨ *For information on car-rental agencies, see Car Travel in Travel Smart.* Maps of Kruger are available at all the park gates and in the camp stores, and gas stations are available at the park gates and at the major camps. Once in the park, observe the speed-limit signs carefully (there are speed traps): 50 kph (31 mph) on paved roads, 40 kph (25 mph) on dirt roads. Leave your vehicle only at designated picnic and view sites, and if you do find animals on the road, allow them to pass before moving on. Sometimes you have to be very patient, especially if a breeding herd of elephants is blocking your way. ■TIP➔ **Animals always have the right-of-way.** Always be cautious. Kruger is not a zoo; you are entering the territory of wild animals, even though many may be habituated to the sights and sounds of vehicles.

If you are planning to go into Kruger, it's worth renting an eight-seater combi (van) or SUV. Though more expensive than a car, they provide more legroom and you'll probably spot more game and see it better from your lofty perch. It's best to reserve well in advance, particularly if you want a bigger vehicle. Opt for the "supercover" insurance; it's not that much more expensive, but if you do get bumped by an elephant, you'll be covered.

TRAIN TRAVEL

If you really like train journeys, the Shosholoza Meyl/Spoornet's *Komati* train travels between Johannesburg and Mbombela (Nelspruit) via Tshwane (Pretoria) on Wednesday and Friday, and although it's comfortable and has a dining car, it's very slow (10 hours). It departs from Johannesburg at 6:10 pm and arrives in Mbombela (Nelspruit) at 4 am, so make sure there's somebody to meet you at that early hour. A one-way, first-class ticket costs R230, round-trip R460. But don't expect the Orient Express. ➪ *For information on trains, see Train Travel in Travel Smart.*

HOTELS

You may be in darkest Africa, but you'll be amazed by the very high standards you'll encounter for both service and accommodations. The latter range from fairly basic in the Kruger Park huts to the ultimate in luxury at most of the private camps. You may forget that you are in the bush until an elephant strolls past. The advantage of a private lodge (apart from superb game-viewing) is that often everything is included—lodging, meals, beverages, including excellent house wines, game drives, and other activities. It's essential to note that there are no elevators in any lodging facility in Mpumalanga or in Kruger.

Prices at most guest establishments on the escarpment include a three- to five-course dinner plus a full English breakfast. Most places have at least one vegetarian course on the menu. Many lodges and hotels offer special midweek or winter low-season rates. If you're opting for a private game lodge, find out whether they accept children (many specify only kids over 12), and stay a minimum of two nights, three if you can.

In Kruger National Park you have the choice between budget self-catering huts from R530 per person per night and much more expensive (but worth it) self-catering cottages in the more remote and exclusive bushveld (*bushveld* is the generic term for the wild indigenous vegetation of the lowveld) camps, which range from R580 to R685 per person. Visit the South African National Parks website (⊕ *www.sanparks.org*)

to get information and book accommodations. ■TIP→ Make sure you book well in advance and, if possible, avoid July, August, and December, which are South African school vacations.

Hotel reviews have been shortened. For full information, visit Fodors. com.

RESTAURANTS

Because Mpumalanga is a sought-after tourist destination, its culinary scene keeps getting better and better, both in *larney* (South African slang for "posh") restaurants and attractive cafés. Cuisines range from Mediterranean to pan-African, and many places serve local delicacies such as fresh trout, venison, Cape Malay favorites such as *bobotie* (a spicy meat-and-egg dish), and curries.

Food is cheap and cheerful in Kruger's cafeterias and restaurants, and usually excellent in the private game lodges. Dinner is eaten 7:30-ish, and it's unlikely you'll get a meal in a restaurant after 9. The more expensive the restaurant, the more formal the dress, with "smart casual" the norm. In Kruger you might put on clean clothes for an evening meal in a restaurant, but that's how formal it gets. After an exciting night game drive in a private reserve, you'll want to change or at least freshen up, but keep the clothes very casual. Wear long sleeves and long pants because of mosquitoes. Many higher-end restaurants close on Monday, and it's always advisable to make reservations at these in advance.

WHAT IT COSTS IN SOUTH AFRICAN RAND			
	$	$$	$$$	$$$$
Restaurants	under R100	R100–R150	R151–R200	over R200
Hotels	under R1,500	R1,500–R2,500	R2,501–R3,500	over R3,500

Restaurant prices are the average cost of a main course at dinner or, if dinner is not served, at lunch. Hotel prices are the lowest cost of a standard double room in high season.

SAFETY

The lowveld area, which stretches from Malelane (east of Mbombela/Nelspruit) to Komatipoort, on the Mozambique border, and up throughout Kruger National Park, is a malarial zone, and you should take antimalarial drugs. Note: malaria prophylactics may be unsuitable for children under six. Consult your doctor about the best options when planning your trip. ■TIP→ Prevention is the best medicine: at dawn and dusk, smother yourself with insect repellent, and wear long sleeves, long pants, socks, and covered shoes. The private camps all have mosquito (mozzie) nets, but not Kruger, so spray yourself again before you go to sleep.

TOUR OPTIONS

All tour operators offer an assortment of trips and tours that cover the Panorama Route, which links the major escarpment sights, as well as game-viewing trips into Kruger National Park and the private reserves. Springbok Atlas, Trips SA, and Welcome Tours are just some of the many operators that lead trips in the area.

Springbok Atlas. An assortment of trips and tours that cover the Panorama Route, which links the major escarpment sights, as well as game-viewing trips into Kruger National Park and the private reserves is offered through Springbok Atlas. ✉ *Head Office, 179 Albert Rd., Woodstock, Cape Town* ☎ *021/460–4700 head office* ⊕ *www.springbokatlas.com.*

Trips SA. As with most of the tour companies in the area, Trips SA offers an excellent variety of trips and tours that cover the spectacularly scenic Panorama Route, which links the major escarpment sights, as well as game-viewing trips into Kruger National Park and the private game reserves. ✉ *90 Main St, Sabie* ☎ *013/764–1177* ⊕ *www.sabie.co.za.*

Welcome Tours. The highly respected Welcome Tours has 30 years service under its belt and offers a wide range of trips and tours ranging from self-drive to fully escorted tours throughout Mpumalanga along the Panorama Route, to Kruger National Park, the private game reserves and beyond. They will tailor a personal itinerary or you can choose from scheduled day or weekly trips. ✉ *Norwich Place West, 2 Norwich Close, 4th fl., Sandton* ☎ *011/676–3300* ⊕ *www.welcome.co.za.*

VISITOR INFORMATION

The Mpumalanga Tourism Authority has a host of information. There are also tourist information offices for Hoedspruit, Mbombela (Nelspruit), and White River. Tours & Tickets in Sabie offers a booking service for places to stay and things to do in the lowveld and escarpment. Their office is open seven days a week. The town of Sabie has a website for additional information.

In Kruger there are information centers at the Letaba, Skukuza, and Berg-en-Dal rest camps.

Contacts Hoedspruit tourist information ✉ *Hoedspruit* ⊕ *www.hoedspruit. co.za.* **Lowveld Info** ⊕ *www.lowveld.info.* **Mpumalanga Tourism Authority** ✉ *Halls Gateway, N4 National Hwy., Nelspruit* ☎ *013/759–5300* ⊕ *www. mpumalanga.com.* **Nelspruit tourist information** ✉ *The Crossing shopping center, N4, Nelspruit* ☎ *013/755–1988* ⊕ *www.krugerlowveld.com.* **SA-Venues** ⊕ *www.SA-Venues.com.* **Sabie** ⊕ *www.sabie.co.za.* **Tours & Tickets** ✉ *Hazyview* ☎ *013/737–8191* ⊕ *www.big5country.com.* **White River tourist information** ✉ *Casterbridge Farm, White River* ☎ *013/751–1540* ⊕ *www.casterbridge.co.za.*

MPUMALANGA

In addition to Cape Town and the Winelands, Mpumalanga should be high on any South African list. Nowhere else in the country can you spend one day seeing spectacular wildlife, the next climbing or gazing over the escarpment, and a third poking around some of the country's most historic towns—all within proximity of each other. The local history is fascinating. In the late 1800s, skirmishes and pitched battles pitted the local Pedi against the Boers (the original Dutch farmers who moved here from the Cape to escape British oppression), as well as the Brits against the Boers (in the First South African War). At the turn of the 20th century, the Brits and Boers fought again (the Second South African War), when England's Queen Victoria brought some of her finest troops from all corners of the British Empire to South Africa, hoping for a final victory over the Boers. Gold and diamonds had been discovered in South Africa, and there was more at stake than political games. The Pilgrim's Rest gold strike of 1873 was minor compared with those in and around Johannesburg, but it nevertheless provided inducement for gold-hungry settlers.

These early gold-mining days have been immortalized by Sir Percy Fitzpatrick in *Jock of the Bushveld,* a classic of South African literature. Jock was a Staffordshire terrier whose master, Percy (he was later knighted by the British crown), worked as a transport rider during the gold rush. Sir Percy entertained his children with tales of his and Jock's adventures braving leopards, savage baboons, and all manner of dangers. Rudyard Kipling, who wandered this wilderness as a reporter covering the First South African War in the early 1880s, encouraged Fitzpatrick to write down the stories. Jock is still a household name in South Africa today. You'll see lots of Jock of the Bushveld signs all over Mpumalanga, seemingly wherever he cocked a leg.

SABIE

355 km (220 miles) east of Johannesburg on the N12.

As you descend Long Tom Pass, the town of Sabie (sah-bee) comes into view far below, in a bowl formed by the surrounding mountains. It's by far the pleasantest and most enjoyable town in the region, with restaurants, shops, and bars. The name Sabie is derived from the Shangaan word *uluSaba,* which described the "fearful river," home to many crocodiles. Today it makes a great base for exploring.

In the 1900s gold provided the community's livelihood, but today it's been replaced by timber, and Sabie sits in the heart of one of the world's largest human-made forests—more than a million acres of exotic pine and eucalyptus. The first forests were planted in 1876 to provide the area's mines with posts and supports. Today much of the timber is still used to prop up shafts in the Gauteng gold mines.

Sabie itself is a busy little town with a farming feel. It boasts some of the biggest traffic humps in South Africa, ensuring that farmers' and visitors' tractors and cars drive slowly through the broad, shady, tree-lined streets. It's easy to walk from one end of the central part of town to the other, taking in sights like **Market Square,** the commercial hub of Sabie in its early days. Here St. Peter's Anglican Church, designed by the famous architect Sir Herbert Baker and built by Italians in 1913, stands in its own pleasant gardens. Also in the square is a Jock of the Bushveld sign, said to commemorate Jock and Percy's arrival in 1885.

GETTING HERE AND AROUND

Travel 355 km (220 miles) east of Johannesburg on the N12. You'll drive on good roads through lovely scenery. Plan to explore the tiny town on foot after parking your vehicle near the main square.

EXPLORING

Komatiland Forestry Museum. Make time to visit the Komatiland Forestry Museum, which provides a wealth of information on South Africa's wood and timber industry in a fun and interesting way. Sabie itself is in the middle of one of the biggest human-made forests in the world. These forests produce more than half of South Africa's timber, and where once the wood was mainly used for pit props in the gold and diamond mines, today they provide the raw material for paper, furniture, and all sorts of consumer products. The museum has some quirky displays, from the matchmaking industry (wood, not people!) to a 100-year-old handcarved Irish gypsy clothes peg. ⊠ *Between 10th Ave. and 4th St.* ☏ *013/764–1058* ✐ *forestrymuseum@klf.co.za* 🖃 *R5* ⊙ *Weekdays 8–1 and 2–4:30, Sat. 8–noon* ⊙ *Public holidays and Sun.*

Lone Creek Falls. This is the prettiest, most peaceful, and last of three local waterfalls on a dead-end road (the others are Bridal Veil Falls and Horseshoe Falls). An easy paved walkway leads to the falls, which plunge 225 feet from the center of a high, broad rock face framed by vines and creepers. The path crosses the river on a wooden bridge and loops through the forest back to the parking lot. If you're feeling energetic, follow the steep steps leading up to the top of the falls. Lone Creek is accessible to the elderly and those with disabilities because of its easy approach. ⊠ *Old Lydenburg Rd.* ⊹ *6½ km (4 miles) down Old Lydenburg Rd., off Main Rd.* 🖃 *R12* ⊙ *Daily 8–5.*

Mac Mac Falls. Set in an amphitheater of towering cliffs, the Mac Mac Falls—a national treasure—is arguably the most famous waterfall in Mpumalanga. The water plunges 215 feet into the gorge as rainbows dance in the billowing spray. A small entry fee gets you through the gate for a closer look. At the gate a number of peddlers sell very well-priced curios. In 1873, President Thomas Burger named the falls after the area's Scottish miners who panned for gold. You can't swim at the falls themselves, but you can at the Mac Mac Pools, about 2 km (½ mile) before you reach the falls. It's worth the small fee to use the picnic and braai facilities there. ⊠ *R532, 15 km (9 miles) northeast of Sabie* ⊕ *www.mpumalanga.com* 🖃 *R5* ⊙ *Daily 8–5.*

WHERE TO EAT

$$$ ✕ **Wild Fig Tree Restaurant and Pub.** This excellent, casual eatery, in the
ECLECTIC shade of a wild fig tree, is open daily from 8:30 to 9 for breakfast, light lunches, and dinner. Although the emphasis is on local specialties ranging from crocodile curry to ostrich kebabs, try the local trout dishes or a home-made burger. Eat on the patio in summer or by the warmth of a cozy log fire in winter. Tourist information and Internet services are available as well as a licensed bar and lounge area. After your meal, pop into the adjoining Wild Fig Tree shops to buy arts, crafts, jewelry, and handmade clothing. ⑤ *Average main: R120* ⊠ *Corner of Main and Louis Trichardt Sts.* ☏ *013/764–2239* ✐ *wildfigtree@gmail.com.*

WHERE TO STAY

$

B&B/INN

FAMILY

Sabie Town House. Built of local Sabie stone, this charming bed-and-breakfast is the perfect base for exploring Mpumalanga's scenic attractions. **Pros:** excellent value for money. **Cons:** bar can get noisy at weekends. $ *Rooms from: R525* ⌂ *27 Power St.* ☎ *013/764–2292, 082/556–7895* ⊕ *www.sabietownhouse.co.za* ↩ *5 rooms, 1 suite, 1 family cottage* ⦿ *Breakfast.*

PILGRIM'S REST

16 km (10 miles) north of Sabie on R533.

The charming (although very touristy) village of Pilgrim's Rest—also a national monument—dates back to the 1870s gold-rush days when it was the first proper gold-mining town in South Africa. Alec "Wheelbarrow" Patterson abandoned the overcrowded Mac Mac diggings and, carting all his belongings in a wheelbarrow, left to search elsewhere for gold. He found it in Pilgrim's Creek, setting off a new gold rush in 1873. Rumors about the richness of the strike spread quickly around the world, bringing miners from California, Australia, and Europe. Within a year 1,500 diggers, living in tents and huts, had moved to the area. Most of the alluvial gold was found by individuals who recovered more than R2 million worth of gold dust and nuggets using pans, sluice boxes, and cradles. It wasn't until about 1876 that most of the tents were replaced by buildings. Most of the beautifully restored houses seen in the village today are from the more staid and elegant period of the early 1900s. It's worth walking up to the cemetery, as the old graves provide an instant history of the village.

> ### THE MPUMALANGA GOLD RUSH
>
> On November 6, 1872, a prospector located deposits of gold in a creek on the Hendriksdal farm, now a small hamlet about 16 km (10 miles) from Sabie. Sabie itself owes its origins to an altogether luckier strike. In 1895 Henry Glynn, a local farmer, hosted a picnic at the Klein Sabie Falls. After a few drinks, his guests started taking potshots at empty bottles on a rock ledge. The flying bullets chipped off shards of rock, revealing traces of gold. Fifty-five years later, when mining operations closed down, more than 1 million ounces of gold had been taken from the Klein Sabie Falls.

GETTING HERE AND AROUND

Pilgrim's Rest is on the R533, 15 km (9 miles) northwest of Graskop. You'll need a vehicle to tour the area, but plan to explore the village on foot, as most of the attractions are on Main Street. There's a great five-hour walking tour through the village with the Friends of Pilgrim's Rest, but this should be booked in advance.

VISITOR INFORMATION

Your first stop should be the Pilgrim's Rest Information Centre, in the middle of town, opposite the Victorian-era Royal Hotel, which is the town's focal point and well worth a visit for its history. The friendly staff at the center will advise you on what to do and what tours to take, such as panning for gold and the Prospector's Hiking Trail, as well as provide maps and tickets for all the museums in the village.

Contacts **Pilgrim's Rest Information Centre** ✉ *Main St., Uptown* ☎ *013/768–1060 reception* ⊕ *www.pilgrims-rest.co.za* ⊗ *Daily 9–12:45 and 1:45–4.*

EXPLORING

TOP ATTRACTIONS

Alanglade. Guided tours, including refreshments, are offered at Alanglade, the former beautiful home of the Transvaal Gold Mining Estates' mine manager, set in a forested grove 2 km (1 mile) north of town. The huge house was built in 1916 for Richard Barry and his family, and is furnished with pieces dating from 1900 to 1930. Look carefully at the largest pieces—you will see that they are segmented, so they could be taken apart and carried on ox wagons. Tour tickets are available at the information center and should be reserved 30 minutes in advance. ✉ *Vaalhoek Rd., off R533* ☎ *Tours R20* ⊗ *Tours Mon.–Sat. at 11 and 2.*

The Diggings. To see how the whole valley looked during gold-rush days, visit the Diggings just outside the village. In the creek where the gold was originally panned, you'll find authentic displays of a water-driven stamp battery, the Gold Commissioner's hut, a transport wagon, a waterwheel, a steam engine, a sluice box, a prison tent, and wattle-and-daub huts typical of the early gold-rush years. The tour lasts about an hour, and you'll watch a gold-panning demonstration (you can even try your own hand at gold-panning). The retired prospector who conducts the tours adds to the atmosphere with yarns about the old days. Tickets are available at the information center. ✉ *R533, 2 km (1 mile) south of Pilgrim's Rest* ⊕ *www.pilgrims-rest.co.za* ☎ *R12* ⊗ *Tours daily at 10, 11, noon, 2, and 3.*

Dredzen Shop and House Museum. Experience life after the heady gold-rush days, and relive the 1930s, when 16 general stores lined the streets of Pilgrim's Rest. By 1950 mine production had taken a nosedive, and most of the businesses had shut down. The Dredzen Shop and House Museum re-creates the look of a general store during those lean years, with shelves displaying authentic items that would have been on sale, from jams and preserves to candles and matches. The attached house belonged to the shopkeeper and re-creates the life of a middle class family in Pilgrim's Rest from 1930 to 1950. ✉ *Main St., Uptown* ⊕ *After you come down hill from cemetery, turn left on Main St.* ⊕ *www.pilgrims-rest.co.za* ☎ *R12* ⊗ *Daily 9–1 and 1:30–4.*

Pilgrim's and Sabie News Printing Museum. The tiny Pilgrim's and Sabie News Printing Museum is full of displays of antique printing presses and old photos. The building, constructed in the late 19th century as a residence, later served as the offices of the weekly *Pilgrim's and Sabie News*. The first newspaper in Pilgrim's Rest was the *Gold News*, published in 1874 and notable for its libelous gossip. The editor, an Irishman by the name of Phelan, felt obliged to keep a pair of loaded pistols on his desk. ✉ *Main St., Uptown* ☎ *R12* ⊗ *Daily 9 am–12:45 pm and 1:45–4 pm.*

Pilgrim's Rest Cemetery. The Pilgrim's Rest Cemetery sits high on the hill above Main Street. The fascinating tombstone inscriptions evoke the dangers and hardship of life in Mpumalanga a century ago. Tellingly, most of the dead were young people from Wales, Scotland, and England. The cemetery owes its improbable setting to the Robber's Grave, the only grave that lies in a north–south direction. It contains the body of a thief banished from Pilgrim's Rest for stealing gold from a tent, after which he was tarred and feathered and chased out of town; he later foolishly returned and was shot dead. Buried where he fell, the area around his grave became the town's unofficial cemetery. ✛ *Follow steep path that starts next to picnic area, near post office.*

WORTH NOTING

House Museum. Originally a doctor's house, the House Museum, across and up the street from the Royal Hotel, re-creates the way of life of a middle-class family in the early part of the 20th century. The house was built in 1913 of corrugated iron and wood and is typical of buildings erected at the time. Check out the late Victorian furnishings, kitchen utensils, and the very grand carved wooden commode (precursor to the toilet). ⊠ *Main St., Uptown* ⊕ *www.pilgrims-rest.co.za* ✉ *R12* ⊘ *Daily 9–12:45 and 1:45–4.*

St. Mary's Anglican Church. Built in 1884, the iron-roofed stone building replaced the original makeshift wattle-and-daub structure. It was an uphill battle for the early ministers to lure miners from the town's 18 canteens. After a backbreaking week spent on the sluices, Holy Communion just didn't pack the punch of a belt of Cape brandy or Squareface gin. ⊠ *Main St.*

WHERE TO EAT

$ ✕ **Scott's Café.** Dozens of varieties of crepes—both savory (stir-fried chicken) and sweet (fried nuts and cinnamon with chocolate sauce)— are the draw at this restaurant. Also on the menu are sandwiches and salads. Meals can be eaten outside on the pleasant wide veranda. There's also an interesting little arts-and-crafts gallery, which, like the café, is open daily from 8 to 6. ⑤ *Average main: R60* ⊠ *Main St., Uptown* ☎ *013/768–1061* ⊘ *Daily 8 am–6 pm.*

CAFÉ

$ ✕ **Vine Restaurant and Pub.** In a former trading store dating from 1910, the Vine uses antique sideboards, sepia photos, and country-style wooden furniture to recapture that heady 1800s gold rush–era feeling. The food is straightforward and hearty. Try traditional South African *bobotie* (curried ground mutton topped with egg), *potjiekos* (lamb stew), digger's stew (beef and veggies) served in a digger's gold-prospecting pan, or *samp* (corn porridge). The pub is a good place to sit outside and watch the world go by. ⑤ *Average main: R80* ⊠ *Main St., Downtown* ☎ *013/768–1080* ⌀ *thevine.pilgrims@gmail.com* ⊘ *Weekdays 10–7, weekends 8–7.*

SOUTH AFRICAN

WHERE TO STAY

$ ⊞ **District 6 Miners' Cottages.** On top of a hill a few minutes' walk from the center of town, these self-catering cottages are very good value. **Pros:** excellent, central location. **Cons:** cold in winter; quite basic. ⑤ *Rooms from: R980* ⊠ *District Six, near Royal Hotel, Uptown* ☎ *072/314–5359* ⊕ *www.pilgrims-rest.co.za* ⤶ *6 cottages* ▭ *No credit cards* ⦿ *No meals.*

RENTAL

9

$ 🔛 **Royal Hotel.** Established in 1873, this hotel dates from the very begin-
HOTEL   ning of the gold rush in Pilgrim's Rest—you'll see its corrugated-iron
facade in sepia photos all over town. **Pros:** step-back-in-time ambience.
Cons: restaurant food unimaginative. ⑤ *Rooms from: R790* ✉ *Main
St., Uptown* ☎ *013/768–1100 reception* 🖷 *013/768–1188* ✐ *royalres@
rhpilgrims.co.za* ⊕ *www.royal-hotel.co.za* ⤴ *50 rooms* ⦿⧵ *Breakfast.*

GRASKOP

*25 km (16 miles) northeast of Sabie; 15 km (9 miles) southeast of Pil-
grim's Rest.*

Graskop (translation: "grass head") was so named because of the abundance of grassveld and few trees. Like so many of the little towns in this
area, it started as a gold-mining camp in the 1880s, on a farm called
Graskop that was owned by Abel Erasmus, who later became the local
magistrate. After the gold mines closed down, the town served as a
major rail link for the timber industry. Today the main features of this
rather featureless little town are its curio shops and eateries. Perched on
the edge of the Drakensberg/Mpumalanga Escarpment, Graskop con-
siders itself the window on the lowveld, and several nearby lookouts do
have stunning views over the edge of the escarpment. It's an ideal base
for visiting scenic hot spots, including Mac Mac Falls and the beauties
in and around the Blyde River (Motlatse) Canyon Nature Reserve.

Traveling east toward Hazyview, you enter the lovely Koewyns Pass,
named for a local Pedi chief. Unfortunately, there are few scenic overlooks, but you'll still get sweeping views of the Graskop gorge. Look for
the turnoff to Graskopkloof on your left as you leave town, and stop to
get a closer view into this deep, surprisingly spectacular gorge, where in
the rainy season two waterfalls plunge to the river below.

GETTING HERE AND AROUND

It's best to approach Graskop from Mbombela (Nelspruit), the biggest
town in the area. It's a pleasant drive (a vehicle is essential) via White
River and Hazyview. But don't hold your breath: the town is hardly
memorable. Still, it's a good base for exploring the region.

WHERE TO STAY

$$ 🔛 **West Lodge.** This attractive Victorian-style B&B is set in a delight-
B&B/INN   ful garden bursting with roses. **Pros:** a wide choice of eateries and the
town center are only minutes away. **Cons:** Graskop not the prettiest of
towns. ⑤ *Rooms from: R2080* ✉ *12/14 Huguenot St.* ☎ *013/767–1390*
⊕ *www.westlodge.co.za* ⤴ *5 rooms* ⦿⧵ *Breakfast.*

BLYDE RIVER CANYON NATURE RESERVE

15 km (9 miles) northeast of Graskop.

Also known as the Motlatse Canyon Nature Reserve, this breathtak-
ingly beautiful 71,660 acres of red sandstone mountains, gorges, and
grassland stretches 60 km (37 miles) north of Graskop, to the Abel
Erasmus Pass. Its spectacular main feature is the canyon itself. Carved

out of almost 2.5 km (1.5 miles) of red sandstone, it's the world's third biggest and greenest canyon, on account of its lush evergreen vegetation.

GETTING HERE AND AROUND

Situated on the scenic Panorama Route, which winds along the edge of the canyon, the Blyde River (Motlatse) Canyon Nature Reserve is easily accessible from Mbombela (Nelspruit) and Sabie, and from the west of Kruger. A vehicle is essential, but if you're keen on hiking, it's hiking heaven.

EXPLORING

Blyde River Canyon Nature Reserve. The world's third-largest canyon is also South Africa's second-most-visited natural attraction (after Table Mountain). Discover spectacular scenery of red cliffs jutting up from the canyon base, quirky mountain formations, indigenous rare Afromontane forest, cascading waterfalls, and an abundance of birds, small animals, and biodiversity. The Treur (sorrow) and Blyde (joy) rivers feed into the canyon, named by early Voortrekkers, and you can try your hand at all sorts of adventure activities, from white-water rafting and abseiling to mountain biking and hiking. The Blyde River (Motlatse) Canyon and Reserve is nearly 30 km (19 miles) long, and stretches for 60 km (37 miles) from its entrance north of Graskop up to the Abel Erasmus Pass. You'll get superb views from the Panorama Route, which winds along the lip of the canyon. ⊠ *Along the R532, Bourke's Luck* 🖾 *R25 (payable at Bourke's Luck Potholes)* ⊙ *Reserve daily 7–5, visitor center daily 7:30–4.*

Bourke's Luck Potholes. The amazing Bourke's Luck Potholes and the Blyde River Canyon Nature Reserve visitor center are 27 km (17 miles) north of Berlin Falls. Named after a gold prospector, the cylindrical and rather alien-looking deep potholes filled with green water are carved into the rock by whirlpools where the Treur (sorrow) and Blyde (joy) rivers converge. The visitor center has interesting information on the flora, fauna, and geology of the canyon. Several long canyon hiking trails start from headquarters, as do shorter walks and trails. A three-hour walk, for example, could take you down into the bottom of the canyon, where you follow a trail marked by rocks painted with animal or bird symbols as the gorge towers above you. ⊠ *Graskop* ✢ *27 km (17 mile) north of Berlin Falls on the R532.*

God's Window. God's Window is the most famous of the lowveld lookouts. It got its name because of the rock "window" that looks out at the sublime view below. Gaze out into seeming infinity from the edge of the escarpment (which drops away almost vertically). Geared to tourists, it has toilet facilities, paved parking areas, curio vendors, and paved, marked walking trails leading to various lookouts. The God's Window lookout has a view back along the escarpment framed between towering cliffs. For a broader panorama, make a 10-minute climb along the paved track through the rain forest to a small area with sweeping views of the entire lowveld. The altitude here is 5,700 feet, just a little lower than Johannesburg. ⊠ *Off R534, Graskop* 🖾 *R10.*

Three Rondawels. This is one of the most spectacular vistas in South Africa—you'll find it in almost every travel brochure. Here the Blyde

9

River, hemmed in by towering buttresses of red rock, snakes through the bottom of the Blyde River Canyon. The Three Rondawels are rock formations that bear a vague similarity to the round, thatch African dwellings of the same name. Before Europeans moved into the area, the indigenous local people named the formations the Chief and His Three Wives. The flat-top peak to the right is Mapjaneng (the Chief), named in honor of a Mapulana chief, Maripe Mashile, who routed invading Swazi at the battle of Moholoholo ("the very great one"). The three "wives," in descending order from right to left, are Maseroto, Mogoladikwe, and Magabolle. ⊠ *Graskop.*

WORTH NOTING

Berlin Falls. A small stream, Waterfall Spruit, runs through a broad expanse of grassland to Berlin Falls. A short walk takes you to the cascade, shaped like a candle, which starts off as a thin stream that drops through a narrow sluice (this looks like the candle wick), and then widens out to drop 150 feet into a deep-green pool surrounded by tall pines. If the weather's good, plan to swim and picnic here. Why the not-very-local-name? The German miners who came here during the gold rush named it nostalgically after their home country. ⊠ *Graskop* ✛ *A little over 2 km (1 mile) north of Lisbon Falls off the R532.*

Lisbon Falls. You'll find more gorgeous waterfalls clustered on the Panorama Route than anywhere else in southern Africa. Just north of Graskop, the dramatic falls are set in a bowl between hills just outside the Blyde (Motlatse) Canyon Nature Reserve, sending cascades 120 feet onto rocks below, throwing up spray over a deep pool. Named nostalgically by European miners who came here looking for gold in the late 1800s, this is a good kick-off point for the whole Panorama Route. Hike down to the pool on a path from the parking area, and enjoy a picnic. ⊠ *Graskop* ✛ *From God's Window turn right on the R534 and continue 6 km (4 miles). At the T with R532, turn right and follow signs.*

Pinnacle. Pinnacle is a 100-foot-high quartzite "needle" that rises dramatically out of the surrounding fern-clad ravine, as it has for countless millennia. Way down below, beneath and to the right of the viewing platform, you can see the plateau beneath the escarpment. The watercourse drops down some 1,475 feet in a series of alternating falls and cascades. Stay away from the edge if you suffer from vertigo. ⊠ *Graskop* ✛ *From Graskop take the R532 north and turn right after 2½ km (1½ miles) onto the R534, marked God's Window. Continue 1½ km (1 mile) and look out for brown sign reading Pinnacle.*

WHERE TO STAY

$$$$
RENTAL
🏠 **Belvedere Guest House.** This self-catering establishment, built in 1915 for the manager of the old Belvedere Power station that provided electricity for the Pilgrim's Rest mining operations, is a great place to experience the awesome beauty of the Blyde River Canyon. **Pros:** superb location; inviting walks for all fitness levels. **Cons:** very popular so book early. ⑤ *Rooms from: R6000* ⊠ *Off the R532, Pilgrim's Rest* ✛ *5 km (3 miles) north of Bourke's Luck Potholes* ☎ *013/759–5432 reservations* 🖶 *086/537–8244* ⊕ *www.mpumalanga.com* 🛏 *1 house, 9 rooms* ⑩ *No meals.*

SPORTS AND THE OUTDOORS

HIKING

Blyde River Canyon Hiking Trail. This breathtakingly scenic 60 km (37 mile) five-day hike runs from God's Window right along the edge of the escarpment. Accommodation ranges from comfortable cottages to sleeping under the stars. You can also take shorter two-day and three-day trails. The mountain scenery is spectacular, making it one of the most popular trails in the country. You'll need to stop—not just to catch your breath—but to drink in the glorious scenery. Several shorter trails explore the canyon from trailheads at Bourke's Luck Potholes. The number of hikers on the multiday trails is controlled, so it's essential to reserve far in advance (contact the nature reserve). There is also a recently developed circular 180 meters (almost 1 mile) trail for disabled visitors. ⊠ *off R534, Graskop.*

EN
ROUTE

Abel Erasmus Pass. The descent out of the nature reserve, down the escarpment, and through Abel Erasmus Pass is breathtaking. (From the Three Rondawels, take the R532 to a T, and turn right onto the R36.) Be careful as you drive this pass. Locals graze their cattle and goats on the verges, and you may be surprised by animals on the tarmac as you round a bend. The J. G. Strijdom Tunnel serves as the gateway to the lowveld. At the mouth of the tunnel are stands where you can buy clay pots, African masks, wooden giraffes, curios of many kinds and subtropical fruit. As you emerge from the dark mouth of the tunnel, the lowveld spreads out below, and the views of both it and the mountains are stunning. On the left, the Olifants River snakes through the bushveld, lined to some extent by African subsistence farms. ⊠ *Graskop.*

HAZYVIEW

45 km (28 miles) east of Sabie.

Named for the heat haze that drifts up from the fruit plantations and bush in the surrounding area, Hazyview is a bustling little town. Situated in the center of the prime tourist attractions, it's also another gateway to Kruger through the nearby Phabeni, Numbi, and Kruger gates. There are plenty of good places to stay and eat, and Hazyview is also the adventure mecca of the region. Here you can try your hand at horseback riding, helicopter trips, river rafting, hiking, ballooning, quad biking, golf, and game-viewing safaris.

GETTING HERE AND AROUND

Hazyview is easily accessible from Mbombela (Nelspruit) on good, well-signposted roads. From here, it's a comfortable drive to the major attractions of the Panorama Route, including God's Window, Bourke's Luck Potholes, and the spectacular Blyde River (Motlatse) Canyon.

EXPLORING

Sabie Valley Coffee. From the moment you enter Sabie Valley Coffee, approximately 10 km (6 miles) from Hazyview, the delicious smell of freshly roasted beans lures you in. A fascinating coffee tour, led by owner Tim Buckland, takes you through the whole coffee-making process—from orchards to roasting to packaging. Find out about a coffee grower's life, and the different kinds of beans that produce different tastes, which is why there are so many (often bewildering) coffees available today. Check out Beatrice, Spong, and Lovelock in the entrance—three old, but still working, coffee mills. Challenge your taste buds with a tasting of homegrown, 100% pure Arabica specialty coffees, before sampling some of the coffee-related goodies for sale: coffee liqueur, cake, and candies. Reservations are essential. ⌧ *R536 ✛ 18 km (11 miles) west of Hazyview* ☎ *013/737–8169* ⊕ *www.sabievalleycoffee. com* ✉ *Tours with tastings R70* ⊙ *Tour: Wed. 2 pm.*

FAMILY **Shangana Cultural Village.** The Shangana Cultural Village is a genuine Shangaan village that's presided over by the incumbent chief, whose family have lived here for decades. An hour-long tour of the *kraal* (traditional rural village) includes a meeting with the chief and a visit to the sangoma (traditional healer who'll throw the bones to predict your future). Enjoy a traditional lunch or a light meal in the tea garden after visiting the Marula Market, where you can stock up on a great variety of good-quality handcrafted items (some made on-site). Don't miss the memorable evening firelight song-and-dance performance hosted by the chief portraying the history of the Shangaan people. A traditional dinner is included. Booking for the performance (5:15 pm in summer, 5 pm in winter) is essential. ⌧ *Graskop Rd. ✛ R535, 5 km (3 miles) northwest of Hazyview* ☎ *013/737–5804* ⊕ *www.shangana.co.za* ✉ *Day tour R182, day tour and meal R280, evening festival R466* ⊙ *Daily 9–5, to 8 for evening shows.*

WHERE TO STAY

$$ ▦ **Böhm's Zeederberg Country House.** Expect a warm, sincere welcome
B&B/INN at this owner-run guesthouse situated on spacious grounds with verdant lawns shaded by indigenous trees. ⑤ *Rooms from: R1848* ⌧ *R536 ✛ R536, 18 km (11 miles) west of Hazyview* ☎ *013/737–8101* ⊕ *www. bohms.co.za* ⤶ *10 rooms* ▯◯▮ *Breakfast.*

$$ ▦ **Rissington Inn.** This lovely reasonably priced lodge offers fine food,
B&B/INN superb hospitality, and all the facilities you'd expect at a top lodge. **Pros:** superb value for money. **Cons:** always busy; book well in advance. ⑤ *Rooms from: R1900* ⌧ *Off the R40 ✛ 1 km (¾ mile) from Hazyview and down dirt road* ☎ *013/737–7700* ⊕ *www.rissington.co.za* ⤶ *14 rooms, 2 suites* ▯◯▮ *Breakfast.*

SHOPPING

Windmill Wine Shop. Stop in at the Windmill Wine Shop, on the same property as Böhm's Zeederberg, to pick up excellent Cape wines, ports, and brandies, local beer made by Hops Hollow Brewery, and local cheeses, olives, olive oil, and coffee grown and processed at nearby Sabie Valley Coffee. You can also get a light meal of local cheese, cold meats, pâté, and olives. You can also stay at the attractive on-site Windmill Cottages. ⌧ *R536 ✛ 18 km (11 miles) west of Hazyview* ☎ *013/737–8175* ⊕ *www.thewindmill.co.za* ⊙ *Closed Sun.*

CLOSE UP

Rock Art

An important key to understanding humankind's past, rock art is a fascinating aspect of the South African and world's heritage. Engravings (made by scratching into the rock surface), paintings, and finger paintings proliferate throughout the province and carry an air of mystery, since relatively little is known about them. Although some archaeologists have attributed the origins of rock art to ancient Egyptians, Phoenicians, and even extraterrestrial races, the rock art found here was created by ancestors of the San. Materials came from the immediate environment. Ocher (red iron-oxide clay) was used to obtain red, charcoal for black, and white clay for white. Blood, egg, and plant juices were used for binding, creating a paint with obvious staying power.

Most rock art illustrates the activities and experiences of the African medicine people, or shamans. Religious rituals, such as those for making rain and healing the sick, involved trances and inspired visions, from which rock-art images were created. The images included large animals, such as the highly regarded eland and rhino, which were believed to possess supernatural power. Half-animal, half-human representations and geometric patterns and grids are also featured. The shamans believed that when an image was drawn, power was transferred to the people and the land.

WHITE RIVER

35 km (22 miles) southeast of Sabie.

This pleasant little town is set amid nut and tropical-fruit plantations and is one of the gateways to the escarpment's major sights. Settled by retired British army officers in the early 20th century, it still retains some of its colonial feel, but it's now much more representative of the "new" South Africa, crowded with people of all backgrounds. Casterbridge is an attractive shopping center, and because White River is home to a resident esoteric community, those who feel like a bit of alternative therapy will find holistic healing hands.

9

GETTING HERE AND AROUND

White River is very conveniently situated on good, well-signposted roads between Mbombela (Nelspruit) and Kruger National Park. You'll need wheels to tour the area, and be sure to shop for fresh fruit and produce at the numerous roadside stalls.

EXPLORING

White River Motor Museum. If you're into automobiles and their history, travel to the Casterbridge Farm shopping and entertainment center for the White River Motor Museum. It has an impressive collection of more than 60 vehicles, dating from as early as 1911, including a 1936 Jaguar SS100, one of only 314 ever built. ⊠ *R40 and Numbi Rd.* ☎ *013/751–1514* ⊕ *www.casterbridge.co.za* ✉ *Free* ☾ *Weekdays 9–4:30, weekends 9:30–3.*

WHERE TO STAY

$$
B&B/INN
⊞ Jatinga Country Lodge and Restaurant. This charming boutique hotel, on the banks of the White River, is only a short drive from Kruger Park, and it was originally a 1920s hunting lodge. **Pros:** good food; friendly staff; old colonial charm. **Cons:** service tends to be slow when lodge is full. $ *Rooms from: R2240* ⊠ *Jatinga Rd.* ☎ *083/235–3460, 083/277–0917* ⊕ *www.jatinga.co.za* ⬗ *13 rooms, 4 suites* ⏲*Some meals.*

$$
B&B/INN
⊞ Oliver's Restaurant and Lodge. This large, white-walled, red-roofed country house situated among pine trees and lush forest overlooks lovely gardens and the 1st hole of the White River Golf Course. **Pros:** gorgeous setting; great food. **Cons:** quite formal. $ *Rooms from: R1850* ⊠ *R40, between Hazyview and White River* ☎ *013/750–0479* ⊕ *www. olivers.co.za* ⬗ *9 rooms, 2 suites* ⏲*Breakfast.*

SHOPPING

Casterbridge Lifestyle Centre. If you need some classy retail therapy, stop off at this upmarket lifestyle center. Once a rambling mango estate, it's now home to art galleries, pottery and sculpture studios, and quirky boutiques selling designer clothes, jewelry, and much more, all set in lovely manicured gardens. The White River Art Gallery always has interesting local and national exhibitions, and when you've shopped till you dropped, tuck into a good meal at one of the eateries that serve everything from tasty pub fare and fine dining to wood-oven pizza. If wheels are your thing, pop into the vintage White River Motor Museum (⇨ *See review*) and feast your eyes on immaculately restored past motoring beauties. ⊠ *R40 and Numbi Rd.* ☎ *013/751–1540 information* ⊕ *www.casterbridge.co.za.*

MBOMBELA (NELSPRUIT)

19 km (12 miles) southwest of White River on the R40.

Mbombela (formerly Nelspruit), the capital of Mpumalanga and home of the provincial government, is a modern, vibrant subtropical city of nearly 600,000 people. Known as the gateway to Kruger and the lowveld, it's also a notable stop on the main route between Gauteng and Maputo, Mozambique. The compact town sits in the middle of a prosperous agricultural community, which farms citrus (a third of South Africa's citrus exports come from here), subtropical fruit, tobacco, and vegetables. It has an international airport, excellent hospitals, great restaurants, superb botanical gardens, and the Riverside Mall, Mpumalanga's biggest shopping center. Nearby is the Jane Goodall Institute's Chimpanzee Eden.

GETTING HERE AND AROUND

Approximately a five-hour drive from Johannesburg, Mbombela (Nelspruit) is easily accessible by road. The Kruger Mpumalanga International Airport (KMIA) is 22 km (13 miles) northeast of the town.

EXPLORING

FAMILY **Lowveld National Botanical Gardens.** The gorgeous Lowveld National Botanical Gardens, just outside Mbombela (Nelspruit), is the only one in the province. It's a must-see if you are at all interested in plant life.

Apart from its collection of more than 2,000 species of plants, it has the largest collection of cycads in Africa. Take great photos from the wooden suspension bridge over a tumbling waterfall where the Crocodile and Nel rivers (which flow through the gardens) join together. In spring and summer, when many of the indigenous plants are flowering, you'll see lots of iridescent sunbirds feasting on the blossoms. But at any time of year, don't miss the lush man-made African rain forest that gives the gardens its "evergreen" moniker. The gardens are wheelchair-friendly. ⊠ *White River Rd.* ⊹ *3 km (2 miles) outside Nelspruit* ☎ *013/752–5531* ⊠ *R24* ⊙ *May–Sept., daily 8–5; Oct.–Apr., daily 8–6.*

KRUGER NATIONAL PARK

561 km (348 miles) from Johannesburg.

Visiting Kruger is likely to be one of the greatest experiences of your life, truly providing ultimate "Wow!" moments. You'll be amazed at the diversity of life forms—the tallest (the giraffe), the biggest (the elephant), the funkiest (the dung beetle), the toothiest (the crocodile), and the glitziest (the lilac-breasted roller).

But it's not all game and safari. If you're into ancient human history, there are also major archaeological sites and fascinating San (Bushman) rock paintings. (There is ample evidence that prehistoric humans—*Homo erectus*—roamed the area between 500,000 and 100,000 years ago.) Founded in 1898 by Paul Kruger, president of what was then the Transvaal Republic, the park is a place to safari at your own pace, choosing between upscale private camps or simple campsites.

Kruger lies in the hot lowveld, a subtropical section of Mpumalanga and Limpopo provinces that abuts Mozambique. The park cuts a swath 80 km (50 miles) wide and 320 km (200 miles) long from Zimbabwe and the Limpopo River in the north to the Crocodile River in the south. It is divided into 16 macro eco-zones, each supporting a great variety of plants, birds, and animals, including 145 mammal species and almost 500 species of birds, some of which are not found elsewhere in South Africa. In 2002 a treaty was signed between South Africa, Zimbabwe, and Mozambique to form a giant conservation area, the Great Limpopo Transfrontier Park. It's a complex ongoing process, but once all the fences between Kruger, the Gonarezhou National Park in Mozambique, and the Limpopo National Park in Zimbabwe are finally removed, the Peace Park will be the largest conservation area in the world.

9

GETTING HERE AND AROUND

You can fly to Kruger Mpumalanga International Airport (KMIA), at Mbombela (Nelspruit); Skukuza Airport in Kruger itself; Hoedspruit Airport, close to Kruger's Orpen Gate; or Phalaborwa Airport (if you're going to the north of Kruger) from either Johannesburg or Cape Town. (⇨ *See Air Travel in Travel Smart.*) You can also drive to Kruger from Johannesburg in about six hours; if you drive, a 4x4 isn't necessary since all roads are paved.

MONEY MATTERS

Kruger accepts credit cards, which are also useful for big purchases, but you should always have some small change for staff tips (tip your cleaning person R20 per hut per day) and for drinks and snacks at the camp shops, although camp shops also accept credit cards.

TIMING

How and where you tackle Kruger will depend on your time frame. With excellent roads and accommodations, it's a great place to drive yourself. If you don't feel up to driving or self-catering, you can choose a private lodge in Kruger itself or just outside the park and take the guided drives—although it's not quite the same as lying in bed and hearing the hyenas prowling around the camp fence or a lion roaring under the stars.

If you can spend a week here, start in the north at the very top of the park at the Punda Maria Camp, then make your way leisurely south to the very bottom at Crocodile Bridge Gate or Malelane Gate. With only three days or fewer, reserve one of the southern camps such as Berg-en-Dal or Lower Sabie and just plan to explore these areas. No matter where you go in Kruger, be sure to plan your route and accommodations in advance (advance booking is essential). Game-spotting isn't an exact science: you might see all the Big Five plus hundreds of other animals, but you could see much less. Try to plan your route to include water holes and rivers, which afford your best opportunity to see game. Old Africa hands claim that the very early morning, when the camp gates open, is the best time for game-viewing, but it's all quite random—you could see a leopard drinking at noon, a breeding herd of elephants midmorning, or a lion pride dozing under a tree in the middle of the afternoon. You could also head out at dawn and find very little wildlife. Be sure to take at least one guided sunset drive; you won't likely forget the thrill of catching a nocturnal animal in the spotlight.

EXPLORING

First-time visitors sometimes feel a little lost driving themselves through the park. They don't know what to look for, and they can't always identify the animals they see. Besides, not everyone knows what to do when a herd of elephants blocks the road. An affordable solution is to hire a game ranger to show you the park and its animal and bird inhabitants. All the major rest camps offer ranger-led bush drives in open-air vehicles (minimum of two people). Not only can rangers explain the finer points of what you're seeing, but they can also take you into areas off-limits to the public. There are also bush walks on offer at the different camps, something else you can't do on your own. Sunrise and sunset drives cost R155 (R80 per child); guided bush walks R230 (no children). Book drives at least two weeks in advance or when you make your park reservations.

Even if you tour the park by yourself (armed with mammal and bird field guides) during the day, don't miss out on a ranger-led night drive, when the park is closed to regular visitors. You'll sit in a large open-air vehicle, scanning the bush with the ranger, who uses a powerful

spotlight to pick out animals, including nocturnal creatures that you would never see otherwise. You might see bush babies (enchanting furry, big-eared, big-eyed little primates that leap from bush to bush), servals (mini-leopard-looking felines), civets (black-and-white possum look-alikes), genets (spotted catlike creatures with bushy tails), or an aardvark ambling along in the moonlight. Scrutinize branches of big trees for the giant eagle owl, with its pink eyelids, or a leopard chewing on its kill. Night is also the time when hyenas and lions hunt. These opportunities alone make a night drive an unforgettable experience. The three- to four-hour trip leaves the rest camps half an hour before the gates close. ■ TIP➜ **Book as far in advance as possible.** Night drives cost R105 per person (depending on the size of the vehicle—smaller vehicles cost more), half price for kids. Don't forget your binoculars, a snack or drink, and a warm jacket whatever the season.

One of the most consistently rewarding drives in the park is along the H4, running along the Sabie River from Skukuza to Lower Sabie. It can be crowded, however, particularly on weekends and public holidays and especially during the July and December school vacations.

Day drives follow the same format as night drives. Choose between sunrise, midmorning, and sunset drives. The cost is approximately the same as for night drives. Check the SANParks' website (⊕ *www.sanparks. org*) for more details.

Kruger National Park. Kruger National Park is undoubtedly one of the world's best game parks, where teeming game roams freely over an area the size of Wales or Israel. The southern and central sections of the park are probably the best for sightings because riverine forests, thorny thickets, and large, grassy plains studded with knobthorn and marula trees, typical vegetation of this region, make ideal habitats for a variety of animals, including black and white rhinos, leopards, giraffes, hyenas, numerous kinds of antelope, lions, and the rare "painted wolf"—a wild dog.

As you drive north to Olifants, Letaba, and Shingwedzi, you enter major elephant country, although you're likely to spot lots of other game, too, including lions and cheetahs. North of Letaba, however, the landscape becomes a monotonous blur of mopane trees, the result of nutrient-poor land that supports smaller numbers of animals, although the lugubrious-looking *tsessebe* (sess-a-bee) antelope and the magnificent and uncommon roan antelope, with its twisty horns, thrive here. Elephants love mopane, and you'll certainly see plenty of them. The Shingwedzi River Drive toward the Kanniedood Dam is one of the park's most rewarding drives, with elephants, leopards, giraffes, and other game. Park your vehicle underneath the lovely hide on this drive, then sit upstairs and take in life on the river, including waterbirds, hippos, and basking crocs. To experience the full richness of the northern Kruger, visit the Pafuri Picnic Site (hot water and braais available), where ancient massive leadwood and jackalberry trees lean over the often dry Luvuvhu River, the haunt of the scarlet-and-green Narina trogon (a bird) and the much-sought-after Pel's fishing owl. But don't leave your picnic unattended while you look for more special birds, such as the wattle-eyed flycatcher, because the vervet monkeys will have it in a flash.

Because the bush is unpredictable, you may get some of your best sightings where and when you least expect them: a pack of wild dogs lying in the road just outside the Skukuza camp gate or a cheetah and two cubs sitting in the middle of the tar road 100 yards inside the Orpen Gate. ■ TIP➔ If you have a week in Kruger, it's worth driving north, as there are always fewer people here. However, if you are short on time, then stick to the south or central sections of the park. But wherever you go, don't get out of your vehicle except at certain well-marked picnic sites or view sites, unless you want to make an international headline.

There are nine entrance gates to Kruger, namely (counterclockwise from the north) Pafuri, Punda Maria, Phalaborwa, Orpen, Paul Kruger, Phabeni, Numbi, Malelane, and Crocodile Bridge. National access roads to all the entrance gates are paved. You can arrange for a late-entry escort until 9 pm for the following gates (and their nearby camps): Paul Kruger (Skukuza), Numbi (Pretoriuskop), Malelane (Berg-en-Dal and Malelane), Crocodile Bridge (Crocodile Bridge), Punda Maria (Punda Maria), and Orpen (Orpen). Always check at your gate for pamphlets, maps, and books (also available in the camp shops).

There is a daily conservation fee, but Wild Cards, available at the gates or online, are more economical for stays of more than a few days. Reservations for all accommodations, bush drives, wilderness trails, and other park activities must be made through South African National Parks (SANParks). ✉ *Kruger National Park* ☎ *012/428–9111 reservations* ⊕ *www.sanparks.org* ⊗ *Gates Apr.–Sept., daily 6–5:30; Oct.–Mar., daily 5:30 am–6:30 pm, but sometimes vary.*

WHERE TO STAY

It's impossible to recommend just one camp in Kruger. One person might prefer the intimacy of Kruger's oldest camp, Punda Maria, with its whitewashed thatch cottages; another might favor big, bustling Skukuza. A great way to experience the park is to stay in as many of the camps as possible. The SANParks website has a comprehensive overview of the different camps. The bushveld camps are more expensive than the regular camps, but offer much more privacy and exclusivity—but no shops, restaurants, or pools. If you seek the ultimate in luxury, stay at one of the private luxury lodges in the concession areas, some of which also have walking trails.

Reservations for park-operated accommodations should be made through **South African National Parks.** (⇨ *For SANParks contact information, see Visitor Information in Travel Smart.*) If air-conditioning is a must for you, be sure to check the website to confirm its availability in the accommodation of your choice. ■ TIP➔ Book your guided game drives and walks when you check in. Opt for the sunset drive. You'll get to see the animals coming to drink plus a thrilling night drive.

WALKING KRUGER

Kruger's seven wilderness trails can accommodate eight hikers each on three-day, two-night hikes. Led by an armed ranger and local tracker, you walk in the mornings and evenings, with an afternoon siesta, approximately 19 km (12 miles) a day.

These trails encourage a sense of companionship among the group, which decides together on speed and length of walks, but this isn't about pushing endurance records. Many hikers can recount face-to-face encounters with everything from rhinos to lions. No one under 12 is allowed; those over 60 must have a doctor's certificate. Hikers sleep in rustic two-bed huts and share a bathroom (flush toilets, bucket showers). Meals are simple (stews and barbecues); you bring your own drinks. Summer is uncomfortably hot (and trails are cheaper), but nights can be freezing in winter—bring warm clothes and an extra blanket. Reserve 13 months ahead. The cost is about R4,000 per person per trail.

Bushman Trail. In the southwestern corner of the park, this trail takes its name from the San rock paintings and sites found here; the camp is in a secluded valley. Watch for white rhinos, elephants, and buffalo. Check in at Berg-en-Dal.

Metsi Metsi Trail. The permanent water of the nearby N'waswitsontso River makes this one of the best trails for winter game-viewing. Midway between Skukuza and Satara, the trail camp is in the lee of a mountain in an area of gorges, cliffs, and rolling savanna. Check in at Skukuza.

Napi Trail. White rhino sightings are common on this trail, which runs through mixed bushveld between Pretoriuskop and Skukuza. Other possibilities are black rhinos, cheetahs, leopards, elephants, and, if you're lucky, nomadic wild dogs. The camp is tucked into dense riverine forest at the confluence of the Napi and Biyamiti rivers. Check in at Pretoriuskop.

Nyalaland Trail. In the far north, this trail camp sits among ancient baobab trees near the Luvuvhu River and has the best birding in the park. Walk at the foot of huge rocky gorges and in dense forest. Hippos, crocs, elephants, buffalo, and the nyala antelope are almost a sure thing. Check in at Punda Maria.

Olifants Trail. This spectacularly sited camp sits on a high bluff overlooking the Olifants River and affords regular sightings of elephants, lions, buffalo, and hippos. The landscape varies from riverine forest to the rocky foothills of the Lebombo Mountains. Check in at Letaba.

Sweni Trail. East of Satara, this trail camp overlooks the Sweni Spruit and savanna. The area attracts large herds of zebras, wildebeests, and buffalo with their attendant predators: lions, spotted hyenas, and wild dogs. Check in at Satara.

Wolhuter Trail. You just might come face-to-face with a white rhino on this trail through undulating bushveld, interspersed with rocky kopjes, midway between Berg-en-Dal and Pretoriuskop. Elephants, buffalo, and lions are also likely. Check in at Berg-en-Dal.

TYPES OF LODGINGS
BUSHVELD CAMPS

Smaller, more intimate, more luxurious, and consequently more expensive than regular rest camps, Kruger's bushveld camps are in remote wilderness areas of the park that are often off-limits to regular visitors. Access is limited to guests only. As a result you get far more bush and fewer fellow travelers. Night drives and day excursions are available in most of the camps. There are no restaurants, gas pumps, or grocery stores, so bring your provisions with you (though you can buy wood for your barbecue). All accommodations have fully equipped kitchens, bathrooms, ceiling fans, and large verandas, most with air conditioning. Cottages have tile floors, cheerful furnishings, and cane patio furniture and are sited in stands of trees or clumps of indigenous bush for maximum privacy. Many face directly onto a river or water hole. There's only a handful of one-bedroom cottages (at Biyamiti, Shimuwini, Sirheni, and Talamati), but it's worth booking a four-bed cottage and paying the extra, even for only two people. The average cottage price for a couple is R1,000 per night, with extra people (up to five or six) paying R290 each. If you have a large group or are planning a special celebration, you might consider reserving one of the two bush lodges, which must be booked as a whole: **Roodewal Bush Lodge** sleeps 16, and **Boulders Bush Lodge** sleeps 12. Reservations should be made with South African National Parks. ⇨ *For SANParks contact information, see Visitor Information in Travel Smart.*

LODGES

There are now nine luxury lodges in Kruger, one of which is operated by the park. You can check them out on the SANParks website (⇨ *For SANParks contact information, see Visitor Information in Travel Smart*). Among the privately operated areas within the boundaries of the park is the 37,000-acre N'wanetsi concession in the extreme northeast of the park. Here two lodges, Singita Lebombo and Sweni, are located at the confluence of the N'wanetsi and Sweni rivers (not to be confused with their sister Singita camps in Sabie Sands private reserve). The area was once the base for the park's foot and horse patrols, and until the building of the lodges, it had never been traversed by vehicles. Today it's home to the Big Five as well as zebras, giraffes, wildebeests, hippos, hundreds of bird species, and varied flora. Twice-daily game drives (dawn and late afternoon) in an open vehicle are led by a highly experienced and knowledgeable ranger. You can also take a bush nature walk, camp out under the stars, or try your hand at archery.

The Rhino Plains Concession, made up of the Rhino Walking Safari, Rhino Post Safari Lodge, and Plains camps, are situated in about 30,000 acres of pristine bushveld in the Mutlumuvi area of Kruger, which is 10 km (6 miles) northeast of Skukuza, the heart of Kruger Park. This location makes the concession easily accessible by road or air and allows for a shared 15-km (9-mile) boundary with MalaMala, in the Sabi Sand Game Reserve, allowing for plenty of game movement between the two. The environmental impact of the lodge and tented camp is minimal; no concrete was used in buildings, battery power is used for lighting, and a special reed-bed system processes bathroom waste. The area is home to the Big Five as well as many other mammals, birds, trees, and other plants. Activities include twice-daily game drives with professional guides in specially adapted open Land Rovers (the camps have access to some of Kruger's public roads at night), a sleep-out on an elevated wooden platform overlooking a water hole, a guided bush walk, a half- or full-day drive on public roads (with picnic lunch), or a game of golf, which can be arranged at the 9-hole Skukuza course. The environmentally friendly Jock Safari Lodge is in a 14,826-acre concession in the southwest of the park. Expect thrilling night drives in Kruger itself.

PERMANENT TENTED CAMPS

Rhino Post Plains Camp is situated in about 30,000 acres of pristine bushveld in the Mutlumuvi area of Kruger, 10 km (6 miles) northeast of Skukuza, the heart of Kruger Park. The area can be easily accessed by road or air. The concession shares a 15-km (9-mile) boundary with MalaMala, in the Sabi Sand Game Reserve, and there's plenty of game movement between the two. Kruger operates a wide variety of permanent tented camps all over the park.

LODGES

$$$$
RESORT
Fodor's Choice
★

Jock Safari Lodge. This lodge, one of South Africa's loveliest, is set among 14,826 acres of private concession in southwest Kruger. **Pros:** authentic safari experience. **Cons:** busy in season. $ *Rooms from: R10200* ⊠ *Kruger National Park* ☎ *041/509–3000 reservations* ✉ *reservations@shamwarigroup.com* ⊕ *www.jocksafarilodge.com* ⊠ *12 suites* ❘❍❘ *All meals.*

$$
HOTEL
FAMILY

Protea Hotel Kruger Gate. Set in its own small reserve 110 yards from the Paul Kruger Gate, this comfortable hotel is a luxury alternative to the sometimes bare-bones accommodations of Kruger's rest camps. **Pros:** good for families. **Cons:** you can't get away from the fact that this is a hotel with a hotel atmosphere. $ *Rooms from: R2100* ⊠ *Kruger Gate, Skukuza* ☎ *013/735–5671* ✉ *sales@phkrugergate.co.za* ⊕ *www.proteahotels.com* ⊠ *96 rooms, 7 suites* ❘❍❘ *Some meals.*

$$$$
RESORT

Rhino Post Safari Lodge. This lodge comprises eight spacious suites on stilts overlooking the Mutlumuvi riverbed. **Pros:** bang in the middle of Kruger Park. **Cons:** canvas makes the suites very hot in summer and very cold in winter; you need to be walking fit for this camp. $ *Rooms from: R7860* ⊠ *Kruger National Park* ☎ *035/474–1473* ⊕ *www.isibindiafrica.co.za* ⊠ *8 suites* ❘❍❘ *All meals.*

$$$$
ALL-INCLUSIVE

Singita Lebombo Lodge. Named for the nearby Lebombo mountain range, the breathtakingly beautiful Singita Lebombo—winner of numerous international accolades and eco-driven in concept—is Bauhaus in the bush, with a uniquely African feel. **Pros:** stunning avant-garde architecture; excellent game; great curio shop and spa; lovely riverside bush breakfasts. **Cons:** avoid if you prefer a traditional safari lodge; very pricey. $ *Rooms from: R34600* ⊠ *Kruger National Park* ☎ *021/683–3424 reservations, 013/735–5471 lodge* ⊕ *www.singita.co.za* ⊠ *15 suites* ❘❍❘ *All-inclusive.*

$$$$
ALL-INCLUSIVE

Sweni Lodge. Built on wooden stilts, Sweni is cradled on a low riverbank amid thick virgin bush and ancient trees. **Pros:** tiny and intimate; great location; lovely riverside bush breakfasts. **Cons:** dim lighting.

⑤ *Rooms from: R34600* ⊠ *Kruger National Park* ☎ *021/683–3424 reservations, 013/735–5500 lodge* ⊕ *www.singita.co.za* ⤴ *12 suites* ⧓ *All-inclusive.*

PERMANENT TENTED CAMPS

$

RESORT

FAMILY

Fodor's Choice

★

⌂ **Berg-en-Dal.** This rest camp lies at the southern tip of the park, in a basin surrounded by rocky hills. **Pros:** you can sit on benches at the perimeter fence and watch game come and go all day. **Cons:** always crowded (although chalets are well spaced out). ⑤ *Rooms from: R1060* ⊠ *Kruger National Park* ☎ *012/428–9111* ⊕ *www.sanparks.org* ⤴ *90 suites* ⧓ *No meals.*

$

RESORT

FAMILY

⌂ **Crocodile Bridge.** Situated in Kruger's southeastern corner, this award-winning small rest camp sits on the scenic Crocodile River and doubles as an entrance gate, which makes it a convenient stopover if you arrive near the park's closing time and are too late to make it to another camp. **Pros:** adjacent to one of best game roads in park. **Cons:** close proximity to the outside world of roads and farms. ⑤ *Rooms from: R1160* ⊠ *Kruger National Park* ☎ *012/428–9111 reservations* ⊕ *www.sanparks.org* ⤴ *28 suites* ⧓ *No meals.*

$

RESORT

FAMILY

⌂ **Letaba.** Overlooking the frequently dry Letaba River, this lovely old camp sits in the middle of elephant country in the park's central section. **Pros:** camp has a real bush feel. **Cons:** far from southern entrance gates, so you'll need more traveling time. ⑤ *Rooms from: R1040* ⊠ *Kruger National Park* ☎ *012/428–9111 reservations* ⊕ *www.sanparks.org* ⤴ *118 suites* ⧓ *No meals.*

$

RESORT

FAMILY

⌂ **Lower Sabie.** One of the most popular camps in Kruger, Lower Sabie has tremendous views over a broad sweep of the Sabie River and sits in one of the best game-viewing areas of the park (along with Skukuza and Satara). **Pros:** great location; superb game in vicinity. **Cons:** camp and restaurant always crowded. ⑤ *Rooms from: R1160* ⊠ *Kruger National Park* ☎ *012/428–9111 reservations* ⊕ *www.sanparks.org* ⤴ *109 suites* ⧓ *No meals.*

$

RESORT

⌂ **Mopani.** Built in the lee of a rocky kopje overlooking a dam, amid surrounding mopane woodlands, this camp in the northern section is one of Kruger's biggest. **Pros:** Attractive accommodation in landscaped camp overlooking big hippo dam. **Cons:** Thick mopane bush around camp and beyond not great for game viewing although elephants love it. ⑤ *Rooms from: R1060* ⊠ *Kruger National Park* ☎ *012/428–9111 reservations* ⊕ *www.sanparks.org* ⤴ *101 suites* ⧓ *No meals.*

$

RESORT

⌂ **Olifants.** In the center of Kruger, Olifants has the best setting of all the camps: high atop cliffs on a rocky ridge with panoramic views of the distant hills and the Olifants River below. **Pros:** stunning location. **Cons:** huts in the middle of the camp have no privacy; high malaria area. ⑤ *Rooms from: R1260* ⊠ *Olifants Camp Rd., Kruger National Park* ☎ *012/428–9111 reservations* ⊕ *www.sanparks.org* ⤴ *109 suites* ⧓ *No meals.*

$

RESORT

⌂ **Orpen.** Don't dismiss this tiny, underappreciated rest camp on Kruger's western border in the center of the park because of its proximity to the Orpen Gate. **Pros:** great game. **Cons:** close to main gate. ⑤ *Rooms from: R1080* ⊠ *Kruger National Park* ☎ *012/428–9111 reservations* ⊕ *www.sanparks.org* ⤴ *15 suites* ⧓ *No meals.*

9

$ ⚏ **Pretoriuskop.** This large, nostalgically old-fashioned camp, close to
RESORT   the Numbi Gate in southwest Kruger, makes a good overnight stop or
FAMILY   touring base. **Pros:** good restaurant for snacks and toasted sandwiches.
Cons: bleak and bare in winter; barracks-style feel. ⑤ *Rooms from:
R1120 ⊠ Kruger National Park* ☎ *012/428–9111 reservations* ⊕ *www.
sanparks.org* ➲ *135 suites* ⑩ *No meals.*

$ ⚏ **Punda Maria.** It's worth visiting this lovely little camp in Kruger's far
RESORT   north, because it offers one of the park's best bush experiences. **Pros:**
very attractive camp; Kruger's best birding area. **Cons:** very far north;
game less abundant than the south. ⑤ *Rooms from: R1030* ⊠ *Punda
Maria Camp Rd., Kruger National Park* ☎ *012/428–9111 reservations*
⊕ *www.sanparks.org* ➲ *31 suites* ⑩ *No meals.*

$$$$ ⚏ **Rhino Post Plains Camp.** Overlooking a water hole amid an acacia
RESORT   knobthorn thicket deep in the heart of the Timbitene Plain, Plains Camp
has four comfortably furnished tents with wooden decks and great
views of the plains. **Pros:** right in the middle of Kruger; great game;
fabulous night drives when everyone else in the Kruger camps is con-
fined to barracks. **Cons:** surroundings a bit bleak, especially in winter;
not much privacy between tents. ⑤ *Rooms from: R7860* ⊠ *Off Marula
Loop, Kruger National Park* ☎ *035/474–1473* ⊕ *www.isibindiafrica.
co.za* ➲ *4 suites* ⑩ *All meals.*

$ ⚏ **Satara.** With some of the best guaranteed game viewing in Kruger
RESORT   (especially on the N'wanetsi River Road, also known as S100), this large
FAMILY   camp sits in the park's central section. **Pros:** good shop, restaurant, pool;
great guided sunset drives. **Cons:** early booking essential. ⑤ *Rooms
from: R1160* ⊠ *Kruger National Park* ☎ *012/428–9111 reservations*
⊕ *www.sanparks.org* ➲ *165 suites* ⑩ *No meals.*

$ ⚏ **Shingwedzi.** This attractive thatch-and-stone camp sits in northern
RESORT   Kruger beside the Shingwedzi River and near the Kanniedood (Never
FAMILY   Die) Dam. **Pros:** game-busy river road; in winter, gorgeous bright pink
impala lilies. **Cons:** some accommodations are grouped in a circle
around a big bare open space that affords little individual privacy.
⑤ *Rooms from: R1030* ⊠ *Kruger National Park* ☎ *012/428–9111 reservations* ⊕ *www.sanparks.org* ➲ *81 suites* ⑩ *No meals.*

$ ⚏ **Skukuza.** Skukuza is highly popular because it lies in an area teeming
RESORT   with game, including lions, cheetahs, and hyenas, and sits on a bank of
FAMILY   the crocodile-infested Sabie River, with good views of dozing hippos,
elephants, and grazing waterbuck. **Pros:** in middle of the park's best
game areas; great river location. **Cons:** usually crowded with regular
visitors and busloads of day-trippers. ⑤ *Rooms from: R1140* ⊠ *Kruger National Park* ☎ *012/428–9111 reservations* ⊕ *www.sanparks.org*
➲ *257 suites* ⑩ *No meals.*

$ ⚏ **Tamboti.** Kruger's first tented camp, close to the Orpen Gate, is
RESORT   superbly sited on the banks of the frequently dry Tamboti River, among
huge trees. **Pros:** great game. **Cons:** always fully occupied; shared bathrooms. ⑤ *Rooms from: R1240* ⊠ *Kruger National Park* ☎ *012/428–
9111 reservations* ⊕ *www.sanparks.org* ➲ *40 suites* ⑩ *No meals.*

BUSHVELD CAMPS

$ **Bateleur.** Hidden in the northern reaches of the park, this tiny camp,
RESORT the oldest of the bushveld camps, is one of Kruger's most remote destinations. **Pros:** private and intimate; guests see a lot at the camp's hide; no traffic jams. **Cons:** long distance to travel; there's a TV, which can be a pro or a con depending on your point of view. $ *Rooms from: R950* ⊠ *Kruger National Park* ☎ *012/428–9111 reservations* ⊕ *www. sanparks.org* ⌁ *7 suites* ¶⊙¶ *No meals.*

$ **Biyamiti.** Close to the park gate at Crocodile Bridge, this larger-than-
RESORT average, beautiful, sought-after bush camp overlooks the normally dry sands of the Biyamiti River. **Pros:** easily accessible; lots of game; variety of drives in area. **Cons:** difficult to book because of its popularity. $ *Rooms from: R1350* ⊠ *Biyamiti Camp Rd., Kruger National Park* ☎ *012/428–9111 reservations* ⊕ *www.sanparks.org* ⌁ *15 suites* ¶⊙¶ *No meals.*

$ **Shimuwini.** Birders descend in droves on this peaceful bushveld camp
RESORT set on a lovely dam on the Letaba River. **Pros:** lovely situation overlooking permanent lake. **Cons:** only one access road so coming and going gets monotonous; game can be sparse. $ *Rooms from: R1120* ⊠ *Shimuwini Camp Rd., Kruger National Park* ☎ *012/428–9111 reservations* ⊕ *www.sanparks.org* ⌁ *15 suites* ¶⊙¶ *No meals.*

$ **Sirheni.** Remote and lovely, Sirheni lies on the edge of the Sirheni
RESORT Dam in an isolated wilderness area in Kruger's far north. **Pros:** permanent waterhole; superb bird-watching. **Cons:** high malaria area; no electrical plug points; no cell-phone reception (which can be a pro or con). $ *Rooms from: R1120* ⊠ *Sirheni Camp Rd., Kruger National Park* ☎ *012/428–9111 reservations* ⊕ *www.sanparks.org* ⌁ *15 cottages* ¶⊙¶ *No meals.*

$ **Talamati.** On the banks of the normally dry N'waswitsontso River
RESORT in Kruger's central section, this peaceful camp in the middle of a wide, open valley has excellent game-viewing. **Pros:** peaceful; good plains game; couple of good picnic spots in vicinity; bigger camps near enough to stock up on supplies. **Cons:** a bit bland. $ *Rooms from: R1200* ⊠ *Talamati-camp Rd., Kruger National Park* ☎ *012/428–9111 reservations* ⊕ *www.sanparks.org* ⌁ *15 suites* ¶⊙¶ *No meals.*

9

SABI SAND GAME RESERVE

This is the most famous and exclusive of South Africa's private reserves. Collectively owned and managed, the 153,000-acre reserve near Kruger is home to dozens of private lodges, including the world-famous MalaMala and Londolozi. Sabi Sand fully deserves its exalted reputation, boasting perhaps the highest game density of any private reserve in southern Africa.

Although not all lodges own vast tracts of land, the majority have traversing rights over most of the reserve. With an average of 20 vehicles watching for game and communicating by radio, you're bound to see an enormous amount of game and almost certainly the Big Five, and since only three vehicles are allowed at a sighting at a time, you can be assured of a grandstand seat. Sabi Sand is the best area for leopard sightings. It's a memorable experience to see this beautiful, powerful, and often elusive cat padding purposefully through the bush at night, illuminated in your ranger's spotlight. There are many lion prides, and occasionally the increasingly rare wild dogs will migrate from Kruger to den in Sabi Sand. You'll also see white and black rhinos, zebras, giraffes, wildebeests, and most of the antelope species, plus birds galore.

The daily program at each lodge rarely deviates from a pattern, starting with tea, coffee, and muffins or rusks (Boer biscuits) before an early-morning game drive (usually starting at dawn, later in winter). You return to the lodge around 10 am, at which point you dine on an extensive hot breakfast or brunch. You can then choose to go on a bush walk with an armed ranger, where you learn about some of the minutiae of the bush (including the Little Five), although you could also happen on giraffes, antelopes, or any one of the Big Five. But don't worry—you'll be well briefed in advance on what you should do if you come face-to-face with, say, a lion. The rest of the day, until the late-afternoon game drive, is spent at leisure—reading up on the bush in the camp library, snoozing, swimming, or having a spa treatment. A sumptuous afternoon tea is served at 3:30 or 4 before you head back into the bush for your night drive. During the drive, your ranger will find a peaceful spot for sundowners (cocktails), and you can sip the drink of your choice and nibble snacks as you watch one of Africa's spectacular sunsets. As darkness falls, your ranger will switch on the spotlight so you can spy nocturnal animals: lions, leopards, jackals, porcupines, servals (small spotted cats like bonsai leopards), civets, and the enchanting little bush babies. You'll return to the lodge around 7:30, in time to freshen up before a three- or five-course dinner, with at least one dinner in a *boma* (open-air dining area) around a blazing fire. Often the camp staff entertains after dinner with local songs and dances—an unforgettable experience. Children under 12 aren't allowed at some of the camps; others have great kids' programs.

GETTING HERE AND AROUND

Kruger Mpumalanga International Airport (KMIA), at Mbombela (Nelspruit), Skukuza Airport, and Hoedspruit Airport, close to Kruger's Orpen Gate, serve Sabi Sand Reserve. You can also drive yourself to the reserve and park at your lodge. Most lodges offer charter flights to and from Johannesburg.

VISITOR INFORMATION

Contacts **Sabi Sand Reserve** ☎ 012/343–1991 ⊕ www.sabisand.co.za.

DJUMA PRIVATE GAME RESERVE

504 km (329 miles) from Johannesburg, via N12.

This 17,297-acre reserve sits right up against Kruger in the northeast corner of the world-famous Sabi Sand Reserve. Expect classic bushveld terrain—dams, rivers, ancient riverine trees, grassland, and plains. There are no fences separating Kruger from Sabi Sand, so game wanders freely back and forth, and no matter where you are in the Sabi Sand Reserve, you'll be treated to some of South Africa's best game-viewing.

Sabi Sand
Game Reserve

KEY

⚠ Camps

🏨 Lodges

✝ Hoedspruit Airstrip

⚠ Djuma Galago

⚠ Djuma Vuyatela

Sand River

🏨 Exeter River Lodge

Kirkman's Camp ⚠

🏨 Singita Ebony Lodge

Singita Boulders Lodge 🏨

🏨 Lodolozi Lodge and Camps

⚠ MalaMala Main Camp

⚠ MalaMala Sable Camp

⚠ Rattray's on MalaMala

Kruger National Park

Sabi Sands Game Reserve

Sand River

Newington ○

0 ___ 5 mi

0 ___ 5 km

🏨 Sabi Sabi Little Bush Camp Lodge

🏨 Sabi Sabi Bush Lodge

🏨 Sabi Sabi Earth Lodge

⚠ Sabi Sabi Selati Camp

Exeter Kirkman's Camp ⚠

🏨 Lion Sands Ivory Lodge & River Lodge

H1-2

Kruger Mpumalanga Airport ✝

Sabi River

Entrance ➤

✝ Paul Kruger Gate

○ Skukuza

Djuma is no exception. The Big Five are all here, plus hundreds of birds. The reserve's rangers are famous for their dedication and knowledge, which they share in a friendly, very informal way.

GETTING HERE AND AROUND

From Johannesburg it's approximately a seven-hour drive north to Hoedspruit via Dullstroom, Ohrigstad. and through the JG Strydom tunnel. Take the R531 to Klaserie and Acornhoek and follow the signs to Sabi Sand, Gowrie Gate. Djuma is signposted from there. You will drive yourself to the camp, and then go on safari in open game vehicles.

There are daily scheduled flights from Johannesburg to Skukuza Airport and Hoedspruit Airport, on SA Express, and Kruger Mpumalanga International Airport on SA Airlink (lodge transfers can be arranged), or you can fly in directly to one of the Sabi Sand airstrips by Fedair charter flight.

EXPLORING

FAMILY **Djuma Private Game Reserve.** Shangaan for "roar of the lion," Djuma is in the northeast corner of the Sabi Sands Game Reserve. Your hosts are husband-and-wife team Jurie and Pippa Moolman, who are passionate about their work (Jurie has a B.S. in ecology). Although there's a good chance of seeing the Big Five during the bush walk after breakfast and the twice-daily game drives, Djuma also caters to those with special bushveld interests, such as bird-watching or tree identification. Djuma's rangers and trackers are also adept at finding seldom-seen animals, such as wild dogs, spotted hyenas, and genets. You'll find none of the formality that sometimes prevails at the larger lodges. For example, members of the staff eat all meals with you and join you around the nighttime fire. In fact, Djuma prides itself on its personal service and feeling of intimacy. ✉ *Sabi Sand Game Reserve* ☎ *013/735–5555 reservations* ⊕ *www.djuma.com* ↪ *Vuyatela: 5 suites; Galago 5 rooms* ⦿ *No meals.*

WHERE TO STAY

$$$$
RESORT

⛺ **Cheetah Plains Private Game Reserve and lodge.** This delightfully unpretentious lodge, one of the oldest in Sabi Sand, is set among huge trees on the banks of an attractive dam that is a magnet for game—particularly elephants. **Pros:** more affordable than many other Sabi Sand lodges. **Cons:** cottages are small. ⑤ *Rooms from: R6990* ✉ *Sabi Sand Game Reserve* ☎ *079/694–8430 lodge, 083/419–1334 reservations* ⊕ *www. cheetahplains.com* ↪ *9 suites* ⦿ *All meals.*

$$
RESORT

⛺ **Galago.** A delightful and affordable alternative to other upscale lodges, Galago, which means "lesser bush baby" in Shangaan, is a converted U-shape farmhouse whose five rooms form an arc around a central fireplace. **Pros:** real value for money. **Cons:** hire a cook or you'll spend your time working. ⑤ *Rooms from: R2300* ✉ *Djuma Private Game Reserve, Sabi Sand Game Reserve* ☎ *013/735–5555 reservations* ⊕ *www.djuma.com* ↪ *5 rooms* ⦿ *No meals.*

$$$
RESORT
FAMILY

⛺ **Vuyatela.** Djuma's vibey, most upscale camp mixes contemporary African township culture with modern Shangaan culture, making it very different from most of the other private camps. **Pros:** amazing African art; legendary hosts; trips to authentic villages. **Cons:** funky township style (corrugated iron, recycled metals, in-your-face glitzy township feel) may not be to everyone's taste. ⑤ *Rooms from: R2900* ✉ *Djuma Private Game Reserve, Sabi Sand Game Reserve* ☎ *013/735–5555 reservations, 013/735–5118 lodge* ⊕ *www.djuma.com* ↪ *5 suites* ⦿ *No meals.*

LION SANDS PRIVATE GAME RESERVE

458 km (284 miles) from Johannesburg.

Situated along the Sabie River, this reserve has one of the best locations in the Sabi Sand Game Reserve. All of the lodges overlook the river, which is a magnet for all kinds of game. You'll be able to peer into Kruger Park, on the other side of the river, and watch game meander along the riverbanks among big riverine trees. You may never want to leave your personal deck, or the big viewing decks even for an exciting game drive or guided walk, because you're bound to spot animals, birds and crocs from camp.

Speaking of camp, Ivory Lodge is the ultimate luxury lodge, with guaranteed privacy. But, there's also the friendly River Lodge; the once-in-a-lifetime Narina Lodge, perched in a treetop canopy; the spacious Tinga Lodge, sited in Kruger Park itself; or the exclusive 1933 African legacy family lodge.

GETTING HERE AND AROUND

If you're coming by car from Hazyview, turn right onto the R536 toward Paul Kruger Gate (Kruger National Park). After 38 km (23 miles), turn left onto a gravel road signposted to Lion Sands, Sabi Sand. At the T-junction, turn right and enter Sabi Sand through Shaw's Gate. Then follow directions to the lodges. There's a vehicle entrance fee of R190 plus R50 per person into the Sabi Sand Reserve, payable on arrival by cash or credit card. The gates close at 10 pm. You can drive yourself to the lodges, but you'll have to park your car and leave it, because while you're at the lodge, you'll be driven around in an open game vehicle.

There are daily scheduled flights from Johannesburg, Durban, and Cape Town to Skukuza Airport and Kruger Mpumalanga International Airport on SA Airlink. Lodge transfers can be arranged.

EXPLORING

Fodor's Choice ★ **Lion Sands Private Game Reserve.** Separated from Kruger National Park by the Sabie River, the reserve has been owned and operated by the More family for four generations. Purchased in 1933 as a family retreat, it was opened to the public in 1978 with two lodges and 10,000 acres of undisturbed wildlife that's available only to its guests. Accommodations range from the ultraluxe Ivory Lodge to the more economical River Lodge, and then there's the once-in-a-lifetime Chalkley Treehouse (yes, it really is a bed on a platform in a tree, but it's nothing like the tree house in your backyard), or the 1933 Lodge, the More family's vacation home that's perfect for larger groups and comes complete with personal chef, guide, pool, gym, and wine cellar. The family is so committed to keeping the reserve as close to its original state as possible that they employ a full-time ecologist, the only reserve in the Sabi Sand group to do so. ⊠ *Lion Sands Private Game Reserve, Sabi Sand Game Reserve* ☎ *013/735–5330* ⊕ *www.lionsands.com* ¶⊙¶ *All meals.*

WHERE TO STAY

$$$$ RESORT **Fodor's Choice** ★ **Lion Sands Ivory Lodge.** Ivory Lodge offers the ultimate in luxury, privacy, and relaxation. **Pros:** exclusivity; great views; brilliant game-viewing. **Cons:** the temptation of abundant great food; it's so decadent, you might forget to leave. ⑤ *Rooms from: R32950* ⊠ *Lion Sands Private Game Reserve, Sabi Sand Game Reserve* ☎ *031/735–5330* ⊕ *www.lionsands.com* ↩ *6 suites* ¶⊙¶ *All meals* ↩ *No children under 12 years old.*

$$$$ RESORT **Lion Sands River Lodge.** Set on one of the longest and best stretches of river frontage in Sabi Sand, you can watch the passing animal and bird show from your deck or from the huge, tree-shaded, wooden viewing area that juts out over the riverbank facing Kruger National Park. **Pros:** fabulous river frontage; well managed. **Cons:** some chalets quite close together so not much privacy. ⑤ *Rooms from: R17560* ⊠ *Lion Sands Private Game Reserve, Sabi Sand Game Reserve* ☎ *013/735–5330* ⊕ *www.lionsands.com* ↩ *20 rooms* ¶⊙¶ *All meals* ↩ *No children under 10 years old.*

9

LONDOLOZI GAME RESERVE

471 km (292 miles) from Johannesburg.

Since its inception in 1974 (it was a family farm and retreat before that), Londolozi has become synonymous with South Africa's finest game lodges and game experiences. (*Londolozi* is the Zulu word for "protector of all living things.") Brother-and-sister Bronwyn and Boyd Varty, the third generation of the Varty family, are now in charge with a mission to reconnect the human spirit with the wilderness and to carry on their family's quest to honor the animal kingdom. The Big Five are all here, as are the world-famous leopards of Londolozi. (You are guaranteed to see at least one.) There are five camps, each representing a different element in nature: Pioneer Camp (water), Tree Camp (wood), Granite Suites (rock), Varty Camp (fire), and Founders Camp (earth). Each is totally private, hidden in dense riverine forest on the banks of the Sand River. The Varty family live on the property, and their friendliness and personal attention, along with the many staff who have been here for decades, will make you feel part of the family immediately. The central reception and curio shop are at Varty Camp.

GETTING HERE AND AROUND

Londolozi is an easy six-hour drive from Johannesburg on the NM12 and N4. Turn right onto R536 from Hazyview toward Paul Kruger Gate. After 37.4 km (23 miles) turn left onto a gravel road signposted "Sabi Sand Wildtuin Shaw's Gate."

There are daily scheduled flights from Johannesburg, Durban, and Cape Town to Skukuza Airport and Kruger Mpumalanga International Airport on SA Airlink (lodge transfers can be arranged), or you can fly in directly to the Londolozi airstrip by Fedair charter flight.

EXPLORING

Fodor's Choice
★

Londolozi Game Reserve. Formerly a family farm and retreat since 1926, Londolozi today is synonymous with South Africa's finest game lodges and game experiences. (*Londolozi* is the Zulu word for "protector of all living things.") Dave and John Varty, grandsons of the original owner, Charles Varty, put the reserve on the map with glamorous marketing and a vision of style and comfort that grandfather Charles could never have imagined. Now younger generation, brother-and-sister team Bronwyn and Boyd Varty, are carrying on their family's quest to honor the animal kingdom. Game abounds; the Big Five are all here, and the leopards of Londolozi are world famous. There are five camps, each representing a different element in nature: Pioneer Camp (water), Tree Camp (wood), Granite Suites (rock), Varty Camp (fire), and Founders Camp (earth). ⊠ *Londolozi Reserve, Sabi Sand Game Reserve* ☎ *011/280-6655 reservations* ⊕ *www.londolozi.com* ⏉ *All meals.*

WHERE TO STAY

$$$$
ALL-INCLUSIVE
FAMILY

Founders Camp. This recently refurbished, inviting camp has 10 stone-and-thatch suites in individual chalets set amid thick riverine bush; some chalets are linked by interconnecting skywalks, which is great for families or groups traveling together. **Pros:** quick, safe access between family rooms; children over 4 welcome. **Cons:** lodges are in quite close proximity to one another. $ *Rooms from: R20900* ✉ *Londolozi Reserve, Sabi Sand Game Reserve* ☎ *011/280–6655* ⊕ *www.londolozi. com* ⤺ *10 suites* ❘❍❘ *All-inclusive.*

$$$$
ALL-INCLUSIVE

🖼 **Granite Suites.** Book all three private suites or just hide yourself away from the rest of the world like the celebrities and royals who favor this gorgeous getaway. **Pros:** one of the best locations in Sabi Sand with truly stunning views; the candelit dinner; Londolozi's unique on-site photographic studio and its user-friendly services. **Cons:** pricey. $ *Rooms from: R32700* ✉ *Londolozi Reserve, Sabi Sand Game Reserve* ☎ *011/280–6655* ⊕ *www.londolozi.com* ⤺ *3 suites* ❘❍❘ *All-inclusive* ⌒ *No children under 16 years old.*

$$$$
ALL-INCLUSIVE

🖼 **Pioneer Camp.** The most secluded of all of Londolozi's camps, Pioneer's three private suites overlook the river and are perfect for getting away from others. **Pros:** authentic romantic-safari atmosphere; only three suites; intimate atmosphere. **Cons:** with only three suites it's best if you know all other guests. $ *Rooms from: R30700* ✉ *Londolozi Reserve, Sabi Sand Game Reserve* ☎ *011/280–6655 reservations* ⊕ *www.londolozi.com* ⤺ *3 suites* ❘❍❘ *All-inclusive* ⌒ *No children under 12 years old.*

$$$$
ALL-INCLUSIVE
Fodor's Choice
★

🖼 **Tree Camp.** The first Relais & Chateaux game lodge in the world, this gorgeous camp (think leopards, lanterns, leadwoods, and leopard orchids) is tucked into the riverbank overlooking indigenous forest. **Pros:** the viewing deck; state-of-the-art designer interiors. **Cons:** stylishness nudges out coziness. $ *Rooms from: R28700* ✉ *Londolozi Reserve, Sabi Sand Game Reserve* ☎ *011/280–6655 reservations* ⊕ *www.londolozi.com* ⤺ *6 suites* ❘❍❘ *All-inclusive.*

$$$$
ALL-INCLUSIVE
FAMILY

🖼 **Varty Camp.** This camp's fire has been burning for more than eight decades, making Varty Camp the very soul and center of Londolozi. **Pros:** friendly atmosphere; great game; all chalets are interleading. **Cons:** lots of kids might not be for you. $ *Rooms from: R17900* ✉ *Londolozi Reserve, Sabi Sand Game Reserve* ☎ *011/280–6655 reservations* ⊕ *www.londolozi.com* ⤺ *10 suites* ❘❍❘ *All-inclusive.*

9

MALAMALA GAME RESERVE

455 km (283 miles) from Johannesburg.

This legendary game reserve (designated as such in 1929) is tops in its field. The first and only community-owned game reserve in Sabi Sand, it continues to be managed by the legendary Rattray family in partnership with the N'wandlamharhi Community. It's the largest privately owned Big Five game area in South Africa, and includes an unfenced 30-km (19-mile) boundary with Kruger National Park, across which game crosses continuously. The variety of habitats range from riverine bush, favorite hiding place of the leopard, to open grasslands, where cheetahs hunt.

You'll be delighted with incomparable personal service, superb food, and discreetly elegant, comfortable accommodations, where you'll rub shoulders with statesmen and stateswomen, aristocrats, celebrities, and returning visitors alike. Mike Rattray, a legend in his own time in South Africa's game-lodge industry, describes MalaMala as "a camp in the bush," but it's certainly more than that, although it still retains that genuine bushveld feel of bygone days. Both the outstanding hospitality and the game-viewing experience keep guests coming back.

MalaMala's animal-viewing statistics are impressive: the Big Five are spotted almost every day. At one moment your well-educated, friendly, articulate ranger will fascinate you with the description of the sex life of a dung beetle, as you watch the sturdy male battling his way along the road pushing his perfectly round ball of dung with wife-to-be perched perilously on top; at another, your adrenaline will flow as you follow a leopard stalking impala in the gathering gloom. Along with the local Shangaan trackers, whose eyesight rivals that of the animals they are tracking, the top-class rangers ensure that your game experience is unforgettable.

GETTING HERE AND AROUND

MalaMala Game Reserve is approximately a six-hour drive from Johannesburg via N12 and N4. From Hazyview, take the R536 toward Skukuza and the Paul Kruger Gate. Turn left at the MalaMala Game Reserve sign onto a gravel road and follow lodge signs. There are daily scheduled flights from Johannesburg, Durban, and Cape Town to Skukuza Airport and Kruger Mpumalanga International Airport on SA Airlink (lodge transfers can be arranged), or you can fly in directly to the MalaMala airstrip by Fedair charter flight.

EXPLORING

Fodor's Choice
★

MalaMala Private Game Reserve. This legendary game reserve (designated as such in 1929), is tops in its field. The first and only community-owned game reserve in Sabi Sand, it continues to be managed by the legendary Rattray family in partnership with the N'wandlamharhi Community. Expect incomparable personal service, superb food, and discreetly elegant, comfortable accommodations where you'll rub shoulders with aristocrats, celebrities, and returning visitors alike. It retains the genuine bushveld feel of bygone days, and its outstanding hospitality and the game-viewing experience keep guests coming back. MalaMala constitutes the largest privately owned Big Five game area in South Africa and includes an unfenced 30-km (19-miles) boundary with Kruger National Park, across which game crosses continuously. MalaMala's animal-viewing statistics are almost unbelievable: the Big Five are spotted almost every day. ⊠ *Mala Mala Game Reserve, Sabi Sand Game Reserve* ☎ *011/442–2267 reservations* ⊕ *www.malamala. com* ⊙ *All meals.*

WHERE TO STAY

$$$$
ALL-INCLUSIVE
FAMILY

⬚ **Main Camp.** Stone and thatch air-conditioned rondavels with separate his-and-her bathrooms are decorated in creams and browns and furnished with cane armchairs, colorful handwoven tapestries and rugs, terra-cotta floors, and original artwork. **Pros:** authentic; sweeping wilderness views, amazing game viewing. **Cons:** rondavels are a bit old-fashioned, but that goes with the ambience. ⑤ *Rooms from: US$1480* ⊠ *Mala Mala Game Reserve, Sabi Sand Game Reserve* ☎ *011/442–2267 reservations, 013/735–9200 lodge* ⊕ *www.malamala.com* ⤢ *8 suites, 9 rooms* ⊙ *All-inclusive.*

$$$$
ALL-INCLUSIVE
Fodor\$Choice
★

MalaMala Sable Camp. This fully air-conditioned, exclusive camp with six ultraluxurious suites lies at the southern end of Main Camp and overlooks the Sand River and surrounding bushveld. **Pros:** small and intimate; privacy guaranteed; unparalleled game-viewing. **Cons:** you might like it so much you never want to leave. $ *Rooms from: US$1700* ⊠ *Mala Mala Game Reserve, Sabi Sand Game Reserve* ☎ *011/442– 2267 reservations* ⊕ *www.malamala.com* ⇌ *6 suites* ⦿ *All-inclusive.*

$$$$
ALL-INCLUSIVE
Fodor\$Choice
★

Rattray's on MalaMala. The breathtakingly beautiful Rattray's merges original bushveld style with daring contemporary ideas. **Pros:** superb game-viewing; tantalizing views over the river. **Cons:** Tuscan villas in the bush may not be your idea of Africa; though this may be a pro for some, no children under 16. $ *Rooms from: US$2050* ⊠ *Mala Mala Game Reserve, Sabi Sand Game Reserve* ☎ *011/442–2267 reservations, 013/735–3000 lodge* ✉ *reception@rattrayscamp.co.za* ⊕ *www. malamala.com* ⇌ *8 suites* ⦿ *All-inclusive.*

SABI SABI PRIVATE GAME RESERVE

500 km (310 miles) from Johannesburg.

Founded in 1978 at the southern end of Sabi Sand, the multi-award-winning Sabi Sabi Game Reserve was one of the first reserves to offer photo safaris and to link ecotourism, conservation, and community. Superb accommodations and abundant game lure guests back to Sabi Sabi in large numbers.

GETTING HERE AND AROUND

Sabi Sabi is an easy six-hour drive from Johannesburg on the N4 and N12. Turn right onto R536 from Hazyview toward Paul Kruger Gate. After 37.4 km (23 miles) turn left onto a gravel road signposted "Sabi Sand Wildtuin Shaw's Gate." There are daily scheduled flights from Johannesburg, Durban, and Cape Town to Skukuza Airport and Kruger Mpumalanga International Airport on SA Airlink (lodge transfers can be arranged), or you can fly in directly to a Sabi Sand airstrip by Fedair charter flight.

EXPLORING

Fodor\$Choice
★

Sabi Sabi Private Game Reserve. There's a strong emphasis on ecology at Sabi Sabi: guests are encouraged to look beyond the Big Five and to become aware of the birds and smaller mammals of the bush. There are four very different lodges, each individually remarkable: Bush Lodge, famous for its friendly hospitality and ever-busy water hole; Little Bush Lodge, an intimate, back-to-nature tented camp; Selati, haunt of celebs and royalty, themed on an old Kruger Park railway line; and the daringly innovative Earth Lodge. ⊠ *Sabi Sand Game Reserve* ☎ *011/447– 7172 reservations* ⊕ *www.sabisabi.com* ⦿ *All meals.*

WHERE TO STAY

$$$$
RESORT
FAMILY

Little Bush Camp. Sabi Sabi's delightful little camp is tucked away in the bushveld on the banks of the Msuthlu River and combines spaciousness with a sense of intimacy. **Pros:** perfect for families. **Cons:** there may be other families. $ *Rooms from: R19400* ⊠ *Sabi Sabi Private*

9

Game Reserve, Sabi Sand Game Reserve ☎ *011/447–7172 reservations, 013/735–5080 lodge* ⊕ *www.sabisabi.com* ⇥ *6 suites* ⦿ *All meals.*

$$$$ 🛏 **Sabi Sabi's Bush Lodge.** Bush Lodge overlooks a busy water hole
RESORT (lions are frequent visitors) and the dry course of the Msuthlu River.
FAMILY **Pros:** always prolific game around the lodge; roomy chalets. **Cons:** big
and busy might not be your idea of relaxing getaway. **$** *Rooms from:
R19400* ⊠ *Sabi Sabi Private Game Reserve, Sabi Sand Game Reserve*
☎ *013/735–5656 lodge* ⊕ *www.sabisabi.com* ⇥ *25 suites* ⦿ *All meals.*

$$$$ 🛏 **Sabi Sabi's Earth Lodge.** This avant-garde, eco-friendly lodge was the
ALL-INCLUSIVE first to break away from the traditional safari style and strive for a contemporary theme. **Pros:** stunning architecture and design. **Cons:** if you
favor traditional safari accommodation, this is not for you. **$** *Rooms
from: R25400* ⊠ *Sabi Sabi Private Game Reserve, Sabi Sand Game
Reserve* ☎ *013/735–5261 lodge* ⊕ *www.sabisabi.com* ⇥ *13 suites*
⦿ *All-inclusive.*

$$$$ 🛏 **Sabi Sabi Selati Camp.** For an *Out of Africa* experience and great game,
RESORT you can't beat Selati, an intimate, stylish, colonial-style camp that was
Fodor's Choice formerly the private hunting lodge of a famous South African opera
★ singer. **Pros:** unique atmosphere; Ivory Presidential Suite superb value
for money; secluded and intimate. **Cons:** some old-timers preferred the
camp when it was just lantern-lit with no electricity. **$** *Rooms from:
R19400* ⊠ *Sabi Sabi Private Game Reserve, Sabi Sand Game Reserve*
☎ *011/447–7172 reservations, 013/735–5771 lodge* ⊕ *www.sabisabi.
com* ⇥ *8 suites* ⦿ *All meals.*

SINGITA

450 km (279 miles) from Johannesburg.

Although Singita (Shangaan for "the miracle") offers much the same
thrilling Sabi Sand bush and game experiences as other lodges, superb
service really puts it head and shoulders above many of the rest of the
herd.

GETTING HERE AND AROUND

Singita is an easy 6½-hour drive from Johannesburg on the N4 and
N12. Turn right onto R536 from Hazyview toward Paul Kruger Gate.
After 37.4 km (23 miles), turn left at the sign that reads "Sabi Sand
Wildtuin Shaw's Gate" onto a gravel road. Follow the signs for Singita.
Singita will arrange scheduled flights or private charters for your trip.
All flights land at Singita's airstrip, 10 minutes from the lodge.

EXPLORING

Fodor's Choice **Singita Sabi Sand.** Expect low-key opulence, a comforting organic atmo-
★ sphere, truly spacious accommodations, superb food and wine with a
resident sommelier (wine can be shipped home), and a variety of public
spaces—little private dining nooks to a huge viewing deck built round
an ancient jackalberry tree, comfortable library with TV and Internet,
and an attractive poolside bar—really do put this gorgeous lodge head
and shoulders above the rest of the herd. Whether you fancy a starlit
private supper, a riverside breakfast, a bike ride though the bush, or
just chilling alone in your megasuite, you've only to ask. Forget the
usual lodge curio shop and take a ride to the on-site Trading Post

where objets d'art, handmade jewelry, classy bush gear, and artifacts from all over Africa are clustered together in a series of adjoiing rooms that seem more like someone's home than a shop. ⊠ *Singita Sabi Sand, Sabi Sand Game Reserve* ☎ *021/683–3424 reservations* ⊕ *www.singita. co.za* ⊠ *All meals.*

WHERE TO STAY

$$$$
ALL-INCLUSIVE
Fodor's Choice
★

🛏 **Boulders Lodge.** Expect traditional Africa at its most luxurious. **Pros:** spacious accommodation; superb food. **Cons:** a bit of a walk from the suites to the main lodge; refuse the crackling log fire if you're at all congested. ⑤ *Rooms from: R34600* ⊠ *Singita Sabi Sand, Sabi Sand Game Reserve* ☎ *021/683–3424 reservations, 013/735–9800 lodge* ⊕ *www. singita.co.za* ⊅ *12 suites* ⊠ *All-inclusive.*

$$$$
ALL-INCLUSIVE

🛏 **Ebony Lodge.** If Ernest Hemingway had built his ideal home in the African bush, this would be it. **Pros:** the mother lodge of all the Singita properties; cozy library. **Cons:** the beds are very high off the ground— if you've short legs or creak a bit, ask for a stool. ⑤ *Rooms from: R34600* ⊠ *Singita Sabi Sand, Sabi Sand Game Reserve* ☎ *021/683– 3424 reservations, 013/735–9800 lodge* ⊕ *www.singita.co.za* ⊅ *9 suites* ⊠ *All-inclusive.*

EXETER PRIVATE GAME RESERVE

500 km (310 miles) from Johannesburg.

Established in 1937, Exeter, at 160,600 acres, was an original part of Sabi Sands when it was incorporated in the 1960s. Its lodges are now operated by @Beyond.

GETTING HERE AND AROUND

Exeter is about a five- to six-hour drive from Johannesburg. Charter flights from Johannesburg land at the Ulusaba Airstrip, which is near the reserve's lodges. Transfers can also be arranged from other nearby airports with regular flights. The lodges generally arrange your transportation.

WHERE TO STAY

$$$$
ALL-INCLUSIVE
Fodor's Choice
★

🛏 **Exeter River Lodge.** One of Sabi Sand's oldest lodges, Exeter scores 10 out of 10 for its gorgeous location—one of the best in the whole reserve—with lush green lawns sweeping down to the Sabi River. **Pros:** more affordable than many of its neighbors; genuine African-bush ambience. **Cons:** no triple rooms for guests with children. ⑤ *Rooms from: R16170* ⊠ *Exeter Private Game Reserve, Sabi Sand Game Reserve* ☎ *011/809–4300 reservations* ⊕ *www.andbeyond.com* ⊅ *8 suites* ⊠ *All-inclusive.*

$$$$
ALL-INCLUSIVE
FAMILY

🛏 **Kirkman's Kamp.** You'll feel as if you've stepped back in time at this camp because rooms are strategically clustered around the original 1920s homestead, which, with its colonial furniture, historic memorabilia, and wrap-around veranda, makes you feel like a family guest the moment you arrive. **Pros:** superb game-viewing. **Cons:** gets tour groups; more of a hotel feel than other lodges. ⑤ *Rooms from: R13200* ⊠ *Exeter Private Game Reserve, Sabi Sand Game Reserve* ☎ *011/809–4300 reservations* ⊕ *www.andbeyond.com* ⊅ *18 suites* ⊠ *All-inclusive.*

9

WEST OF KRUGER

Manyeleti, Timbavati, Thornybush, and Kapama, along with a couple of other smaller game reserves, all lie north of Sabi Sand Game Reserve, but also border Kruger's western boundary. Although the reserves are less well known, they offer much the same game experiences, often at more affordable prices. The best-known ones are Manyeleti and Timbavati with lovely lodges set among typical bushveld, both adjoining Kruger, so you stand a good chance of seeing the Big Five and lots more. A big bonus is that because they are less frequently visited and have fewer lodges than Sabi Sand, there are fewer people and fewer vehicles. Some lodges have no electricity, so no email or Internet, but this will free you from the pressures of everyday life.

MANYELETI GAME RESERVE

502 km (311 miles) from Johannesburg.

North of Sabi Sand, Manyeleti Private Game Reserve ("the place of the stars" in Shangaan) covers 59,280 acres that border Kruger, Sabi Sand, and Timbavati, but it's something of a Cinderella reserve compared with its more famous neighbors. Away from the major tourist areas, it's amazingly underused; you'll probably see very few vehicles while you're here.

GETTING HERE AND AROUND

Travel north from Johannesburg on the N12 to Ohrigstad and continue toward Hoedspruit via the Abel Erasmus Pass and the JG Strijdom Tunnel. Cross the Blyde River, and turn right at the R531 to the Orpen Gate sign. Turn left here and continue until you see the Manyeleti Reserve sign.

There are daily scheduled flights from Johannesburg to Hoedspruit Airport by SA Express. There are also daily scheduled flights from Johannesburg, Durban, and Cape Town to Skukuza Airport and Kruger Mpumalanga International Airport on SA Airlink (lodge transfers can be arranged).

EXPLORING

Manyeleti Game Reserve. The park's grassy plains and mixed woodland attract good-size herds of general game and their attendant predators. You have a strong chance of seeing the Big Five, but the Manyeleti lodges and tented camps, which are owned and operated by two separate companies (one for the lodge, one for the tented camps), focus more on providing an overall bush experience than simply rushing after big game. You'll learn about trees, birds, and bushveld ecosystems as you go on guided bush walks. ☒ *Manyeleti Game Reserve* ⊕ *www.manyeleti.com.*

WHERE TO STAY

$$$$ ⌨ **Khoka Moya.** This delightful, value-priced camp owned and operated
RESORT by Honeyguide is situated on both sides of a riverbed within Manyeleti
FAMILY Game Reserve. **Pros:** excellent value for money; great kids' programs.
Cons: no a/c; usually lots of kids around so if you aren't childproof, stay

away. $ *Rooms from: R8000* ✉ *Manyeleti Game Reserve* ☎ *021/424–3122 reservations* ✇ *cres@albatros.co.za* ⊕ *www.honeyguidecamp.com* ⇱ *12 suites* ⦿ *All meals.*

$$$$
RESORT
🛖 **Mantobeni.** This tented camp, built on wooden platforms, minimalist but with surprising luxury touches (owned and operated by Honey Guide within Manyeleti Game Reserve), gives you the total bush experience at half the price of some of the more upscale lodges. **Pros:** superb value for money; complimentary bar and well-stocked wine cellar; can watch ellies from the pool deck. **Cons:** canvas structure may not be to everyone's taste; very comfortable but far from five star. $ *Rooms from: R8000* ✉ *Manyeleti Game Reserve* ☎ *021/424–3122 reservations* ✇ *cres@albatros.co.za* ⊕ *www.honeyguidecamp.com* ⇱ *12 suites* ⦿ *All meals.*

$$$$
ALL-INCLUSIVE
🛖 **Tintswalo Safari Lodge.** This gorgeous ultraluxurious lodge, sited under huge jackalberry and fig trees, overlooks a seasonal river, where game come down to drink and bathe. **Pros:** drop-dead luxury; kids' program on request; suites overlook water hole. **Cons:** potentially overattentive staff. $ *Rooms from: R13960* ✉ *Manyeleti Game Reserve* ☎ *011/300–8888 reservations* ⊕ *www.tintswalo.com* ⇱ *7 suites* ⦿ *All-inclusive.*

TIMBAVATI GAME RESERVE

515 km (320 miles) from Johannesburg.

The 185,000-acre Timbavati, the northernmost of the private reserves, is collectively owned and managed by the Timbavati Association, a non-profit organization that strives to conserve the biodiversity of the area.

GETTING HERE AND AROUND

Travel north from Johannesburg on the N12 to Ohrigstad and continue toward Hoedspruit via the Abel Erasmus Pass and the J G Strijdom Tunnel. Drive through Hoedspruit and take the R40 to Klaserie. Turn left at the Timbavati/East Gate signs. Go through the security gate, and drive straight for 17 km (10.5 miles), cross the Klaserie River, and enter through the Timbavati Control Gate. Roads can be rough in the reserve, particularly in the rainy season, so a 4x4 is recommended.

There are daily scheduled flights from Johannesburg to Hoedspruit Airport by SA Express. There are also daily scheduled flights from Johannesburg, Durban, and Cape Town to Skukuza Airport and Kruger Mpumalanga International Airport on SA Airlink (lodge transfers can be arranged).

EXPLORING

Ngala. *Ngala* means "the place of the lion" and certainly lives up to its name. This private concession within Timbavati but adjacent to Kruger has wall-to-wall game, and you'll almost certainly see the King of Beasts as well as leopards, rhinos, elephants, and buffalo, among others. Ngala lies in Timbavati's mopane shrubveld, and its main advantage over Sabi Sand is its proximity to four major ecozones—mopane shrubveld, marula combretum, acacia shrub, and riverine forest—which provide habitats for a wide range of animals. Ngala welcomes kids and puts on a range of activities for them with rangers, trackers, and general

9

staff who are specially trained to look after children and their needs. After the morning game drive, kids are whisked away to go on a bug hunt, visit a local village, or bake cookies. ⊠ *Timbavati Game Reserve* ☎ *011/809–4300 reservations* ⊕ *www.andBeyond.com* |◎| *Some meals.*

Timbavati Game Reserve. Timbavati, a collectively managed private reserve, is home to more than 40 mammal species, including the Big Five, and more than 360 species of birds. It's famed for its rare white lions; if you miss them here, you can see more at the National Zoological Gardens in Tshwane. Timbavati also has a large population of "regular" lions, and there's a good chance of finding leopards, elephants, buffalo, and spotted hyenas. Rhinos are scarcer, however, but you might get lucky and see wild dogs, as they migrate regularly to this region from Kruger. ⊠ *Timbavati Game Reserve* ⊕ *www.timbavatigamereserve. co.za.*

WHERE TO STAY

$$$$
ALL-INCLUSIVE
FAMILY

📷 **Ngala Safari Lodge.** Guests return again and again to this classic safari lodge with its timeless Out of Africa ambience. **Pros:** great kids' programs; superb game and a bird-watcher's paradise. **Cons:** always busy; kids dine with adults. ⑤ *Rooms from: R10130* ⊠ *Timbavati Game Reserve* ☎ *011/809–4300 reservations* ⊕ *www.andBeyond.com* ⇨ *20 rooms, 1 suite* |◎| *All-inclusive.*

$$$$
ALL-INCLUSIVE
Fodor's Choice
★

📷 **Ngala Tented Safari Camp.** Marula seeds softly falling on the tents seem to be applauding this gorgeous little camp shaded by a canopy of giant trees. **Pros:** exclusivity. **Cons:** if you're nervous of too-close game, this is not for you, as hippos (and other game) wander freely around the tents; no a/c. ⑤ *Rooms from: R33000* ⊠ *Timbavati Game Reserve* ☎ *011/809–4300 reservations* ⊕ *www.andBeyond.com* ⇨ *6 suites* |◎| *All-inclusive.*

$$$$
ALL-INCLUSIVE

📷 **Tanda Tula Safari Camp.** Tanda Tula has a well-deserved reputation as one of the best bush camps in Mpumalanga. **Pros:** emphasis on the whole bush experience, not just the Big Five; moonlit bush barbeques. **Cons:** if you don't like being under canvas, stay away; no a/c. ⑤ *Rooms from: R11200* ⊠ *Timbavati Game Reserve* ☎ *015/793–3191* ⊕ *www. tandatula.com* ⇨ *13 suites* |◎| *All-inclusive.*

THORNYBUSH NATURE RESERVE

504 km (313 miles) from Johannesburg.

Situated within 34,594 acres of pristine wilderness, adjacent to the Greater Kruger National Park in Limpopo, Thornybush Nature Reserve is set among classic bushveld scenery. There are nine comfortable, unpretentious lodges offering friendly service, excellent food, and great game. Thornybush was the first lowveld reserve to implement rhino horn treatments (injecting poison that is harmless to the rhinos) as a form of anti-poaching (some disproven but popular traditional Asian medical treatments use rhino horn), and one of the first to introduce elephant contraception as an alternative to culling.

GETTING HERE AND AROUND

Take the R40 from Hazyview to Acornhoek. Turn right after 7.4 km (4.6 miles) and take the Guernsey turnoff. Check in at the security gate, drive approximately 11 km (6.8 miles), and turn left at the T-junction. You'll find the Thornybush Nature Reserve Gate on your right after approximately 4 km (2.5 miles). There are daily scheduled flights from Johannesburg to Hoedspruit Airport by SA Express. There are also daily scheduled flights from Johannesburg, Durban, and Cape Town to Skukuza Airport and Kruger Mpumalanga International Airport on SA Airlink (lodge transfers can be arranged).

WHERE TO STAY

$$$$
RESORT
FAMILY

☷ **Jackalberry Lodge.** This lodge offers understated luxury, excellent food, superb guiding, and the Big Five at half the price of some of the better-known lodges. **Pros:** excellent value for money; very friendly staff and super-knowledgeable rangers. **Cons:** no children under six on game drives (babysitters available, however); game not quite as prolific as Sabi Sand and Timbavati. ⑤ *Rooms from: R7932* ✉ *Thornybush Game Reserve, Limpopo* ☎ *011/253–6500 reservations* ✐ *sales@thornybush. co.za* ⊕ *www.jackalberrylodge.co.za* ⇄ *8 rooms* ⑩ *All meals.*

KAPAMA PRIVATE GAME RESERVE

481 km (315 miles) from Johannesburg on N4 and R36.

The 32,123-acre Kapama Private Game Reserve, the area's largest single-owned private reserve, sits between the northern Drakensberg Mountains and the Greater Kruger Park. The Big Five is all here, and it boasts some high-end luxury lodges, but it lacks some of the genuine wilderness feel of other nearby reserves because of its proximity to roads and electrical towers. Its trump card, however, is that it is home to the Hoedspruit Endangered Species Centre, where rescued and endangered animals like cheetahs are to be found.

9

GETTING HERE AND AROUND

Drive north from Johannesburg on the N4 and R36 to Hoedspruit via Dullstroom and Lydenburg (Mashishing).Turn right at the R40 to Klaserie/Bushbuck Ridge. Follow signs to Kapama. Report to the gate, where your ranger will meet you.

There are daily scheduled flights from Johannesburg to Hoedspruit Airport by SA Express. There are also daily scheduled flights from Johannesburg, Durban, and Cape Town to Skukuza Airport and Kruger Mpumalanga International Airport on SA Airlink (lodge transfers can be arranged).

EXPLORING

FAMILY **Hoedspruit Endangered Species Centre.** This center, which cares for, breeds, and protects endangered species, is in the Kapama Game Reserve, outside the little Mpumalanga town of Hoedspruit. It started in a small way, when South African Lente Roode, who owns the reserve, decided to dedicate herself to saving cheetahs—a highly endangered species. The center quickly gained credibility and fame when other animals and birds were brought to her, nursed back to health, and returned to the wild (when possible). It now has a state-of-the-art veterinary center, a highly respected research program, outreach programs for schools, international volunteer programs, a restaurant, and a shop, and is a great day destination. You'll meet Baby G, a white rhino calf found beside his mother, who had been brutally slaughtered for her horn, and Crunchy, the first cheetah ever born in the center. You can also watch wild vultures feast at a vulture restaurant or see wild dogs being fed. The center also rents out a three-bedroom, self-catering cottage on the grounds, and the staff can help you arrange guided game drives; alternatively, you can visit and do things on your own. ⊠ *R40, just outside of Hoedspruit, Kapama Private Game Reserve* ☎ *015/793–1633* ⊕ *www. hesc.co.za* ⊠ *Adults R130* ⊙ *Daily 9–3.*

WHERE TO STAY

$$$$ ⛨ **Camp Jabulani.** This sumptuous Relais & Châteaux lodge, a cross
ALL-INCLUSIVE   between a Hollywood set designer's and an Arab prince's idea of colonial Africa, sits in the 32,123-acre Kapama Game Reserve, only 40 km (25 miles) from Kruger. **Pros:** ultraluxurious accommodation. **Cons:** all this opulence could be excessive. ⑤ *Rooms from: R20900* ⊠ *R40, Kapama Private Game Reserve* ☎ *015/793–1265 lodge, 012/460–5605 reservations* ⊕ *www.campjabulani.com* ⥢ *6 suites, 1 villa* ⏐⏐ *All-inclusive.*

VICTORIA FALLS

Updated by
Christopher
Clark

Roughly 1,207 km (750 miles) from its humble origins as an insignificant spring in northern Zambia, the Zambezi River has grown more than a mile wide. Without much warning the river bends south, the current speeds up, and the entire mass of water disappears into a single fissure. More than 1 million gallons of water rush over a vertical, 328-foot-high drop in the time it takes an average reader to reach the end of this paragraph. The resulting spray is astounding, the brute force forming a cloud of mist visible 64 km (40 miles) away on a clear day.

The settlements of Livingstone in Zambia and Victoria Falls in Zimbabwe both owe their existence to the Zambezi and the Falls. Though they're located in different countries and intriguingly diverse in character, they function almost like two sides of one town. Crossing the border is a formality that generally happens with minimum fuss. Although the Zimbabwean town of Victoria Falls has escaped the political strife that has dogged the country in recent years, Livingstone on the Zambian side is determined to remain the favored destination. Zambia spoils guests with an overabundance of top-class safari lodges along the Zambezi, and this strong competition has resulted in an emphasis on personalized service, which enables you to tailor your visit.

On the other hand, Zimbabwe is slowly rebuilding itself and severe shortages of basic necessities are a thing of the past. The relative absence of large numbers of travelers is a luxury in itself, and this area currently provides good value for money.

The region as a whole deserves its reputation as an adventure center and offers adrenaline-inducing activities by the bucketful. The backdrop for any of these is stunning, and the safety record nothing less than spectacular.

PLANNING

WHEN TO GO

If you're at all sensitive to heat and humidity, visit from May through August, when it's dry and cool, with pleasant days and cool to cold nights. The winter bush is dry, with most of the grass having died down, and the leaves fallen from the trees. The advantage is improved game-viewing, and most other adventure activities are more comfortable in the cooler weather. This is also the time when the mosquitoes are less active, although it remains a malaria area year-round, and precautions should always be taken.

The rainy season starts sometime around late October or early November and generally stretches well into April. As the heavens open up the bug population explodes with mosquitoes, and the harmless but aptly named stink bug seemingly runs the show for brief periods of the day. Of course, the abundance of insect life also leads to great bird-watching. Although the rain showers tend to be of the short and spectacular kind, they can interfere with some activities, especially if your visit to the area is brief. Try to arrange excursions for the early hours of the day, as the rain generally falls in the late afternoon.

Peak flow for Victoria Falls occurs in late April and May, when rafting and visiting Livingstone Island might not be possible. If your visit coincides with school vacations in South Africa, the area can become quite crowded.

HOTELS AND RESTAURANTS

WHAT IT COSTS IN U.S. DOLLARS				
	$	$$	$$$	$$$$
Restaurants	under $12	$12–$20	$21–$30	over $30
Hotels	under $250	$250–$450	$451–$600	over $600

Restaurant prices are per person for a main course at dinner, a main course equivalent, or a prix-fixe meal. Hotel prices are for a standard double room in high season, including 17.5% value-added tax (V.A.T.) in Zambia and 15% V.A.T. in Zimbabwe and service charge.

Hotel reviews have been shortened. For full information, visit Fodors.com.

LIVINGSTONE, ZAMBIA

This marvelous old town, once the government capital of Northern Rhodesia (now Zambia), boasts a wealth of natural beauty and a surplus of activities. After a few decades of neglect it's recently recast itself as Zambia's tourism and adventure capital.

There's a tangible whiff of the past here: historic buildings outnumber new ones, and many local inhabitants live a life not that dissimilar to the one they would have experienced 50 years ago. Livingstone handles the surge of tourists with equal parts grace, confidence, banter, and nuisance.

Many visitors to this side of the Falls opt to stay in one of the secluded safari-style lodges on the Zambezi River. The Zambian experience sprawls out along the many bends of the large river and time ticks in a very deliberate African manner.

10

GETTING HERE AND AROUND

South African Airways and Comair/British Airways regularly fly from Johannesburg into Livingstone International Airport, 5 km (3 miles) out of town. The flight is a comfortable hop, less than two hours in duration, and the airport is small and friendly, with helpful staff to speed you on your way. ■TIP→ **If at all possible, don't check your luggage in**

TOP REASONS TO GO

A World-Class Phenomenon. Not only can you experience Victoria Falls and the Batoka Gorge from every angle—the sheer size of this wonder fosters the delightful illusion of exclusivity.

The Adrenaline Rush. Looking for an adventure to get your heart pounding? From bungee jumping to elephant-back riding and skydiving, Victoria Falls truly has it all.

Perfectly Indulgent Relaxation. Massages are offered on the banks of the Zambezi River, sumptuous food is served wherever you turn, and there are few sights on earth that rival watching the spray of the Falls fade from rainbow to starlight while enjoying cocktails at the end of the day.

Intact Africa. The warm, rich heart of Africa is proudly showcased in a region governed by people who have lived here for centuries, adeptly utilizing the very latest in ecotourism and benefiting from environmentally conscious development.

Johannesburg and always lock suitcases securely, as luggage theft in South Africa is an everyday occurrence.

There's a perfectly reasonable traffic code in Zambia. Unfortunately, not many people have ever heard of it. You would do well to leave the driving to your local guides or negotiate an all-inclusive rate with a taxi driver recommended by your hotel or lodge for the duration of your stay. Note that taxis are generally not allowed to cross the border, so if you want to visit Zimbabwe, you'll have to book a tour that includes transfers. Once at the border, it's feasible to walk into and around Victoria Falls town or rent a bicycle.

If you insist on renting a car, you should know that some of the roads have more potholes than tar. You don't necessarily need a 4x4, but it's not a bad idea, especially if you want to go off-road at all. Voyagers has two offices in Livingstone: Mosi-oa-Tunya Road (opposite Ngolide Lodge) and Livingstone Airport. Hemingway's rents out Toyota Hilux Double Cabs (similar to the Toyota Tacoma), fully equipped with tents and other camping equipment—you can even hire a driver! Costs start from US$220 per day for an unequipped vehicle.

■ **TIP**➜ **If you plan to add the popular Kafue and Lower Zambezi camps to your trip, you should book your transfers together with your accommodation through a travel agent or with your camp reservations, as air-transfer companies change hands and/or minds quite often in Zambia.** A travel agent or camp will also assure that connection times work to your best advantage if they're responsible for the transfers.

Car Rental Contacts Hemingway's ☏ *0213/32–3097, 0977/86–6492* ⊕ *www. hemingwayszambia.com.* **Voyagers** ☏ *0213/32–2753, 0213/32–3259* ⊕ *www. voyagerszambia.com.*

HOTELS

It's advisable to make both flight and lodge reservations ahead of time. Lodges tend to have all-inclusive packages; hotels generally include breakfast only. All hotels and lodges quote in U.S. dollars but accept

ZAMBIA

Mukuni
Village

TO
LUSAKA

Livingstone
Airport

SEE LIVINGSTONE
MAP

Livingstone

Livingstone
Train Station

Kubu Crafts

Prana
Tented Camp

The Royal
Livingstone

Mosi-oa-Tunya Rd.

Sichango Rd.

Mosi-oa-Tunya
National
Park

Siloka Island

Zambezi River

Waterfront

SEE VICTORIA
FALLS (TOWN) MAP

Park Way

Mosi-oa-Tunya
(Victoria Falls)

Border
(Victoria Falls)
Post

Victoria Falls
Train Station

Victoria
Falls

Mosi-oa-Tunya
National
Park

Livingstone Way

Pioneer Rd.

TO
VICTORIA FALLS
AIRPORT

Kazangula Rd.

Mulamba

Sankaia

Simonga

TO
BOVU

River Club

Sindabezi
Island

Tongabezi

Elephant
Back Safaris

Zambezi
National
Park

ZIMBABWE

Victoria Falls
Area

0   2 miles

0   2 kilometers

payment in other major currencies at unfriendly exchange rates. It might be best to take an all-inclusive package tour because meals can be exorbitantly expensive. A 10% service charge is either included or added to the bill (as is the value-added tax) in both countries, which frees you to include an extra tip only for exceptional service. Although air-conditioning can be expected in the hotels, lodges tend to have fans. ■TIP→ Travel with a sarong (locally available as a chitenge), which you can wet and wrap around your body, guaranteeing a cooler siesta.

MONEY MATTERS

The Zambian government is curbing the use of U.S. dollars, and increasingly, places accept only Zambian *kwacha (ZMW)*. ■TIP→ Tipping is less common in Zambia because service charges are included, but it's appreciated. Small notes or 10% is appropriate. Gas-station attendants can be tipped, but tip a taxi driver only on the last day if you've used the same driver for a number of days.

Zambia has a 17.5% V.A.T. and a 10% service charge, which is included in the cost or itemized on your bill. International banks along Mosi-oa-Tunya Road in Livingstone have ATMs and exchange services (lines can be long). Many bank ATMs accept only Visa. Don't use black-market currency exchanges; if you can't change money easily, you can use a credit card at many businesses in Livingstone (but ask first).

PASSPORTS AND VISAS

You'll need a valid passport and visa to enter Zambia. Nationals of any country not on the Zambian Immigration Referred Visa list can simply purchase a visa on entering the country. At this writing a standard U.S. single-entry visa costs US$50, and a single-entry and transit visa cost the same. Day-trip visas cost US$20 (often included in the cost of pre-booked activities, so check with your booking agent).

RESTAURANTS

In Zimbabwe, game meat can be found on almost any menu, but it's something of a delicacy in Zambia; superior free-range beef and chicken are available everywhere. The local bream, filleted or whole, is excellent, and the staple starch, a thick porridge similar to polenta—*sadza* in Zimbabwe and *nsima* in Zambia—is worth a try; use your fingers to eat it (you'll be given a bowl for washing afterward). Adventurous? Try *macimbi* or *vinkuvala* (sundried mopane worms) or *inswa* (flash-fried flying ants) during the flood season.

Meals are taken at regular hours, but during the week, restaurants close around 10. Dress is generally casual, but this part of Africa easily lends itself to a little bling, so you'll never be out of place in something more glamorous.

SAFETY AND PRECAUTIONS

Wild animals abound throughout this area (even in the center of town from time to time) and must be given a lot of physical space and respect. You must also remember that Zambia is relatively poor. There are tourism police, but opportunistic thieving still happens occasionally. Although crime in this area is generally nonviolent, losing your money, belongings, or passport will result in spending the remainder of your trip with various officials in stuffy, badly decorated offices instead of sitting back on the deck of your sunset cruise with drink in hand.

As for the water, it's always advisable to drink bottled water, although the tap water in Zambia is generally considered safe.

TOUR OPTIONS

Livingstone Walking Safaris. Many park guides are well informed, but the ultimate Mosi-oa-Tunya National Park experience is this three-hour guided walking safari. Not only can you see the endangered white rhino and other plains game, but your professional guide and park scout will impart detailed information on birding, flora, and the modern use of plants by local people. Walks are conducted early in the morning and late in the afternoon and cost US$75, including transfers within Livingstone, park fees and refreshments. ☎ 213/32–2267 ✉ gecko@zamnet.zm ⊕ www.livingstonerhinosafaris.com.

VISITOR INFORMATION

Although the Zambia National Tourist Board (next to the museum; open weekdays 8–1 and 2–5, Saturday 8–noon) is very helpful and friendly, you might be better off visiting Jollyboys (behind the Livingstone Museum; open daily 7 am–10 pm) for comprehensive and unbiased advice.

Contacts Jollyboys ✉ *34 Kanyanta Rd.* ☎ *213/32–4229* ⊕ *www.backpackzambia.com.* **Zambia National Tourist Board** ✉ *Tourist Centre, Mosi-Oa-Tunya Rd.* ☎ *0213/321–487* ⊕ *www.zambiatourism.com.*

EXPLORING

FAMILY **Batoka Gorge.** Just below the Falls, the gorge forms an abyss between the countries with edges that drop away from the cliffs of both Zambia and Zimbabwe. Each successive sandstone gorge is numbered in sequence starting from the youngest (First Gorge to the Fifth Gorge), followed by Songwe Gorge and finally the official Batoka Gorge; it is common for all these gorges to be referred to collectively as The Gorge or Batoka Gorge. Batoka Gorge is more than 120 km (75 miles) long with vertical walls that are an average of 400 feet high (the Zambezi river water levels fluctuates up to 65 feet between the wet and dry season). Batoka lies mostly within the Hwange Communal Land and is covered with mopane and riparian forests that are interspersed with grassland. On the Zambian side, the gorge is surrounded by the Mosi-oa-Tunya National Park, which contains a tropical rain forest that thrives on the eternal rainfall from the Falls. Victoria Falls National Park in Zimbabwe surrounds the other side of the gorge. Operators from both countries offer excursions to what is reputed to be the world's best one-day white-water rafting, with rapids rated between Class I and Class VI (amateurs can do only Class V and down commercially) that have been given evocative nicknames like "The Ugly Sisters" and "Oblivion." If you're "lucky" enough to experience what locals call a "long swim" (falling out of the raft at the start of a rapid and body surfing through), your definition of the word *scary* will surely be redefined. The walk in and out of the gorge is quite strenuous on the Zimbabwe side, but as long as you are

10

reasonably fit and looking for adventure, you need no experience. On the Zambian side though, operators use a cable car to transport you from the bottom of the gorge to your waiting transportation (and beverage) at the top. Also on the Zambian side, travelers can walk down into the Boiling Pot (the first bend of the river after the Falls) in the First Gorge. It's an easy walk down and slightly more challenging walk out of the gorge (lots of steps), but even young children enjoy it—be sure to carry extra sun protection and water.

FAMILY **Livingstone Museum.** The country's oldest and largest museum contains history, ethnography, natural history, archaeology sections, and materials ranging from newspaper clippings to photographs of Queen Elizabeth II dancing with Kenneth Kaunda (Zambia's first president) to historical information dating back to 1500. Among the priceless David Livingstone memorabilia is a model of the mangled arm bone used to identify his body and various journals and maps from the period when he explored the area and claimed the Falls for the English queen. ⊠ *Mosi-oa-Tunya Rd., between civic center and post office* ☎ *213/32–0495* ⊠ *USD$5* ⊘ *Daily 9–4:30.*

FAMILY **Mosi-oa-Tunya (The Victoria Falls).** Literally translated as "the Smoke that Fodor's Choice Thunders," the Falls more than lives up to its reputation as one of the ★ world's greatest natural wonders. Words can never do these incredible

Falls justice, and it's a difficult attraction to fully appreciate in a single visit, as it's constantly changing. The Zimbabwean side offers famously panoramic views, while the Zambian side of the Falls features the Knife Edge bridge, which allows guests to stand virtually suspended over the Boiling Pot (the first bend of the river after the Falls), with the deafening water crashing everywhere around you. From around May through August the Falls are a multisensory experience, and there may be too much spray to see the bottom of the gorge. In high season the entire experience can be summed up in two words: power shower! Prepare to get soaked. If you stand with your back to the sun, you'll be surrounded by a symphony of rainbows. A network of paths leads to the main viewing points; some are not well protected, so watch your step and wear sensible shoes, especially at high water, when you are likely to get dripping wet. You will have dramatic views of the full 1½ km (1 mile) of the ironstone face of the Falls, the Boiling Pot directly below, the railway bridge, and Batoka Gorge. During low water levels, it's possible to take a guided walk to Livingstone Island and swim in the **Devils Pool,** a natural pond right on the lip of the abyss. ⊠ *Mosi-oa-Tunya Rd., just before border post* 🎫 *USD$10* ☯ *Daily 6–6, later at full moon.*

FAMILY **Mosi-oa-Tunya National Park.** This park is a quick and easy option for viewing plains game. In fact, you are almost guaranteed to spy white rhinos. You can also visit the Old Drift graveyard, as the park marks the location of the original settlement of Livingstone. The park's guides are very knowledgeable, and while you're free to explore on your own, the roads do get seriously muddy in the rainy season, and a guide who knows where to drive becomes a near-necessity. ⊠ *Sichanga Rd., off Mosi-oa-Tunya Rd., 3½ km (2 miles) from Livingstone* 🎫 *$10 per person per day and $16 per vehicle per day* ☯ *Daily 6–6.*

FAMILY **Mukuni Village.** Fascinated by the history, customs, and traditions of the area? Local guides can escort you on an intimate visit inside a house and explain the customs of the village. This is not a stage set but a very real village, so your tour will be different depending on the time of day. It is customary to sign in the visitors' book and to pay a small fee to your guide. ⇨ *See Bushtracks, in Sport and the Outdoors, for information on booking a trip.* ☯ *Daily 8–5.*

10

WHERE TO EAT

$$ ✕ **Golden Leaf.** The Moghuls themselves might declare a meal here a
INDIAN feast. Spicy but not hot, the curries are lovingly prepared from ingredients imported from India. The chicken *tikka masala* is a house specialty, and the handmade saffron *kulfi* is an inspired dessert at the end of another hot day in Africa. You'll do well to find better curry anywhere in Zambia, and portions and prices are reasonable. Ⓢ *Average main: $18* ⊠ *110 Mosi-oa-Tunya Rd., opposite Ngolide Lodge* ☎ *213/32–1266* ☯ *No dinner Mon.*

$$$$ ╳**Livingstone Island Picnic.** Available throughout the year whenever the
ECLECTIC water levels are low enough, this is a spectacular dining option. Living-
FAMILY stone Island is perched right on the edge of the void, where you'll dine
Fodor's Choice at a table dressed with linen and gleaming silver on a delicious organic
★ lunch (with salads) served by attentive waiters. You get there by boat
(two engines, just in case). Brunch and afternoon tea are US$90 and
US$120, respectively, and lunch is US$150, including transfers and a
dip in Devil's Pool. The trips are run by Tongabezi Lodge, and there is
a maximum of 16 guests. Ⓢ *Average main: $120* ⊠ *Livingstone Island*
☎ *213/32–7450* ⌂ *Reservations essential* ☾ *Closed a couple of months
around Feb.–June, depending on water levels. No dinner.*

$ ╳**Olga's Italian Corner.** This restaurant delivers a double whammy. Not
ITALIAN only does it serve genuine homemade Italian food prepared from fresh
FAMILY local ingredients, it's also part of an NGO project that trains and benefits the local youth. Open six days a week, Olga's features homemade
croissants and muffins with Italian espresso for breakfast and seasonal
delights for lunch and dinner. All the Italian pastas and pizzas are prepared on the premises and served with flavorful sauces made to order.
Ⓢ *Average main: $9* ⊠ *20 Mokambo Rd.* ☎ *213/32–4160* ⊕ *www.
olgasproject.com* ▭ *No credit cards.*

$$$$ ╳**Royal Livingstone Express.** Walking the long stretch of red carpet along-
SOUTH AFRICAN side Locomotive 156 while it blows steam and rumbles in preparation
Fodor's Choice for the journey is undeniably exciting and romantic. Dinner guests
★ are seated in either the Wembley or Chesterfield dining carriage (both
exquisitely restored) while the historic steam train pulls you through
a bustling, charming, shanty town, over the Sinde River Bridge, and
then back through Mosi-oa-Tunya National Park at sunset, or on
Wednesday and Saturday the train stops to watch the sunset on the
magnificent Victoria Falls Bridge. The gourmet dinner is beautifully
presented and meticulously prepared, offering guests no fewer than
five set courses (special dietary requests can be catered to with advance
notice). And yes, the train gives right-of-way to giraffes, elephants,
and any other plains game who might decide to cross the tracks during dinner! ■TIP➜ **Dress code is "smart casual." No shorts are allowed.**
Ⓢ *Average main: $165* ⊠ *Km 0 of Mulobezi line on Mosi-oa-Tunya Rd.*
☎ *27/11–469–9300* ⊕ *www.royal-livingstone-express.com* ⌂ *Reservations essential* ☾ *Closed Mon. and Tues.*

WHERE TO STAY

$ ▦**Bovu.** The vibe of California and Marrakesh in the '60s and '70s is
B&B/INN alive and well at this collection of thatch huts and campsites along the
FAMILY banks of the Zambezi, 52 km (32 miles) upstream of the Falls. **Pros:**
Bovu is *the* Zambian chill-out zone; a great way to combine an educational canoe trip with a basic overnight camp; the perfect balance
between comfort and a real commune with nature. **Cons:** this might be
too basic for travelers who like their little luxuries; meals, fishing, and
transfers are charged separately; guests have to bring their own towels.
Ⓢ *Rooms from: $50* ⊠ *52 km (32 miles) upstream from Victoria Falls,
on Zambezi River* ☎ *097/872–5282* ⊕ *www.junglejunction.info* ⤳ *8
huts* ▭ *No credit cards* ⧄*No meals.*

$$$$
ALL-INCLUSIVE
Fodor's Choice
★

Islands of Siankaba. The lodge, located on two beautiful forested islands in the Zambezi River about 48 km (30 miles) upstream from Victoria Falls, was awarded the Environmental Certificate by the Environmental Council of Zambia in 2002. **Pros:** beautifully secluded location; innovative design; easy access to Chobe National Park just across the border into Botswana **Cons:** 40-minute transfer from Livingstone might be daunting for visitors planning to partake in many of the activities based in town and around the Falls. ⑤ *Rooms from: $1070* ⊠ *40 km (25 miles) from Livingstone along Nakatindi road on Zambezi* ☎ *097/772–0530 cell* ⊕ *www.siankaba.net* ⟿ *7 tented chalets* ⦿ *All-inclusive.*

$
B&B/INN

Jollyboys. The entire design of this small establishment is user-friendly, inviting, and certainly aimed at both private relaxation and easy interaction with other travelers. **Pros:** very central location; free daily transfers to the Falls. **Cons:** the lodge and camp are for backpackers, so are pretty basic; the location of the lodge right in the middle of town might not be exactly where you'd like to spend your holiday. ⑤ *Rooms from: $45* ⊠ *Kanyanta Rd.* ☎ *213/324–229, 213/324–756* ⊕ *www.backpackzambia.com* ⟿ *24 rooms* ▭ *No credit cards* ⦿ *No meals.*

$
B&B/INN
FAMILY

Prana Cottage & Tented Camp. Taking its name from the Sanskrit for breathing, this exclusive camp offers the perfect opportunity for taking just that, a breather. **Pros:** this is the best value for an exclusive stay in the area; you are assured of personal attention and being completely off the beaten track yet only 10 minutes from Livingstone and 10 minutes from the entry to Mosi-oa-Tunya Park at the Falls. **Cons:** if you don't have a car, you can feel a little isolated ⑤ *Rooms from: $116* ⊠ *Off Mosi-oa-Tunya Rd.* ☎ *213/32–7120* ⊕ *www.pranazambia.com* ⟿ *1 house, 9 tented chalets* ▭ *No credit cards* ⦿ *Breakfast.*

$$$$
HOTEL

The River Club. With split-level rooms that cling to the edge of the great Zambezi, The River Club puts a modern spin on a Victorian house party. **Pros:** beautiful location with stunning views of the Zambezi; a/c and enclosed rooms are pluses for those who don't want to give up too many modern conveniences. **Cons:** colonial decor may not be Zambian enough for some travelers; 20-minute drive from town for any activities that are not in-house. ⑤ *Rooms from: $780* ⊠ *About 18 km (11 miles) upstream from Victoria Falls town, on Zambezi River, down same road as Tongabezi* ☎ *213/32–7457* ⊕ *www.theriverclubafrica.com* ⟿ *7 rooms, 4 suites* ⦿ *Multiple meal plans.*

$$$$
HOTEL

The Royal Livingstone. This high-volume, high-end hotel has an incredibly gorgeous sundowner deck, arguably on the best spot on the river, just upstream from the Falls. **Pros:** Location, location, location; the level of service here is definitely that of a five-star international hotel; there is direct access to the Falls via a resort gate that opens onto the eastern cataract. **Cons:** volume of people can lead to occasional problems, omissions, and errors; it can feel a little impersonal; stay clear if colonial nostalgia isn't your thing. ⑤ *Rooms from: $827* ⊠ *Livingstone Way* ☎ *27/11–780–7810* ⊕ *www.suninternational.com* ⟿ *173 rooms* ⦿ *Breakfast.*

10

Naming the Falls

Dr. David Livingstone, a Scottish medical doctor and missionary, visited Victoria Falls in 1855 and is widely credited with being the first European to document the existence of this natural wonder. He named it Victoria Falls in honor of his queen, although the Makololo name, Mosi-oa-Tunya (literally, "the Smoke that Thunders"), remains popular. Livingstone fell madly in love with the Falls, describing them in poignant prose. Other explorers had slightly different opinions. E. Holub could not contain

his excitement and spoke effusively of "a thrilling throb of nature," A. A. de Serpa Pinto called them "sublimely horrible" in 1881, and L. Decle (1898) declared ominously that he expected "to see some repulsive monster rising in anger" at any moment. The modern traveler has the luxury of exploring every one (or all) of these perspectives. There's so much to do around the Falls that the only limitations will be your budget and sense of adventure or your lack thereof.

$$$$
ALL-INCLUSIVE
Fodor's Choice
★

Sindabezi Island. This is the most environmentally friendly property on the Zambezi. **Pros:** lovely views of the national park on the Zimbabwean side from parts of the island; if you're lucky, elephants might swim across the Zambezi and graze a few meters from your bed; service is top notch. **Cons:** it's very open, so if you are a bit nervous in the African bush, this might not suit you; there's no pool; it's difficult to get to. $ *Rooms from: $1190* ⊠ *About 19 km (12 miles) upstream from Victoria Falls, on Zambezi River* ☎ *213/32–7450, 213/32–7468* ⊕ *www.tongabezi.com* ⇔ *5 chalets* ⦿ *All-inclusive.*

$$$$
ALL-INCLUSIVE

Toka Leya Camp. Spread out along the banks of the Zambezi River, the tents are set up on stilts, surrounded by a wooden deck that you can sit on and watch the world and the Zambezi River go by. **Pros:** the camp is close to Livingstone and all of the activities offered in the area; there's a small spa on the banks of the river; almost all your activities in included in the rates. **Cons:** the decor makes it feel a bit like a hotel as opposed to a camp in the middle of the bush. $ *Rooms from: $1408* ⊠ *On the Zambezi River, 12 km (7.5 miles) upstream from Victoria Falls* ☎ *0027–11/807–1800, 0027–21/702–7500* ⊕ *www.wilderness-safaris.com* ⇔ *12 tent suites* ⦿ *All-inclusive.*

$$$$
ALL-INCLUSIVE
Fodor's Choice
★

Tongabezi Lodge. If you're looking for a truly African experience, this owner-run open-fronted lodge on the Zambezi River was designed to complement the Africa you have come to see, without trying to upstage it—but you'll still find indulgent offerings and personalized service at every turn. **Pros:** the original open-fronted lodge; owner offers personal service and thoughtful touches; management is environmentally focused and community aware. **Cons:** the use of local materials for building and decoration might not meet luxury standards for some; interaction with others is limited—though some might count this as a pro; a bit of a distance from town and most activities. $ *Rooms from: $1190* ⊠ *About 19 km (12 miles) upstream from Victoria Falls,* *on Zambezi River* ☎ *213/32–7468* ⊕ *www.tongabezi.com* ⮐ *6 houses, 5 cottages* ⧚ *All-inclusive.*

$$ ⛱ **Victoria Falls Waterfront.** There's
RESORT   a hive of happy activity here rang-
ing from opportunistic monkeys
relieving unsuspecting tourists of
their lunch to serious late-night
boozing. **Pros:** great location right
on the river with beautiful sunsets;
many of the adventure activities
in the area are managed from the

> **GOOD SOUVENIRS**
>
> Shona stone carvings from
> Zimbabwe, woven baskets from
> Botswana and Zambia, and soap-
> stone from Zambia and Zimbabwe
> make great souvenirs. Make sure
> you pack these things carefully,
> especially the soapstone, as it's
> extremely fragile.

Waterfront, so this is an excellent choice for travelers who like social-
izing and one-stop convenience. **Cons:** can be very noisy as it caters to
campers and backpackers; food can still be inconsistent. ⑤ *Rooms from:
$200* ⊠ *Sichango Rd., just off Mosi-oa-Tunya Rd.* ☎ *260/96–832–0606*
⊕ *www.safpar.net* ⮐ *23 chalets, 24 tents* ⧚ *Breakfast.*

SPORTS AND THE OUTDOORS

Livingstone can compete with the best as far as indulging the wildest
fantasies of adrenaline junkies and outdoor enthusiasts goes. You can
reserve activities directly with the operators, let your hotel or lodge
handle it, or book through a central booking agent.

Bushtracks. This operator runs one-day excursions to Botswana's Chobe
National Park. The trip includes transfers from Livingstone, a morning
boat cruise, lunch with a drink, and an afternoon game drive. Bush-
tracks is also your best bet for a visit to the Mukuni Village. Reser-
vations must be prepaid for both. ☎ *213/32–3232, 27–11/469–0484
in Johannesburg* ⊕ *www.gotothevictoriafalls.com* ⊠ *Chobe National
Park, US$189; Mukuni Village , US$45.*

BOATING

African Queen. Truly the monarch of the river, the African Queen—
no relation to the movie—is an elegant colonial-style riverboat. Their
sunset cruises offer the maximum style and splendor. ☎ *213/323–589*
✉ *reservations@livingstonesadventure.com* ⊠ *Two-hour sunset cruise
with an open bar and snacks from US$75.*

BUNGEE JUMPING

Zambezi Adrenaline Company. Bungee jumping off the 346-foot-high Vic-
toria Falls Bridge with Zambezi Adrenaline Company is a major adrena-
line rush, with 65 feet and three seconds of free fall and a spectacular
view. It's worth it to pay additional for the photo and video, complete
with *Top Gun* music track! ☎ *213/32–4231* ⊕ *www.victoriafallsbungee.
com* ⊠ *From US$135; photo and video, US$50.*

CANOEING

A gentle canoeing trip on the upper Zambezi is a great opportunity
to see birds and a variety of game. Many of the lodges upriver have
canoeing as an inclusive activity, but trips are also run by a number of
companies, which are all reputable.

10

Bundu Adventures. Bundu Adventures offers custom-made canoe trips that range from half-day outings to multiday excursions. ⊠ *Office is at Maramba River Lodge* ☎ *213/32–4407* ⊕ *www. bunduadventures.com* ✉ *From US$116 for a ½- day cruise.*

ELEPHANT-BACK RIDING

FAMILY **Elephant-Back Safaris.** Fancy the idea of meandering through the bush along the shores of the Zambezi courtesy of your own ellie? Very lucky clients might even have the opportunity to ride through the river! Not only does this operation keep clients happy enough to forget their sore thighs the next day, it also has the elephants happy enough to keep having babies! ⊠ *Safpar office at David Livingstone Safari Lodge, for bookings* ⊕ *www.safpar.net.*

FLYING

Batoka Sky. Batoka Sky offers weight-shift Aerotrike twin-axis microlighting (flying jargon for what resembles a motorized hang glider) and helicopter flights over the Falls and through the gorges. There's a minimum of two passengers for helicopters. You are issued a flight suit (padded in winter) and a helmet with a headset, before you board the microlight, but you may not bring a camera for safety reasons. Batoka Sky has been operating since 1992, and has a 100% microlighting safety record. Flights are booked for early morning and late afternoon and are dependent on the weather. Transfer and a day visa, if you are coming from Victoria Falls, are included. The Helicopter Gorge picnic includes lunch and drinks for a minimum of six people. ⊠ *Riverside Dr., off Mosi-Oa-Tunya Rd. toward Waterfront and David Livingstone Safari Lodge* ☎ *213/32– 0058* ⊕ *www.livingstonesadventure.com* ✉ *US$150–US$300, depending on length of flight and aircraft; Helicopter Gorge, US$400.*

HORSEBACK RIDING

Ride Zambezi Horse Trails. You can take a placid horseback ride through the bush along the banks of the Zambezi with Chundukwa Adventure Trails. If you are comfortable enough to keep your cool while riding through the African hinterland, you may want to book a horseback bush trail. Half-day trips include lunch and refreshments. Fully-inclusive overnight camping options are also available. ⊠ *Chundukwa Horse, 25 km (15 miles) from Livingstone along Nakatindi Rd.* ☎ *213/32–7064* ⊕ *www.ridezambezi.com* ✉ *From US$75.*

PERUSING THE MARKETS

Original African art is hard to come by in curio markets, and unfortunately most of the pieces are replicas. Explore the markets with an open mind and feel free to indulge in something simply because it tickles your fancy. Try to resist an actual purchase until you've walked the length of the market. This will give you a sense of what's on offer and the standard of workmanship. Look for objects carved from one solid piece of wood. Those made from more than one piece of wood are often stuck together using very dodgy processes. Within a year you could find your beloved treasure in pieces.

JETBOATING

FAMILY **Jet Extreme.** If you want some thrills and speed but rafting seems a bit daunting, or you can't face the walk in and out, you'll probably enjoy jetboating with Jet Extreme. A new cable-car ride, included in the cost of the jetboat ride, means no more strenuous walking out of the gorge. Jetboating can be combined with a rafting excursion, as the jetboat starts at the end of the rafting run, or with a helicopter trip out of the gorge. ■TIP→ **The rafting and helicopter must be booked separately, although big operators like Safari Par Excellence and Livingstone's Adventure offer combinations.** Children over seven can jetboat if they are accompanied by an adult. ✉ *Safpar at David Livingstone Safari Lodge, for bookings* ☎ *213/32–1375* ⊕ *www.livingstonesadventure. com* 🌐 *US$125 for 30 minutes.*

RAFTING AND RIVERBOARDING

Safari Par Excellence. Safari Par Excellence offers half- and full-day rafting excursions to Batoka Gorge. The cable car transports rafters out of the gorge, so you only have to climb down. You can also do a combination helicopter-and-rafting trip. Bring secure shoes, dry clothes for the long drive home, a baseball cap to wear under your helmet, and plenty of sunscreen. You can also try river-boarding in which you hop off the raft onto a body board and surf suitable rapids. ✉ *Booking office, Safpar at David Livingstone Safari Lodge* ☎ *213/32–0606* ⊕ *www.safpar. net* 🌐 *Rafting, US$150 ½-day; US$175 full-day; river-boarding from US$185.*

RAPPELLING AND SWINGING

Abseil Zambia. For something completely different, Abseil Zambia has taken some specially designed heavy-duty steel cables, combined them with various pulleys and rigs, one dry gorge, and a 100% safety record to entertain both the fainthearted and the daring. The full day is great value, as it includes lunch, refreshments, and as many repeats of the activities as you like. ⚠ **Keep in mind that you will have to climb out after the gorge swing and the rappel. A half day is advised during the hot months of October–December.** Work up an appetite for more daring drops by starting on the zip line (or flying fox). You run off a ramp while attached to the line, and the sensation is pure freedom and surprisingly unscary, as you are not moving up or down. Next rappel down into the 175-foot gorge, and, after you climb out, try it again facing forward. It's called a rap run. You're literally walking down the cliff face. End the day with the king of adrenaline activities, a whopping 175-foot, 3½-second vertical free-fall swing into the gorge. Payment is only accepted in Kwacha ✉ *Batoka Gorge* ☎ *213/32–1188* ⊕ *www.thezambeziswing. com* 🌐 *From US$139; swing, US$95 for one swing.*

10

SHOPPING

Kubu Crafts. This stylish home-decor shop features locally made furniture in hardwood and wrought iron. There's also a selection of West African masks and weavings and the work of numerous local artists. Local curios are attractively displayed and screened for quality. Kubu Crafts also provides both fair employment and training opportunities for the community. ⊠ *Mosi-O-Tunya Sq., 133 Mosi-Oa-Tunya Rd.* ☎ *213/32–0230* ⊕ *www.kubucrafts.com.*

Mukuni Park Market. Although the park at the entrance to the Falls has stalls where you can find stone and wood carvings and simple bead and semiprecious-stone jewelry, the real gem of an African bazaar lies in the center of town, at Mukuni Park Market. ■ TIP➔ **This is the place to try your hand at bargaining.** You'll be quoted top dollar initially, but shop around. Look out for individual and unusual pieces, as it is occasionally possible to find valuable antiques. The market is open daily approximately 7–6. ⊠ *Mosi-oa-Tunya Rd. and Libala Dr.*

VICTORIA FALLS, ZIMBABWE

Victoria Falls started with a little curio shop and slowly expanded until the 1970s, when it became the mecca around which the tourist phenomenon of Victoria Falls pivoted. The political problems following independence have been well documented in the world press and have certainly taken their toll, as has poaching in Zambezi National Park to the northwest (if you really want to have the African game experience, take a day trip to Chobe National Park, only 70 km [44 miles] away in Botswana). However, the country is currently regaining political stability, and the town of Victoria Falls enjoys the happy coincidence of being a curio shopper's paradise inside a national park. This means you can literally buy an elephant carving while watching the real McCoy march past the shop window. The town has an easygoing feel and is extremely compact. Almost all the hotels are within walking distance, and the Falls are only 10 minutes away on foot. The main road that runs through town and goes to the Falls in one direction and to the airport in the other is called Livingstone Way. Park Way is perpendicular. Most of the shops, banks, and booking agents can be found on these two streets, and this part of town is also where most of the hawkers operate. ■ TIP➔ **Give these vendors a clear berth, as their wares are cheap for a reason (the boat cruise is substandard, it's illegal to change money, etc.).**

PLANNING

GETTING HERE AND AROUND
Tourists are slowly returning to Victoria Falls. If you choose to fly in and out of Victoria Falls Airport, most hotels will provide free shuttle service; book in advance.

Hotels can summon reputable taxis quickly and advise you on the cost. Tipping isn't mandatory, but change is always appreciated.

Airport **Victoria Falls Airport** ⊠ *Livingstone Way, Victoria Falls, Zimbabwe* ☎ *013/4–4428.*

HOTELS
It's advisable to make both flight and lodge reservations ahead of time. Lodges tend to have all-inclusive packages; hotels generally include breakfast only. All hotels and lodges quote in U.S. dollars but accept payment in other major currencies at unfriendly exchange rates. It might

be best to take an all-inclusive package tour because meals can be exorbitantly expensive. A 10% service charge is either included or added to the bill (as is the value-added tax), which frees you to include an extra tip only for exceptional service. Although air-conditioning can be expected in the hotels, lodges tend to have fans.

MONEY MATTERS

Zimbabwe's currency used to be the Zimbabwe dollar, but now foreign currency is the only acceptable method of payment. Carry U.S. dollars in small denominations and stick to U.S. dollars for all activity payments to Zimbabwe-based operators (all activities are quoted in U.S. dollars). Credit cards are not widely accepted. (You'll also find Western Union banks in Victoria Falls and Livingstone, should you need to do cash transfers.)

PASSPORTS AND VISAS

It's possible to buy point-of-entry visas for Zimbabwe for US$60 for a single entry.

RESTAURANTS

In Zimbabwe, game meat can be found on almost any menu, but it's something of a delicacy in Zambia; superior free-range beef and chicken are available everywhere. The local bream, filleted or whole, is excellent, and the staple starch, a thick porridge similar to polenta—*sadza* in Zimbabwe and *nsima* in Zambia—is worth a try; use your fingers to eat it (you'll be given a bowl for washing afterward). Adventurous? Try *macimbi* or *vinkuvala* (sundried mopane worms) or *inswa* (flash-fried flying ants) during the flood season.

Meals are taken at regular hours, but during the week, restaurants close around 10. Dress is casual, but this part of Africa easily lends itself to a little bling, and you'll never be out of place in something more glamorous.

SAFETY AND PRECAUTIONS

The political situation in Zimbabwe is currently fairly stable, but the damage from the lengthy dictatorship and internal strife is still very apparent. Prices have stabilized and basic goods have reappeared on the shelves, but the tourist capital of Victoria Falls has not yet regained its status as a prime international destination. ■ TIP→ **The Victoria Falls town and tourism industry has managed to build itself up in a remarkably short time. The political situation is still not 100% resolved, but for now, Zimbabwean lodges offer good value and service.**

VISITOR INFORMATION

The Victoria Falls Publicity Association is fairly well stocked with brochures. It's open weekdays 8–1 and 2–4 and Saturday 8–1. You could also choose to seek advice from one of the many safari companies in town.

Contacts Victoria Falls Publicity Association ✉ *412 Park Way, Victoria Falls, Zimbabwe* ☎ *013/4–4202* ✐ *vfpa@mweb.co.zw.*

EXPLORING

Victoria Falls. The first European to set eyes on the Falls was the Scots explorer and missionary Dr. David Livingstone in the mid-1850s. Overcome by the experience he named them after the English queen, Victoria.

On a clear day the spray generated by the Falls is visible from 50 km (31 miles) away—the swirling mist rising above the woodland savanna looks like smoke from a bush fire, inspiring their local name, Mosi-Oa-Tunya, or the "Smoke that Thunders." The rim of the Falls is broken into separate smaller falls with names like the Devil's Cataract, Rainbow Falls, Horseshoe Falls, and Armchair Falls.

The Falls, which are more than 300 feet high, are one of the world's seven natural wonders and were named a UNESCO World Heritage Site in 1989. Upon seeing Victoria Falls for the first time Dr. David Livingstone proclaimed, "Scenes so lovely must have been gazed upon by angels in their flight." Truer words were never spoken.

A basaltic plateau once stood where the Falls are today. The whole area was once completely submerged, but fast-forward to the Jurassic Age and the water eventually dried up. Only the Zambezi River remained flowing down into the gaping 1.6-km-long (1-mile) continuous gorge that was formed by the uneven cracking of the drying plateau.

The Falls are spectacular at any time, but if you want to see them full, visit during the high water season (April–June) when more than 2 million gallons hurtle over the edge every second. The resulting spray is so dense that, at times, the view can be obscured. Don't worry, though, the frequent gusts of wind will soon come to your aid and your view will be restored. If you're lucky to be there during a full moon, you might be able to catch a moonbow or lunar rainbow (a nighttime version of a rainbow) in the spray.

Sorry, Zambia, but the view from your side just doesn't stack up to the view from the Zimbabwean side. Only on the Zim side do you see infamous Devil's Cataract racing through the gorge, the entire width of the world's most spectacular waterfall, and the most rainbows dancing over the rapids. Both countries have commissioned a statue in remembrance of Dr. Livingstone's first sight of the Falls. You'll also get to walk through the glorious rain forest that borders the cliff edges, where wild flowers glow from greenery and monkeys chatter in ancient trees. This is also where accessible, flat-stone pathways—found immediately after you pass through the Zimbabwe entrance to the Falls—will take even the most unfit, tottery, or wheelchair-bound visitor right up to all the viewpoints. You don't need a map or a guide, as each path to the viewpoints is clearly marked.

On the Zambian side it is possible to cross the Knife Edge bridge to the very middle of the Gorge, and during low water guests can swim in the Devil's Pool on Livingstone Island. The Zambian side has many levels and steps making it practically inaccessible for anyone in a wheelchair.

Built in 1905, Victoria Falls Bridge is a monument to explorer, adventurer, empire-builder, and former South African Prime Minister Cecil Rhodes and his dream of creating a Cape-to-Cairo railway. Though the line was never completed, steam-powered trains still chug over the bridge, re-creating a sight seen here for more than a century. From the bridge you get a knockout view of the Falls, as well as the Zambezi River raging through Batoka Gorge. An added bonus: watching adrenaline junkies hurl themselves off the 364-foot-high Victoria Falls Bridge.

Victoria Falls is renowned for the plethora of adventure activities that can be organized on either side. It's best to arrange activities through your hotel or a safari adventure shop, but if you want to go it alone, know that some operators serve only one side of the Falls, and operators have a tendency to come and go quickly. ⊠ *Victoria Falls, Zimbabwe.*

FAMILY **Victoria Falls Bridge.** A veritable monument to Cecil Rhodes's dream of completing a Cape-to-Cairo rail line, this graceful structure spans the gorge formed by the Zambezi River. It would have been far easier and less expensive to build the bridge upstream from the Falls, but Rhodes was captivated by the romance of a railway bridge passing over this natural wonder. A net was stretched across the gorge under the construction site, which curiously prompted the construction workers to go on strike for a couple of days. They resumed work only when it was explained that they would not be expected to leap into it at the end of every workday. Although the workers did not share the current adrenaline-fueled obsession with jumping into the abyss, the net probably had a lot to do with the miraculous fact that only two people were killed during construction. The bridge was completed in only 14 months, and the last two cross-girders were defiantly joined on April 1, 1905.

To get onto the bridge, you first have to pass through Zimbabwean immigration and customs controls, so bring your passport. Unless you decide to cross into Zambia, no visa is necessary, though you will need a gate pass.

Depending on crowds, the simple procedure can take from five minutes to a half hour. The border posts are open daily from 6 am to 10 pm, after which the bridge is closed to all traffic. From the bridge you are treated to a fabulous view of the river raging through Batoka Gorge, as well as a section of the Falls on the Zambian side. An added bonus is watching the bungee jumpers disappear over the edge. ⊠ *Livingstone Way, Victoria Falls, Zimbabwe* ⊕ *www.victoriafallsbridge.com.*

FAMILY
Fodor's Choice
★
Victoria Falls National Park. Plan to spend at least two hours soaking in the splendors of this park. Avoid the crowds and the heat by getting there as early as possible. Bring snacks and water, and supervise children extremely well, as the barriers are by no means safe. Babies and toddlers can be pushed in a stroller. If you visit the Falls during the high-water peak, between April and June, you'd do well to carry a raincoat or umbrella (you can rent them at the entrance) and to bring along a waterproof, disposable camera because you *will* be drenched in the spray from the Falls, which creates a permanent downpour. Be prepared for limited photo opportunities due to the mist. ■ TIP➔ **Leave expensive cameras, cell phones, and wristwatches in your hotel or lodge safe.**

The constant drizzle has created a small rain forest that extends in a narrow band along the edge of the Falls. A trail running through this dripping green world is overgrown with African ebony, Cape fig, Natal

10

mahogany, wild date palms, ferns, and deep-red flame lilies. A fence
has been erected to keep non-fee-paying visitors at bay. Clearly signposted side trails lead to viewpoints overlooking the Falls. The most
spectacular is **Danger Point,** a perilous rock outcropping that overlooks
the narrow gorge through which the Zambezi River funnels out of the
Boiling Pot, but be careful, as this viewpoint is hazardously wet and
precarious. In low-water months (September–November) most of the
water goes over the Falls through the **Devil's Cataract,** a narrow and
mesmerizingly powerful section of the Falls visible from **Livingstone's
statue.** Around the full moon the park stays open late so you can see
the lunar rainbow formed by the spray—a hauntingly beautiful sight.
Early morning and late afternoon are the best times to see the daylight
rainbows most vividly. A booklet explaining the formation and layout of the Falls is available from the Victoria Falls Publicity Association for a small fee. ⊠ *Off Livingstone Way, Victoria Falls, Zimbabwe*
☎ *263/470–6077* 🖃 *US$30* 🕙 *Daily 6–6; open later around full moon.*

WHERE TO EAT

At the peak of Zimbabwe's political problems, shortages of even the
most basic foods, like vegetables, were an everyday occurrence. Since
the adoption of the USD as the official currency, however, hotels and

restaurants have been able to restore some sanity, and in a short time, have been able to reestablish their unique flair for first-rate hospitality while maintaining a healthy dose of local flavor.

IN THE SAFARI CAMPS

$$ ✕**MaKuwa Kuwa.** Perched above a game-rich watering hole at the Victoria Falls Safari Lodge, a spectacular view awaits diners at this memorable dining spot. On offer at breakfast is a combination of both cold and hot dishes; lunch ranges from great salads to huge gourmet burgers; dinnertime guests are treated to local a cappella performers. The à la carte supper menu has quality local and international fare with dishes such as grilled fresh bream (recommended) and, if you aren't too squeamish, crocodile simmered in red curry. Service can be a bit brisk, but it's friendly and the bar is well-stocked. Though it's a bit of a drive from the town center, you would do well to find a better location anywhere on this side of the Falls. ⑤ *Average main: $18* ✉ *Victoria Falls Safari Lodge, 471 Squire Cummings Rd., Victoria Falls, Zimbabwe* ☎ *013/432–1120* ⊕ *www.africaalbidatourism.com* ⌣ *Reservations essential* ⑪ *Jacket required.*

AFRICAN

$$ ✕**The Palm Restaurant.** With tables flowing out onto the deep veranda of Ilala Lodge, the Palm has old-world grandeur with delicious modern cuisine. Lunches are light, including daring crocodile kebabs and the more familiar toasted panini sandwiches with french fries. Dinner is a more formal affair with familiar and exotic dishes. ■**TIP➜ Reservations aren't necessary, but advisable for dinner.** From the outside tables you can see and hear the tumbling waters of the Falls. ⑤ *Average main: $20* ✉ *Ilala Lodge, 411 Livingstone Way, Victoria Falls, Zimbabwe* ☎ *013/4–4737, 013/4–4739* ⊕ *www.ilalalodge.com.*

AFRICAN

$$$$ ✕**Stanley's Terrace.** A trip to Victoria Falls isn't complete without high tea (3–6 pm) on the Victoria Falls Hotel's terrace. A multilayered cake stand filled with an array of delicious treats, including cakes, tarts, and sandwiches, is served with a pot of tea or coffee. ■**TIP➜ Don't have a big lunch beforehand!** The hotel is very grand, and although some of the furnishings are a little tired, the view out over the gorge and onto the bridge and falls is unforgettable. Also at the hotel is the more formal Livingstone Room Restaurant where you can make a reservation for their seven-course degustation meal ($$$$). ⑤ *Average main: $38* ✉ *The Victoria Falls Hotel, 2 Mallet Dr., Victoria Falls, Zimbabwe* ☎ *013/4–4751* ⊕ *www.victoria-falls-hotels.net* ⌣ *Reservations essential.*

MODERN BRITISH
Fodor'sChoice
★

10

IN TOWN

$ ✕**The Africa Cafe.** Find refuge on a hot day at the Africa Cafe in the Elephant's Walk Shopping and Artist's Village. The chef creates simple, delicious food, using ingredients freshly picked from the Happy Hippo Organic Herb and Veggie Garden, found just behind the restaurant. Dishes are varied—from crisp organic salads to buffalo or crocodile burgers to warthog ciabattas—and inspired by the fresh produce of the day with the influence of local Zimbabwean specialties. Elephant's Walk is set in a lush garden shopping center where you'll find local craft and design, with artists working in situ. At dinnertime group bookings are by reservation only. There are plenty of shaded areas and comfy couches around, too, making it a good spot to escape the midday heat.

CAFÉ

⑤ *Average main: $10* ✉ *Adam Stander Rd., Victoria Falls, Zimbabwe* ☎ *771/402–081* ⊕ *www.elephantswalk.com* ⟀ *Reservations essential.*

$$ ✕ **Lola's Tapas and Bar.** One of the town's newer restaurants, Lola's offers
TAPAS   authentic Spanish flair in its cuisine and decor and is popular with the younger backpacker crowd. It's cool and open with tables and chairs spilling out onto a shaded courtyard. Choose from the reasonably-priced tapas menu, or dine à la carte. The restaurant offers an array of dishes, from salad to steak and plenty of local game options. Try the crocodile meat if you feel like something different, or if you are really adventurous give the local "delicacy" of fried mopane worms a go. If you can't get enough, it's open for breakfast, lunch, and dinner. The coffee is probably the best in town. ■ TIP→ **Bookings aren't essential but advisable for larger groups, especially for dinner during the busy season.** Lola's is open until the last drum beat from the group of musicians who provide entertainment on occasion. The food is tasty and reasonably priced. ⑤ *Average main: $18* ✉ *8 Landela Complex, Livingstone Way, in tourist center, Victoria Falls, Zimbabwe* ☎ *013/4–2994.*

$$ ✕ **Mama Africa Eating House.** This a good local food experience as the
AFRICAN   menu offers typical Zimbabwean dishes along with other African food and the atmosphere is colorful and celebratory. Tuesday and Friday nights are "Africa Nights" with a buffet dinner and live music from the local jazz band. There's usually some kind of live music every night of the week except Monday. There's a good selection of vegetarian and meat dishes, too; the Mama Africa Hot Pots are especially popular. There's a biltong and peanut butter stew, chicken with peanut butter (*huku nedove*), and the Hunter's Hot Pot, which is the "catch of the day" game dish. All dishes are accompanied by either *sadza* (cooked cornmeal, a Zimbabwean staple) or rice. ⚠ **The chef prepares several dishes with peanuts, so if you have a severe allergy, it might be best to just enjoy the music and the atmosphere!** ■ TIP→ **It's advisable to make a reservation, especially for large groups and the Africa Nights.** ⑤ *Average main: $15* ✉ *Landela Complex, Matcalfe Rd., Victoria Falls, Zimbabwe* ☎ *013/4–1725* ⊕ *www.mamaafricaeatinghouse.com* ⟀ *Reservations essential* ⊙ *10 am–11 pm daily.*

WHERE TO STAY

With the introduction of the U.S. dollar as the official currency, there's no longer the rocketing inflation. However, an all-inclusive package tour is still a good bet in this area. Electricity and voltage are the same in Zimbabwe and South Africa.

$$$$ 🏕 **The Elephant Camp.** From the deck of your luxurious tented suite,
ALL-INCLUSIVE   you gaze out across the bush and down to the Batoka Gorge and the
Fodor's Choice   "smoke" rising up from the Victoria Falls, just 10 km (6 miles) away.
★   **Pros:** every suite has a plunge pool that's most welcoming in the summer months, although if you're feeling more social, the main lodge has a big pool, too. **Cons:** even though it's in the middle of a national game park, you'll be disappointed if you're there to see a variety of animals. ⑤ *Rooms from: $880* ✉ *10 km (6 miles) outside of Victoria Falls, on Livingstone Way (road to airport), Victoria Falls, Zimbabwe* ☎ *013/4–4571* ⊕ *www.wildhorizons.co.za* ⇗ *12 tented suites* ⦿| *All-inclusive.*

$$ ⬚ **Ilala Lodge.** The lodge's elegant interior design is tempered with thatch
HOTEL roofs, giving it a graceful African look. **Pros:** great central location;
FAMILY family-friendly; only 10 minutes from the Falls by foot. **Cons:** the loca-
tion in town can ruin expectations if you are keen on the peace of
the African bush; the noise from the helicopters can be disturbing.
⑤ *Rooms from: $426* ✉ *411 Livingstone Way, Victoria Falls, Zim-
babwe* ☎ *013/4–47379* ⊕ *www.ilalalodge.com* ⤴ *32 rooms, 2 suites*
⊙ *Breakfast.*

$$$$ ⬚ **Imbabala Zambezi Safari Lodge.** Imbabala is a charming lodge an hour's
ALL-INCLUSIVE drive from Victoria Falls Airport, set about a hundred meters from
the river's edge, close to where Zimbabwe, Namibia, Botswana, and
Zambia converge. **Pros:** authentic Zambezi River and bush experience
Cons: the chalets all look out onto the main lawn, so other guests walk
past the front of them; the lodge isn't far from Kazungula and the noise
from the late-night revelers on the Zambian side can detract a little
from the experience, unless it's your kind of music. ⑤ *Rooms from:
$600* ✉ *Kazungula Rd., 70 km (43 miles) from Victoria Falls, Victoria
Falls, Zimbabwe* ☎ *013/4–4571* ⊕ *www.imbabalazambezisafarilodge.
com* ⤴ *9 chalets* ⊙ *All-inclusive.*

$$ ⬚ **Victoria Falls Hotel.** Hotels come and go, but this landmark built in
HOTEL 1904 has retained its former glory as a distant, stylish outpost in empire
days, while pandering to today's modern tastes, needs, and wants.
Pros: one of the very best views of the Falls—it does not come closer
than this! **Cons:** hotel is slightly run down following the Zimbabwean
political crises. ⑤ *Rooms from: $350* ✉ *2 Mallet Dr., Victoria Falls,
Zimbabwe* ☎ *013/4–4751* ⊕ *www.africansunhotels.com* ⤴ *161 rooms*
⊙ *Breakfast.*

$$ ⬚ **Victoria Falls Safari Lodge.** The lodge's location is atop a natural plateau
HOTEL that perfectly frames the African sunset against a private water hole
FAMILY frequented by various game throughout the entire year. **Pros:** fabulous
Fodor's Choice architecture; beautiful location; great African sunsets are guaranteed.
★ **Cons:** can get quite busy; a little bit of a distance from the town's ameni-
ties. ⑤ *Rooms from: $398* ✉ *471 Squire Cummings Rd., Victoria Falls,
Zimbabwe* ☎ *013/4–3211* ⊕ *www.victoria-falls-safari-lodge.com* ⤴ *72
rooms* ⊙ *Breakfast.*

10

SPORTS AND THE OUTDOORS

The town of Victoria Falls was the epicenter of extreme adventures
for many years. But at the peak of Zimbabwe's civil unrest, many of
the adventure operators either closed down or moved to the Zambian
side. Livingstone took over as the gateway to the Victoria Falls, the
Zambezi River, and all the activities associated with them. Over the
last few years, however, the Zimbabwean side has made a remarkable
comeback, with companies such as Adventure Zone, Wild Horizons,
and the original Shearwater offering all manner of thrills.

Adventure Zone. This is a one-stop booking agent for bungee jump-
ing, upper Zambezi River canoeing, white-water rafting, Victoria
Falls Bridge tour, transfers, and many other activities Victoria Falls

has to offer. ✉ *Shop No.4, Phumula Centre, Victoria Falls, Zimbabwe* ☎ *013/4–4424* ⊕ *www.adventurezonevicfalls.com.*

Shearwater. One of the oldest operating companies in Victoria Falls (thrill seeking since 1982) and unique in that it owns and operates the majority of activities available in Victoria Falls, Shearwater can put you in a helicopter or raft, or on an elephant or boat cruise. ✉ *Park Way and West Dr., Victoria Falls, Zimbabwe* ☎ *013/4–4471* ⊕ *www. shearwatervictoriafalls.com.*

Wild Horizons. Need to get around? Wild Horizons runs transfers in and around Victoria Falls, Livingstone, and Chobe, including airport pick-ups and drop-offs as well as multiday tours and cross-border transfers between Zambia, Zimbabwe, and Botswana. They also operate a range of adrenaline activities in and around the falls. ✉ *Livingstone Way, Victoria Falls, Zimbabwe* ☎ *013/4–4571* ⊕ *www.wildhorizons.co.za.*

SAFARI PRIMER

Updated
by Claire
Baranowski

In choosing to take a safari, you'll embark on one of the biggest travel adventures of your life. It's a big investment of both time and money—and planning well is crucial to ensure you have a good time. Even a basic question like "What should I wear?" is extremely important. In this safari section, we'll cover all the special considerations and lingo you'll need, with plenty of insider tips along the way.

Most people start planning a safari six to nine months in advance, but it's never too soon to start planning your trip. In fact, planning your trip 12 months in advance isn't unreasonable, especially if you want to travel during peak season—November through February in South Africa, July through October elsewhere—and have your heart set on a particular lodge.

If you're keen to see big game, particularly the Big Five (Lion, Elephant, Rhinoceros, Leopard, and Cape Buffalo), then South Africa is a good choice. South Africa, Kruger National Park and the private Sabi Sand game reserve just outside of Kruger (⇨ *Chapter 9*) are ideal places to observe the Big Five as well as hundreds of other species. In Kruger alone, there are an estimated 1,200 species of flora and fauna. You'll see the African elephants everywhere in the park, with lions more abundant in the central and eastern regions; rhinos and buffaloes make their home in the woods of southwest Kruger, though many rhinos are being moved out of Kruger in an attempt to protect them from poachers.

Deciding where you want to go and choosing the safari operator in whose hands you'll place your trip are the most important things you need to do. Start planning for your safari the way you would any trip. Read travel books about the areas that most interest you. Talk to people who have been on a similar trip; word-of-mouth advice can be invaluable. Surf the Net. Get inspired. Line up your priorities. And find someone you trust to help plan your trip.

GETTING STARTED

AIR TRAVEL

Traveling by plane is the best and most viable means of transportation to most safari destinations. If you're visiting a game lodge deep in the bush, you'll be arriving by light plane—and you really will be restricted in what you can bring. Excess luggage can usually be stored with the operator until your return. Don't just gloss over this: charter operators take weight very seriously, and some will charge you for an extra ticket if you insist on bringing excess baggage. ⇨ *For airline contact information, see Air Travel in Travel Smart.*

11

CHARTER FLIGHTS

Charter flights are a common mode of transportation when getting to safari lodges and remote destinations throughout southern Africa. These aircraft are well maintained and are almost always booked by your lodge or travel agent.

On-demand flights, those made at times other than those scheduled, are very expensive for independent travelers, as they require minimum passenger loads. If it's just two passengers, you'll be charged for the vacant seats. Keep in mind that you probably won't get to choose the charter company you fly with. The aircraft you get depends on the number of passengers flying and can vary from very small (you'll sit in the copilot's seat) to a much more comfortable commuter plane. Those with a severe fear of small planes might consider road travel instead.

Luggage limits: Because of the limited space and size of the aircraft, charter carriers observe strict luggage regulations: luggage must be soft sided, preferably with no wheels, and weigh no more than 15 kg (33 pounds). Weight allowances may vary by company, so be sure to ask what the limits are before packing.

⇨ *For information about charter companies see the Air Travel in Travel Smart.*

CUSTOMS AND DUTIES

Everyone is limited with regard to the amount of tobacco or alcohol they bring into a country, but in most cases you won't be carrying enough that you will hit those limits. What's more important is the value and type of goods you bring home.

The United States is a signatory to CITES, a wildlife protection treaty, and therefore doesn't allow the importation of living or dead endangered animals, or their body parts, such as rhino horns or ivory. If you purchase an antique that's made partly or wholly of ivory, you must obtain a CITES preconvention certificate that clearly states that the item is at least 100 years old. The import of zebra skin or other tourist products also requires a CITES permit.

U.S. Information U.S. Customs and Border Protection ⊕ *www.cbp.gov.* **U.S. Fish and Wildlife Service** ⊕ *www.fws.gov.*

MONEY MATTERS

Most safaris are paid for in advance, so you need money only to cover personal purchases and gratuities. (Tips in rand are usually preferred in South Africa, so obtain appropriate small bills on arrival.) If you're driving yourself, also note that many places prefer to be paid in rand, so make sure you change money where you can. *For more information, see* ⇨ *Credit Cards in Money Matters in Travel Smart.*

FIGURING YOUR BUDGET

When setting a budget, consider how much you want to spend and keep in mind three things: your flight, the actual safari costs, and extras. You can have a low-budget self-catering trip in one of South Africa's national parks or spend a great deal of money in one of the small, pampering, exclusive camps in Sabi Sand. Almost every market has high-priced options as well as some economical ones.

Besides airfare and safari costs, make sure you budget for tips, medications, and other sundries such as souvenirs. Plan to stay at a city hotel on your first and last nights in Africa—it'll help you adjust to jet lag and makes things altogether easier. Expect to pay from US$50 for basic accommodations to US$750 a night in the most luxurious hotels. If you do splash out on your safari, but want to keep costs down elsewhere, look out for special offers—sometimes South African lodges will throw in a free night's accommodation in Cape Town, for example, and this can turn out to be a great bargain.

Plan to spend about US$25 a day (per traveler) on gratuities. In South Africa, tips are usually paid in rand; you may also use U.S. dollars for tips, however.

The most popular option is to book with a tour operator and stay in private lodges, which are owned and run by an individual or company rather than the South African government. Prices at these lodges include all meals and, in some cases, alcoholic beverages, as well as two three- to five-hour-long game-viewing expeditions a day. Occasionally high-end lodges offer extra services such as spa treatments, boat trips, or special-occasion meals served alfresco in the bush. Prices range approximately from US$500 to US$1,800 per person per night sharing a double room. If you travel alone, expect to pay a single supplement, because all safari-lodge rooms are doubles.

But safaris don't have to cost $1,000 a day. Some safaris provide accommodations in less luxurious surroundings and include overland travel instead of flights. These can all be cheaper. Other safaris are strictly walking safaris, and while you may stay in more primitive bush camps, these aren't necessarily cheap options.

MONEY-SAVING TIPS

Drive yourself and/or self-cater. The least expensive option is to choose a public game park—Kruger National Park in South Africa, for example—where you drive yourself and self-cater (shop for and prepare all meals yourself). Most South Africans travel this way. The price of this type of trip is approximately a tenth of that for private, fully inclusive lodges.

Rates for national-park camps, called rest camps, start at about US$80 a day for a two-bed *rondavel* (a round hut modeled after traditional African dwellings) and go up to $175 for a four-bed bungalow. The South African National Parks website (⊕ *www.sanparks.org*) has photos and prices for all their different accommodations around the country. Budget about $6 for breakfast, $8 for lunch, and $12 for dinner per person for each day on the trip (less if you're self-catering). You'll need to factor in park entry fees, however, and these can add quite considerably to the cost of your trip.

Driving yourself can be enjoyable, but keep in mind that you'll have to identify all the animals yourself, and you can't go off-road. Hire a guide from the main office of the park or opt for a game drive in a national park vehicle; it's inexpensive and will add a great deal to your experience.

Stay in accommodations outside the park or in a nearby town. This cuts down on the "mark-ups" that you may experience for the convenience of staying inside a park, and you can come into the park on day trips, so you won't miss anything.

Stick to one park, or visit a lesser-known one, and keep your trip short. The high-end safari-goer may visit up to four different parks in different terrains and areas of the country, but the budget traveler would do well to stick to just one. Lesser-known parks can be just as good as famous ones, and sometimes being far from the madding crowds is a luxury in itself. Many travelers tack a two- or three-day safari on to the end of a beach vacation; this is enough time to see the Big Five and get a good understanding of the animals you'll encounter.

Book a private lodge in the off-season. Many lodges—South Africa's Sabi Sands area, for example—cost about US$800 per person per night during the high season but can drop to about US$500 a night during the slower months of July and August; on average, savings can be 30%–40%. In the rainy season, however, roads may be impassable in some areas and the wildlife hard to spot, so do your research beforehand. Sometimes, the high season merely correlates with the European long vacation. In South Africa, the low season is from May to September, mostly because Cape Town is cold and wet during this time. Regions in the northern part of the country, such as Kruger, are excellent for game-viewing during this time, as the winter is the dry season and grasses are short. Early mornings and nighttime can get cold, but the daytime is usually dry and sunny. You'll also have the benefit of fewer crowds, although if you're very social, you may find the off-season too quiet. If you're a honeymooner, it's perfect.

Cheap flights are out there, but you'll have to work for them. Aggregators such as Skyscanner.net and ebookers.com can help you search for the best fares that meet your requirements. American travelers can save money by flying through Europe. Book a flight to a regional hub like Johannesburg, and then catch a connecting flight to your destination. You'll add extra time to your flight, but you could save big. Always book at least two months in advance, especially during the high season.

Budget for all aspects of your trip and watch out for hidden extras. Most safaris are all-inclusive, so you don't think about the cost of your sundowner drink, snacks on your game drive, or cocktails at mealtime. However, some lodges charge extra for drinks and excursions. You can keep your costs down by going to a place where things are à la carte and pay only for the things you deem important.

When you book your trip, be clear about whether extras such as airport transfers, use of equipment (including sleeping bags on some mobile-camping safaris), and entry fees are included in the price.

Book your trip locally, or at the last minute. Last-minute deals can offer massive discounts, as long as you're prepared to be flexible about everything to do with your trip. Alternatively, book a trip locally once you're at your destination. You can also gather a group of people at your lodging and do a group booking. This way you'll have the benefit of a guide, too, with the cost shared among a number of people. You can also save money by booking with a tour operator based in South Africa, as you will be cutting out the commission charged by an American agent. Make sure that you thoroughly research your prospective tour operator first, however, to ensure they have a consistently good reputation.

TIPPING

Most tipping in South Africa is done in rand. Most tipping in other African countries is done in U.S. dollars.

Ranger/Guide: About R200 (US$20) per person, per day.

General staff: R250 (US$25) is sufficient for a couple staying two days. A general guide is roughly R150 (US$15) a day (per couple) into the general tip box, and R150 (US$15) each to your tracker and butler (if applicable), and R150 (US$15) per trip for a vehicle transfer. (Note that some safari operators, such as Micato, include tips in their price, so you don't have to worry about carrying around the correct denominations.)

It's also nice if you bring thank-you cards from home to include with the tip as a personal touch. Fodor's Forum member atravelynn adds, "Put bills in an envelope for your guide and in a separate envelope with your name on it for the camp staff. Sometimes the camps have envelopes, but bringing some from home is also a good idea."

PASSPORTS AND VISAS

A valid passport is a must for travel to any African country. ⚠ **South Africa will not let you enter with a soon-to-expire passport; also, you need two blank pages in your passport to enter South Africa.** If you have a passport, check the expiration date. If it's due to expire within six months of your return date, you need to renew it at once. Allow six weeks for a passport renewal.

U.S. Passport Information U.S. Department of State ☎ 877/487–2778 ⊕ *www.travel.state.gov.*

SAFETY AND PRECAUTIONS

Although South Africa is relatively stable and safe, it's a good idea to do your homework and be fully aware of the areas you'll be traveling to before planning that once-in-a-lifetime trip.

The CIA's online *World Factbook* has maps and facts on the people, government, economy, and more for countries from Afghanistan to Zimbabwe. It's the fastest way to get a snapshot of a nation. It's also updated regularly and, obviously, well researched.

The U.S. State Department's advice on the safety of a given country is probably the most conservative you'll encounter. That said, the information is updated regularly, and nearly every nation is covered. Just try to parse the language carefully. For example, a warning to "avoid all travel" carries more weight than "avoid nonessential travel," and both are much stronger than a plea to "exercise caution." A travel warning is

DOCUMENT CHECKLIST

- Passport
- Visas, if necessary
- Airline tickets
- Proof of yellow-fever inoculation, if necessary
- Accommodation and transfer vouchers
- Car-rental reservation forms
- International driver's license
- Copy of information page of your passport

- Copy of airline tickets
- Copy of medical prescriptions
- List of credit-card numbers and international contact information for each card issuer
- Copy of travel insurance and medical-emergency evacuation policies
- Travel agent's contact numbers
- Notarized letter of consent from one parent if the other parent is traveling alone with their children

more permanent (though not necessarily more serious) than a so-called public announcement, which carries an expiration date.

Travel Warnings Central Intelligence Agency (*CIA*). ⊕ *www.cia.gov.* **U.S. State Department** ⊕ *www.travel.state.gov.*

TRAVEL INSURANCE

You may want to consider a comprehensive travel-insurance policy in addition to any primary insurance you already have. Travel insurance incorporates trip cancellation; trip interruption or travel delay; loss or theft of, or damage to, baggage; baggage delay; medical expenses; emergency medical transportation; and a collision damage waiver if renting a car. These policies are offered by most travel-insurance companies in one comprehensive policy and vary in price based on both your total trip cost and your age. ⇨ *For more information, see Trip Insurance in Travel Smart.*

VACCINATIONS AND HEALTH CONCERNS

Traveling overseas is daunting enough without having to worry about all the scary illnesses you could contract. But if you do your research and plan accordingly, you will have no reason to worry.

The Centers for Disease Control, or CDC, has an extremely helpful and informative website where you can find out country by country what you'll need. Remember that the CDC is going to be extremely conservative, so it's a good idea to meet with a trusted health-care professional to decide what you'll really need, which will be determined by your itinerary.

Keep in mind that there's a time frame for vaccines. You should see your health provider four to six weeks before you leave for your trip. Also keep in mind that vaccines and prescriptions could run you anywhere

SAFARI PLANNING TIMELINE

SIX MONTHS AHEAD

- Research destinations and options, and make a list of sights you want to see.

- Start a safari file to keep track of information.

- Set a budget.

- Search the Internet. Post questions on bulletin boards and narrow your choices. Watch out for fake trip reviews posted by unscrupulous travel agents.

- Choose your destination and make your reservations.

- Apply for a passport, or renew yours if it's due to expire within six months of travel time. Many countries now require at least two empty pages in your passport.

- Buy travel insurance.

THREE TO SIX MONTHS AHEAD

- Find out which travel documents you need.

- Confirm whether your destination requires visas and certified health documents.

- Arrange vaccinations or medical clearances.

- Research malaria precautions.

- Book excursions, tours, and side trips.

ONE TO THREE MONTHS AHEAD

- Create a packing checklist. ⇨ *See our list below.*

- Fill prescriptions for antimalarial and regular medications. Buy mosquito repellent.

- Shop for safari clothing and equipment.

- Arrange for a house- and pet sitter.

ONE MONTH AHEAD

- Get copies of any prescriptions and make sure you have enough of any needed medicine to last you a few days longer than your trip.

- Confirm international flights, transfers, and lodging reservations directly with your travel agent.

- Using your packing list, start buying articles you don't have. Update the list as you go.

ONE WEEK AHEAD

- Suspend newspaper and mail delivery.

- Check antimalarial prescriptions to see whether you need to start taking medication now.

- Arrange transportation to the airport.

- Make two copies of your passport's data page. Leave one copy, and a copy of your itinerary, with someone at home; pack the other separately from your passport. Make a PDF of these pages and email them to yourself for access.

from $1,000 to $2,000. It's important to factor this into your budget when planning, especially if your plans include a large group.

You must be up-to-date with all of your routine shots such as the measles/mumps/rubella (MMR) vaccine, diphtheria/pertussis/tetanus (DPT) vaccine, and so on. If you're not up to date, usually a simple booster shot will bring you up to par.

We can't stress enough the importance of taking malaria prophylactics. But be warned that all malaria medications aren't equal. Chloroquine is not an effective antimalarial drug. And halofantrine (marketed as Halfan), which is widely used overseas to treat malaria, has serious heart-related side effects, including death. The CDC recommends that you not use halofantrine. Their website has a comprehensive list of the different malaria medications available and which ones are recommended for each country. The Travel Health Online website is a good source to check out before you travel because it compiles primarily health and some safety information from a variety of official sources, and was created by a medical publishing company. ⇨ *For more information on malaria, or other health issues while on safari, see Health below.*

Health Warnings Centers for Disease Control (*CDC*). ☏ *800/232–4636 international travelers' health line* ⊕ *wwwnc.cdc.gov/travel.* **Travel Health Online** ⊕ *www.tripprep.com.*

HEPATITIS A AND B

Hepatitis A can be transmitted via contaminated seafood, water, or fruits and vegetables. According to the CDC, hepatitis A is the most common vaccine-preventable disease in travelers. Immunization consists of a series of two shots received six months apart. You only need to have received the first one before you travel. This should be given at least four weeks before your trip.

The CDC recommends vaccination for hepatitis B only if you might be exposed to blood (if you're a health-care worker, for example), have sexual contact with the local population, stay longer than six months, or risk exposure during medical treatment. As needed, you should receive booster shots for tetanus-diphtheria (every 10 years), measles (you're usually immunized as a child), and polio (you're usually immunized as a child).

YELLOW FEVER

Yellow fever isn't endemic in South Africa.

FINDING A TOUR OPERATOR

Before you entrust your trip to a tour operator or travel agent, do your best to determine the extent of his or her knowledge as well as the level of enthusiasm he or she has for the destination. There are many travel companies claiming to specialize in South Africa, so it's especially important to determine which operators and agents are up to the challenge. We recommend the companies we feel are the best.

After choosing a tour operator or travel agent, it's a good idea to discuss with him or her the logistics and details of the itinerary so you know what to expect each day. Ask questions about lodging, even if you're traveling on a group tour. A lodge that's completely open to the elements may be a highlight for some travelers and terrifying for others, particularly at night when a lion roars nearby. Also ask about the amount of time you'll spend with other travelers. If you're planning a safari honeymoon, find out if you can dine alone when you want to, and ask about honeymoon packages.

RECOMMENDED OPERATORS

Our list of tour operators hardly exhausts the number of reputable companies, but the following operators, sorted alphabetically, were selected because they're well-established firms that offer a good selection of itineraries ranging from overland safaris, walking and fly-in safaris, and under-canvas safaris, to safari lodges. They all offer fully customizable trips, too.

TOP OUTFITTERS

&Beyond. This luxury tour operator offers ready-made trips and tours to all parts of Southern or East Africa, or can tailor a safari to your needs. They offer some of the best destinations and accommodations in Africa (and manages 33 of its own highly regarded properties), from the Okovango Delta to remote Indian Ocean islands. Unique trips for the discerning traveler can be planned around learning, conservation, and sustainability, or "luxury in the bush," which includes more holistic activities, such as yoga safaris. They also offer active adventures such as rhino darting for conservation, walking safaris, and turtle-hatching expeditions. **What they do best:** Luxury in the bush; impeccable attention to detail, honeymoons. ⊠ *Pinmill Farm, 164 Katherine St., Sandton, South Africa* ☎ *27/11809–4300 in South Africa, 888/882–3742 in U.S.* ⊕ *www.andbeyond.com.*

Abercrombie & Kent. In business since 1962, this company is considered one of the best in the business and is consistently given high marks by former clients. From your first decision to go on safari to its successful conclusion, A&K offers seamless service. Their tailor-made safaris hearken back to days past when intrepid adventurers such as Teddy Roosevelt and Ernest Hemingway relied on private guides to create a safari program and escort them through the bush from start to finish. The company has a professional network of local A&K offices in all its destination countries, staffed by full-time A&K experts, and maintains its own fleet of four-wheel-drive safari vehicles and trains its own drivers. The head office in the U.S. is in Illinois. **What they do best:** Destination knowledge—they have some of the most experienced guides on the continent. ⊠ *1411 Opus Pl., Downer's Grove, Illinois, United States* ☎ *888/611–4711* ⊕ *www.abercrombiekent.com.*

African Portfolio. African Portfolio's team members visit each in-country operator annually and are on a first-name basis with the managers of the properties they use. They pride themselves on discovering the best places, whether they're hidden gems, up-and-coming properties, or well-established classics. With each client, they're committed to providing a safari reminiscent of what captivates them about Africa. Their mission is to provide unique and memorable experiences through nature-based travel that educate, entertain, inspire, and provide participants with opportunities to directly contribute to conservation. **What they do best:** Assisting travelers with "off the beaten path" trips. ⊠ *146 Sound Beach Ave., Greenwich, Connecticut, United States* ☎ *800/700–3677* ⊕ *www. onsafari.com.*

Gamewatchers Safaris. This Nairobi-based company specializes in delivering luxury tailor-made safaris to small camps and lodges in the top game-viewing areas of East Africa. Every traveler is guaranteed a personal, authentic safari and the opportunity to experience the magic of the African bush while helping protect Africa's wildlife, ecosystems, and cultures. Gamewatchers run their own ground operations, ensuring guests are well looked after from the start of their trip to the finish. Guests often add beach trips to the end of their safaris. **What they do best:** A personal, authentic experience, as far from mass-market tourism as it's possible to get. ☎ *877/710–3014* ⊕ *www.porini.com.*

Micato Safaris. Family-owned and -operated, this New York–based operator offers ultraluxurious trips driven by a sustainable ethos. Safari lodges enchant with such unadulterated luxuries as private plunge pools and personal butlers. Cultured safari guides educate, instruct, and amuse, while itineraries offer an irresistible array of experiences from the sophisticated pleasures of Cape Town to the celebrated savannas of the Serengeti and the near-spiritual beauty of the Kalahari. Micato has been long praised for its ability to deliver seamless personalized "un-group-like" service and over-the-top luxury without sacrificing true immersion in the "real Africa." Stand-out inclusions on Micato programs include time-saving bush flights between lodges and an "all tips included" policy. **What they do best:** Impeccable service from start to finish alongside excellent community projects. ⊠ *15 W. 26th St., New York, New York, United States* ☎ *212/545–7111* ⊕ *www. micatosafaris.com.*

Natural Habitat Adventures. Nicknamed "The Nature People," this operator is known for its focus on wildlife and conservation. Nat Hab's headquarters are in Colorado, and although they organize trips to destinations around the world they have a good reputation for arranging incredible safari itineraries. They always choose the best destinations for viewing wildlife in its natural habitat and focus on small groups and intimate lodges in secluded, off-the-beaten-track settings. Their online safari-building tool, iSafari.com, is a useful starting point for getting an idea of what's possible before speaking to one of the experts in their team. They can also arrange photo expeditions and family safaris. **What they do best:** Sustainable ecotourism for small groups with a focus on wildlife and conservation. ⊠ *833 W., South Boulder Rd., Boulder, Colorado, United States* ☎ *800/543–8917* ⊕ *www.nathab.com.*

Wilderness Safaris. One of Africa's most respected and innovative tour operators, Wilderness Safaris assures you impeccable service, pristine wilderness destinations, spacious safari camps and wildlife galore. The company operates a wide array of safari camps and lodges, from "seven star" premier accommodation to mobile safaris known as Explorations, to tailor-made itineraries and honeymoon packages. Wilderness has more than 70 lodges and camps, all with different styles, so there is something for everyone. They have a regional office in each country in which they operate, as well as a head office in Gaborone, Botswana, ensuring that their ground operations run very smoothly. **What they do best:** Incredible destinations, authentic experiences and seamless service from start to finish. ✉ *373 Rivonia Blvd., Rivonia, South Africa* ☎ *27–11/807–1800* ⊕ *www.wilderness-safaris.com.*

HIGHLY RECOMMENDED OUTFITTERS

Africa Adventure Company. Based in Florida, Africa Adventure Company is renowned for arranging low-impact and personalized travel. Their experienced staff listen closely to what kind of experience their clients are after and match it with a suitable itinerary. Owner Mark Nolting has spent more than 25 years exploring and researching Africa and has written several guidebooks. His partner Alison managed safari camps for many years and now works on developing new safari programs for both repeat and new clients as well organizing community and volunteer programs. They promote camps that are symbiotic with nature and the community, and offer exquisite game viewing with top notch guides. They also offer add-on tours, such as beach escapes and honeymoon packages. ✉ *2601 E. Oakland Blvd., Suite 600, Fort Lauderdale, Florida, United States* ☎ *800/882–9453* ⊕ *www.africa-adventure.com.*

Big Five. Offering more than 100 tours to Africa, this Florida-based operator promises its clients a trip of a lifetime—if you're not happy with the choices given, Big Five will custom create one for you. You can be assured that whatever trip you choose, your knowledgeable agent will be able to draw on personal experience to assist you. Since its inception in 1973, the company has been committed to responsible travel that fosters the preservation of natural and cultural heritage and, equally importantly, the well being of local communities. ✉ *1551 S.E. Palm Ct., Stuart, Florida, United States* ☎ *800/244–3483* ⊕ *www.bigfive.com.*

Cheli & Peacock. Born out of a passion to conserve Kenya's wildlife and wilderness areas, this upmarket company is owner-managed and has offices in Nairobi, Nanyuka, and Arusha, Tanzania. It has developed over the years to become one of Kenya's leading destination-management companies and inbound tour operators, specializing in East Africa. The variety of locations covers a broad selection of ecosystems, game, and conservation, and features small luxury camps and lodges in top national parks and reserves. Their trips are very creative; for example, helicopter rides across the Great Rift Valley, or walking with camels across the Laikipia plateau. They manage all ground arrangements themselves. Beach escapes can be added to safari trips. ✉ *Lengai House, Wilson Airport, Nairobi, Kenya* ☎ *254–20/600–3090* ⊕ *www.chelipeacock.com.*

Deeper Africa. This small, hands-on company, based in Colorado, specializes in East Africa, Botswana and Namibia. Their focus is on wildlife and guiding. If you want to catch the Serengeti wildebeest migration, explore the Okavango Delta, trek mountain gorillas, or scout for desert-adapted animals in the Namib desert, they have very detailed knowledge of these areas and can get you privileged access to places you'd never find on your own. Their guide-to-guest ratio is high: one guide for every four or five guests. Ethical tourism is a cornerstone of their approach and they aim to educate as well as entertain and indulge their guests. They can deliver a fully customized itinerary within an hour of conversation. ✉ *5353 Manhattan Circle, Suite 202, Boulder, Colorado, United States* ☎ *303/415–2574* ⊕ *www.deeperafrica.com.*

Eyes on Africa. Whether you're a honeymooner, wildlife enthusiast, or photographer, Chicago-based Eyes on Africa will find a trip to match your budget. A wide range of interests and preferences can be catered to, and they have a long list of budget options, too. Along with safaris, they also cover mountainous destinations and beaches. They are becoming well known for their occasional group photography trips, and are planning to expand out of Africa in order to service requests from their existing customer base. ✉ *1743 W. Fletcher St., Chicago, Illinois, United States* ☎ *888/450–9247* ⊕ *www.eyesonafrica.net.*

Ker & Downey. One of the oldest and most respected safari companies in Africa (it's been operating since 1946), Ker & Downey also has an office in Texas. The company utilizes its exclusive camps to provide luxury safari experiences and offers in-house expertise for all destinations as well as excellent on-the-ground service. They work hard to get to know all clients to match them with the ultimate itineraries. They pioneered the concept of the photographic safari and often organize trips for film crews as well as corporations and private clients. ✉ *6703 Highway Blvd., Katy, Texas, United States* ☎ *800/423–4236* ⊕ *www. kerdowney.com.*

Premier Tours. Although it's based in Philadelphia, Premier Tours is owned and managed by people born and raised in Africa who have organized all kinds of safaris, from basic camping trips to celebrity vacations. CEO Julian Harrison specializes in the development of ecotourism on the continent and is the founding member (and first USA tour operator) of The UN's Environment Program's Initiative on Sustainable Tourism Development. Other team members lead tour groups as naturalist guides, and participate in research projects in various African countries. Beach escapes can be added to safaris. ✉ *21 S. 12th St., Philadelphia, Pennsylvania, United States* ☎ *800/545–1910* ⊕ *www. premiertours.com.*

Pulse Africa. More than 75% of Pulse Africa's clients are repeats or have been recommended by others. The company is based in South Africa, so it has up-to-date information on travel in Southern Africa, East Africa, and the Indian Ocean Islands. Every member of the team has personally visited each place that they recommend. "Pulse Packages" are trips primarily to one destination (either beach or safari); as a result they're more affordable than a tailor-made trip. ✉ *2nd fl., Hyde Sq., Jan Smuts Ave., Johannesburg, South Africa* ☎ *2711/325–2290* ⊕ *www. pulseafrica.com.*

ROAR Africa. ROAR Africa offers a one-of-a-kind travel service for personalized, custom tours. The founder's family dates back to 1688, ensuring a wealth of information and well-established network that can only come from years of actually living in Africa. Clients have had memorable and life-changing adventures, such as meeting with artists and tribesmen, sleeping under the stars in the Kalahari, dinner with a CEO from their industry, participation in rhino conservation efforts, the opportunity to meet wildlife documentary producers Dereck and Beverly Joubert, VIP wine tours by helicopter, and visiting township schools. ROAR is headquartered in New York but also has offices in South Africa. They run their own ground operation, which enables concierge-level service and support during both the planning phase and travel. They also meet clients at the door of the airplane upon arrival, whisk them through customs, and can offer their own plane for private flights. ⊠ *1111 Lexington Ave., New York, New York, United States* ☎ *855/666–7627* ⊕ *www.roarafrica.com.*

Tauck. A slightly different safari: Tauck operates its African safaris in cooperation with the award-winning documentary filmmakers BBC Earth, and clients can view a number of short documentaries during their trip, thus adding insight and context to their experience. Clients have the opportunity to use the same equipment as the filmmakers, such as infrared cameras, night-vision goggles, and long-distance microphones to immerse themselves in their surroundings in new and exciting ways. Premium-quality trips are virtually all-inclusive, with all excursions, most meals and gratuities, airport transfers, luggage handling, and other expenses built into the price. ⊠ *10 Norden Pl., Connecticut, United States* ☎ *203/899–6814* ⊕ *www.tauck.com.*

PACKING

You'll be allowed one duffel-type bag, approximately 36 inches by 18 inches and a maximum of 26 kg (57 pounds)—less on some airlines, so it's essential you check ahead—so that it can be easily packed into the baggage pods of a small plane. A personal-effects bag can go on your lap. Keep all your documents and money in this personal bag. Note above, that many charter flights have more restrictive limits.

■TIP→ At O. R. Tambo International Airport in Johannesburg and Cape Town International Airport you can store your bags at Bagport (⊕ *www. bagport.co.za*). The cost is approximately US$8 per bag per day, and the facility is open 24 hours a day, 7 days a week. Many travelers also pay to have their luggage wrapped in shrink-wrap, but locking your suitcase should be sufficient.

BINOCULARS

Binoculars are essential and come in many types and sizes. You get what you pay for, so avoid buying a cheap pair—the optics will be poor and the lenses usually don't stay aligned for long, especially if they get bumped, which they will on safari. Whatever strength you choose, pick the most lightweight pair; otherwise you'll be in for neck and shoulder strain. Take them with you on a night drive; you'll get great visuals of nocturnal animals and birds by the light of the tracker's spotlight. Many

PACKING CHECKLIST

Light, khaki, or neutral-color clothes are universally worn on safari and were first used in Africa as camouflage by the South African Boers, and then by the British Army that fought them during the First and Second South African Wars. Light colors also help to deflect the harsh sun and are less likely than dark colors to attract mosquitoes. Don't wear camouflage gear. Do wear layers of clothing that you can strip off as the sun gets hotter and put back on as the sun goes down.

- Three cotton T-shirts

- Two long-sleeve cotton shirts

- Two pairs shorts or two skirts in summer

- Two pairs long pants (three pairs in winter)

- Optional: sweatshirt and sweatpants, which can double as sleepwear

- One smart-casual dinner outfit

- Underwear and socks

- Walking shoes or sneakers

- Sandals

- Bathing suit

- Warm thigh-length padded jacket and sweater in winter

- Windbreaker or rain poncho

- Camera equipment, extra batteries or charger, and memory cards

- Contact lenses, including extras

- Eyeglasses

- Binoculars

- Small flashlight

- Personal toiletries

- Malaria tablets

- Sunscreen and lip balm with SPF 30 or higher, moisturizer, and hair conditioner

- Antihistamine cream

- Insect repellent

- Basic first-aid kit (aspirin, bandages, antidiarrheal, antiseptic cream, etc.)

- Tissues and/or premoistened wipes

- Warm hat, scarf, and gloves in winter

- Sun hat and sunglasses (Polaroid and UV-protected ones)

- Documents and money (cash, credit cards), etc.

- A notebook and pens

- Travel and field guides

- A couple of large white plastic garbage bags

- Ziplock bags to keep documents dry and protect electronics from dust people find that when they start using binoculars and stop document-ing each trip detail on film, they have a much better safari experience.

CAMERAS

Cameras with eight megapixels of resolution can print high-quality, smooth A4 or letter-size prints; images with five-megapixel resolution are fine as well. Any iPhone work pretty well as digital cameras for snapshots. Invest in a telephoto lens to shoot wildlife, as you tend to be too far away from the animals to capture any detail with the zoom lens generally built into most point-and-shoot cameras. This may mean upgrading to a more robust camera. A tripod or beanbag is another must-have; it'll stabilize your camera, especially when a zoom lens is extended.

Bring a tripod or a beanbag to rest the camera on while in a vehicle. When using a long lens (upward of 200 mm), you can't hand-hold a steady shot; you must have some support if you want your photos to be clear.

Buy or borrow as many memory cards as you can—you'll use them. You may want to use multiple smaller memory cards to minimize the risk of losing an entire card's worth of images. And, as always, remember to bring extra batteries or your battery charger.

■ TIP→ **No matter what kind of camera you bring, be sure to keep it tightly sealed in plastic bags while you're traveling to protect it from dust.** Tuck your equipment away when the wind kicks up. You should have one or more cloth covers while you're working, and clean your equipment every day if you can.

CLOTHING

You should need only three changes of clothing for an entire trip; almost all safaris include laundry as part of the package. If you're driving your-self, you can carry more, but washing is still easy, especially if you use drip-dry fabrics that need no ironing. On mobile safaris you can wear tops and bottoms more than once, and either bring enough underwear to last a week between lodges or wash as you go in the bathroom sink. Unless there's continual rain (unlikely), clothes dry overnight in the hot, dry African air.

For game walks, pack sturdy but light walking shoes or boots—in most cases durable sneakers suffice for this option. For a walking-based safari, you need sturdy, lightweight boots. Buy them well in advance of your trip so you can break them in. If possible, isolate the clothes used on your walk from the remainder of the clean garments in your bag. Bring a couple of plastic garbage bags to segregate your dirty laundry.

ELECTRICITY

Most of southern Africa is on 220/240-volt alternating current (AC). The plug points are round. However, there are both large 15-amp three-prong sockets (with a ground connection) and smaller two-prong 5-amp sockets. Most lodges have adapter plugs, and some hotels and lodges even have hair dryers and electric-razor sockets. Lodges on limited generator and solar power are usually able to charge cameras, as long as you have the right plug.

TOILETRIES AND SUNDRIES

Most hotels and game lodges provide toiletries such as soap, shampoo, and insect repellent, so you don't need to overpack these items. In the larger lodges in South Africa's national parks and private game reserves, stores and gift shops are fairly well stocked with clothing and guidebooks; in self-drive and self-catering areas, shops also carry food and drink. Many lodges have small shops with a selection of books, clothing, and curios.

⚠ **The African sun is harsh, and if you're even remotely susceptible to burning, especially coming from a northern winter, don't skimp on sunscreens and moisturizers.**

ON SAFARI

Your safari will be one of the most memorable trips you'll ever take, and it's essential that your African experience matches the one you've always imagined. Nothing should be left to chance, and that includes where you'll stay and how you'll get around.

ACCOMMODATIONS

The days are long gone when legendary 19th-century explorer Dr. David Livingstone pitched his travel-stained tent under a tree and ate his sparse rations. But whether you go simple in a basic safari tent with an adjacent bucket shower and long-drop toilet, choose ultracomfort in a mega-tent or canvas-and-thatch chalet, or go totally over the top in a glass-walled aerie-cum-penthouse with a state-of-the-art designer interior, you'll still feel very much part of the bush.

LUXURY LODGES
Some would say that using the word luxury with safari lodge is redundant, because all such lodges fall into this category. But there's luxurious, and then there's *luxurious*. Options in the latter category range from Out of Africa–type accommodations with antique furniture, crystal, and wrought-iron chandeliers to thatch-roofed stone chalets, Tuscan villas, and suites that wouldn't seem out of place in midtown Manhattan. In nearly all, you can expect to find air-conditioning; in many there will be a small library, a spa, a gift shop, and Internet service—often in a "business center" (a computer in the main lodge) or Wi-Fi. You may even have your own plunge pool.

PERMANENT TENTED CAMPS
Think luxurious, oh-so-comfortable, and spacious . . . in a tent. This is no ordinary tent, though. Each has its own bathroom, usually with an outdoor shower; a wooden deck with table and chairs that overlooks the bush; carpet or wooden floors; big "windows"; and an inviting

four-poster (usually) bed with puffy pillows and fluffy blankets (for those cold winter months). The public space will comprise a bar, a lounge, dining areas, viewing decks, usually a pool, and a curio shop. Some will have Wi-Fi, air-conditioning, and private plunge pools.

MOBILE TENTED CAMPS

This option varies enormously. You could have the original, roomy walk-in dome tent (complete with canvas bedrolls, crisp cotton bedding on GI stretchers, open-air flush toilets, and bucket showers) that's ready and waiting for you at day's end. Or you could have luxury tents (with crystal chandeliers, antique rugs, and shining silver) that stay in one place for a few months during peak seasons. They're all fully serviced (the staff travels with the tents), and you'll dine under the stars or sip coffee as the sun rises.

NATIONAL PARK ACCOMMODATIONS

What you'll get in this category depends on which park you're in and what type of lodgings you're looking for. Accommodations can vary from campsites to simple one-room rondavels, or round huts, with en-suite bathrooms; safari tents to two- to four-bed cottages; or possibly a top-of-the-range guesthouse that sleeps eight people. With the exception of some camping sites, and some places in South Africa, all national-park accommodations are fully serviced with staff to look after you.

CHILDREN ON SAFARI

Most safari operators and private game reserves don't accept children under a certain age, usually under 8, but sometimes the age limit is as high as 12. This age limit is largely for safety reasons. Animals often respond, not in a positive manner, to something that is younger, slower, or smaller than they are. And even though you might think your six- or seven-year-old adores all sorts of animals and bugs, you'd be surprised how overwhelmed kids can become, out of the comfort of their home and backyard, by the size and multitude of African insects and wildlife.

Take into account, also, that when you're following a strange schedule (with jet lag) and getting in and out of small planes, safari vehicles, boats, and the like with other people whom you probably won't know, there often is no time to deal with recalcitrant children—and fussing will, you can be guaranteed, annoy the other people in your plane or lodge, who have spent a great deal of money for what may be a once-in-a-lifetime safari trip.

One option, if you can afford it, is to book a private safari where no other people are involved and you dictate the schedule. Many private lodges will rent you the entire property for the length of your stay; this is often the only way these camps allow children under age eight on safari. At the very least, a camp will require that you pay for a private safari vehicle and guide if you have children under 12. Be advised that, even if you're renting the whole camp, babies and toddlers still aren't allowed out on game-viewing trips.

One great family option is to stay with &Beyond, a safari operator with children's programs at several of its upscale camps. While you follow your own program, your kids pursue their own wilderness activities, and you all meet up later for meals and other activities.

A much cheaper alternative is also one of the most enjoyable for a safari as a family: a self-driving trip where you stay at national parks. No destination is better in this regard than Kruger National Park, where there are comfortable accommodations and lots of other families around. You'll be able to set your own schedule, rent a cottage large enough for the entire family, and buy and prepare food you know your children will eat.

It's best not to visit malarial areas with children under age 10. Young kidneys are especially vulnerable to both the effects of malaria and the side effects of malaria prophylactics. You might opt to practice stringent nonchemical preventive measures, but know the risks: malaria's effects on young children are much worse than they are on older people.

Babies aren't allowed in safari vehicles. Some lodges provide babysitting services for infants. The sound of an infant crying puts most predators on alert—dangerous to other passengers as well as the child. Keep in mind also that the bush is often a hot and dusty place with little in the way of baby-friendly amenities. You'd have to bring all your own supplies, and if something were to go wrong, there would be no way to get immediate help until a flight could be arranged.

COMMUNICATIONS

You will notice that pretty much everyone in Africa has a cell phone, and areas with 3G reception are increasing rapidly and can include pretty remote areas. Don't count on it, though. This is Africa, and networks can be down. If you urgently need to get in touch with home, most camps have a radio or satellite phone.

Most lodges will have a computer with Internet access, but remember that there's often one computer for all the guests to use, and service is probably coming via satellite so availability may be limited. Many have Wi-Fi, too, although the service can be erratic and slow.

GAME DRIVES

In most regions the best time to find game is in the early morning and early evening, when the animals are most active, although old Africa hands will tell you that you can come across good game at any time of day. Stick to the philosophy "you never know what's around the next corner," and keep your eyes and ears wide open all the time. If your rest camp offers guided night drives on open vehicles with spotlights—go for it. You'll rarely be disappointed, seeing not only big game but also a lot of fascinating little critters that surface only at night. Book your night drive in advance or as soon as you get to camp.

Arm yourself with specialized books on mammals and birds rather than a more general one that tries to cover too much. Airports, lodges, and camp shops stock a good range, but try to bring one with you and do a bit of boning up in advance. Any bird guide by Ken Newman (Struik Publishers) and the *Sasol Guide to Birds* are recommended.

Many national parks have reception areas with charts that show the most recent sightings of wildlife in the area. To be sure you see everything you want to, stop at the nearest reception and ask about a spotting chart, or just chat with the other drivers, rangers, and tourists you may encounter there, who can tell you what they've seen and where.

BATHROOM BREAKS

On your game drive you'll very likely be pointed to a nearby bush (which the ranger checks out before you use it). Tissues and toilet paper are usually available in the vehicle (but you may want to make sure). Sometimes there might be a toilet—well, actually, it'll very likely be a hole in the ground below a toilet seat—called a drop toilet. Bury any paper you use. If you have an emergency, ask your ranger to stop the vehicle and he or she will scout a suitable spot.

GAME RANGERS AND TRACKERS

Game rangers (sometimes referred to as guides) tend to be of two types: those who've come to conservation by way of hunting and those who are professional conservationists. In both cases they have vast experience with and knowledge of the bush and the animals that inhabit it. Rangers often work in conjunction with trackers, who spot animals and advise the rangers where to go. Often a tracker will be busy searching out animal tracks, spoor, and other clues to nearby wildlife while the ranger drives and discusses the animals and their environment. Rangers often communicate with each other via radio when there's been a good sighting.

The quality of your bush experience depends heavily on your guide or game ranger and tracker. A ranger wears many hats while on safari: he's there to entertain you, protect you, and put you as close to the wilderness as possible while serving as bush mechanic, first-aid specialist, and host. He'll often eat meals with you, will explain animal habits and behavior while out in the bush, and, if you're on foot, will keep you alive in the presence of an excitable elephant, buffalo, hippo, or lion. This is no small feat, and each ranger has his particular strengths. Because of the intensity of the safari experience, with its exposure to potentially dangerous animals and tricky situations, your relationship with your guide or ranger is one of trust, friendliness, and respect. Misunderstandings may sometimes occur, but you're one step closer to ensuring that all goes well if you know the protocols and expectations.

INTERACTING WITH YOUR RANGER

Acknowledge that your guide is a professional and an expert in the field, and defer to his knowledge. Instead of trying to show how much you know, follow the example of the hunter, which is to walk quietly and take notice of all the little signs around you. Save social chatter with the guide for when you're back at camp, not out on a game drive. Rangers appreciate questions, which give them an idea of your range of knowledge and of how much detail to include in their animal descriptions. However, if you like to ask a lot of questions, save some for later, especially as several other people are likely to be in the safari vehicle with you. Carry a pocket notebook on game drives and jot down questions as they occur; you can then bring them up at dinner or around the campfire, when your ranger has more time to talk and everyone can participate in the discussion.

Don't let your ranger "guide by the numbers"—providing only a list of an animal's attributes. Politely ask questions and show you'd like to know more. Even the best guides may experience "bush burnout" by the end of a busy safari season with demanding clients, but any guide worthy of the title always goes out of his way to give you the best possible experience. If you suspect yours has a case of burnout, or just laziness, you have a right to ask for certain things. There's never any harm in asking, and you can't expect your guide to read your mind about what you like. If, for example, you have a preference for birds, insects, or whatever, ask your guide to spend time on these subjects. You may be surprised by how happy he is to oblige.

BUSH WALKS

Guided bush walks vary, but usually a maximum of eight guests walk in single file with the armed ranger up front and the tracker at the back. A bush walk is a more intimate experience than a drive. You're up close with the bush and with your fellow walkers and guides. Your guide will brief you thoroughly about where and how to walk, emergency procedures, and the like. If you're in a national park, you'll most likely have to pay an additional fee to have an armed park ranger escort you on your walk.

VEHICLES ON GAME DRIVES

Your safari transportation is determined by your destination and could range from custom-made game-viewing vehicles (full-service safari) to a combi or minivan (basic safari or self-drive). There shouldn't be more than six people per vehicle. To make sure you experience every view, suggest to your ranger that visitors rotate seats for each drive. Be warned if you're going it alone: roads in Africa range from superb to bone crunching. Plan your route carefully, arm yourself with reliable maps, and get up-to-date road conditions before you go.

In closed vehicles, which are used by private touring companies operating in Kruger National Park, sit as close to the driver-guide as possible so you can get in and out of the vehicle more easily and get the best views.

The most common game-viewing vehicle, especially in **South Africa**, is usually a Land Rover or a Land Cruiser. Each vehicle seats six to eight people. Vehicles that have raised, stepped seating—meaning the seats in back are higher than the ones in front—are used for game drives. There are usually three rows of seats after the driver's row; the norm at a luxury lodge is to have two people per row. The more expensive the camp, the fewer people in the vehicle. Sit beside the ranger/driver if you're a bit unsteady, because you won't have to climb up into the rear. In the front row you'll have the clearest conversations with the ranger, but farther back you'll have a clearer, elevated view over the front of the car. The back seats tend to be bumpy, but you get great views.

HEALTH

Of all the horror stories and fantastic nightmares about meeting your end in the bush, the problem you're most likely to encounter will be of your own doing: dehydration. Also be wary of malaria, motion sickness, and intestinal problems. By taking commonsense precautions, your safari will be uneventful from a health perspective but memorable in every other way.

The CDC has information on health risks associated with almost every country on the planet, as well as what precautions to take. The World Health Organization (aka the WHO) is the health arm of the United Nations and has information by topic and by country. Its clear, well-written publication *International Travel and Health,* which you can download from the website, covers everything you need to know about staying healthy abroad.

DEHYDRATION AND OVERHEATING

The African sun is hot and the air is dry, and sweat evaporates quickly in these conditions. You might not realize how much bodily fluid you're losing as a result. Wear a hat, lightweight clothing, and sunscreen—all of which will help your body cope with high temperatures. If you're prone to low blood sugar or have a sensitive stomach, consider bringing along rehydration salts, available at camping stores, to balance your body's fluids and keep you going when you feel listless.

Drink at least 2 to 3 quarts of water a day, and in extreme heat conditions as much as 3 to 4 quarts of water or juice. Drink more if you're exerting yourself physically. Alcohol is dehydrating, so try to limit consumption on hot or long travel days. If you do overdo it at dinner with wine or spirits, or even caffeine, you need to drink even more water to recover the fluid lost as your body processes the alcohol. Antimalarial medications are also very dehydrating, so it's important to drink water while you're taking this medicine.

Don't rely on thirst to tell you when to drink; people often don't feel thirsty until they're a little dehydrated. At the first sign of dry mouth, exhaustion, or headache, drink water, because dehydration is the likely culprit. ■TIP→ **To test for dehydration, pinch the skin on the back of your hand and see if it stays in a peak; if it does, you're dehydrated.** Drink a solution of ½ teaspoon salt and 4 tablespoons sugar dissolved in a quart of water to replace electrolytes.

Heat cramps stem from a low salt level caused by excessive sweating. These muscle pains usually occur in the abdomen, arms, or legs. When a child says he can't take another step, ask if he has cramps. When cramps occur, stop all activity and sit quietly in a cool spot and drink water. Don't do anything strenuous for a few hours after the cramps subside. If heat cramps persist for more than an hour, seek medical assistance.

DON'T SWIM IN LAKES OR STREAMS

Many lakes and streams, particularly east of the watershed divide (i.e., in rivers flowing toward the Indian Ocean), are infected with *bilharzia* (schistosomiasis), a parasite carried by a small freshwater snail. The microscopic fluke enters through the skin of swimmers or waders, attaches itself to the intestines or bladder, and lays eggs. Avoid wading in still waters or in areas close to reeds. If you've been wading or swimming in dubious water, dry yourself off vigorously with a towel immediately upon exiting the water, as this may help to dislodge any flukes before they can burrow into your skin. Fast-moving water is considered safe. If you've been exposed, pop into a pharmacy and purchase a course of treatment and take it to be safe. If your trip is ending shortly after your exposure, take the medicine home and have a checkup once you get there. Bilharzia is easily diagnosed, and it's also easily treated in the early stages.

INSECTS
In summer ticks may be a problem, even in open areas close to cities. If you intend to walk or hike anywhere, use a suitable insect repellent. After your walk, examine your body and clothes for ticks, looking carefully for pepper ticks, which are tiny but may cause tick-bite fever. If you're bitten, keep an eye on the bite. Most people suffer no more than an itchy bump, so don't panic. If the tick was infected, however, the bite will swell, itch, and develop a black necrotic center. This is a sure sign that you'll develop tick-bite fever, which usually hits after about 8 to 12 days. Symptoms may be mild or severe, depending on the patient. This disease isn't usually life-threatening in healthy adults, but it's horribly unpleasant. ■TIP➔ **Check your boots for spiders and other crawlies and shake your clothes out before getting dressed.**

Always keep a lookout for mosquitoes. Even in nonmalarial areas they're extremely irritating. When walking anywhere in the bush, watch out for snakes. If you see one, give it a wide berth and you should be fine. Snakes really bite only when they're taken by surprise, so you don't want to step on a napping mamba.

INTESTINAL UPSET
Micro-fauna and micro-flora differ in every region of Africa, so if you drink unfiltered water, add ice to your soda, or eat fruit from a roadside stand, you might get traveler's diarrhea. All reputable hotels and lodges have filtered, clean tap water or provide sterilized drinking water, and nearly all camps and lodges have supplies of bottled water. If you're traveling outside organized safari camps in rural Africa or are unsure of local water, carry plenty of bottled water and follow the CDC's advice for fruits and vegetables: boil it, cook it, peel it, or forget it. If you're going on a mobile safari, ask about drinking water.

MALARIA
The most serious health problem facing travelers is malaria. The risk is medium at the height of the summer and very low in winter. All travelers heading into malaria-endemic regions should consult a health-care professional at least one month before departure for advice. Unfortunately, the malarial agent *Plasmodium sp.* seems to be able to develop a hardy resistance to new prophylactic drugs pretty quickly, so the best prevention is to avoid being bitten by mosquitoes in the first place.

After sunset, wear light-colored (mosquitoes and tsetse flies are attracted to dark surfaces), loose, long-sleeve shirts, long pants, and shoes and socks, and apply mosquito repellent (that contains DEET) generously.

Always sleep in a mosquito-proof room or tent, and if possible, keep a fan going in your room. If you're pregnant or trying to conceive, some malaria medicines are safe to use, but in general it's best to avoid malaria areas entirely.

Generally speaking, the risk is much lower in the dry season (May–October) and peaks immediately after the first rains, which should be in November, but El Niño has made that a lot less predictable.

If you've been bitten by an infected mosquito, you can expect to feel the effects anywhere from 7 to 90 days afterward. Typically you'll feel like you have the flu, with worsening high fever, chills and sweats, headache, and muscle aches. In some cases this is accompanied by abdominal pain, diarrhea, and a cough. If it's not treated, you could die. It's possible to treat malaria after you've contracted it, but this shouldn't be your long-term strategy for dealing with the disease. ⚠ **If you feel ill even several months after you return home, tell your doctor that you've been in a malaria-infected area.**

MEDICAL CARE AND MEDICINE

As a foreigner, you'll be expected to pay in full for any medical services, so check your existing health plan to see whether you're covered while abroad, and supplement it if necessary. South African doctors are generally excellent. The equipment and training in private clinics rival the best in the world, but public hospitals tend to suffer from overcrowding and underfunding and are best avoided.

OVER-THE-COUNTER REMEDIES

You can buy over-the-counter medication in pharmacies and supermarkets. For expediency, however, you should bring your own supply for your trip and rely on pharmacies just for emergency medication.

MOTION SICKNESS

If you're prone to motion sickness, be sure to examine your safari itinerary closely. Though most landing strips for chartered planes aren't paved but rather grass, earth, or gravel, landings are smooth most of the time. If you're not sure how you'll react, take motion-sickness pills just in case. Most of the air transfers take an average of only 30 minutes and the rewards will be infinitely greater than the pains.

■ TIP➔ **When you fly in small planes, take a sun hat and a pair of sunglasses.** If you sit in the front seat next to the pilot, or on the side with the sun, you'll experience harsh glare that could give you a severe headache and exacerbate motion sickness.

SEASONS

The seasons in sub-Saharan Africa are opposite of those in North America. Summer is December through March, autumn is April and May, winter is June through September, and spring is October and November.

HIGH SEASON

High season, also called **dry season**, refers to the winter months in southern Africa when there's little to no rain at all. Days are sunny and bright, but the nights are cool. In the desert, temperatures can plummet to below freezing, but you'll be snug and warm in your tent wherever

CLOSE UP

Safari Do's and Don'ts

11

Do observe animals silently. Talking loudly frightens animals and disturbs their activities.

Don't attempt to attract an animal's attention. Don't imitate sounds, clap hands, pound the vehicle, or throw objects.

Do respect your driver and guide's judgment. They have more knowledge and experience than you. If they say no, there's a good reason for it.

Don't leave your vehicle. On self-drives, drive slowly, and keep ample distance between you and the wildlife.

Do dress in neutral tones. If everyone is wearing earth tones, the animal sees one large vegetation-colored mass.

Don't litter. Any tossed item can choke or poison animals.

Don't attempt to feed or approach animals. This is especially important at lodges and campgrounds where animals are accustomed to humans.

Don't smoke. The bush ignites easily.

---

you stay. The landscape will be barren and dry (read: not very attractive), but vegetation is low and surface water is scarce, making it easier to spot game. This is the busiest tourist time.

High season is linked with the summer vacation schedules of South Africans (December through mid-January).

LOW SEASON

When we say "low season," we're saying that this is the **rainy season**. Although the rains are intermittent—often occurring in late afternoon—the bush and vegetation are high and it's more difficult to spot game. It can also get very hot and humid during this time. However, the upside is that there are far fewer tourists, lodge rates are much cheaper (often half price), and the bush is beautifully lush and green. Plus there are lots of baby animals, and if you're a birder, you'll appreciate that all the migrant species are back from their winter habitats.

SHOULDER SEASON

The shoulder season occurs between summer and winter; it's fall in the United States. The rains are just beginning, tourist numbers are decreasing, and the vegetation is starting to die off. Lodges will offer cheaper rates.

To find out exactly what the weather will be for your destination, **African Weather Forecasts** (⊕ *www.africanweather.net*) lists weather information for the entire continent.

WILDLIFE SAFETY AND RESPECT

Nature is neither kind nor sentimental. Don't be tempted to interfere with the natural processes. The animals are going about the business of survival in a harsh environment, and you can unwittingly make this business more difficult. Don't get too close to the animals, and don't try to help them cross some perceived obstacle; you have no idea what it's really trying to do or where it wants to go. If you're intrusive, you could drive animals away from feeding and, even worse, from drinking at water holes, where they're very skittish and vulnerable to predators. That time at the water hole may be their only opportunity to drink that day.

Never feed any wild creature. Not a cute monkey, not an inquisitive baboon, not a baby tree squirrel, or a young bird out of its nest. In some camps and lodges, however, animals have gotten used to being fed or steal food. The most common animals in this category are baboons and monkeys; in some places they sneak into huts, tents, and even occupied vehicles to snatch food. If you see primates around, keep all food out of sight, and keep your windows rolled up. (If a baboon manages to get into your vehicle, he will trash the interior as he searches for food and use the vehicle as a toilet.)

Never try to get an animal to pose with you. This is probably the biggest cause of death and injury on safaris, when visitors don't listen to or believe the warnings from their rangers or posted notices in the public parks. Regardless of how cute or harmless they may look, these animals aren't tame. An herbivore hippo, giraffe, or ostrich can kill you just as easily as a lion, elephant, or buffalo can.

Immersion in the African safari lands is a privilege. To preserve this privilege for later generations, it's important that you view wildlife with minimal disturbance and avoid upsetting the delicate balance of nature at all costs. You're the visitor, so act like you would in someone else's home: respect their space. Caution is your most trusted safety measure. Keep your distance, keep quiet, and keep your hands to yourself, and you should be fine.

NIGHTTIME SAFETY

Never sleep out in the open in any area with wildlife. If you're sleeping in a tent, make sure it's fully closed as in zipped or snapped shut; if it's a small tent, place something between you and the side of the wall to prevent an opportunistic bite from the outside. Also, if you're menstruating, be sure to dispose of your toiletries somewhere other than in or near your tent. All in all, if you're in your tent and not exposed, you should be quite safe. Few people lose their lives to lions or hyenas. Malaria is a much more potent danger, so keep your tent zipped up tight at night to keep out mosquitoes.

Never walk alone. Most camps and lodges insist that an armed ranger accompany you to and from your accommodation at night, and rightly so.

TRAVEL SMART
SOUTH AFRICA

GETTING HERE AND AROUND

Countless cities, towns, streets, parks, and more have gotten or will get new monikers, both to rid the country of names that recall the apartheid era and to honor the previously unsung. The names in this book were accurate at time of writing but may still change.

▌ AIR TRAVEL

Some South Africa–bound flights from United States cities have refueling stops en route, and sometimes those stops can be delayed. Don't plan anything on the ground too rigidly after arriving; leave yourself a cushion for a connecting flight to a game lodge. At this writing, only South African Airways and Delta provide direct service from the United States to South Africa, but flights routed through Europe may be more pleasant since they allow you a stop en route.

In peak season (midsummer, which is from December to the end of February, and South African school vacations), give yourself at least a half hour extra at the airport for domestic flights, as the check-in lines can be endless—particularly on flights to the coast at the start of vacations and back to Johannesburg's O. R. Tambo International Airport at the end.

If you are returning home with souvenirs, leave time for a V.A.T. (Value-Added Tax) inspection before you join the line for your international flight check-in. And it's always a good idea to check what you can and cannot carry onto the plane. ▌TIP→ There are fairly long distances between gates and terminals at Johannesburg's O. R. Tambo, particularly between the international and domestic terminals, so clear security before stopping for a snack or shopping, as you don't want to scramble for your flight.

The longest domestic flight within South Africa is only two hours.

If you are visiting a game lodge deep in the bush, you will be arriving by light plane—and you will be restricted in what you can bring. Excess luggage can usually be stored with the operator until your return. Don't just gloss over this: charter operators take weight very seriously, and some will charge you for an extra ticket if you insist on bringing excess baggage (⇨ *Charter Flights, below*).

Airline Security Issues Transportation Security Administration ⊕ *www.tsa.gov.*

AIRPORTS

Most international flights arrive at and depart from Johannesburg's O. R. Tambo International Airport, 19 km (12 miles) from the city. The country's other major airports are in Cape Town and Durban, but international flights departing from Cape Town often stop in Johannesburg. O.R. Tambo has a tourist information desk, a V.A.T. refund office, several ATMs, and a computerized accommodations service. Porters, who wear a bright-orange-and-navy-blue uniform with an Airports Company of South Africa badge, work exclusively for tips (R5 or R10 a bag). If you're leaving O. R. Tambo's international terminal (Terminal A), the domestic terminal (Terminal B) is connected by a busy and fairly long walkway. ▌TIP→ Allow 10–15 minutes' walking time between international and domestic terminals.

The Cape Town and Durban airports are much smaller and more straightforward. Cape Town International is 19 km (12 miles) southeast of the city, and Durban International is 16 km (10 miles) north of the city. If you are traveling to or from either Johannesburg or Cape Town airport (and, to a lesser extent, Durban) be aware of the time of day. Traffic can be horrendous between 7 and 9 in the morning and between about 3:30 and 6 in the evening.

Just 40 km (25 miles) outside Johannesburg's city center in the northern suburbs, Lanseria International Airport is closer to Sandton than O. R. Tambo and handles executive jets, company jets, domestic scheduled flights to and from Cape Town, and some charter flights to safari camps. It has a 24-hour customs and immigration counter, a café, and a high-end flight store. It's a popular alternative for visiting dignitaries and other VIPs.

The other major cities are served by small airports that are really easy to navigate. Port Elizabeth is the main airport for the Eastern Cape, George serves the Garden Route, and the closest airports to Kruger National Park are the small airports at Nelspruit, Hoedspruit, and Phalaborwa. Most airports are managed by the Airports Company of South Africa. *For more information, see individual destination chapters.*

Airport Information **Airports Company of South Africa** ☎ 086/727–7888 *flight information* ⊕ *www.acsa.co.za.*

Domestic Airports **Bram Fischer International Airport** (*BFN*). ✉ *Bloemfontein* ☎ *051/407–2200* ⊕ *www.acsa.co.za.*

International Airports **Cape Town International Airport** (*CPT*). ✉ *Matroosfontein, Cape Town* ☎ *021/937–1200* ⊕ *www. capetown-airport.com.* **Durban International Airport** (*DUR*). ✉ *King Shaka Dr., La Mercy, Durban* ☎ *032/436–6585* ⊕ *www. kingshakainternational.co.za.* **Lanseria International Airport** (*HLA*). ✉ *Airport Rd., Lanseria, Johannesburg* ☎ *011/367–0300* ⊕ *www.lanseria.co.za.* **O. R. Tambo International Airport** (*JNB*). ✉ *OR Tambo Airport Rd., Johannesburg* ☎ *011/921–6911* ⊕ *www. johannesburg-airport.com.*

⇨ *For more information about airports and ground transportation, see Getting Here and Around, in each chapter.*

FLIGHTS

South Africa's international airline is South African Airways (SAA), which offers nonstop service between Johannesburg and New York–JFK (JFK) and Washington–Dulles (IAD), though some flights from Dulles make a stopover in Dakar, Senegal. Delta also offers nonstop service from the United States to South Africa. Flight times from the U.S. East Coast range from 15 hours (from Atlanta to Johannesburg on Delta) to almost 20 hours (on Delta via Amsterdam). When booking flights, check the routing carefully; some involve stopovers of an hour or two, which may change from day to day. European airlines serving South Africa are British Airways, KLM, Virgin Atlantic, Lufthansa, and Air France.

Three major domestic airlines have flights connecting South Africa's principal airports. SA Airlink and SA Express are subsidiaries of SAA, and Comair is a subsidiary of British Airways. Comair and SAA serve Livingstone, Zambia (for Victoria Falls); Air Zimbabwe and SAA serve Victoria Falls airport in Zimbabwe.

Recent years have seen an explosion of low-cost carriers serving popular domestic routes in South Africa with regularly scheduled flights. Kulula.com and Mango provide reasonably priced domestic air tickets if you book in advance. Phakalane Airways provides service to airports in the Northern Cape. The only downside is that they have fewer flights per day and aren't always cheaper than SAA.

Airlines **Air France** ☎ *0861/340–340 in South Africa, 800/237–2747 in U.S.* ⊕ *www. airfrance.co.za.* **British Airways** ☎ *011/441–8600 in South Africa, 800/247–9297 in U.S.* ⊕ *www.britishairways.com.* **Delta** ☎ *800/241–4141 in U.S., 011/408–8200 in South Africa* ⊕ *www.delta.com.***KLM** ☎ *0860/247–747 in South Africa, 866/434–0320 in U.S.* ⊕ *www. klm.com.* **Lufthansa** ☎ *0861/842–538 in South Africa, 800/645–3880 in U.S.* ⊕ *www.lufthansa. com.* **South African Airways** ☎ *800/521–4845 in U.S., 0860/003–146 in South Africa* ⊕ *www.flysaa.com.* **United** ☎ *800/864–8331 in U.S., 011/463–1170 in South Africa* ⊕ *www. united.com.* **Virgin Atlantic** ☎ *011/340–3400 in South Africa, 800/862–8621 in U.S.* ⊕ *www. virgin-atlantic.com.*

Domestic Airlines Air Zimbabwe
☎ 263/457–5021 ⊕ www.airzimbabwe.aero.
British Airways Comair ☎ 011/921–0222
in South Africa, 0860/435–922 toll-free in
South Africa, 800/247–9297 in U.S. ⊕ www.
britishairways.com. **Kulula** ☎ 086/158–5852
in South Africa ⊕ www.kulula.com. **Mango**
☎ 011/086–6100 in Johannesburg, 021/815–
4100 in Cape Town, 086/101–0002 toll-free in
South Africa ⊕ www.flymango.com. **Phakalane Airways.** Phakalane Airways provides air
connections between Kimberley, Upington, and
Springbok in conjunction with the Northern
Cape Provincial Department. ✉ Springbok
☎ 053/492–0001 ⊕ www.phakalaneairways.
co.za. **SA Airlink** ☎ 011/451–7300 in South
Africa, 010/590–3170 in South Africa ⊕ www.
flyairlink.com. **SA Express** ☎ 086/172–9227
toll-free in South Africa ⊕ www.flyexpress.aero.

CHARTER FLIGHTS

Charter companies are a common mode
of transportation when getting to safari
lodges and remote destinations throughout southern Africa. These aircraft are
well maintained and are almost always
booked by your lodge or travel agent.
The major charter companies run daily
shuttles from O. R. Tambo to popular
tourism destinations, such as Kruger Park.
On-demand flights are very expensive for
independent travelers, as they require
minimum passenger loads. If it's just two
passengers, you will be charged for the
vacant seats. Keep in mind that you probably won't get to choose the charter company you fly with. The aircraft you get
depends on the number of passengers flying and can vary from very small (you will
sit in the copilot's seat) to a much more
comfortable commuter plane.

Because of the limited space and size of
the aircraft, charter carriers observe strict
luggage regulations: luggage must be soft-
sided and weigh no more than 57 pounds
(and often less); on many charter flights
the weight cannot exceed 33 pounds.

African Ramble flies out of Plettenberg Bay
and Port Elizabeth and will take direct
bookings. **Federal Air** is the largest charter
air company in South Africa; it's based

at Johannesburg's O. R. Tambo International Airport and has its own efficient
terminal with a gift shop, refreshments,
and a unique, thatched-roof outdoor
lounge. It also has branches in Cape
Town, Durban, and Nelspruit (near Kruger). Wilderness Air (previously **Sefofane**)
is a Botswana-based fly-in charter company that will take you anywhere there's
a landing strip from its base in Jo'burg's
Lanseria Airport.

Charter Companies African Ramble
☎ 084/359–2929, 083/375–6514 ⊕ www.
aframble.co.za. **Federal Air** ☎ 011/395–9000
⊕ www.fedair.com. **Wilderness Air** ⊕ www.
wilderness-air.com.

▌ BUS TRAVEL

Greyhound, Intercape Mainliner, and
Translux operate extensive bus networks
that serve all major cities. The buses are
comfortable, sometimes there are videos,
and tea and coffee are served on board.
Travel times can be long; for example,
Cape Town to Johannesburg takes 19
hours. Johannesburg to Durban, at
about seven hours, is less stressful. The
Garden Route is less intense if you take
it in stages, but the whole trip from Cape
Town to Port Elizabeth takes 12 hours.
Buses are usually pretty punctual. Greyhound and Intercape buses can be booked
directly or through Computicket.

For travelers with a sense of adventure,
a bit of time, and not too much money,
the Baz Bus runs a daily hop-on/hop-off
door-to-door service between backpackers' hostels around South Africa and other
countries in the region. The rates are a
bit higher than for the same distance on a
standard bus, but you can break the journey up into a number of different legs,
days or weeks apart, and the bus drops
you off at some hostels so you don't need
to find taxis, shuttles, or lifts. The Baz Bus
offers both 7-day and 14-day unrestricted
packages, an especially useful service if
you're planning a long leg followed by a

few short ones before returning to your starting point.

■ **TIP→** It is illegal to smoke on buses in South Africa.

Approximate one-way prices for all three major bus lines are R530–R630 Cape Town to Tshwane (Pretoria), R320–R360 Cape Town to Springbok, R260–R370 Cape Town to George, R380–R510 Cape Town to Port Elizabeth, R250–R350 Johannesburg to Durban, and R600–R750 Cape Town to Durban. Baz Bus also runs direct routes between cities, with prices comparable to those of major bus lines.

Contacts Baz Bus ☎ *021/422-5202, 086/122-9287 toll-free* ⊕ *www.bazbus.com.* **Computicket** ☎ *0861/915-8000* ⊕ *www. computicket.co.za.* **Greyhound** ☎ *083/915-9000* ⊕ *www.greyhound.co.za.* **Intercape Mainliner** ☎ *021/380-4400* ⊕ *www.intercape. co.za.* **Translux** ☎ *0861/589-282* ⊕ *www. translux.co.za.*

■ CAR TRAVEL

South Africa has a superb network of multilane roads and highways, so driving can be a pleasure. Remember, though, that distances are vast, so guard against fatigue, which is an even bigger killer than alcohol. Toll roads, scattered among the main routes, charge anything from R10 to R60.

You can drive in South Africa for up to six months on any English-language license.

South Africa's Automobile Association publishes a range of maps, atlases, and travel guides, available for purchase on its website. Maps and map books are also available at all major bookstores.

The commercial website Drive South Africa has everything you need to know about driving in the country, including road safety and driving distances.

⚠ **Carjackings can and do occur with such frequency that certain high-risk areas are marked by permanent carjacking signs** (⇨ *Safety*).

Maps and Information Drive South Africa ☎ *021/423-6957* ⊕ *www.drivesouthafrica. co.za.*

GASOLINE

Service stations (open 24 hours) are positioned at regular intervals along all major highways in South Africa. There are no self-service stations. In return, tip the attendant R2–R5 (more if you've filled the tank). South Africa has a choice of unleaded or leaded gasoline, and many vehicles operate on diesel—be sure you get the right fuel. Gasoline is measured in liters, and the cost is higher than in the United States. When driving long distances, check your routes carefully, as the distances between towns—and hence gas stations—can be more than 100 miles.

DRIVING FROM	TO	RTE./ DISTANCE
Cape Town	Port Elizabeth	769 km (478 miles)
Cape Town	Johannesburg	1,402 km (871 miles)
Johannesburg	Durban	583 km (361 miles)
Johannesburg	Kruger National Park	355 km (220 miles)
Kruger National Park	Victoria Falls, Zimbabwe	1,090 km (677 miles)
Johannesburg	Pretoria	58 km (36 miles)

PARKING

In the countryside, parking is mostly free, but you will almost certainly need to pay for parking in cities, which will probably run you about R5–R8 per hour. Many towns have an official attendant (who should be wearing a vest of some sort) who will log the number of the spot you park in; you're asked to pay up front for the amount of time you expect to park. If the guard is unofficial, acknowledge them on arrival, ask them to look after your car, and pay a few rand when you return (they depend on these tips). At pay-and-display parking lots you pay in advance;

other garages expect payment at the exit. Many (such as those at shopping malls and airports) require that you pay for your parking before you return to your car (at kiosks near the exits to the parking areas). Your receipt ticket allows you to exit. Just read the signs carefully.

ROAD CONDITIONS

South African roads are mostly excellent, but it's dangerous to drive at night in some rural areas, as roads are not always fenced and animals often stray onto the road. In very remote areas only the main road might be paved, whereas many secondary roads are of high-quality gravel. Traffic is often light in these areas, so be sure to bring extra water and carry a spare, a jack, and a tire iron (your rental car should come with these).

RULES OF THE ROAD

South Africans drive on the left-hand side of the road, British-style. That may be confusing at first, but having the steering wheel on the right helps to remind you that the driver should be closer to the middle of the road.

Throughout the country, the speed limit is 100 kph (60 mph) or 120 kph (about 75 mph) on the open road and usually 60 kph (35 mph) or 80 kph (about 50 mph) in towns. Of course, many people drive far faster than that. Wearing seat belts is required by law, and the legal blood-alcohol limit is 0.08 mg/100 ml, which means about one glass of wine puts you at the limit. It is illegal to talk on a handheld mobile phone while driving.

South African drivers tend to be aggressive and reckless, thinking nothing of tailgating at high speeds and passing on blind rises. Traffic accidents are a major problem.

If it's safe to do so, it's courteous for slow vehicles to move over onto the shoulder, which is separated from the road by a solid yellow line. (In built-up areas, however, road shoulders are occasionally marked by red lines. This is a strict "no-stopping" zone.) The more aggressive drivers expect this and will flash their lights at you if you don't. Where there are two lanes in each direction, remember that the right-hand lane is for passing.

In towns, minibus taxis can be quite unnerving, swerving in and out of traffic without warning to pick up customers. Stay alert at all times. Many cities use mini-traffic circles in lieu of four-way stops. These can be dangerous, particularly if you're not used to them. In theory, the first vehicle to the circle has the right-of-way; otherwise yield to the right. In practice, keep your wits about you at all times. In most cities traffic lights are on poles at the side of the street. In Johannesburg the lights are only on the far side of each intersection, so don't stop in front of the light or you'll be in the middle of the intersection.

In South African parlance, traffic lights are known as "robots," and what people refer to as the "pavement" is actually the sidewalk. Paved roads are just called roads. Gas is referred to as petrol, and gas stations are petrol stations.

RENTAL CARS

Renting a car gives you the freedom to roam freely and set your own timetable. Most of Cape Town's most popular destinations are an easy drive from the City Bowl. Many people enjoy the slow pace of exploring South Africa's Garden Route by car, or a few days meandering through the Winelands on their own.

Roads in South Africa are generally good, and rates are similar to those in the United States. Some companies charge more on weekends, so it's best to get a range of quotes before booking your car. Request car seats and extras such as GPS when you book, and ask for details on what to do if you have a mechanical problem or other emergency.

For a car with automatic transmission and air-conditioning, you'll pay slightly less for a car that doesn't have unlimited mileage. When comparing prices, make sure you're getting the same thing.

Some companies quote prices without insurance, some include 80% or 90% coverage, and some quote with 100% protection. Get all terms in writing before you leave on your trip.

Most major international companies have offices in tourist cities and at international airports, and their vehicle types are the same range you'd find at home. There's no need to rent a 4x4 vehicle, as all roads are paved, including those in Kruger National Park.

Maui Motorhome Rentals offers fully equipped motor homes, camper vans, and 4x4 vehicles, many of which come totally equipped for a bush sojourn. Prices start at around R1,500 per day, not including insurance, and require a five-day minimum.

You can often save some money by booking a car through a broker, who will access the car from one of the main agencies. Smaller, local agencies often give a much better price, but the car must be returned in the same city. This is pretty popular in Cape Town but not so much in other centers.

To rent a car you need to be 23 years or older and have held a driver's license for three years. Younger international drivers can rent from some companies but will pay a penalty. You need to get special permission to take rental cars into neighboring countries (including Lesotho and Swaziland). Most companies allow additional drivers, but some charge.

Leave ample time to return your car when your trip is over. You shouldn't feel rushed when settling your bill. Be sure to get copies of your receipt.

CAR-RENTAL INSURANCE

In South Africa it's necessary to buy special insurance if you plan to cross borders into neighboring countries, but CDW and TDW (collision damage waiver and theft-damage waiver) are optional on domestic rentals. Any time you are considering crossing a border with your rental vehicle, you must inform the rental company

ahead of time to fulfill any paperwork requirements and pay additional fees.

Emergency Services General emergency number ☎ *112 from mobile phone, 10111 from landline, 107 for Cape Town only.*

Local Agencies Car Mania ☎ *021/447–3001* ⊕ *www.carmania.co.za.* **Maui Motorhome Rental** ☎ *011/396–1445, 021/385–1616* ⊕ *www.maui.co.za.* **Value Car Hire** ☎ *021/386–7699* ⊕ *www.valuerentalcar.com.*

Major Agencies Avis ☎ *0861/021–111, 011/387–8431* ⊕ *www.avis.co.za.* **Budget** ☎ *800/472–3325* ⊕ *www.budget.co.za.* **Europcar** ☎ *0861/131–000, 011/479–4000* ⊕ *www.europcar.co.za.* **Hertz** ☎ *021/935–4800* ⊕ *www.hertz.co.za.* **National Car Rental** ☎ *877/222–9058* ⊕ *www.nationalcar.com.*

▋ TRAIN TRAVEL

Shosholoza Meyl operates an extensive system of passenger trains along eight routes that connect all major cities and many small towns in South Africa. Departures are usually limited to one per day, although trains covering minor routes leave less frequently. Distances are vast, so many journeys require overnight travel. The service is good and the trains are safe and well maintained, but this is far from a luxury option, except in Premier Classe, the luxury service that runs between Cape Town and Johannesburg or Port Elizabeth and between Jo'burg and Durban. In Premier Classe, sleeping compartments accommodate two to four travelers, and single compartments are also available. Compartments include a/c, bedding, and limited room service (drinks only). The Jo'burg–Cape Town and Jo'burg–Durban routes have a compartment for vehicles (including 4x4s).

Tourist Class (the old first class) has four-sleeper (bunks) and two-sleeper compartments. Don't expect a/c, heat, or a shower in either class. Bathrooms are shared, compartments have a sink, and bedding can be rented. The dining car serves pretty ordinary food, but it's inexpensive.

We do not recommend Third class or Economy Class (aka "sitter class") because that's what you do—up to 25 hours on a hard seat with up to 71 other people in the car, sharing two toilets and no shower.

You must reserve tickets in Premier Classe and Tourist Class, whereas sitter-class tickets require no advance booking. You can book up to three months in advance by telephone, with travel agents, at reservations offices in major cities, and at railway stations.

A fun way to see the country is on the Shongololo Express. The train is as basic as the Shosholoza Meyl trains, but while you sleep at night, it heads to a new destination. After breakfast, tour buses are loaded, and you explore the surroundings. In the evening, you reboard the train, have supper, and sleep while the train moves to the next stop. Trips include the Dune Adventure (the dunes of Namibia), the Good Hope Adventure (Cape attractions), and the Southern Cross Adventure (six African countries). Rates start at about R1,500 per person per night. By the way, a *shongololo* is a millipede.

Contacts Premier Classe ☎ 011/733–9247 ⊕ www.premierclasse.co.za. **Shongololo Express** ☎ 0861/777–014, 0027/11 486–4357 (Outside South Africa) ⊕ www.shongololo.com. **Shosholoza Meyl** ☎ 086/000–8888 ⊕ www.shosholozameyl.co.za.

LUXURY TRAIN TRIPS
South Africa's leisurely and divine luxury trains come complete with gold-and-brass-plated fixtures, oak paneling, and full silver service for every meal. The elegant Blue Train travels several routes, but the main one is between Cape Town and Tshwane (Pretoria). It departs once a week in each direction, takes 28 hours, and starts from R17,030 per person sharing one way (peak season). The fare includes all meals (extravagant three-course affairs), drinks (a full bar and great selection of South African wines), and excursions (usually a two-hour stop in Kimberley). Only caviar and French Champagne are excluded. The Blue Train also goes to Durban from Tshwane for from R6,740 per person sharing.

Rovos Rail's *Pride of Africa* runs from Cape Town to Tshwane every Monday (and sometimes other days). Fares are R15,200 for the 72-hour trip in Pullman Class; fancier suites cost up to R30,500. Rovos also includes all excursions, sumptuous meals, all drinks (except French Champagne), and excellent butler service, but whereas the Blue Train excels in modern luxury, the *Pride of Africa* creates an atmosphere of Victorian colonial charm (no cell phones or laptops in public spaces), and is the only luxury train in the world in which you can open the windows. Rovos also has a nine-day Cape Town–Swakopmund round-trip in April and May, and a 14-day epic Cape Town–Dar es Salaam loop in January, July, and September. Prices per person can reach R32,800 for the Royal Suite on the three-night, four-day trip from Cape Town to Victoria Falls.

All prices are for double occupancy; the single-occupancy supplement is 50%.

Contacts Blue Train ☎ 012/334–8459 in Pretoria, 021/449–2672 in Cape Town, 973/832–4384 in U.S. ⊕ www.bluetrain.co.za. **Rovos Rail** ☎ 012/315–8242 ⊕ www.rovos.com.

ESSENTIALS

∎ ACCOMMODATIONS

The Tourism Grading Council of South Africa is the official accreditation and grading body for accommodation in South Africa. However, you may still find some establishments clinging to other grading systems. Hotels, bed-and-breakfasts, guesthouses, and game lodges are graded on a star rating from one to five. Grading is not compulsory, and there are many excellent establishments that are not graded. Those that are given a grade are revisited annually; however, these marks are purely subjective and reflect the comfort level and quality of the surroundings.

Be warned that in southern Africa, words do not necessarily mean what you think they do. The term *lodge* is a particularly tricky one. A guest lodge or a game lodge is almost always an upmarket, full-service facility with loads of extra attractions. But the term *lodge* when applied to city hotels often indicates a minimum-service hotel, like the City and Town Lodges and Holiday Inn Garden Courts. A backpacker lodge, however, is essentially a hostel.

A *rondavel* can be a small cabin, often in a rounded shape, and its cousin, the *banda,* can be anything from a basic stand-alone structure to a Quonset hut. Think very rustic.

We always list the facilities that are available—but we don't specify whether they cost extra: when pricing accommodations, always ask what's included. Price categories are based on a property's least expensive standard double room in high season (excluding holidays). We do not review rustic campgrounds (as opposed to the fairly luxurious safari tents at many private game lodges), but we may mention where they exist alongside other accommodations.

Be sure you understand the hotel's cancellation policy. Some places allow you to cancel without any kind of penalty—even if you prepaid to secure a discounted rate—if you cancel at least 24 hours in advance. Others require you to cancel a week in advance or penalize you the cost of one night. Small inns and B&Bs are most likely to require you to cancel far in advance. Always have written confirmation of your booking when you check in.

∎ **TIP→** Most hotels allow children under a certain age to stay in their parents' room at no extra charge, but others charge for them as extra adults, and some don't allow children under 12 at all. Ask about the policy on children before checking in, and make sure you find out the cutoff age for discounts.

In South Africa, most accommodations from hotels to guesthouses do include breakfast in the rate. Most game lodges include all meals, or they may be all-inclusive (including alcohol as well). All hotels listed have private bath unless otherwise noted.

BED-AND-BREAKFASTS

B&Bs are ubiquitous in South Africa. Many are very small and personalized. For more information, contact the Bed and Breakfast Association of South Africa (BABASA) or the Portfolio Collection, which represents more than 700 lodging options in South Africa and publishes a respected list of South Africa's best B&Bs that may also be useful; it offers a similar guide to small hotels and lodges.

Contacts **BABASA** ☎ *082/239–2111, 012/480–4012* ⊕ *www.babasa.co.za.* **Portfolio Collection** ☎ *021/701–9632* ⊕ *www. portfoliocollection.com.* **SA-Venues** ⊕ *www. sa-venues.com.*

FARM STAYS

The Farm Stay website lists a range of farms with self-catering or bed-and-breakfast accommodation in rural areas. Activities on offer include game-viewing, bird-watching, hiking, biking, and horse riding.

Contact **Farm Stay** ☎ 039/313–0770 ⊕ www. farmstay.co.za.

GAME LODGES

Game lodges in South Africa are often designed to fulfill your wildest wildlife fantasy. Top designers have created magical worlds in styles from African chic to throwback bush romance. At the highest end, you can enjoy dinner under starlight on your own deck, or swap stories around the boma (outdoor eating area) at night. For some people the first glimpse of their accommodations is a thrill to rival the best game-viewing.

GUESTHOUSES

The term *guesthouse* may conjure up the image of a flophouse, but in South Africa guesthouses are a cross between an inn and a B&B. Usually in residential neighborhoods, they offer an intimate experience that benefits from the proprietor's tastes and interests, often at a vast savings over hotels. A guesthouse manager might make special arrangements to drive you to an attraction, whereas a hotel might charge extra transportation fees. Long-term visitors tend to choose guesthouses, where they can meet other like-minded travelers who are interested in experiencing the country, not just checking off sites.

Contacts **Guest House Accommodation of South Africa** ☎ 021/762–0880 ⊕ www.ghasa. co.za. **Sleeping Out** ☎ 021/762–1543 ⊕ www. sleeping-out.co.za.

HOTELS

Your hotel in South Africa will be similar to one at home; the more you pay, the better the quality and amenities. As at home, peak seasons mean peak prices. There are many international chains represented in South Africa, so check with your frequent-stay program to see if you can get a better room or better rate. It might be more fun, though, to experience a local, or African, establishment.

Most hotel rates will include breakfast in the hotel's dining room, and in South Africa that means a full array of meats,

cheeses, and eggs cooked to order—a little bonus that makes it easier to ease into your touring day.

▮ COMMUNICATIONS

INTERNET

Most hotels have Wi-Fi. Stores such as Woolworths, restaurants such as Wimpy, and most airports offer a countrywide Wi-Fi service called AlwaysOn that allows you 30 minutes of free Wi-Fi per day. If you need more time, you can pay for it.

If you bring your laptop or tablet, you'll have no problem finding Wi-Fi service in the cities, but it's unlikely you'll find anyone to service a Mac outside of Cape Town and Jo'burg.

Contacts **Always On** ⊕ www.alwayson.co.za.

PHONES

There are toll-free numbers in South Africa. There's also something called a share-call line, for which the cost of the call is split between both parties.

The country code for South Africa is 27. When dialing from abroad, drop the initial 0 from local area codes.

CALLING WITHIN SOUTH AFRICA

Local calls (from landline to landline) are very cheap, although all calls from hotels add a hefty premium. Calls between a mobile phone and a landline are relatively expensive (up to R5 per minute). Pay phones may be coin- or card-operated (the former are being phased out). Phone cards are available at newsstands, convenience stores, and telephone company offices.

When making a phone call in South Africa, always use the full 10-digit number, including the area code, even if you're in the same area. For directory assistance in South Africa, call 1023. For operator-assisted national long-distance calls, call 1025. For international operator assistance, dial 10903#. These numbers are free if dialed from a Telkom (landline) phone but are charged at normal cell-phone rates from a mobile—and they're busy call centers. Directory inquiries numbers are different for each cell-phone network. Vodacom is 111, MTN is 200, and Cell C is 146. These calls are charged at normal rates, but the call is timed only from when it is actually answered.

CALLING OUTSIDE SOUTH AFRICA

When dialing out from South Africa, dial 00 before the international code. So, for example, you would dial 001 for the United States, since the country code for the United States is 1.

Internet calling like Skype also works well from the United States, but it's not always functional in South Africa, unless you're on a reliable high-speed Internet connection, which isn't available everywhere. However, if you have a South African "free" cell phone (meaning you can receive calls for free; all phones using an SA SIM card do this), someone in the United States can call you from their Skype account, for reasonable per-minute charges, and you won't be charged.

Access Codes AT&T Direct ☎ 800/288–2020 from South Africa ⊕ www.att.com. **MCI Worldwide Access** ☎ 0800/990–011 from South Africa. **Sprint International Access** ☎ 0800/990–001 from South Africa.

MOBILE PHONES

Cell phones are ubiquitous and have quite extensive coverage. There are four cell-phone service providers in South Africa—Cell C, MTN, Virgin Mobile, and Vodacom—and you can buy these

SIM cards, as well as airtime, in supermarkets for as little as R10 for the SIM card. (If you purchase SIM cards at the airport, you will be charged much more.) Bear in mind that your U.S. cell phone may not work with the local GSM system and/or that your phone may be blocked from using SIM cards outside of your plan if your phone is not unlocked. Basic but functional GSM cell phones start at R100, and are available at the mobile carrier shops as well as major department stores like Woolworths.

Cell phones also can be rented by the day, week, or longer from the airport on your arrival, but this is an expensive option. If you plan to bring a U.S. cell phone while you're traveling, know what your own company will charge both for calls and data use. Texts cost a fraction of a call and are the handiest option for meeting up with local friends, but for calling a hotel reservations line, it's best to make the call.

Cellular Abroad rents and sells GMS phones and sells SIM cards that work in many countries, but they cost a lot more than local solutions. Mobal rents mobiles and sells GSM phones (starting at $49) that will operate in 150 countries. Per-call rates vary throughout the world. Vodacom is the country's leading cellular network.

The least complicated way to make and receive phone calls is to obtain international roaming service from your cell-phone service provider before you leave home, but this can be expensive. Any phone that you take abroad must be unlocked by your company for you to be able to use it.

Contacts Cell C ☎ 084/140 ⊕ www.cellc. co.za. **Cellular Abroad** ☎ 800/287–5072 in U.S., 800/3623–3333 International ⊕ www. cellularabroad.com. **Mobal** ☎ 888/888–9162 in U.S. ⊕ www.mobal.com. **MTN** ☎ 083/173 ⊕ www.mtn.co.za. **Virgin Mobile** ☎ 0741/000–123 ⊕ www.virginmobile.co.za. **Vodacom** ☎ 082/111 ⊕ www.vodacom.co.za.

▮ CUSTOMS AND DUTIES

Visitors may bring in new or used gifts and souvenirs up to a total value of R3,000 duty-free. Duty-free allowances of tobacco and alcoholic beverages are also limited.

The United States is a signatory to CITES, a wildlife protection treaty, and therefore does not allow the importation of living or dead endangered animals, or their body parts, such as rhino horns or ivory. If you purchase an antique that is made partly or wholly of ivory, you must obtain a CITES preconvention certificate that clearly states that the item is at least 100 years old. The import of zebra skin or other tourist products also requires a CITES permit.

U.S. Information **U.S. Customs and Border Protection** ⊕ www.cbp.gov. **U.S. Fish and Wildlife Service** ⊕ www.fws.gov.

▮ EATING OUT

South Africa's cities and towns are full of dining options, from chain restaurants like the popular Nando's to chic cafés. Indian food and Cape Malay dishes are regional favorites in Cape Town, and traditional smoked meats and sausages are available countrywide. Children are allowed in all restaurants, but don't expect toys and games as in American restaurants.

The restaurants we list are the cream of the crop in each price category. Price categories are based on the average cost of a main course at dinner (or at lunch if that is the only option). If you love seafood, you should make a point of visiting one of the casual West Coast beach restaurants in the Western Cape, where you sit on the beach in a makeshift structure and eat course after course of seafood cooked on an open fire.

⇨ *For food-related health issues, see Health, below.*

MEALS AND MEALTIMES

In South Africa dinner is eaten at night and lunch at noon. Breakfast generally consists of something eggy and hot, but many people are moving over to muesli and fruit. South Africans may eat muffins for breakfast but draw the line at doughnuts, so don't expect too many breakfast sweets. Restaurants serve breakfast until about 11:30; a few serve breakfast all day.

If you're staying at a game lodge, your mealtimes will revolve around the game drives—usually coffee and rusks (similar to biscotti) early in the morning, more coffee and probably muffins on the first game drive, a huge brunch in the late morning, no lunch, tea and something sweet in the late afternoon before the evening game drive, cocktails and snacks on the drive, and a substantial supper, or dinner, about 8 or 8:30.

If you're particularly interested in food, stay at a guesthouse selected by Good Cooks and Their Country Houses, which are noted for superior cuisine. For a guesthouse to qualify for inclusion, the chef must be the owner (or one of them).

Unless otherwise noted, the restaurants listed in this guide are open daily for lunch and dinner.

Contacts **Good Cooks and Their Country Houses** ⊕ www.goodcooks.co.za.

PAYING

Many restaurants accustomed to serving tourists accept credit cards, usually Visa and American Express, with MasterCard increasingly accepted.

⇨ *For guidelines on tipping, see Tipping, below. For restaurant price charts, see Planning, at the beginning of each chapter.*

RESERVATIONS AND DRESS

Most restaurants welcome casual dress, including jeans and sneakers. Very expensive restaurants and old-fashioned hotel restaurants (where colonial traditions die hard) may welcome nicer dress, but other

LOCAL DO'S AND TABOOS

GREETINGS

The first words you should say to anyone in South Africa, no matter the situation, are "Hello, how are you?" It doesn't matter if you are in a hurry—African conversations begin with a greeting. To skip this and jump to the question, as we often do in the United States, is considered rude. Slow down and converse, then ask for what you need. After a few weeks you'll get used to it and miss it when you return home to instant demands.

SIGHTSEEING

South Africa, unlike the rest of the continent, is relatively casual. Aside from top-end restaurants and houses of worship, you can dress fairly casually (shorts and sandals). In national parks and by the beach, rules are even more flexible, and many people stroll into cafés right off the beach, wearing only cover-ups.

If you're visiting a house of worship, dress modestly. This is especially true at mosques, where women should bring scarves to cover their heads, wear skirts below the knees, and cover their shoulders. Some mosques prefer that non-Muslims remain outside.

OUT ON THE TOWN

When out at a restaurant or a club, behave as you would at home. Be polite to waitstaff, and don't call out.

HOUSE CALLS

If you are invited to someone's home, it's a good idea to bring a small gift. If you know your hosts' habits, you can bring a bottle of wine, chocolates, or flowers. If you've been invited to a very humble home—as can happen in rural areas—and your hosts are struggling to feed their children, they may prefer something a bit more pragmatic than a bunch of flowers. This is delicate territory, so when in doubt, ask a trustworthy, knowledgeable third party. Dress nicely and modestly when visiting homes, especially in the townships or Muslim areas.

DOING BUSINESS

Arrive on time for appointments, and hand over a business card during introductions. Handshakes are the proper form of greeting in a business setting. Gifts are not part of the business culture. Address colleagues by their titles and surnames.

It's not uncommon for business to be conducted over a meal. You may be inclined to rush proceedings along and force decisions, but this is not the African way. Slow down and relax.

Men generally wear a jacket and tie to meetings, but a suit isn't necessary, unless it's a really high-powered meeting. Women can get away with anything from a pretty floral dress to a suit, but take your cue from the general purpose of the meeting and other participants. Trousers are perfectly acceptable for women.

LANGUAGE

⚠ **Although many Americans consider the term coloured offensive, it's widely used in South Africa to describe South Africans who are descended from imported slaves, the San, the Khoekhoen, and European settlers. Over the years the term has lost any pejorative connotations.**

South Africa has 11 official languages: Afrikaans, English, Ndebele, North Sotho, South Sotho, Swati, Tsonga, Tswana (same as Setswana in Botswana), Venda, Xhosa, and Zulu. English is widely spoken, although road signs and other important markers often alternate between English and Afrikaans.

than the Blue Train, few require a jacket and tie.

WINES, BEER, AND SPIRITS

You can buy wine in supermarkets and many convenience stores. Beer is available only in "bottle shops," which are licensed to sell spirits. Most restaurants are licensed to sell wine and beer, and many also sell spirits. From Saturday at 8 pm through Sunday, you can buy alcohol only in restaurants and bars. You may not take alcohol onto beaches, and it's illegal to walk down the street with an open container. You can, however, drink with a picnic or enjoy sundowners (cocktails at sunset) in almost any public place, such as Table Mountain or Kirstenbosch. The beach rule is also somewhat relaxed at sundowner time, but be careful.

⇨ *For more information on food and drink, see "Flavors of South Africa," in Chapter 1.*

■ ELECTRICITY

The electrical current is 220 volts, 50 cycles alternating current (AC); wall outlets in most of the region take 15-amp plugs with three round prongs (the old British system), some take the European two narrow prongs, and a few take the straight-edged three-prong plugs, also 15 amps.

If your appliances are dual voltage, you'll need only an adapter. In remote areas (and even in some lodges) power may be solar or from a generator; this means that delivery is erratic both in voltage and supply. In even the remotest places, however, lodge staff will find a way to charge video and camera batteries, but you will receive little sympathy if you insist on using a hair dryer or electric razor.

Consider making a small investment in a universal adapter, which has several types of plugs in one lightweight, compact unit. Most laptops and mobile phone chargers are dual voltage (i.e., they operate equally well on 110 and 220 volts), so require only an adapter. These days the same

is true of small appliances such as hair dryers. Always check labels and manufacturer instructions to be sure. Don't use 110-volt outlets marked FOR SHAVERS ONLY for high-wattage appliances such as hair dryers.

■ EMERGENCIES

The U.S. embassy is in Pretoria; there's a consulate in Cape Town.

If you specifically need an ambulance, you can get one by calling the special ambulance number or through the general emergency number. If you intend to do scuba diving in South Africa, make sure you have DAN membership, which will be honored by Divers Alert Network South Africa (DANSA).

Embassies U.S. Consulate, Cape Town ⊠ *2 Reddam Ave., Westlake, Cape Town* ☎ *021/702–7300 in Cape Town, 703/439–2301 in U.S.* ⊕ *southafrica.usembassy.gov* ⊘ *Mon.–Thurs. 8–5, Fri 8–noon.* **U.S. Embassy to South Africa** ⊠ *877 Pretorius St., Pretoria* ☎ *012/431–4000.*

Emergency Contacts DANSA ☎ *0800/020–111 Emergency hotline, 27/828–106010 from outside S.A.* ⊕ *www.dansa.org.* **General emergency** ☎ *10111 from landline, 112 from mobile phone, 107 for Cape Town only.*

▮ GEAR

Goods in South Africa's pharmacies and grocery stores are very similar to those in the States. If you have a favorite brand of toiletry, bring it; otherwise expect to pay average prices for items you may have left at home. Minimarts at gas stations also stock the same range of candies and sodas you would expect of a roadside shop.

Take care to bring enough prescription medicines and a copy of your prescription if you anticipate needing a refill. Ask your doctor to write down the ingredients so that a pharmacist will find a suitable substitute if necessary. Obtain your antimalarials at home.

Incidents of theft from checked baggage in Cape Town and Johannesburg airports make luggage wrapping a popular option. For a few rand, the process of wrapping a bag in impenetrable cellophane is a great deterrent against crime. ⚠ **Fragile items in soft-sided bags can be crushed in the wrapping process, so remove breakable items or place them in the center of the bag to prevent their getting squeezed.** The wrapping can be removed by hand or with a knife. Security accepts wrapped bags.

In southern Africa it's possible to experience muggy heat, bone-chilling cold, torrential thunderstorms, and scorching African sun all within a couple of days. The secret is to pack lightweight clothes that you can wear in layers, and at least one lightweight fleece pullover or sweater. Take along a warm jacket, too, especially if you're going to a private game lodge. It can get mighty cold sitting in an open Land Rover at night or on an early-morning game drive. It really and truly does get very cold in almost every part of southern Africa, so don't fall into the it's-Africa-so-it-must-always-be-hot trap.

South Africans tend to dress casually. Businessmen still wear suits, but dress standards have become less rigid and more interesting since the late Nelson Mandela redefined the concept of sartorial elegance with his Madiba shirts. You can go almost anywhere in neat, clean, casual clothes, but you can still get dolled up to go to the theater or opera.

It's easy to get fried in the strong African sun, especially in mile-high Johannesburg or windy Cape Town, where the air can feel deceptively cool. Pack plenty of sunscreen (SPF 30 or higher), sunglasses, and a hat. An umbrella comes in handy during those late-afternoon thunderstorms but is almost useless in Cape Town in the winter, as it will get blown inside out. But do take a raincoat. ⇨ *For more details on what to pack for a safari, see Chapter 11, Safari Primer.*

Some hotels do supply washcloths; some don't. It's always a good idea to have at least a couple of tissues in your bag, and moist towelettes, because there may not be a restroom (or toilet paper) just when you need it. Even an hour in a safari vehicle on a dry day can cover you with dust.

Make copies of all your important documents. Leave one set in one bag, another at home, and try to save them online in a PDF file, which may be the fastest way to access data if you need to replace anything. Consider carrying a small card with emergency contact numbers on it, such as the local U.S. embassy, in case things go terribly wrong.

If your luggage does get lost, your best bet for replacing staple items will be Woolworths (a high-quality brand in South Africa, with both department and food stores). Edgars and Truworths are also fine. You can find all three in most big shopping malls. Mr. Price is South Africa's Target equivalent, but with less-reliable quality. Cape Union Mart is great for safari stuff. You'll find a wide supply of toiletries in Clicks.

▮ HEALTH

South Africa is a modern country, but Africa still poses certain health risks even in the most developed areas.

These days everyone is sun sensitive (and sun can be a big issue in South Africa), so pack plenty of your favorite SPF product from home, and use it generously. And drink plenty of water to avoid dehydration.

The drinking water in South Africa is treated and, except in rural areas, is absolutely safe to drink. Many people filter it, though, to get rid of the chlorine, as that aseptic status does not come free. You can eat fresh fruits and salads and have ice in your drinks.

It is always wise for travelers to have medical insurance for travel that will also help with emergency evacuation (most safari operators require emergency evacuation coverage and may ask you to pay for it along with your tour payments). If you don't want general travel insurance, many companies offer medical-only policies.

COMMON ISSUES
MALARIA
Although there are some nonmalarial safari regions in South Africa, the most serious health problem facing travelers is malaria, which occurs in the prime South African game-viewing areas of Mpumalanga, Limpopo Province, and northern KwaZulu-Natal and in the countries farther north. The risk is medium at the height of the summer and very low in winter. All travelers heading into malaria-endemic regions should consult a healthcare professional at least one month before departure for advice. Unfortunately, the malarial organism *Plasmodium sp.* seems to be able to develop a hardy resistance to new prophylactic drugs pretty quickly, so even if you are taking the newest miracle drug, the best prevention is to avoid being bitten by mosquitoes in the first place. After sunset wear light-color, loose, long-sleeve shirts, long pants, and shoes and socks, and apply mosquito repellent generously. Always sleep in a mosquito-proof room or tent, and if possible, keep a fan going in your room. If you are pregnant or trying to conceive, avoid malaria areas entirely.

Generally speaking, the risk is much lower in the dry season (May–October) and peaks immediately after the first rains, which should be in November, but El Niño has made that a lot less predictable.

BILHARZIA
Many lakes and streams, particularly east of the watershed divide (i.e., in rivers flowing toward the Indian Ocean), are infected with *bilharzia* (schistosomiasis), a parasite carried by a small freshwater snail. The microscopic fluke enters through the skin of swimmers or waders, attaches itself to the intestines or bladder, and lays eggs. Avoid wading in still waters or in areas close to reeds. If you have been wading or swimming in doubtful water, dry yourself off vigorously with a towel immediately upon exiting the water, as this may help to dislodge any flukes before they can burrow into your skin. Fast-moving water is considered safe. If you have been exposed, pop into a pharmacy and purchase a course of treatment and take it to be safe. If your trip is ending shortly after your exposure, take the medicine home and have a checkup once you get there. Bilharzia is easily diagnosed, and it's also easily treated in the early stages.

HIV
Be aware of the dangers of becoming infected with HIV (which is a big problem in Africa) or hepatitis. Make sure you use a condom during a sexual encounter; they're sold in supermarkets, pharmacies, and most convenience stores. If you feel there's a possibility you've exposed yourself to the virus, you can get antiretroviral treatment (post-exposure prophylaxis or PEP) from private hospitals, but you must do so within 48 hours of exposure.

RABIES
Rabies is extremely rare in domesticated animals in South Africa but is more common in wild animals—one more reason you should not feed or tease them. If you are bitten by a monkey or other wild animal, seek medical attention immediately. The chance of contracting rabies is extremely small, but the consequences are

so horrible that you really don't want to gamble on this one.

INSECTS AND OTHER PESTS

In summer ticks may be a problem, even in open areas close to cities. If you intend to walk or hike anywhere, use a suitable insect repellent. After your walk, examine your body and clothes for ticks, looking carefully for pepper ticks, which are tiny but may cause tick-bite fever. If you find a tick has bitten you, do not pull it off. If you do, you may pull the body off, and the head will remain embedded in your skin, causing an infection. Rather, smother the area with petroleum jelly, and the tick will eventually let go, as it will be unable to breathe; you can then scrape it off with a fingernail. If you are bitten, keep an eye on the bite. If the tick was infected, the bite will swell, itch, and develop a black necrotic center. This is a sure sign that you will develop tick-bite fever, which usually hits after about 8 to 12 days. Symptoms may be mild or severe, depending on the patient. This disease is not usually life-threatening in healthy adults, but it's horribly unpleasant. Most people who are bitten by ticks suffer no more than an itchy bump, so don't panic.

Also, obviously, keep a lookout for mosquitoes. Even in nonmalarial areas they are extremely irritating. When walking anywhere in the bush, keep a lookout for snakes. Most will slither away when they feel you coming, but just keep your eyes peeled. If you see one, give it a wide berth and you should be fine. Snakes really bite only when they are taken by surprise, so you don't want to step on a napping adder.

■TIP➔ If on safari or camping, check your boots and shake your clothes out for spiders and other crawlies before getting dressed.

OVER-THE-COUNTER REMEDIES

You can buy over-the-counter medication in pharmacies and supermarkets, and you will find the more general remedies in Clicks, a chain store selling beauty products, some OTC medication, and housewares. Your body may not react the same way to the South African version of a product, even something as simple as a headache tablet, so bring your own supply for your trip and rely on pharmacies just for emergency medication.

SHOTS AND MEDICATIONS

South Africa does not require any inoculations for entry. Travelers entering South Africa within six days of leaving a country infected with yellow fever require a yellow-fever vaccination certificate. The South African travel clinics and the U.S. National Centers for Disease Control and Prevention (CDC) recommend that you be vaccinated against hepatitis A and B if you intend to travel to more isolated areas. Cholera injections are widely regarded as useless, so don't let anyone talk you into having one, but the newer oral vaccine seems to be more effective.

If you are coming to South Africa for a safari, chances are you are heading to a malarial game reserve. Only a handful of game reserves are nonmalarial. Millions of travelers take oral prophylactic drugs before, during, and after their safaris. It's up to you to weigh the risks and benefits of the type of antimalarial drug you choose to take. If you're pregnant or traveling with small children, consider a nonmalarial region for your safari.

The CDC provides up-to-date information on health risks and recommended vaccinations and medications for travelers to southern Africa. In most of South Africa you need not worry about any of these, but if you plan to visit remote regions, check with the CDC's traveler's health line. For up-to-date, local expertise, contact Netcare Travel Clinics.

MEDICAL CARE IN SOUTH AFRICA

South African doctors are generally excellent. The equipment and training in private clinics rivals the best in the world, but public hospitals tend to suffer from overcrowding and underfunding. So if you need to seek medical treatment, ask your hotel or safari operator to get you to a private hospital. In South Africa, foreigners are expected to pay in full for any medical services, so check your existing health plan to see whether you're covered while abroad, and supplement it if necessary.

On returning home, if you experience any unusual symptoms, including fever, painful eyes, backache, diarrhea, severe headache, general lassitude, or blood in urine or stool, be sure to tell your doctor where you have been. These symptoms may indicate malaria, tick-bite fever, bilharzia, or—if you've been traveling north of South Africa's borders—some other tropical malady.

Health Warnings National Centers for Disease Control and Prevention (*CDC*). ☎ 800/232–4636 international travelers' health line ⊕ www.cdc.gov/travel. **World Health Organization** (*WHO*). ⊕ www.who.int.

Medical-Only Insurers International Medical Group ☎ 866/368–3724 ⊕ www. imglobal.com. **International SOS** ☎ 011/541–1000, 011/541–1300 24-hr emergency, 800/523–8662 in U.S. (sales) ⊕ www. internationalsos.co.za. **Wallach & Company** ☎ 800/237–6615 ⊕ www.wallach.com.

∎ HOURS OF OPERATION

The most surprising aspect of South Africa's business hours, especially for tourists who come to shop, is that shopping centers, including enclosed secure indoor malls, almost always close by 6 pm. This is starting to change in Cape Town's malls, with summer hours increased until 7 or 8, but don't expect it. It's rare for a store to remain open after dinner.

Business hours in major South African cities are weekdays from about 9 to 5. Most banks close in midafternoon, usually about 3:30, but dedicated currency exchange offices usually stay open longer. In addition, post offices and banks are open briefly on Saturday morning from about 9, so get there early. In rural areas and small towns things are less rigid. Post offices often close for lunch, and in very

small towns and villages, banks may have very abbreviated hours.

Most museums are open during usual business hours, including Saturday morning, but some stay open longer.

Most pharmacies close about 6, but there's generally an all-night pharmacy in towns of a reasonable size. If not, look for an emergency number posted on a pharmacy.

Many gas stations are open 24 hours, and urban gas stations have 24-hour convenience stores, some of which have an impressive range of goods.

HOLIDAYS

National holidays in South Africa are New Year's Day (January 1), Human Rights Day (March 21), Good Friday, Easter, Family Day (sometime in March or April), Freedom Day (April 27), Workers Day (May 1), Youth Day (June 16), National Women's Day (August 9), Heritage Day (September 24), Day of Reconciliation (December 16), Christmas Day (December 25), and Day of Goodwill (December 26). If a public holiday falls on a Sunday, the following Monday is also a public holiday. Election days are also public holidays, so check calendars closer to your time of travel for those, which are not on fixed dates.

In Cape Town, January 2 is also a holiday, known as *tweede nuwe jaar* (second new year). School vacations vary with the provinces, but usually comprise about 10 days over Easter, about three weeks around June or July, and then the big summer vacation from about December 10 to January 10.

∎ MAIL

The mail service in South Africa is reasonably reliable, but mail can take weeks to arrive, and money and other valuables may be stolen from letters and packages. You can buy stamps at post offices, open weekdays 8:30 to 4:30 and Saturday 8 to noon. Stamps for local use only, marked "standardized post," may be purchased from newsstands in booklets of 10 stamps. PostNet franchises—a combined post office, courier service, business services center, and Internet café—are in convenient places like shopping malls and are open longer hours than post offices.

All overseas mail costs the same. At the post office a postcard is about R6.05, and a letter ranges from R5.90 to about R26.90, depending on size and weight.

ADDRESSES

Note that the first floor of a building is the one between the ground floor and the second floor. Mailing addresses are pretty straightforward. If they're not a street address, they're either a P.O. Box or a Private Bag—essentially the same, just differing in size. The only vaguely tricky variation is a postnet suite, which consists of a number, followed by a private bag and then a post office (e.g., Postnet Suite 25, Private Bag X25, name of town, postal code). Even the smallest town has its own postal code, and suburbs may have different postal codes—one for a street address and one for P.O. boxes.

SHIPPING PACKAGES

If you make a purchase, try your best to take it home on the plane with you, even if it means packing your travel clothes and items into a box and shipping those to your home, or buying a cheap piece of luggage and paying the excess weight fees. If you buy something from a store accustomed to foreign visitors, it will likely already have a system for getting your items to you, often in a surprising few weeks' time.

Federal Express and DHL offer more reliable service than regular mail, as do the new Fast Mail and Speed Courier services, yet even these "overnight" services are subject to delays. PostNet, South Africa's version of Kinko's, also offers courier services. A parcel of up to about a pound (half a kilogram) will cost around R360 to send to the United States, and a one-kilogram parcel (2.2 pounds) will cost around R700.

Express Services DHL ☎ *0860/345–000* ⊕ *www.dhl.co.za.* **FedEx** ☎ *87/742–8000, 080/00–3339 toll-free in South Africa* ⊕ *www. fedex.com.* **PostNet** ☎ *0860/767–8638* ⊕ *www.postnet.co.za.*

▌ MONEY

Because of inflation and currency fluctuations, it's difficult to give exact exchange rates. It's safe to say, though, that the region is a good value, with high-quality accommodations and food at about two-thirds or half the cost they would be at home.

A bottle of good South African wine costs about the equivalent of $9 (double or triple in a restaurant), and a meal at a prestigious restaurant won't set you back more than $50 per person; an average restaurant, with wine, might be about $40 for two. Double rooms in the country's finest hotels may cost $400 a night, but $200 is more than enough to secure high-quality lodging in most cities, and charming, spotless B&Bs or guesthouses with full breakfasts can be less than $80 in many areas.

Not everything in South Africa is cheap. Expect to pay international rates and more to stay in one of the exclusive private game lodges in Mpumalanga, Limpopo Province, or KwaZulu-Natal—with a fly-in charter figured into the price, expect to pay between $2,000 and $3,000 per couple per night. Flights to South Africa are expensive, but the rash of new low-cost carriers makes popular domestic routes less expensive, with most trips less than $150 one way. Taxis are uncharacteristically expensive, compared with other vacation needs.

ATMS AND BANKS

South Africa has a modern banking system, with branches throughout the country and ubiquitous ATMs, especially at tourist attractions, in gas stations, and in shopping malls. Banks open at 9 in the morning weekdays and close at 3:30 in the afternoon; on Saturday they close at 11 in the morning, and they are closed Sunday (with the exception of Standard Bank branches in shopping malls, some of which are open on Sunday, 9:30–1). Many banks can perform foreign-exchange services or international electronic transfers, but you will always get a better exchange rate from an ATM. The major South African banks are ABSA, First National Bank, Nedbank, and Standard.

If your card gets swallowed, *stay at the ATM* and call the help line number displayed. If possible, withdraw money during the day and choose ATMs with security guards present or those inside stores.

CREDIT CARDS

MasterCard, Visa, and American Express are accepted almost everywhere, but Diners Club and Discover are not.

It's a good idea to inform your credit-card company before you travel, especially if you're going abroad and don't travel internationally very often. Otherwise, the credit-card company might put a hold on your card owing to unusual activity—not a good thing halfway through your trip. Record all your credit-card numbers—as well as the phone numbers to call if your cards are lost or stolen—in a safe place, so you're prepared should something go wrong. MasterCard, Visa, and American Express all have general numbers you can call collect if you're abroad.

If you plan to use your credit card for cash advances, you'll need to apply for a PIN at least two weeks before your trip. Although it's usually cheaper (and safer) to use a credit card abroad for large purchases (so you can cancel payments or be reimbursed if there's a problem), note that some credit-card companies *and* the banks that issue them add substantial percentages to all foreign transactions, whether they're in a foreign currency or not. Check on these fees before leaving home, so there won't be any surprises when you get the bill.

Reporting Lost Cards American Express ☎ 800/528–4800 in U.S. ⊕ www. americanexpress.com. **Diners Club** ☎ 0860/346–377, 011/358–8500 outside S.A. ⊕ www.dinersclub.com. **MasterCard** ☎ 800/990–418 ⊕ www.mastercard.com. **Visa** ☎ 0800/990–475 toll-free in South Africa, 1303/967–1090 collect from abroad ⊕ www. visa.com.

ITEM	AVERAGE COST
Cup of coffee	$2
Glass of beer	$1.70–$2
Quarter of roasted chicken with salad and drink at a fast-food restaurant	$5–$7
Room-service sandwich in a hotel	$5–$7
2-km (1-mile) taxi ride	$6–$8

Prices throughout this guide are given for adults. Substantially reduced fees are almost always available for children, students, and senior citizens.

CURRENCY AND EXCHANGE

The unit of currency in South Africa is the rand (R), with 100 cents (¢) equaling R1. Bills come in R10, R20, R50, R100, and R200 denominations, which are differentiated by color (beware of the similar color of the R50 and R200 notes). Coins are minted in 5¢, 10¢, 20¢, 50¢, R1, R2, and R5 denominations.

At this writing, the rand is trading at about R11 to $1. It's a good bargain given the quality of lodgings, which cost probably two-thirds the price of comparable facilities in the United States.

To avoid administrative hassles, keep all foreign-exchange receipts until you leave the region, as you may need them as proof when changing any unspent local currency back into your own currency. You may not take more than R25,000 or US$10,000 in cash in or out of South

Africa. For more information you can contact the South African Reserve Bank.

■TIP→ **Even if a currency-exchange booth has a sign promising no commission, rest assured that there's some kind of huge, hidden fee. And as for rates, you're almost always better off getting foreign currency at an ATM or exchanging money at a bank.**

Currency Conversion Oanda.com ⊕ *www.oanda.com.* **XE.com** ⊕ *www.xe.com.*

▌ PASSPORTS

American citizens need only a valid passport to enter South Africa for visits of up to 90 days; this includes infants. Check the expiration date. If your passport will expire within six months of your return date, you need to renew it in advance, as South Africa won't let you enter with a soon-to-expire passport. ⚠ **You will be denied entry to the country if you do not have two blank, facing pages in your passport.**

Before your trip, make two copies of your passport's data page (one for someone at home and another for you to carry separately). Or scan the page and email it to someone at home and/or yourself.

U.S. Passport Information U.S. Department of State ☎ 877/487-2778 ⊕ *travel.state.gov.*

▌ RESTROOMS

All fuel complexes on the major roads have large, clean, well-maintained restrooms. In cities you can find restrooms in shopping malls, at some gas stations, and in restaurants—most of which are quite happy to allow you to use them.

▌ SAFETY

South Africa is a country in transition, and as a result experiences growing pains that reveal themselves in economic inequities, which result in high crime rates. Although the majority of visitors experience a crime-free trip to South Africa, it's essential to practice vigilance and extreme care.

Crime is a major problem in the whole region, particularly in large cities, and all visitors should take precautions to protect themselves. Do not walk alone at night, and exercise caution even during the day. Avoid wearing jewelry (even costume jewelry), don't invite attention by wearing an expensive camera around your neck, and don't flash a large wad of cash. If you are toting a handbag, wear the strap across your body; even better, wear a money belt, preferably hidden from view under your clothing. When sitting at airports or at restaurants, especially outdoor cafés, make sure to keep your bag on your lap or between your legs—otherwise it may just quietly "walk off" when you're not looking. Even better, loop the strap around your leg, or clip the strap around the table or chair.

Carjacking is another problem, with armed bandits often forcing drivers out of their vehicles at traffic lights, in driveways, or during a fake accident. Always drive with your windows closed and doors locked, don't stop for hitchhikers, and park in well-lighted places. At traffic lights, leave enough space between you and the vehicle in front so you can pull into another lane if necessary. In the unlikely event you are carjacked, don't argue, and don't look at the carjacker's face. Just get out of the car, or ask to be let out of the car. Do not try to keep any of your belongings—they are all replaceable, even that laptop with all that data on it. If you aren't given the opportunity to leave the car, try to stay calm, ostentatiously look away from the hijackers so they can be sure you can't identify them, and follow all instructions. Ask again, calmly, to be let out of the car.

Many places that are unsafe in South Africa will not bear obvious signs of danger. Make sure you know exactly where you're going. Purchase a good map and obtain comprehensive directions from your hotel, rental-car agent, or a trusted local. Taking the wrong exit off a highway into a township could lead you straight to disaster. Many cities are ringed by "no-go" areas. Learn from your hotel or the locals which areas to avoid. If you sense you have taken a wrong turn, drive toward a public area, such as a gas station, or building with an armed guard, before attempting to correct your mistake, which could just compound the problem. When parking, don't leave anything visible in the car; stow it all in the trunk—this includes clothing or shoes. As an added measure, leave the glove box open, to show there's nothing of value inside (take the rental agreement with you).

Before setting out on foot, ask a local, such as your hotel concierge or a shopkeeper, which route to take and how far you can safely go. Walk with a purposeful stride so you look like you know where you're going, and duck into a shop or café if you need to check a map, speak on your mobile phone, or recheck the directions you've been given. ⚠ **Don't walk while speaking on a cell phone.**

Lone women travelers need to be particularly vigilant about walking alone and locking their rooms. South Africa has one of the world's highest rates of rape. If you do attract someone who won't take a firm but polite *no* for an answer, appeal immediately to the hotel manager, bartender, or someone else who seems to be in charge. If you have to walk a short distance alone at night, such as from the hotel reception to your room in a dark motel compound or back from a café along a main street, have a plan, carry a whistle, and know what you'll do if you are grabbed.

⇨ *For destination-specific information, see Safety in each chapter.*

▌ TAXES

All South African hotels pay a bed tax, which is included in quoted prices. In South Africa the Value-Added Tax (V.A.T.), which at this writing is 14%, is included in the price of most goods and services, including hotel accommodations and food. To get a V.A.T. refund, foreign visitors must present their receipts (minimum of R250) at the airport and be carrying any purchased items with them or in their luggage. You must fill out Form V.A.T. 255, available at the airport V.A.T. refund office. Whatever you buy, make sure that your receipt is an original tax invoice, containing the vendor's name and address, V.A.T. registration number, and the words "tax invoice." Refunds are paid by check, which can be cashed immediately at an airport bank or refunded directly onto your credit card, with a small transaction fee. Be sure you visit the V.A.T. refund desk in the departures hall before you go through check-in procedures, and try to organize your receipts as you go, to make for easy viewing. Officials will go through your receipts and randomly ask to view your purchases.

Contacts V.A.T. Refund Office ☎ 011/979–0055 ⊕ *www.taxrefunds.co.za.*

▌ TIME

South Africa operates on SAST (South African Standard Time). That makes it seven hours ahead of North American eastern standard time. South Africa doesn't follow any daylight saving time, so when U.S. clocks spring forward, it's only 6 hours ahead.

▌ TIPPING

Tipping is an integral part of South African life, and it's expected that you'll tip for services that you might take for granted at home. Most notable among these is getting gas, as there are no self-service stations. If the attendant simply fills your tank, tip R2–R3; if he or she offers to clean your windshield, checks your tires, oil, or water, and is generally helpful, tip R5–R10. In restaurants the size of the tip should depend on the quality of service, but 10% is standard, unless, of course, a service charge has already been added to the bill. Give the same percentage to bartenders, taxi drivers, and tour guides.

TIPPING GUIDELINES FOR SOUTH AFRICA	
Bartender	10% of your bill is common
Bellhop	R5 per item
Hotel concierge	Hotel managers say it's not necessary to tip a concierge. If one goes out of his way for you, getting tickets to a sold-out event, say, then anything from R70 to R175 would be appropriate.
Hotel doorman	R5, but it's not expected
Hotel maid	Tips are not expected for maids in South Africa, as hotels add service charges to the bill that are distributed to staff
Hotel room-service waiter	R5 per delivery is nice but not expected
Porter at airport or train station	R5 per bag
Skycap at airport	R5 per bag checked
Taxi driver	10%, but round up the fare to the next dollar amount.
Tour guide	10% of the cost of the tour
Valet parking attendant	R5 when you get your car
Waiter	10%; nothing additional if a service charge is added to your bill
Car guards	R2–R5

At the end of your stay at a game lodge, you're expected to tip both the ranger and the tracker and the general staff. Different lodgings handle it differently, and checking with the management is one way to make sure you tip properly. However, a good model to follow is to factor 10% of your total room bill. Fifty percent of this figure should go to your ranger/tracker, and 50% should go to the general staff. If you have a personal butler, factor an

additional 10% (of your total tip figure). If you have your laundry done, leave R5–R10 for the laundress in a special envelope. Envelopes are usually provided in safari rooms and tents for tipping, but it's a nice touch to bring your own note cards to write a personal message.

Informal parking attendants operate in the major cities in South Africa and even in some tourist areas. Although they often look a bit seedy, they do provide a good service, so tip them R2–R5 if your car is still in one piece when you return to it.

▋ TRIP INSURANCE

Comprehensive trip insurance is valuable if you're booking a very expensive or complicated trip (particularly to an isolated region) or if you're booking far in advance. Comprehensive policies typically cover trip cancellation and interruption, letting you cancel or cut your trip short because of illness, or, in some cases, acts of terrorism in your destination. Such policies might also cover evacuation and medical care. For trips abroad you should have at least medical-only coverage (⇨ *Health, above*). Some also cover you for trip delays because of bad weather or mechanical problems as well as for lost or delayed luggage.

Another type of coverage to consider is financial default—that is, when your trip is disrupted because a tour operator, airline, or cruise line goes out of business. Generally you must buy this when you book your trip or shortly thereafter, and it's available to you only if your operator isn't on a list of excluded companies.

Always read the fine print of your policy to make sure that you're covered for the risks that most concern you. Compare several polices to be sure you're getting the best price and range of coverage available.

Comprehensive Insurers **Allianz Travel Insurance** ☎ 866/884-3556 ⊕ *www. allianztravelinsurance.com.* **CSA Travel Protection** ☎ 877/243-4135 *toll-free in U.S.,* 240/330-1529 *outside U.S.* ⊕ *www. csatravelprotection.com.* **HTH Worldwide** ☎ 610/254-8700, 888/243-2358 *toll-free in U.S.* ⊕ *www.hthworldwide.com.* **Travelex Insurance** ☎ 800/228-9792 ⊕ *www.travelex-insurance.com.* **Travel Guard** ☎ 800/826-4919 ⊕ *www.travelguard.com.* **Travel Insured International** ☎ 800/243-3174 ⊕ *www. travelinsured.com.*

Insurance Comparison Information **Insure My Trip** ☎ 800/487-4722 ⊕ *www.insuremytrip. com.* **Square Mouth** ☎ 800/240-0369, 727/564-9203 *(International Customer Service)* ⊕ *www.squaremouth.com.*

▌ VISITOR INFORMATION

See the individual chapter Essentials sections for details on local visitor bureaus.

ONLINE TRAVEL TOOLS

All About South Africa **South Africa National Parks** ⊕ *www.sanparks.org.* **SouthAfrica.info** ⊕ *www.southafrica.info.*

Culture **Artslink.co.za** ⊕ *www.artslink.co.za.* **Iziko South African Museum** ⊕ *www.iziko. org.za.* **Mail & Guardian** ⊕ *www.mg.co.za.*

Media **Independent Newspapers** ⊕ *www.iol. co.za.*

Visitor Information **Cape Town Tourism** ⊕ *www.capetown.travel.* **South African Tourism** ☎ 800/593-1318 *in U.S.,* 011/895-3000 *in South Africa* ⊕ *www.southafrica.net.*

INDEX

PHOTO CREDITS

Cover credit: Dereje/Shutterstock [Description: Cape Town].1, Andrea Willmore / Shutterstock. 2, Miguel Sobreira/age fotostock. 4, InnaFelker / Shutterstock. 5 (top), Adstock\UIG/age fotostock. 5 (bottom), espiegle / istockphoto. 6 (top left), Frank Kahts / Alamy. 6 (top right), michaeljung / istockphoto. 6 (bottom left), Fabian von Poser/imageBROKER/age fotostock. 6 (bottom right), Ken C Moore / Shutterstock. 7 (top), Shaen Adey/age fotostock. 7 (bottom), Johan Swanepoel / Shutterstock. 8 (top left), Hel080808 | Dreamstime.com. 8 (top right), Neil Overy/age fotostock. 8 (bottom), AfriPics. com / Alamy. Chapter One: Experience South Africa. 13, michaeljung / Shutterstock. 14, Flatscreen | Dreamstime.com. 15 (left), Johan Swanepoel / Shutterstock. 15 (right), Bruce Amos / Shutterstock. 20, BarryTuck / Shutterstock. 21, Timwege | Dreamstime.com. 22, michaeljung / Shutterstock. 23, e2dan / Shutterstock. 24, francesco de marco / Shutterstock. 26, Andre van der Veen / Shutterstock. 27, Photosky | Dreamstime.com. Chapter Two: Cape Town and Peninsula. 35, David Ryznar / Shutterstock. Chapter Three: The Western Cape. 129, PhotoSky / Shutterstock. Chapter Four: The Northern Cape. 225, francesco de marco / Shutterstock. Chapter Five: The Garden Route and the Little Karoo. 267, Domossa | Dreamstime.com. Chapter Six: The Eastern Cape. 303, David Steele / Shutterstock. Chapter Seven: Durban and KwaZulu-Natal. 339, 2630ben / Shutterstock. Chapter Eight: Johannesburg. 411, Ratmandude | Dreamstime.com. Chapter Nine: Mpumalanga & Kruger National Park. 467, Delpixel / Shutterstock. Chapter Ten: Victoria Falls. 515, Libux77 | Dreamstime.com. Chapter Eleven: Safari Primer. 539, Neil Burton / Shutterstock. Back cover (from left to right): espiegle/iStockphoto; Delpixel / Shutterstock; AnetaPics / Shutterstock. Spine: Johan Swanepoel / Shutterstock.

About Our Writers: All photos are courtesy of the writers except for the following: Christopher Clark, courtesy of Nicola Cernik.

Fodor's SOUTH AFRICA

Publisher: Amanda D'Acierno, *Senior Vice President*

Editorial: Arabella Bowen, *Editor in Chief*; Linda Cabasin, *Editorial Director*

Design: Tina Malaney, *Associate Art Director*; Chie Ushio, *Senior Designer*; Ann McBride, *Production Designer*

Photography: Jennifer Arnow, *Senior Photo Editor*; Mary Robnett, *Photo Researcher*

Production: Linda Schmidt, *Managing Editor*; Evangelos Vasilakis, *Associate Managing Editor*; Angela L. McLean, *Senior Production Manager*

Maps: Rebecca Baer, *Senior Map Editor*; David Lindroth, Mark Stroud (Moon Street Cartography), *Cartographers*

Sales: Jacqueline Lebow, *Sales Director*

Marketing & Publicity: Heather Dalton, *Marketing Director*; Katherine Punia, *Publicity Director*

Business & Operations: Susan Livingston, *Vice President, Strategic Business Planning*; Sue Daulton, *Vice President, Operations*

Fodors.com: Megan Bell, *Executive Director, Revenue & Business Development*; Yasmin Marinaro, *Senior Director, Marketing & Partnerships*

Copyright © 2015 by Fodor's Travel, a division of Random House LLC

Writers: Claire Baranowski, Angus Begg, Christopher Clark, Karena du Plessis, Christine Marot, Lee Middleton, Kate Turkington, Tara Turkington, Andrea Weiss

Editors: Doug Stallings (lead editor), Alexis Kelly, Denise Leto, Penny Phenix, Amanda Theunissen

Production Editor: Elyse Rozelle

6th edition

ISBN 978–1–101–87813–2

ISSN 1091–4757

SPECIAL SALES

This book is available at special discounts for bulk purchases for sales promotions or premiums. For more information, e-mail specialmarkets@penguinrandomhouse.com

PRINTED IN THE UNITED STATES OF AMERICA

10 9 8 7 6 5 4 3 2 1

ABOUT OUR WRITERS

Travel Smart updater **Claire Baranowski** spent an idyllic childhood in a small town in Zimbabwe before moving to South Africa. Today, she splits her time between London and Cape Town as a travel writer and editor. Her favorite experiences have included backpacking in Laos and beach escapes in Sri Lanka, but the most magical have been on safari in Africa.

A CNN award-winning television producer, **Angus Begg** was the first South African broadcast journalist to report from the chaos of Somalia in 1992. He went on to cover the Rwandan genocide of 1994 and South Africa's first democratic elections the same year, for which he was nominated for the national public service radio awards. It was these episodes in Somalia and Rwanda that took him the roundabout route to the fields of travel and environment, in which he now writes, produces, and photographs. He updated Northern Cape and parts of Cape Town for this edition and wrote our new itineraries.

Christopher Clark, who updated the Eastern Cape, is a freelance dreamer, writer, and wanderer based in Cape Town. Afflicted with itchy feet from a young age, he has traveled to and written from more than 50 countries across Africa and beyond. His work has been published by a number of regional and international publications including *Africa Geographic*, *News24*, *The Big Issue*, *Nkwazi Magazine*, *This Is Africa*, and more. He has twice been named as one of South Africa's best young writers by *The Big Issue*.

Writer **Karena du Plessis** lives in an old-fashioned stone house overlooking the Kalk Bay harbor with her husband and two children. She's passionate about the Western Cape, which she updated for this edition, and has written two books, *The Overberg—Inland From the Tip of Africa* and *West Coast—Cederberg to Sea*, which document the province's history and beauty. Apart from writing, Karena has a small vineyard producing around 700 bottles of wine a year, runs a horse livery yard, teaches at the local school, and sings in an a capella group. She wants to travel more and learn to play polo.

Our Durban updater **Christine Marot** is a KwaZulu-Natal-based online communications editor who loves sharing the beauty and diversity of South Africa with prospective visitors elsewhere in the world. She has more than 30 years of experience in print and online media. She believes that South Africa, with its unique mix of culture, adventure, history, wildlife, and cuisine, offers the tourist incredible value for money. Christine has written copy for many of South Africa's tourism-based organizations.

Focusing on environment, development, and humanitarian features—and having been writing in Africa since 2005, and based in South Africa since 2006—American journalist **Lee Middleton** has written for *Time*, the *Mail & Guardian*, *Africa Geographic*, *Men's Health*, and IRIN News, among others. Having also lived in Thailand, India, and Mexico as a wildlife researcher, Himalayan adventurer, and human rights worker, her penchant for exploration now manifests in food and travel writing from across the continent, with a focus on Southern and Eastern Africa. She updated Cape Town dining and lodging.

Kate Turkington is one of South Africa's best known travel writers and broadcasters and updated Mpumalanga & Kruger National Park and KwaZulu-Natal for this edition. Her live

Sunday night radio show, "Believe it or Not," is South Africa's longest-running radio talk show. She travels the world on a regular basis, but her heart and home are in Africa, where she lives in Johannesburg. She specializes in safari destinations, but in the last few years she has found herself at Everest Base Camp in Tibet, deep in the Amazon jungle, high in the Andes, being held up by heavily armed tribesmen in the Rift Valley, and shedding tears at Hiroshima.

Our Johannesburg updater **Tara Turkington** is well known on Twitter (@taraturk1) for her tweets about travel in and around South Africa and further afield. She's CEO of Flow Communications, which specializes in digital communications, including websites and social media for travel-related clients, including South African Tourism and many of the country's top attractions. Also a journalist, she is a mother of four. She grew up in Johannesburg, where she now lives, but has also called Cape Town, Durban, and Kimberley home. Top of her bucket list? The ultimate journey—Space, of course!

Andrea Weiss started her journalism career on the Cape Town daily newspaper *The Cape Argus,* had a stint at the University of Cape Town as media and communications manager, and was the founding editor of *go!* (a South African travel and outdoor publication). She currently works as an editor, writer, and blogger with Flow Communications with clients such as the World Wide Fund for Nature in South Africa and South African Tourism. She loves nothing more than the great open road and planning her next adventure into the wilderness. She updated the Garden Route & Little Karoo for this edition.